NOW
LET
ME FLY

NOW LET ME FLY

A PORTRAIT OF EUGENE BULLARD

Written by
Ronald WIMBERLY

Art by
Brahm REVEL

First Second
New York

To my grandfather John Wimberly
—R.W.

To my lovely and brilliant wife, Giulia
—B.R.

MADISON AV

HEY, PHIL!

HERE'S OKAY.

ALL RIGHT, MR. CASEY.

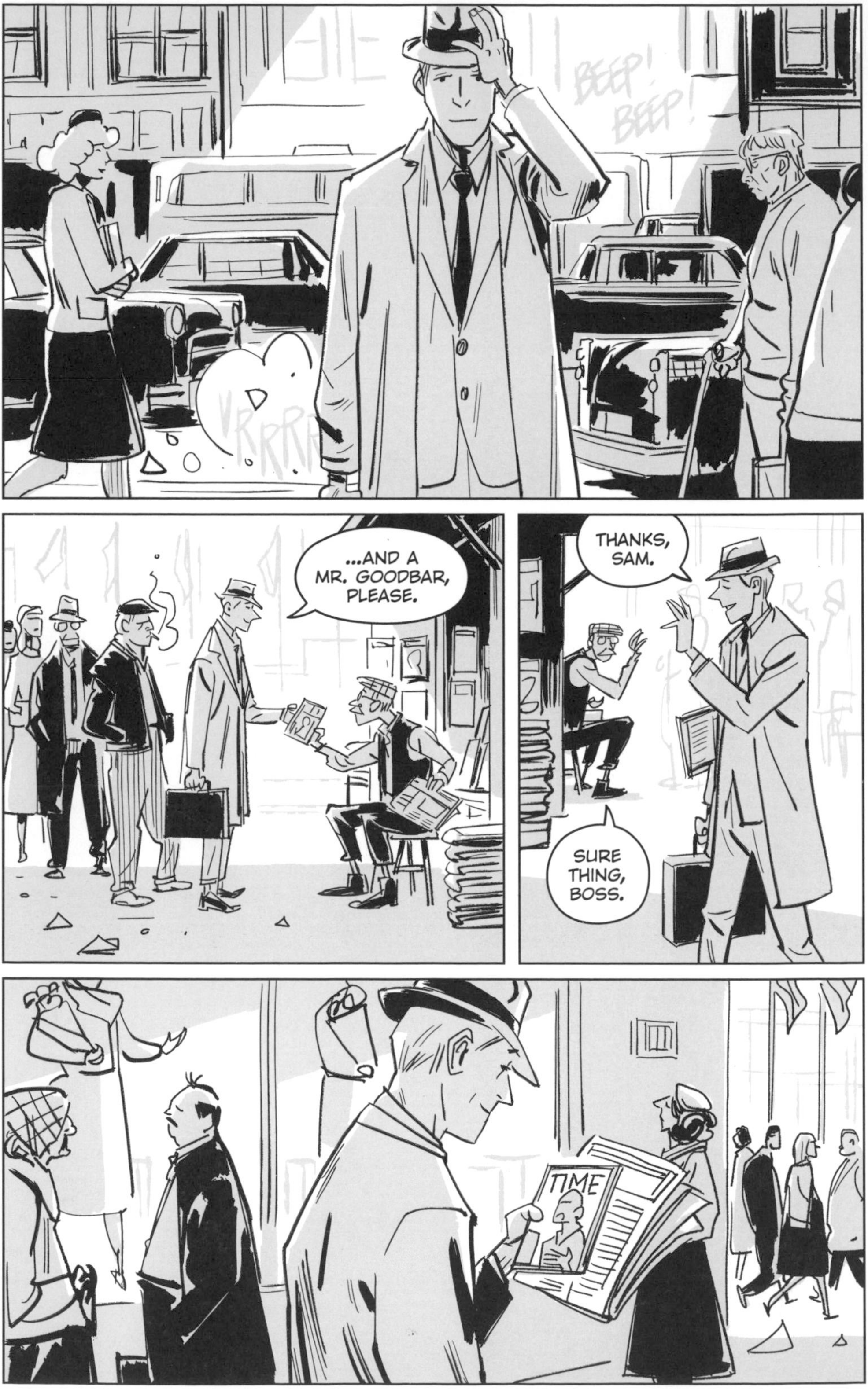
BEEP! BEEP!
VRRRR
...AND A MR. GOODBAR, PLEASE.
THANKS, SAM.
SURE THING, BOSS.
TIME

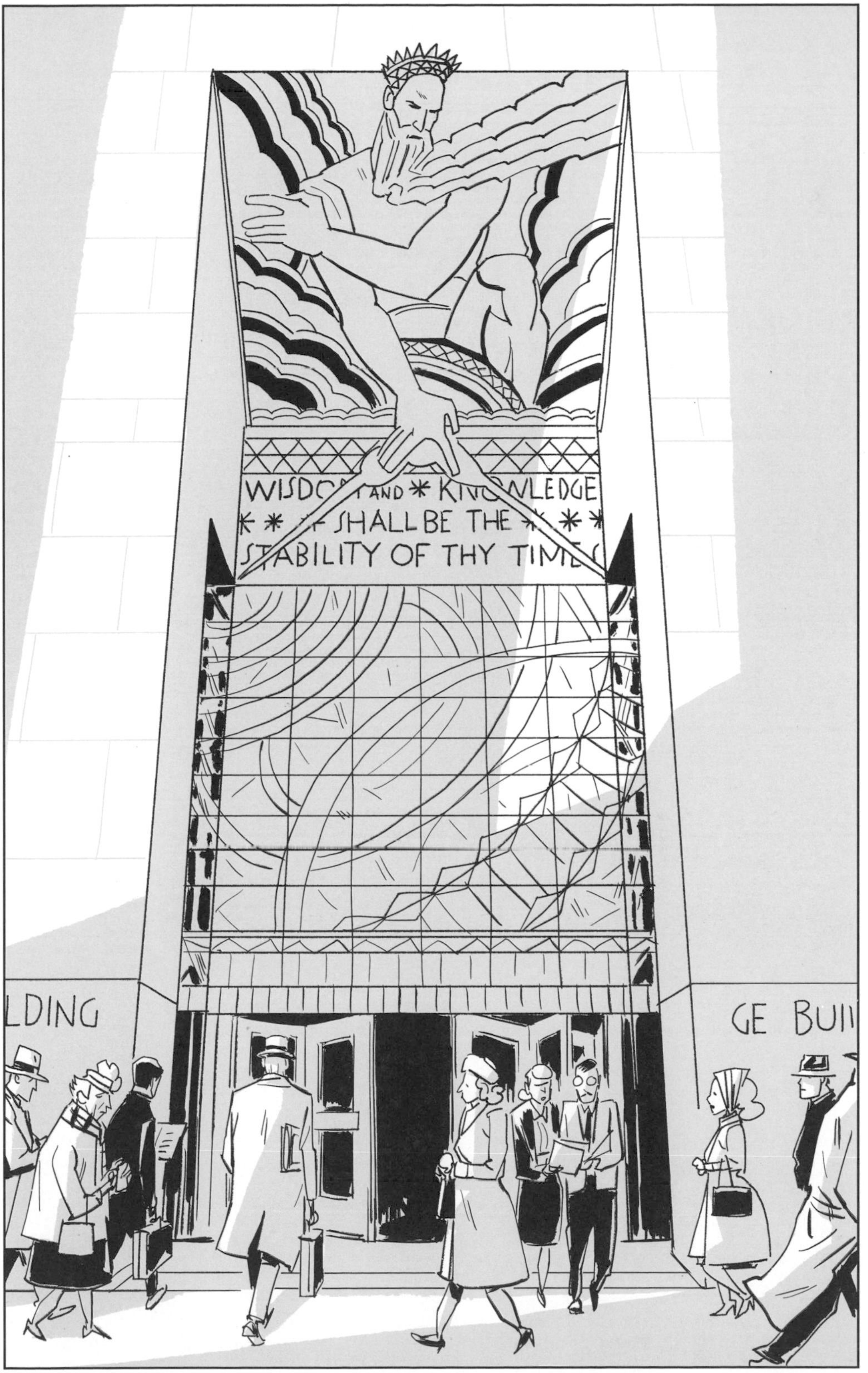
WISDOM AND KNOWLEDGE SHALL BE THE STABILITY OF THY TIMES
LDING
GE BUI

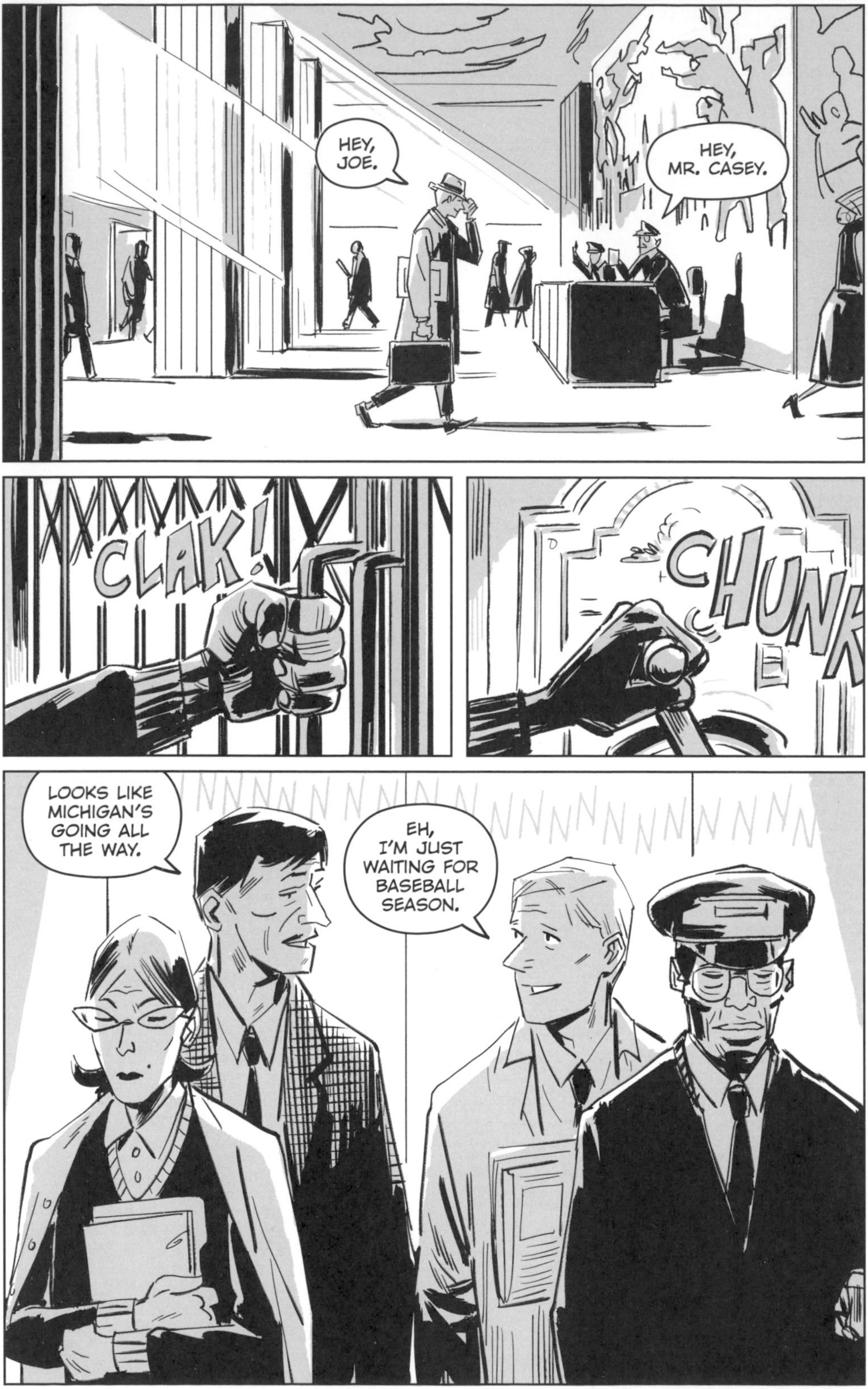
HEY, JOE.
HEY, MR. CASEY.
CLAK!
CHUNK
LOOKS LIKE MICHIGAN'S GOING ALL THE WAY.
EH, I'M JUST WAITING FOR BASEBALL SEASON.

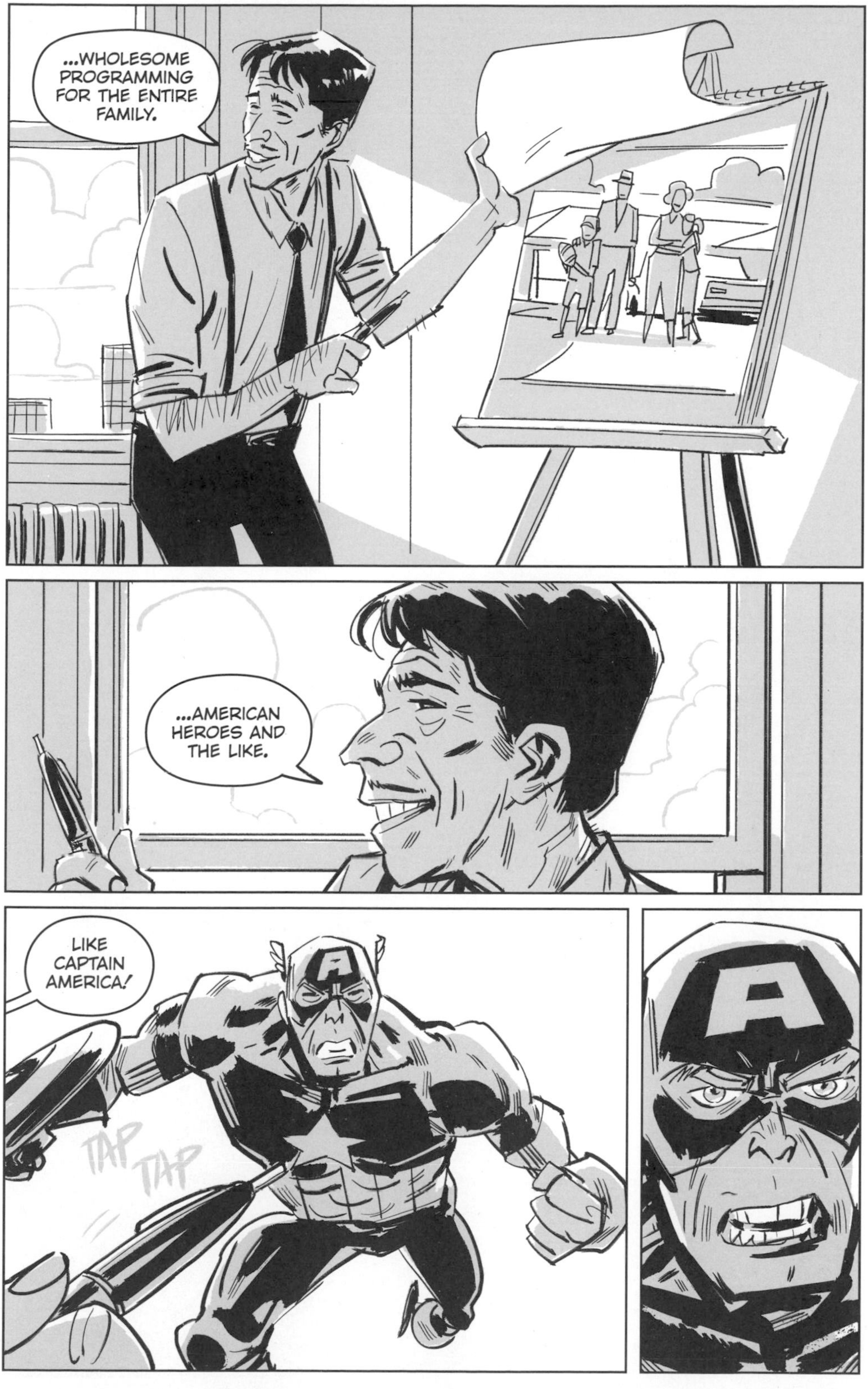
...WHOLESOME PROGRAMMING FOR THE ENTIRE FAMILY.
...AMERICAN HEROES AND THE LIKE.
LIKE CAPTAIN AMERICA!
TAP TAP

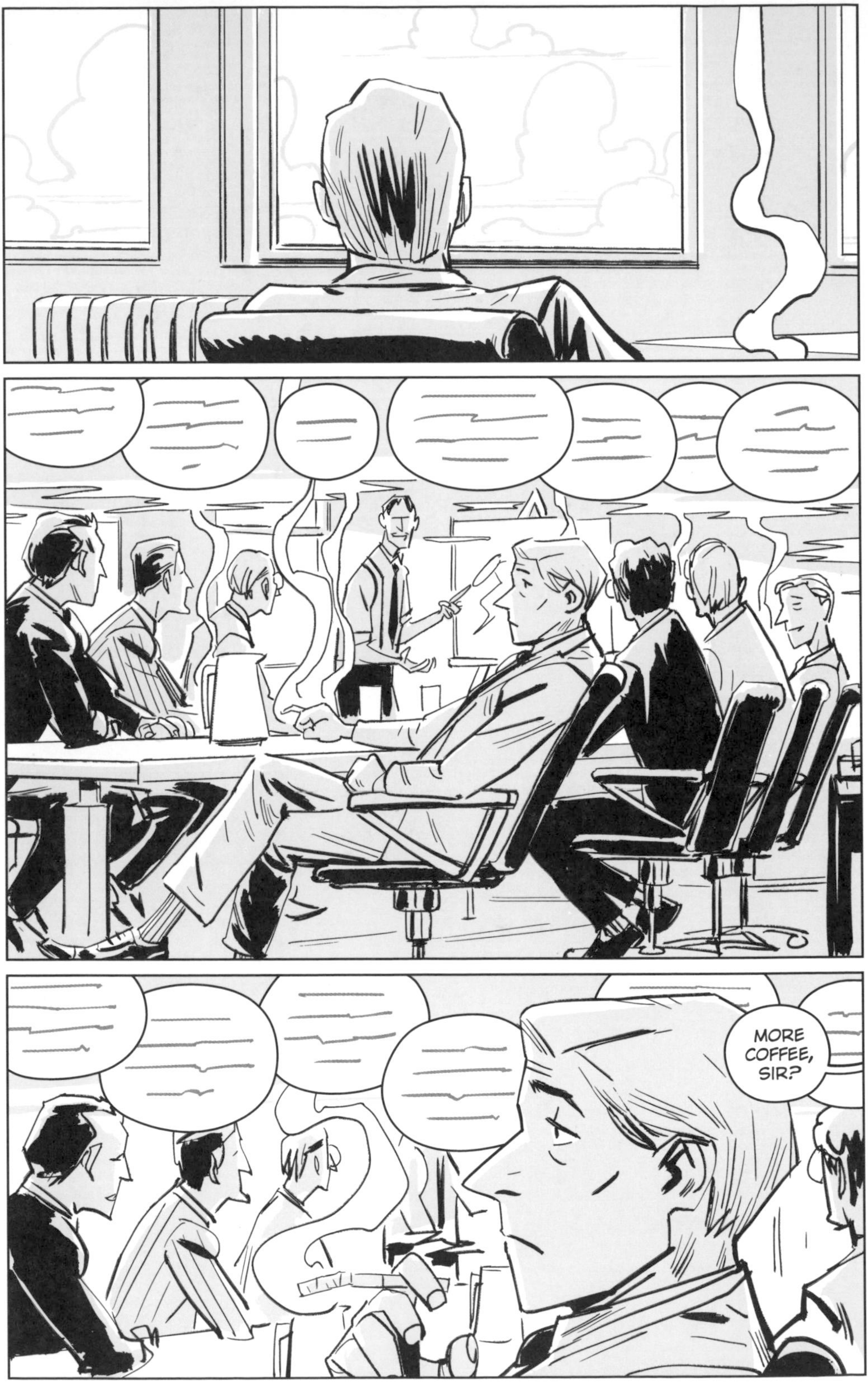
MORE COFFEE, SIR?

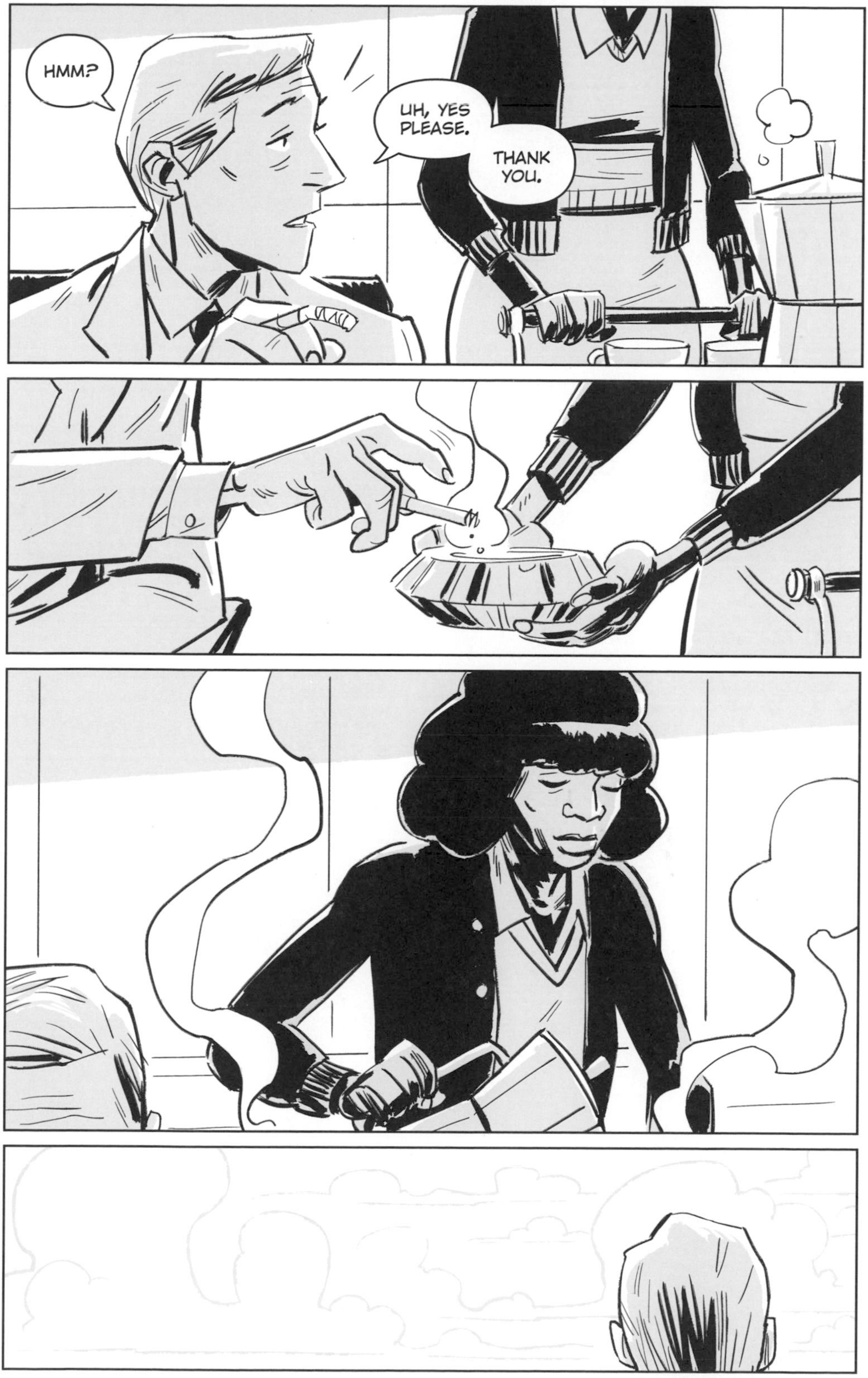
HMM?
UH, YES PLEASE.
THANK YOU.

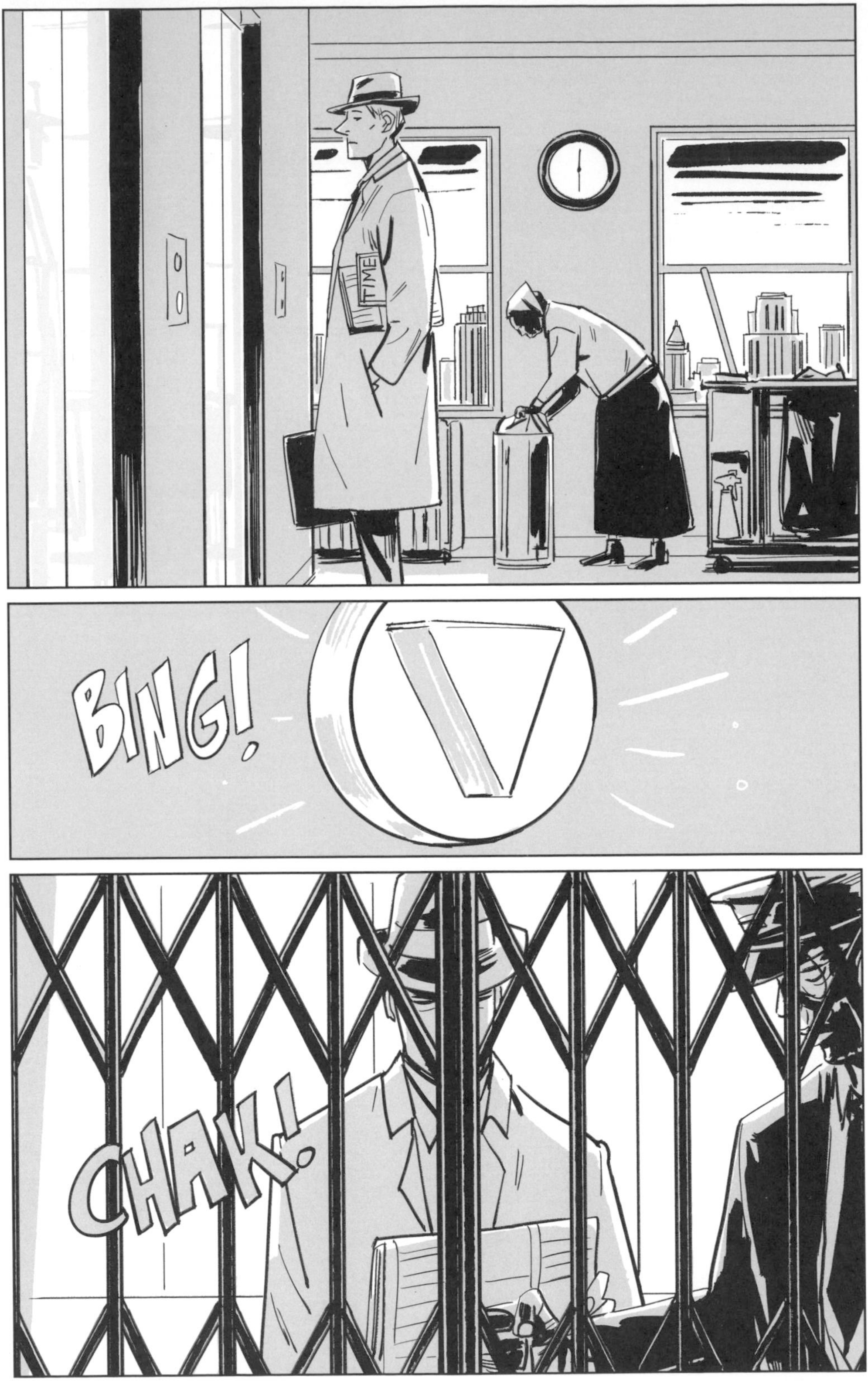
TIME
BING!
CHAK!

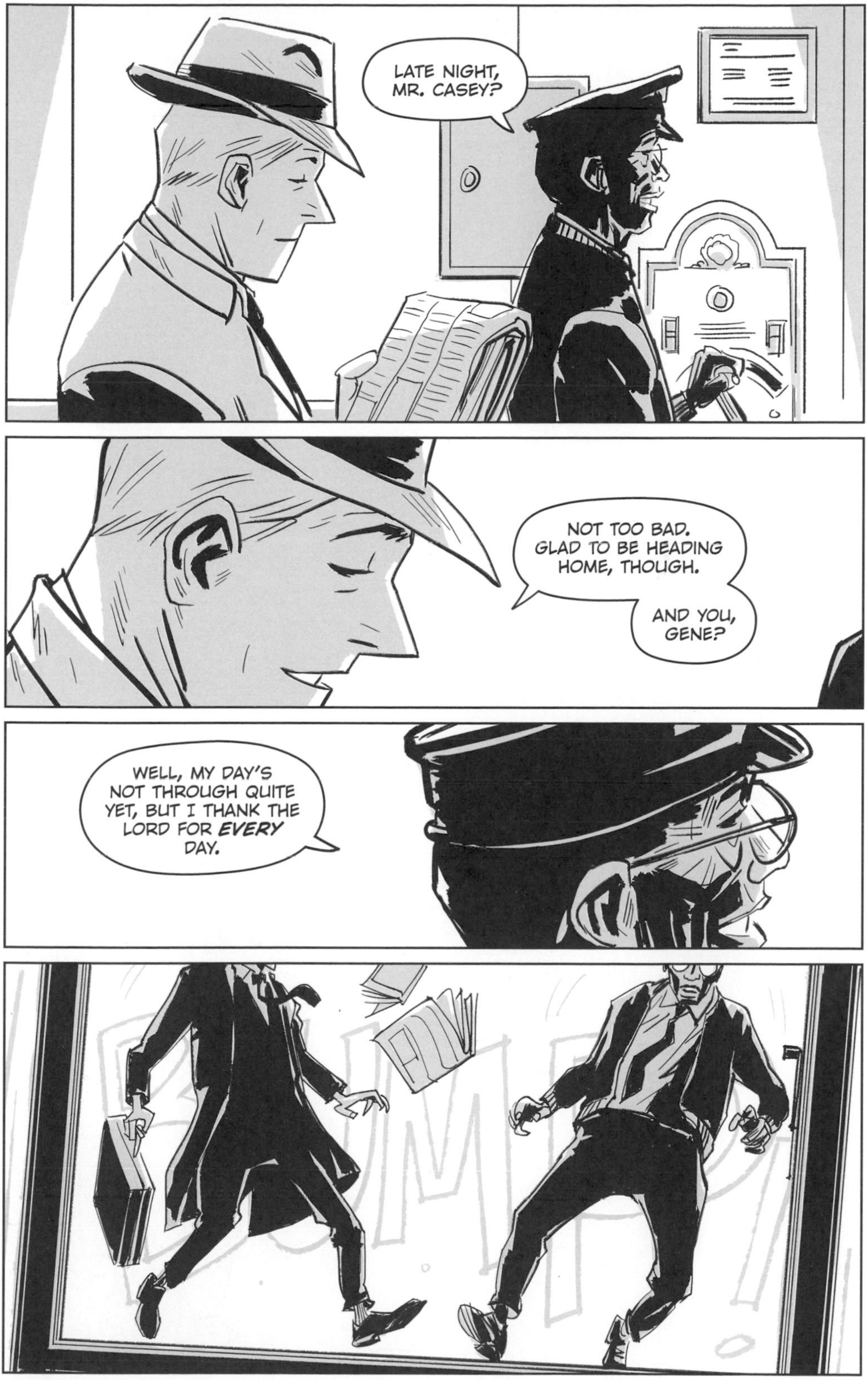
LATE NIGHT, MR. CASEY?
NOT TOO BAD. GLAD TO BE HEADING HOME, THOUGH.
AND YOU, GENE?
WELL, MY DAY'S NOT THROUGH QUITE YET, BUT I THANK THE LORD FOR ***EVERY*** DAY.
BUMP!

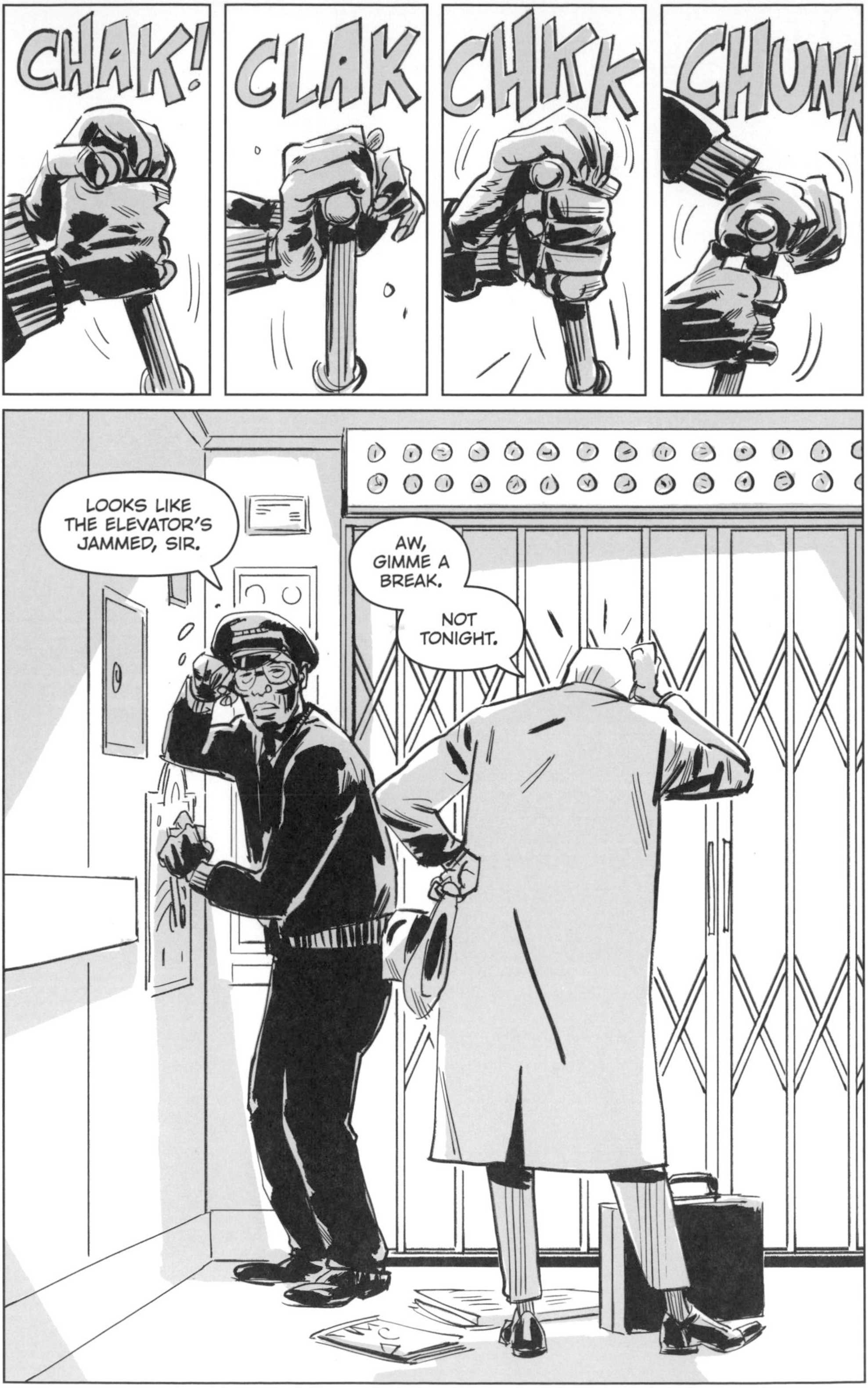
CHAK!
CLAK
CHKK
CHUNK
LOOKS LIKE THE ELEVATOR'S JAMMED, SIR.
AW, GIMME A BREAK.
NOT TONIGHT.

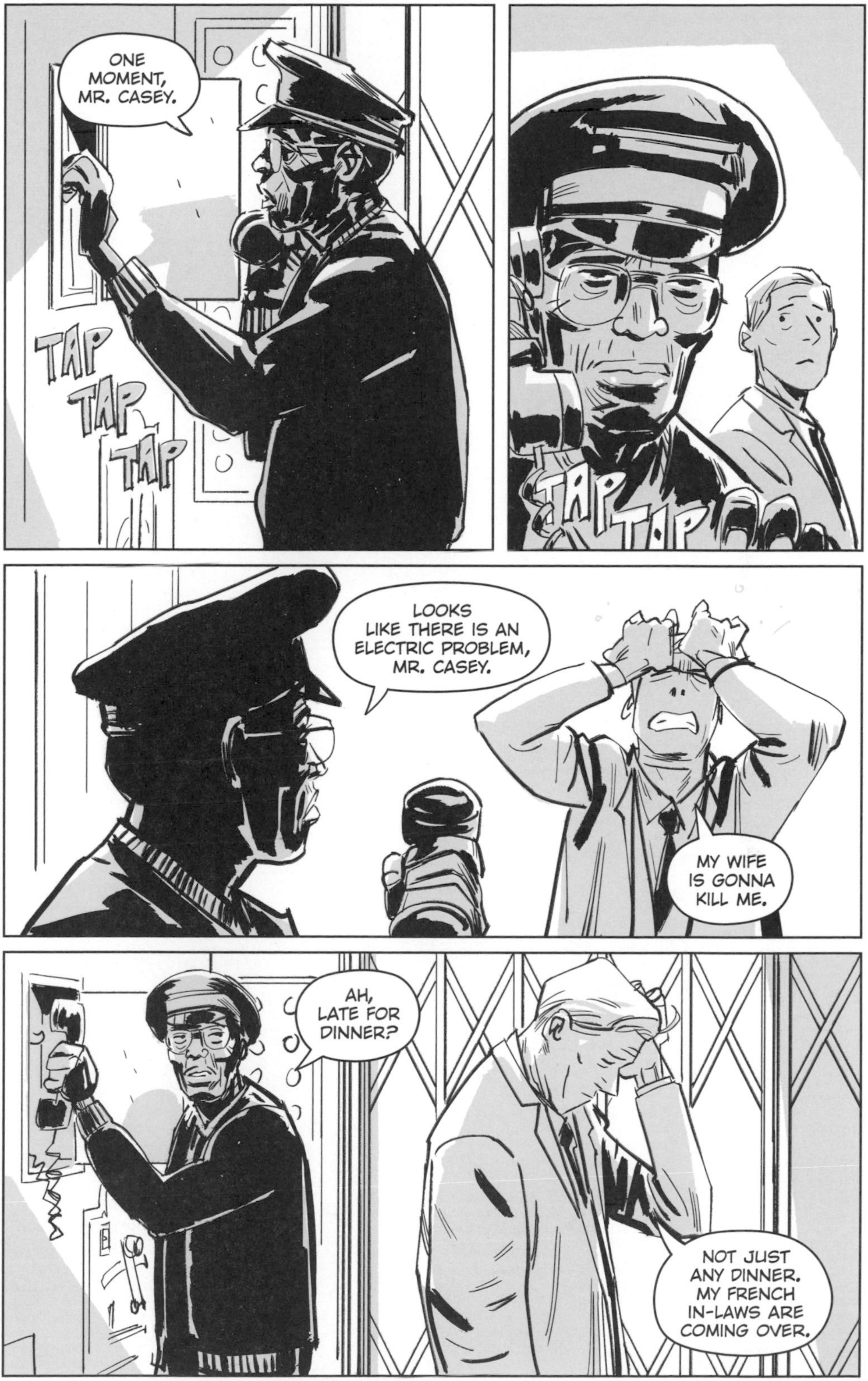
ONE MOMENT, MR. CASEY.
TAP TAP TAP
TAP TAP
LOOKS LIKE THERE IS AN ELECTRIC PROBLEM, MR. CASEY.
MY WIFE IS GONNA KILL ME.
AH, LATE FOR DINNER?
NOT JUST ANY DINNER. MY FRENCH IN-LAWS ARE COMING OVER.

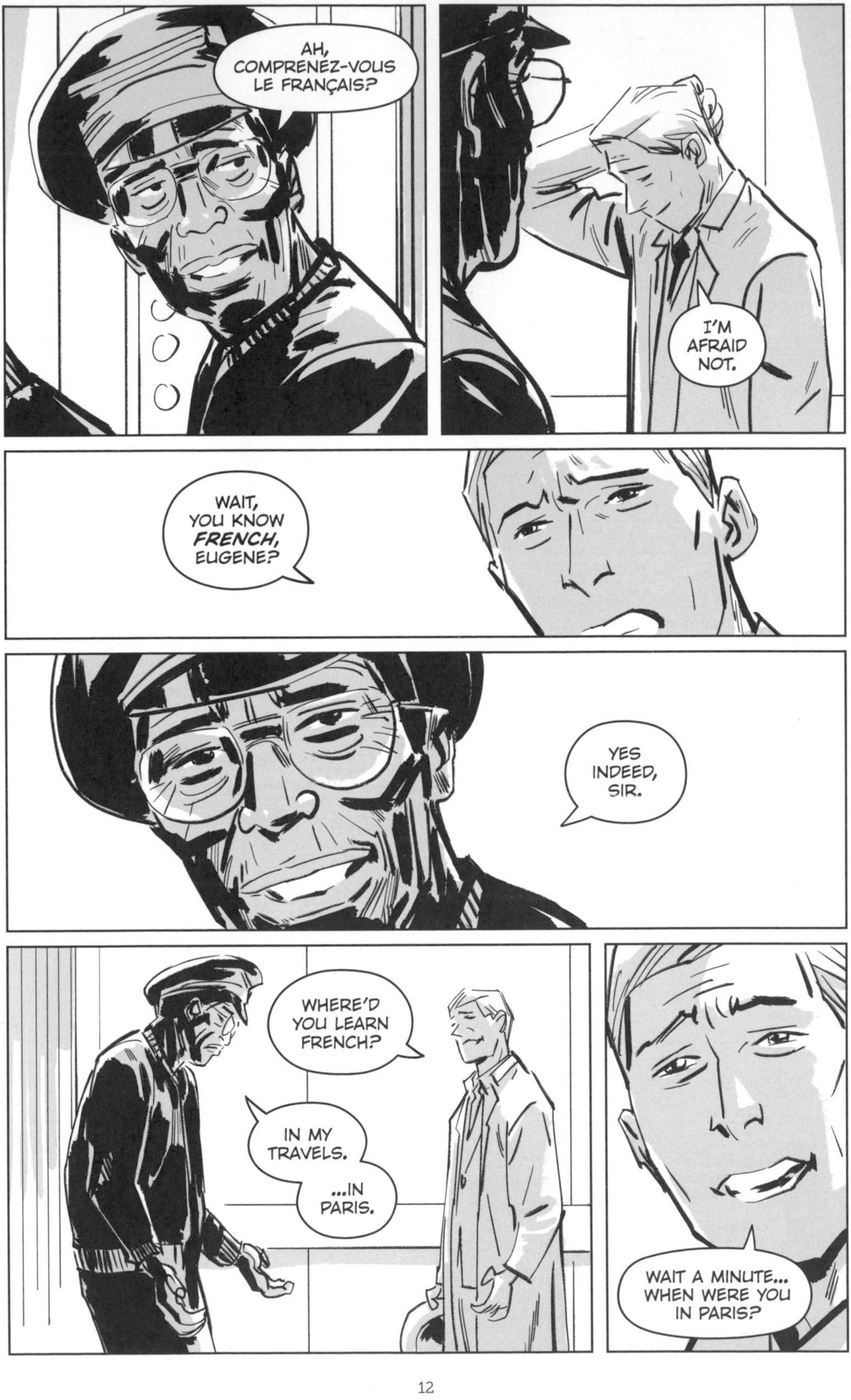
AH, COMPRENEZ-VOUS LE FRANÇAIS?
I'M AFRAID NOT.
WAIT, YOU KNOW *FRENCH*, EUGENE?
YES INDEED, SIR.
WHERE'D YOU LEARN FRENCH?
IN MY TRAVELS.
...IN PARIS.
WAIT A MINUTE... WHEN WERE YOU IN PARIS?

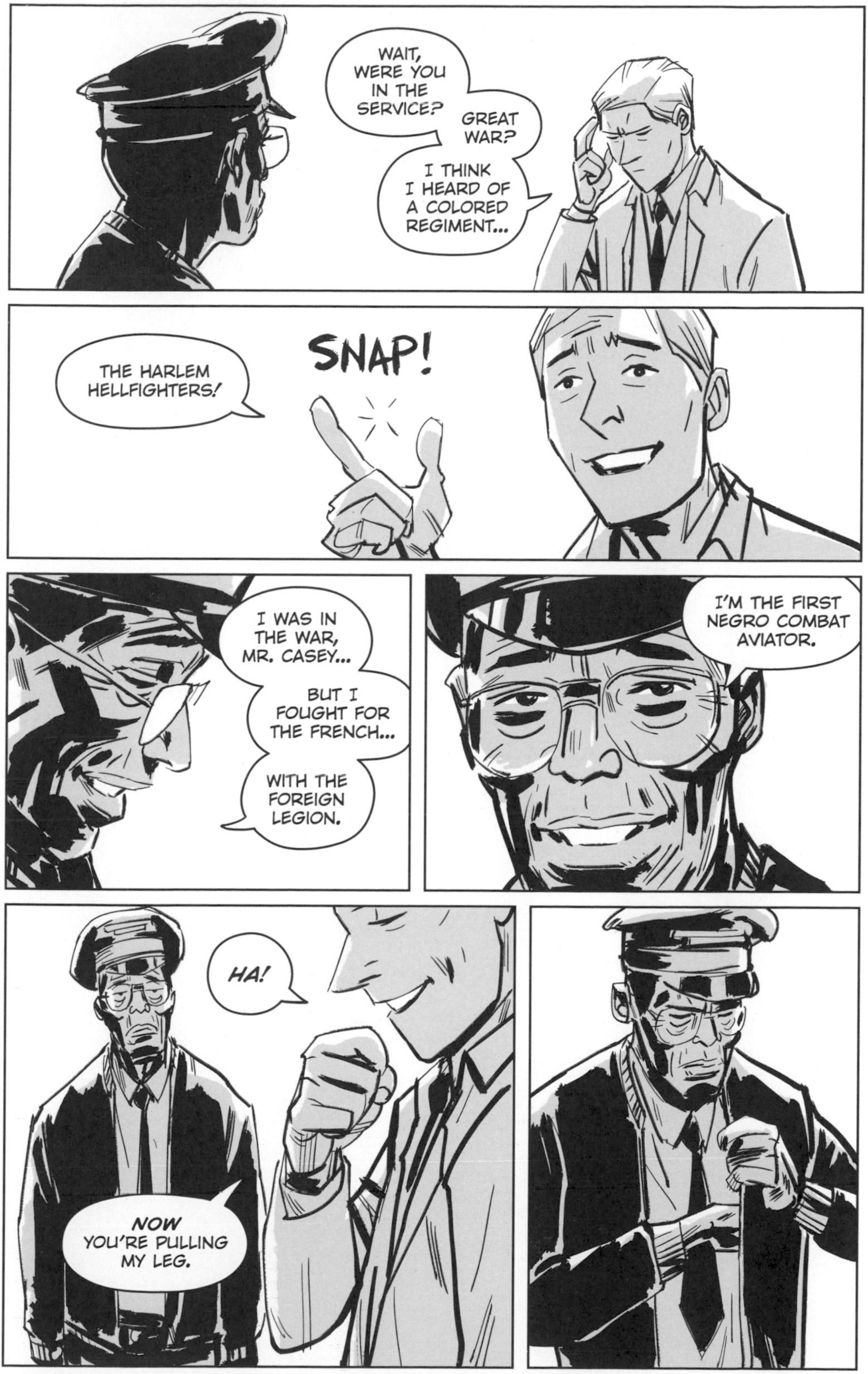
WAIT, WERE YOU IN THE SERVICE?
GREAT WAR?
I THINK I HEARD OF A COLORED REGIMENT...
THE HARLEM HELLFIGHTERS!
SNAP!
I WAS IN THE WAR, MR. CASEY...
BUT I FOUGHT FOR THE FRENCH...
WITH THE FOREIGN LEGION.
I'M THE FIRST NEGRO COMBAT AVIATOR.
HA!
NOW YOU'RE PULLING MY LEG.

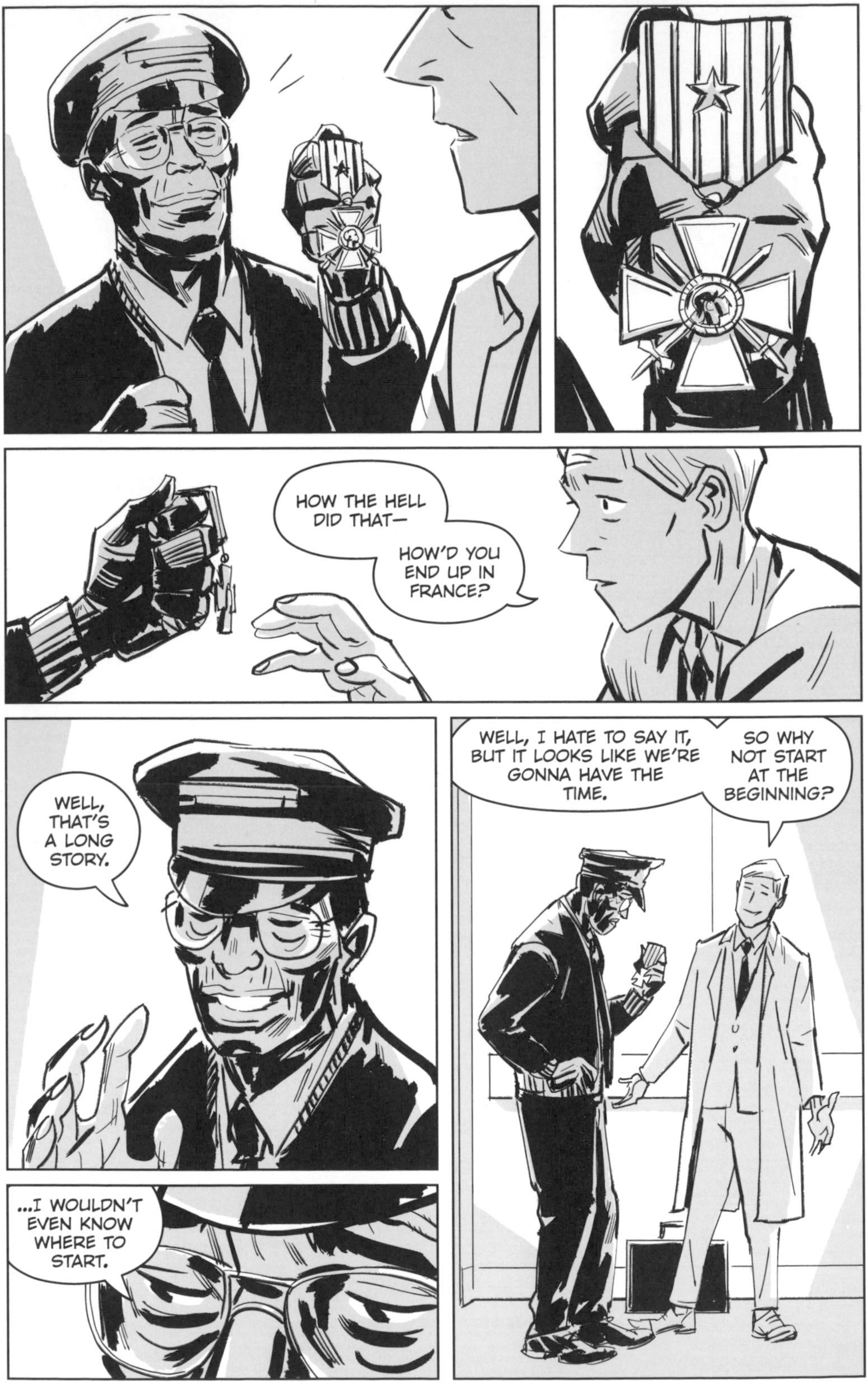
HOW THE HELL DID THAT—
HOW'D YOU END UP IN FRANCE?
WELL, THAT'S A LONG STORY.
...I WOULDN'T EVEN KNOW WHERE TO START.
WELL, I HATE TO SAY IT, BUT IT LOOKS LIKE WE'RE GONNA HAVE THE TIME.
SO WHY NOT START AT THE BEGINNING?

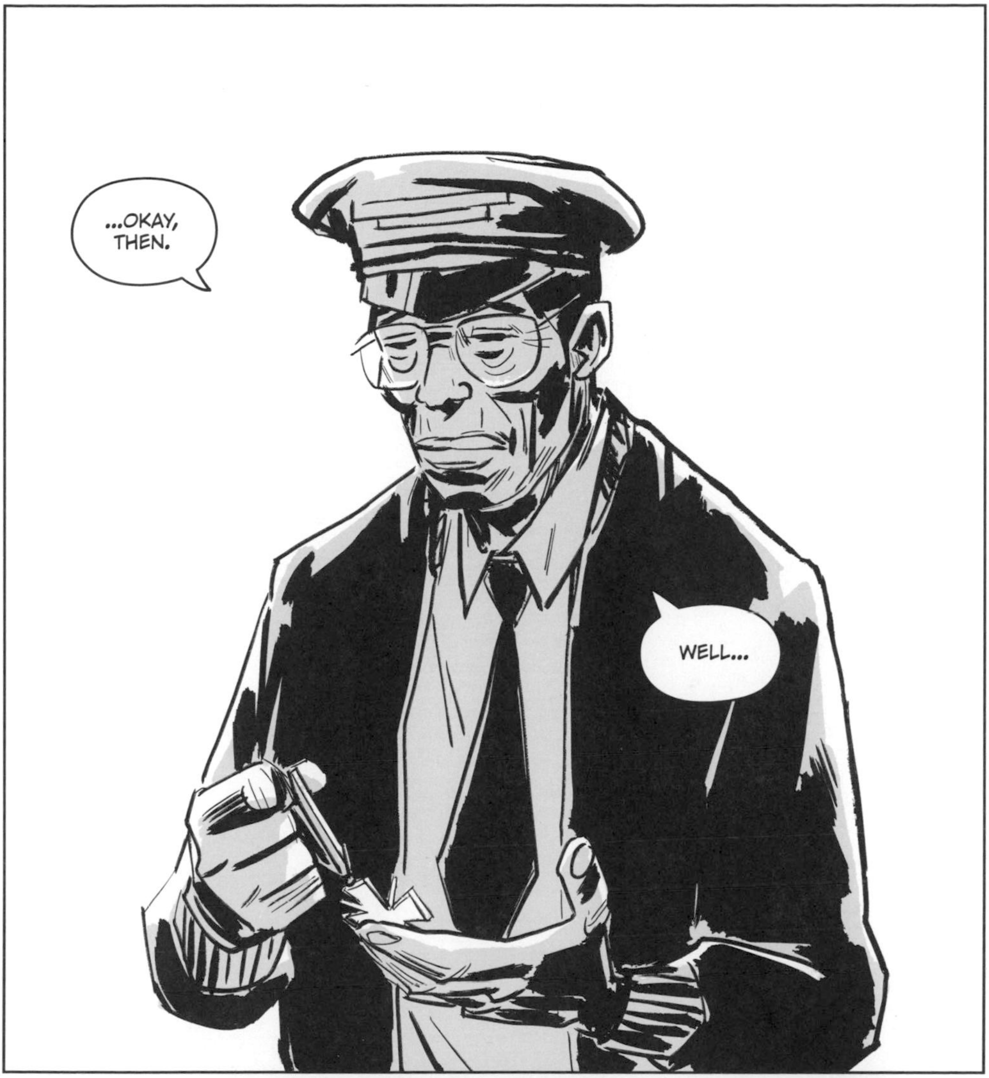
...OKAY, THEN.
WELL...

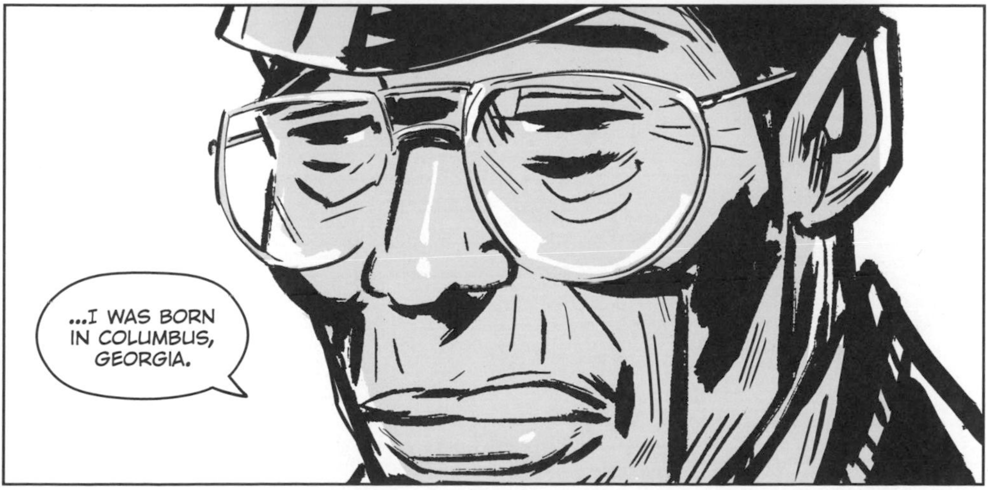
...I WAS BORN IN COLUMBUS, GEORGIA.

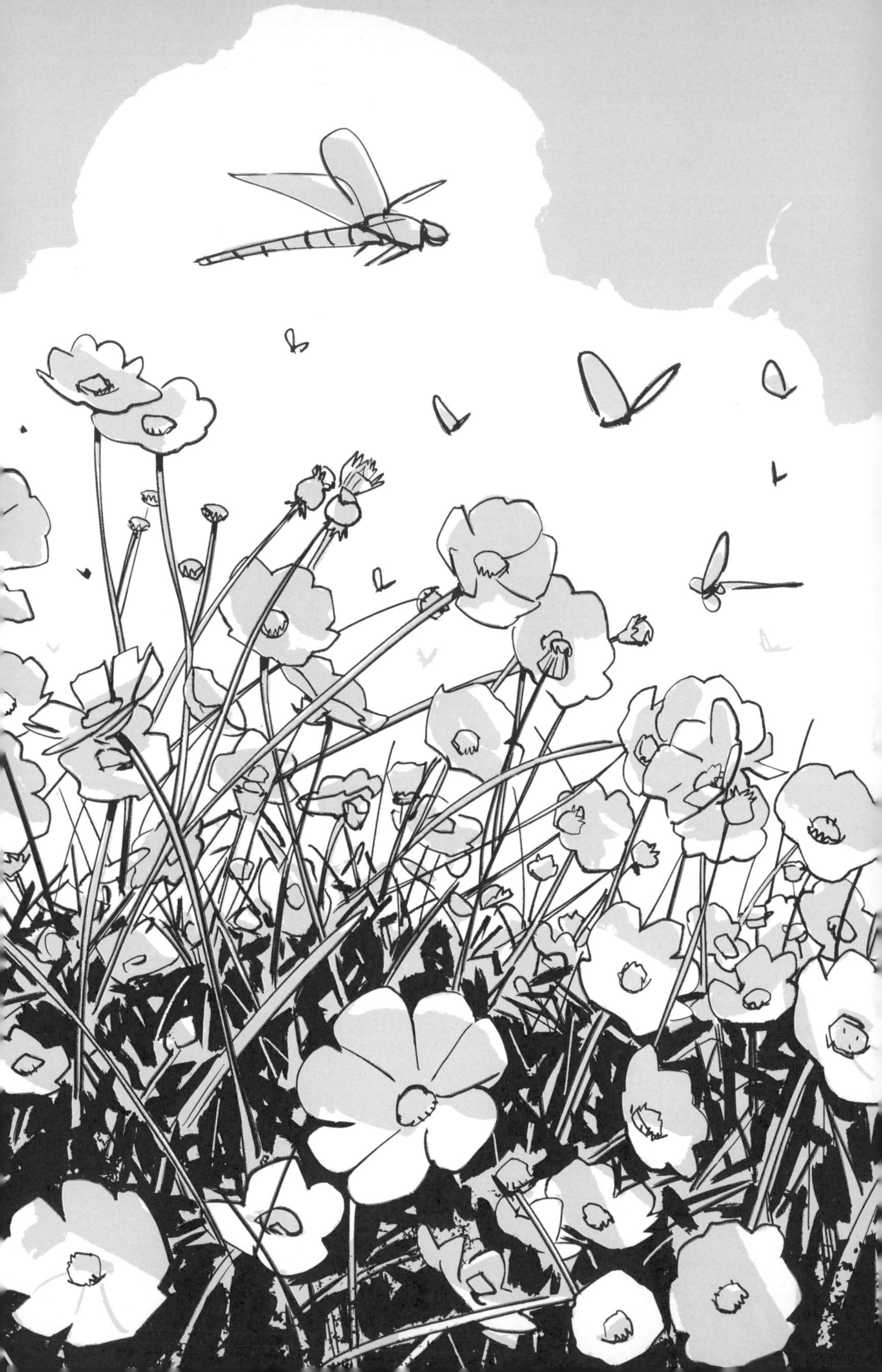

CHAPTER 1

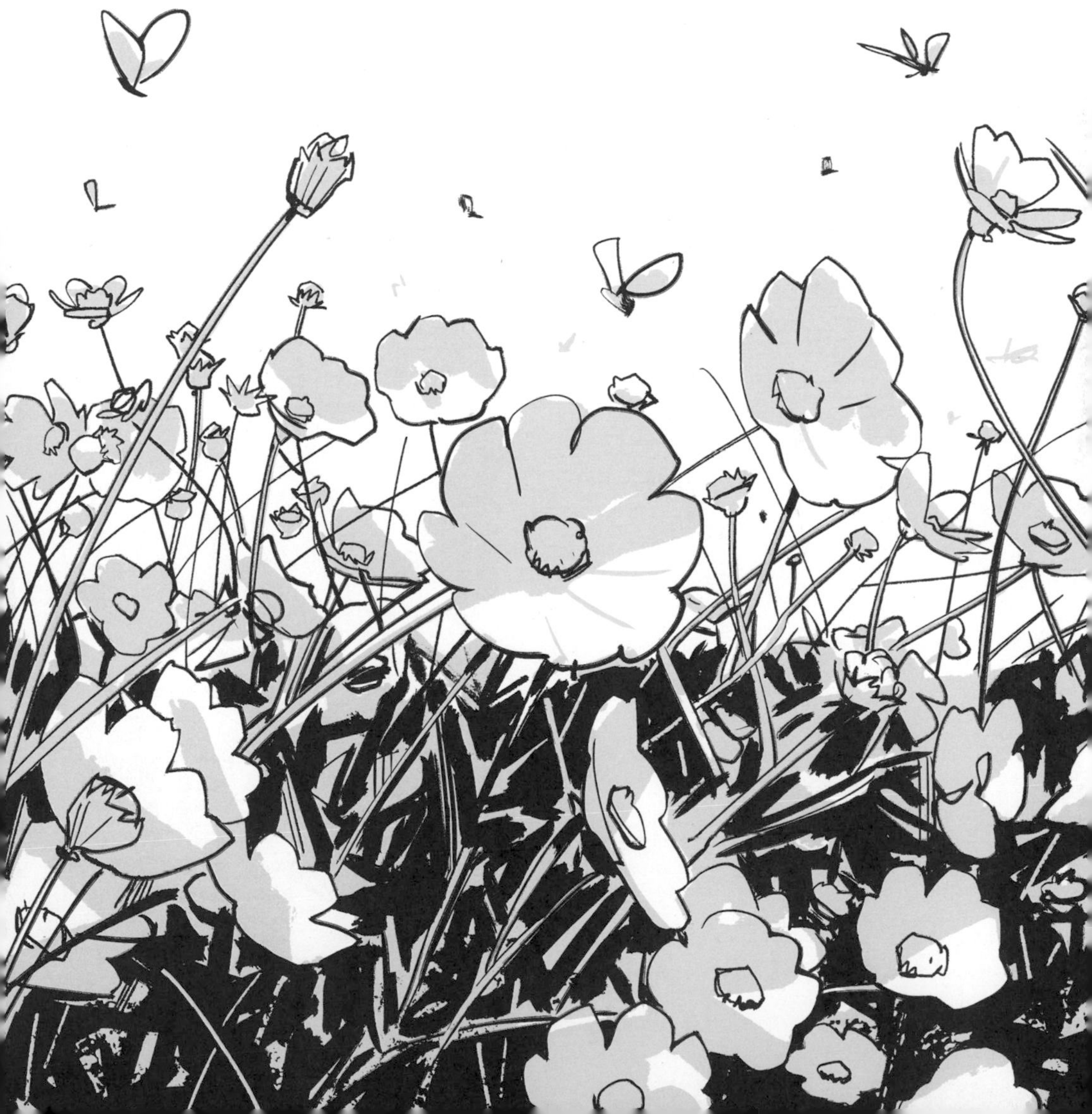

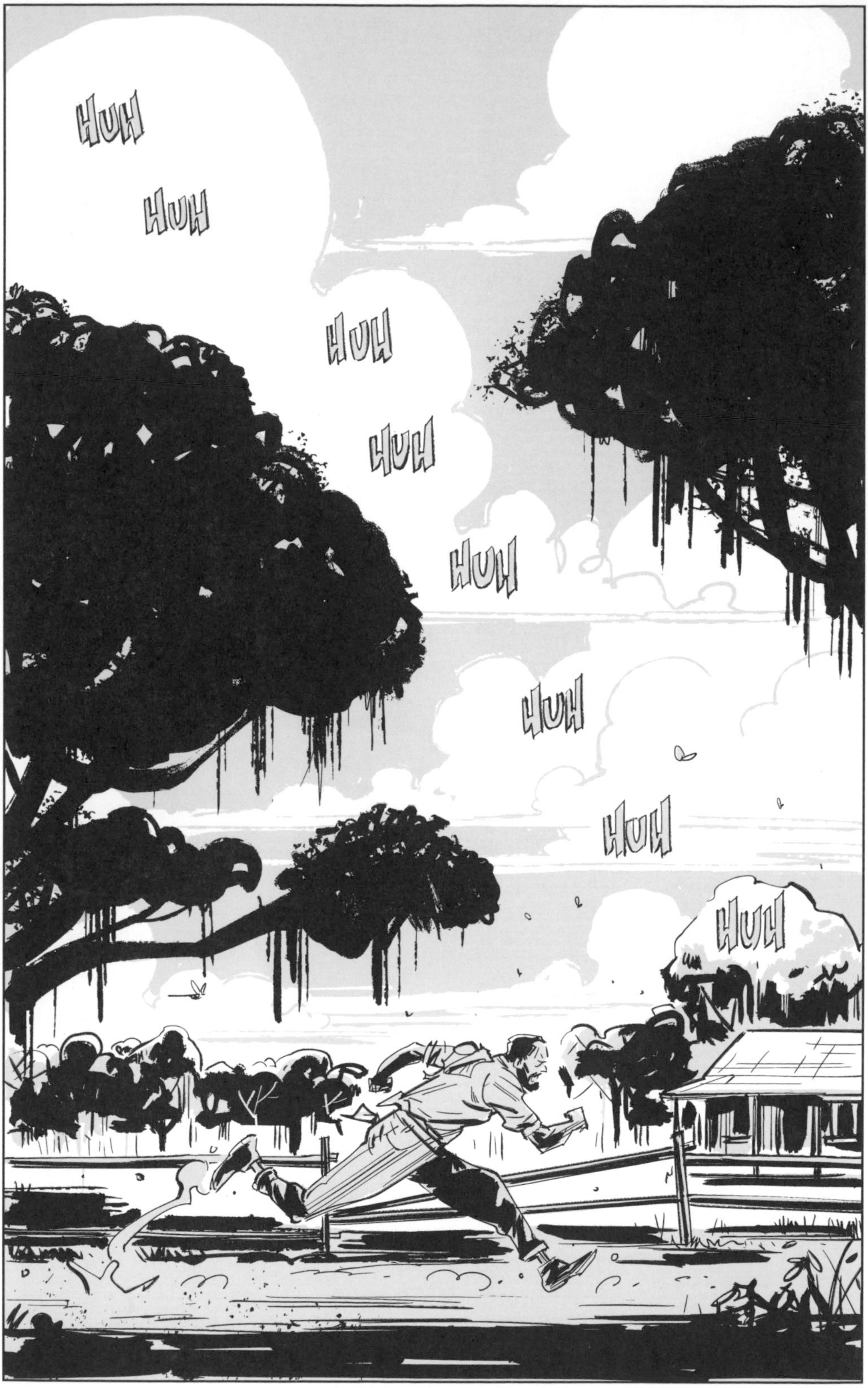
HUH
HUH
HUH
HUH
HUH
HUH
HUH
HUH

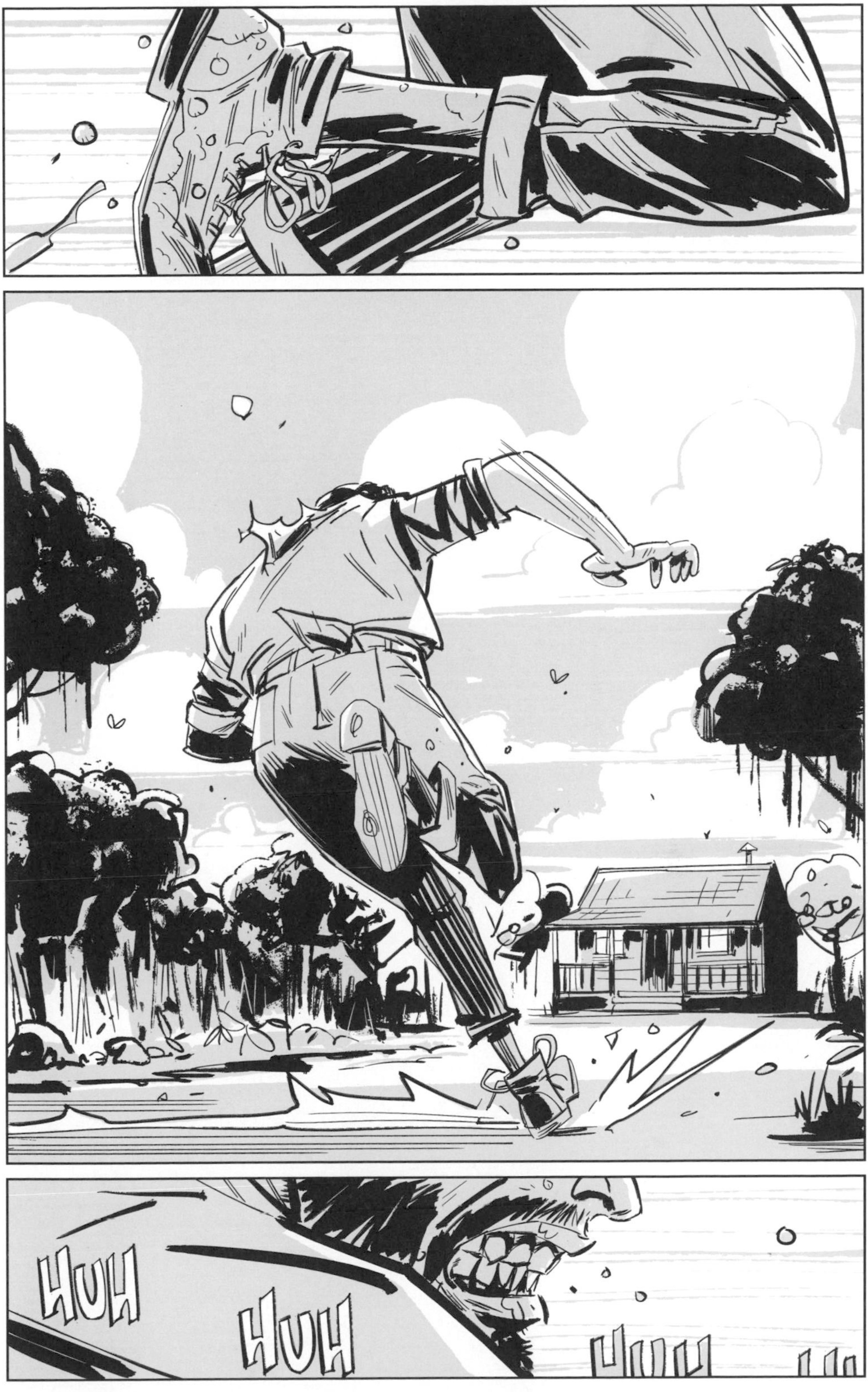
HUH
HUH

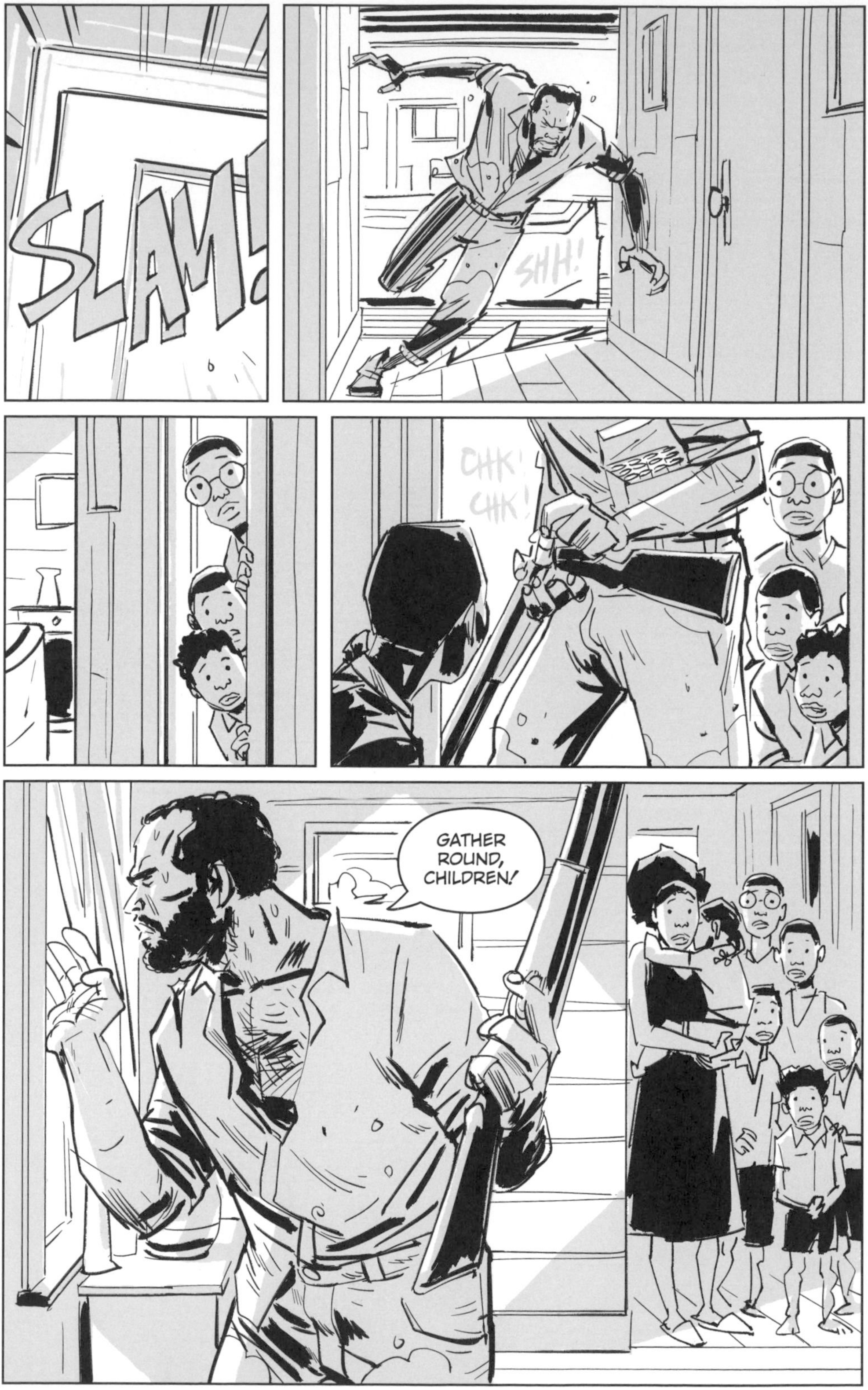
SLAM!
SHH!
CHK! CHK!
GATHER ROUND, CHILDREN!

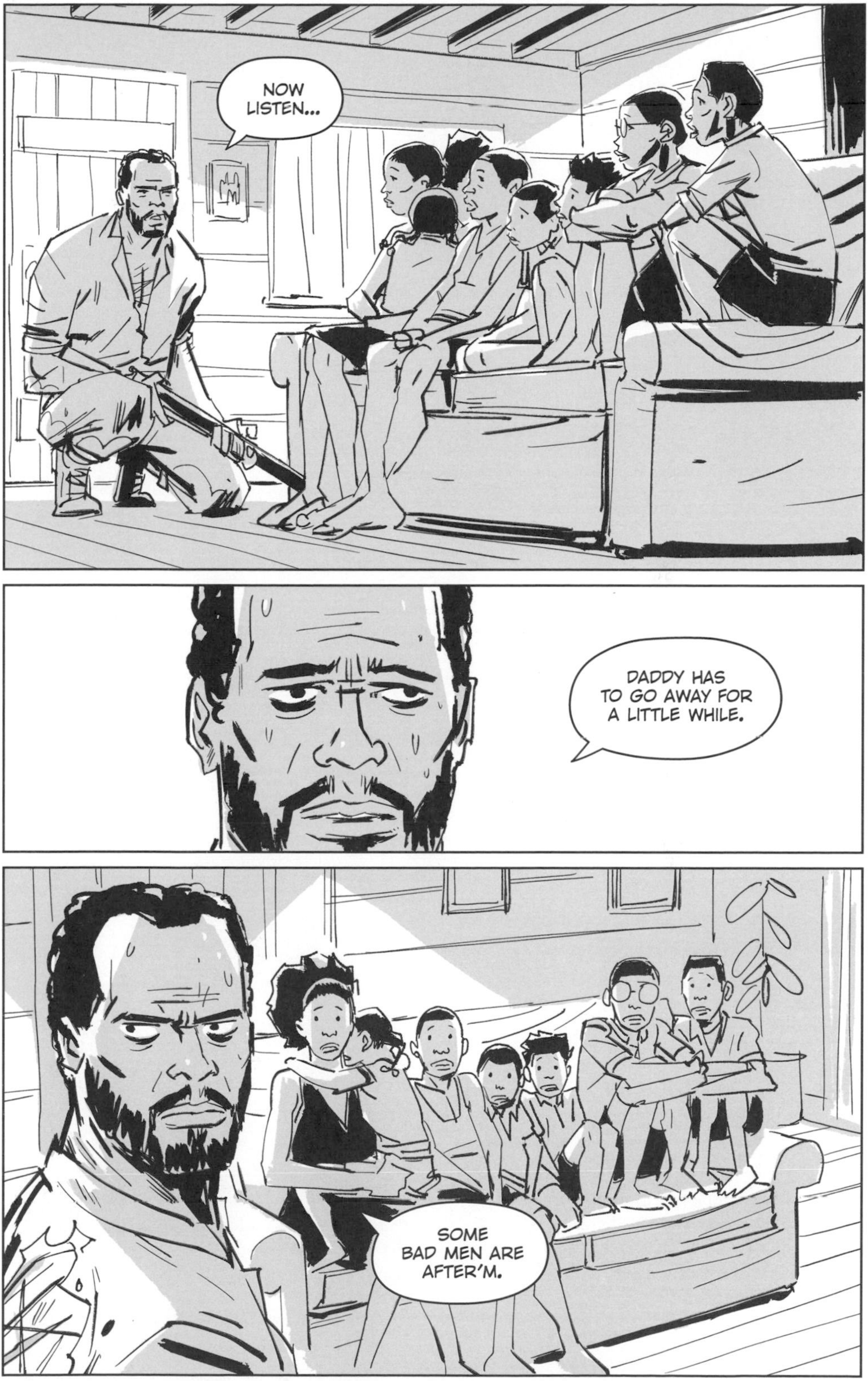
NOW LISTEN...
DADDY HAS TO GO AWAY FOR A LITTLE WHILE.
SOME BAD MEN ARE AFTER'M.

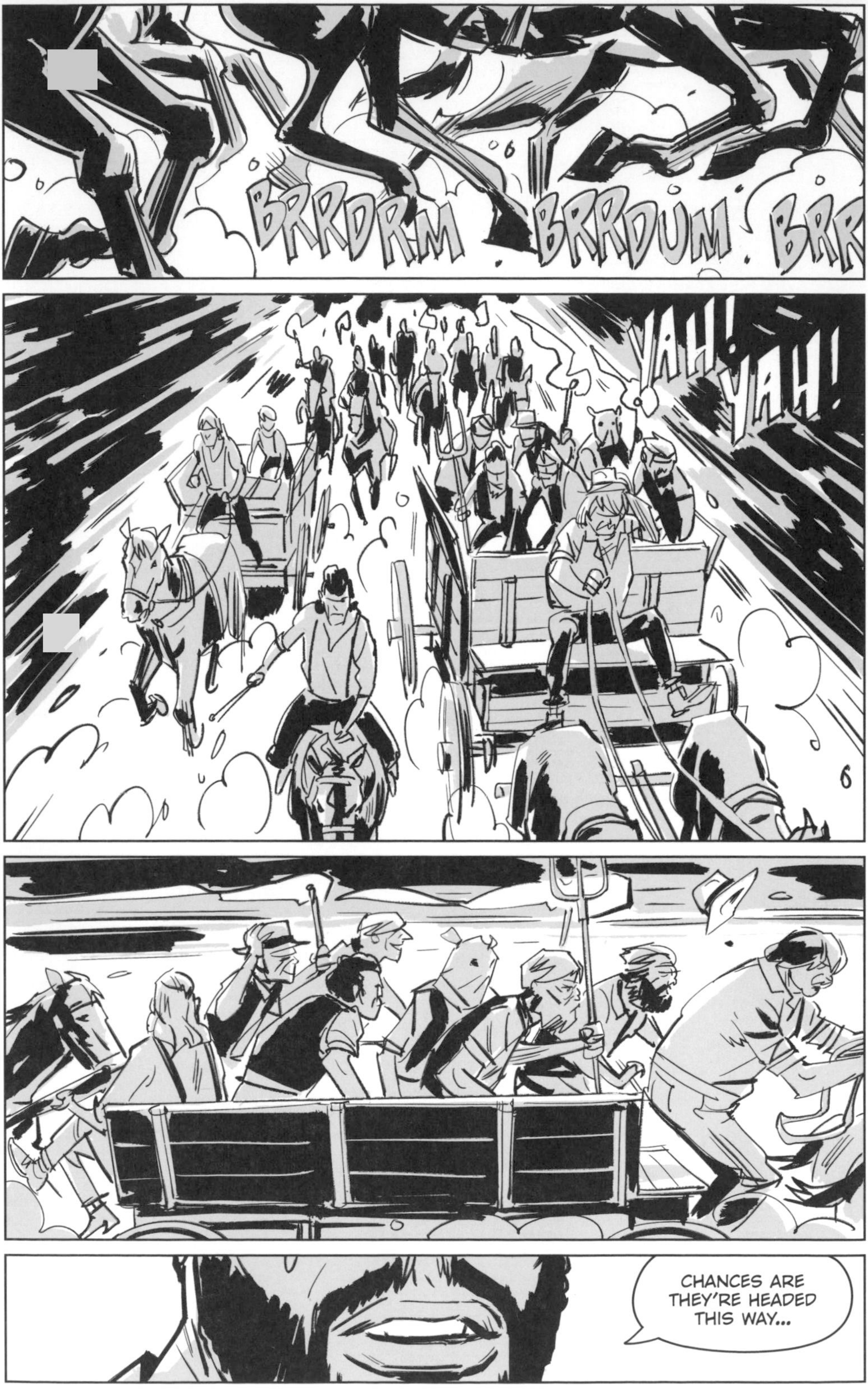
BRRDRM BRRDUM BRR
YAH! YAH!
CHANCES ARE THEY'RE HEADED THIS WAY...

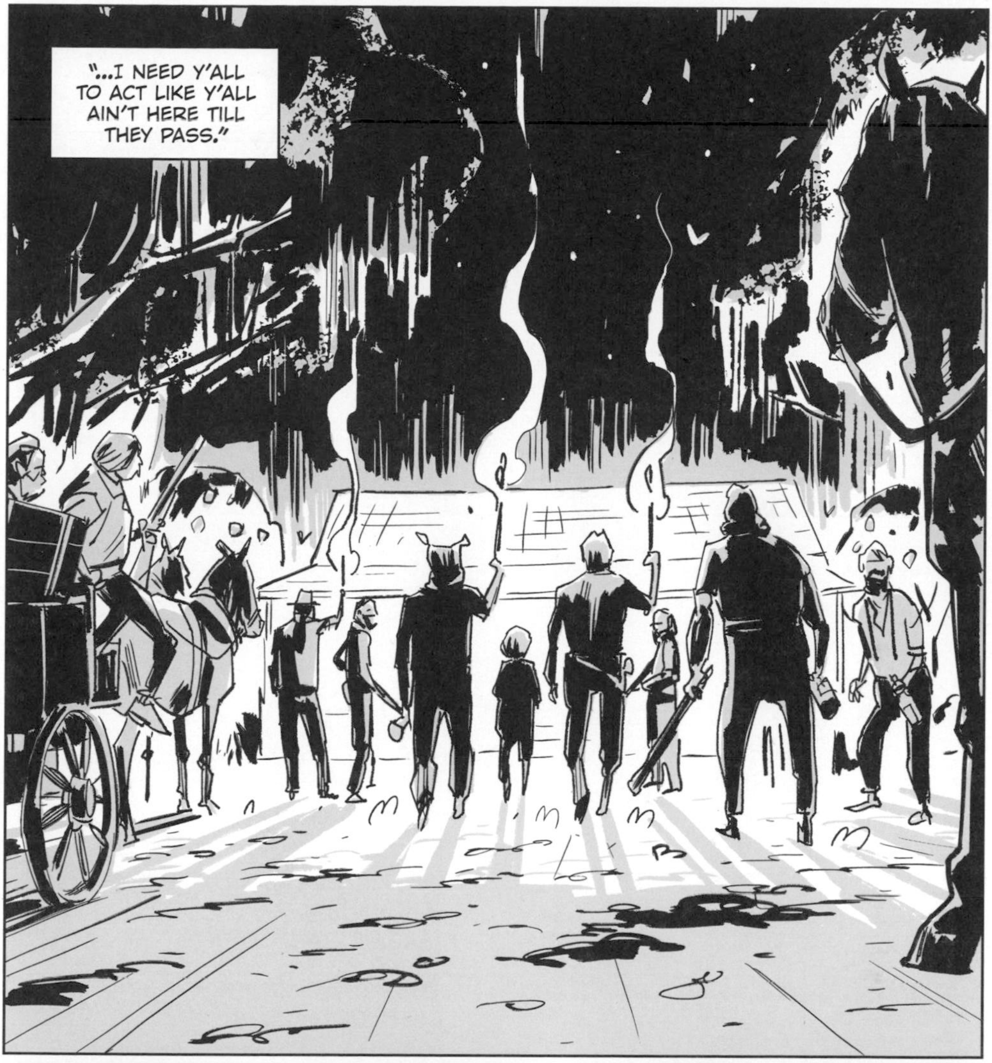
"...I NEED Y'ALL TO ACT LIKE Y'ALL AIN'T HERE TILL THEY PASS."

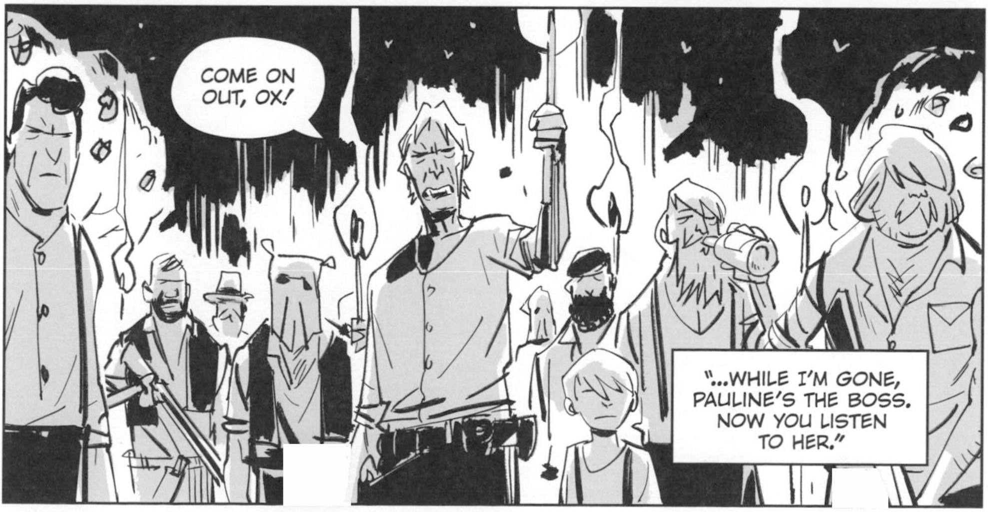
COME ON OUT, OX!
"...WHILE I'M GONE, PAULINE'S THE BOSS. NOW YOU LISTEN TO HER."

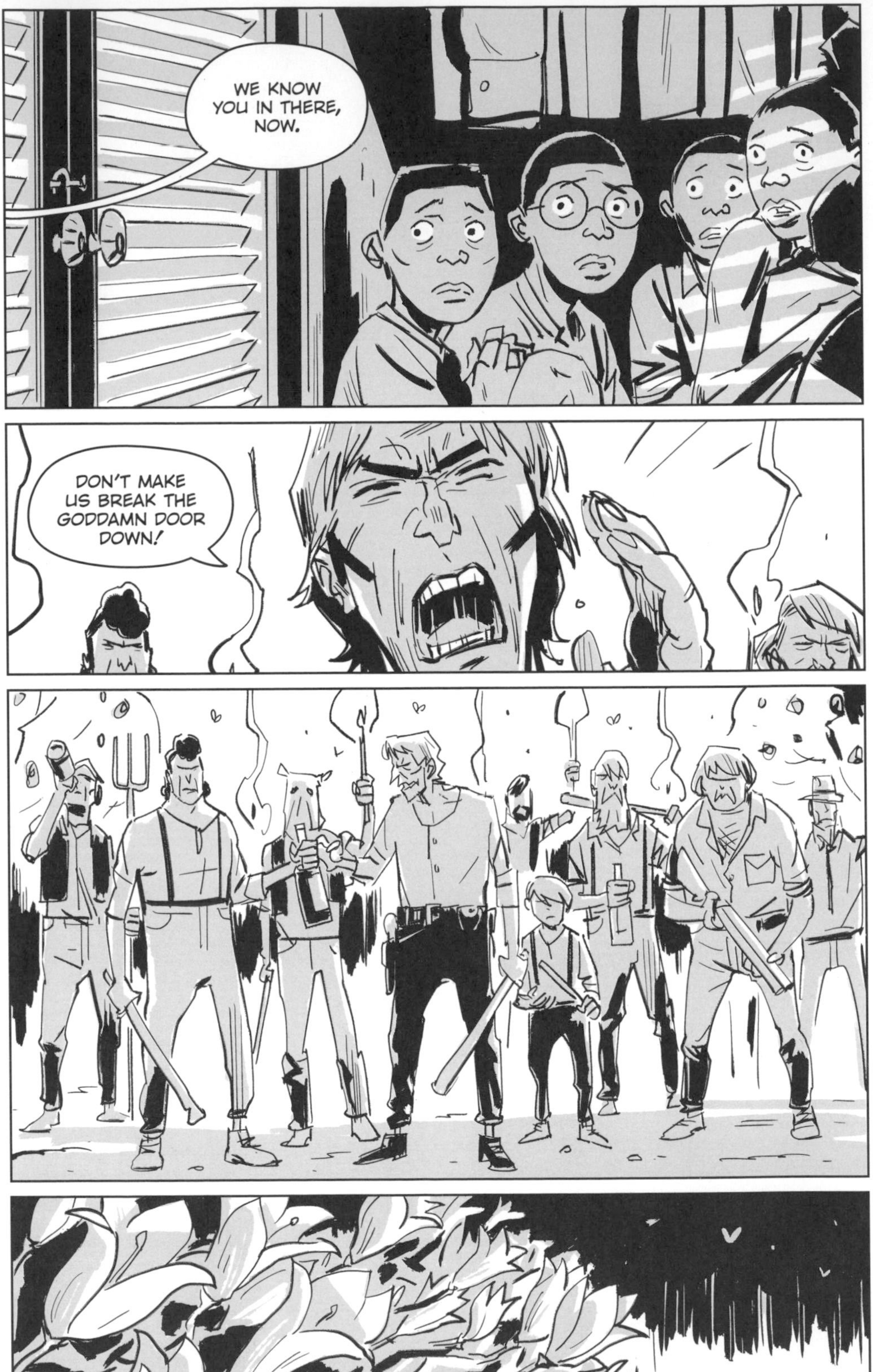
WE KNOW YOU IN THERE, NOW.
DON'T MAKE US BREAK THE GODDAMN DOOR DOWN!

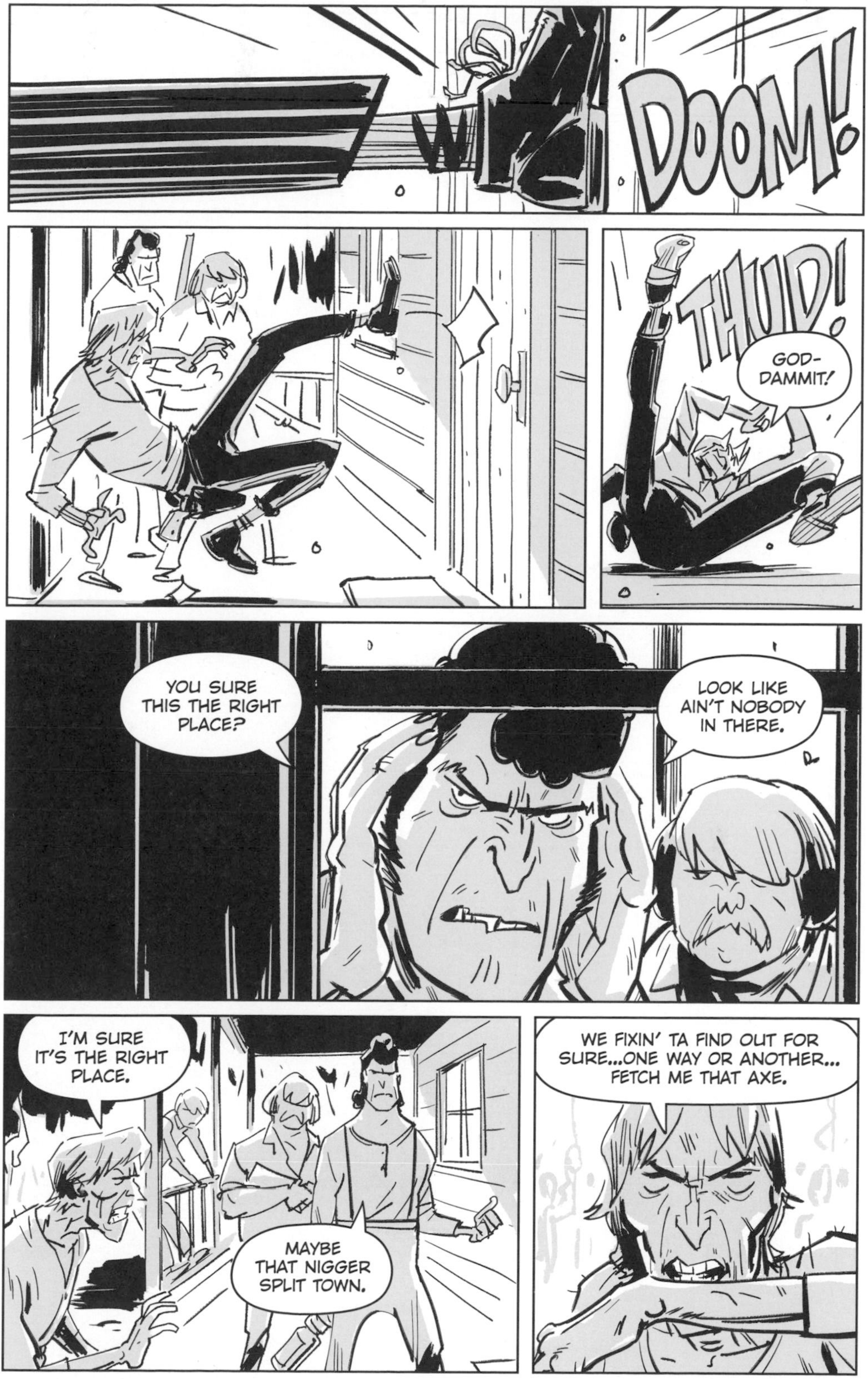
DOOM!
THUD!
GOD-DAMMIT!
YOU SURE THIS THE RIGHT PLACE?
LOOK LIKE AIN'T NOBODY IN THERE.
I'M SURE IT'S THE RIGHT PLACE.
MAYBE THAT NIGGER SPLIT TOWN.
WE FIXIN' TA FIND OUT FOR SURE...ONE WAY OR ANOTHER... FETCH ME THAT AXE.

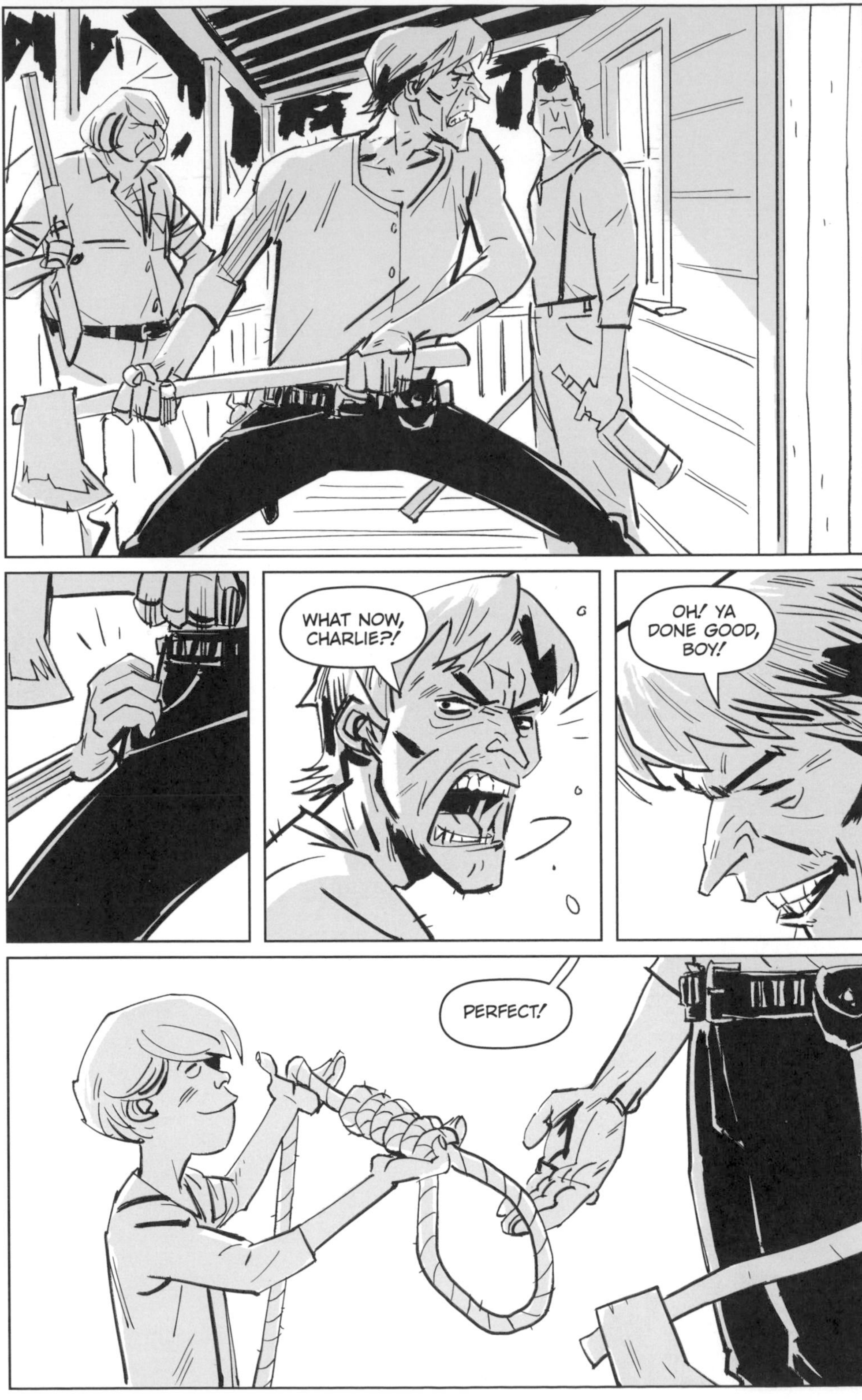
WHAT NOW, CHARLIE?!
OH! YA DONE GOOD, BOY!
PERFECT!

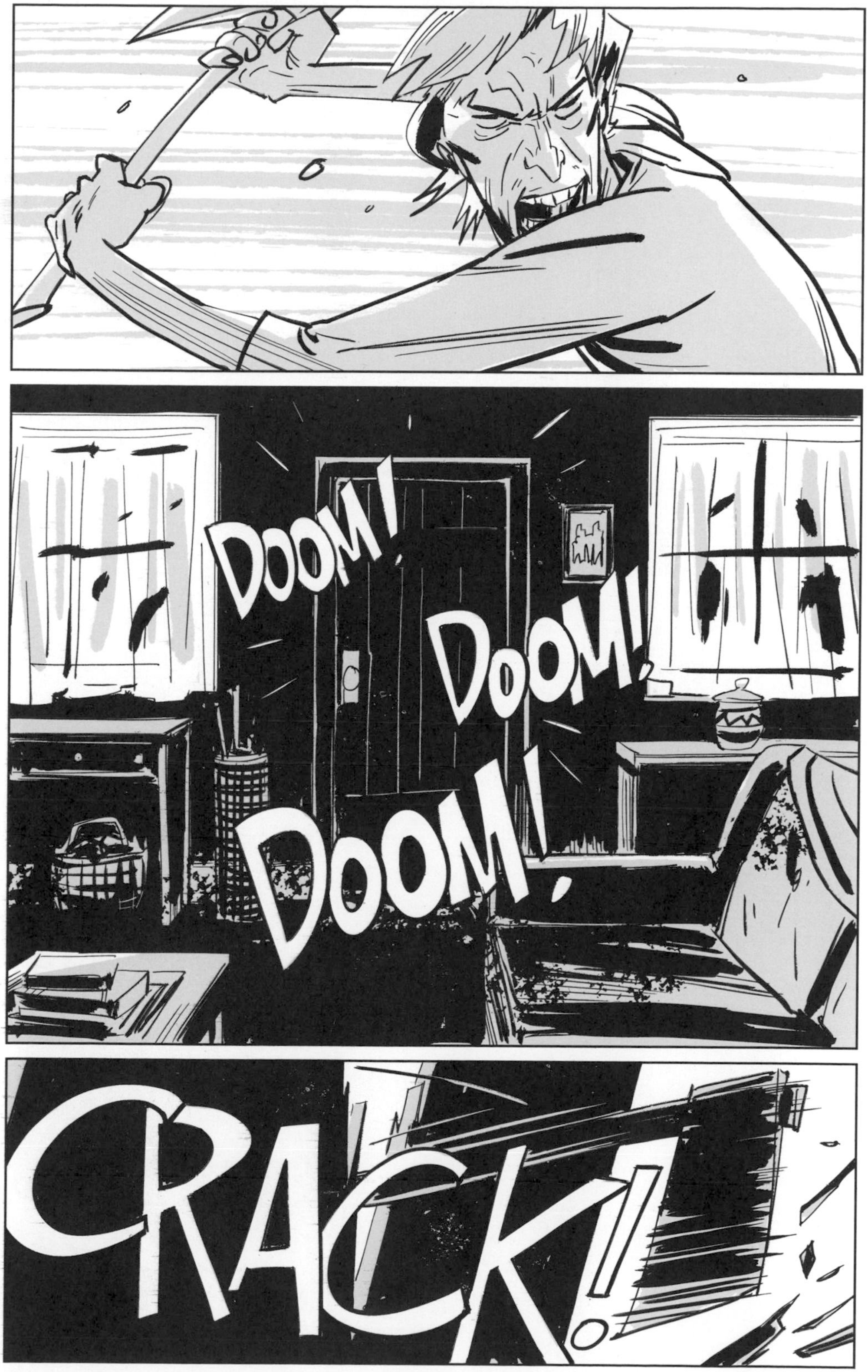
DOOM!
DOOM!
DOOM!
CRACK!

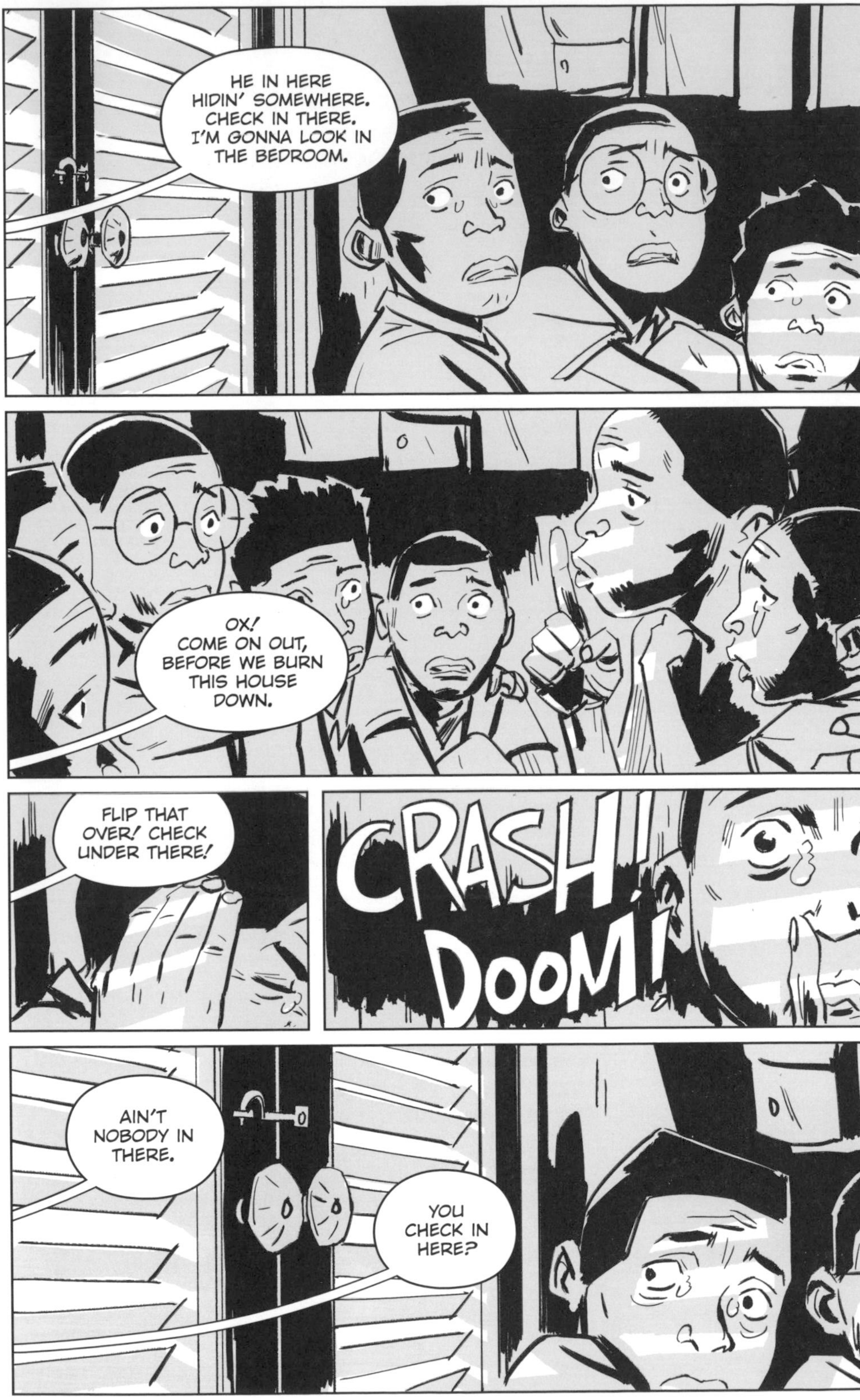
HE IN HERE HIDIN' SOMEWHERE. CHECK IN THERE. I'M GONNA LOOK IN THE BEDROOM.
OX! COME ON OUT, BEFORE WE BURN THIS HOUSE DOWN.
FLIP THAT OVER! CHECK UNDER THERE!
CRASH!
DOOM!
AIN'T NOBODY IN THERE.
YOU CHECK IN HERE?

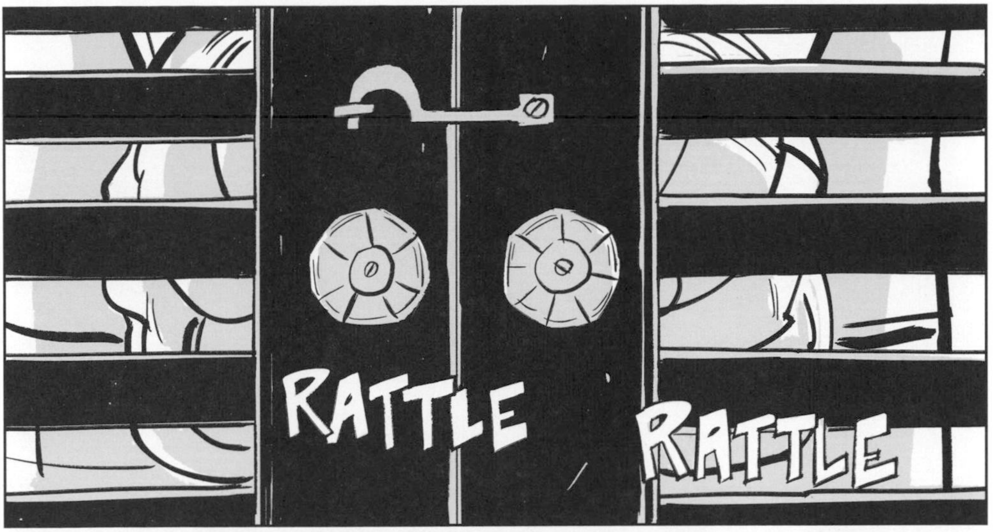
RATTLE
RATTLE

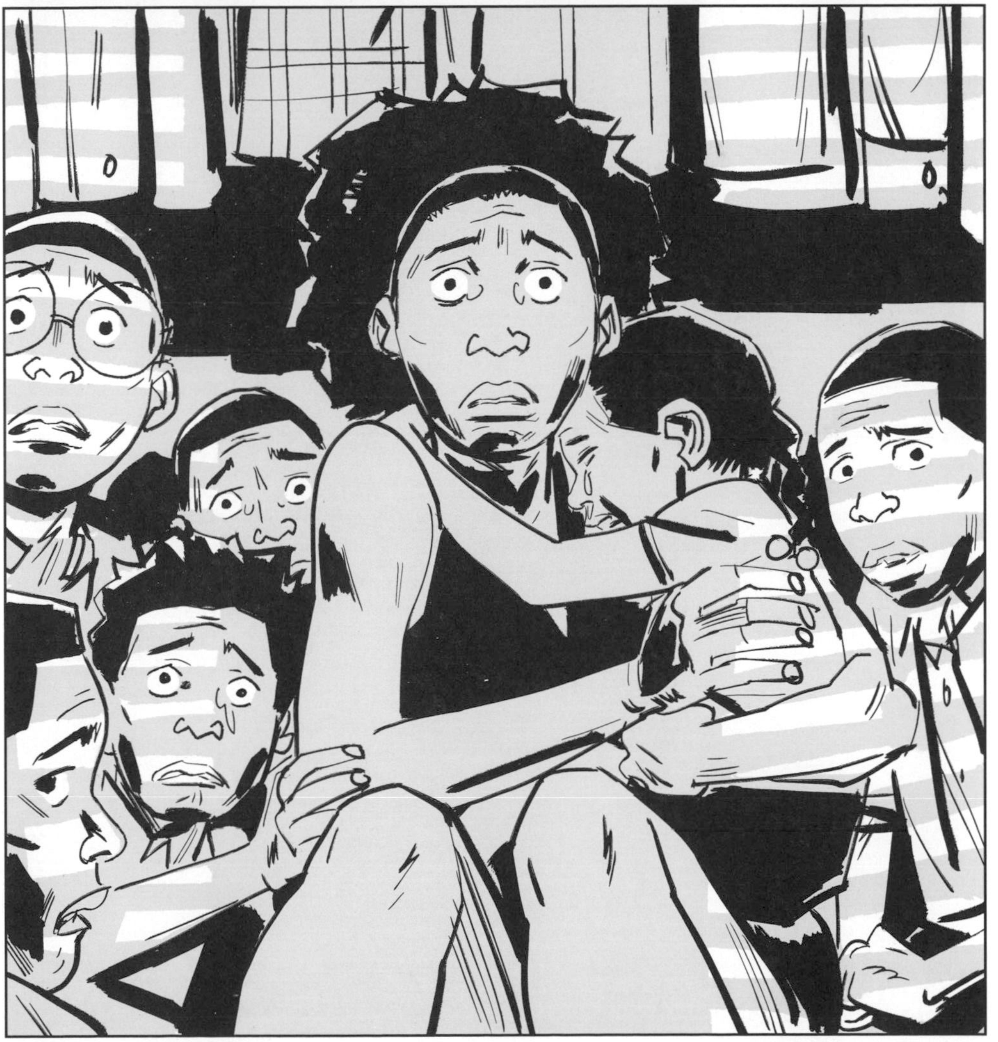

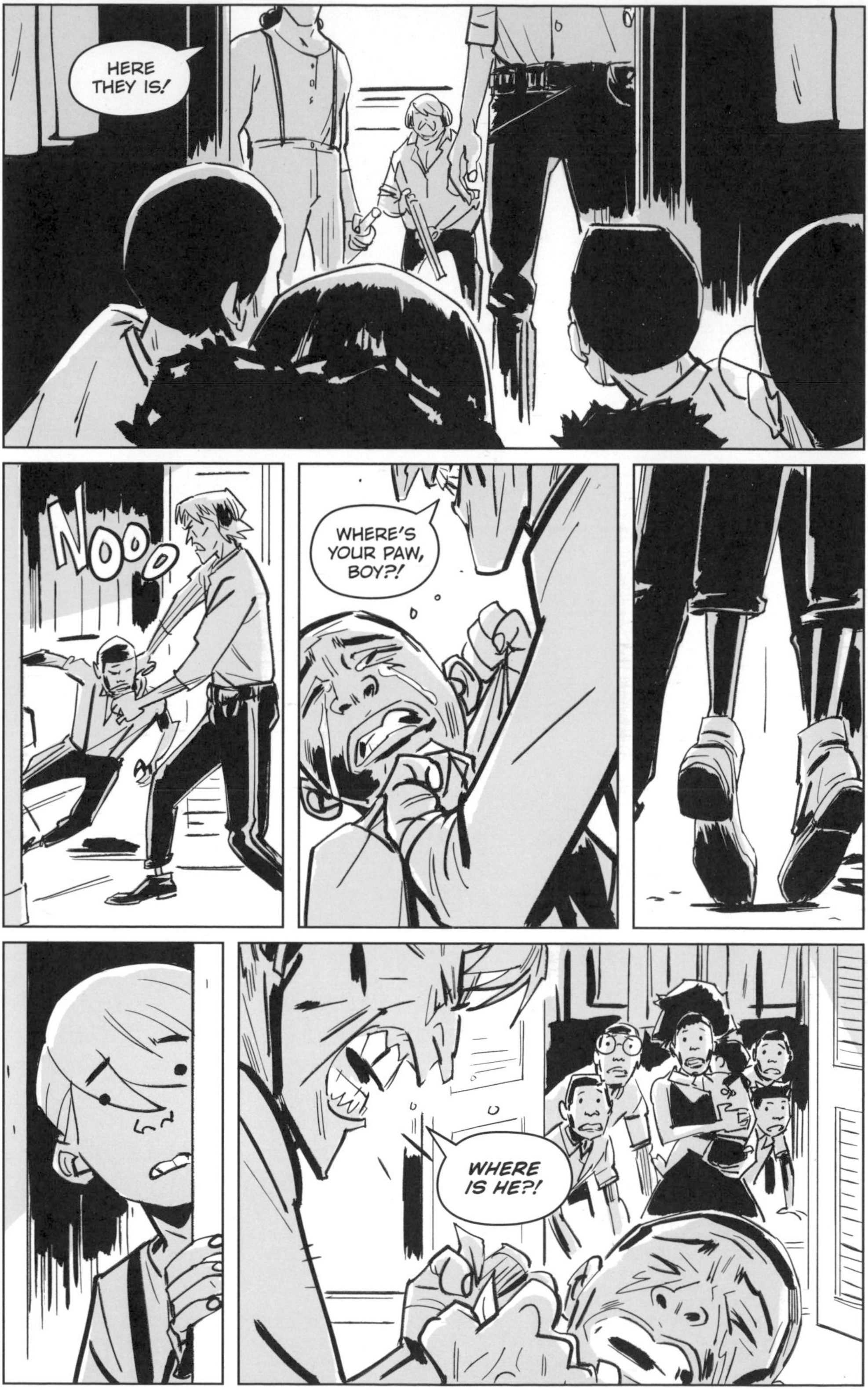
HERE THEY IS!
NOOO
WHERE'S YOUR PAW, BOY?!
WHERE IS HE?!

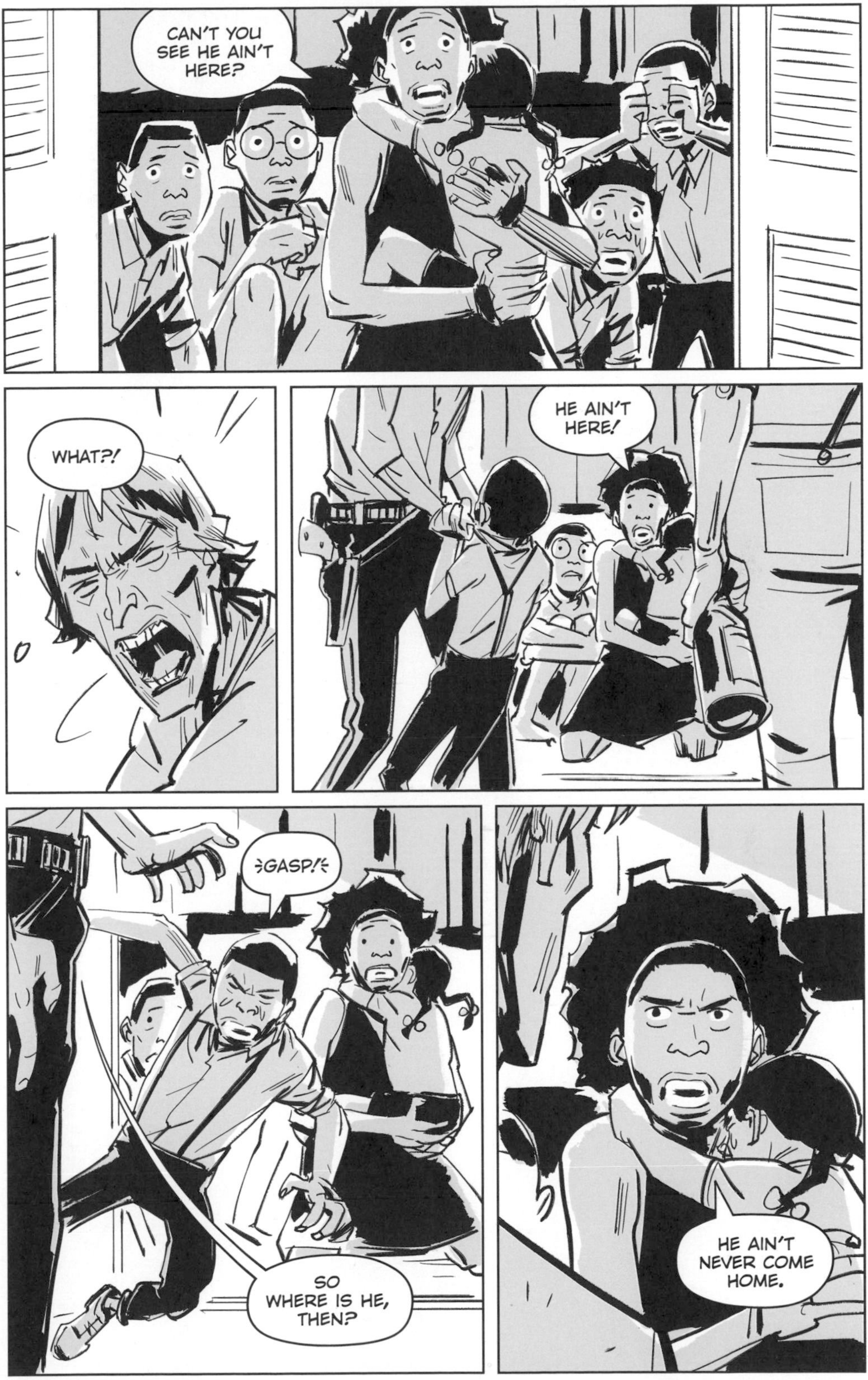
CAN'T YOU SEE HE AIN'T HERE?
WHAT?!
HE AIN'T HERE!
GASP!
SO WHERE IS HE, THEN?
HE AIN'T NEVER COME HOME.

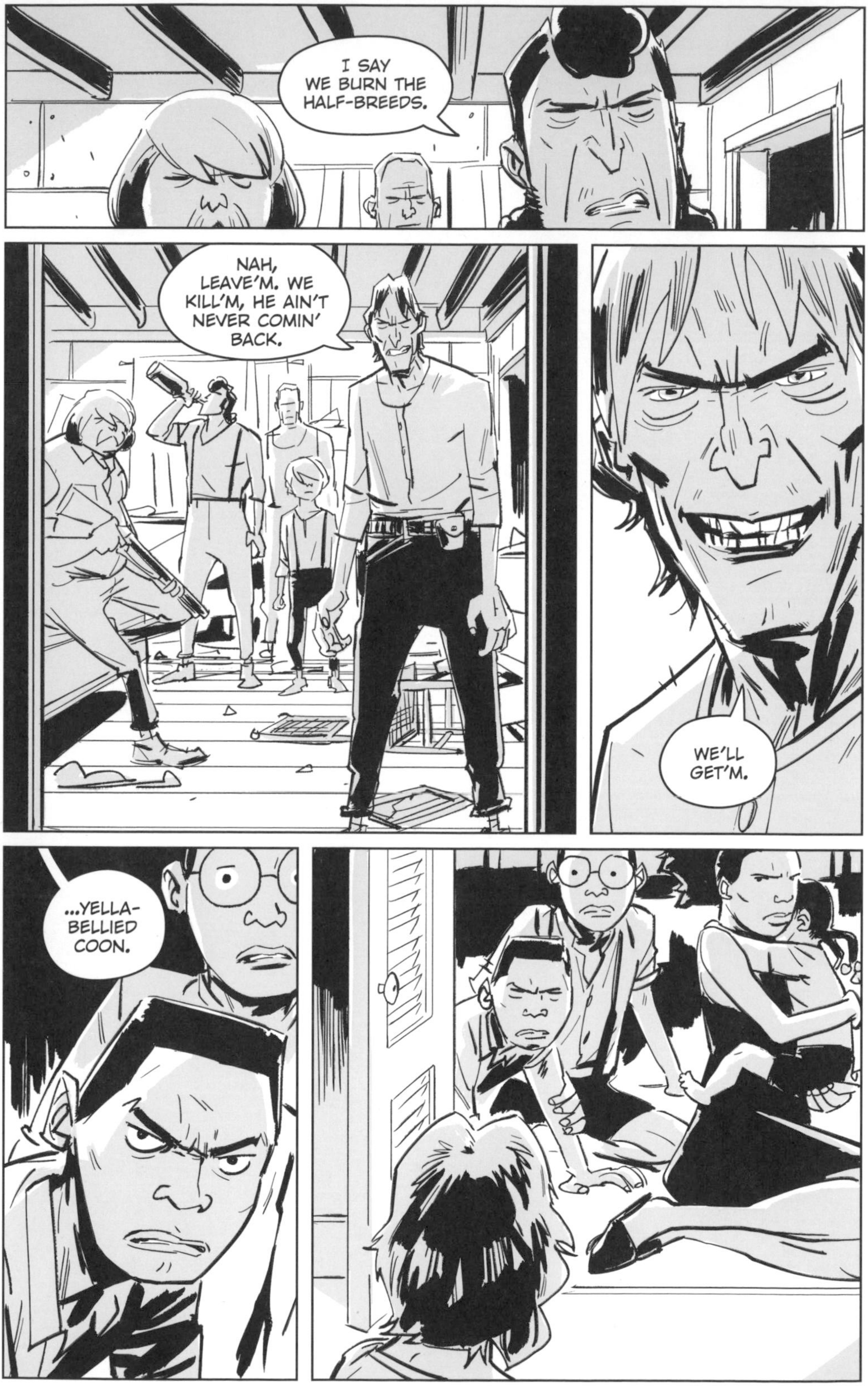
I SAY WE BURN THE HALF-BREEDS.
NAH, LEAVE'M. WE KILL'M, HE AIN'T NEVER COMIN' BACK.
WE'LL GET'M.
...YELLA-BELLIED COON.

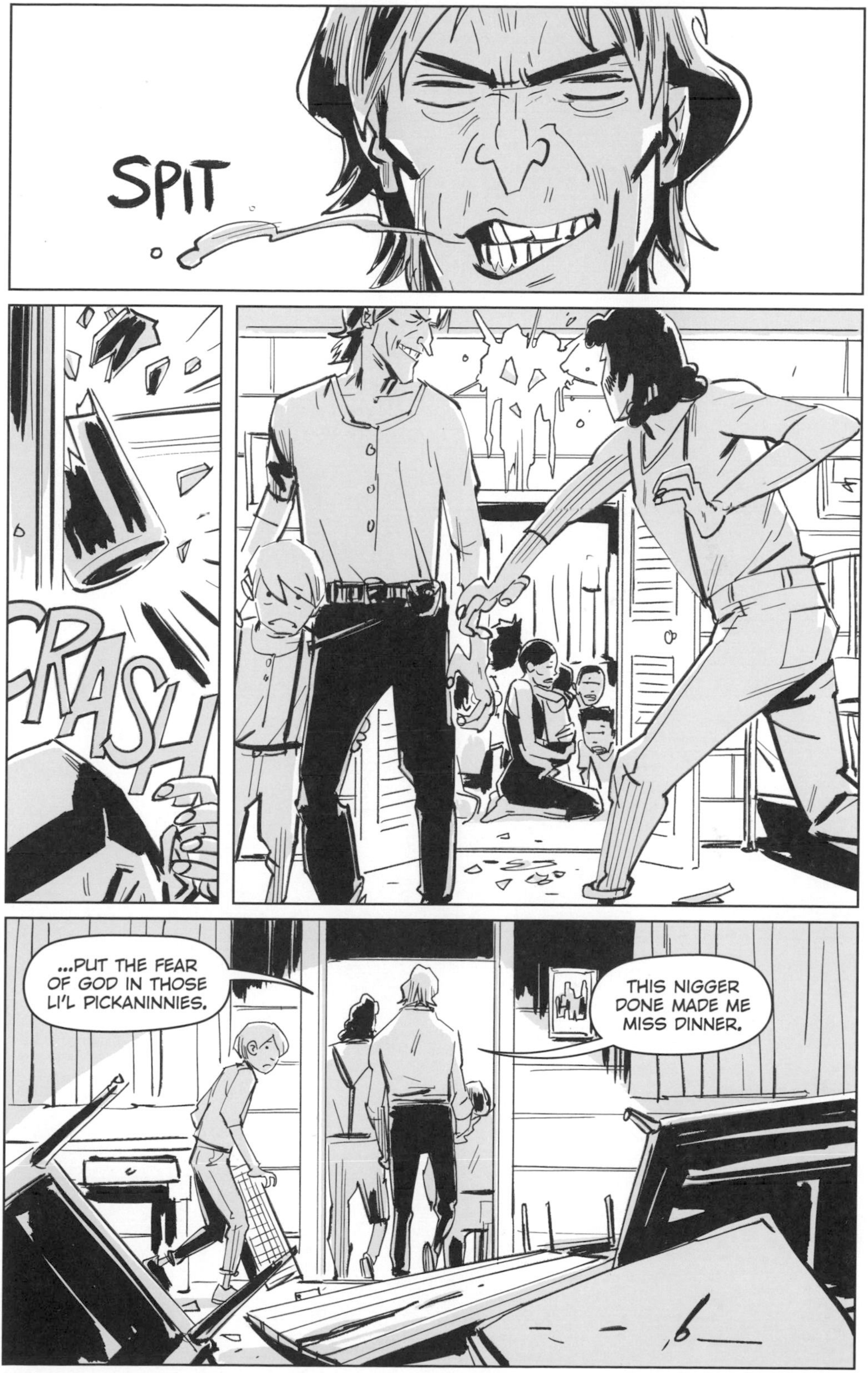
SPIT
CRASH
...PUT THE FEAR OF GOD IN THOSE LI'L PICKANINNIES.
THIS NIGGER DONE MADE ME MISS DINNER.

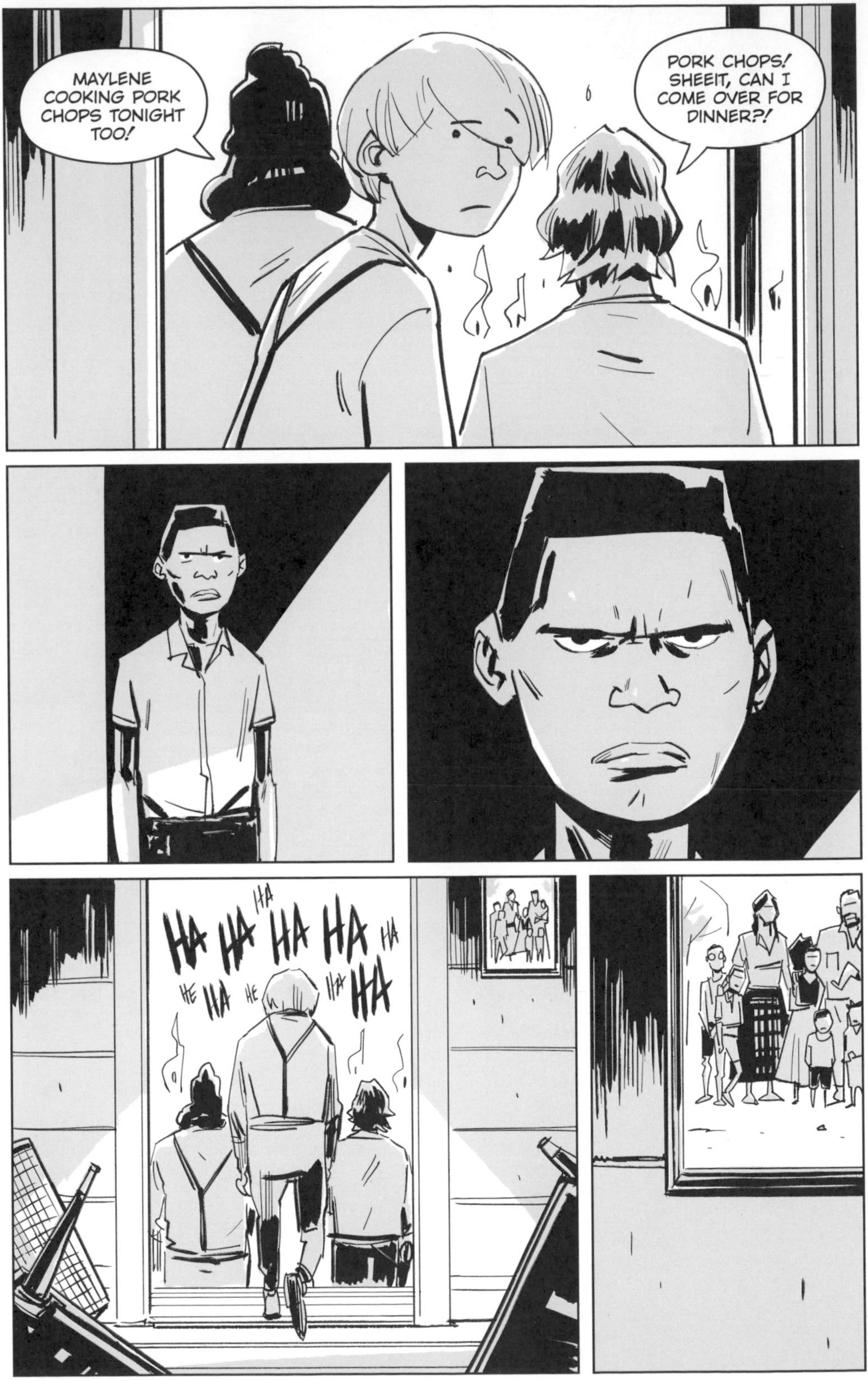
MAYLENE COOKING PORK CHOPS TONIGHT TOO!
PORK CHOPS! SHEEIT, CAN I COME OVER FOR DINNER?!
HA HA HA HA HA HA HA
HE HA HE HA HA

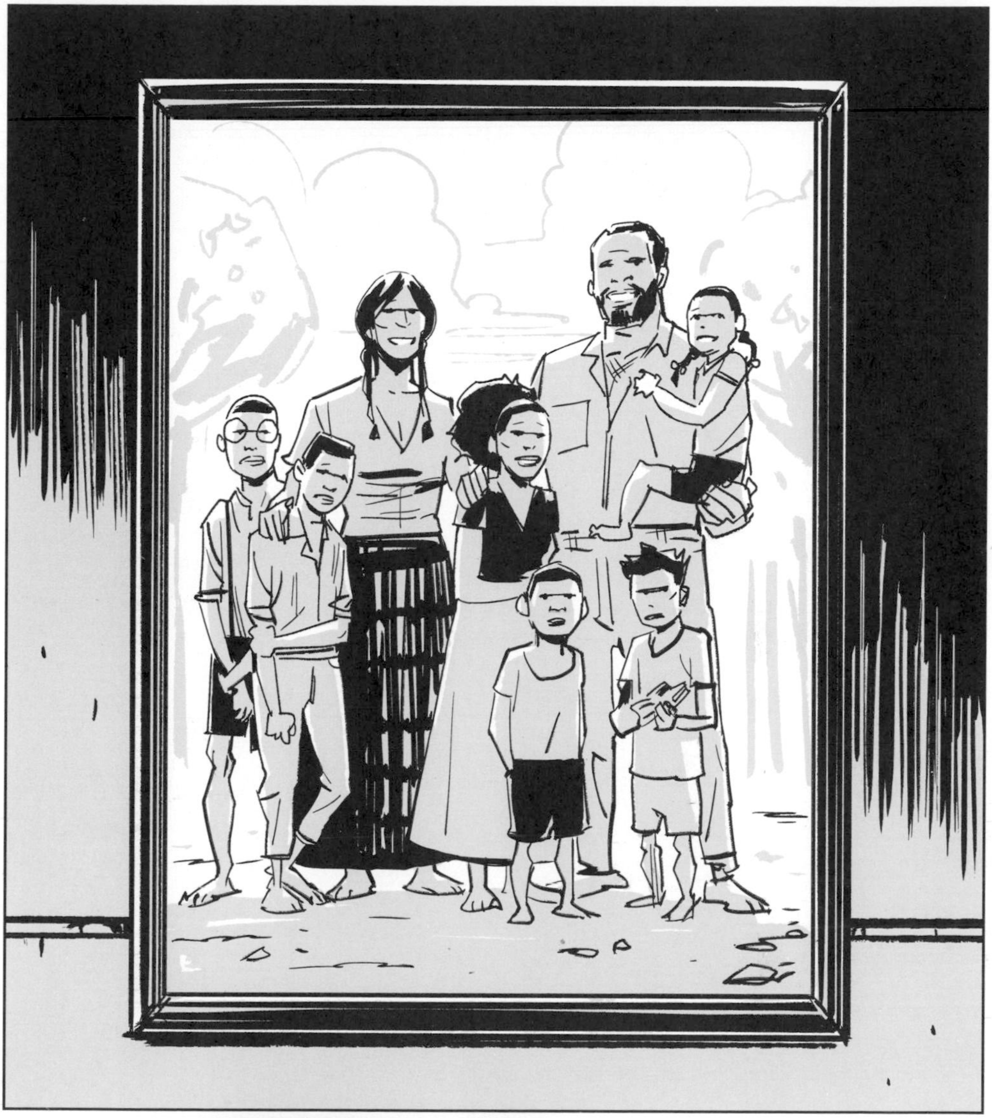

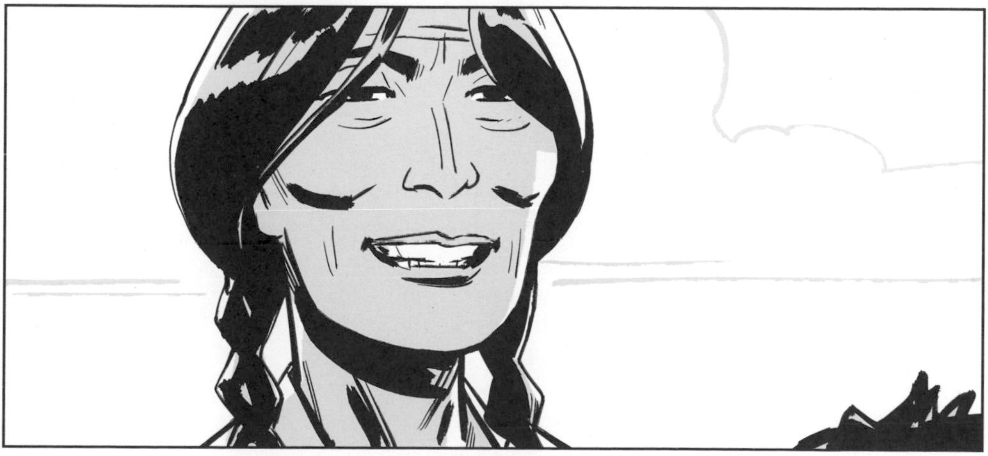

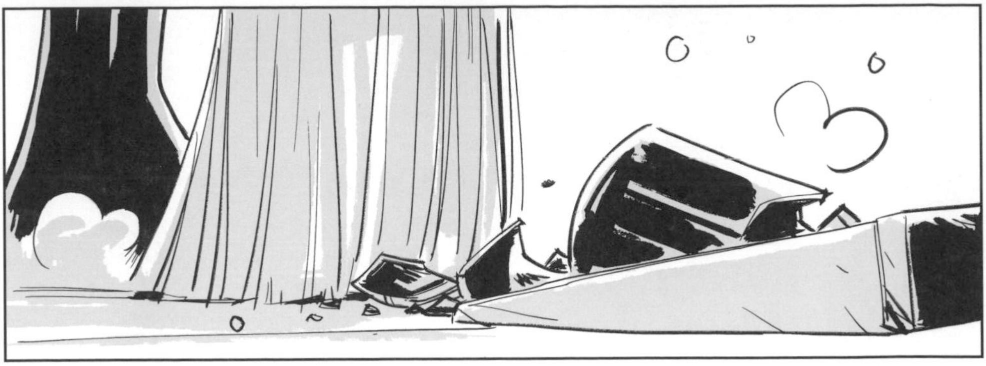

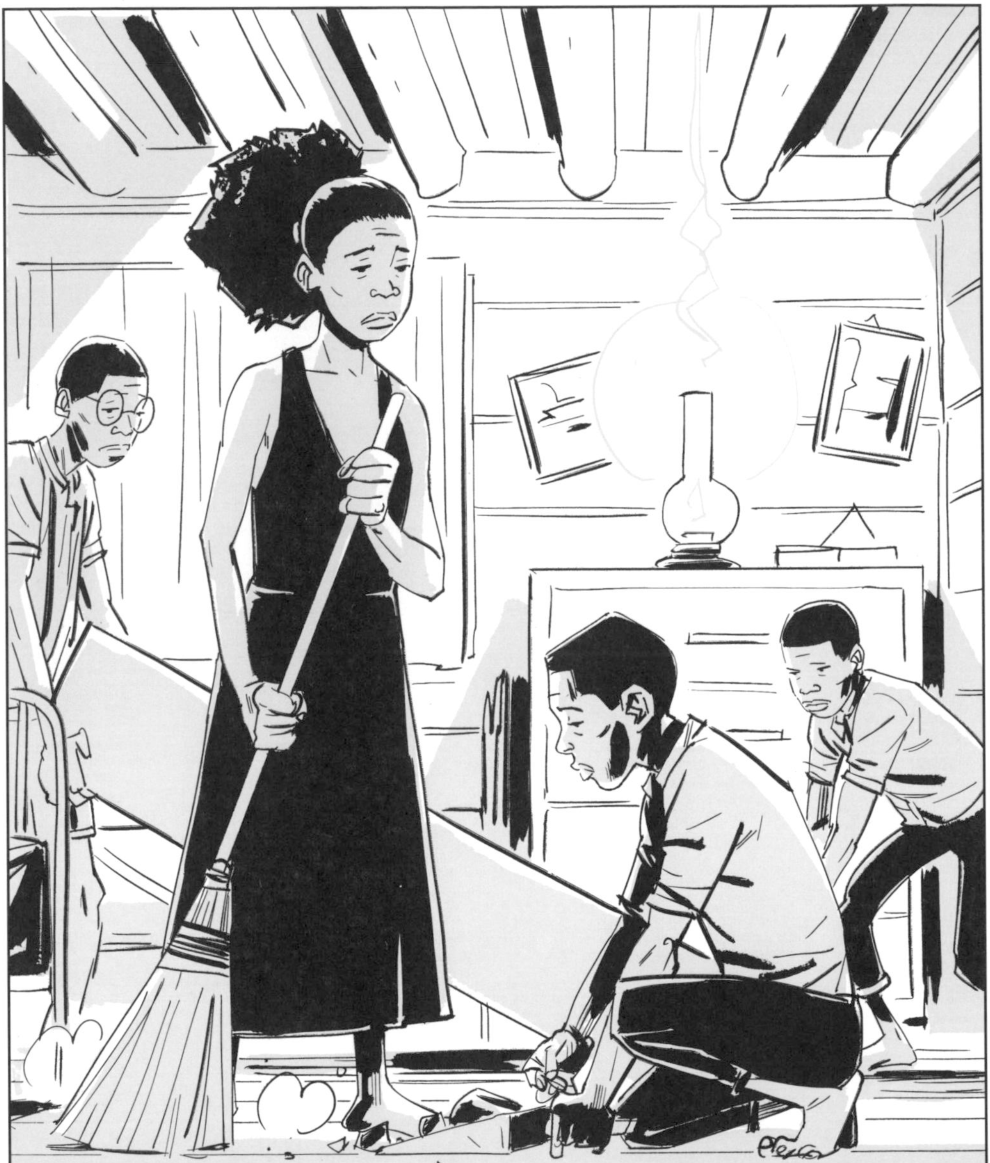

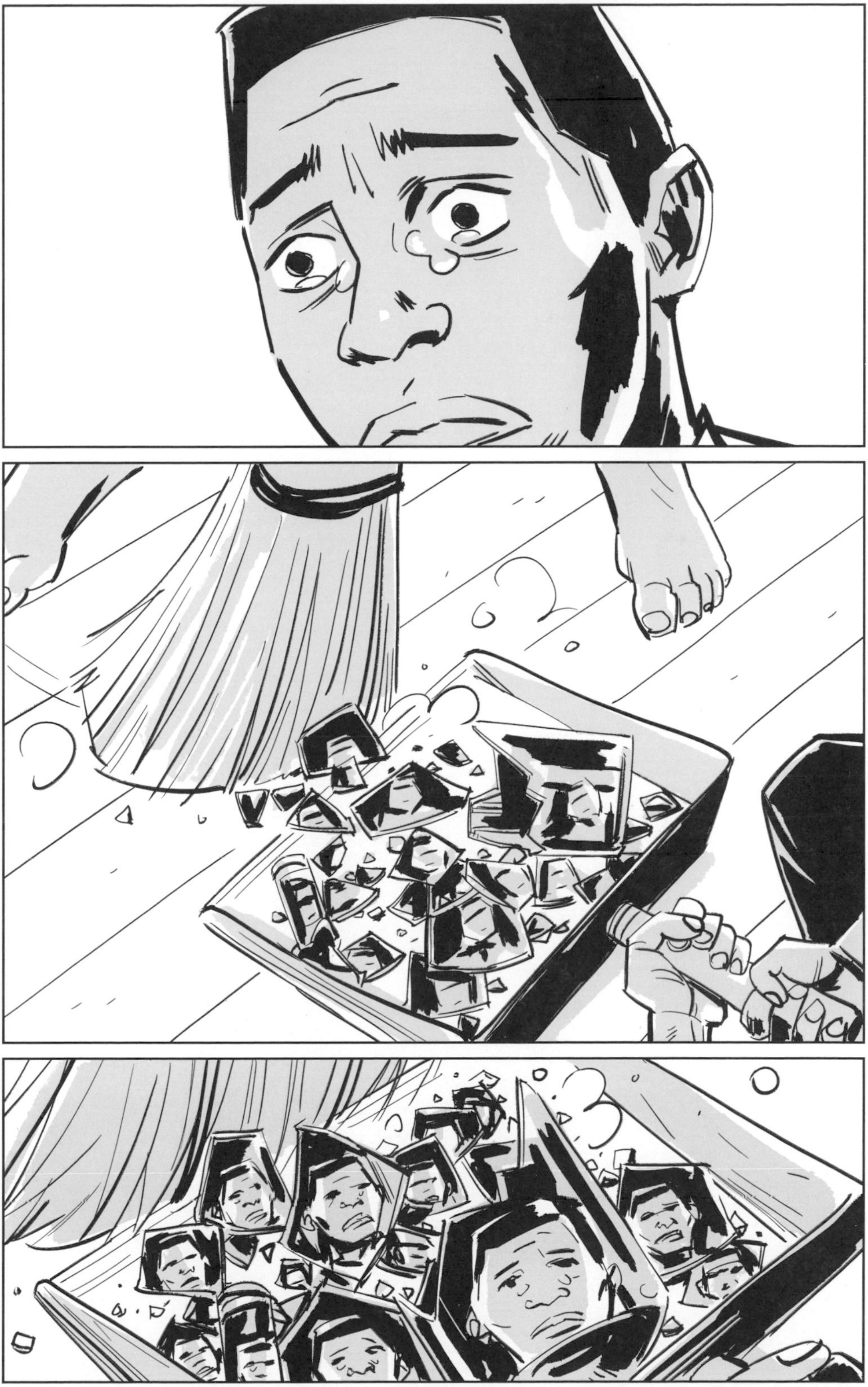

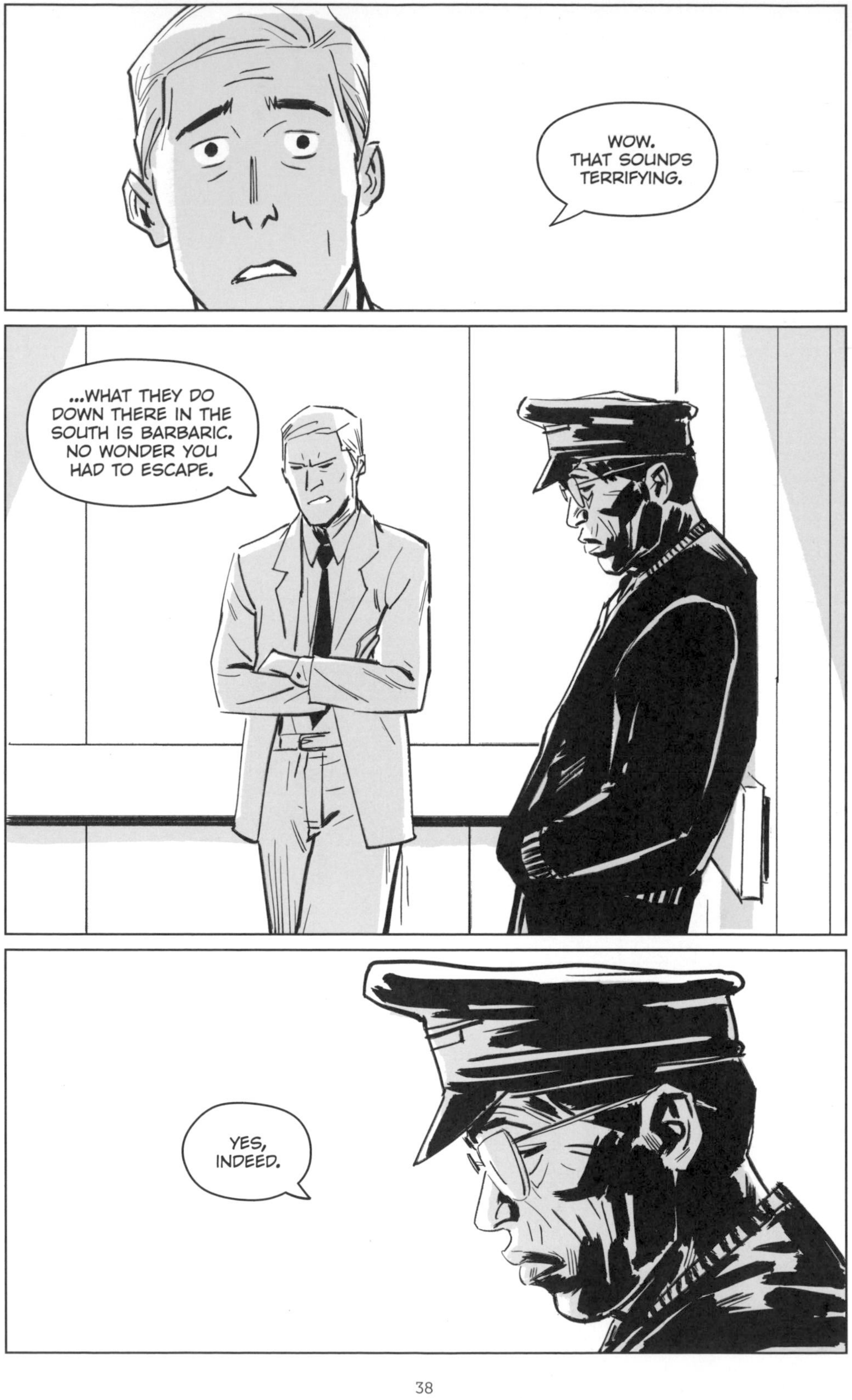
WOW. THAT SOUNDS TERRIFYING.
...WHAT THEY DO DOWN THERE IN THE SOUTH IS BARBARIC. NO WONDER YOU HAD TO ESCAPE.
YES, INDEED.

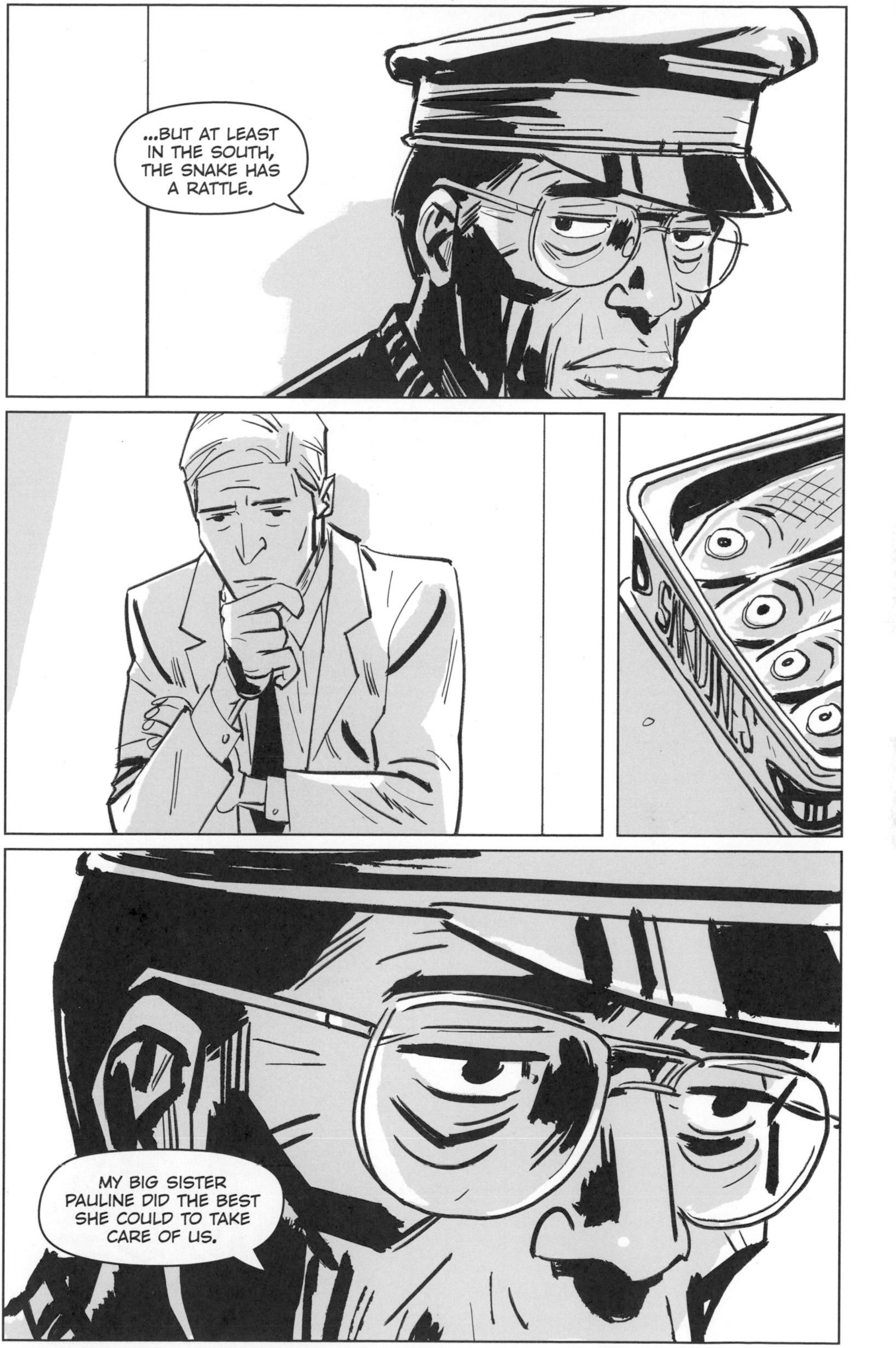
...BUT AT LEAST IN THE SOUTH, THE SNAKE HAS A RATTLE.
SARDINES
MY BIG SISTER PAULINE DID THE BEST SHE COULD TO TAKE CARE OF US.

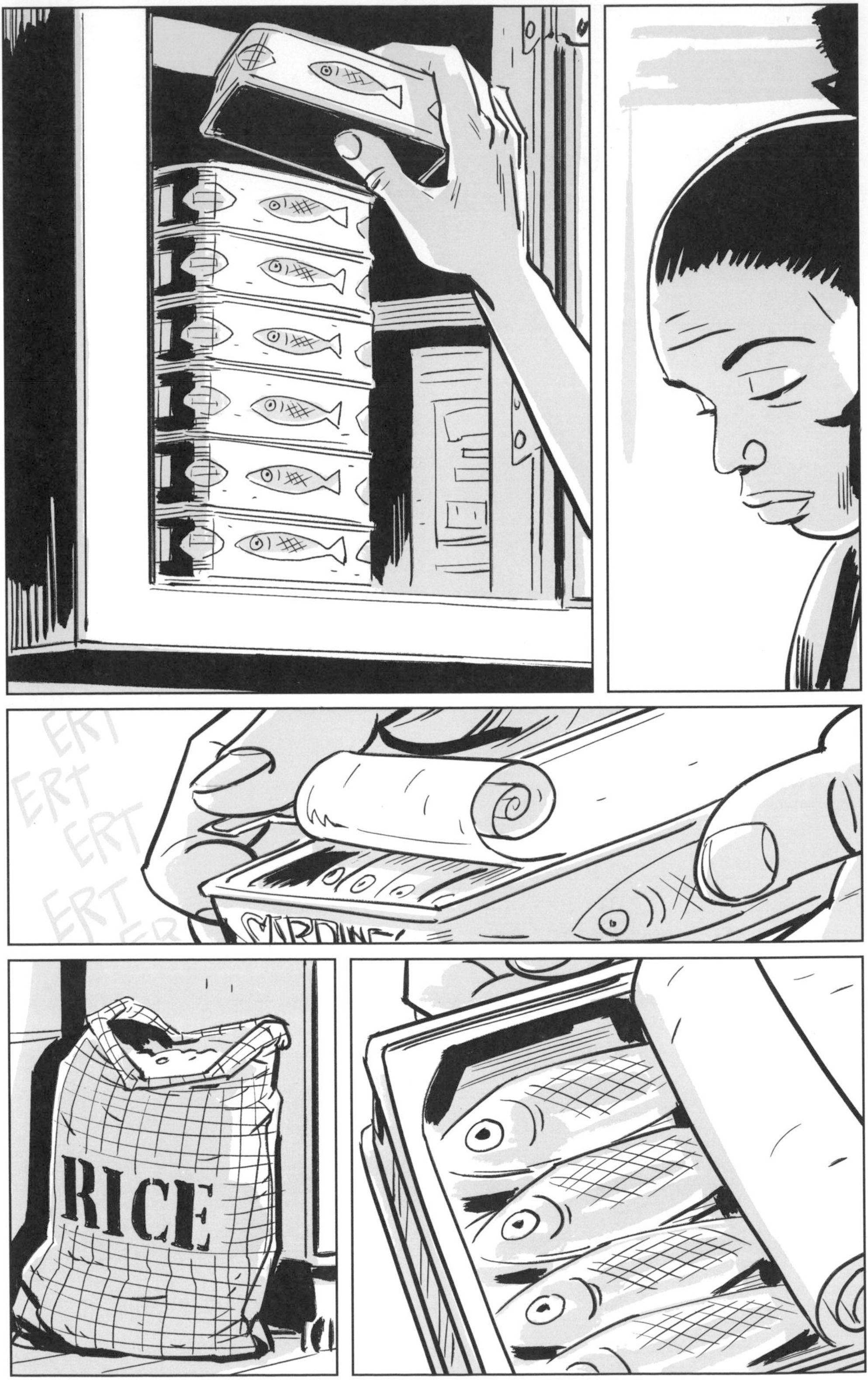
ERT
ERT
ERT
ERT
RICE

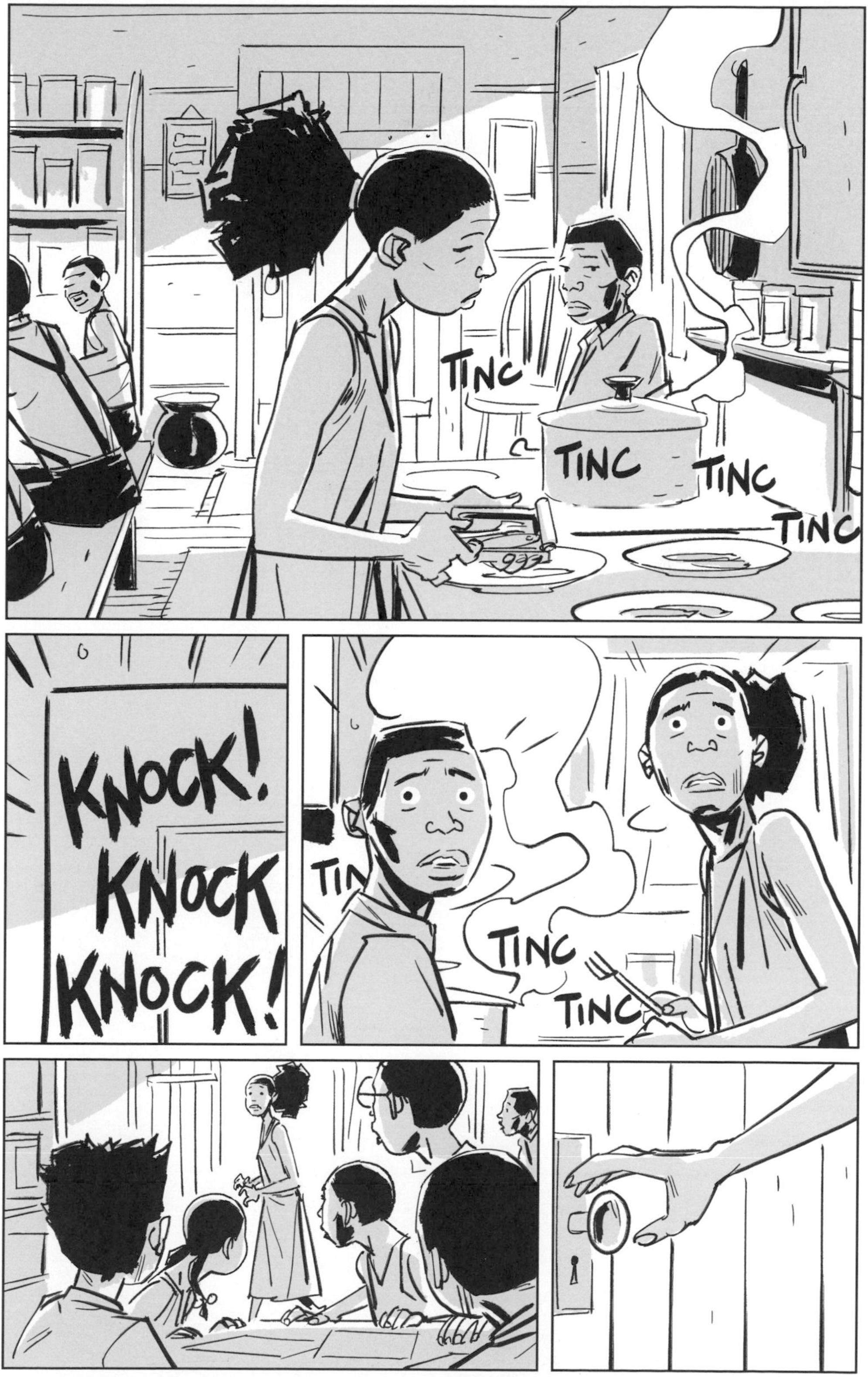
TINC
TINC
TINC
TINC
KNOCK!
KNOCK
KNOCK!
TIN
TINC
TINC

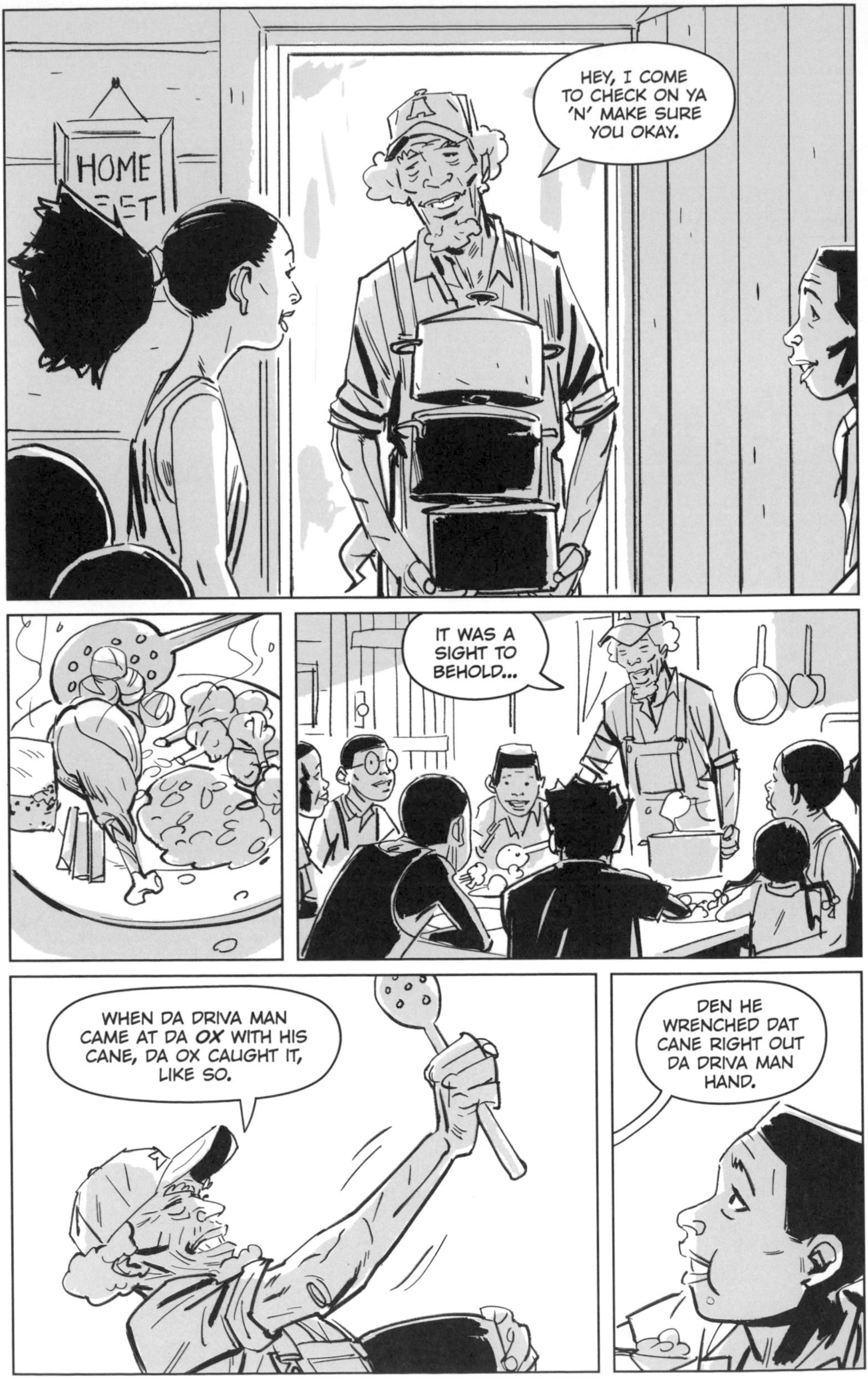
HOME
HEY, I COME TO CHECK ON YA 'N' MAKE SURE YOU OKAY.
IT WAS A SIGHT TO BEHOLD...
WHEN DA DRIVA MAN CAME AT DA *OX* WITH HIS CANE, DA OX CAUGHT IT, LIKE SO.
DEN HE WRENCHED DAT CANE RIGHT OUT DA DRIVA MAN HAND.

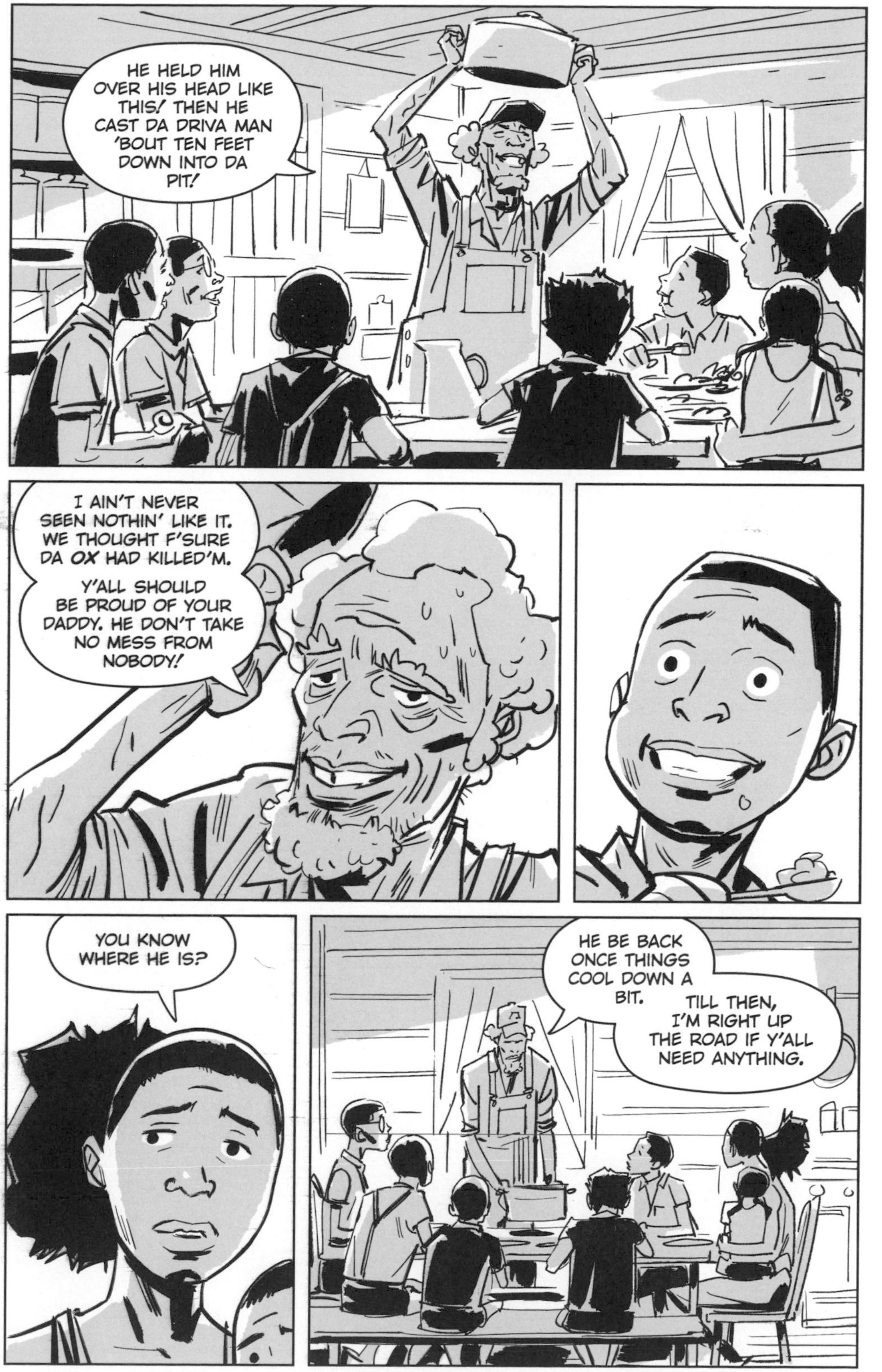
HE HELD HIM OVER HIS HEAD LIKE THIS! THEN HE CAST DA DRIVA MAN 'BOUT TEN FEET DOWN INTO DA PIT!
I AIN'T NEVER SEEN NOTHIN' LIKE IT. WE THOUGHT F'SURE DA OX HAD KILLED'M.
Y'ALL SHOULD BE PROUD OF YOUR DADDY. HE DON'T TAKE NO MESS FROM NOBODY!
YOU KNOW WHERE HE IS?
HE BE BACK ONCE THINGS COOL DOWN A BIT.
TILL THEN, I'M RIGHT UP THE ROAD IF Y'ALL NEED ANYTHING.

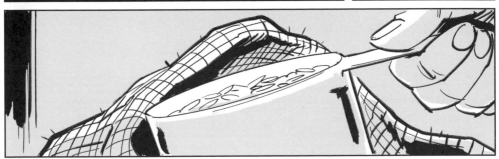

TINC TINC TINC

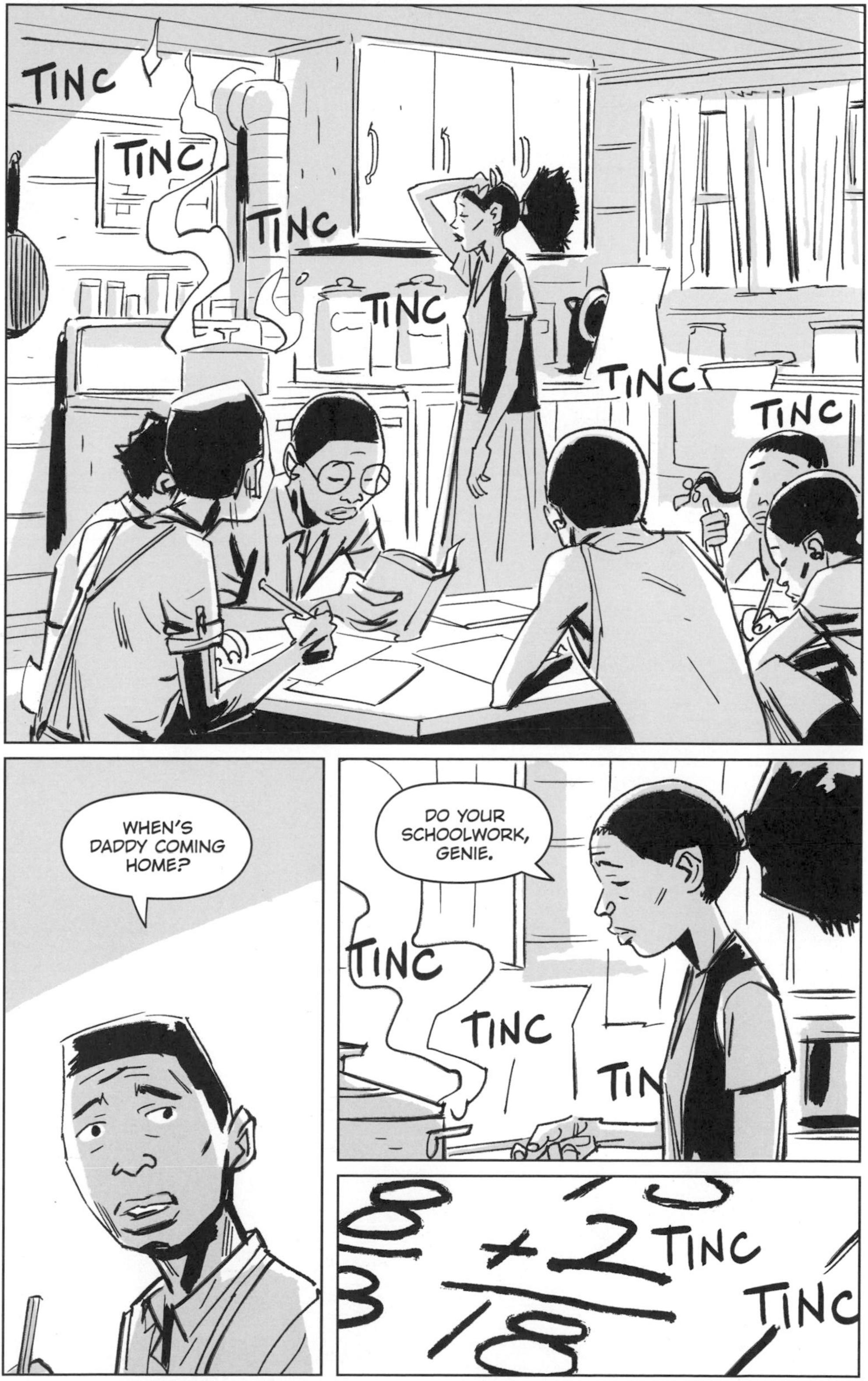

TINC
TINC
TINC
TINC
TINC
TINC
WHEN'S DADDY COMING HOME?
DO YOUR SCHOOLWORK, GENIE.
TINC
TINC
+2
18
TINC
TINC

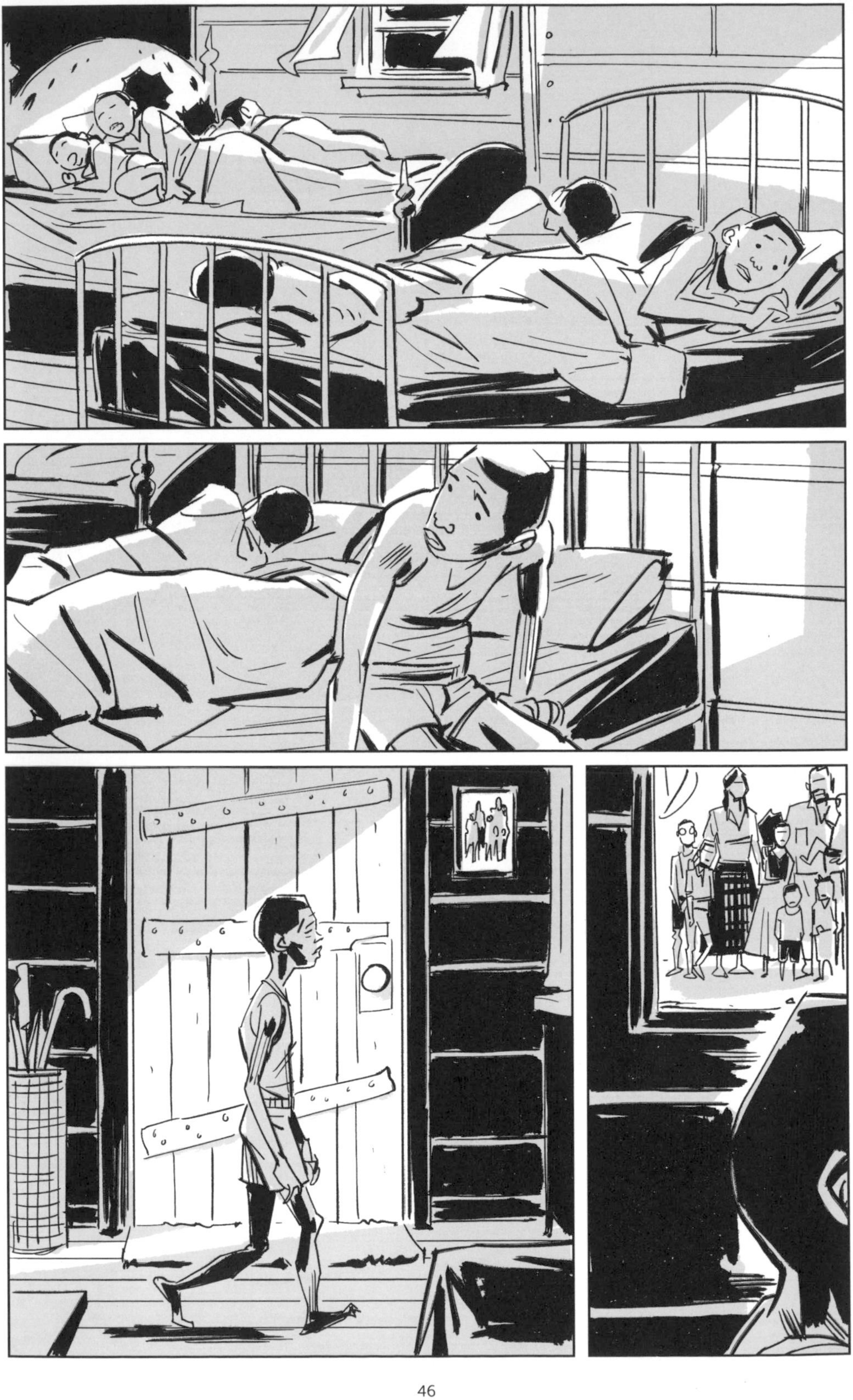

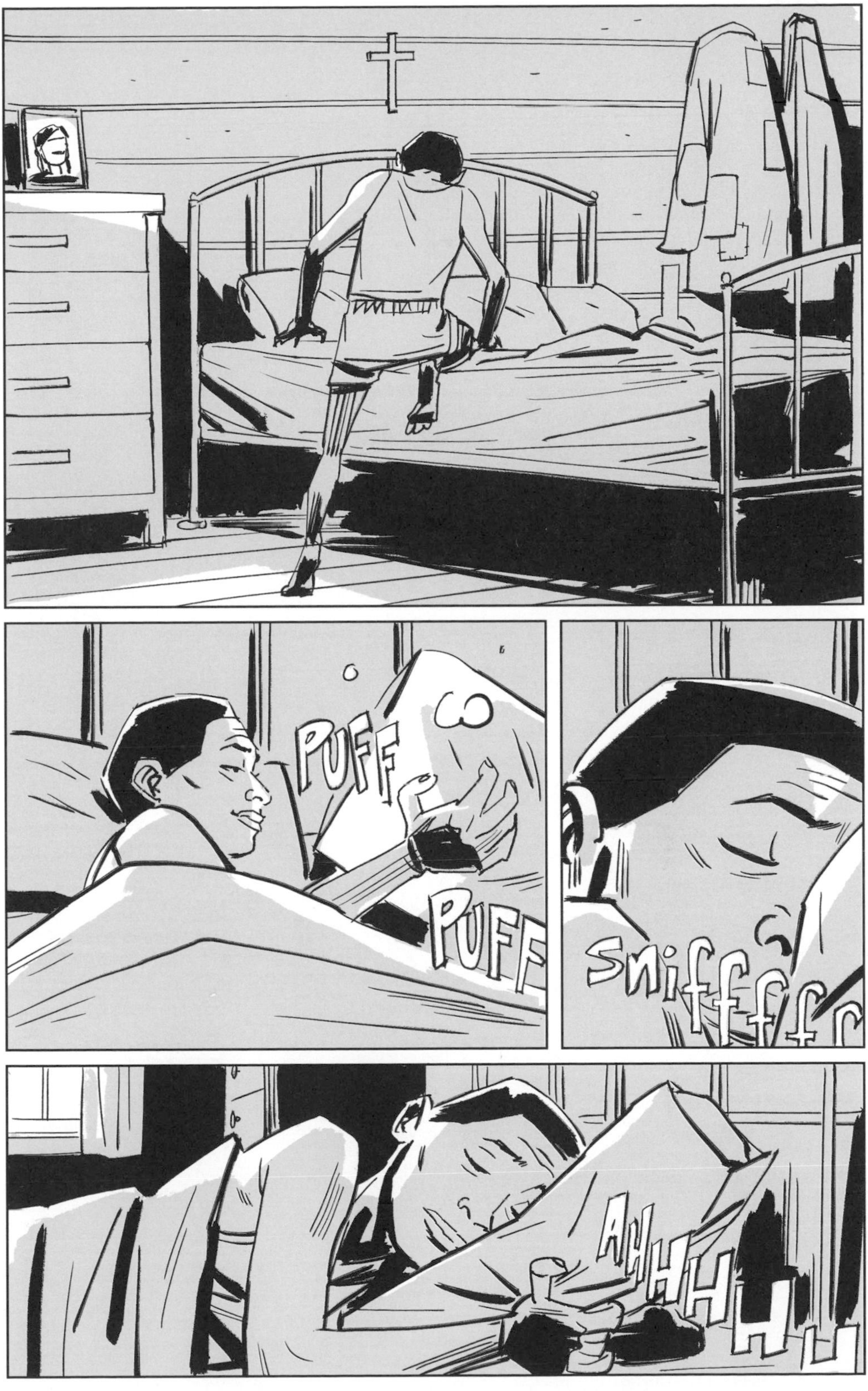
PUFF
PUFF
Sniffffff
AHHHHHH

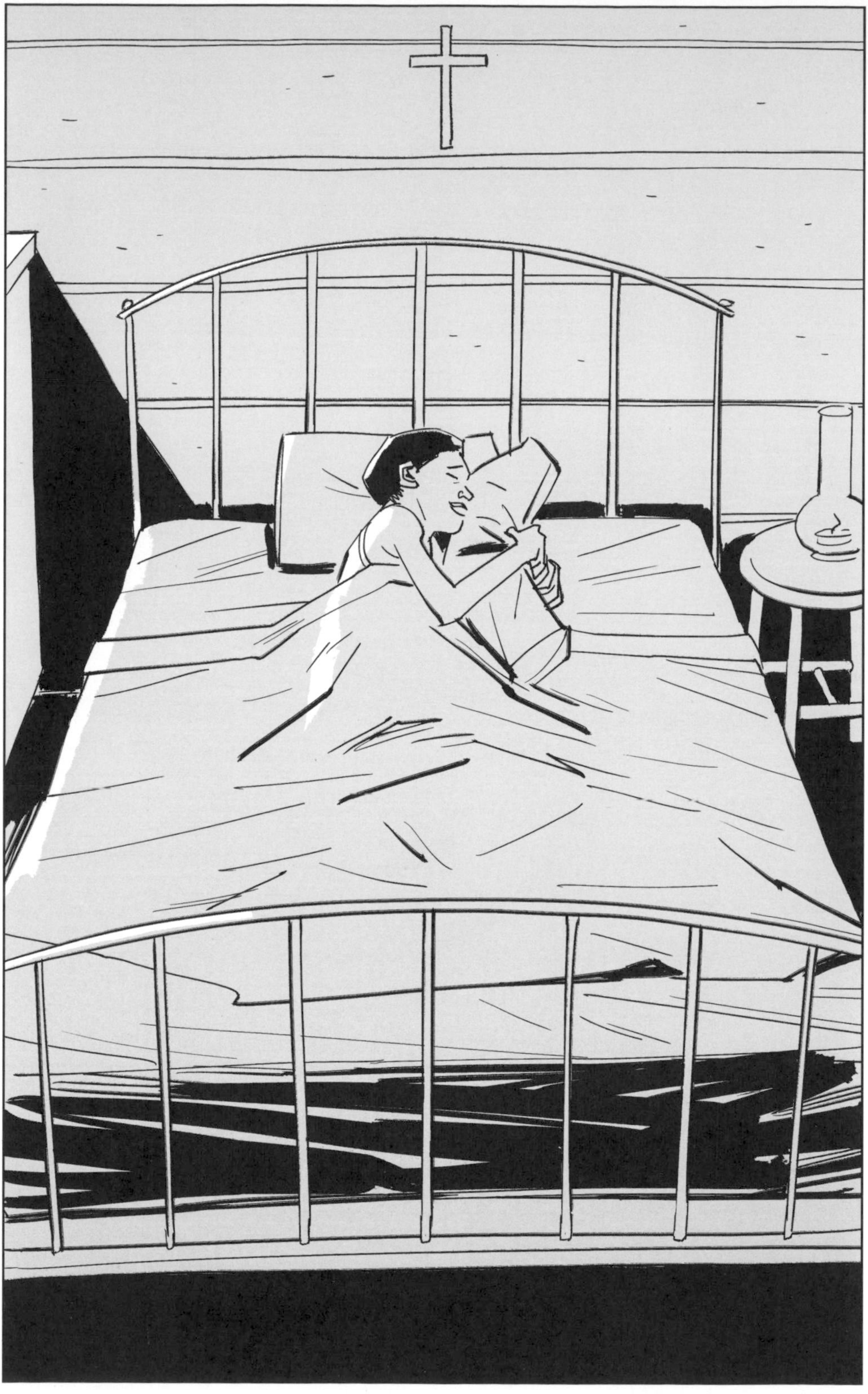

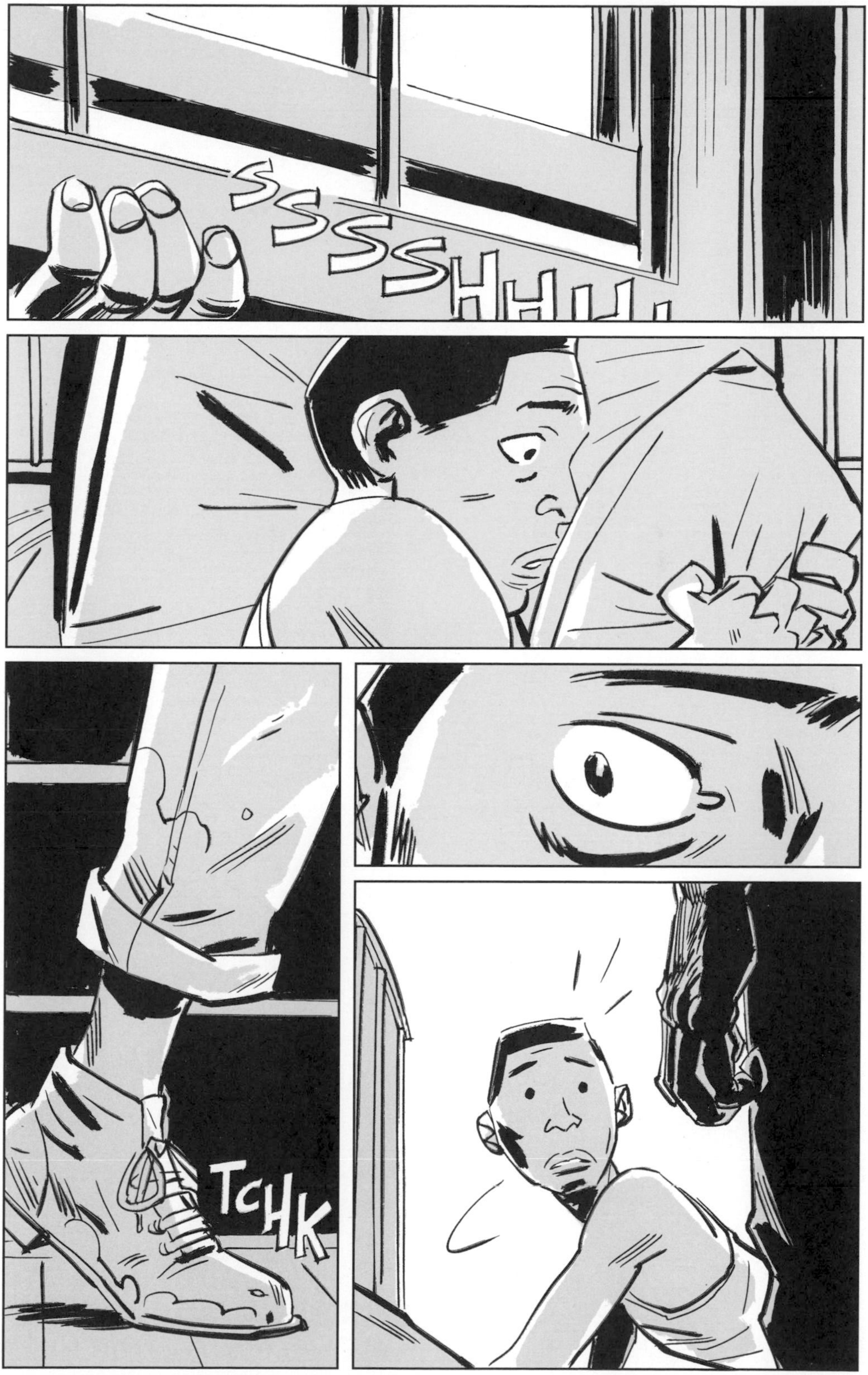
SSSSHHH
TCHK

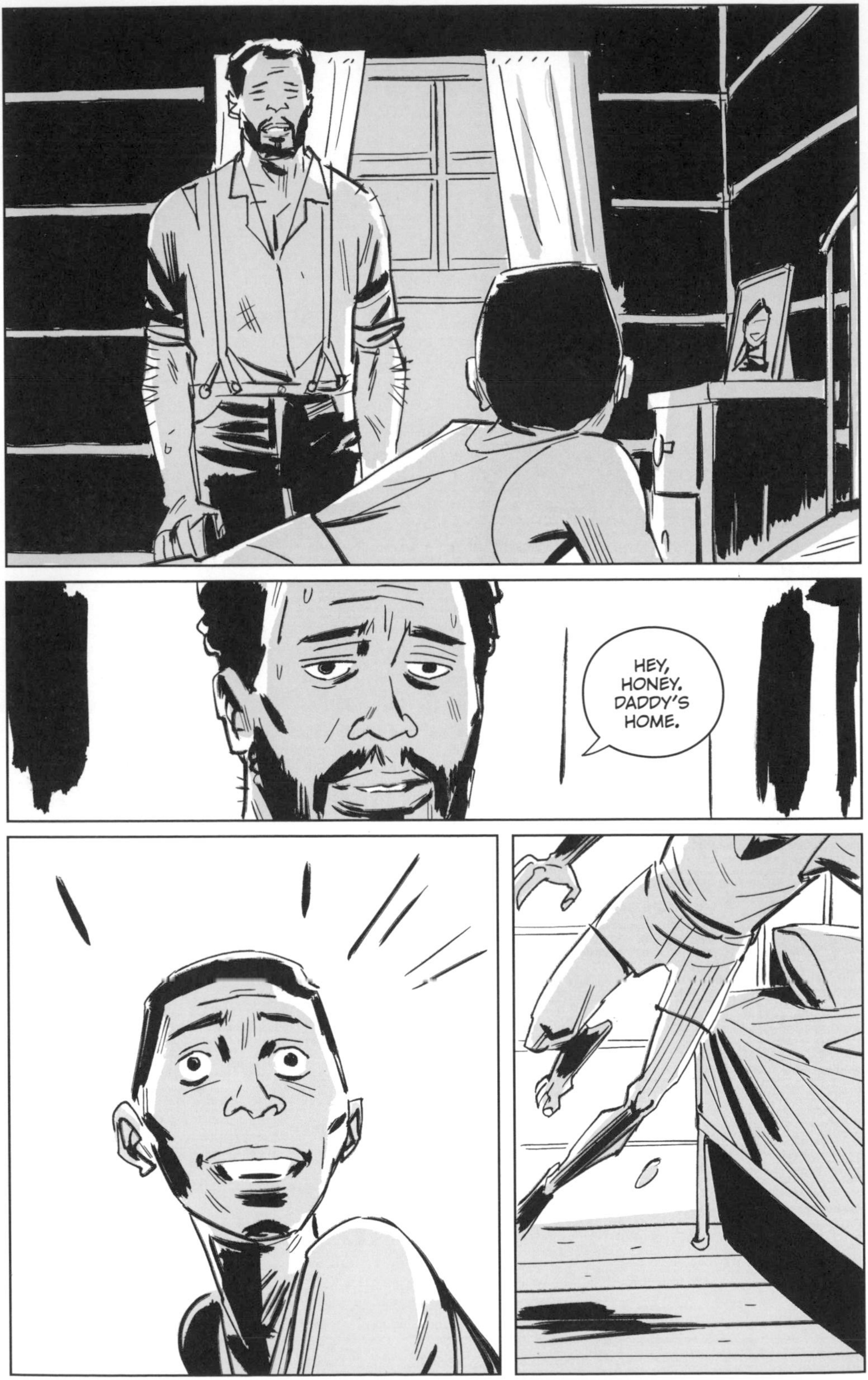
HEY, HONEY. DADDY'S HOME.

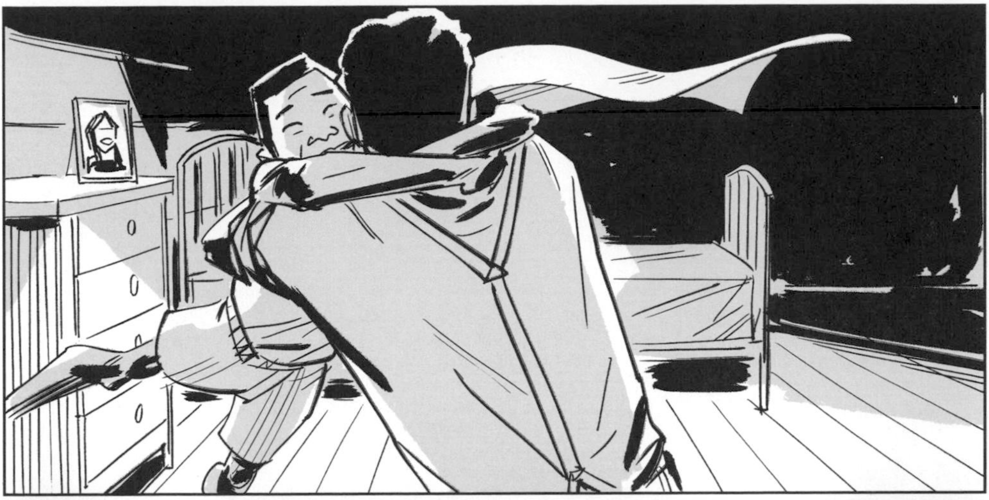

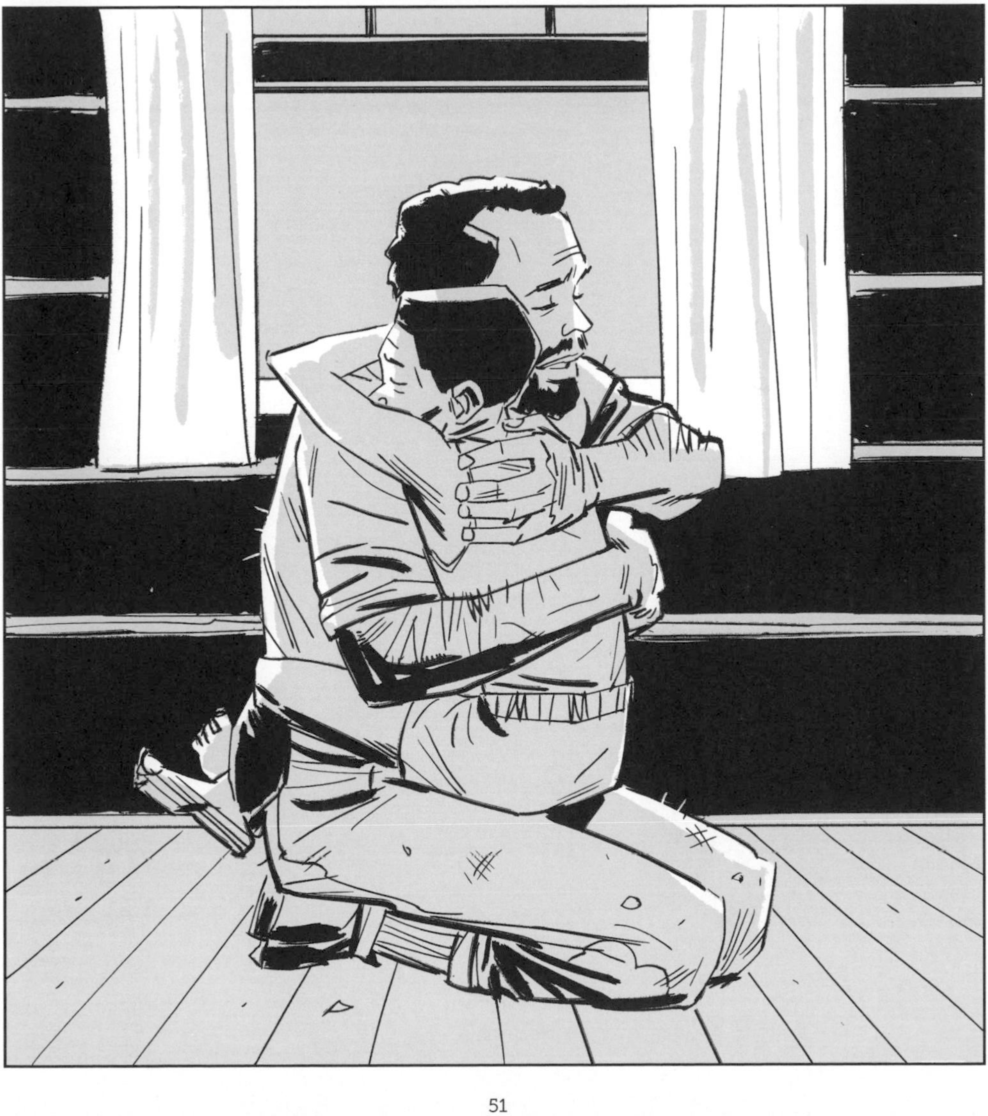

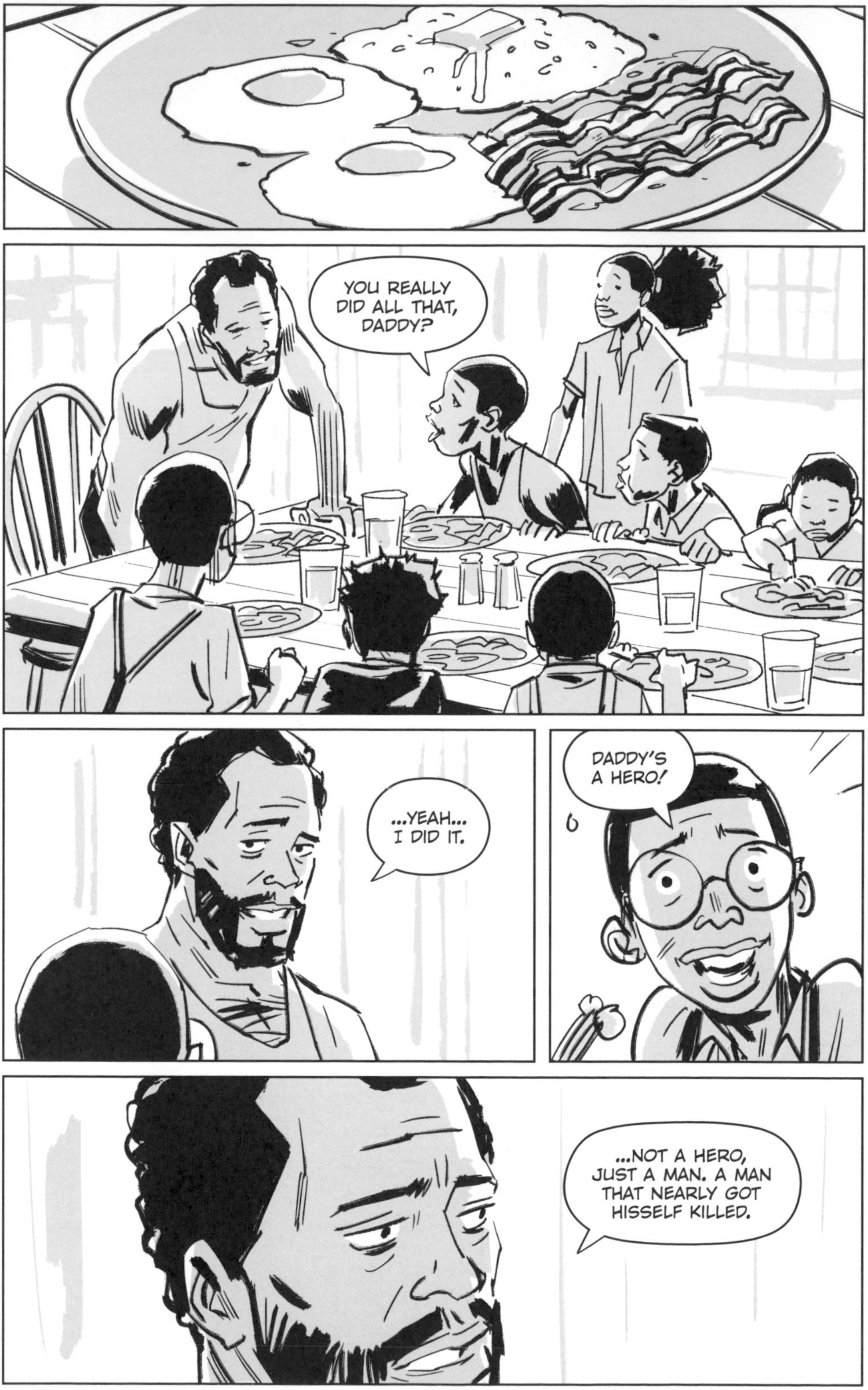
YOU REALLY DID ALL THAT, DADDY?
...YEAH... I DID IT.
DADDY'S A HERO!
...NOT A HERO, JUST A MAN. A MAN THAT NEARLY GOT HISSELF KILLED.

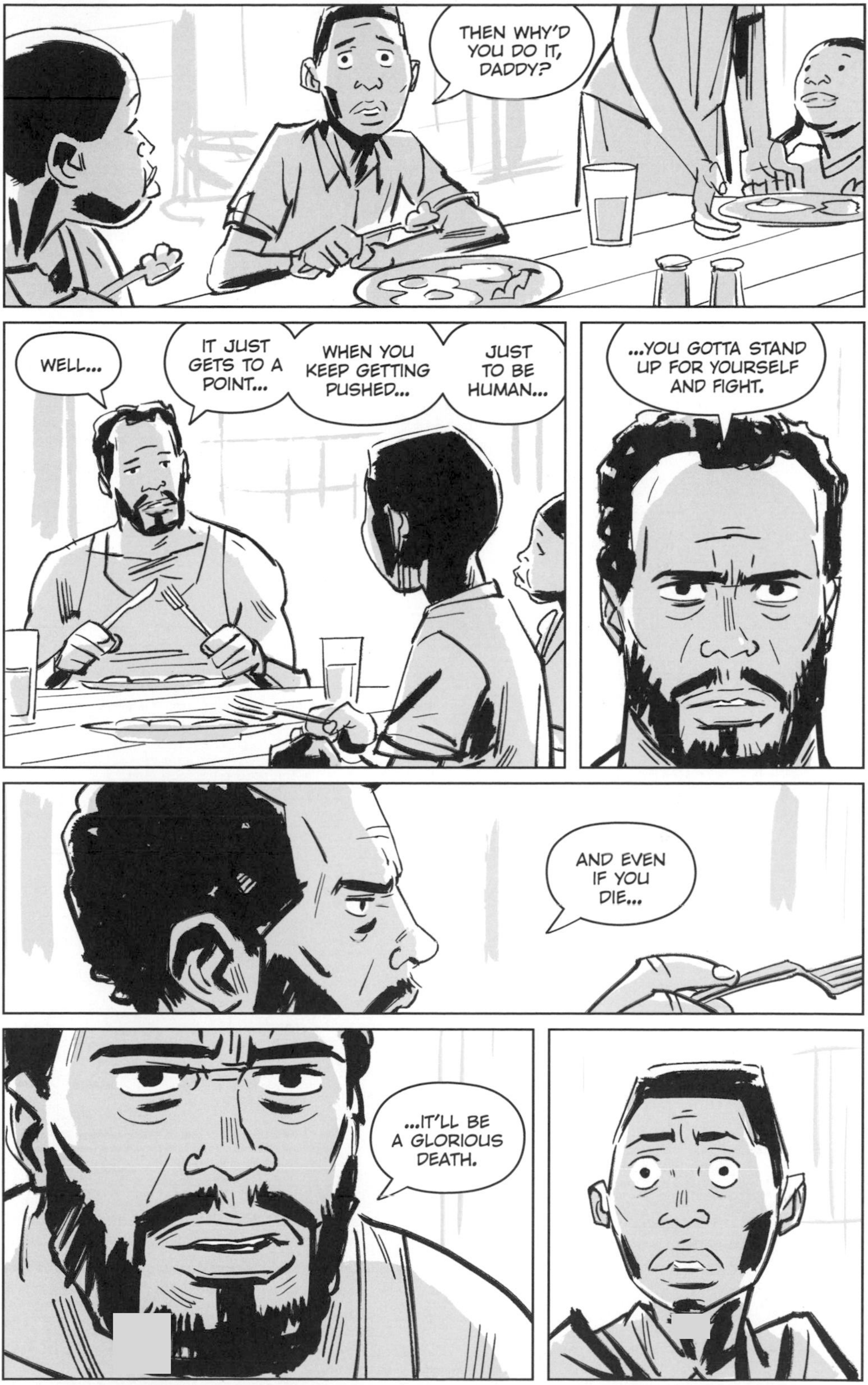
THEN WHY'D YOU DO IT, DADDY?
WELL...
IT JUST GETS TO A POINT...
WHEN YOU KEEP GETTING PUSHED...
JUST TO BE HUMAN...
...YOU GOTTA STAND UP FOR YOURSELF AND FIGHT.
AND EVEN IF YOU DIE...
...IT'LL BE A GLORIOUS DEATH.

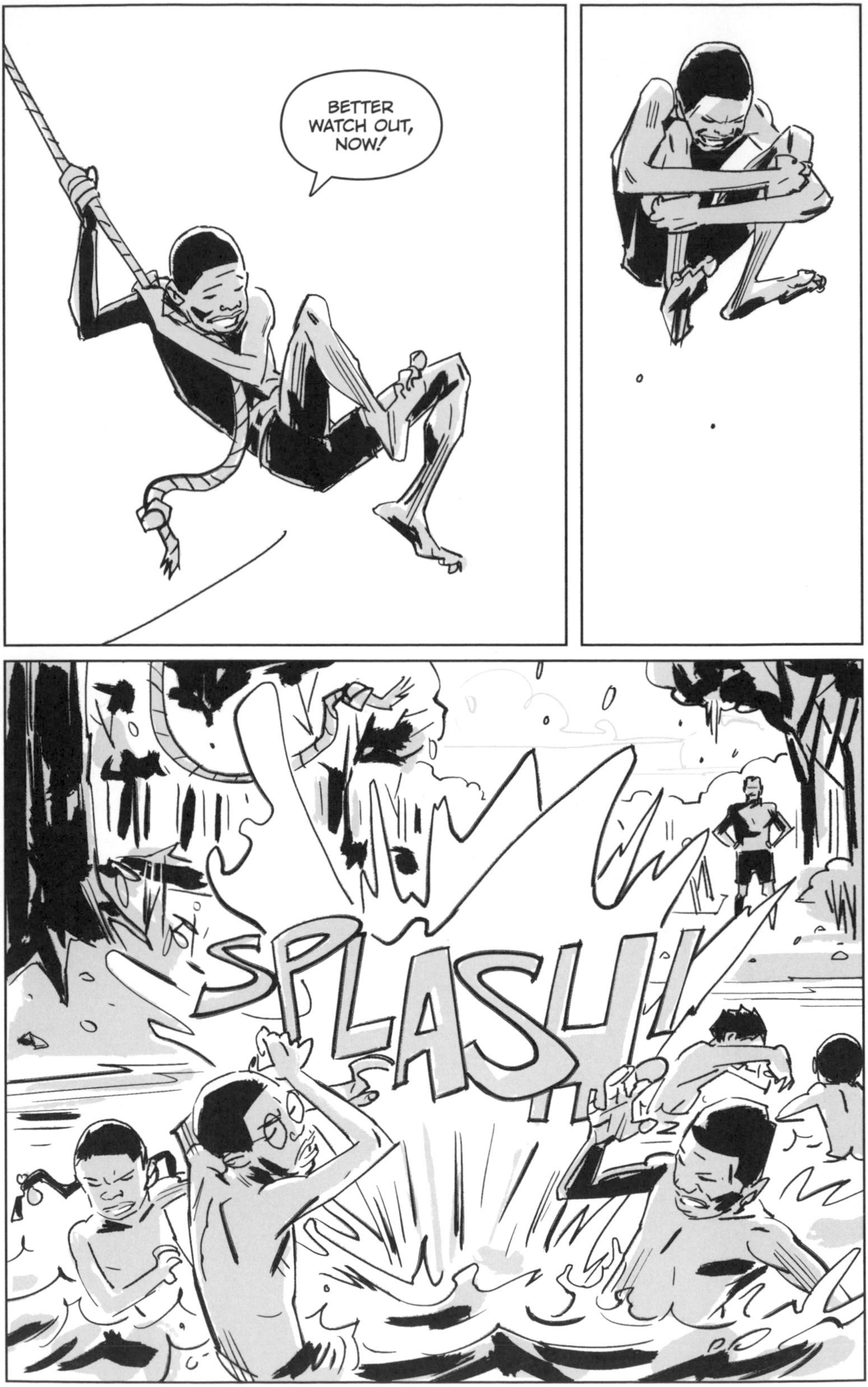
BETTER WATCH OUT, NOW!
SPLASH!

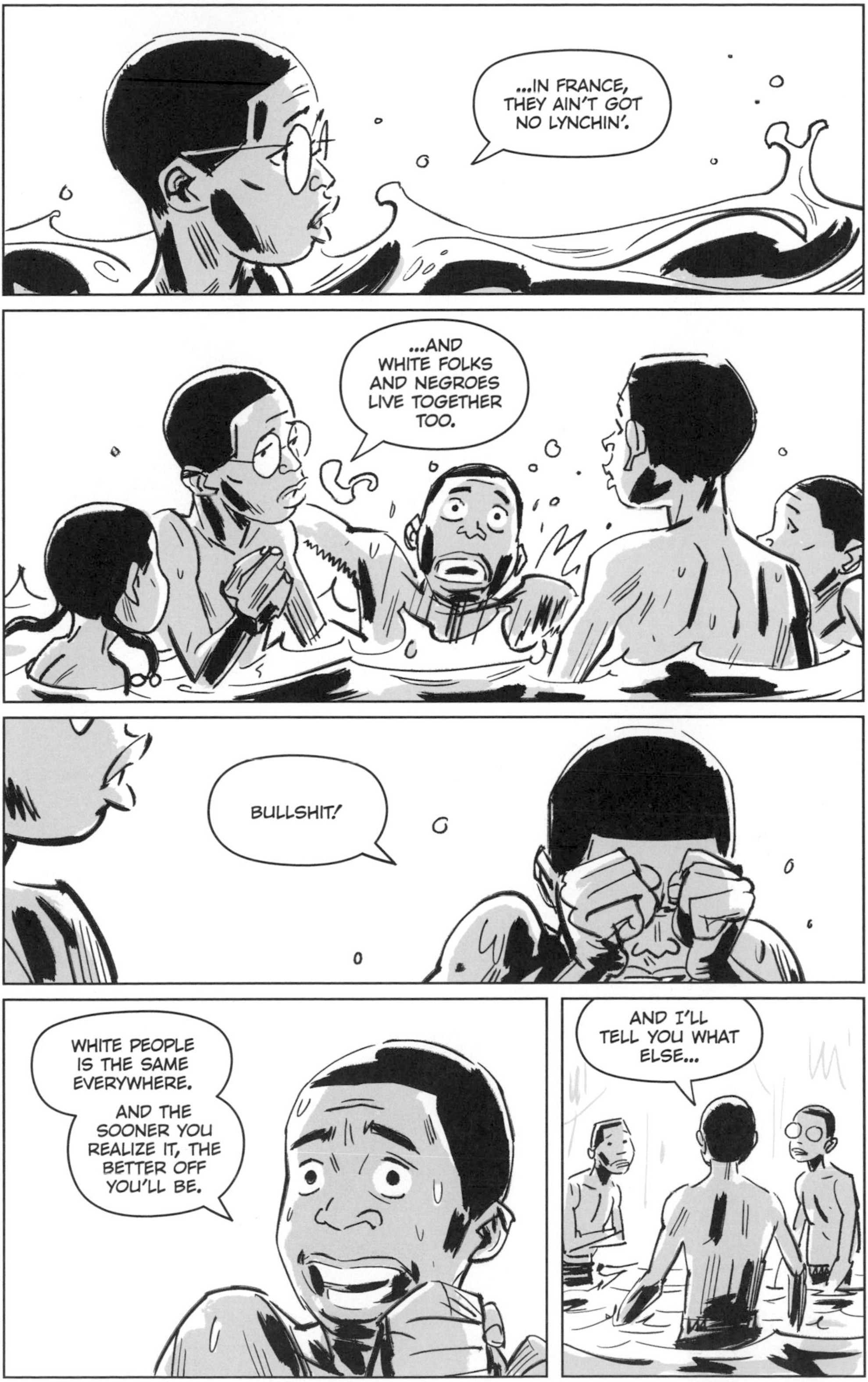
...IN FRANCE, THEY AIN'T GOT NO LYNCHIN'.
...AND WHITE FOLKS AND NEGROES LIVE TOGETHER TOO.
BULLSHIT!
WHITE PEOPLE IS THE SAME EVERYWHERE.
AND THE SOONER YOU REALIZE IT, THE BETTER OFF YOU'LL BE.
AND I'LL TELL YOU WHAT ELSE...

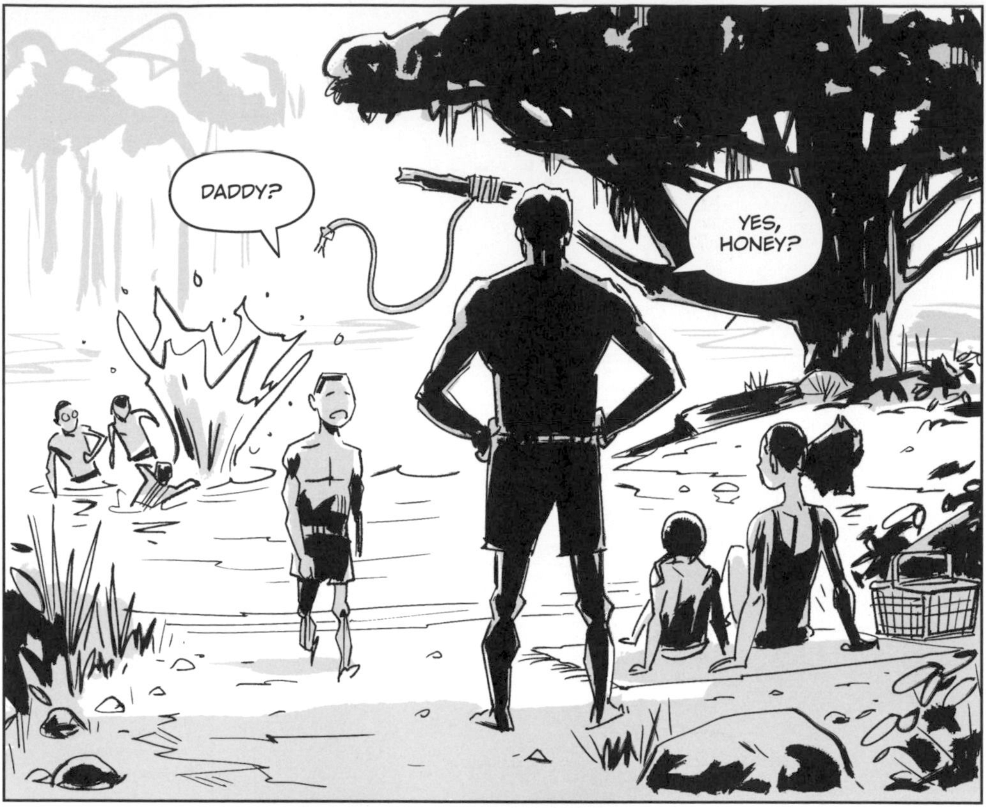
DADDY?
YES, HONEY?

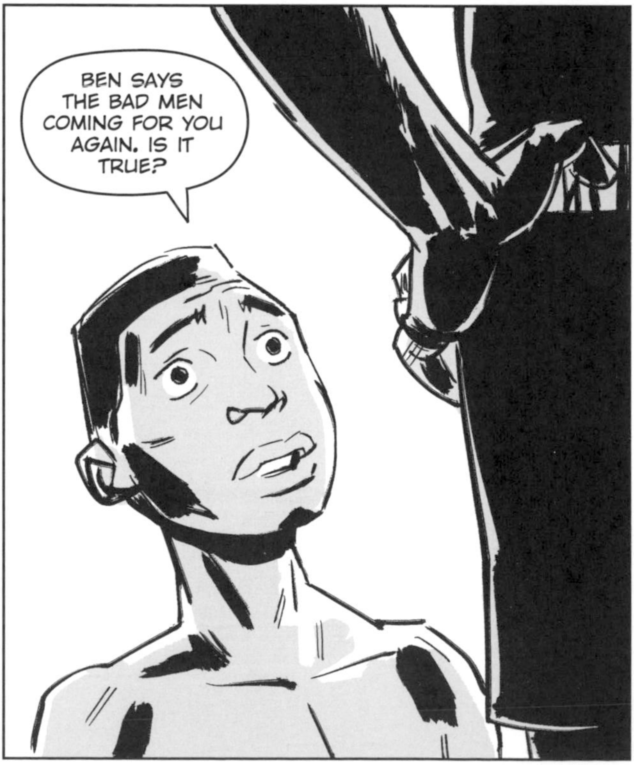
BEN SAYS THE BAD MEN COMING FOR YOU AGAIN. IS IT TRUE?

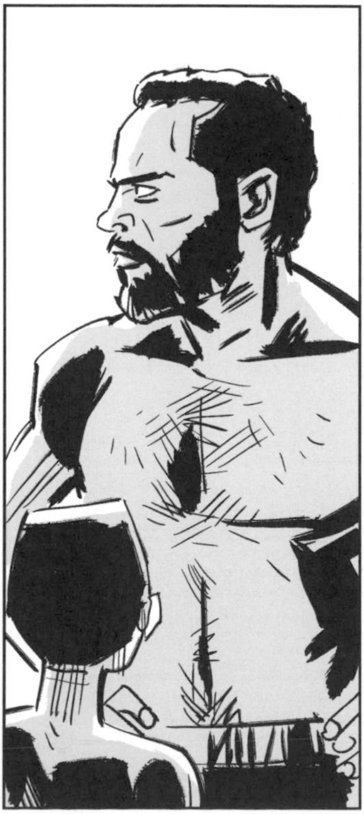

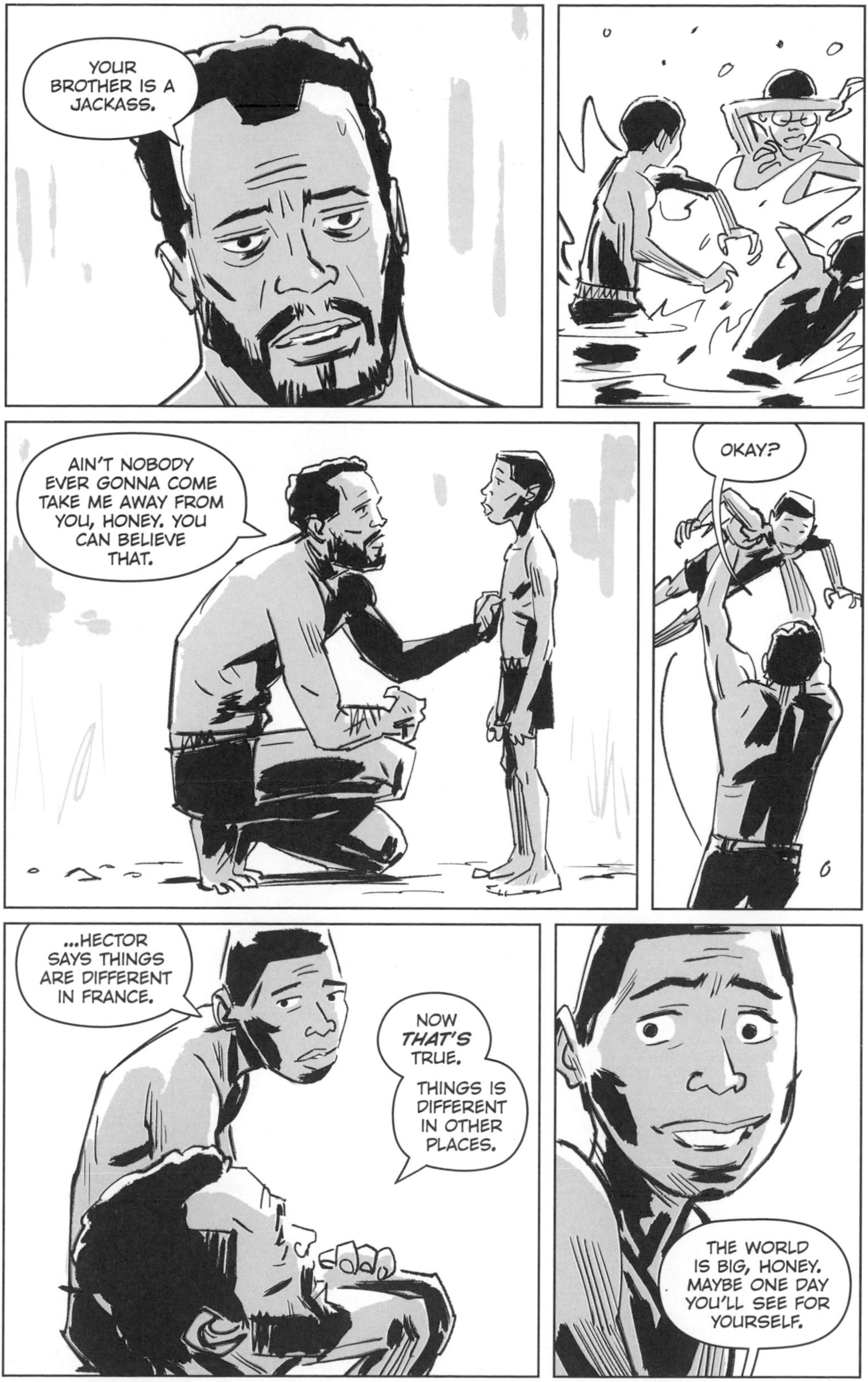
YOUR BROTHER IS A JACKASS.
AIN'T NOBODY EVER GONNA COME TAKE ME AWAY FROM YOU, HONEY. YOU CAN BELIEVE THAT.
OKAY?
...HECTOR SAYS THINGS ARE DIFFERENT IN FRANCE.
NOW *THAT'S* TRUE.
THINGS IS DIFFERENT IN OTHER PLACES.
THE WORLD IS BIG, HONEY. MAYBE ONE DAY YOU'LL SEE FOR YOURSELF.

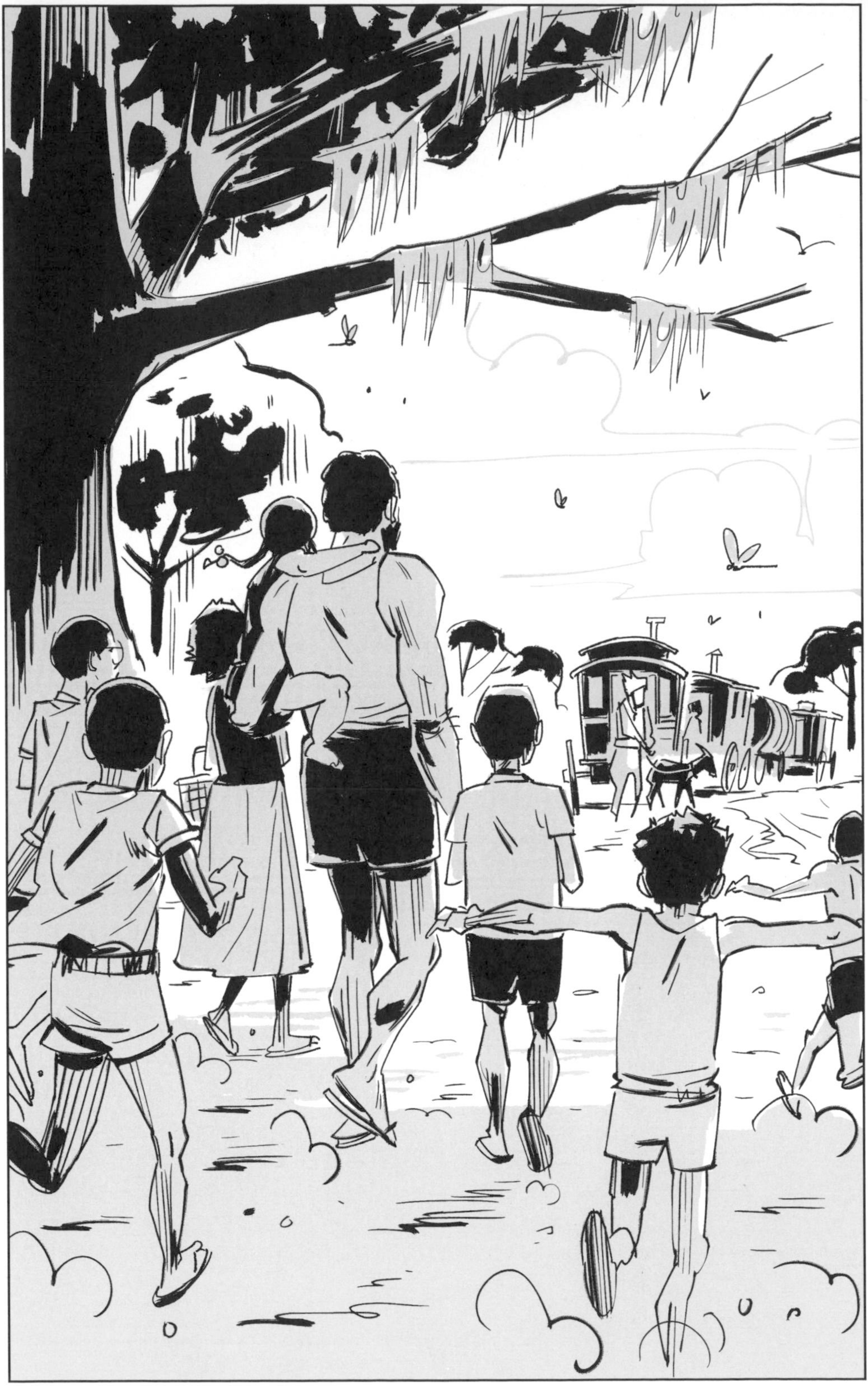

GOAT 4 SALE

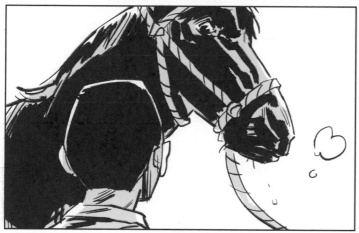

YOU BETTER WATCH OUT.

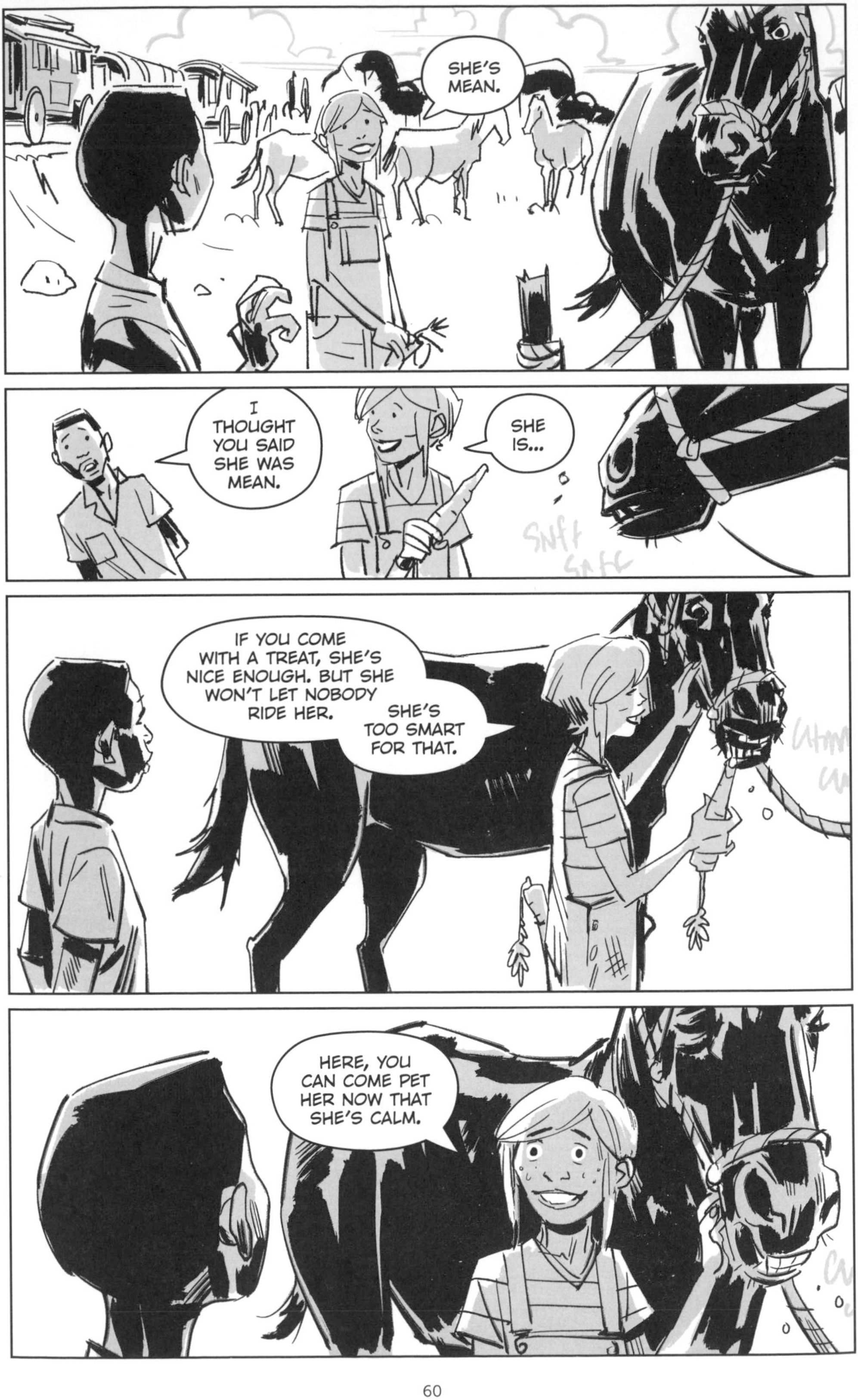
SHE'S MEAN.
I THOUGHT YOU SAID SHE WAS MEAN.
SHE IS...
IF YOU COME WITH A TREAT, SHE'S NICE ENOUGH. BUT SHE WON'T LET NOBODY RIDE HER.
SHE'S TOO SMART FOR THAT.
HERE, YOU CAN COME PET HER NOW THAT SHE'S CALM.

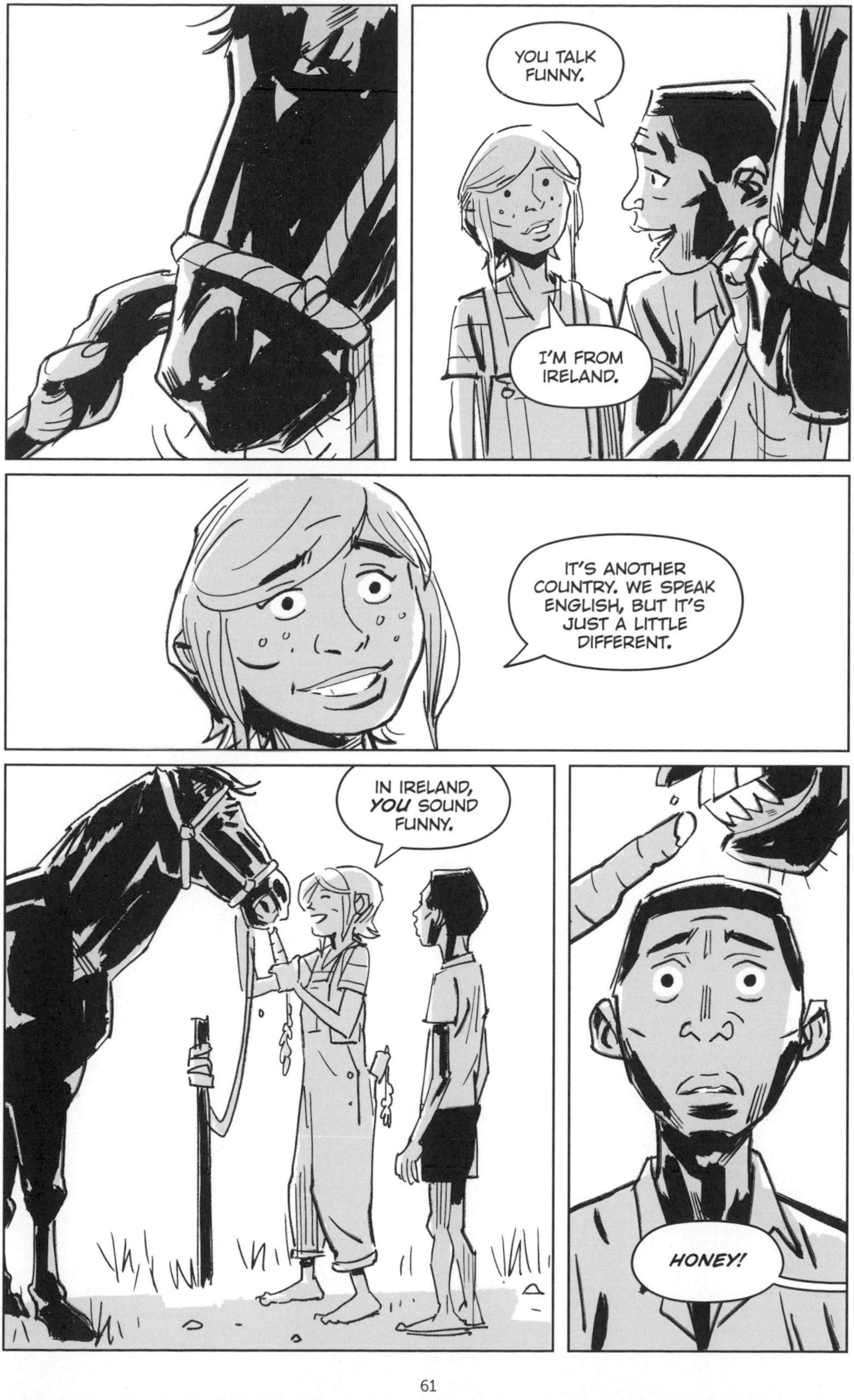
YOU TALK FUNNY.
I'M FROM IRELAND.
IT'S ANOTHER COUNTRY. WE SPEAK ENGLISH, BUT IT'S JUST A LITTLE DIFFERENT.
IN IRELAND, ***YOU*** SOUND FUNNY.
HONEY!

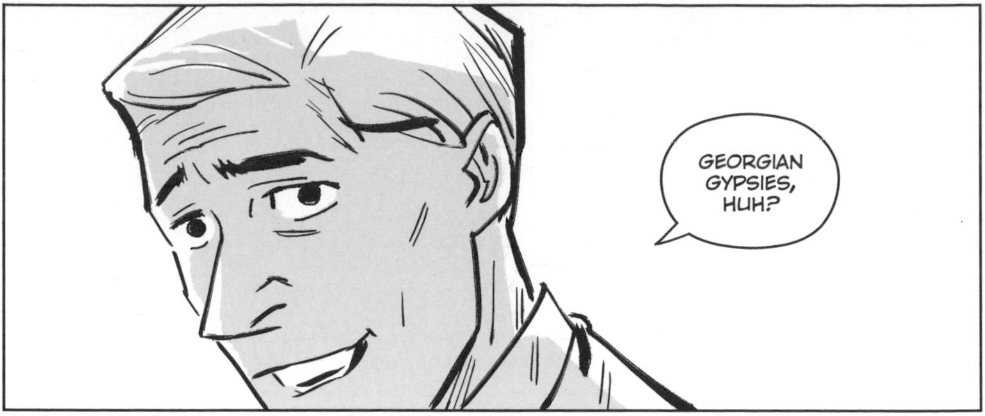
GEORGIAN GYPSIES, HUH?

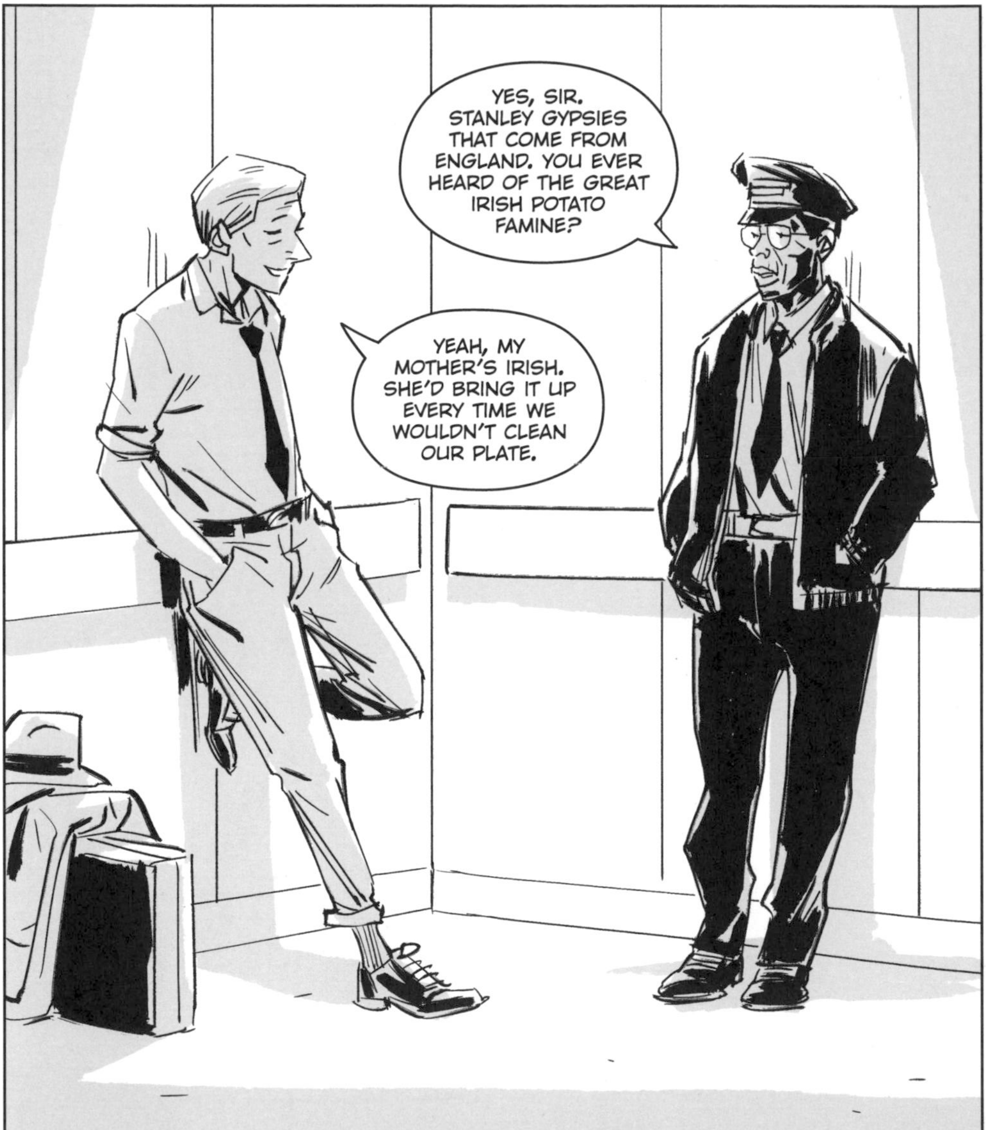
YES, SIR. STANLEY GYPSIES THAT COME FROM ENGLAND. YOU EVER HEARD OF THE GREAT IRISH POTATO FAMINE?
YEAH, MY MOTHER'S IRISH. SHE'D BRING IT UP EVERY TIME WE WOULDN'T CLEAN OUR PLATE.

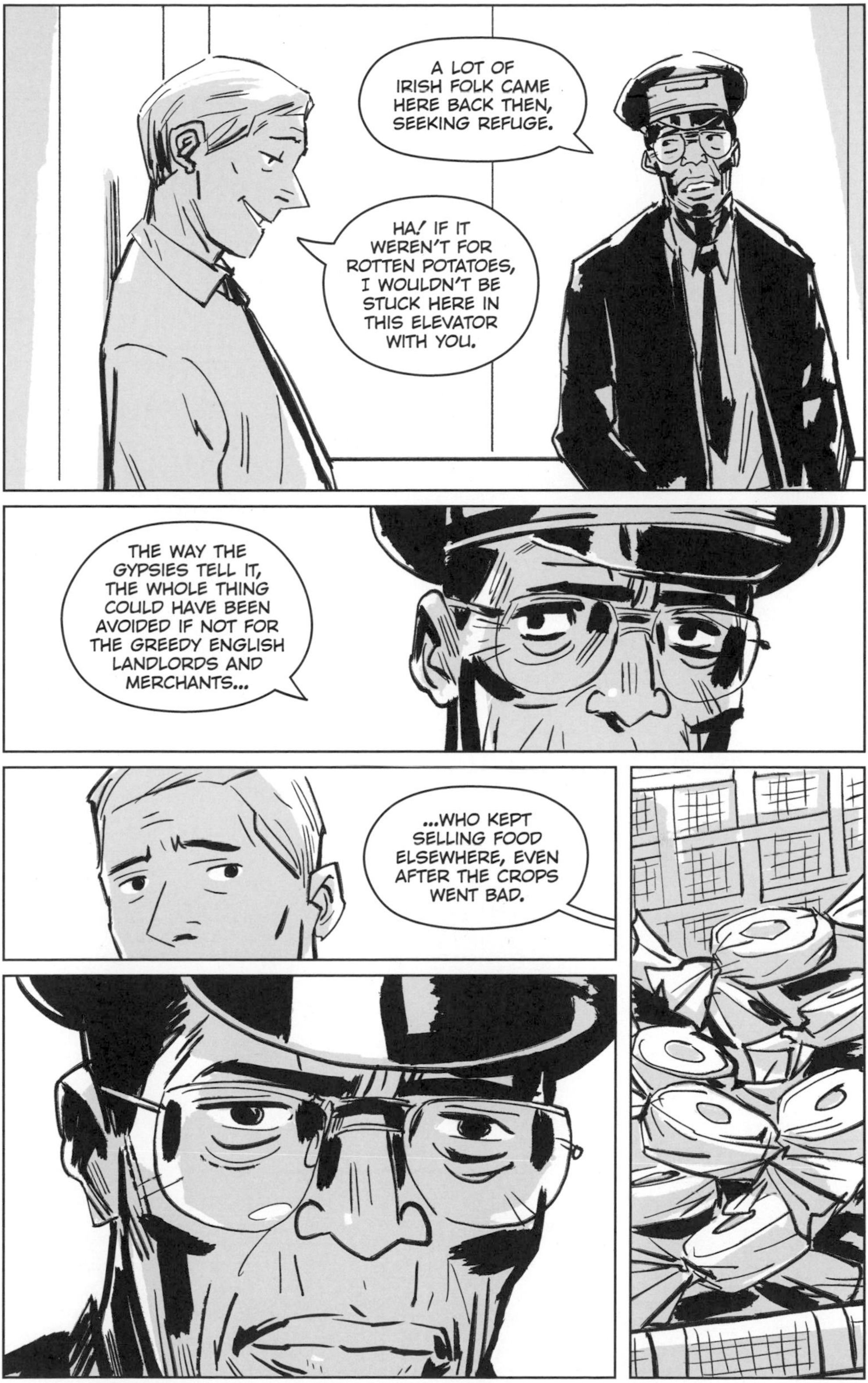
A LOT OF IRISH FOLK CAME HERE BACK THEN, SEEKING REFUGE.
HA! IF IT WEREN'T FOR ROTTEN POTATOES, I WOULDN'T BE STUCK HERE IN THIS ELEVATOR WITH YOU.
THE WAY THE GYPSIES TELL IT, THE WHOLE THING COULD HAVE BEEN AVOIDED IF NOT FOR THE GREEDY ENGLISH LANDLORDS AND MERCHANTS...
...WHO KEPT SELLING FOOD ELSEWHERE, EVEN AFTER THE CROPS WENT BAD.

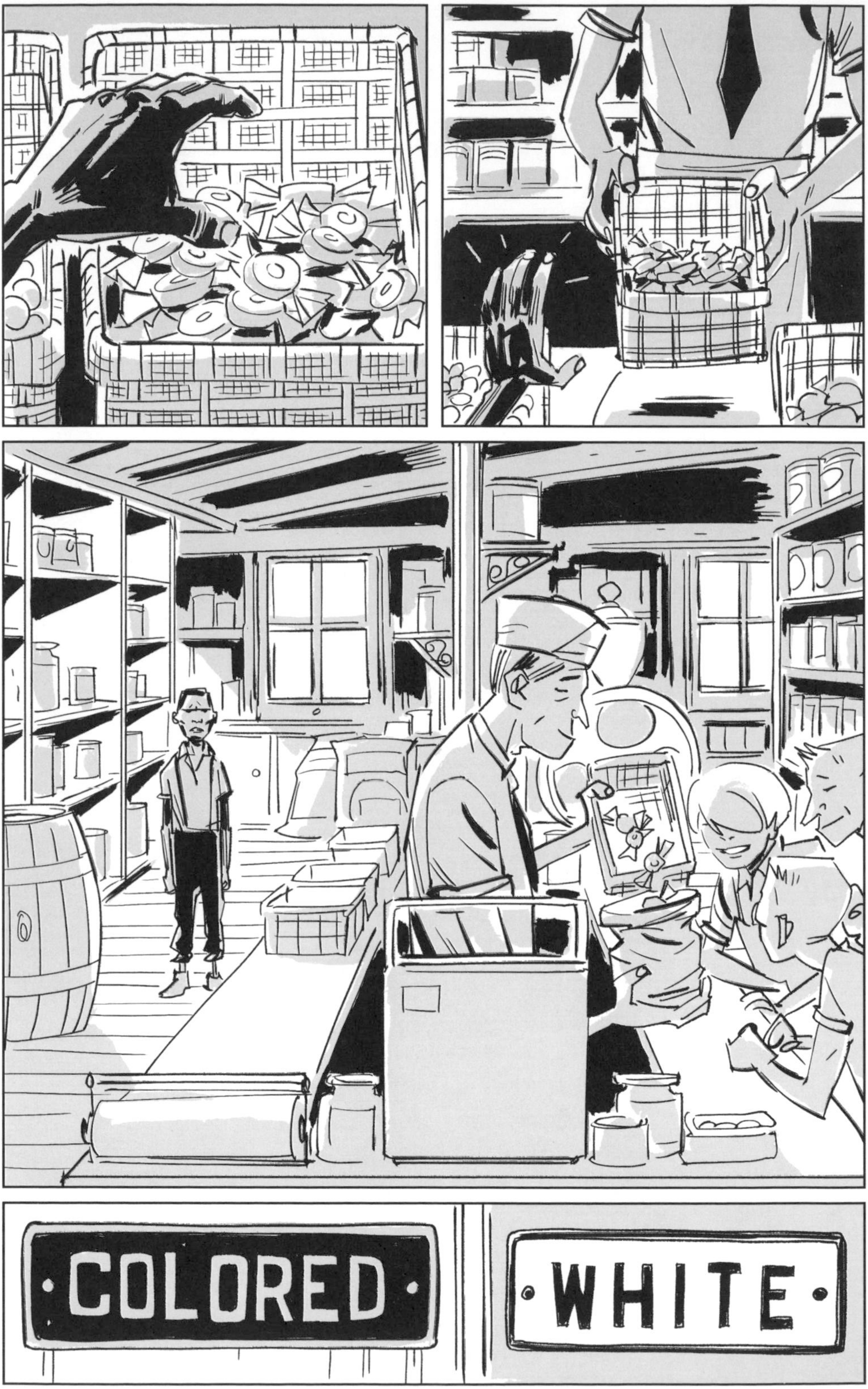
COLORED
WHITE

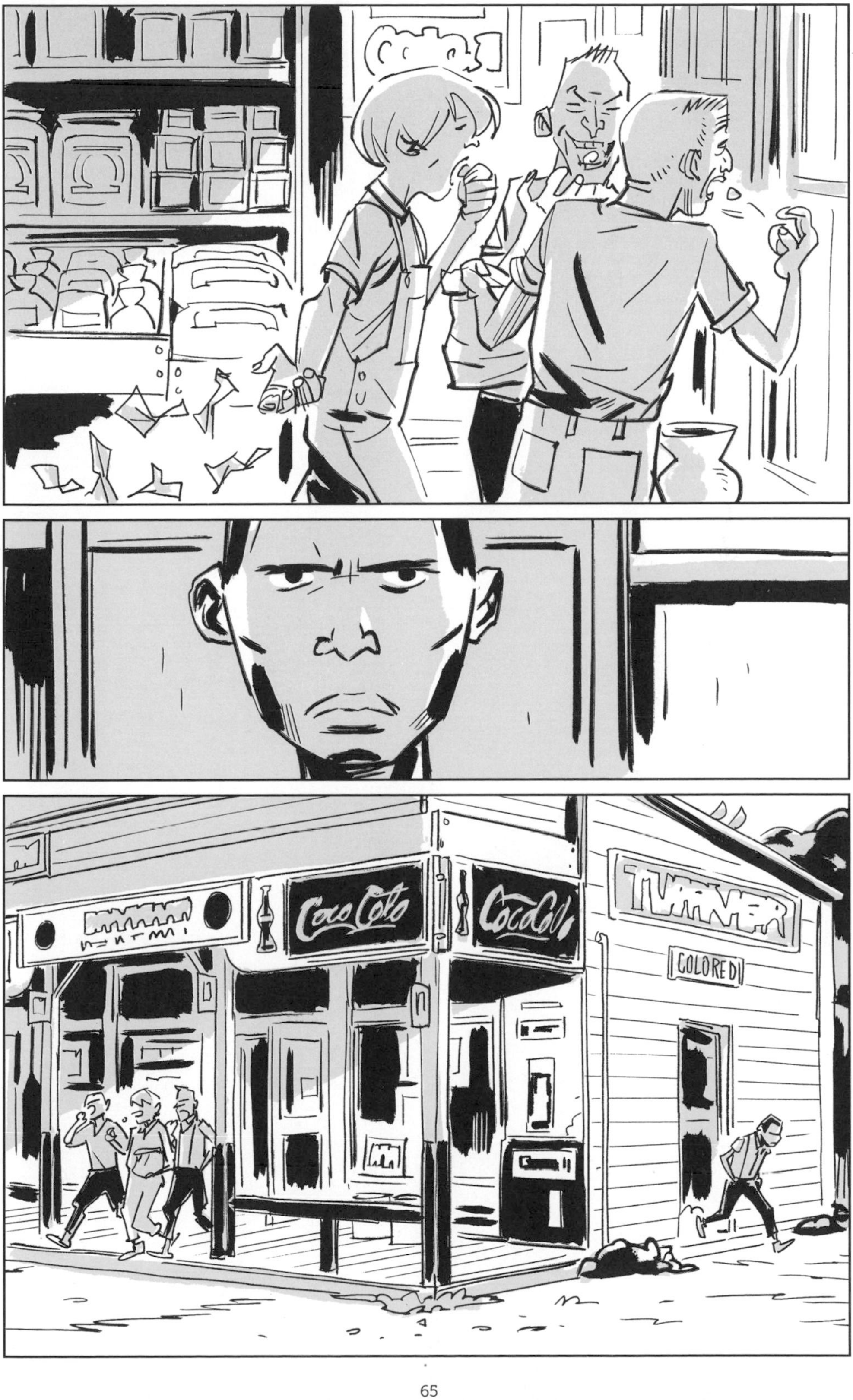
TURNER
COLORED

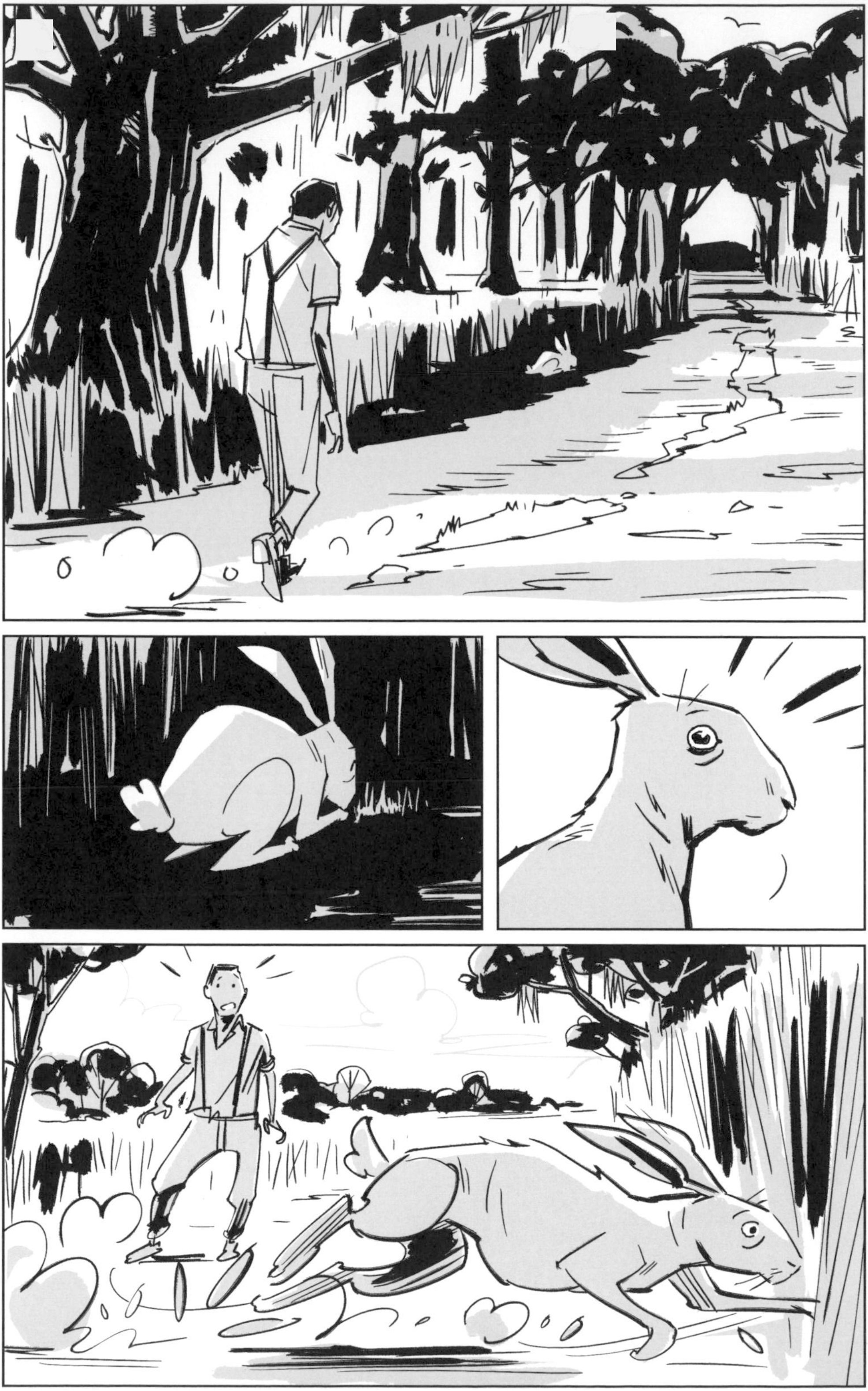

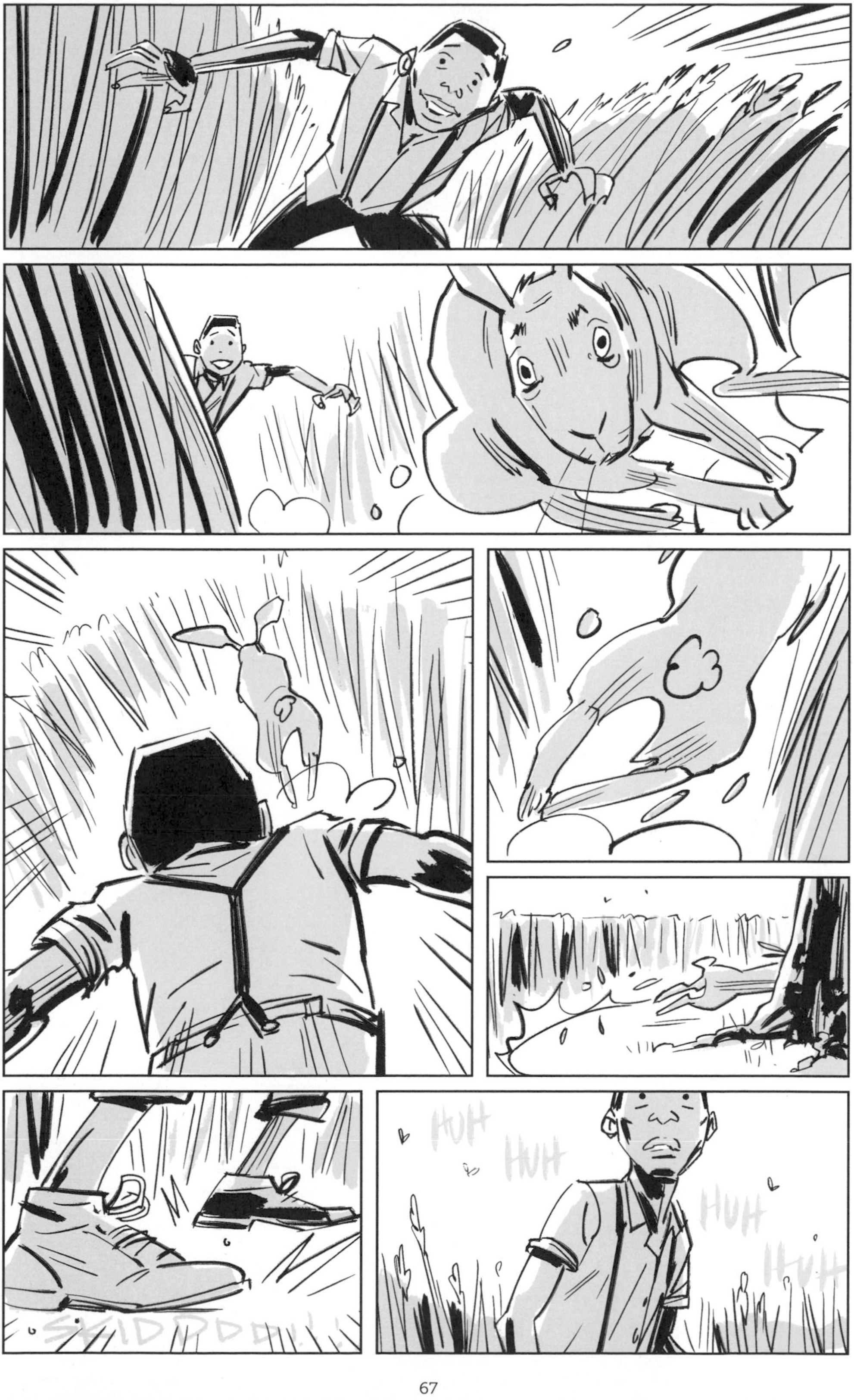
SKIDDDD!!
HUH
HUH
HUH
HUH

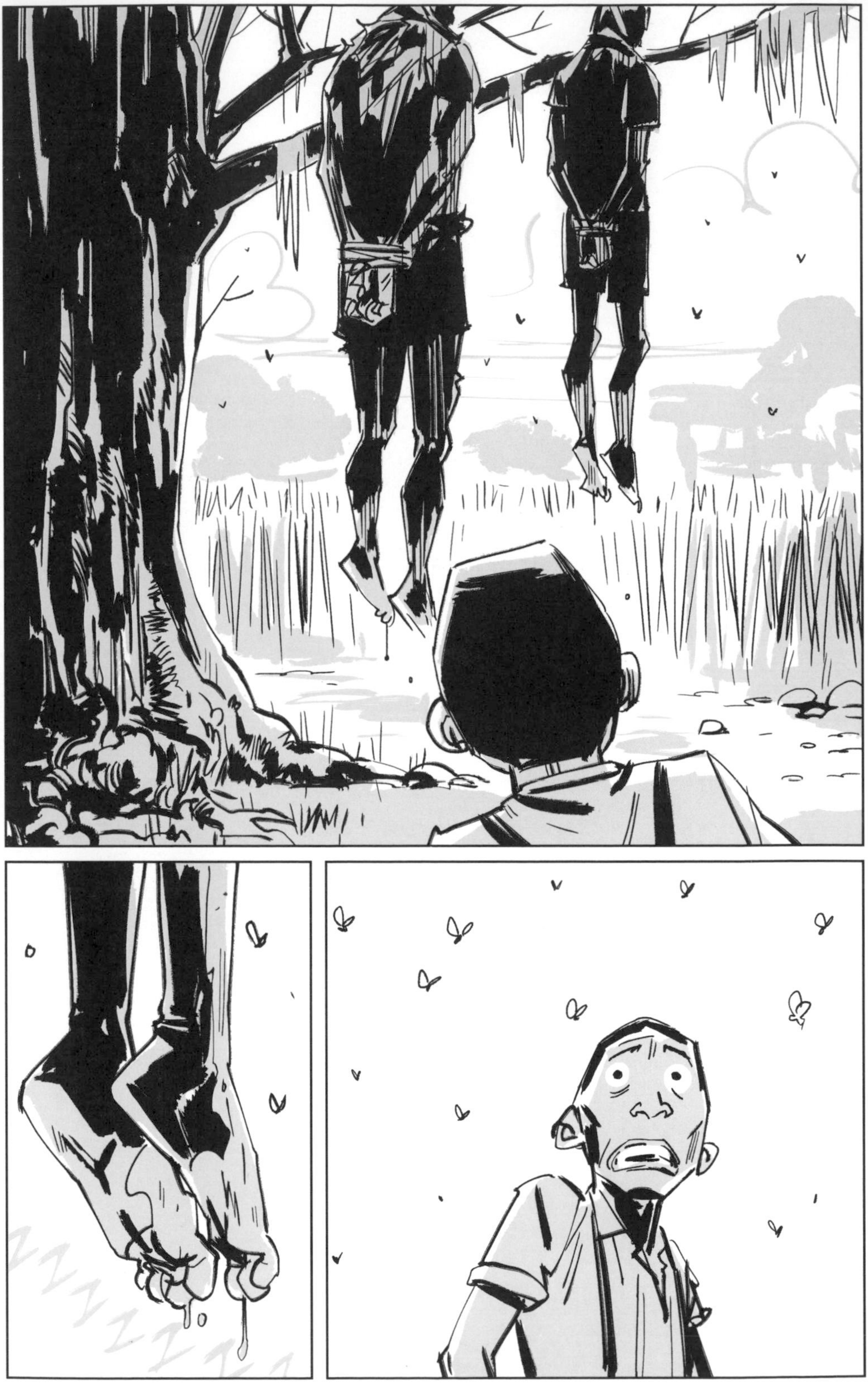

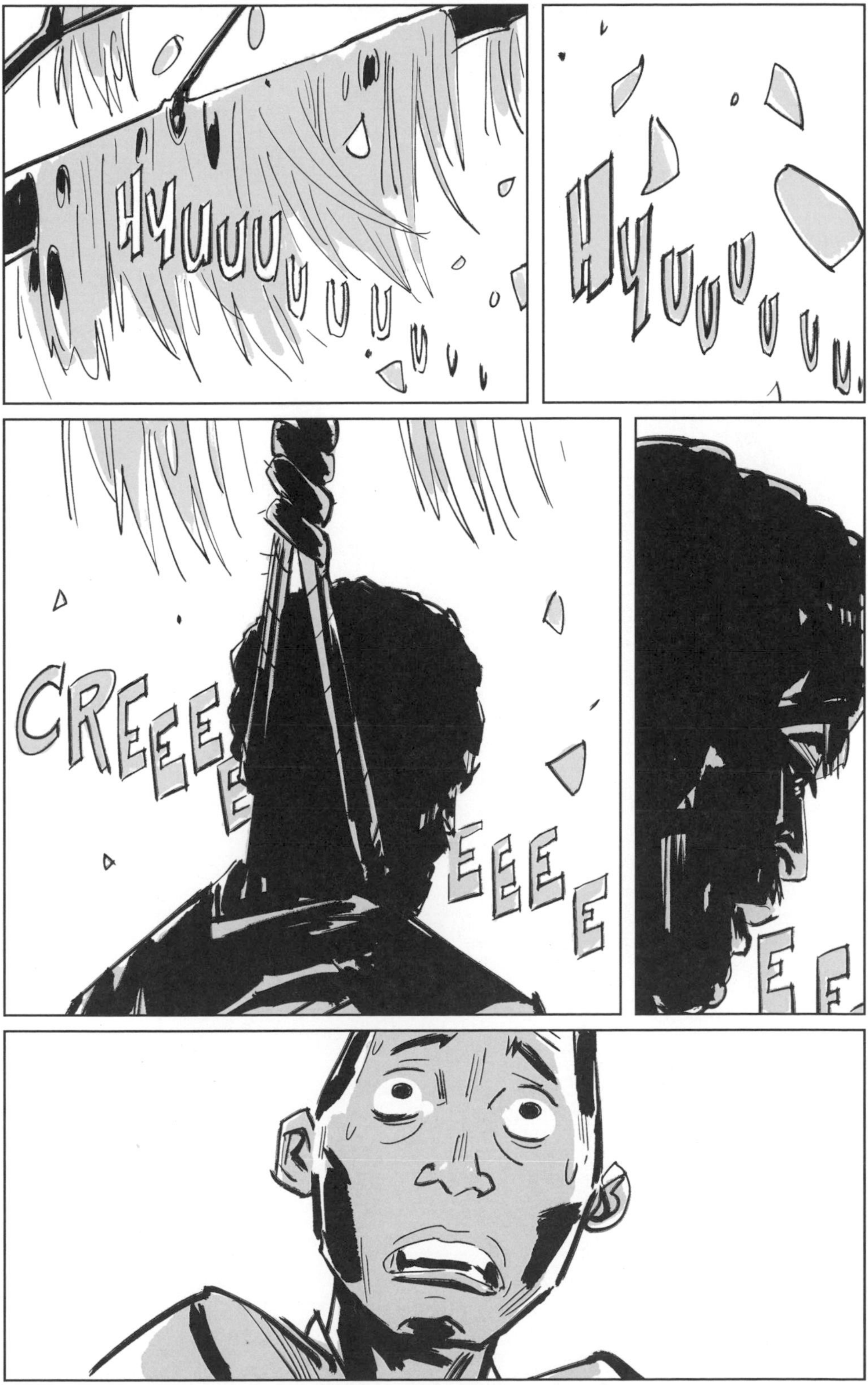
HYUUUUUUUU
HYUUUUUUU
CREEEEEEEEE
EE

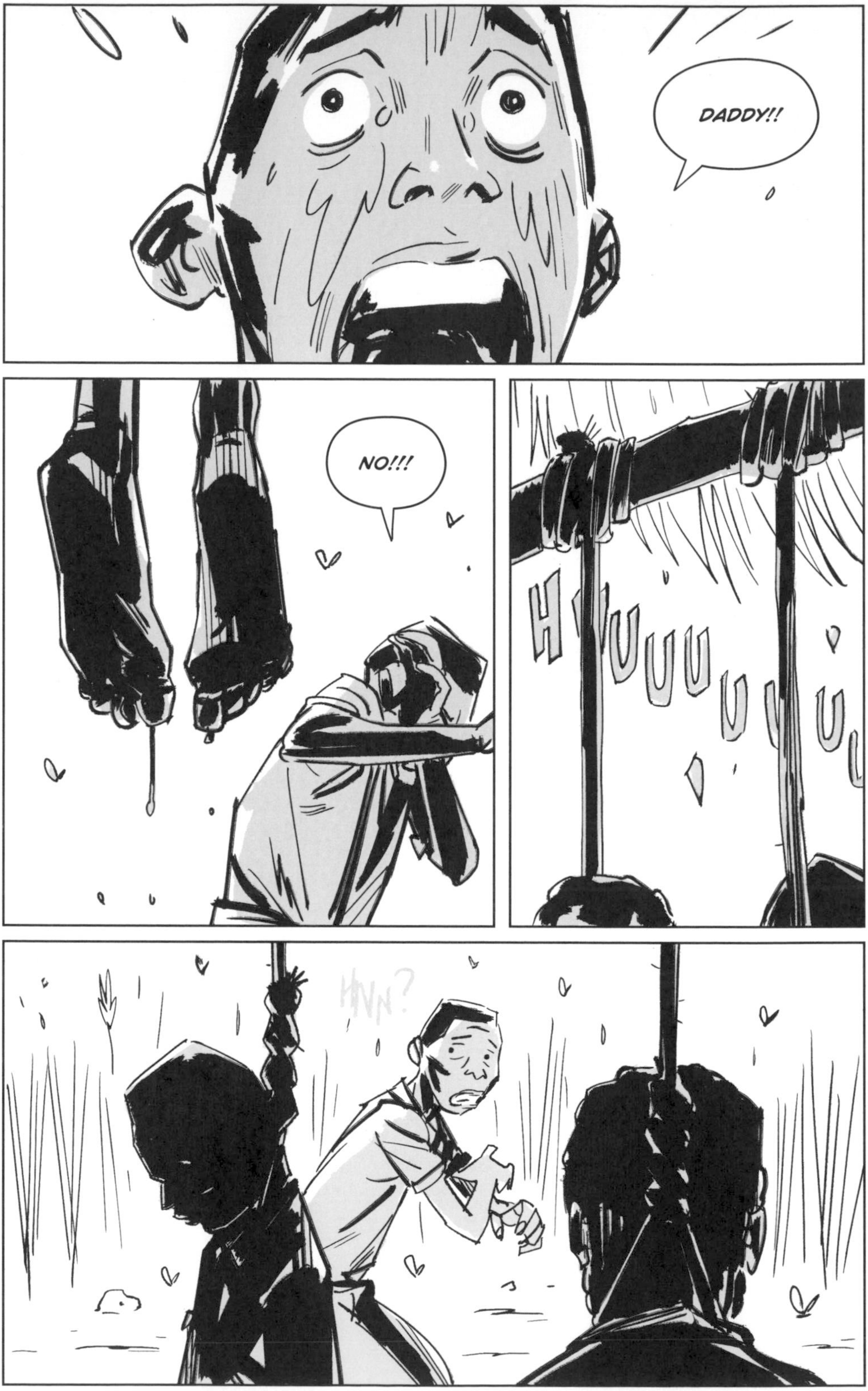
DADDY!!
NO!!!
HUUUUUUUU
HNN?

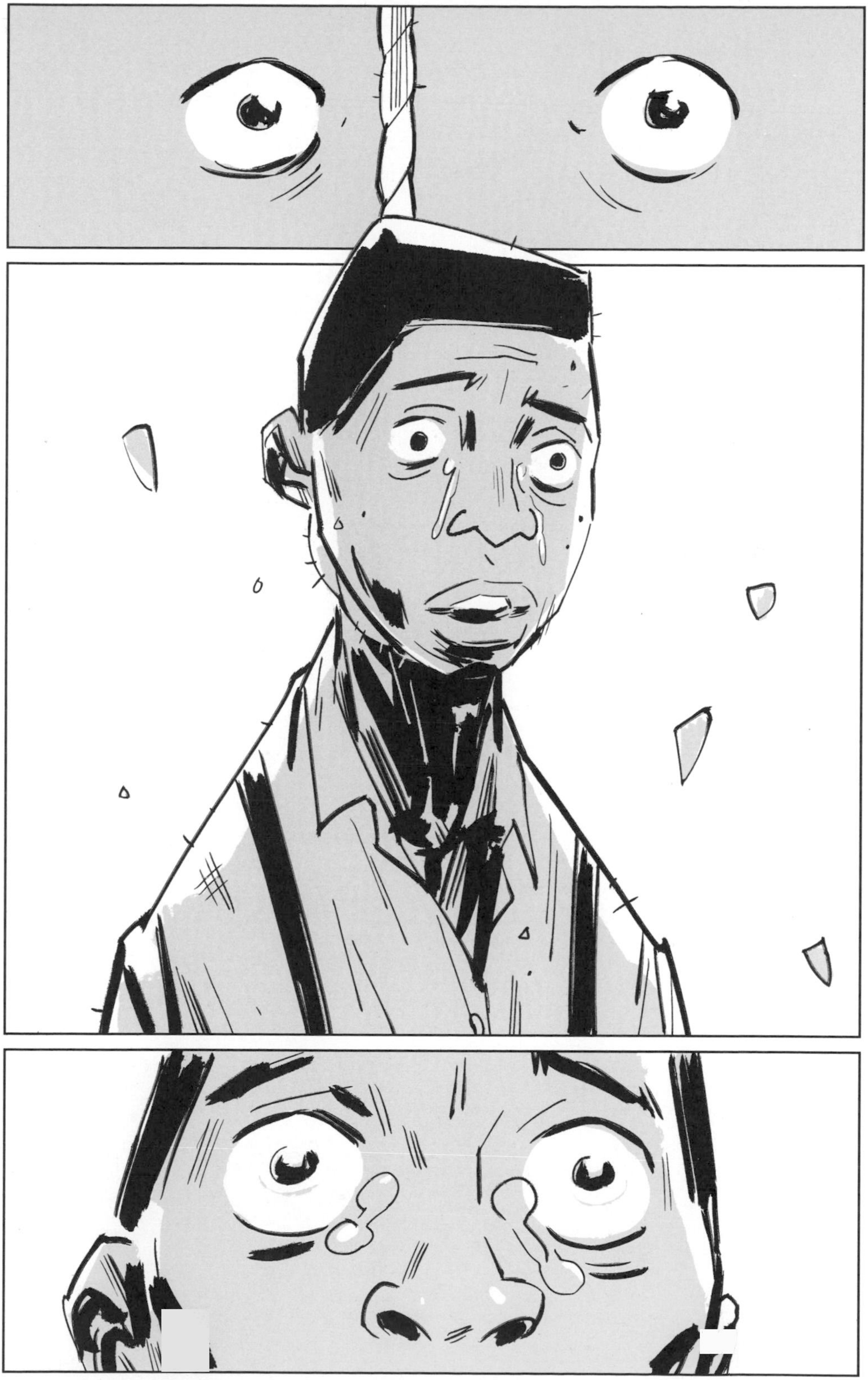

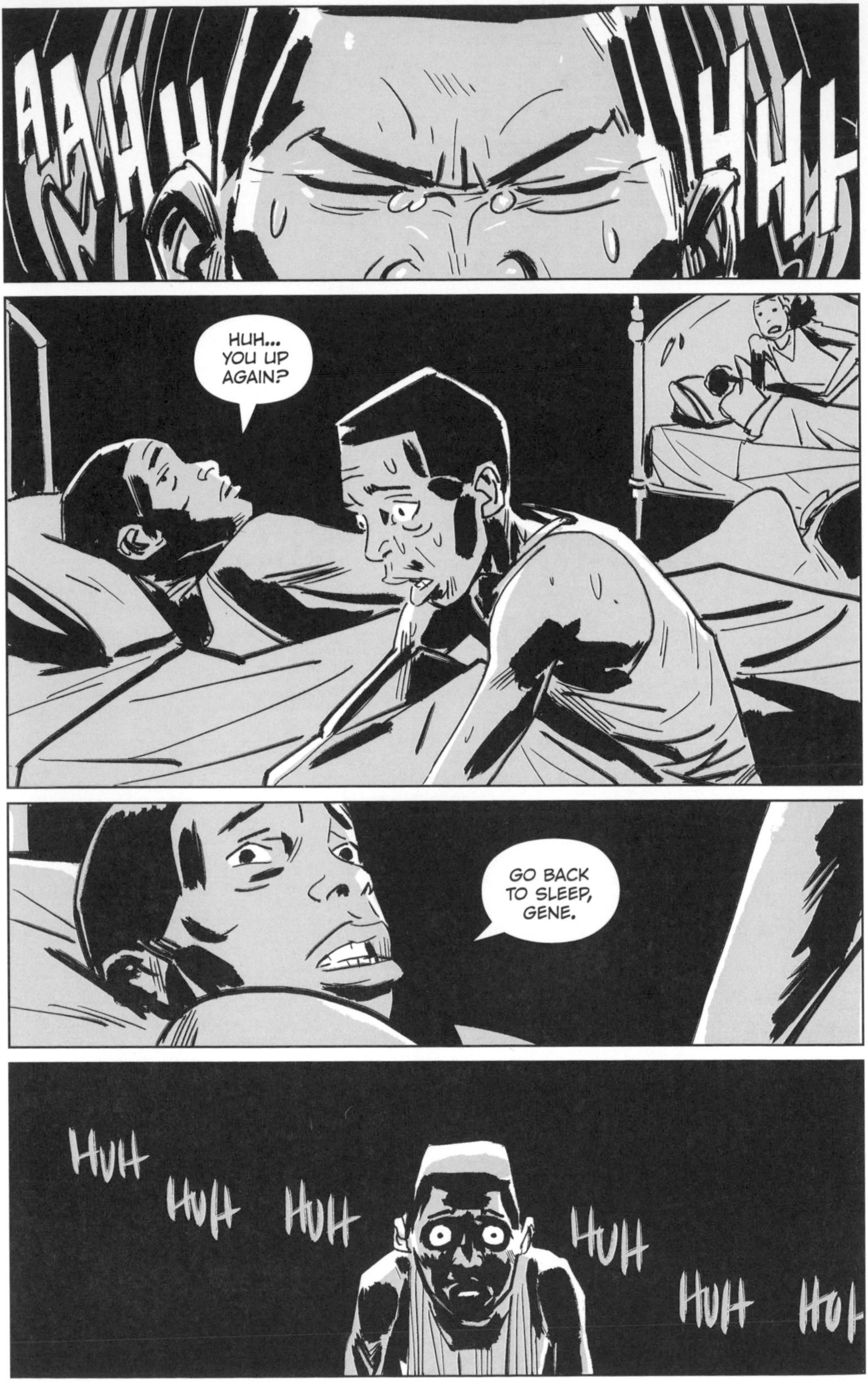
AAHH
HHH
HUH... YOU UP AGAIN?
GO BACK TO SLEEP, GENE.
HUH HUH HUH HUH HUH HUH

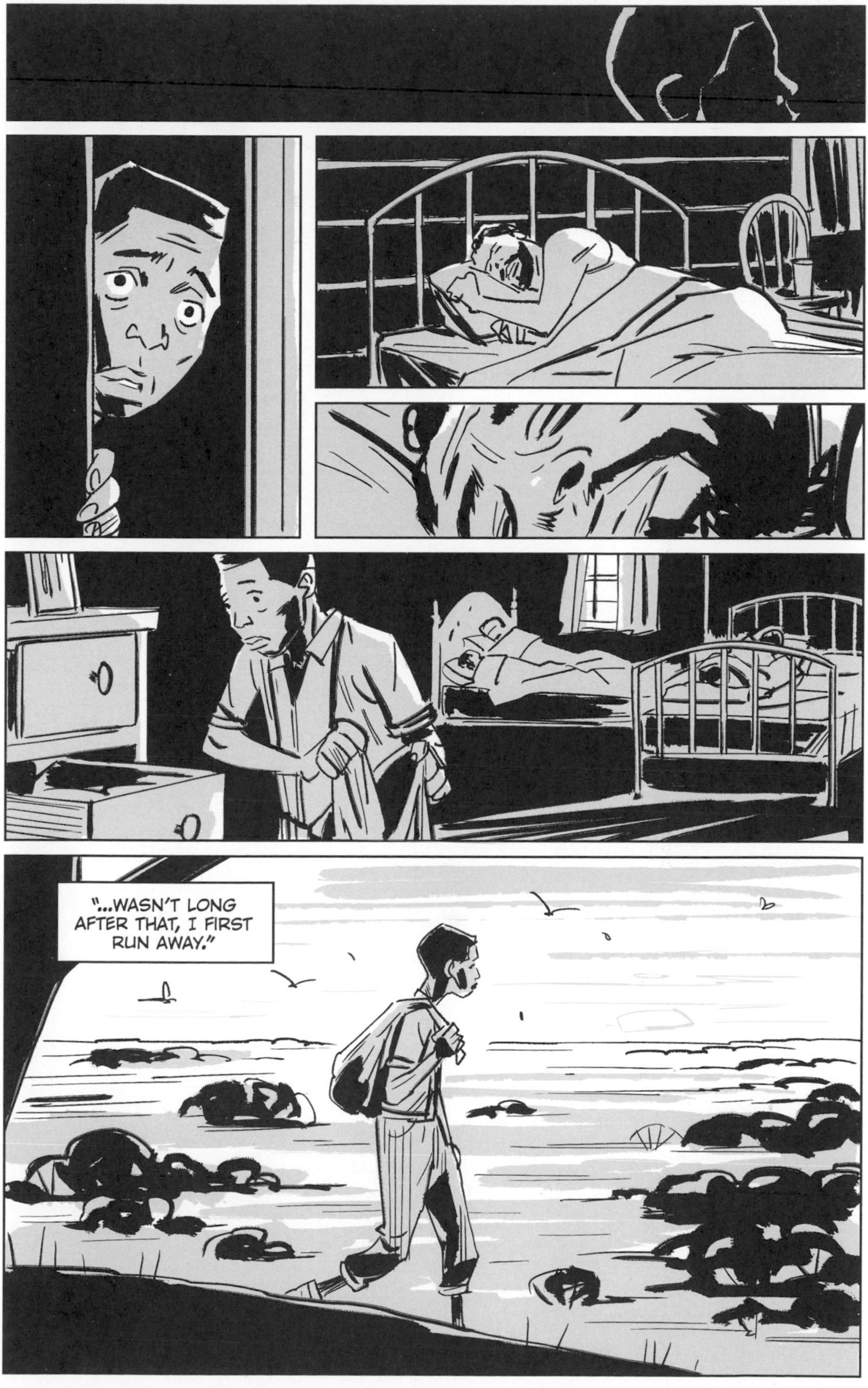
"...WASN'T LONG AFTER THAT, I FIRST RUN AWAY."

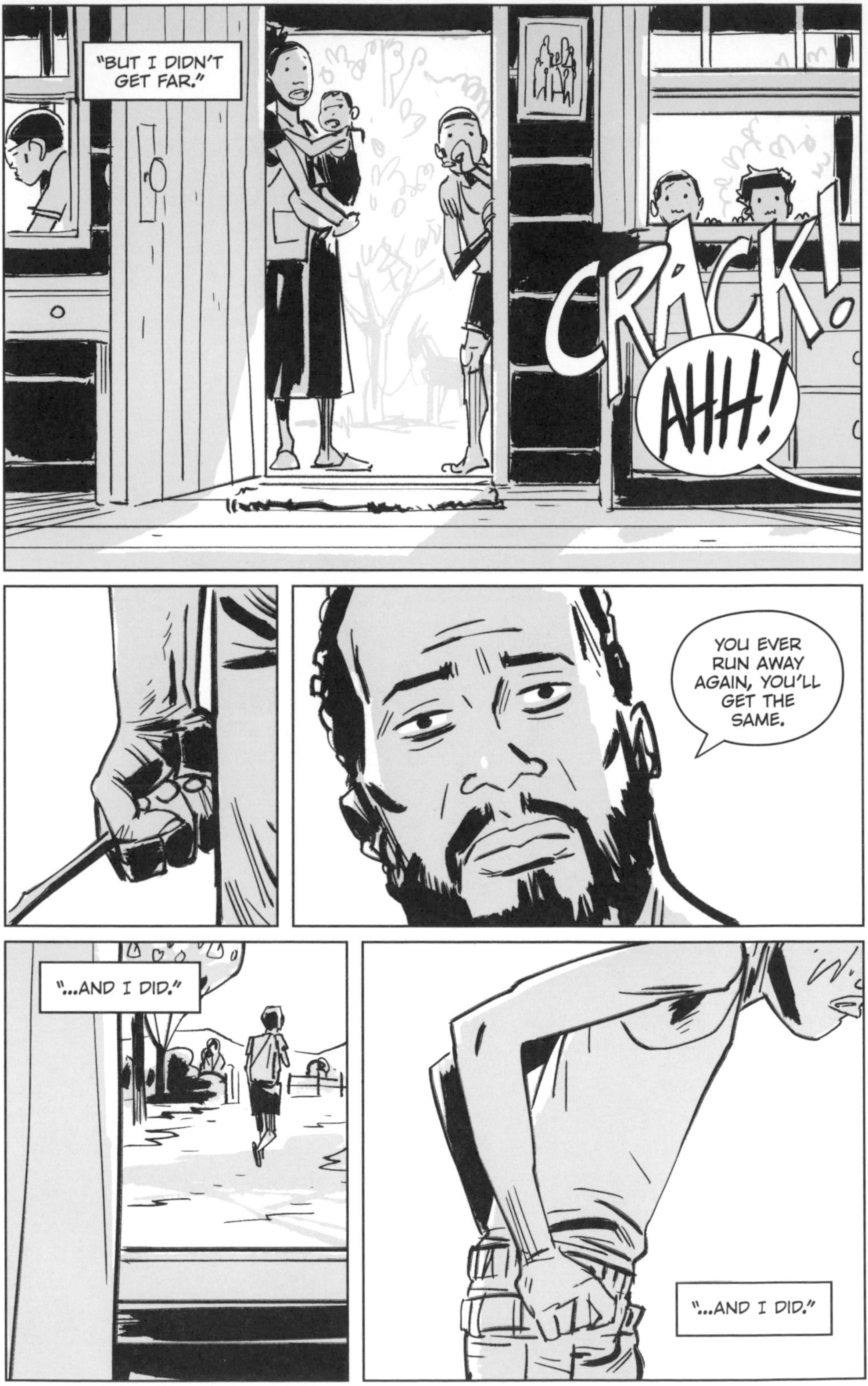
"BUT I DIDN'T GET FAR."
CRACK!
AHH!
YOU EVER RUN AWAY AGAIN, YOU'LL GET THE SAME.
"...AND I DID."
"...AND I DID."

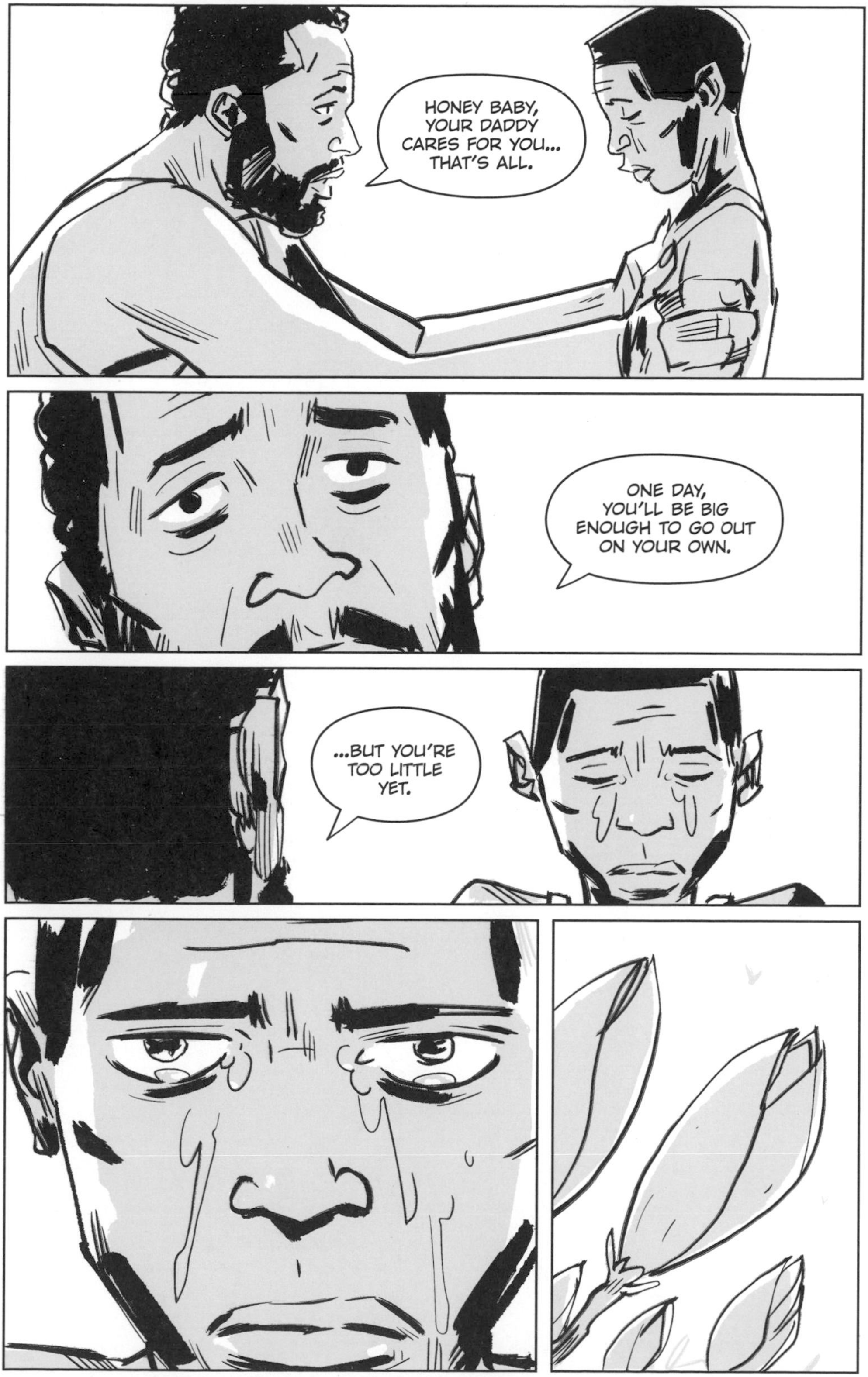
HONEY BABY, YOUR DADDY CARES FOR YOU... THAT'S ALL.
ONE DAY, YOU'LL BE BIG ENOUGH TO GO OUT ON YOUR OWN.
...BUT YOU'RE TOO LITTLE YET.

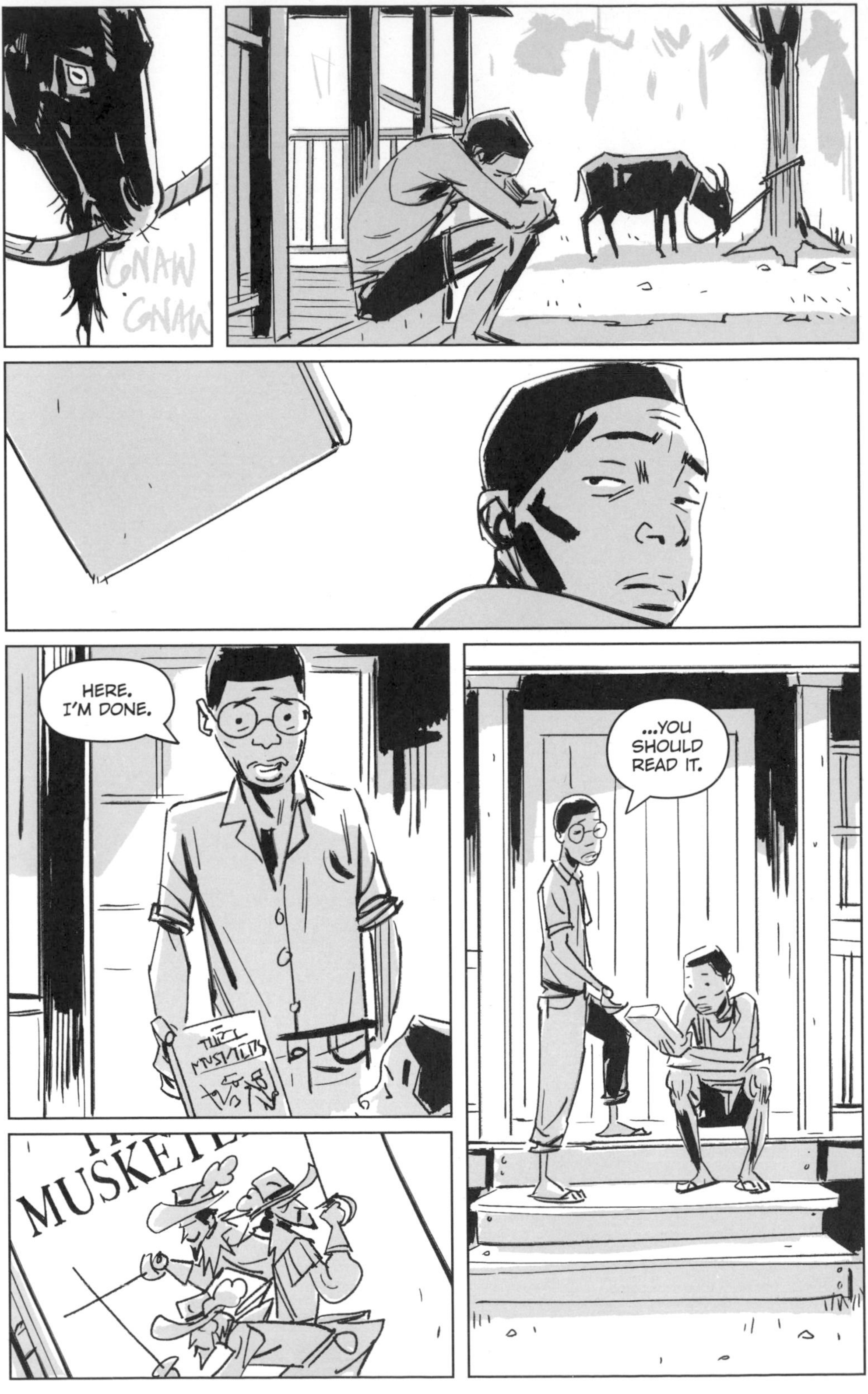
GNAW
GNAW
HERE. I'M DONE.
...YOU SHOULD READ IT.
MUSKETE

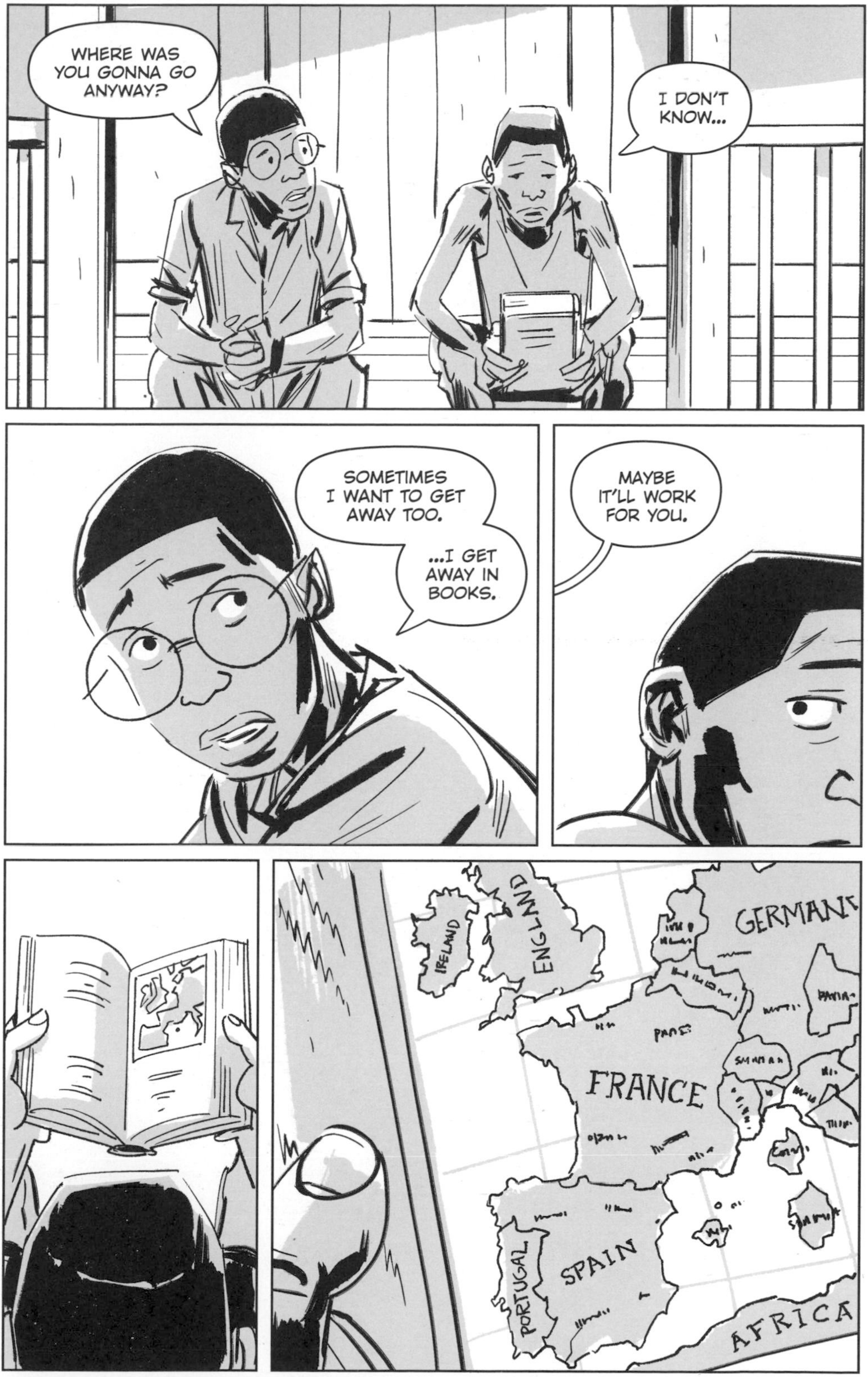
WHERE WAS YOU GONNA GO ANYWAY?
I DON'T KNOW...
SOMETIMES I WANT TO GET AWAY TOO.
...I GET AWAY IN BOOKS.
MAYBE IT'LL WORK FOR YOU.
IRELAND
ENGLAND
GERMAN
FRANCE
SPAIN
PORTUGAL
AFRICA

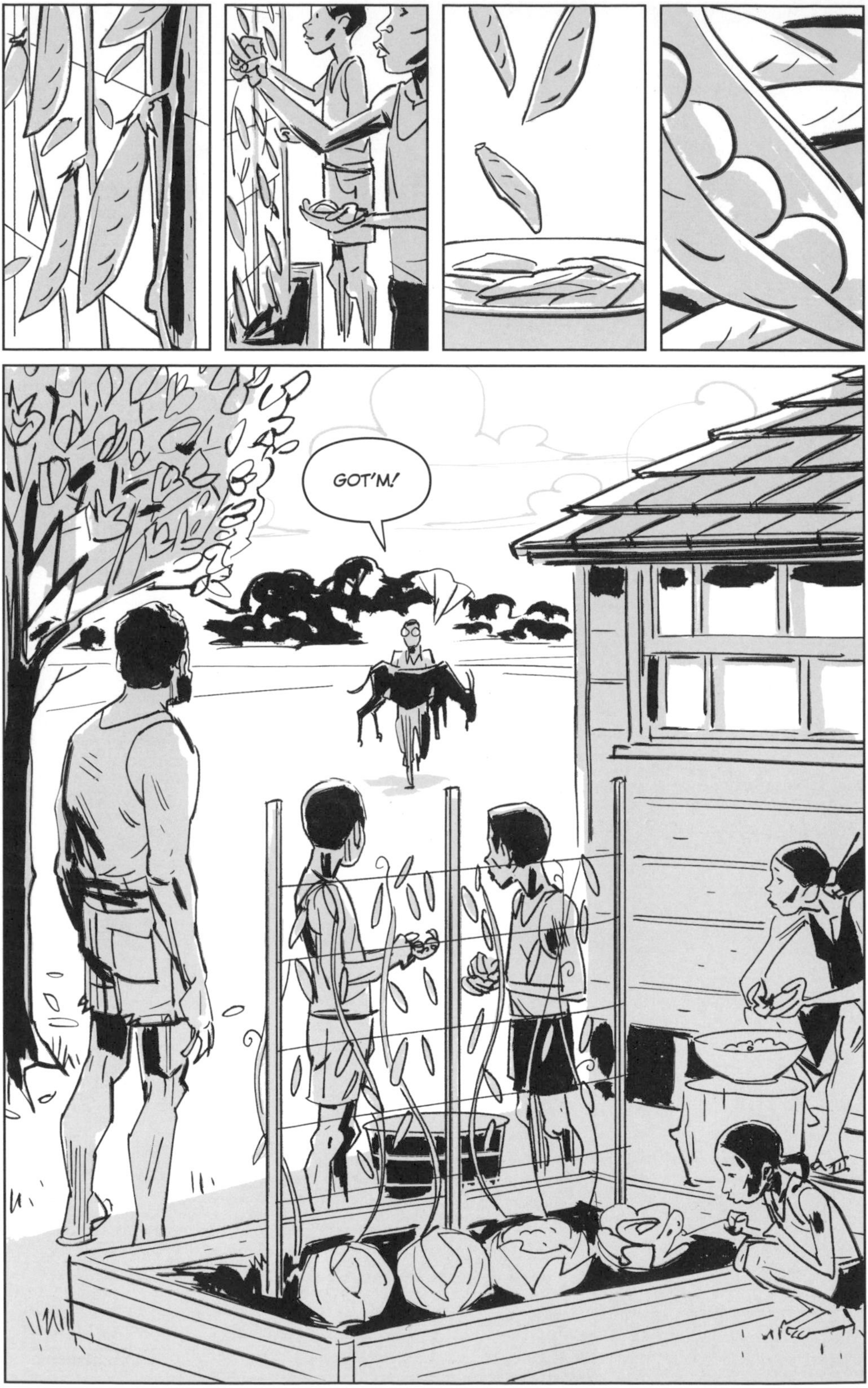
GOT'M!

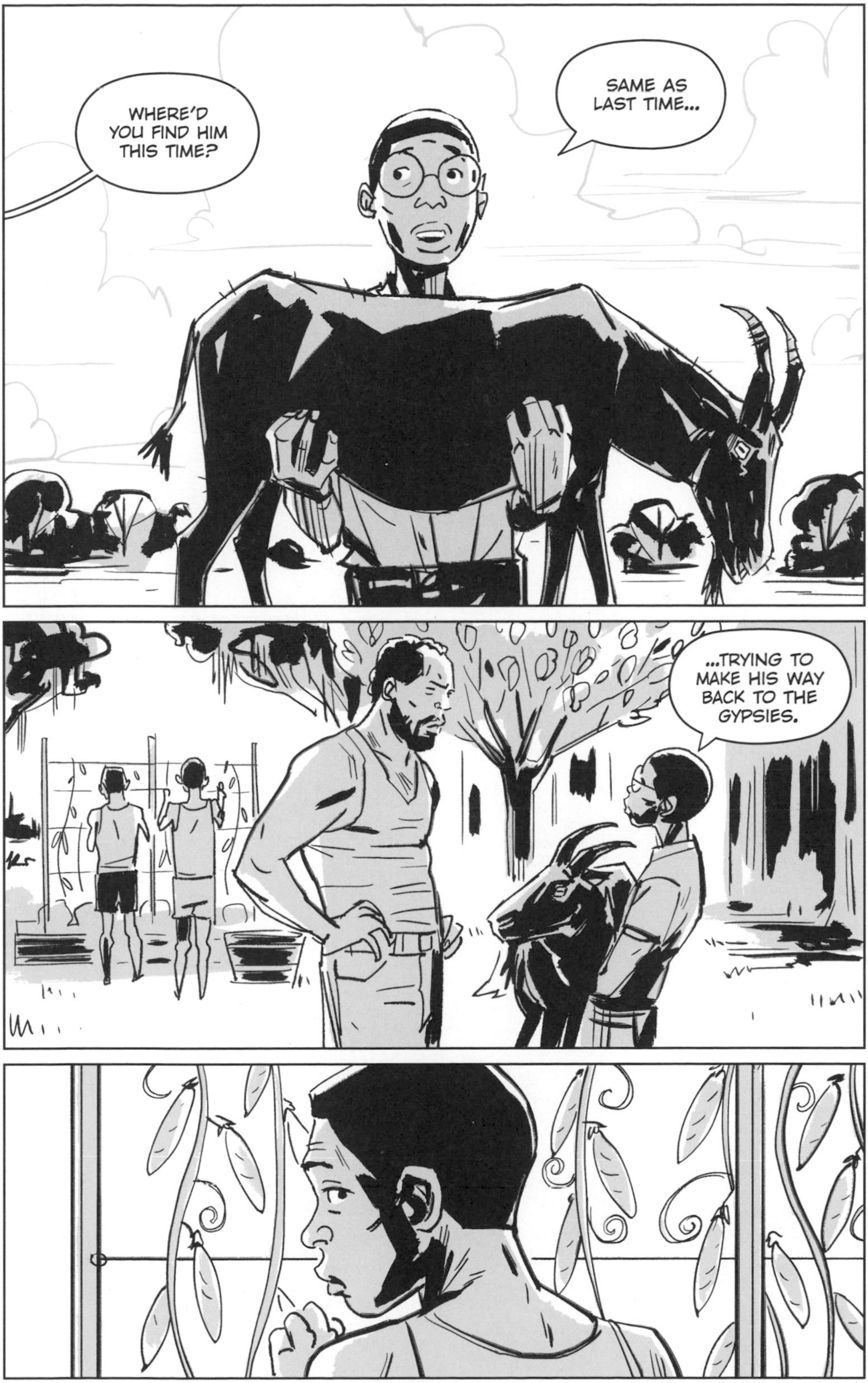
WHERE'D YOU FIND HIM THIS TIME?
SAME AS LAST TIME...
...TRYING TO MAKE HIS WAY BACK TO THE GYPSIES.

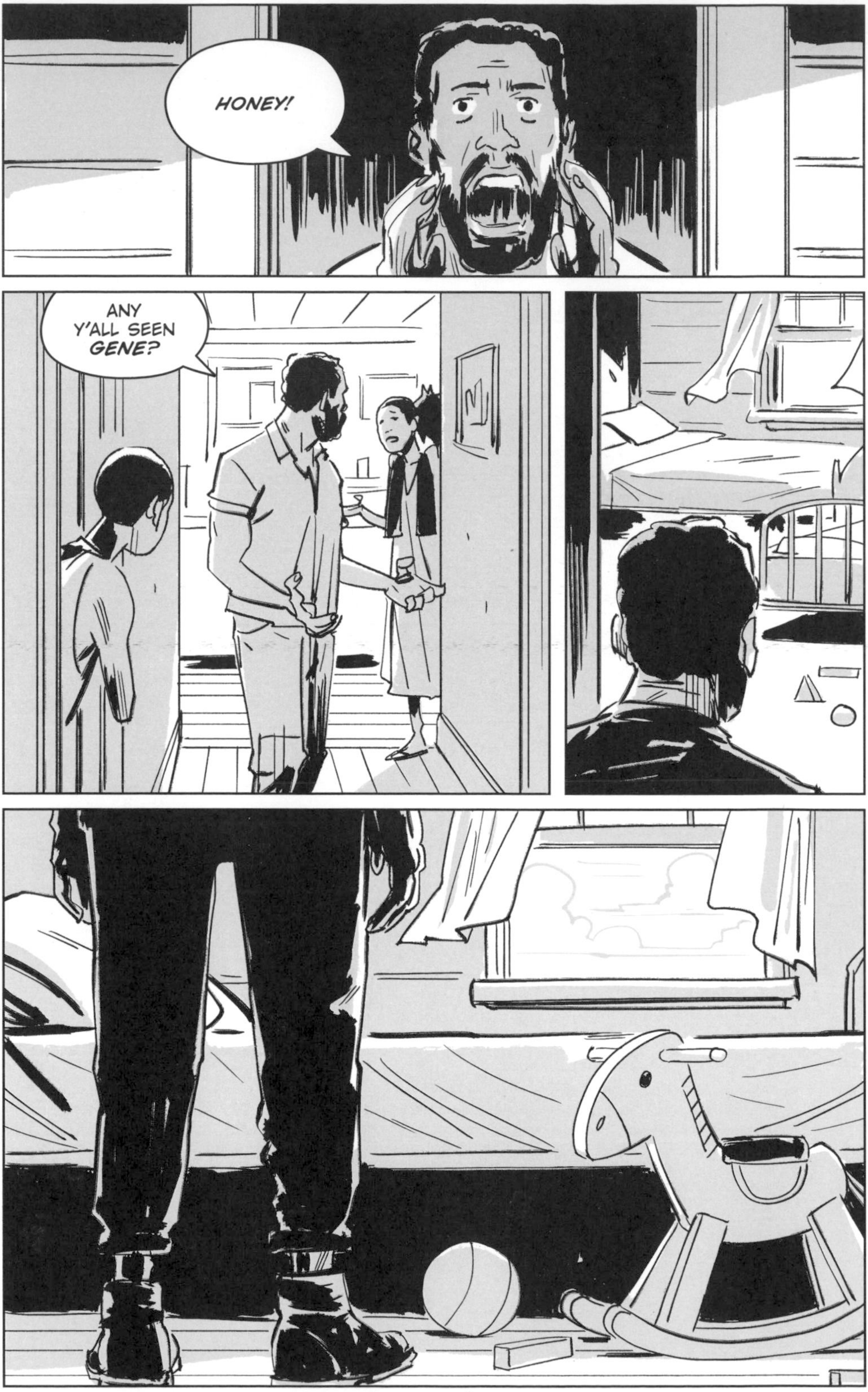
HONEY!
ANY Y'ALL SEEN GENE?

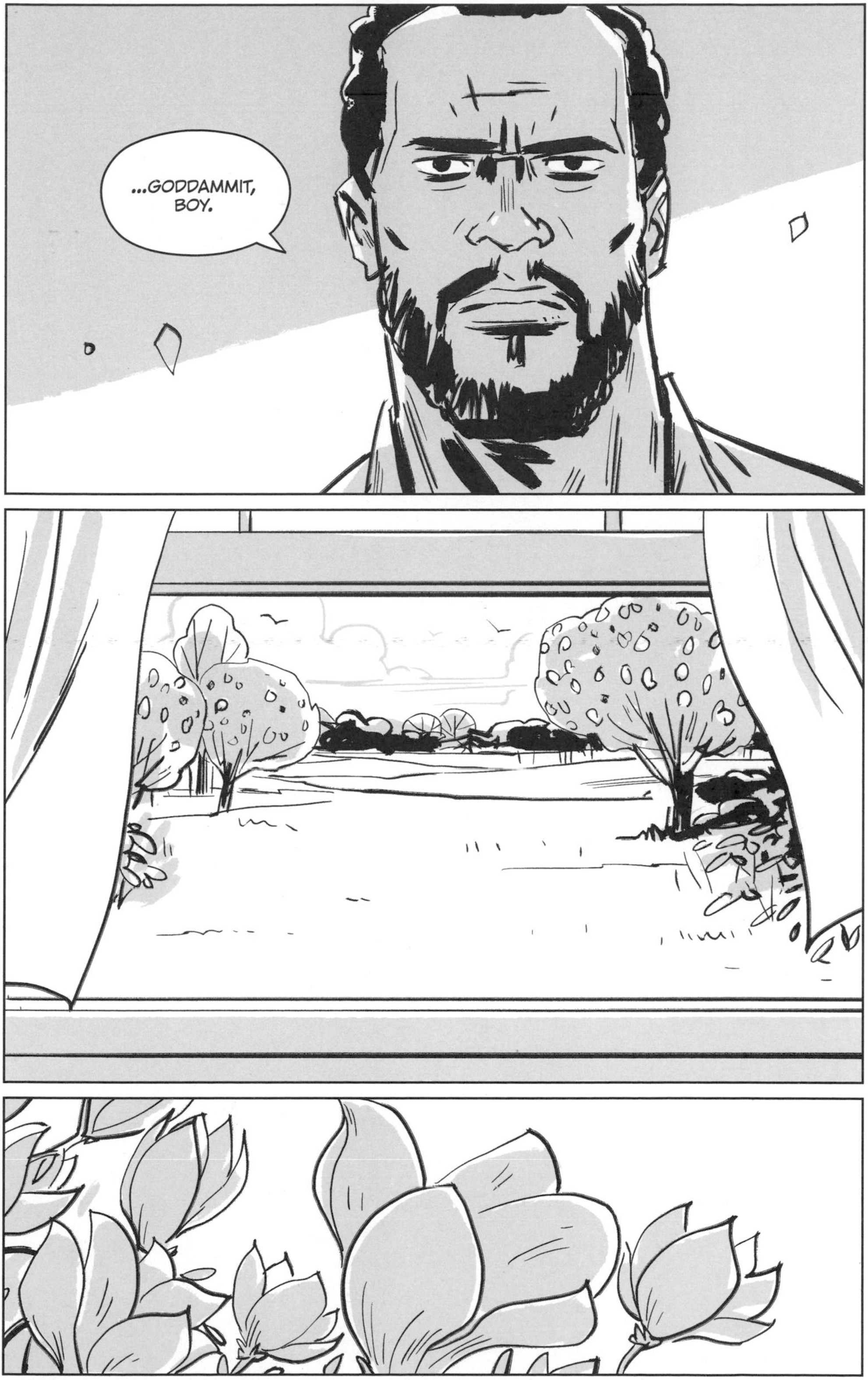
...GODDAMMIT, BOY.

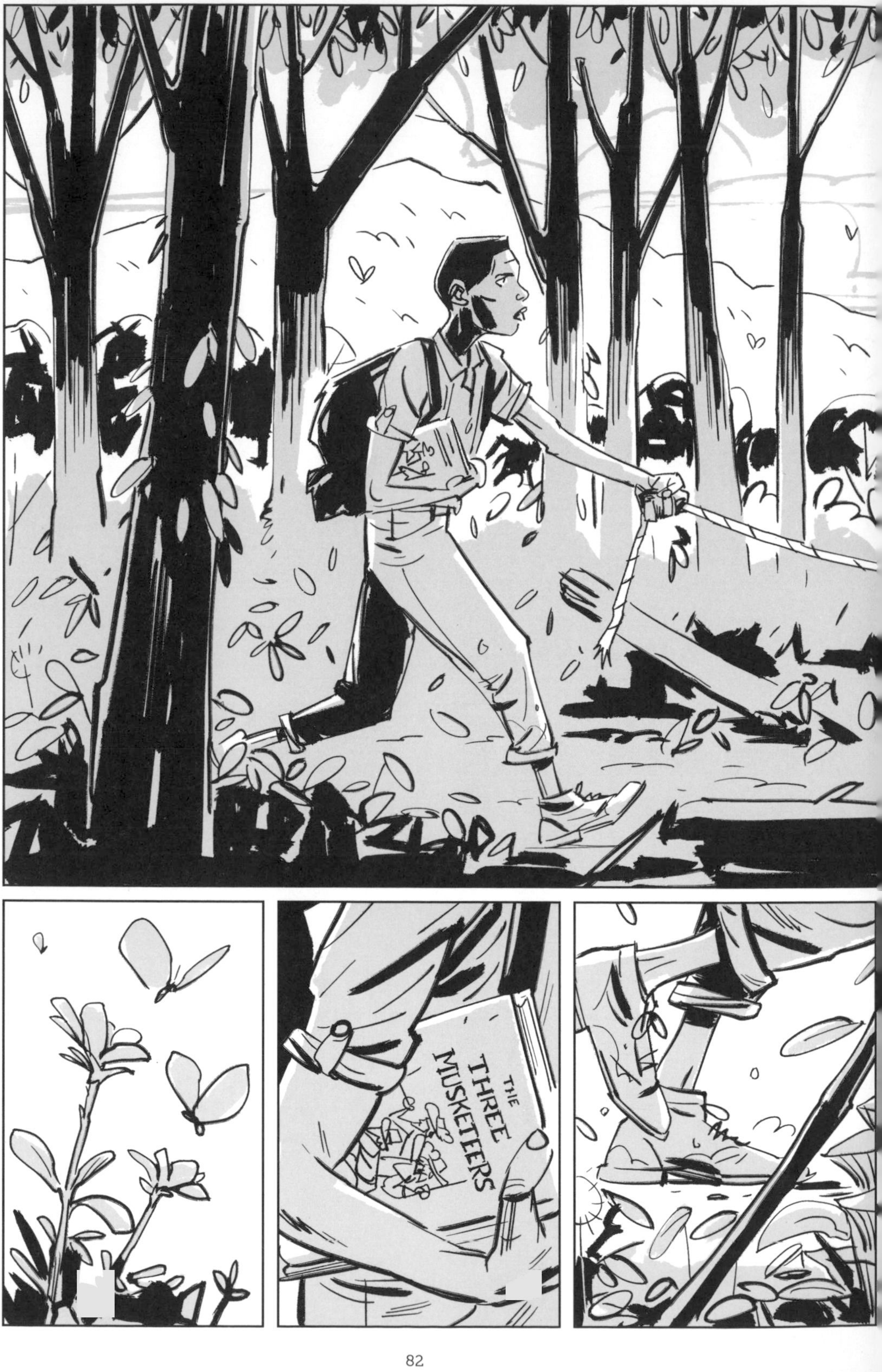
THE THREE MUSKETEERS

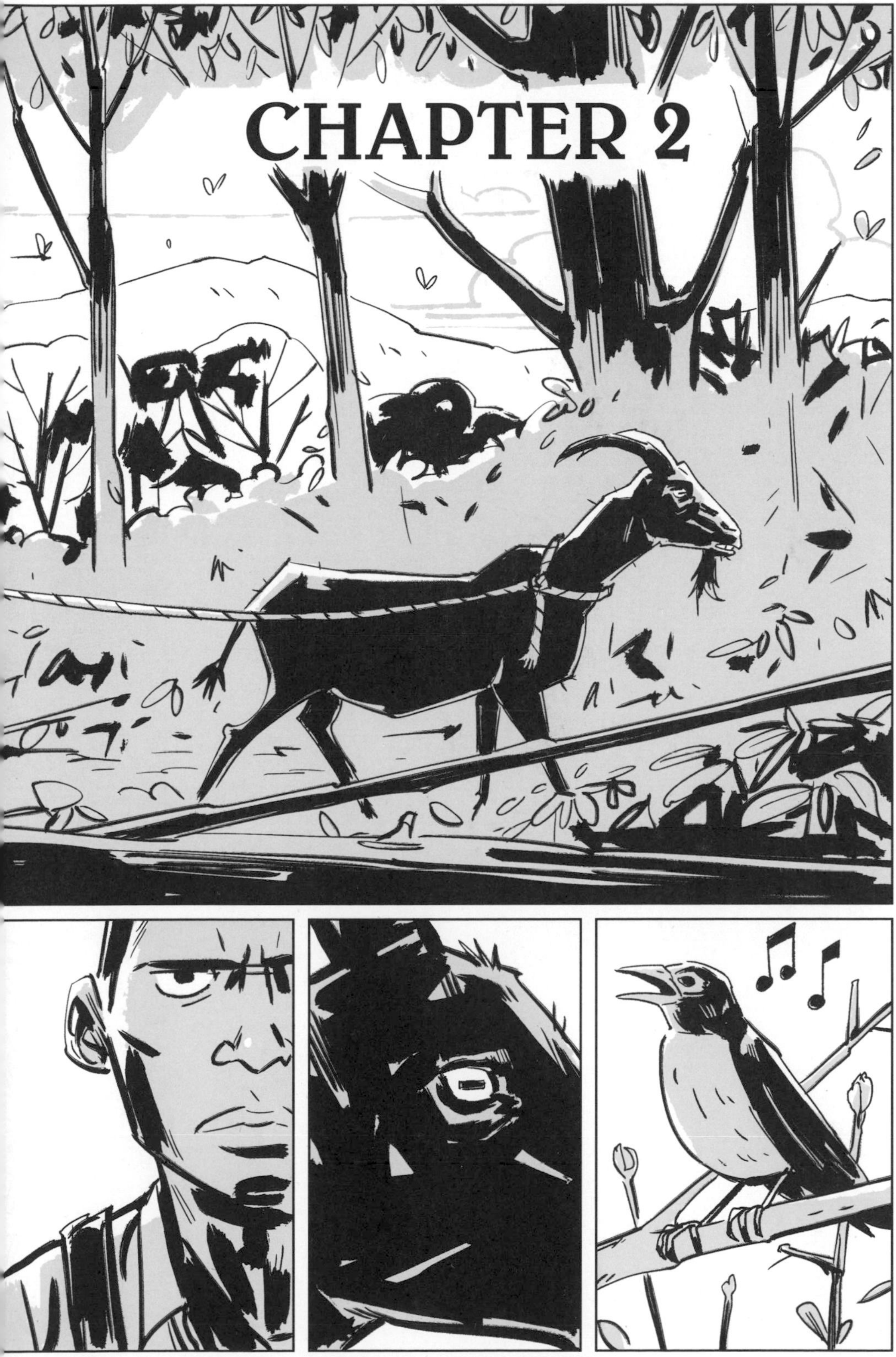
CHAPTER 2

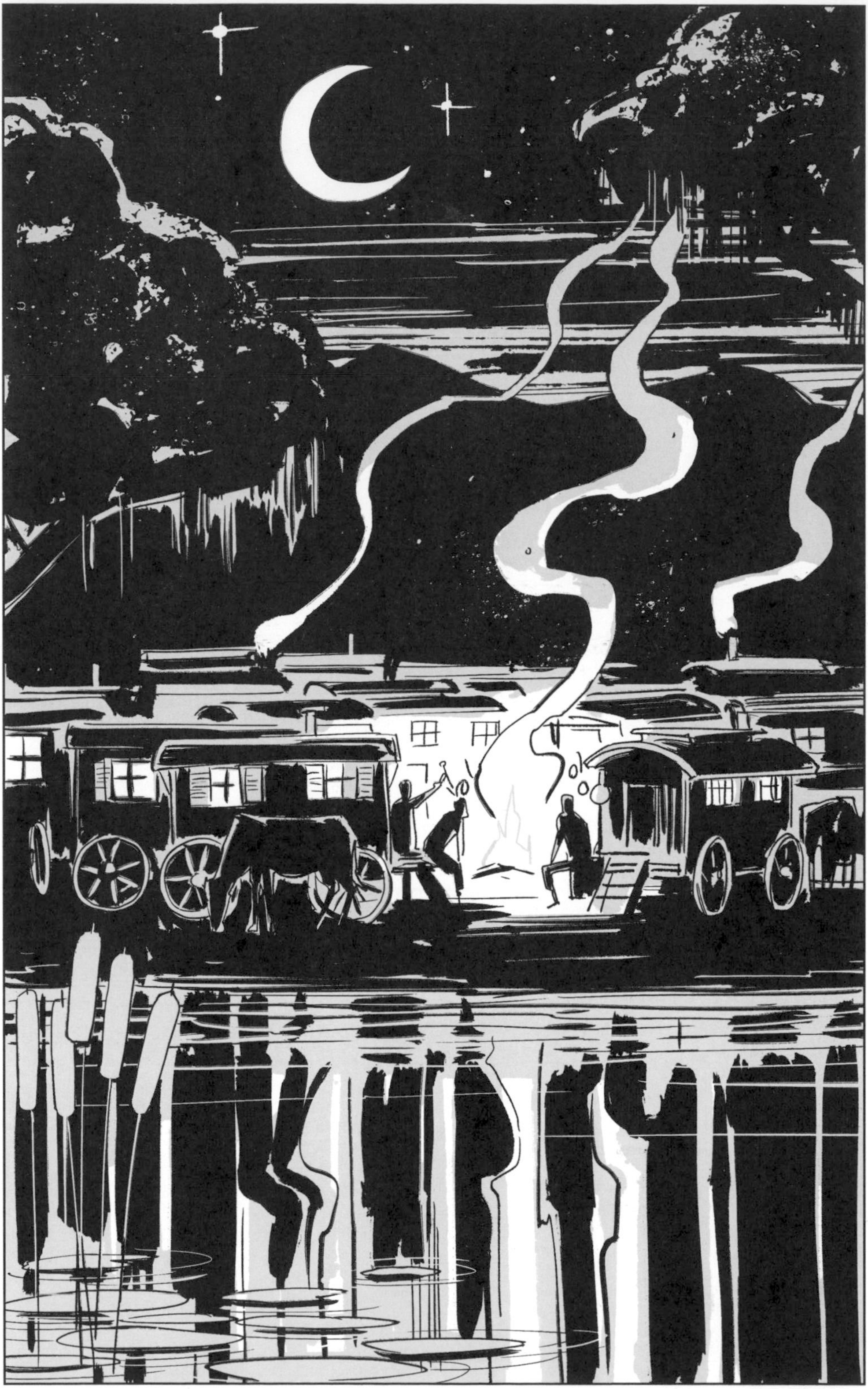

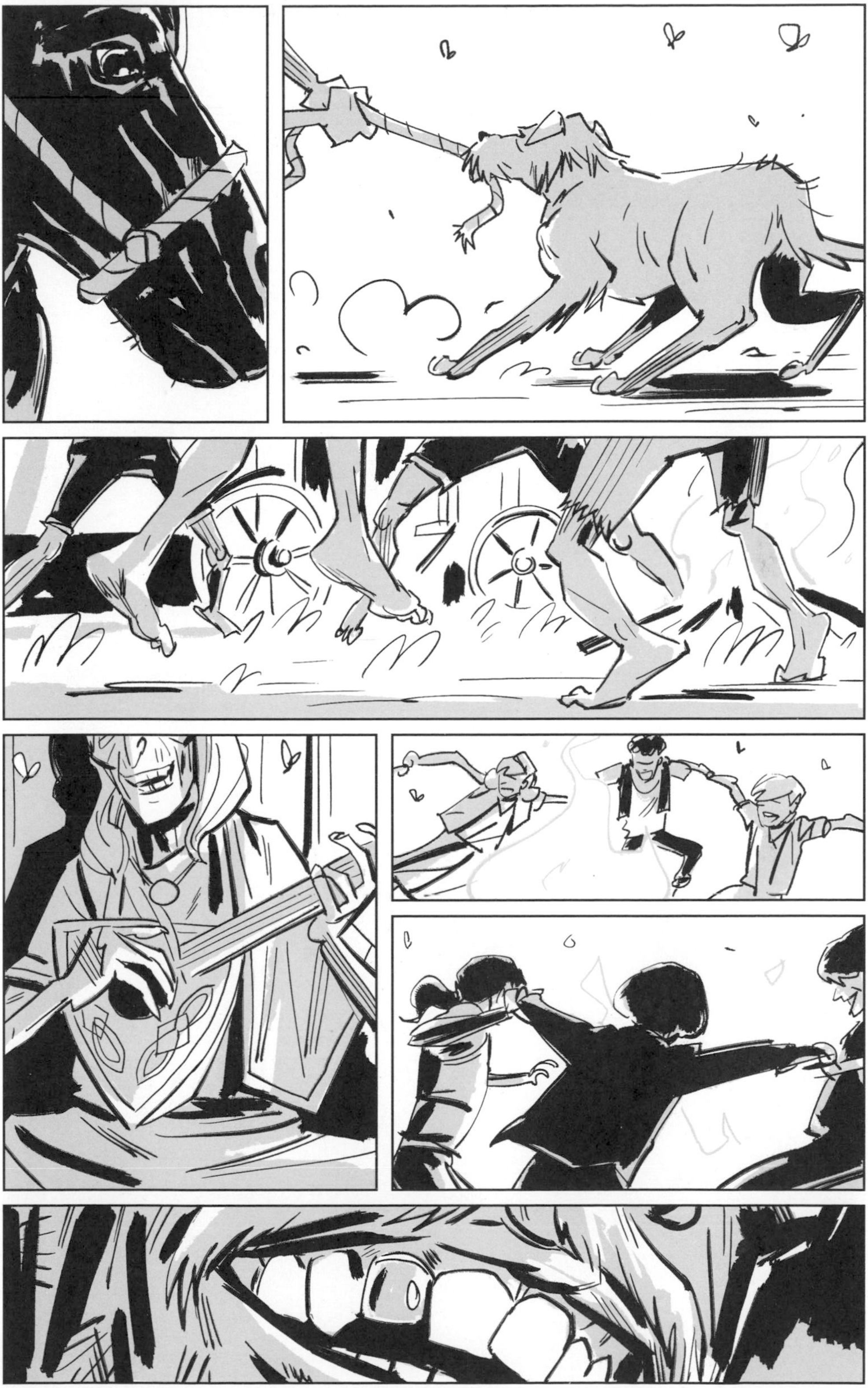

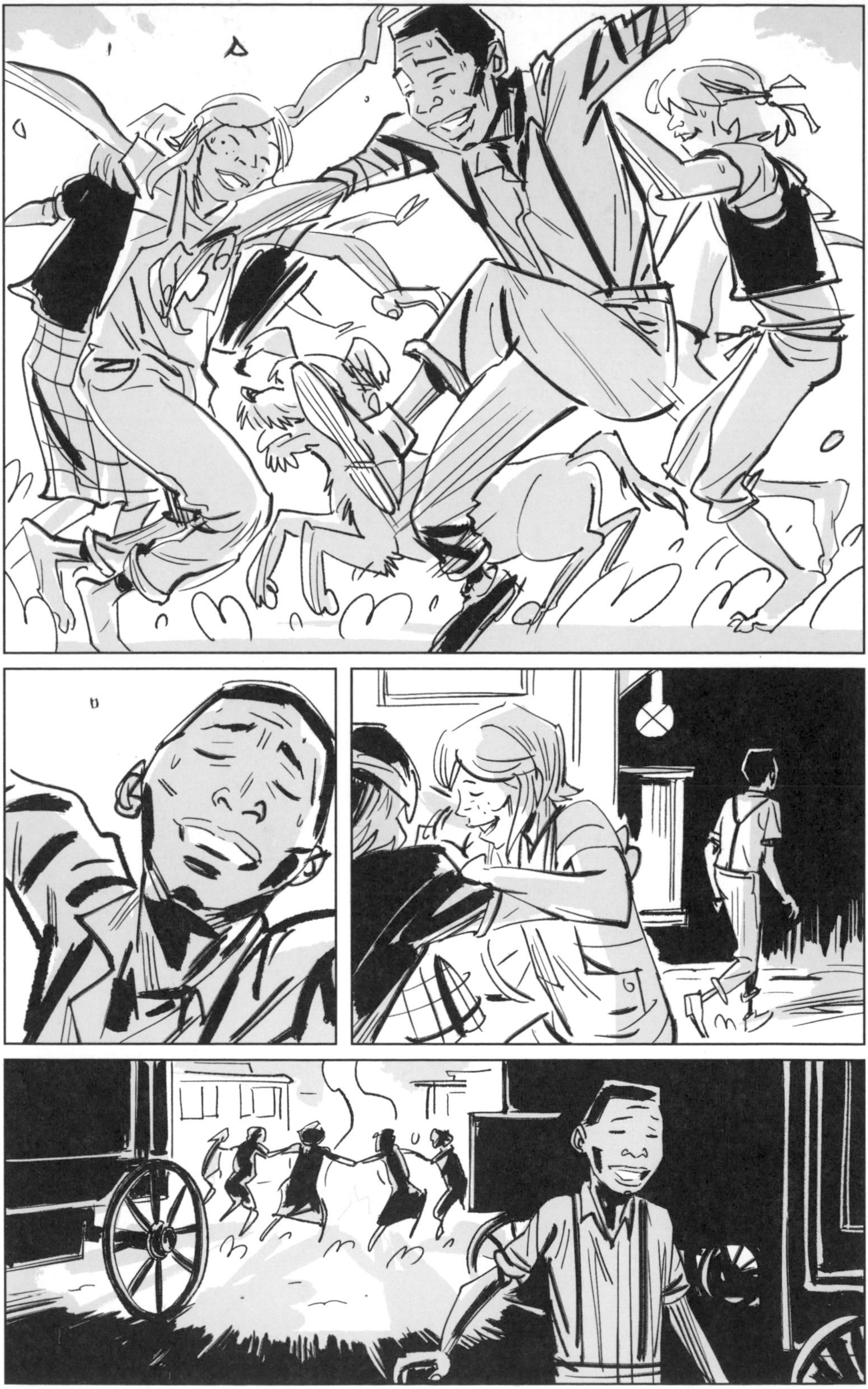

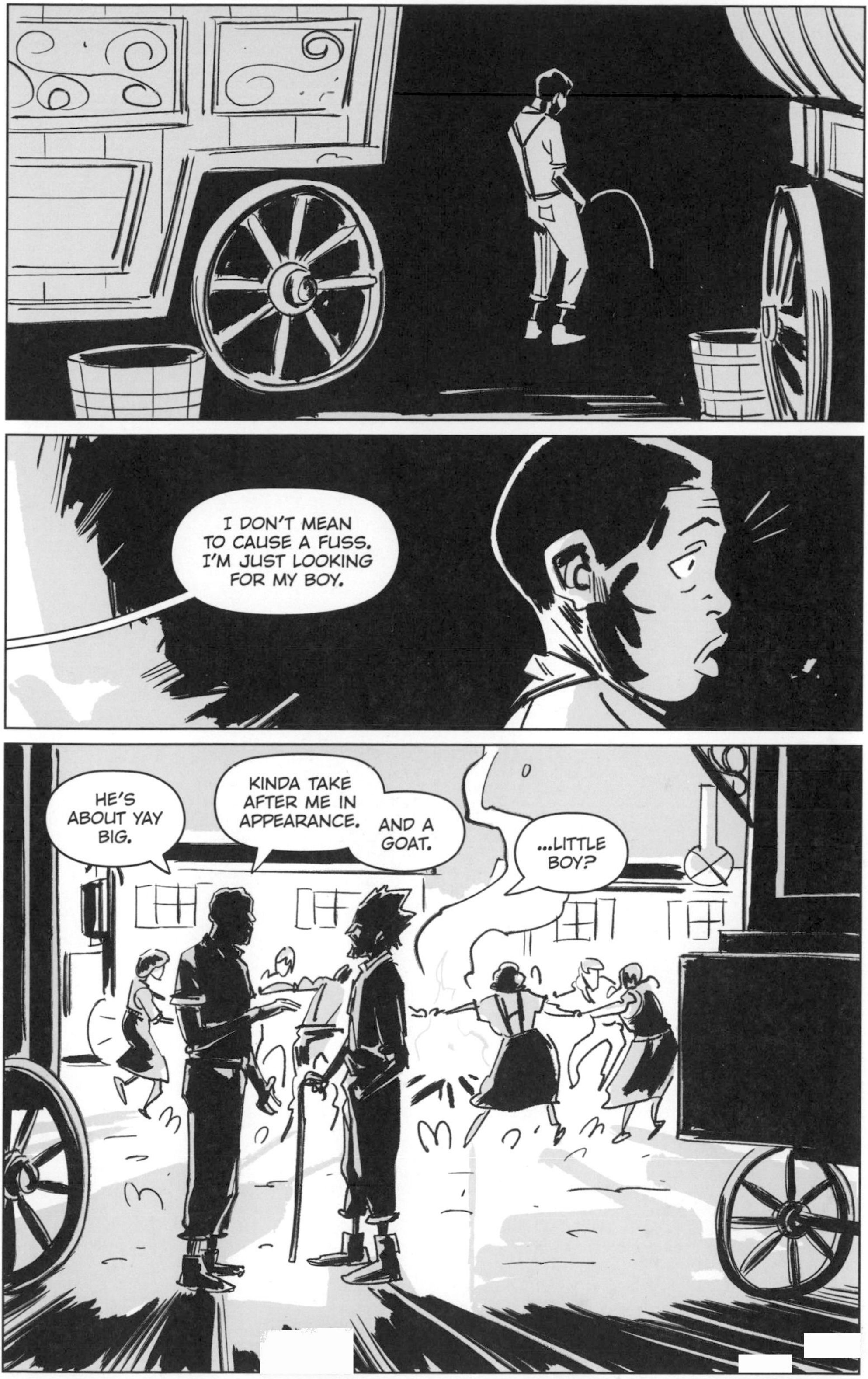
I DON'T MEAN TO CAUSE A FUSS. I'M JUST LOOKING FOR MY BOY.
HE'S ABOUT YAY BIG.
KINDA TAKE AFTER ME IN APPEARANCE.
AND A GOAT.
...LITTLE BOY?

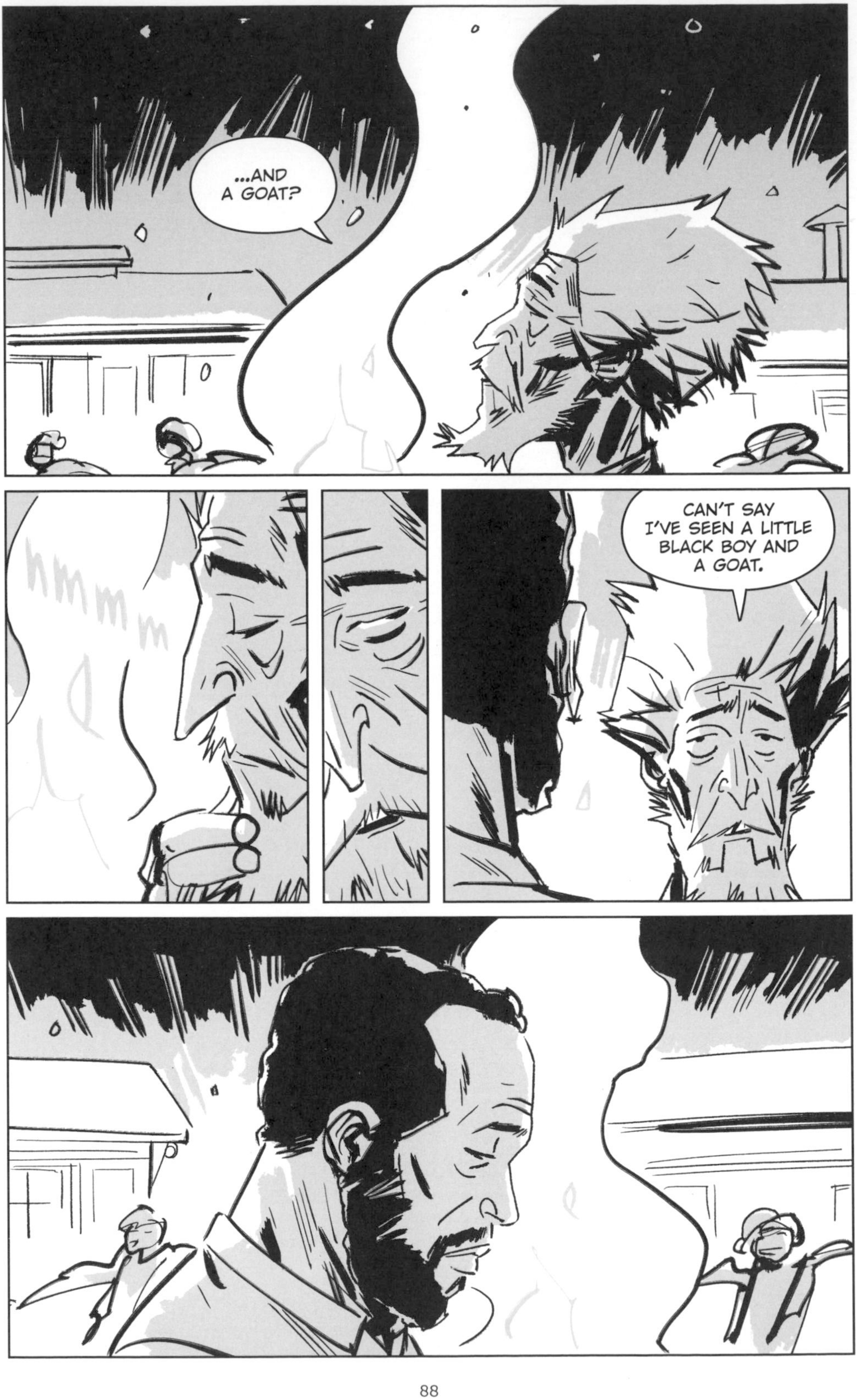
...AND A GOAT?
CAN'T SAY I'VE SEEN A LITTLE BLACK BOY AND A GOAT.

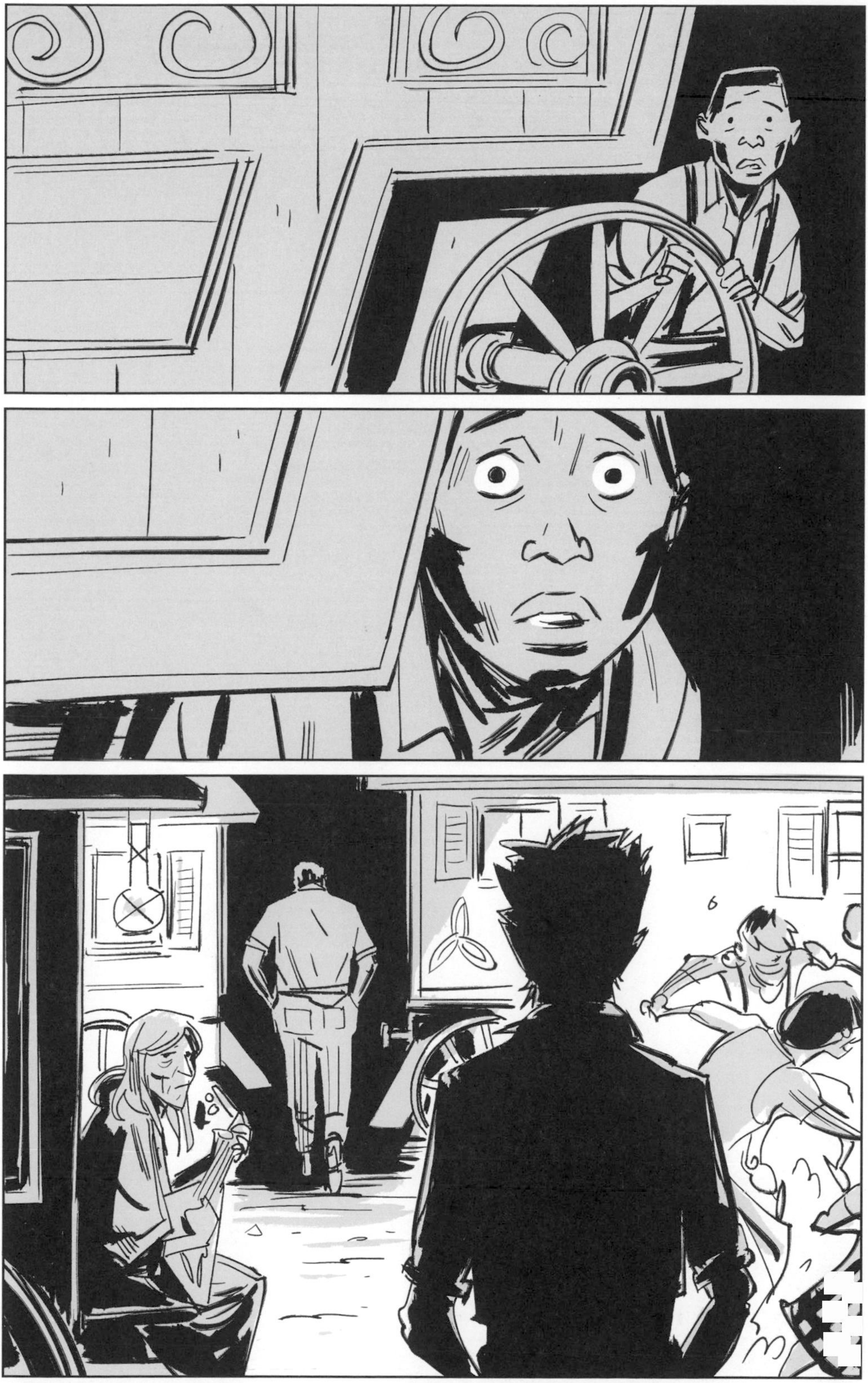

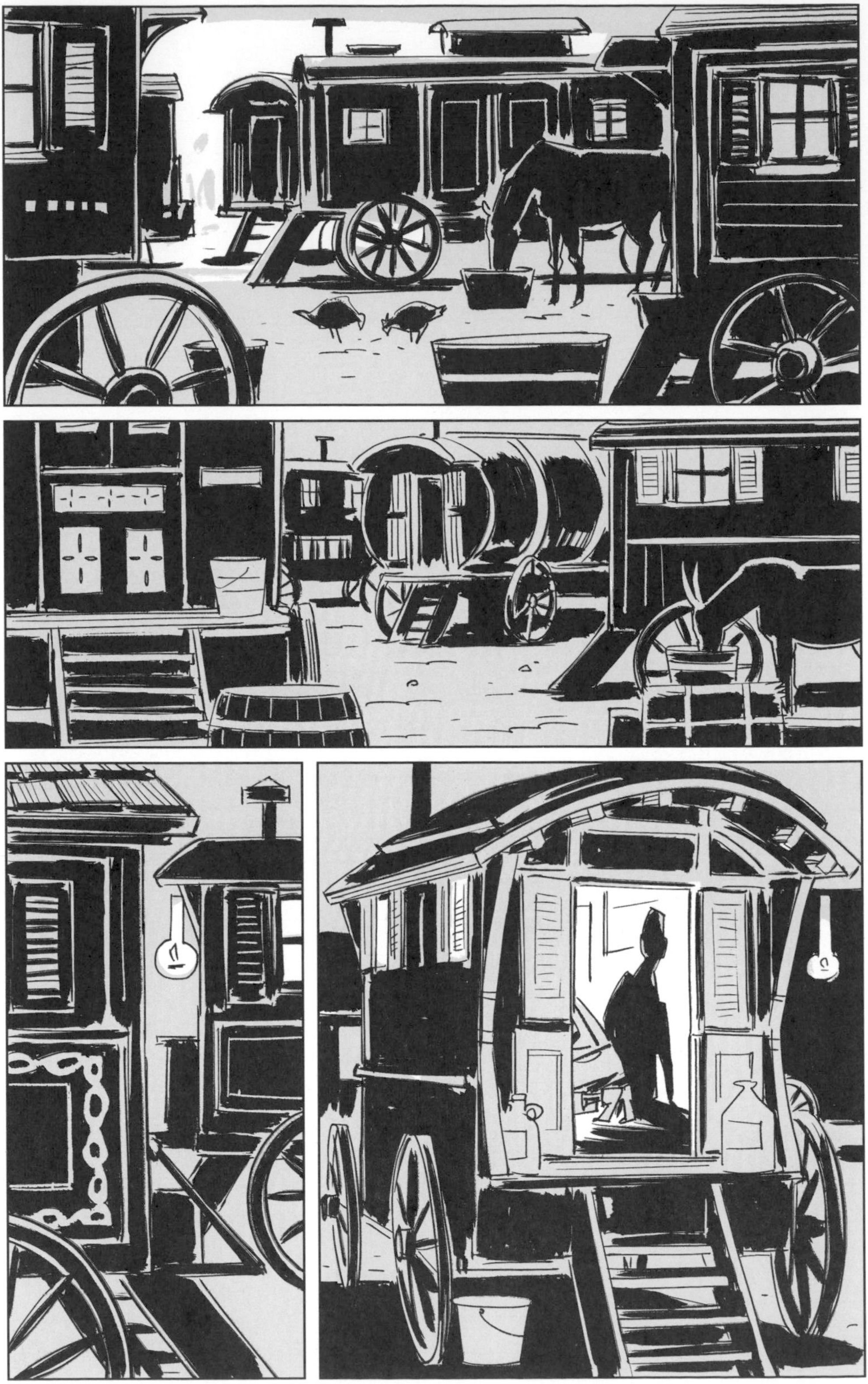

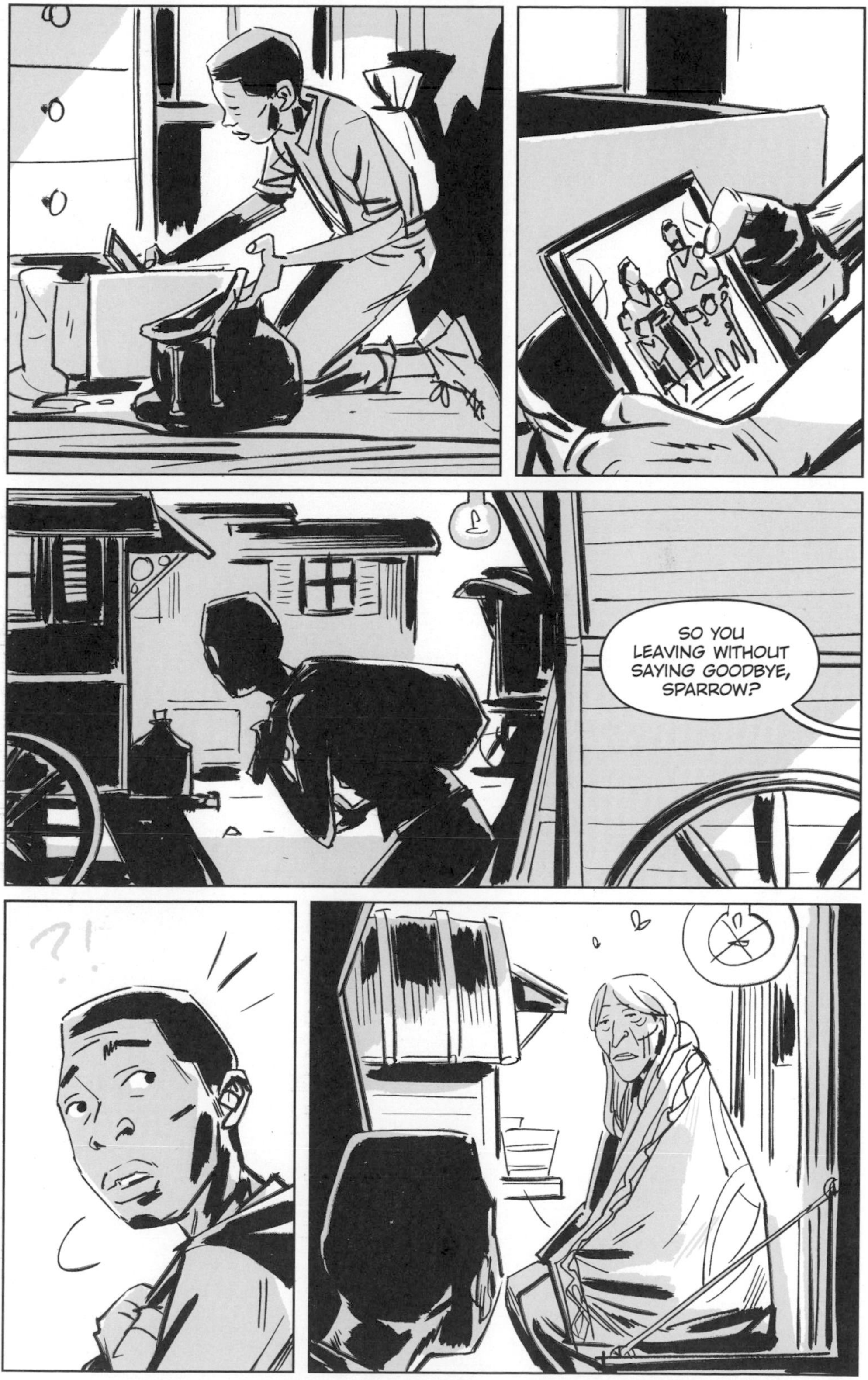
SO YOU LEAVING WITHOUT SAYING GOODBYE, SPARROW?
?!

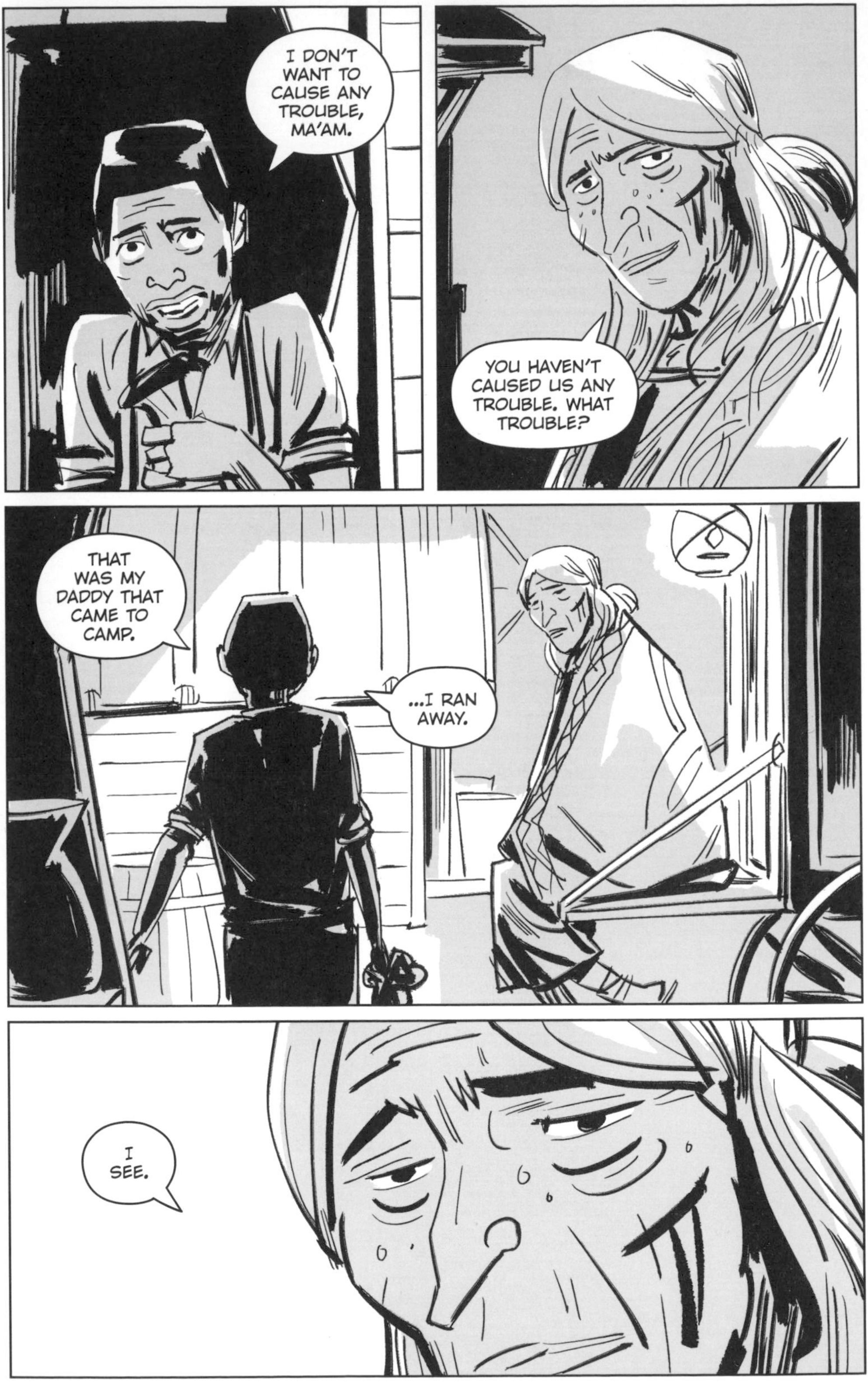
I DON'T WANT TO CAUSE ANY TROUBLE, MA'AM.
YOU HAVEN'T CAUSED US ANY TROUBLE. WHAT TROUBLE?
THAT WAS MY DADDY THAT CAME TO CAMP.
...I RAN AWAY.
I SEE.

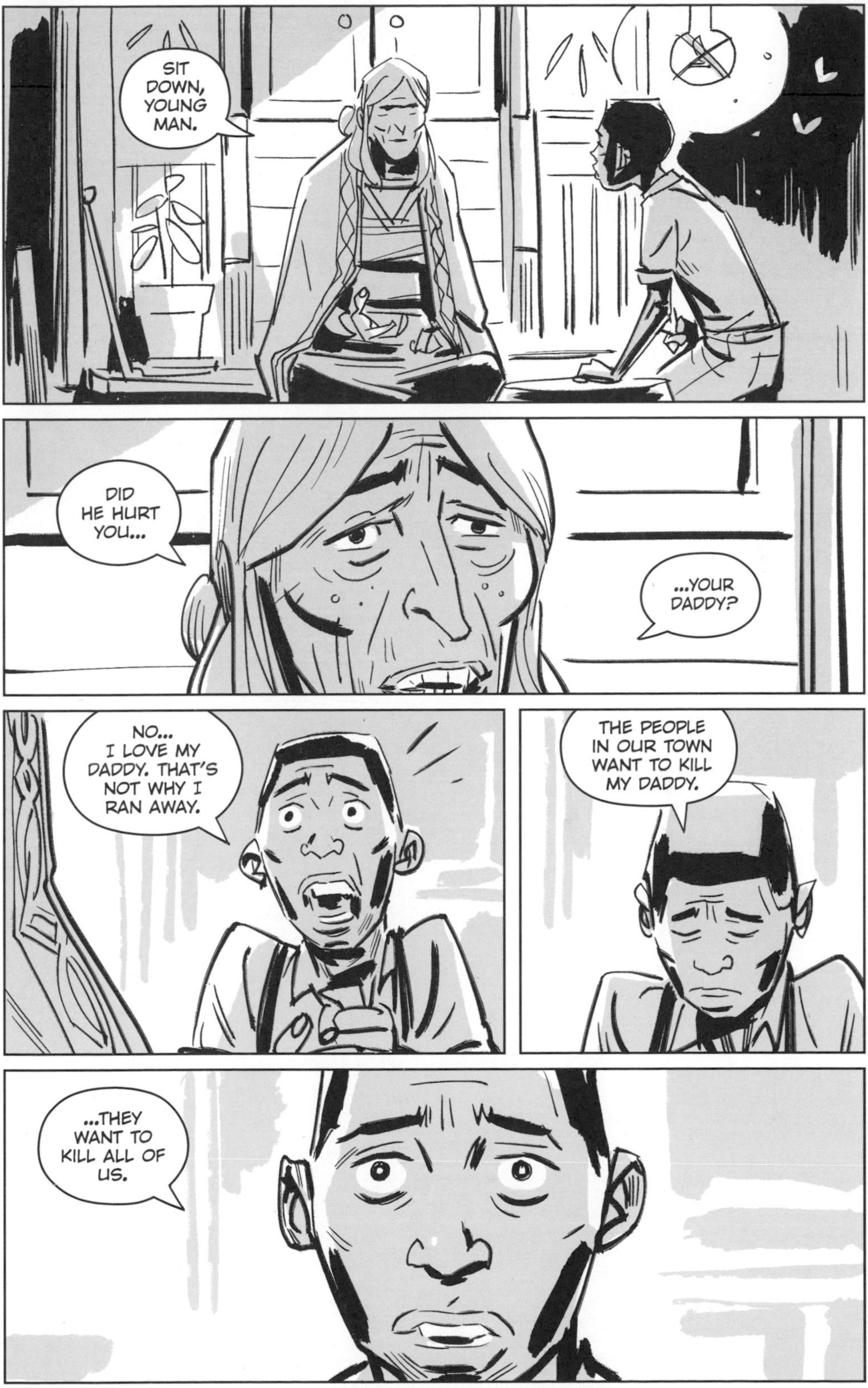
SIT DOWN, YOUNG MAN.
DID HE HURT YOU...
...YOUR DADDY?
NO... I LOVE MY DADDY. THAT'S NOT WHY I RAN AWAY.
THE PEOPLE IN OUR TOWN WANT TO KILL MY DADDY.
...THEY WANT TO KILL ALL OF US.

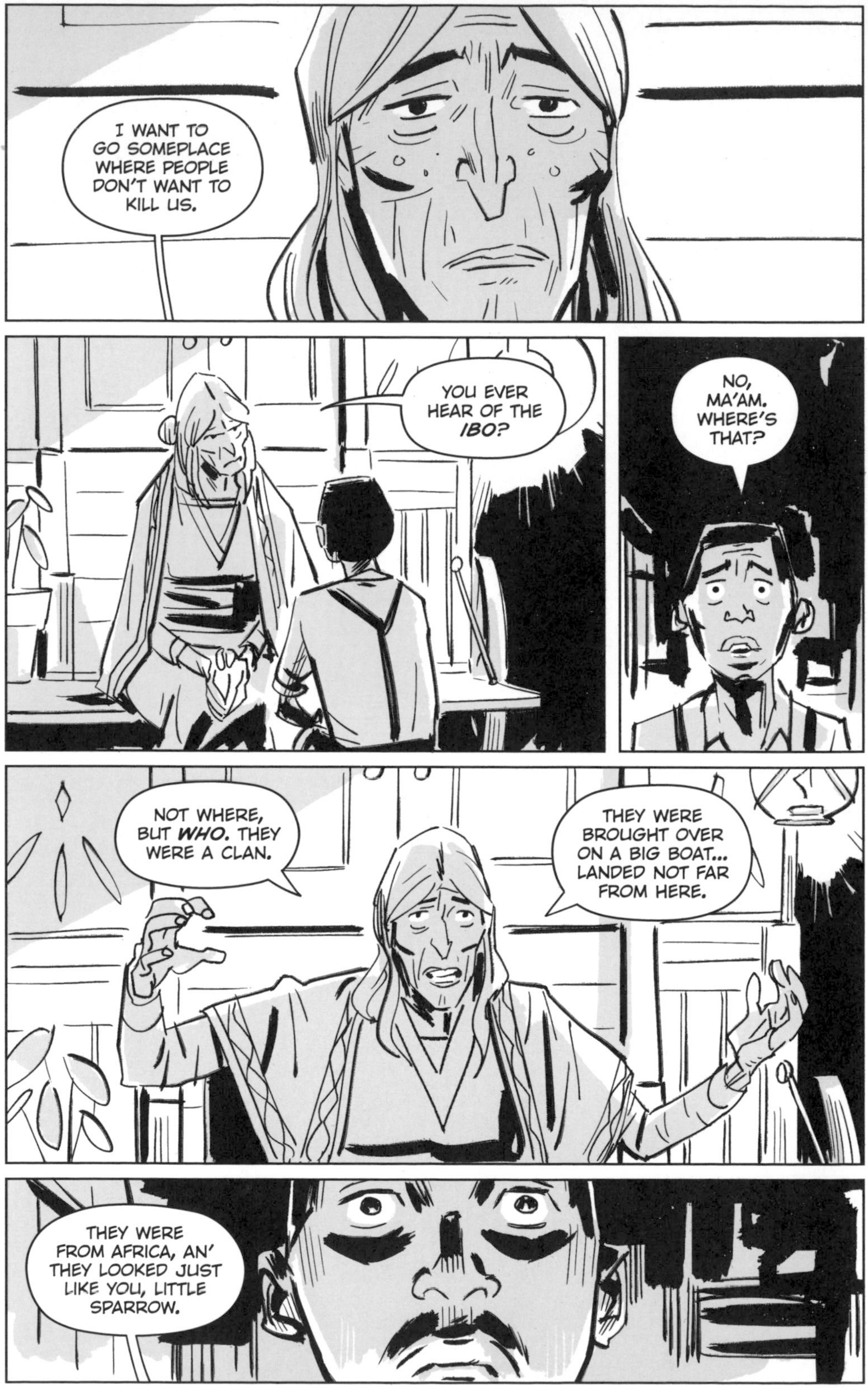
I WANT TO GO SOMEPLACE WHERE PEOPLE DON'T WANT TO KILL US.
YOU EVER HEAR OF THE *IBO*?
NO, MA'AM. WHERE'S THAT?
NOT WHERE, BUT ***WHO***. THEY WERE A CLAN.
THEY WERE BROUGHT OVER ON A BIG BOAT... LANDED NOT FAR FROM HERE.
THEY WERE FROM AFRICA, AN' THEY LOOKED JUST LIKE YOU, LITTLE SPARROW.

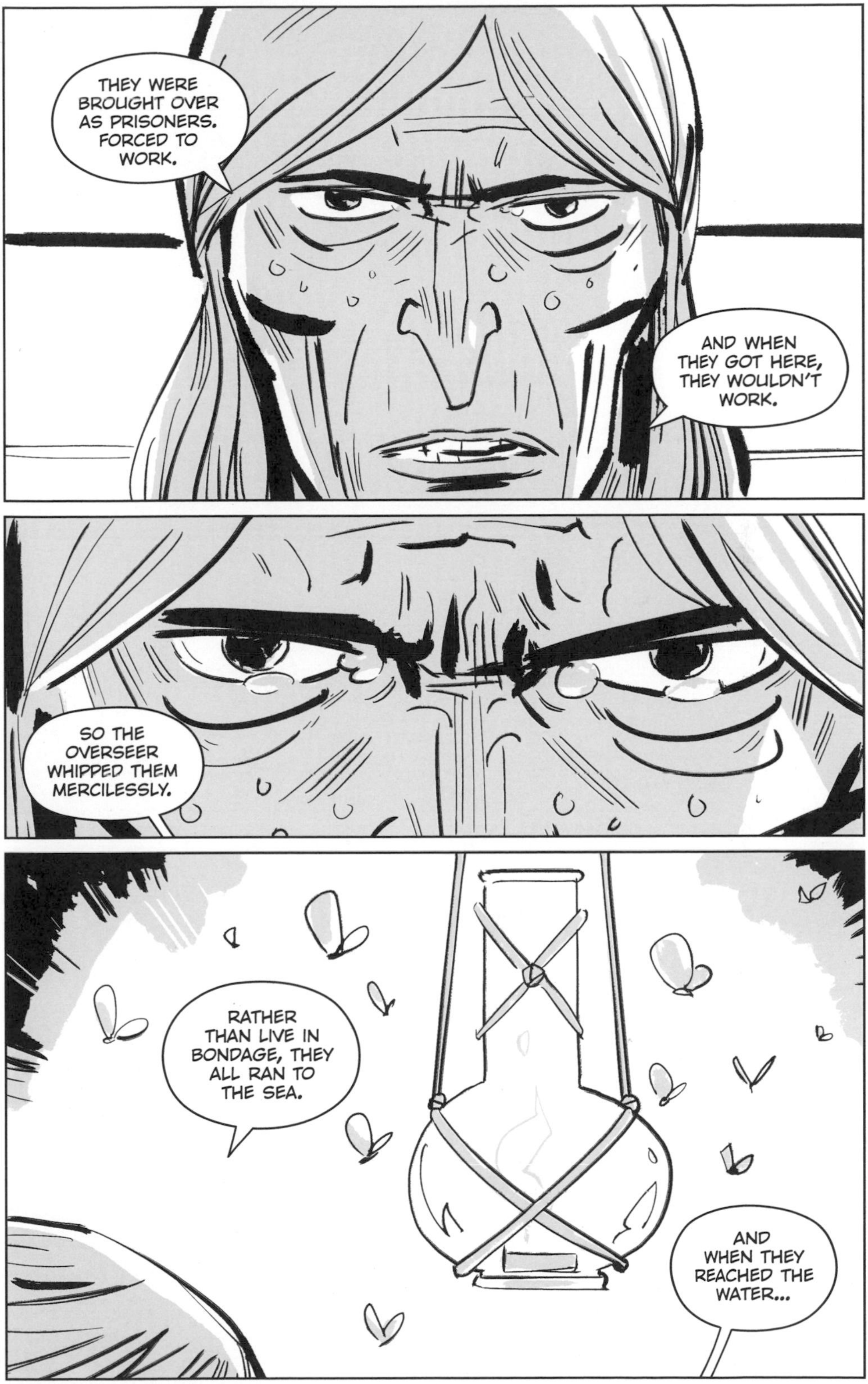
THEY WERE BROUGHT OVER AS PRISONERS. FORCED TO WORK.
AND WHEN THEY GOT HERE, THEY WOULDN'T WORK.
SO THE OVERSEER WHIPPED THEM MERCILESSLY.
RATHER THAN LIVE IN BONDAGE, THEY ALL RAN TO THE SEA.
AND WHEN THEY REACHED THE WATER...

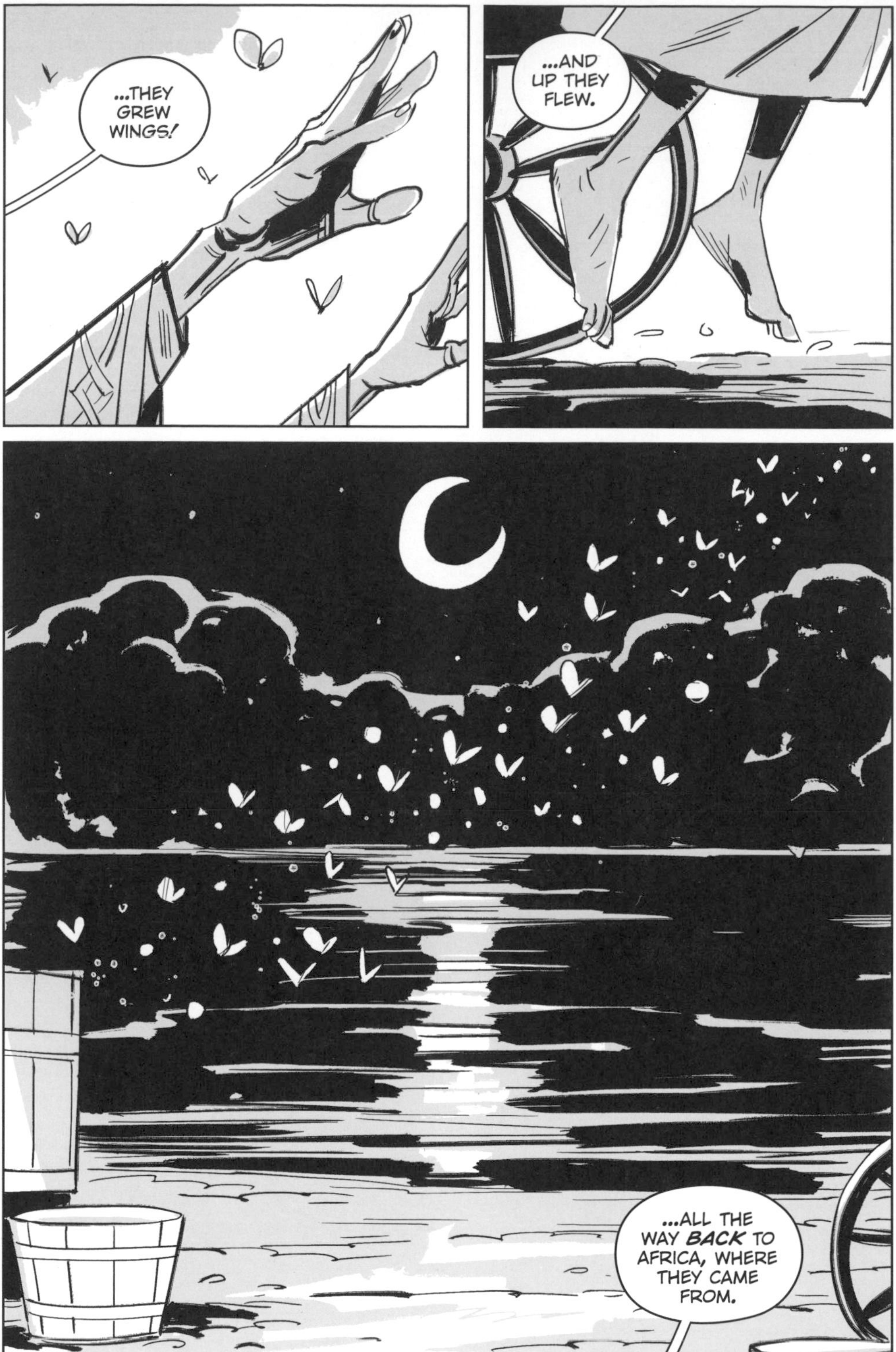
...THEY GREW WINGS!
...AND UP THEY FLEW.
...ALL THE WAY BACK TO AFRICA, WHERE THEY CAME FROM.

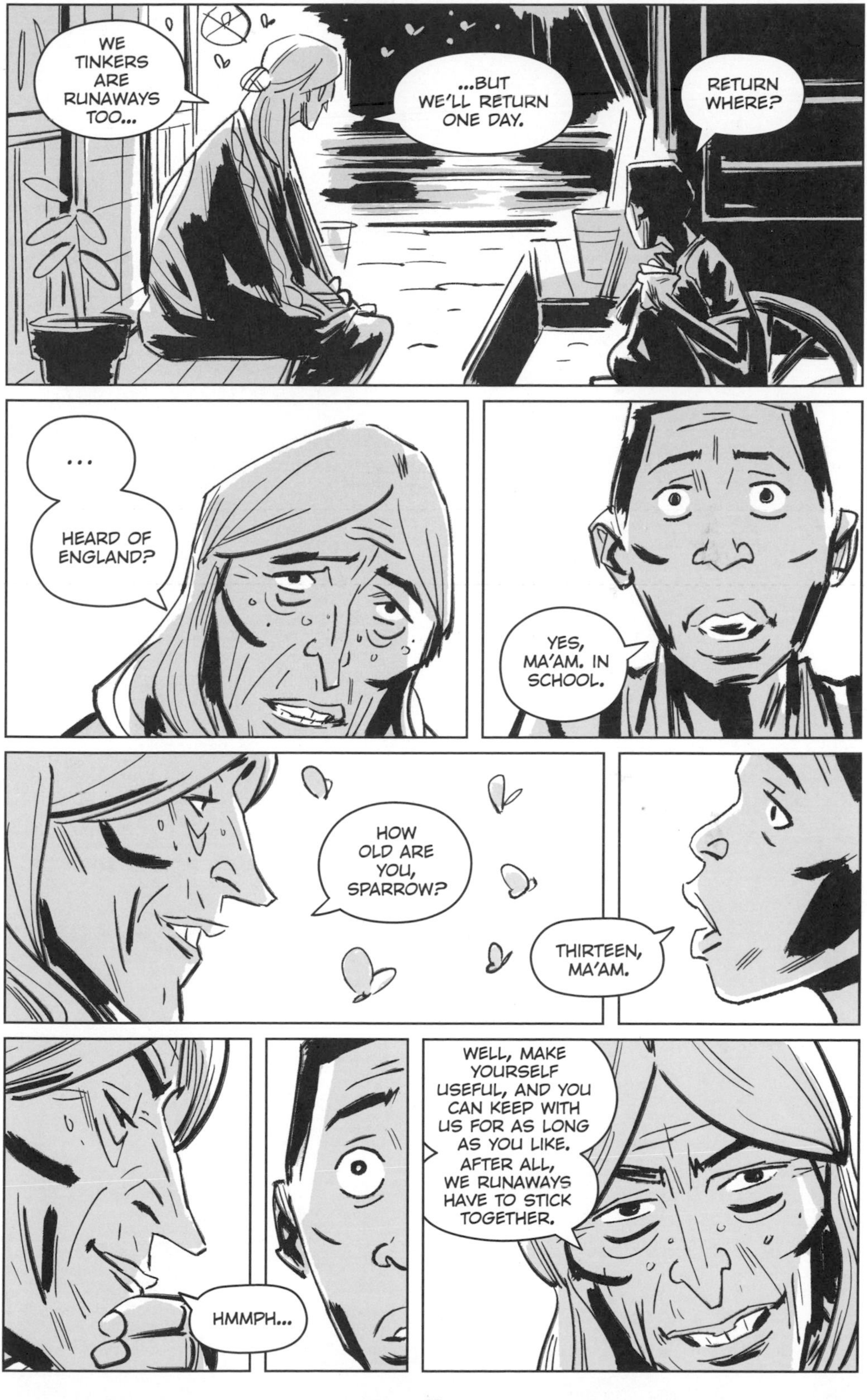

WE TINKERS ARE RUNAWAYS TOO...
...BUT WE'LL RETURN ONE DAY.
RETURN WHERE?
...
HEARD OF ENGLAND?
YES, MA'AM. IN SCHOOL.
HOW OLD ARE YOU, SPARROW?
THIRTEEN, MA'AM.
HMMPH...
WELL, MAKE YOURSELF USEFUL, AND YOU CAN KEEP WITH US FOR AS LONG AS YOU LIKE. AFTER ALL, WE RUNAWAYS HAVE TO STICK TOGETHER.

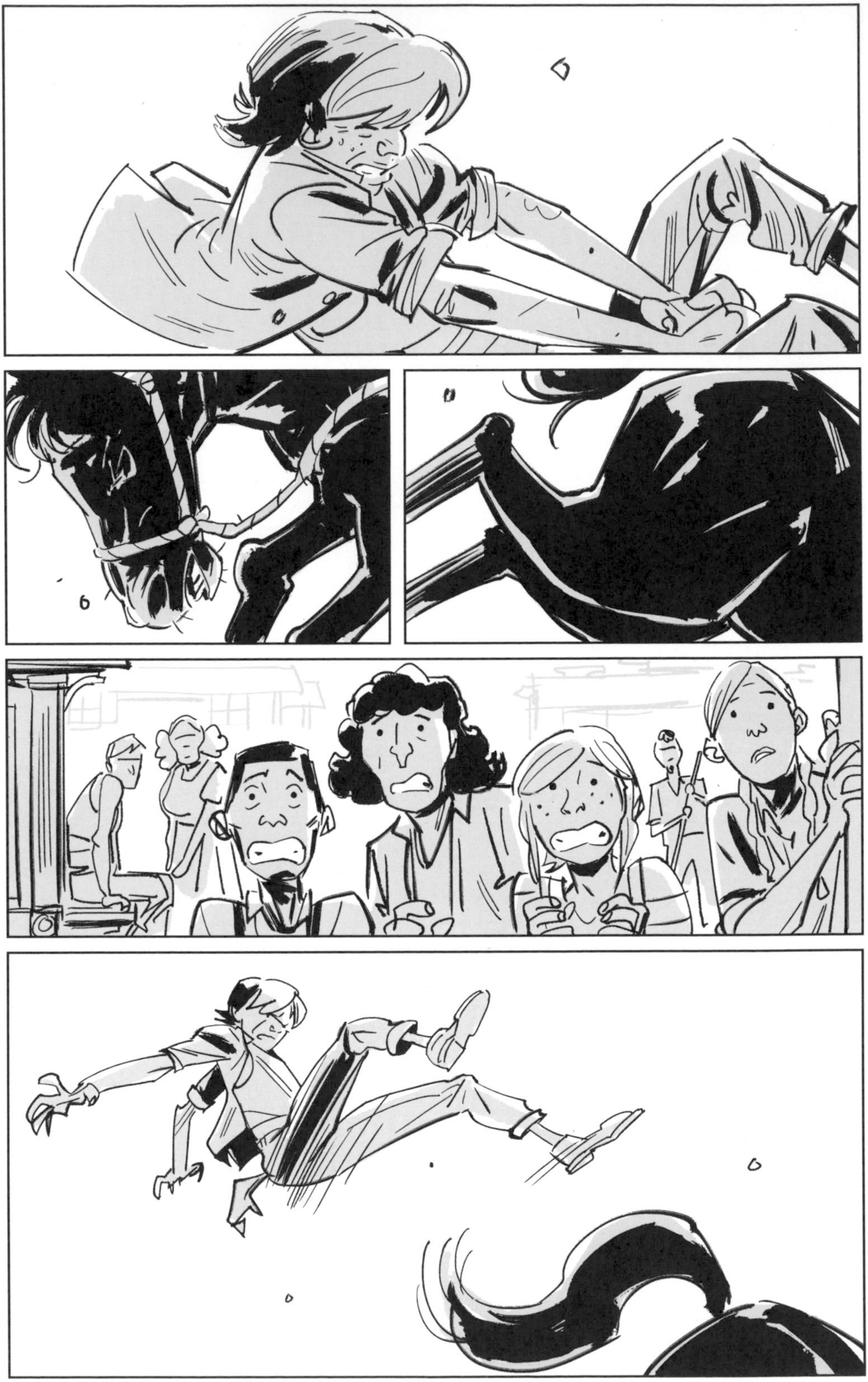

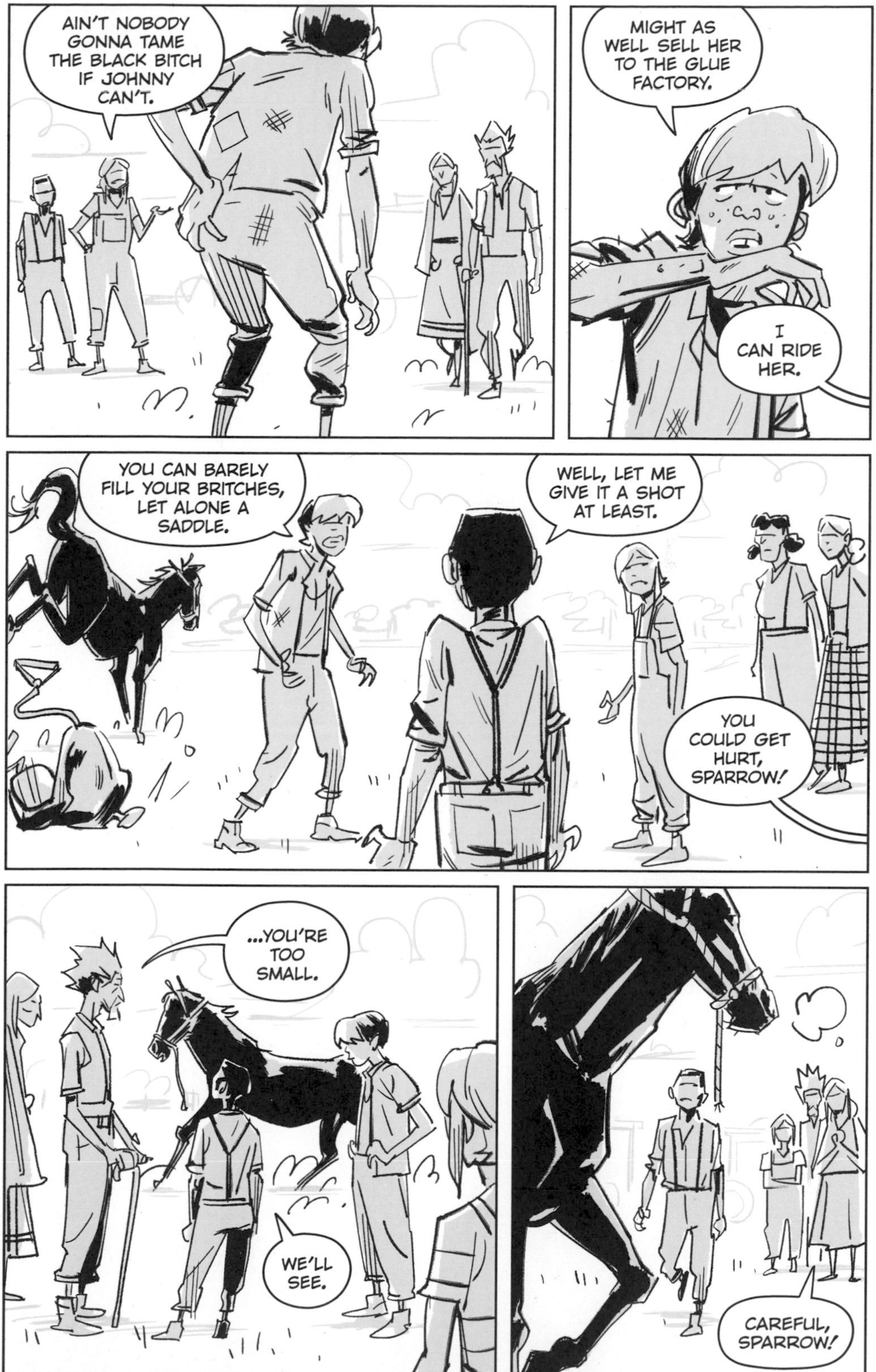
AIN'T NOBODY GONNA TAME THE BLACK BITCH IF JOHNNY CAN'T.
MIGHT AS WELL SELL HER TO THE GLUE FACTORY.
I CAN RIDE HER.
YOU CAN BARELY FILL YOUR BRITCHES, LET ALONE A SADDLE.
WELL, LET ME GIVE IT A SHOT AT LEAST.
YOU COULD GET HURT, SPARROW!
...YOU'RE TOO SMALL.
WE'LL SEE.
CAREFUL, SPARROW!

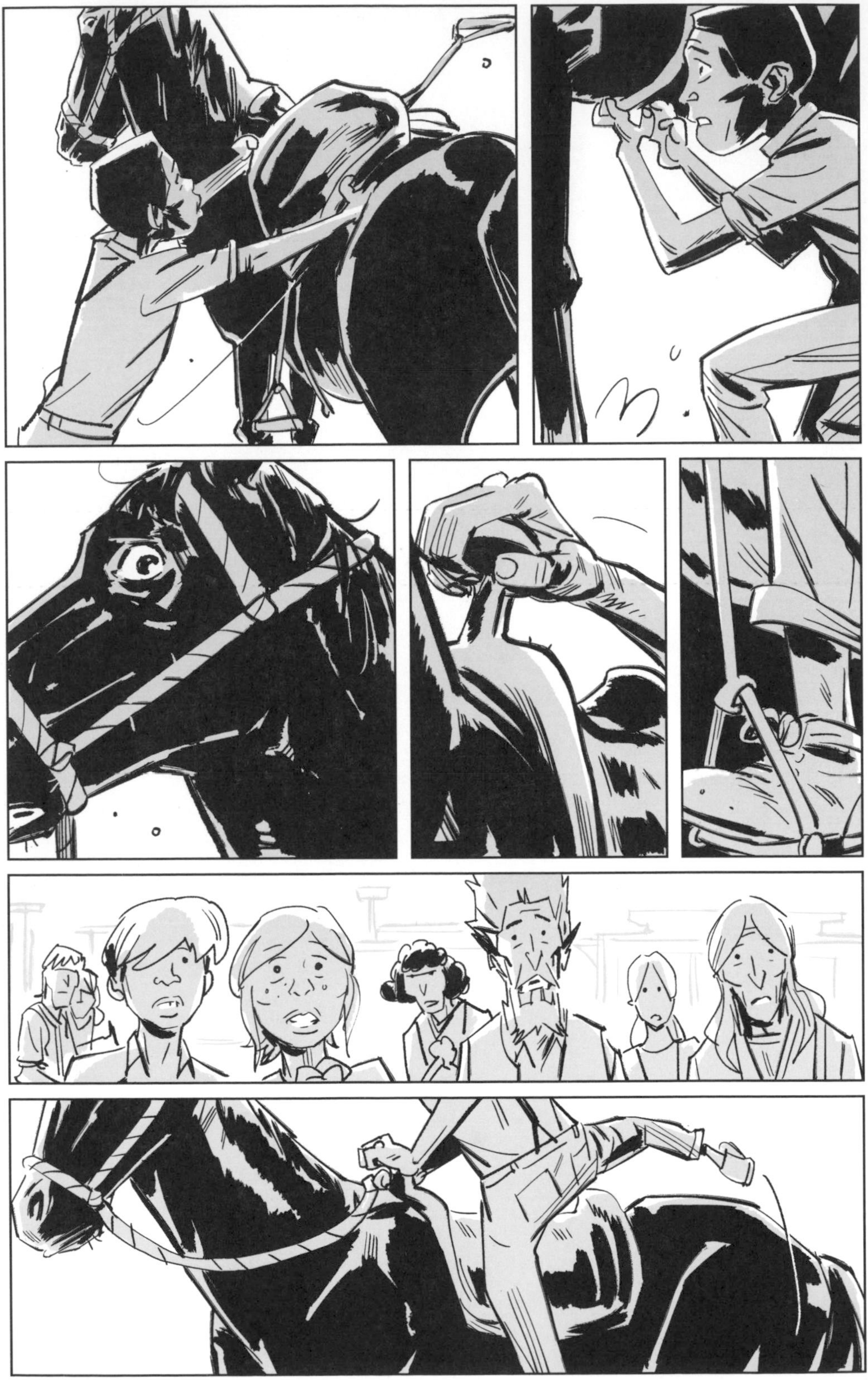

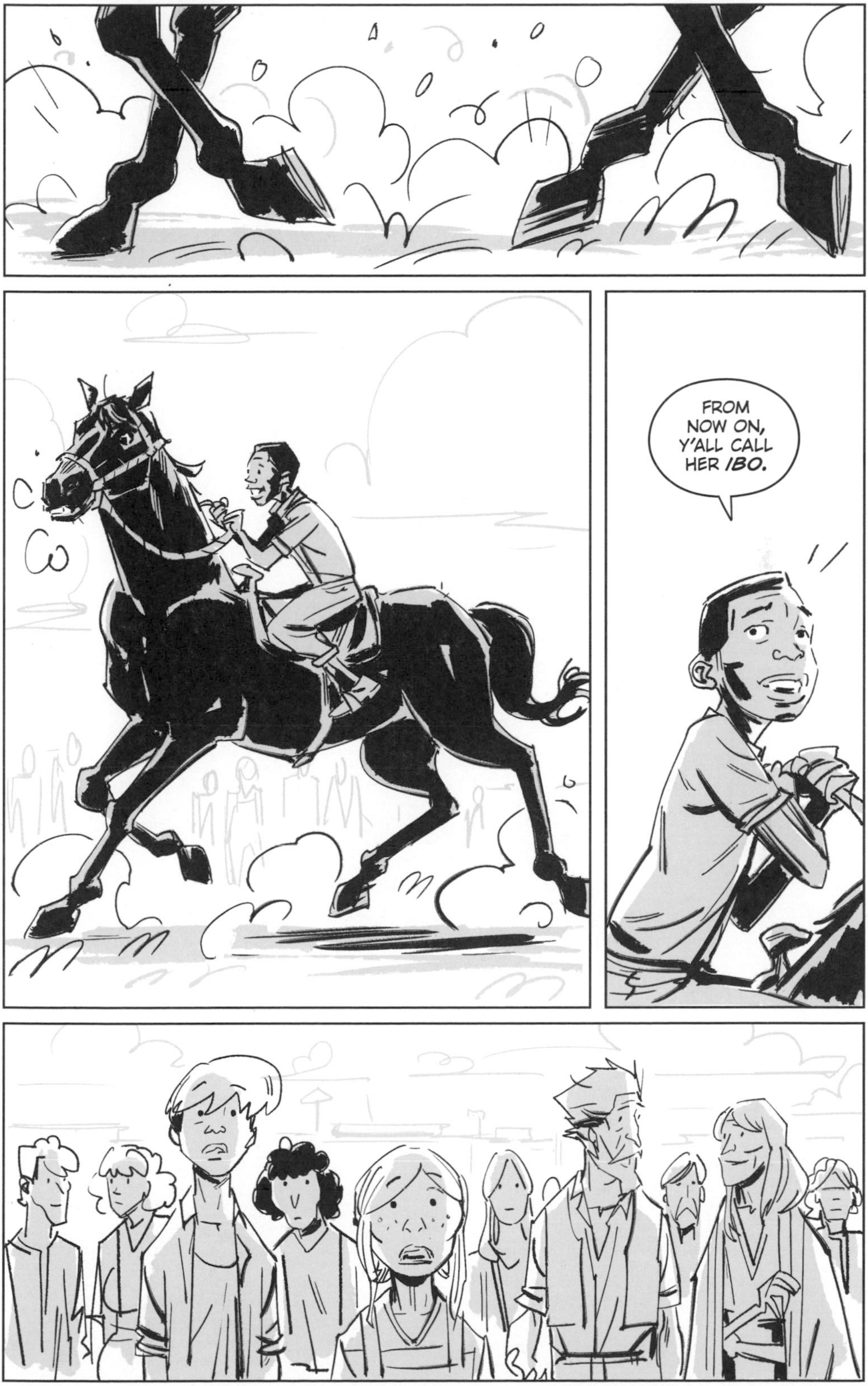
FROM NOW ON, Y'ALL CALL HER *IBO*.

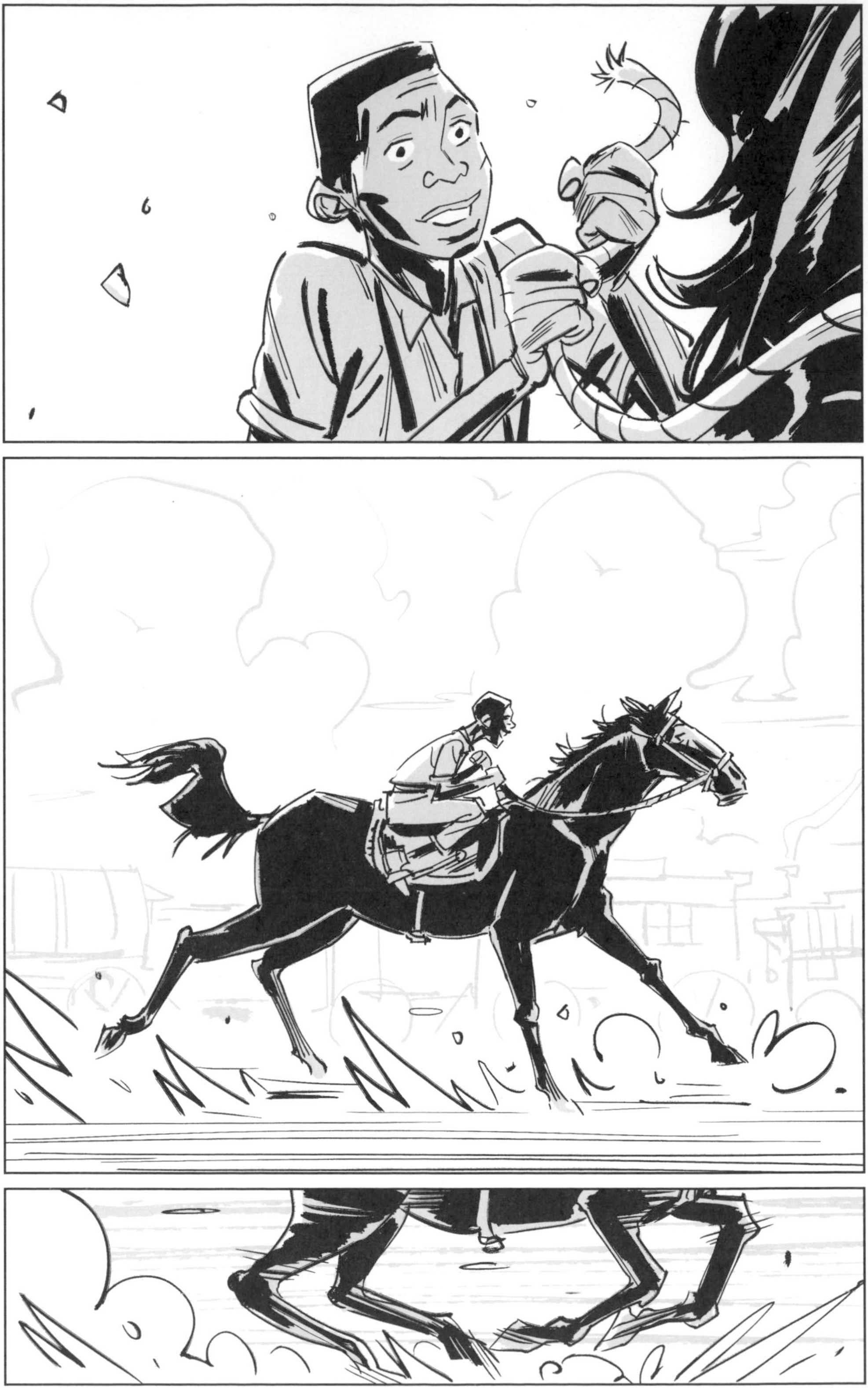

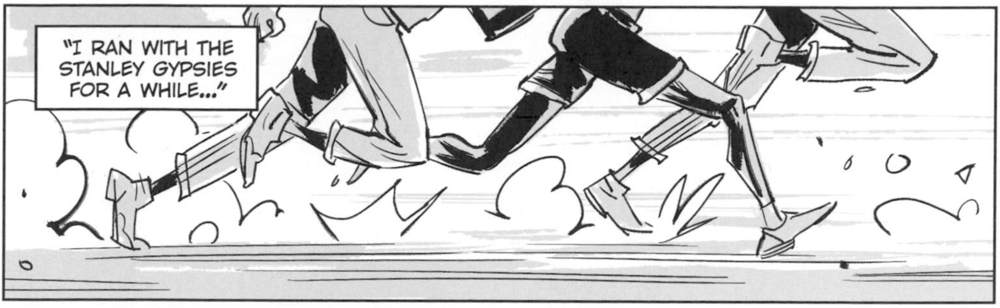
"I RAN WITH THE STANLEY GYPSIES FOR A WHILE..."

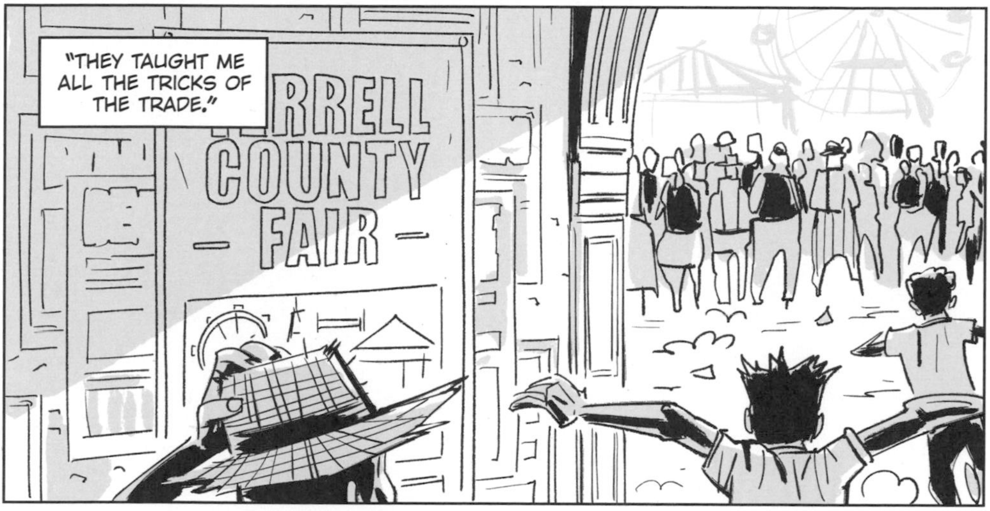
"THEY TAUGHT ME ALL THE TRICKS OF THE TRADE."
RRELL
COUNTY
FAIR

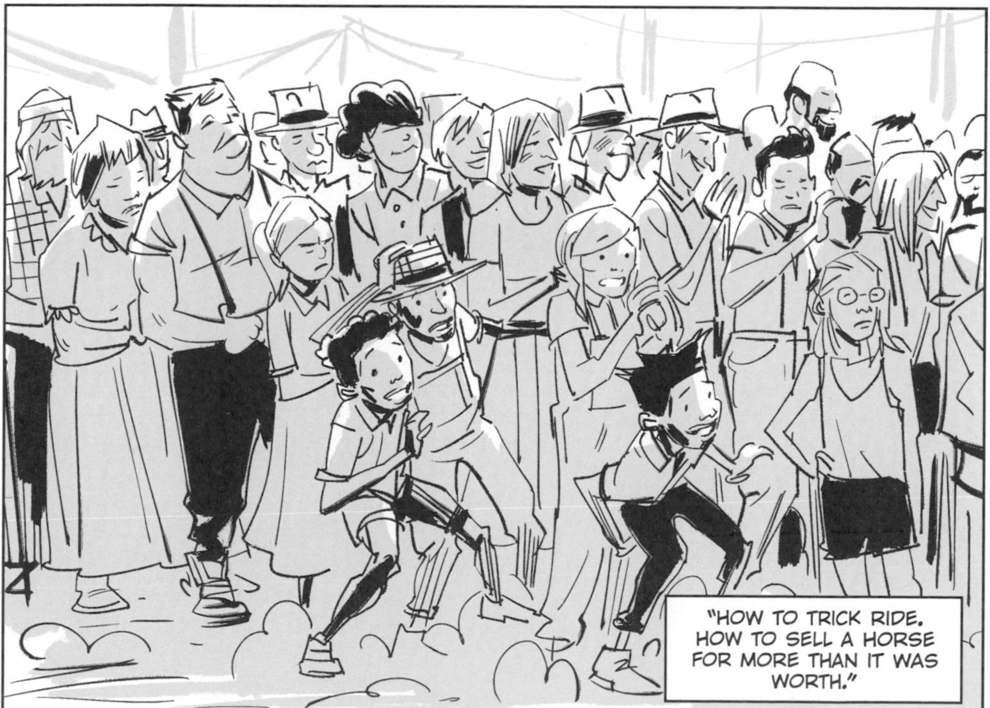
"HOW TO TRICK RIDE. HOW TO SELL A HORSE FOR MORE THAN IT WAS WORTH."

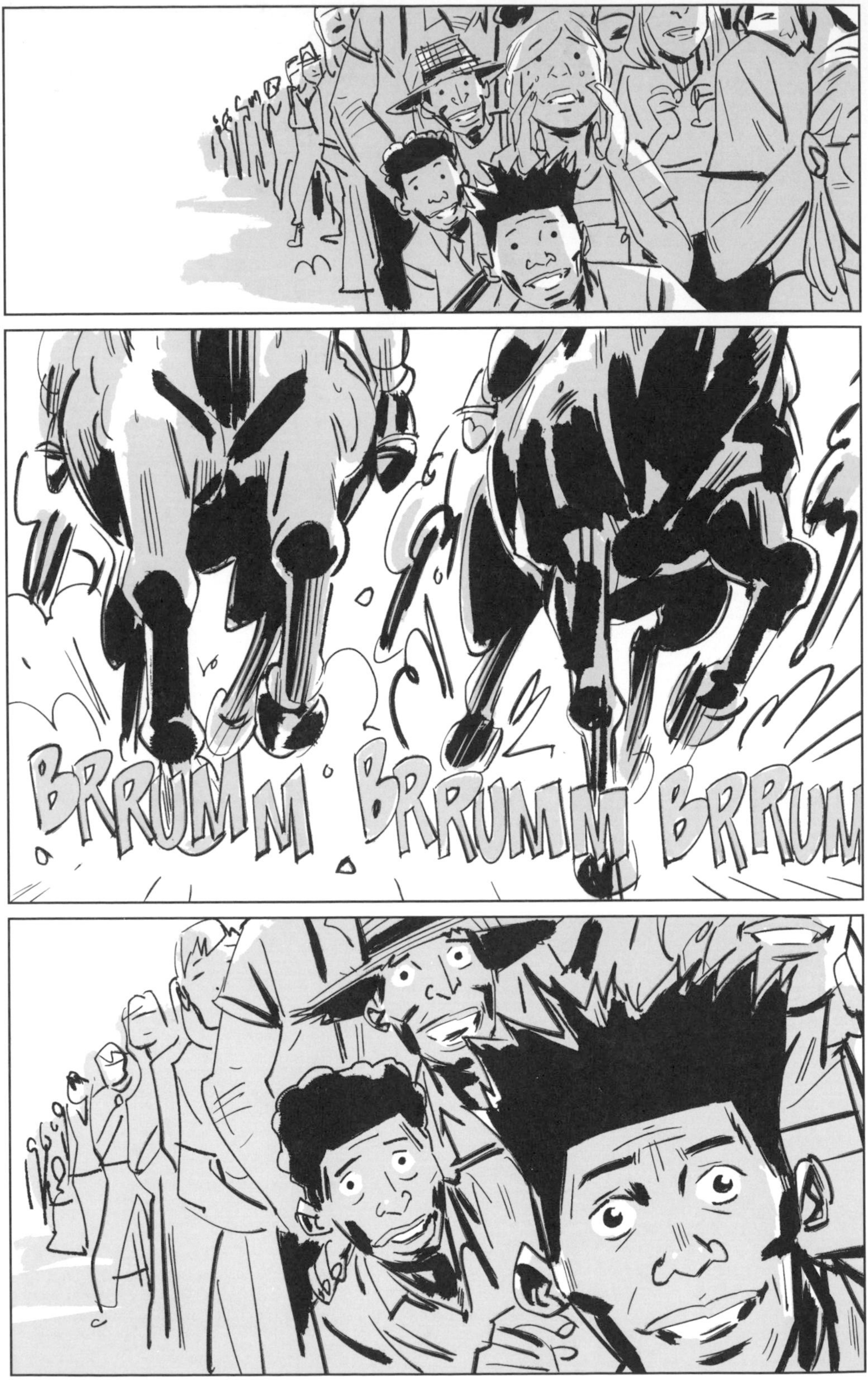
BRRUMM BRRUMM BRRUM

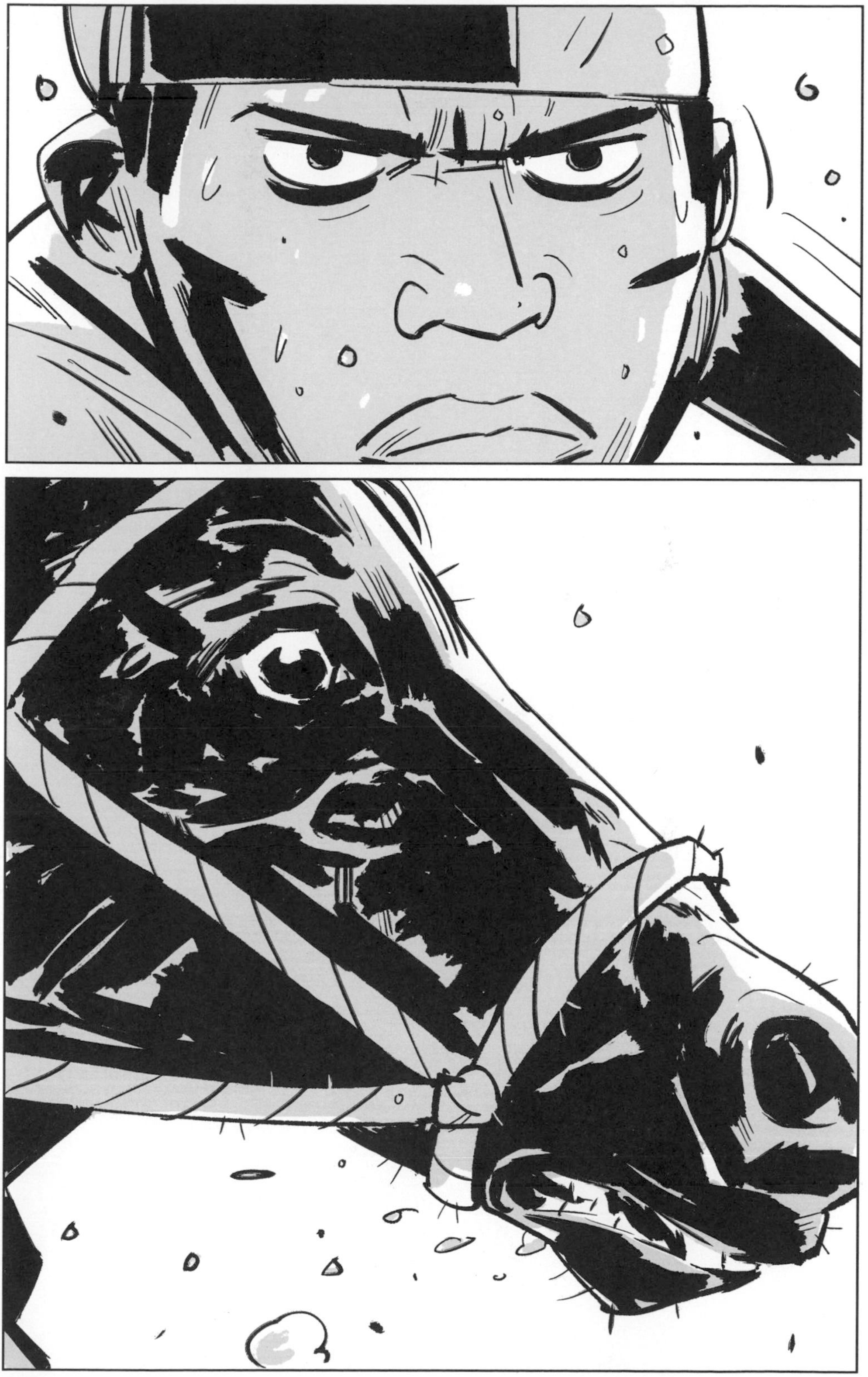

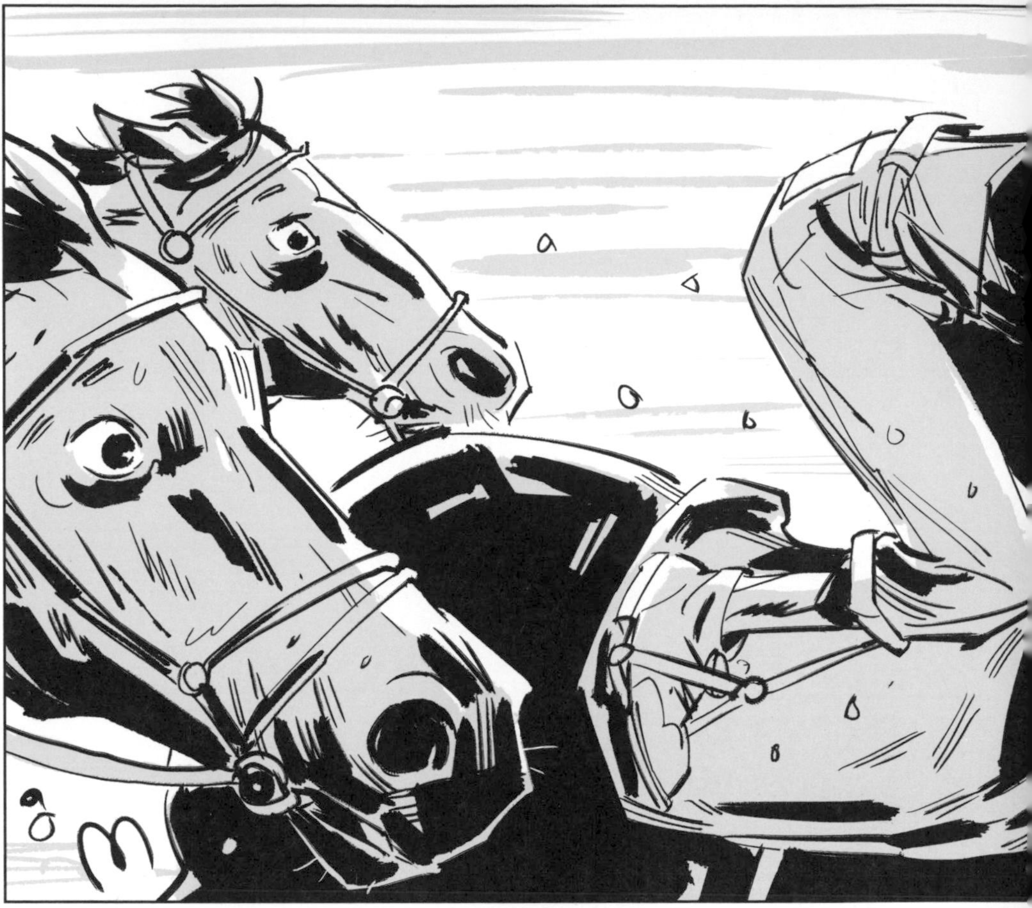

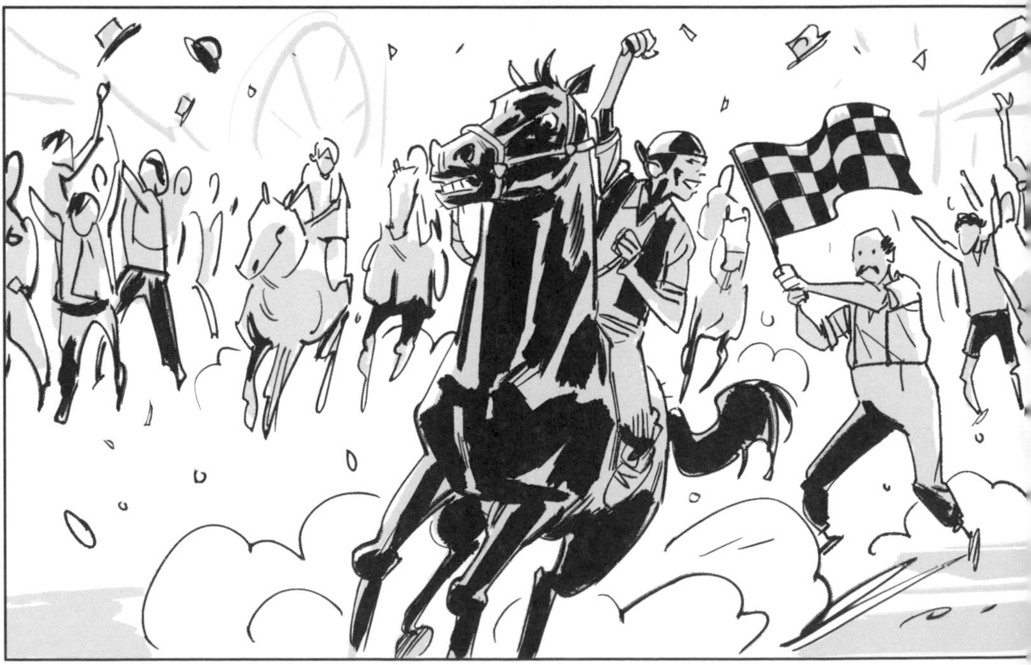

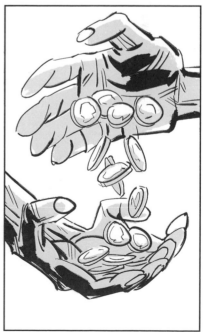

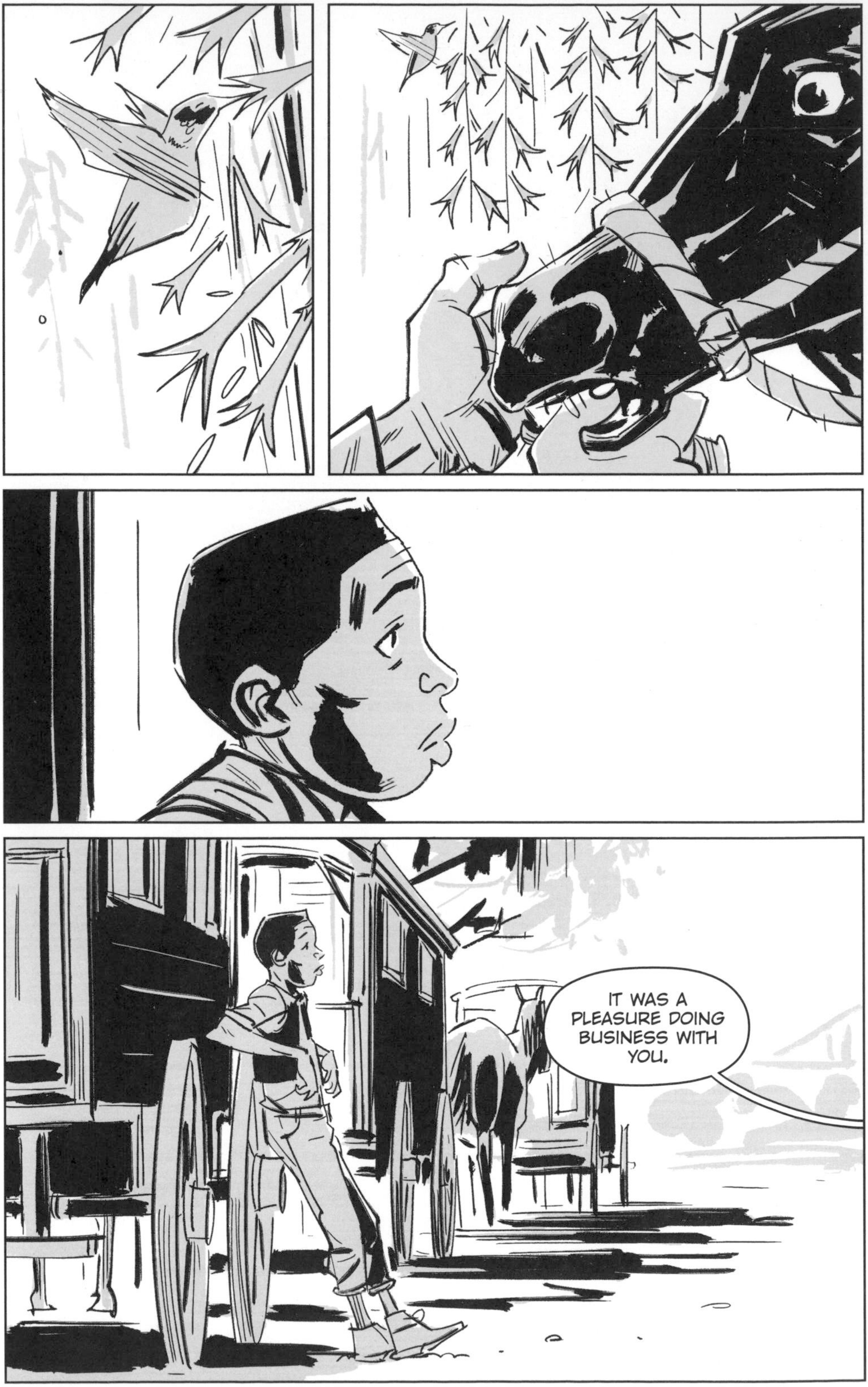
IT WAS A PLEASURE DOING BUSINESS WITH YOU.

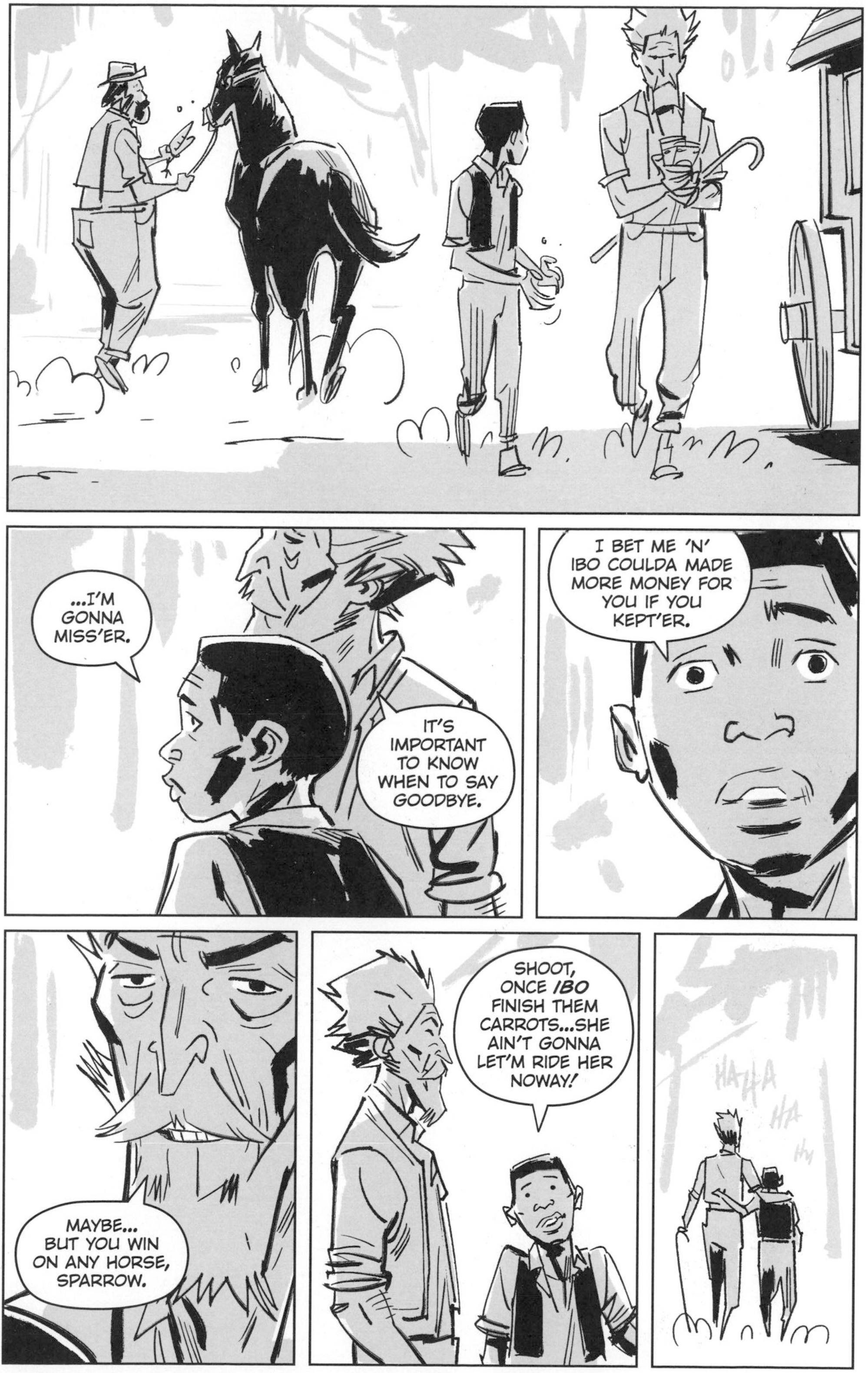
...I'M GONNA MISS'ER.
IT'S IMPORTANT TO KNOW WHEN TO SAY GOODBYE.
I BET ME 'N' IBO COULDA MADE MORE MONEY FOR YOU IF YOU KEPT'ER.
MAYBE... BUT YOU WIN ON ANY HORSE, SPARROW.
SHOOT, ONCE *IBO* FINISH THEM CARROTS...SHE AIN'T GONNA LET'M RIDE HER NOWAY!
HA HA HA

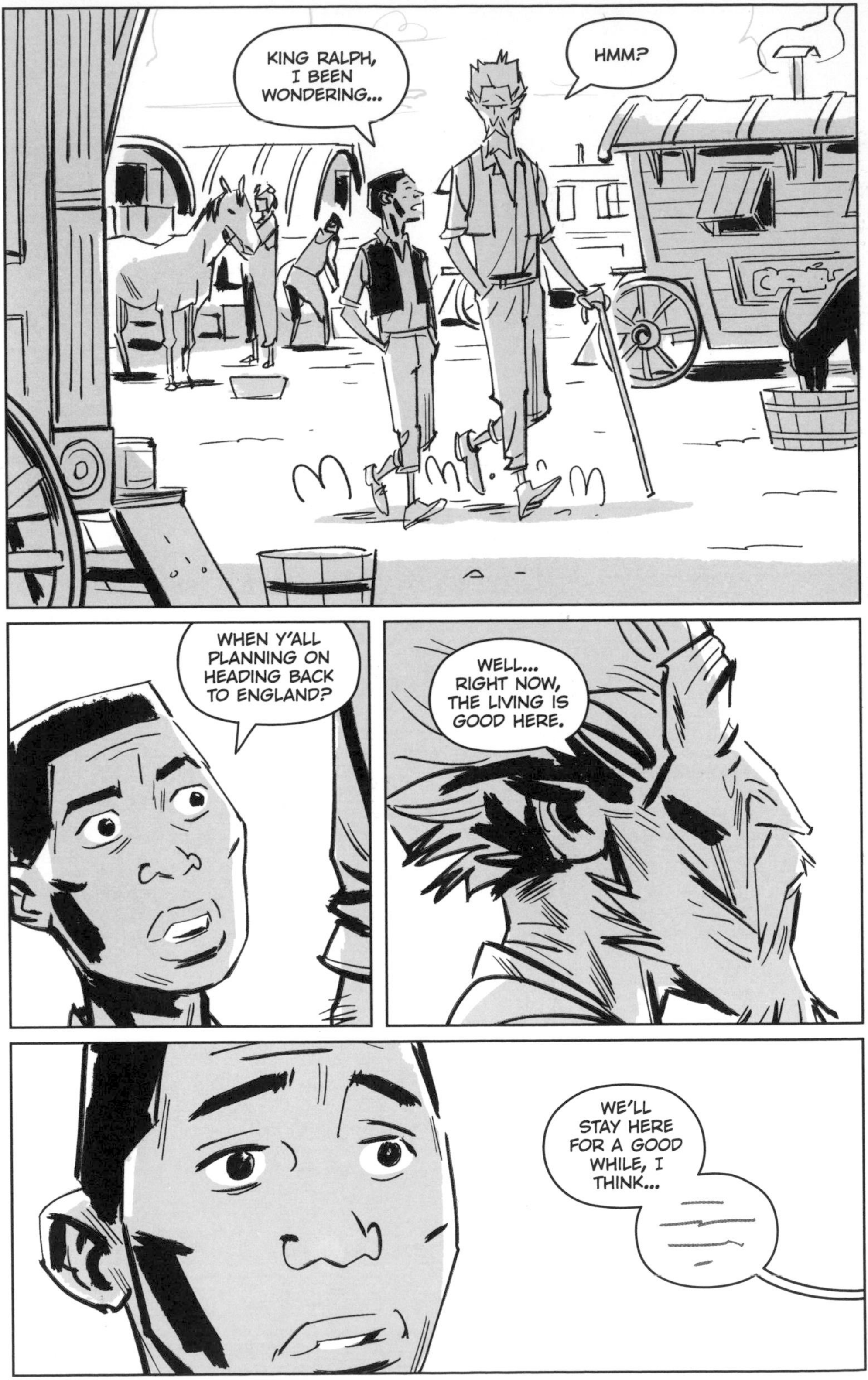
KING RALPH, I BEEN WONDERING...
HMM?
WHEN Y'ALL PLANNING ON HEADING BACK TO ENGLAND?
WELL... RIGHT NOW, THE LIVING IS GOOD HERE.
WE'LL STAY HERE FOR A GOOD WHILE, I THINK...

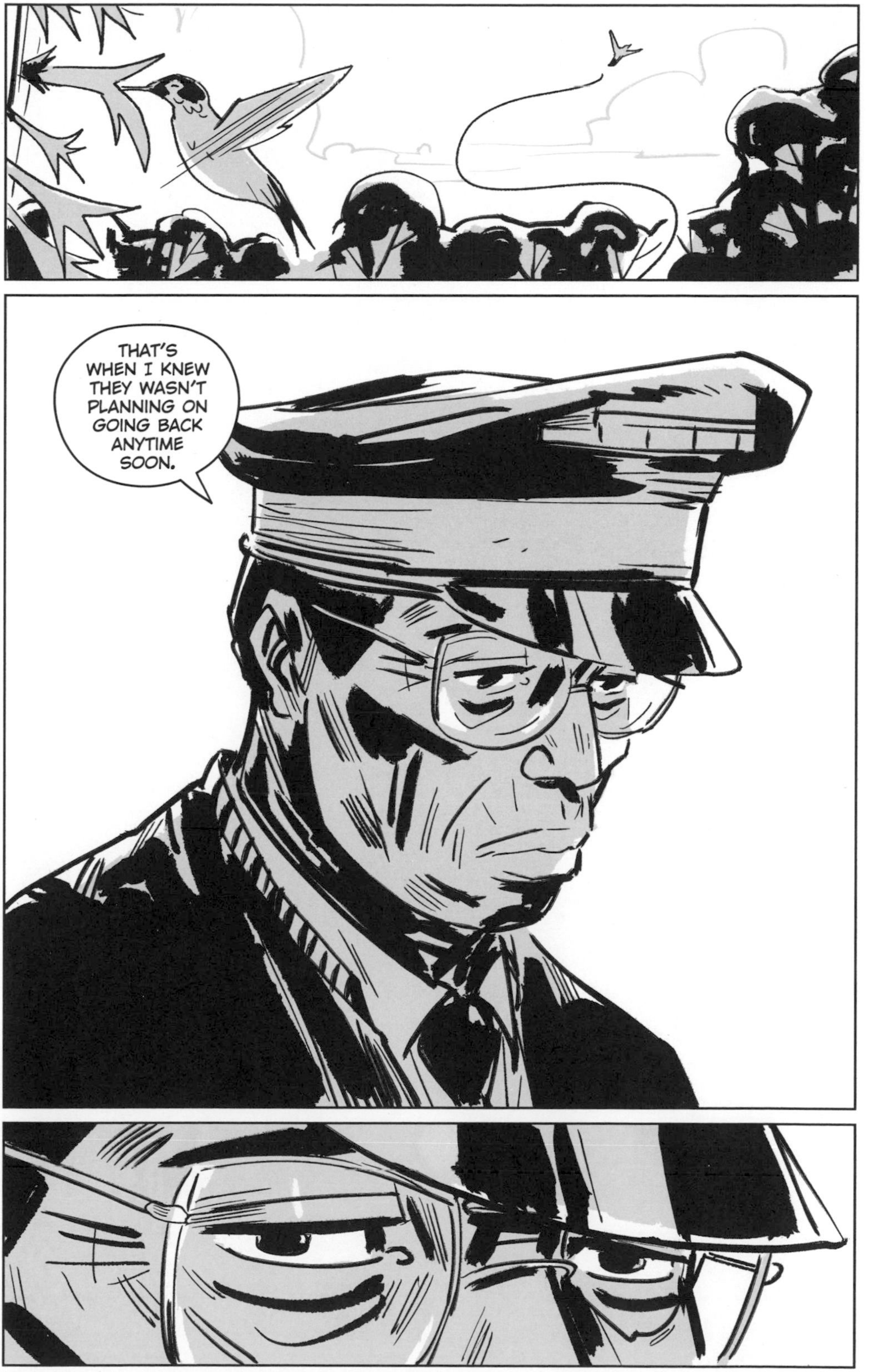
THAT'S WHEN I KNEW THEY WASN'T PLANNING ON GOING BACK ANYTIME SOON.

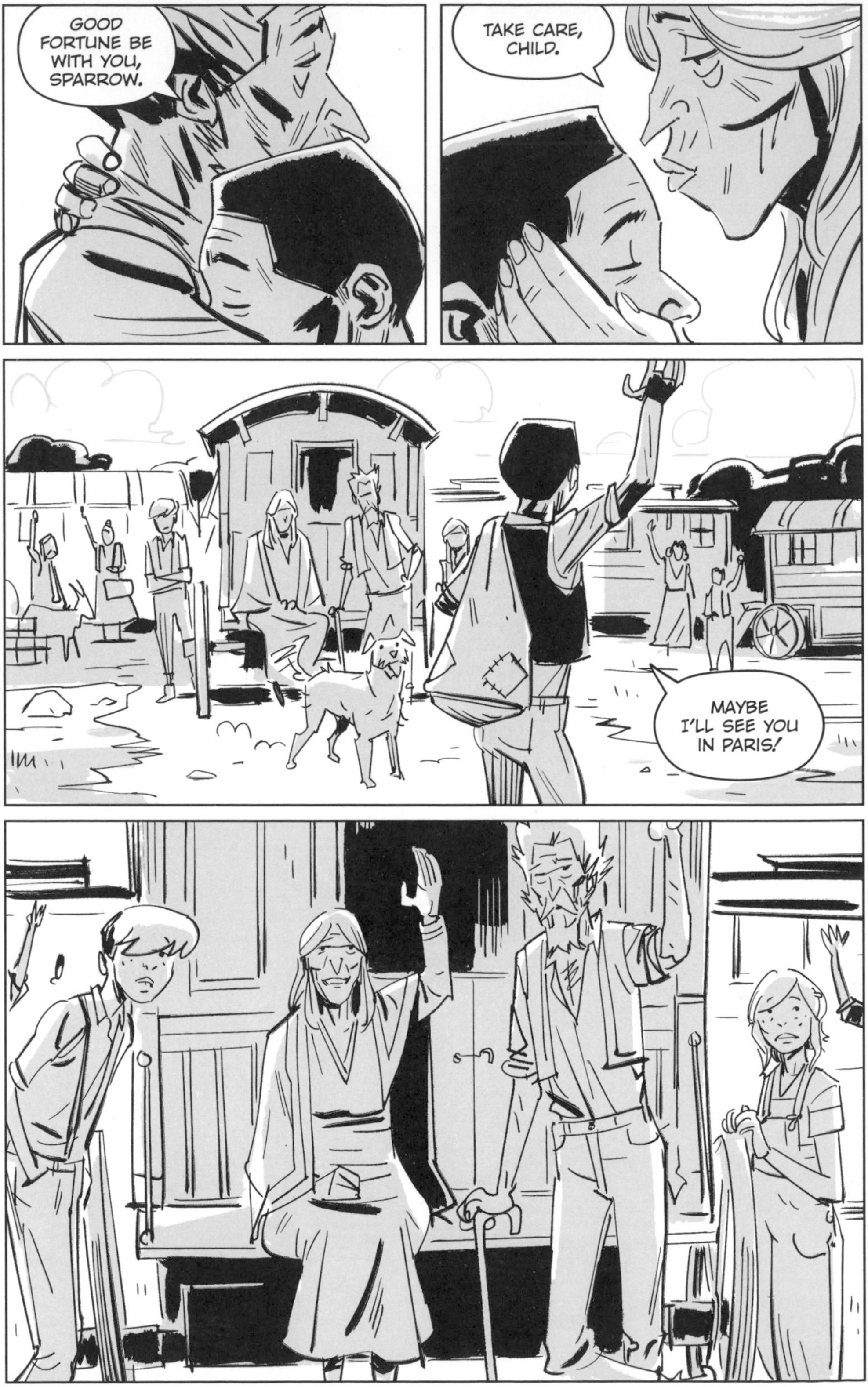
GOOD FORTUNE BE WITH YOU, SPARROW.
TAKE CARE, CHILD.
MAYBE I'LL SEE YOU IN PARIS!

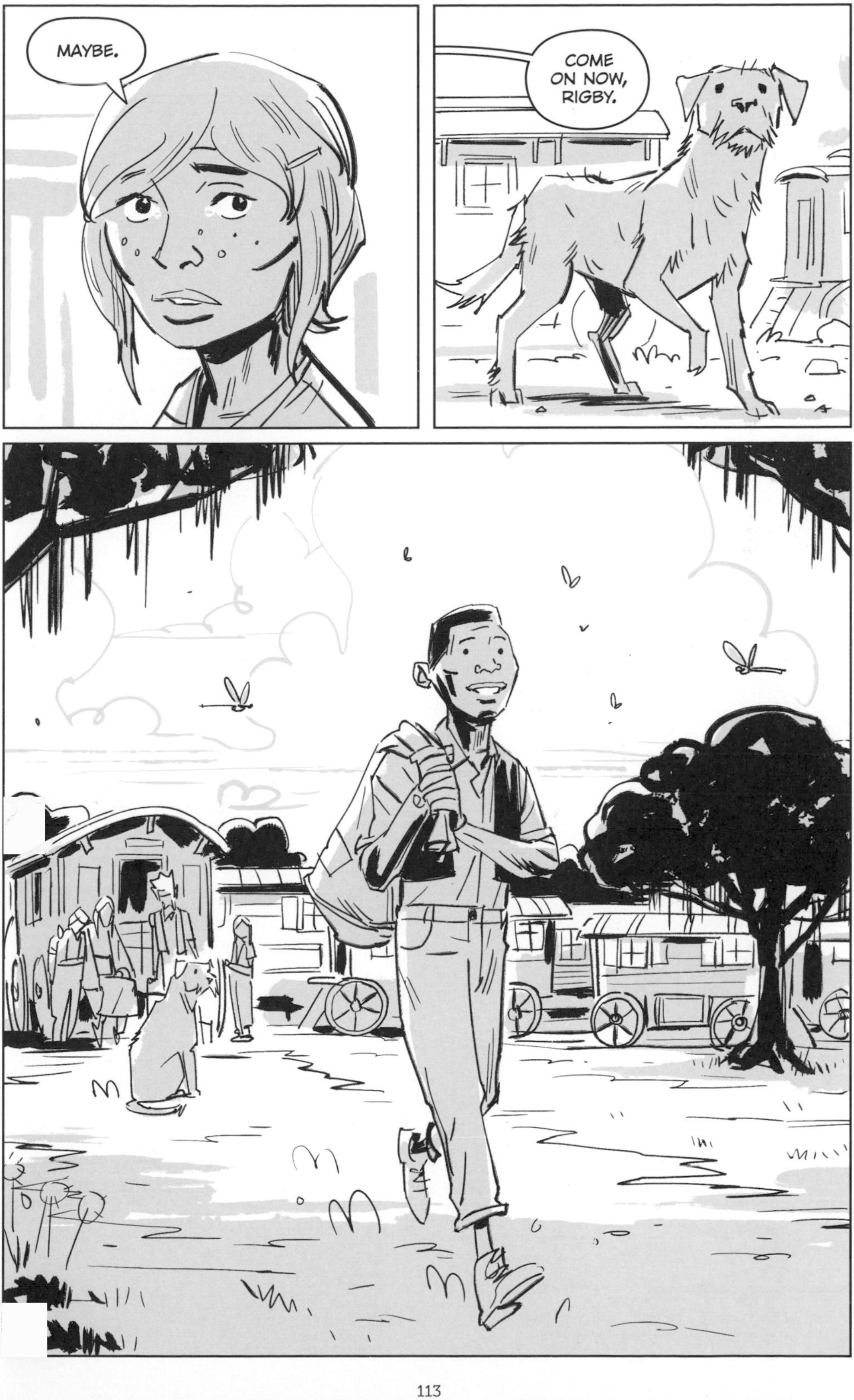
MAYBE.
COME ON NOW, RIGBY.

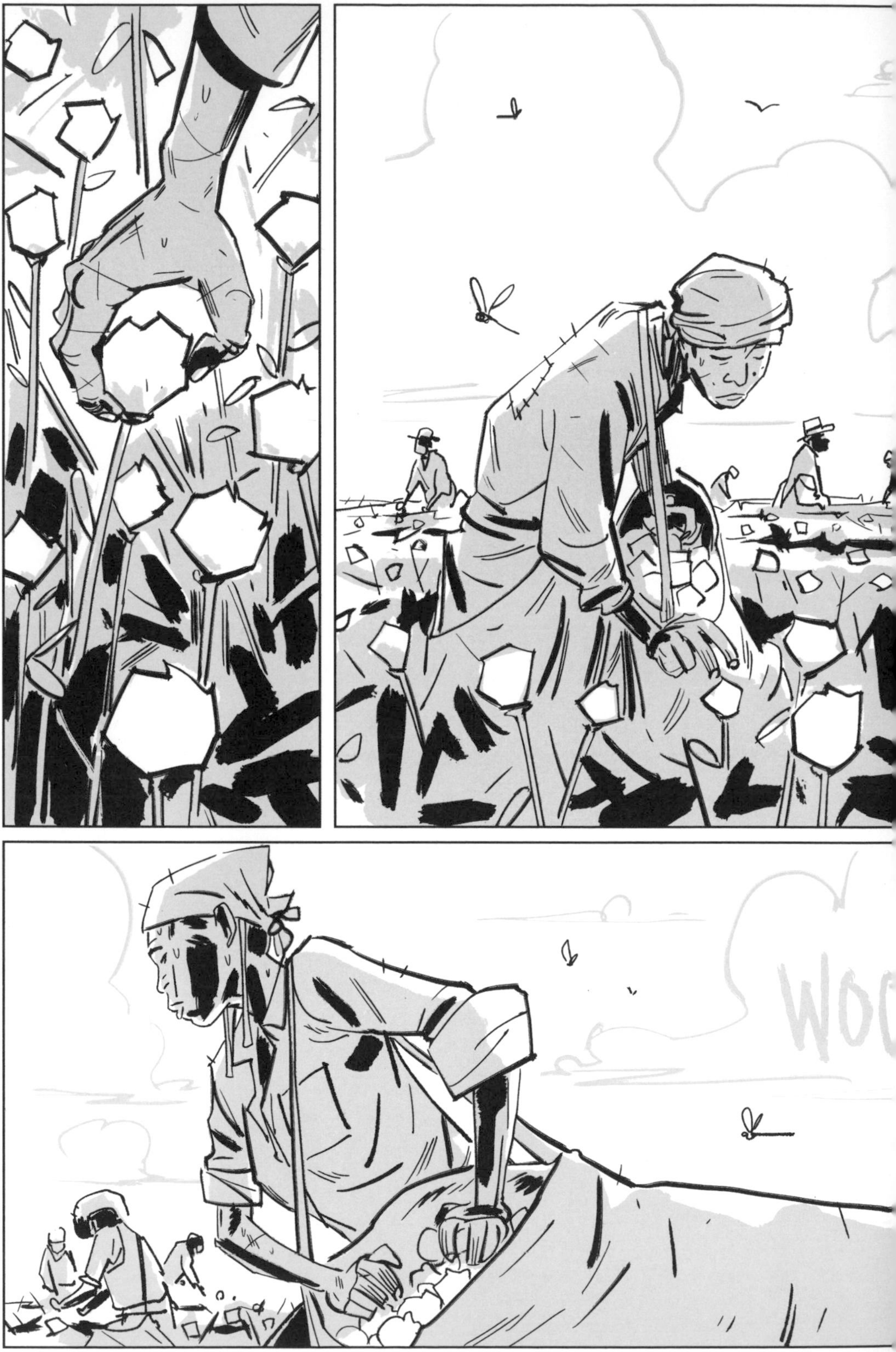
WOO

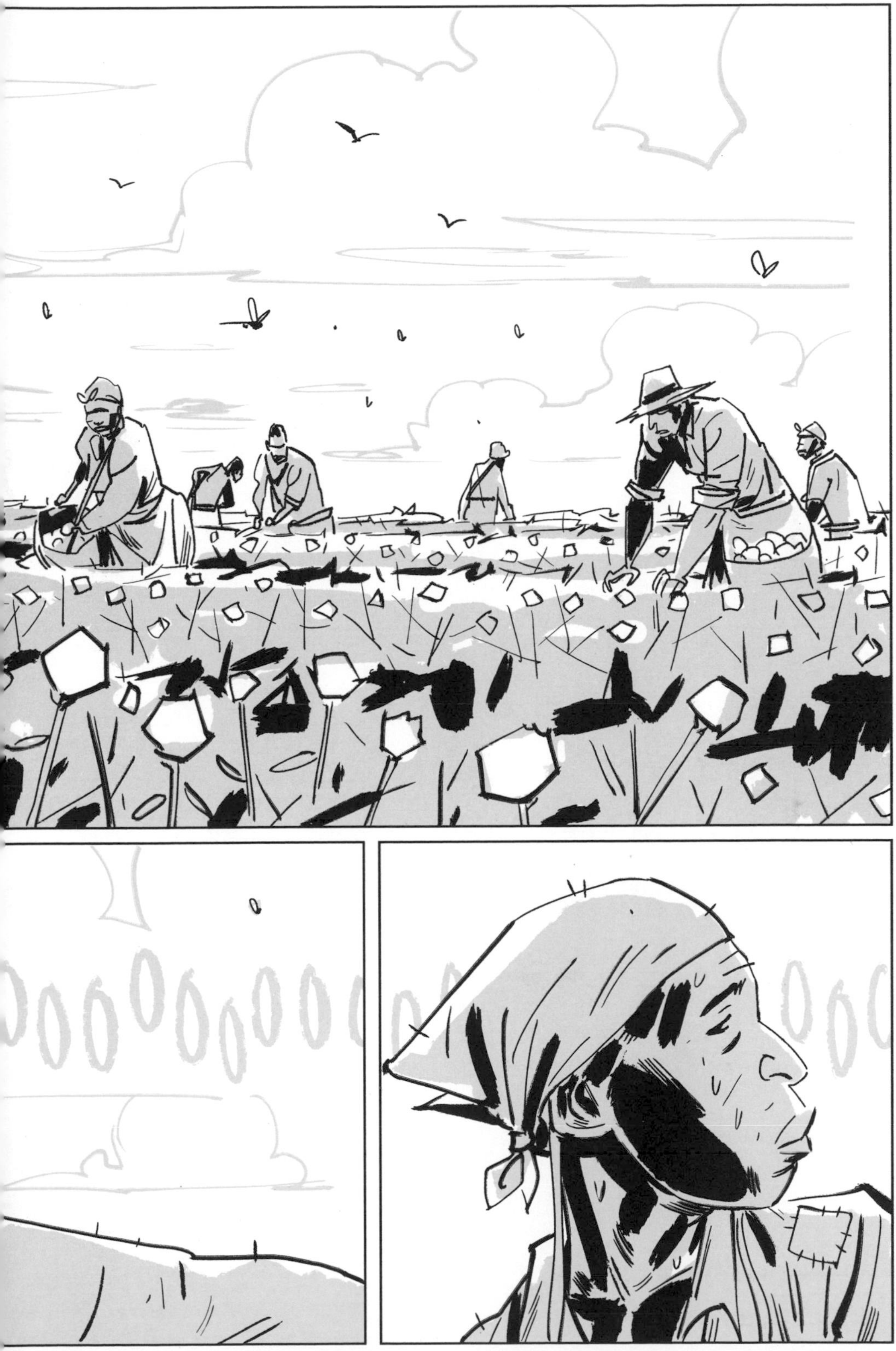

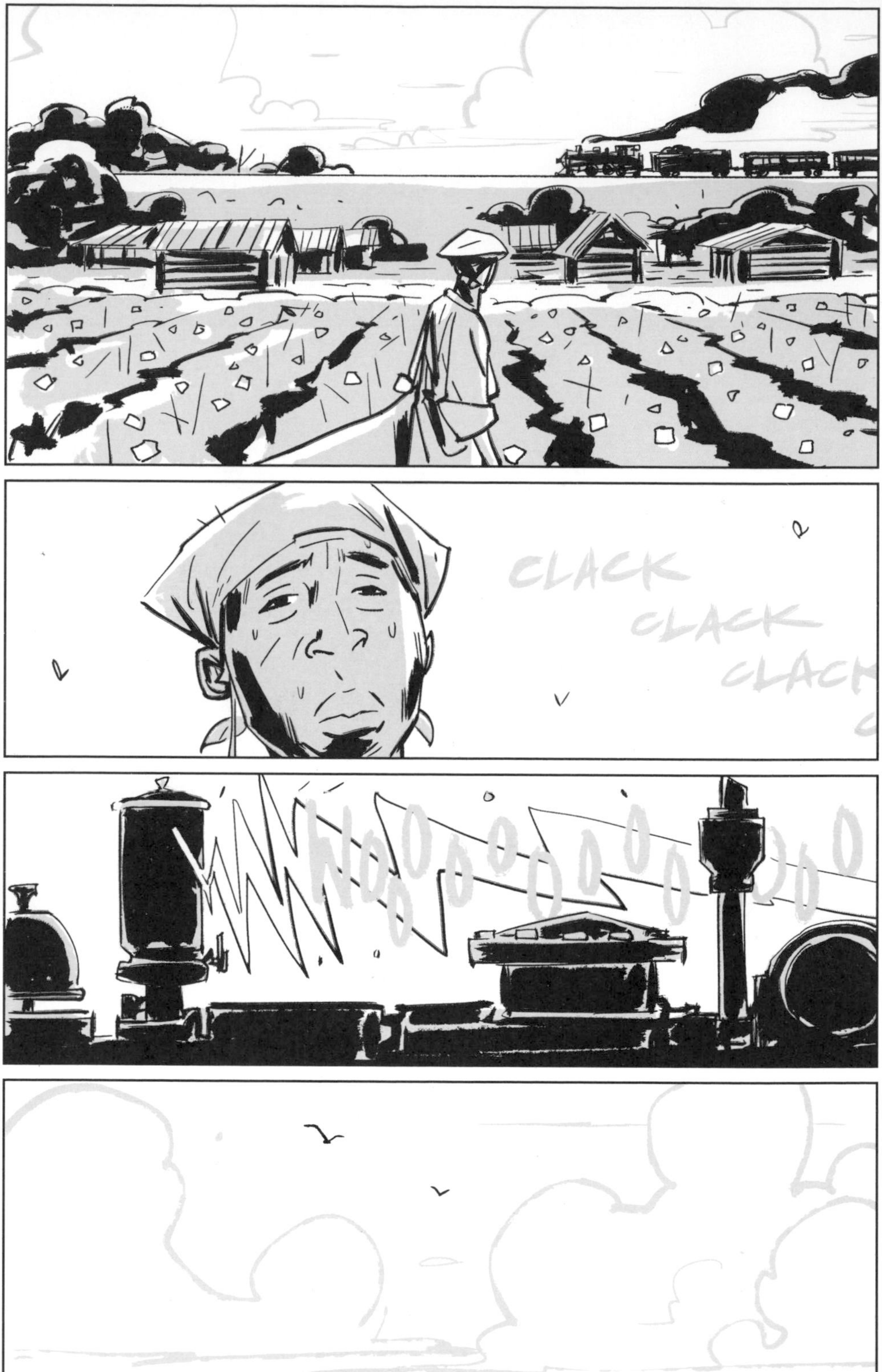
CLACK
CLACK
CLACK

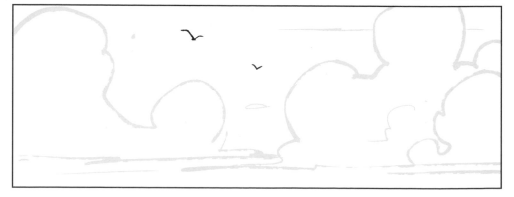

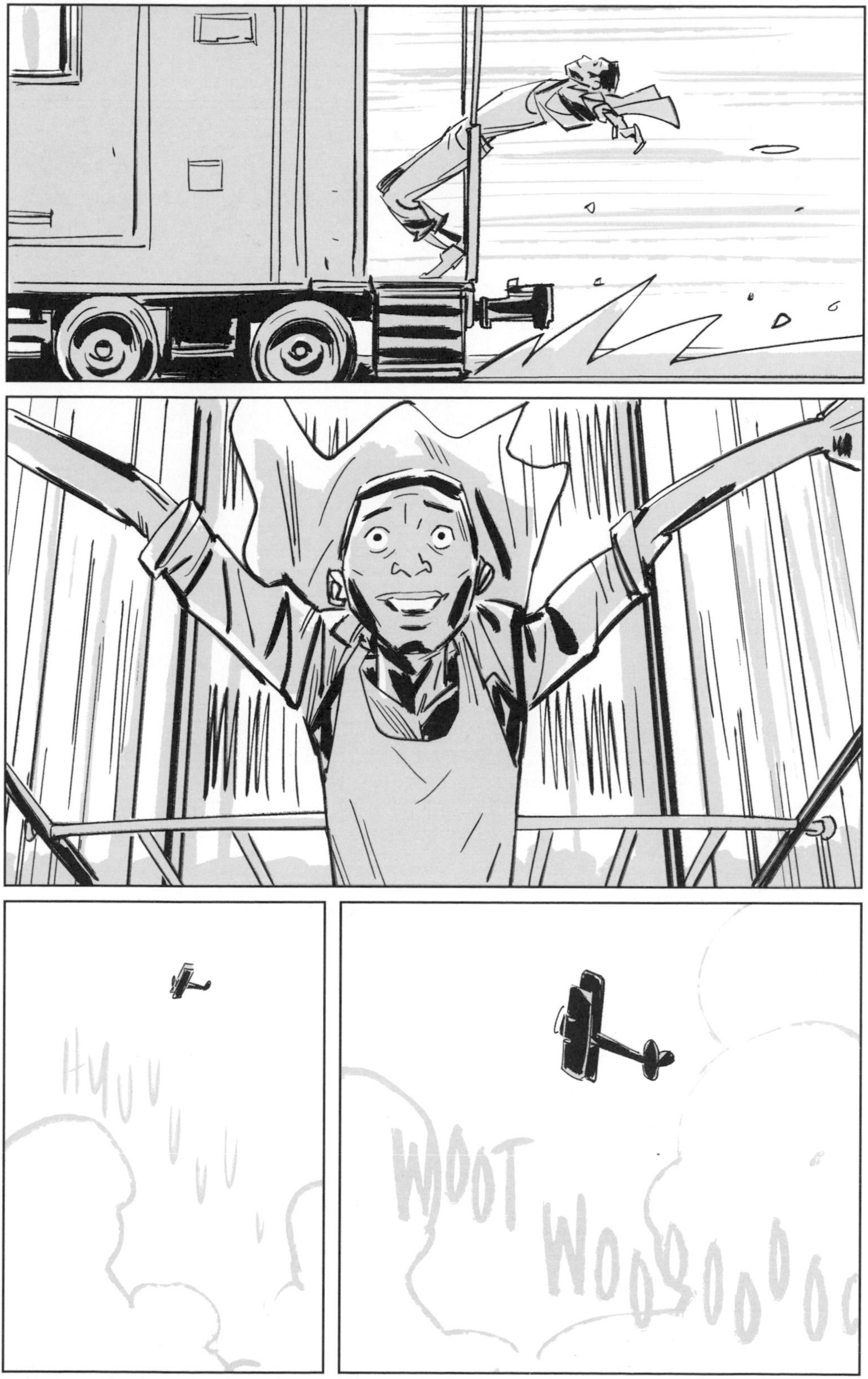
HYUUUUUU
WOOT
WOOOOOOOOO

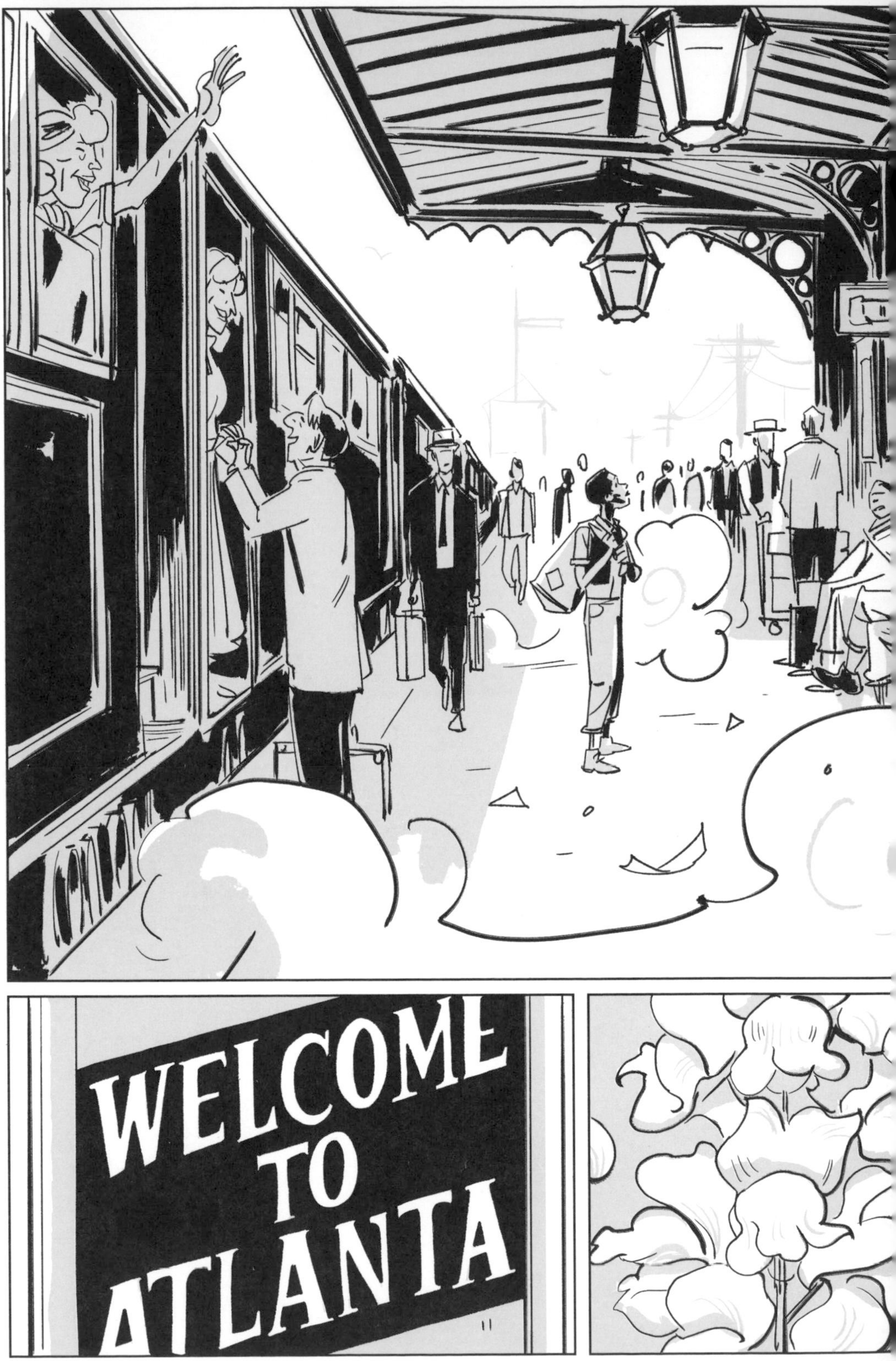
WELCOME
TO
ATLANTA

CHAPTER 3

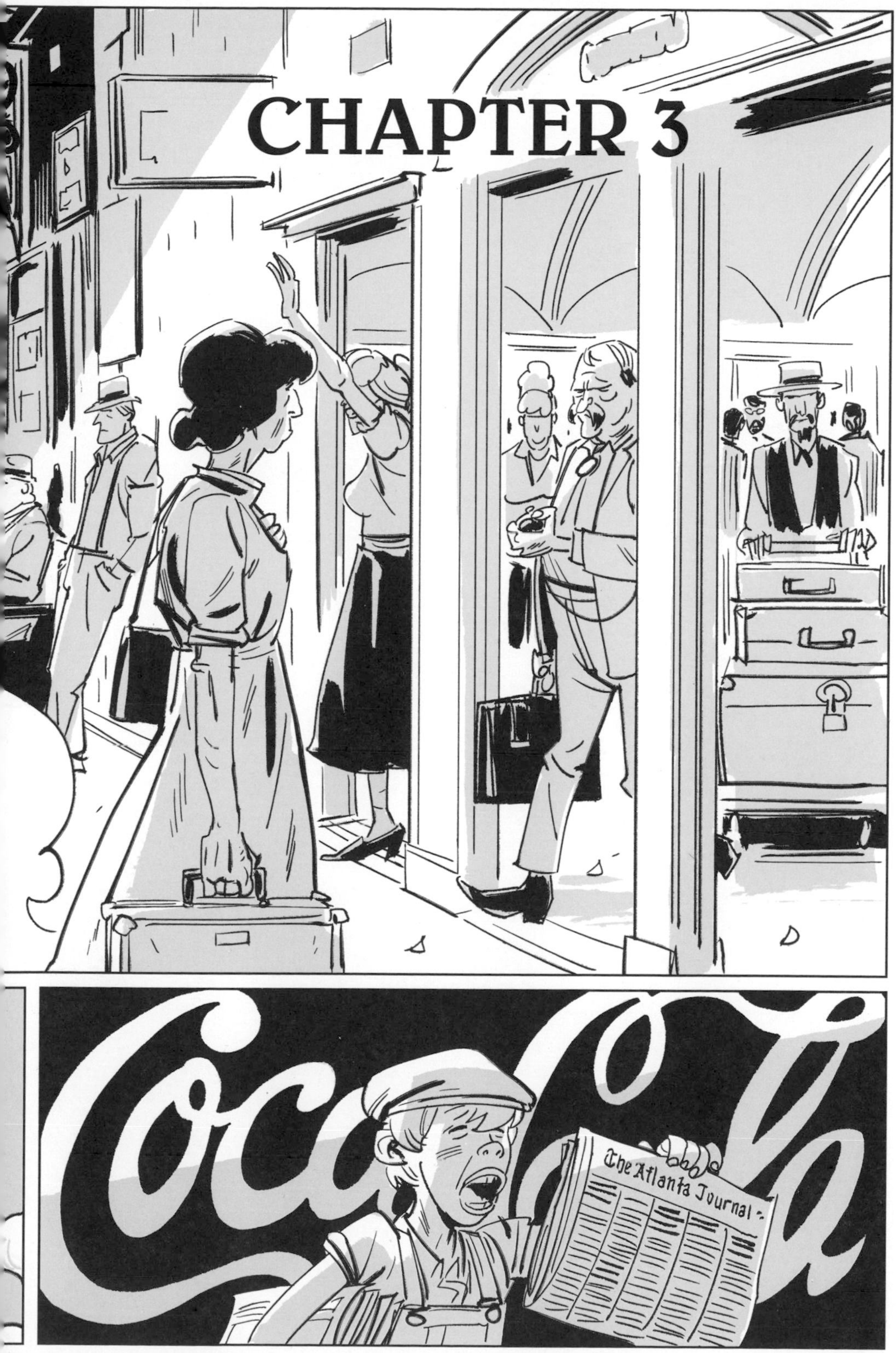
Coca-Cola
The Atlanta Journal

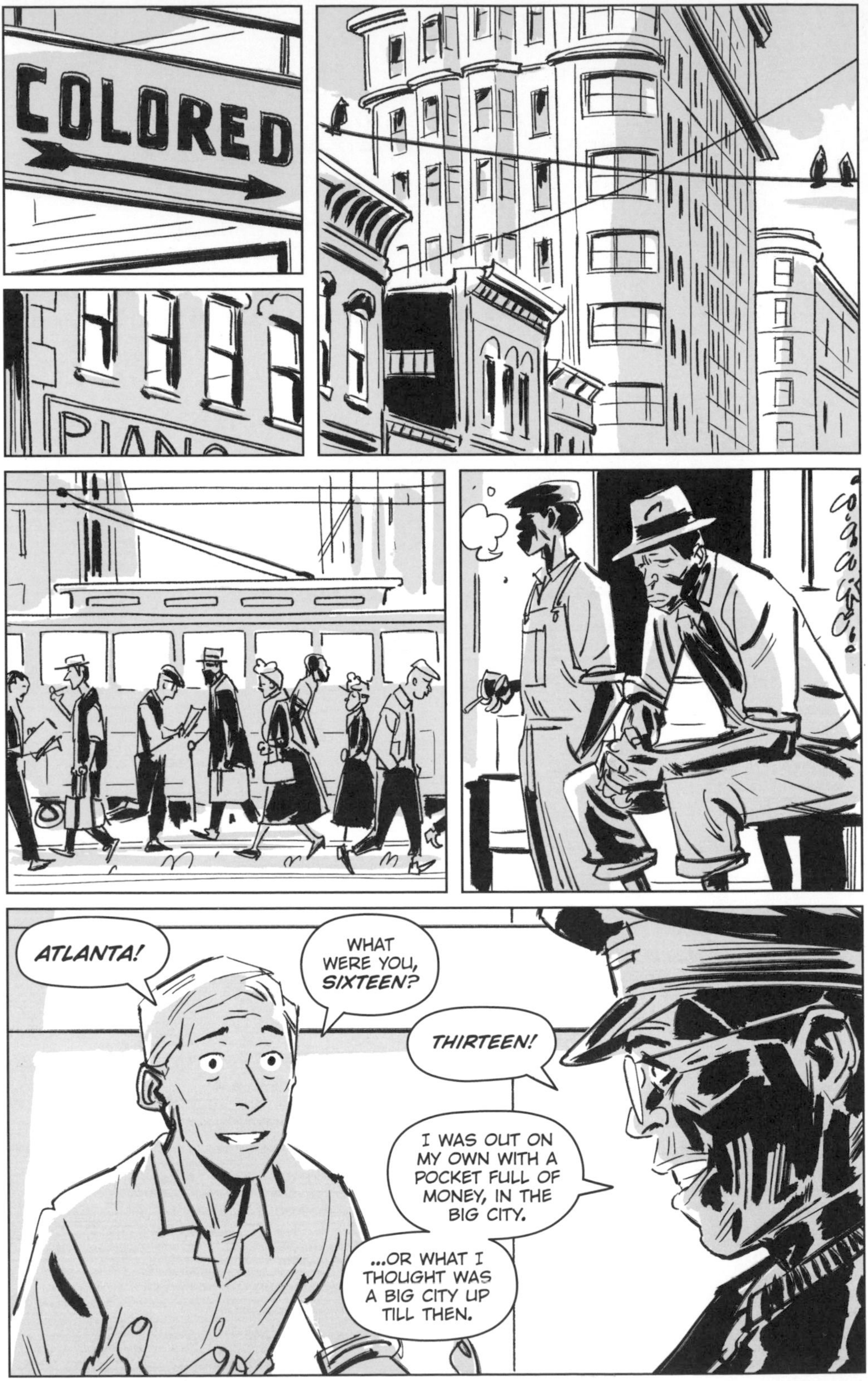
COLORED
PIANO
ATLANTA!
WHAT WERE YOU, SIXTEEN?
THIRTEEN!
I WAS OUT ON MY OWN WITH A POCKET FULL OF MONEY, IN THE BIG CITY.
...OR WHAT I THOUGHT WAS A BIG CITY UP TILL THEN.

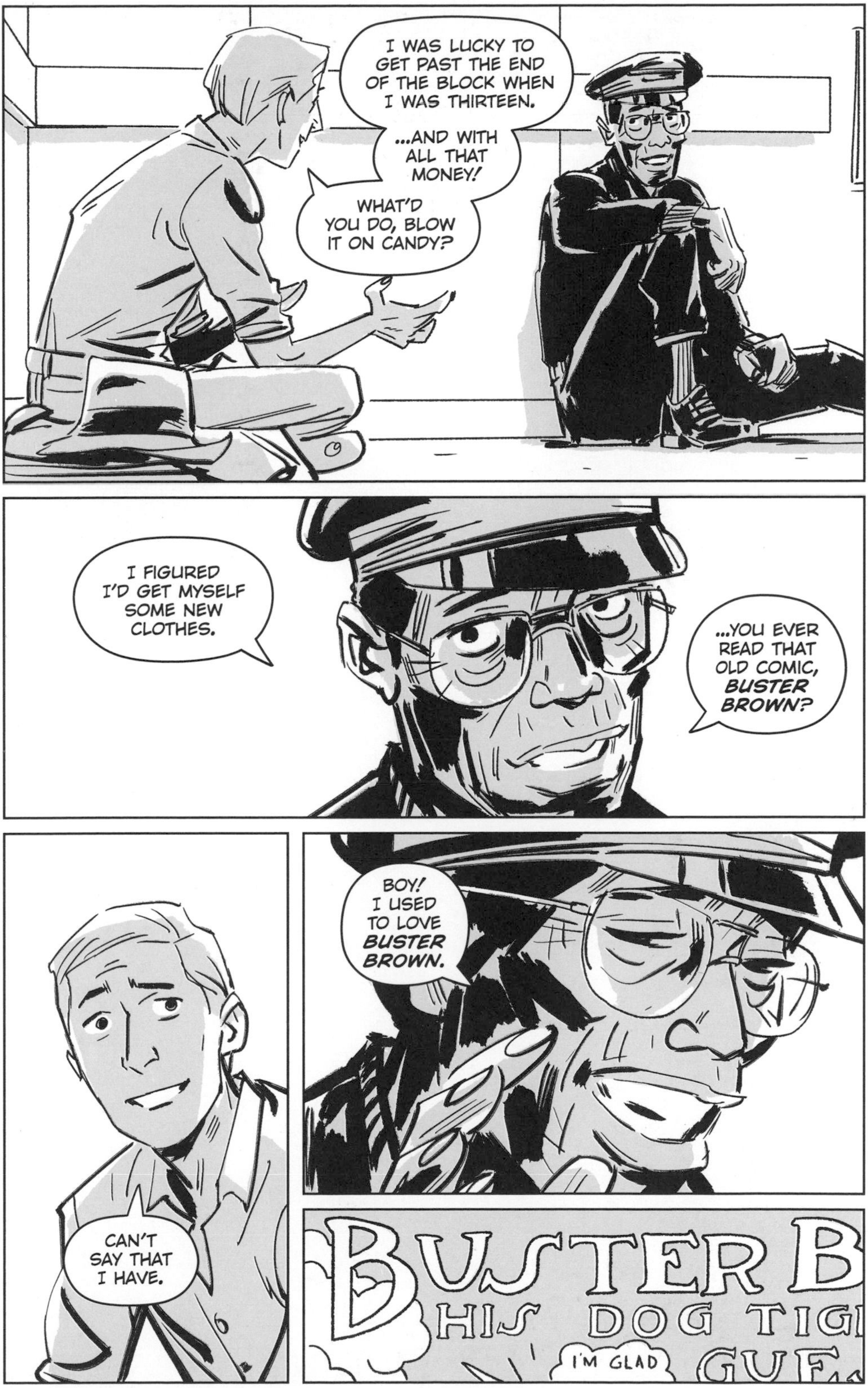
I WAS LUCKY TO GET PAST THE END OF THE BLOCK WHEN I WAS THIRTEEN.
...AND WITH ALL THAT MONEY!
WHAT'D YOU DO, BLOW IT ON CANDY?
I FIGURED I'D GET MYSELF SOME NEW CLOTHES.
...YOU EVER READ THAT OLD COMIC, *BUSTER BROWN?*
CAN'T SAY THAT I HAVE.
BOY! I USED TO LOVE *BUSTER BROWN.*
BUSTER B
HIS DOG TIG
I'M GLAD
GUE

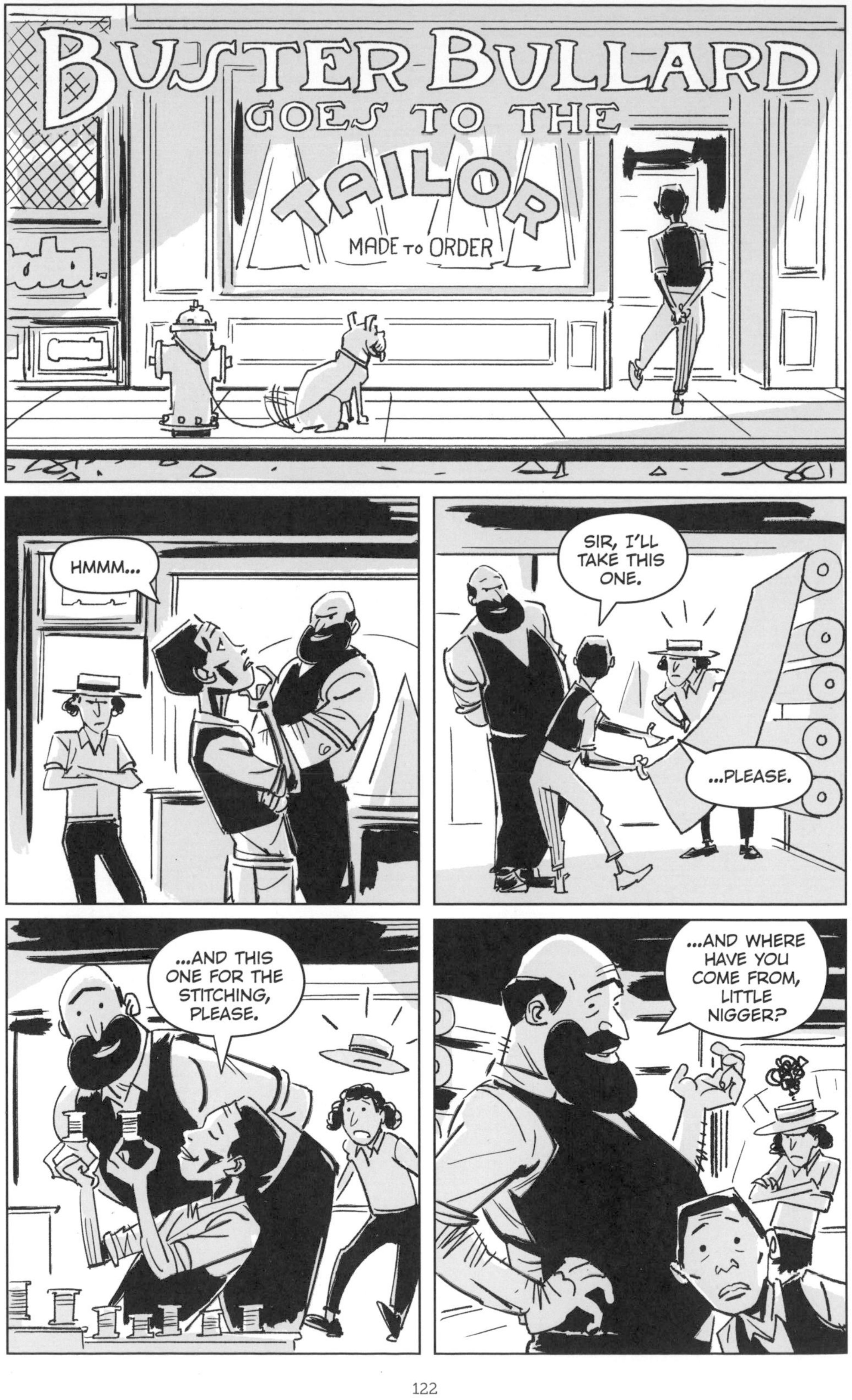
BUSTER BULLARD
GOES TO THE
TAILOR
MADE TO ORDER
HMMM...
SIR, I'LL TAKE THIS ONE.
...PLEASE.
...AND THIS ONE FOR THE STITCHING, PLEASE.
...AND WHERE HAVE YOU COME FROM, LITTLE NIGGER?

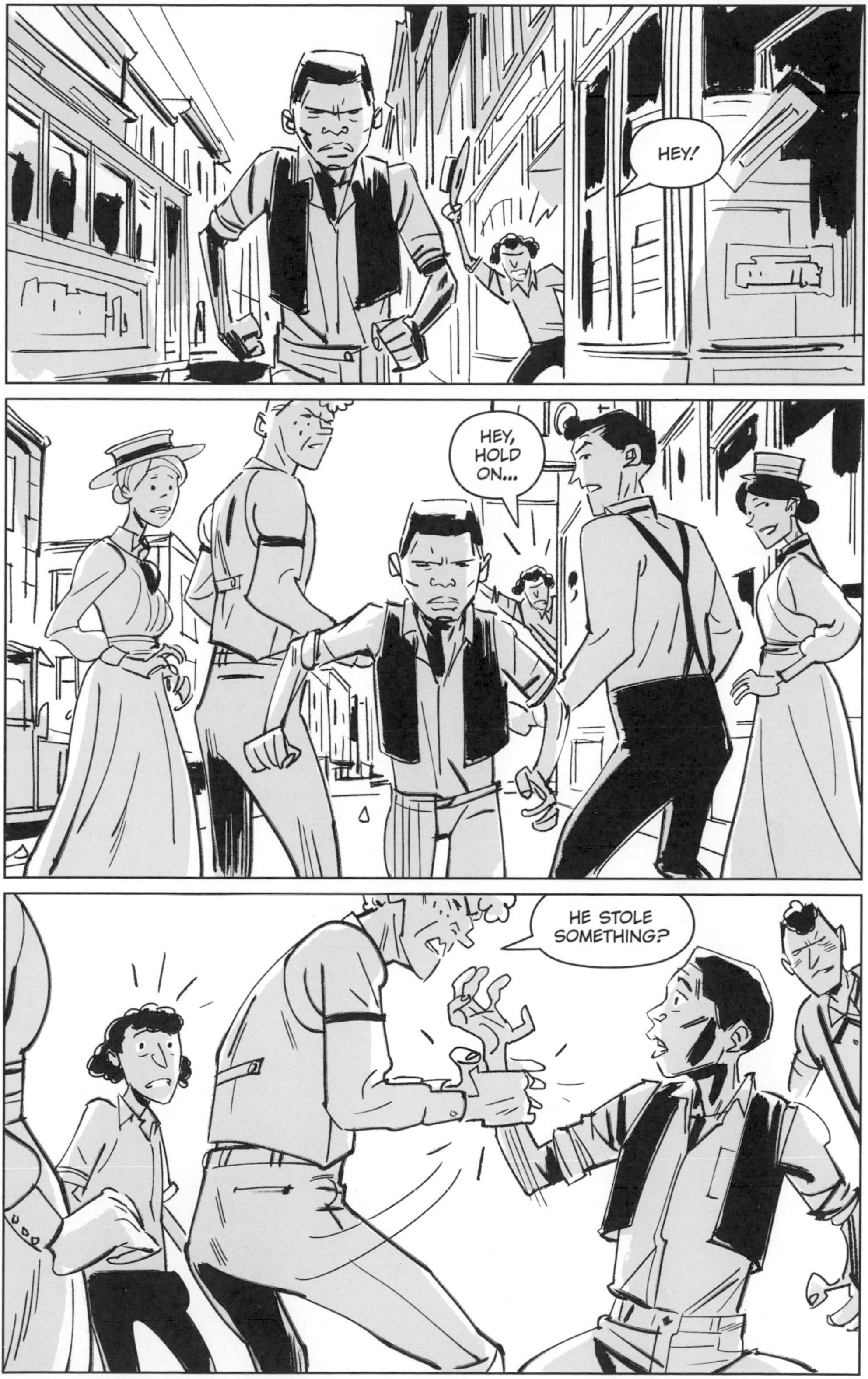
HEY!
HEY, HOLD ON...
HE STOLE SOMETHING?

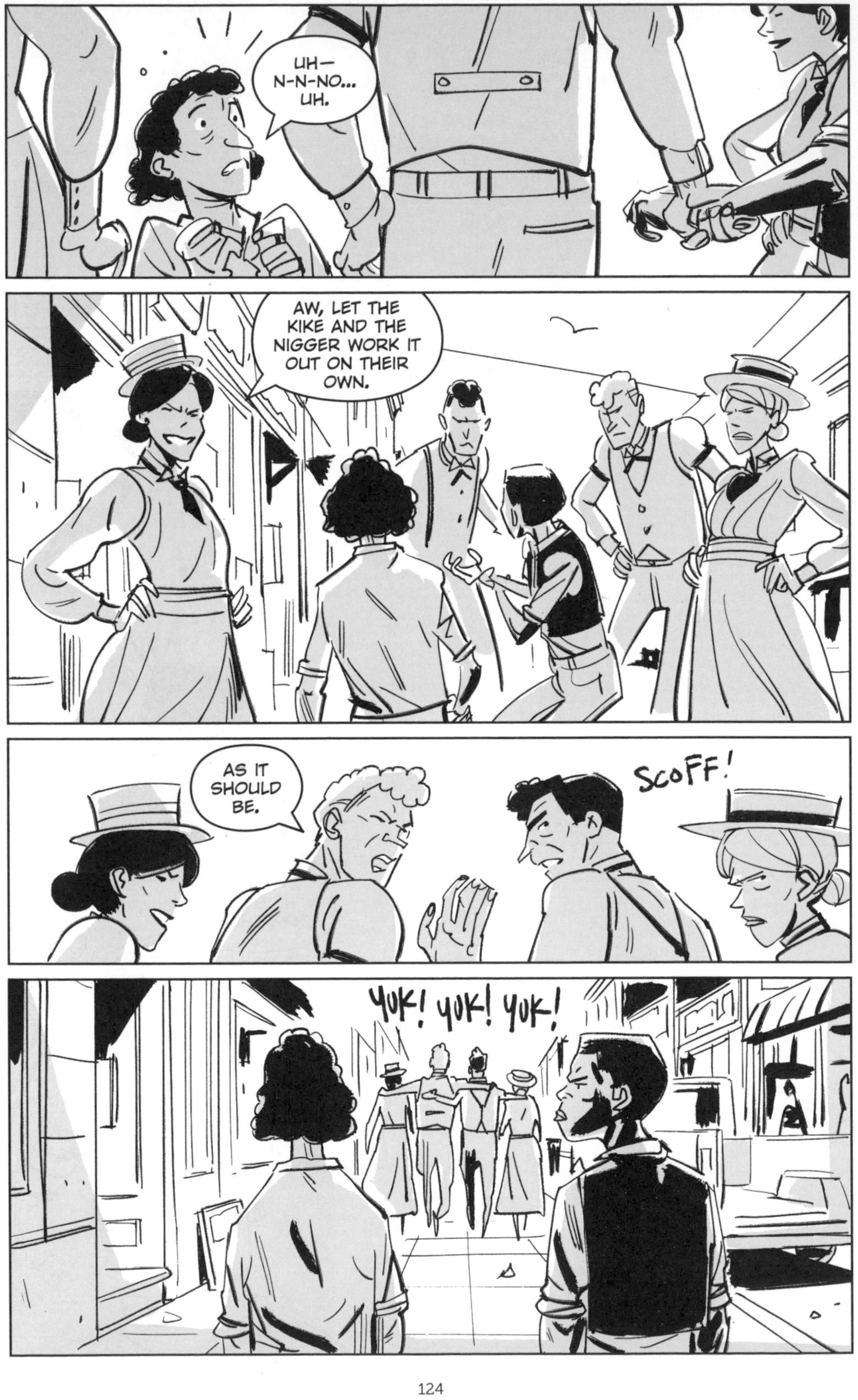
UH—
N-N-NO...
UH.
AW, LET THE KIKE AND THE NIGGER WORK IT OUT ON THEIR OWN.
AS IT SHOULD BE.
SCOFF!
YUK! YUK! YUK!

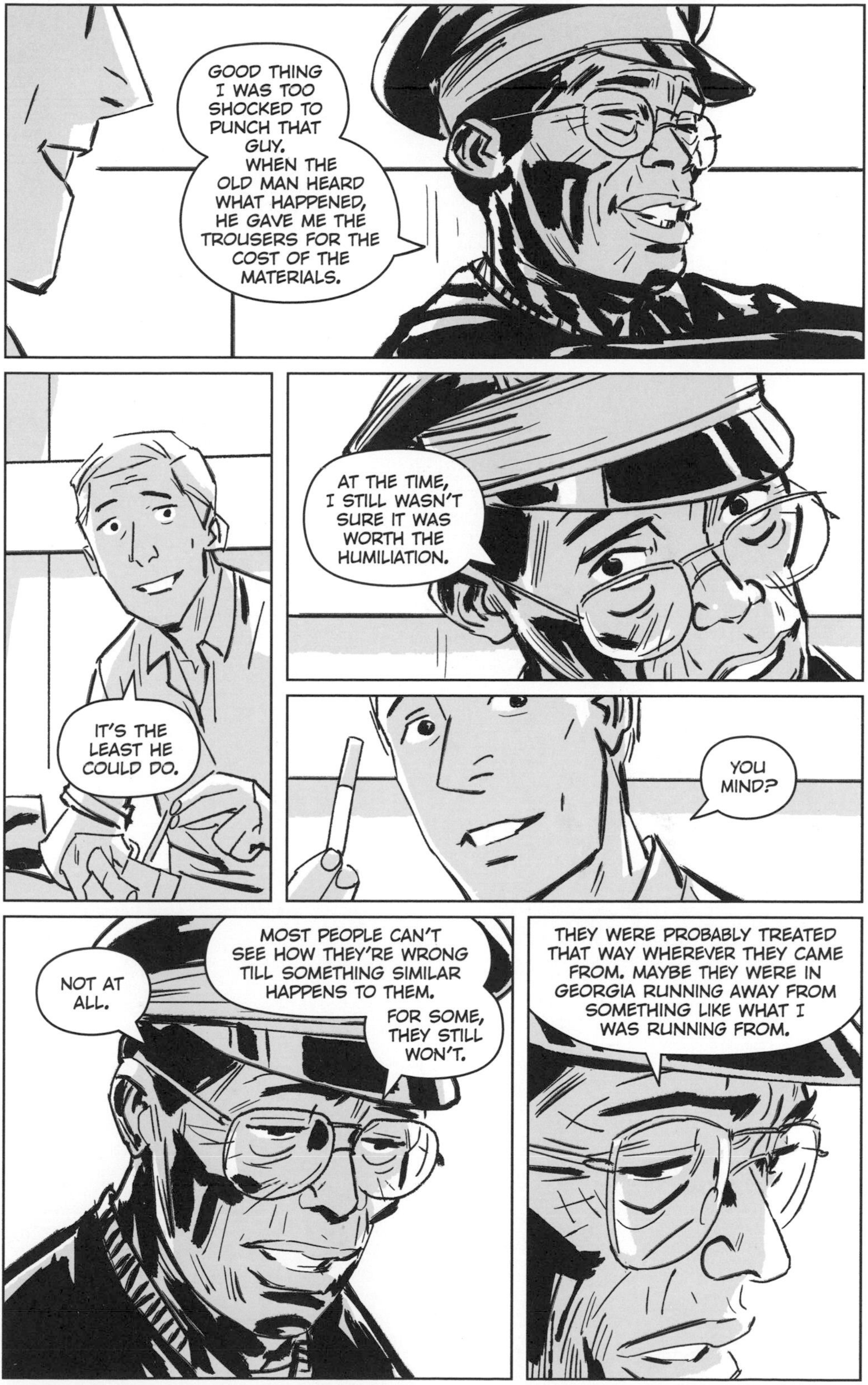
GOOD THING I WAS TOO SHOCKED TO PUNCH THAT GUY.
WHEN THE OLD MAN HEARD WHAT HAPPENED, HE GAVE ME THE TROUSERS FOR THE COST OF THE MATERIALS.
IT'S THE LEAST HE COULD DO.
AT THE TIME, I STILL WASN'T SURE IT WAS WORTH THE HUMILIATION.
YOU MIND?
NOT AT ALL.
MOST PEOPLE CAN'T SEE HOW THEY'RE WRONG TILL SOMETHING SIMILAR HAPPENS TO THEM.
FOR SOME, THEY STILL WON'T.
THEY WERE PROBABLY TREATED THAT WAY WHEREVER THEY CAME FROM. MAYBE THEY WERE IN GEORGIA RUNNING AWAY FROM SOMETHING LIKE WHAT I WAS RUNNING FROM.

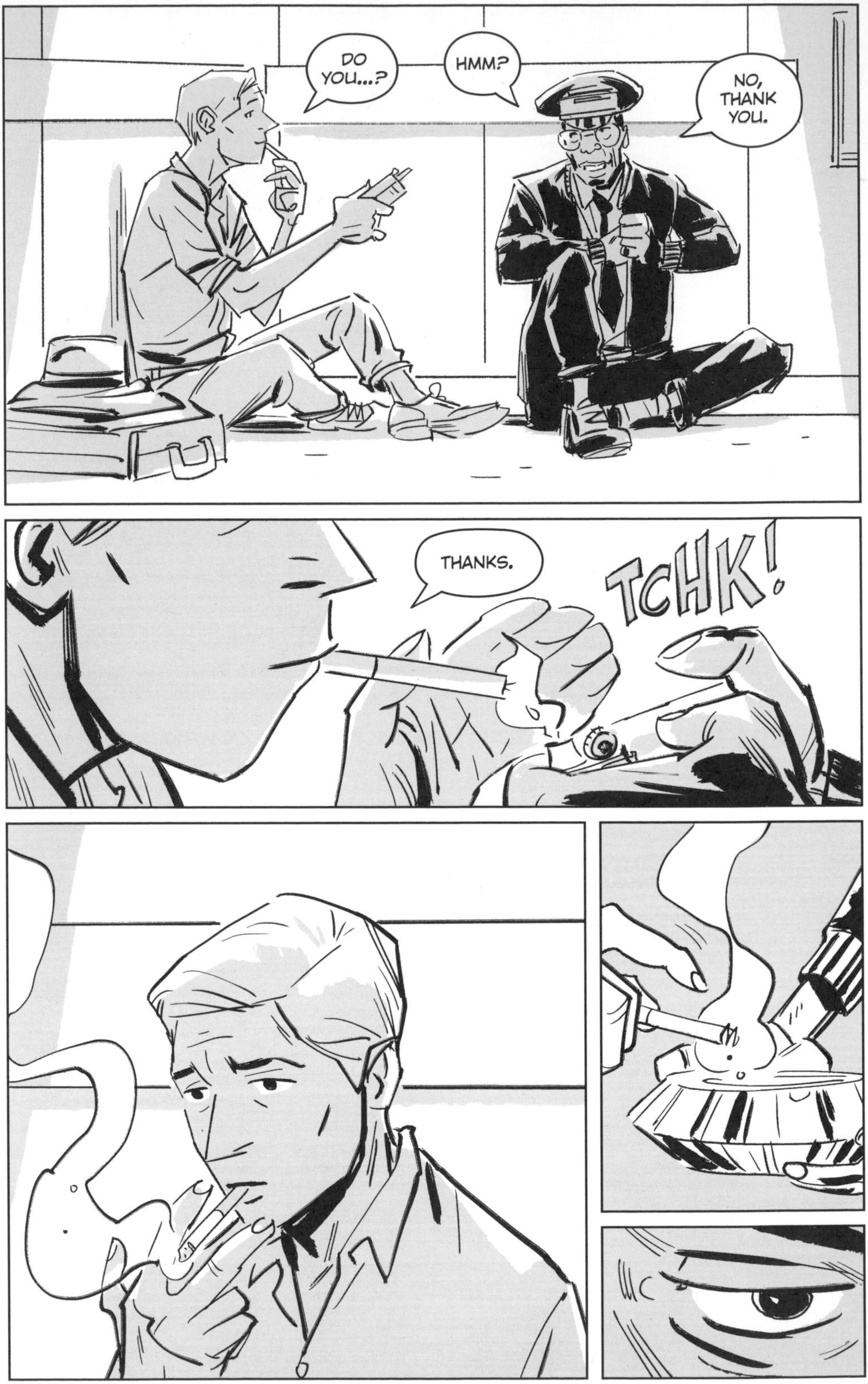
DO YOU...?
HMM?
NO, THANK YOU.
THANKS.
TCHK!

SO HOW'D YOU END UP GETTING OUT OF THE SOUTH?

HISSSSSSSSSSSSS

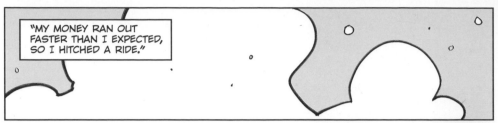

"MY MONEY RAN OUT FASTER THAN I EXPECTED, SO I HITCHED A RIDE."

"I FIGURED I'D HEAD TO THE COAST AND CATCH A BOAT TO FRANCE."

"...TO TELL THE TRUTH, I HAD NO IDEA WHERE I WAS GOING."

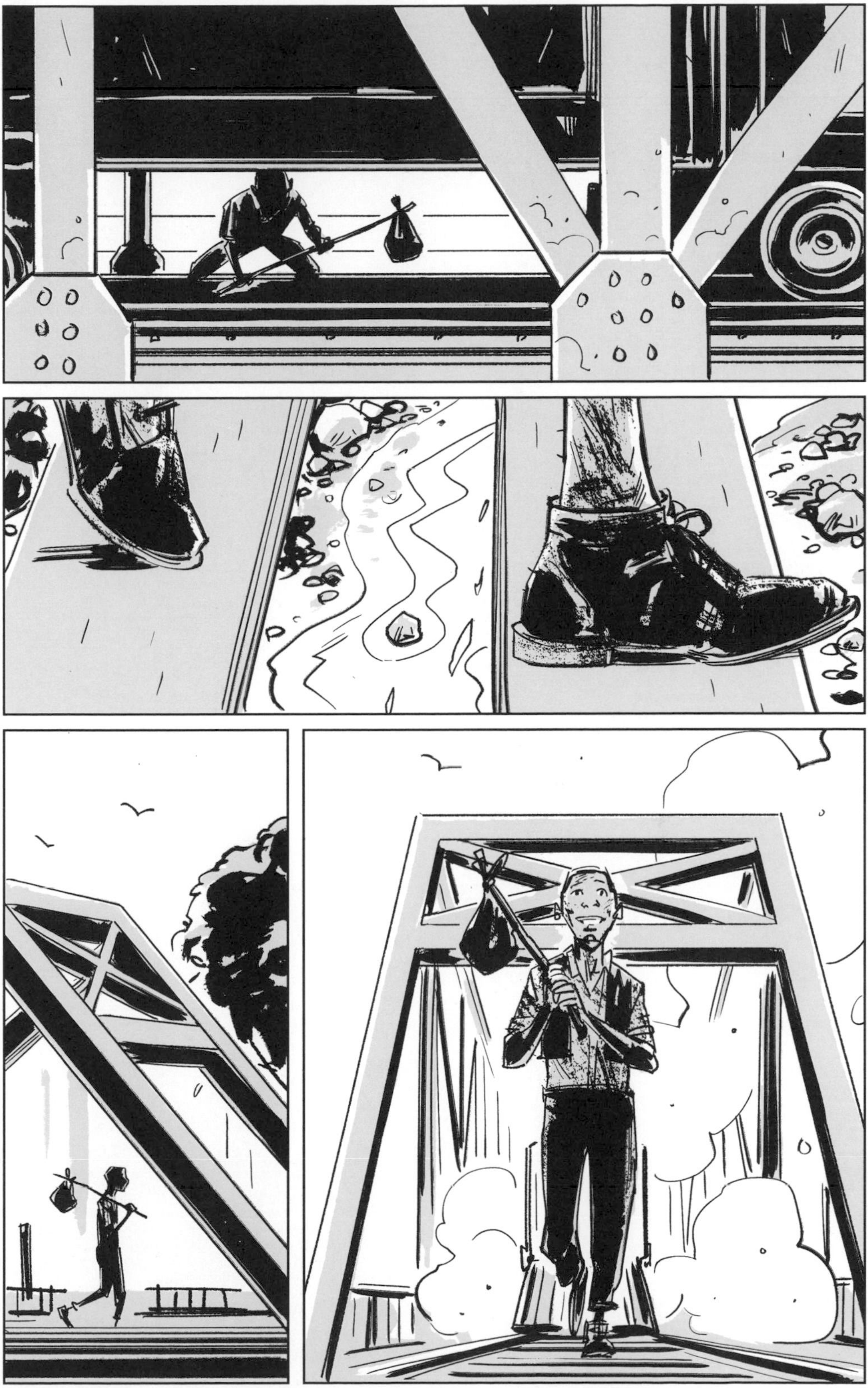

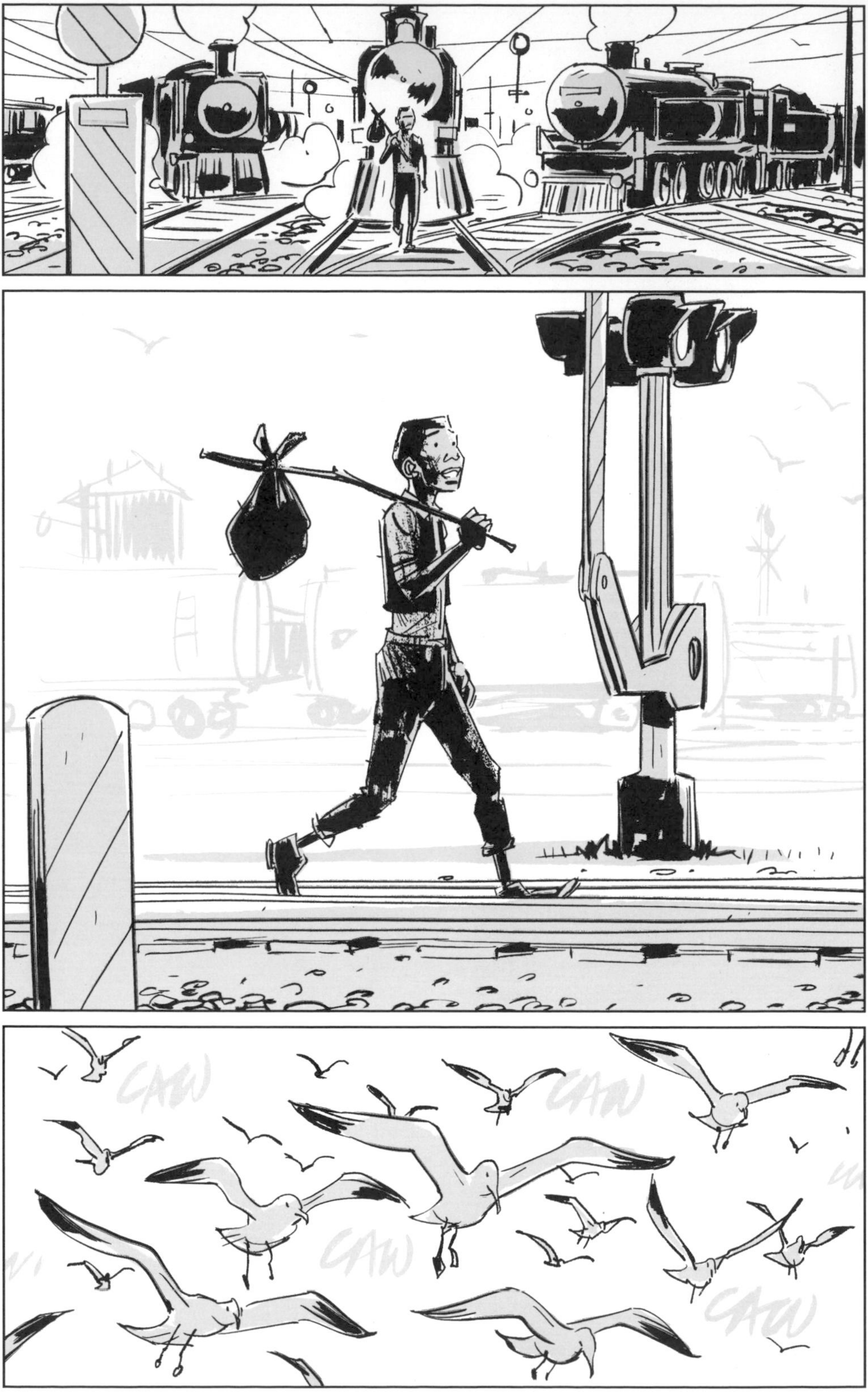
CAW
CAW
CAW
CAW

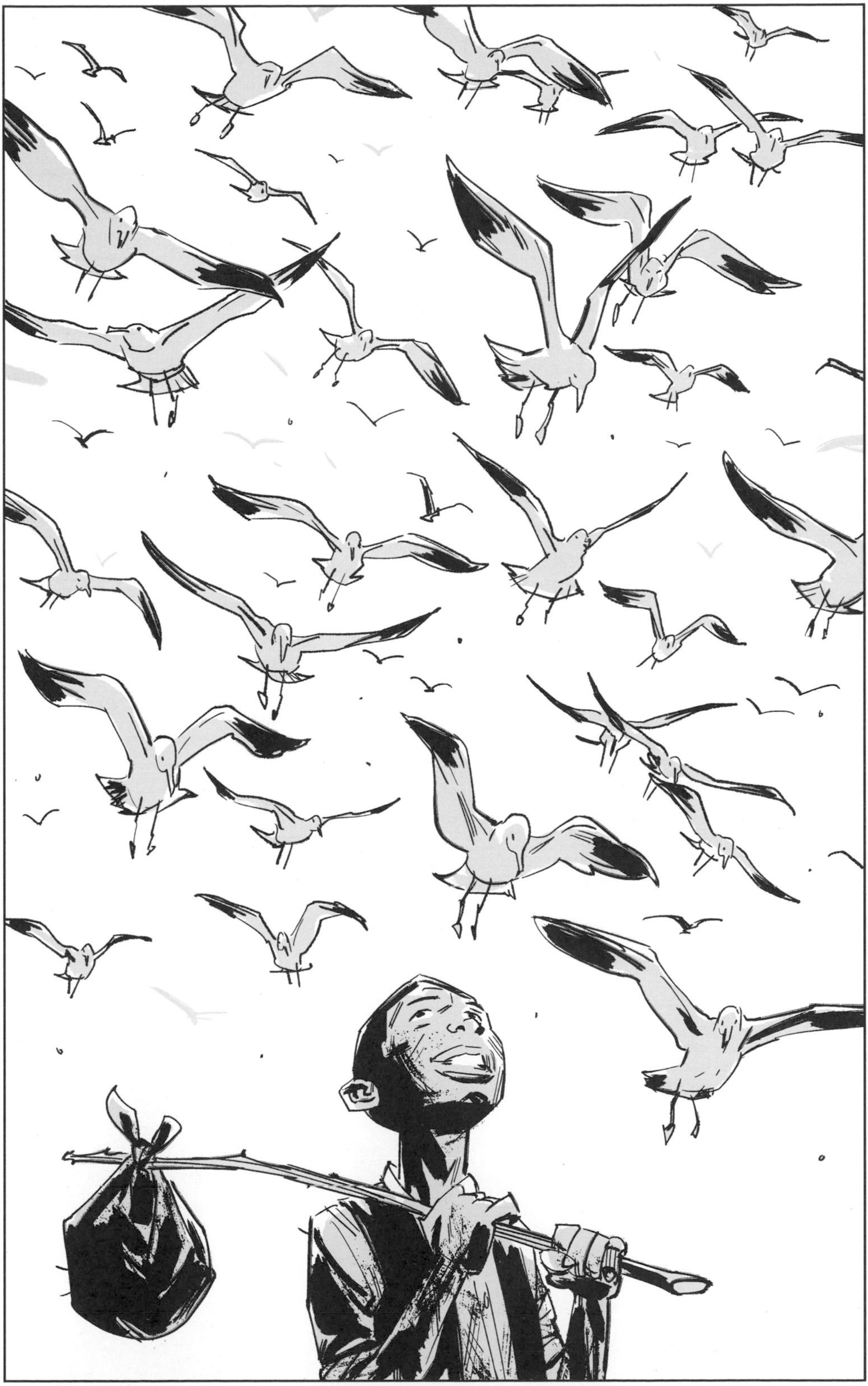

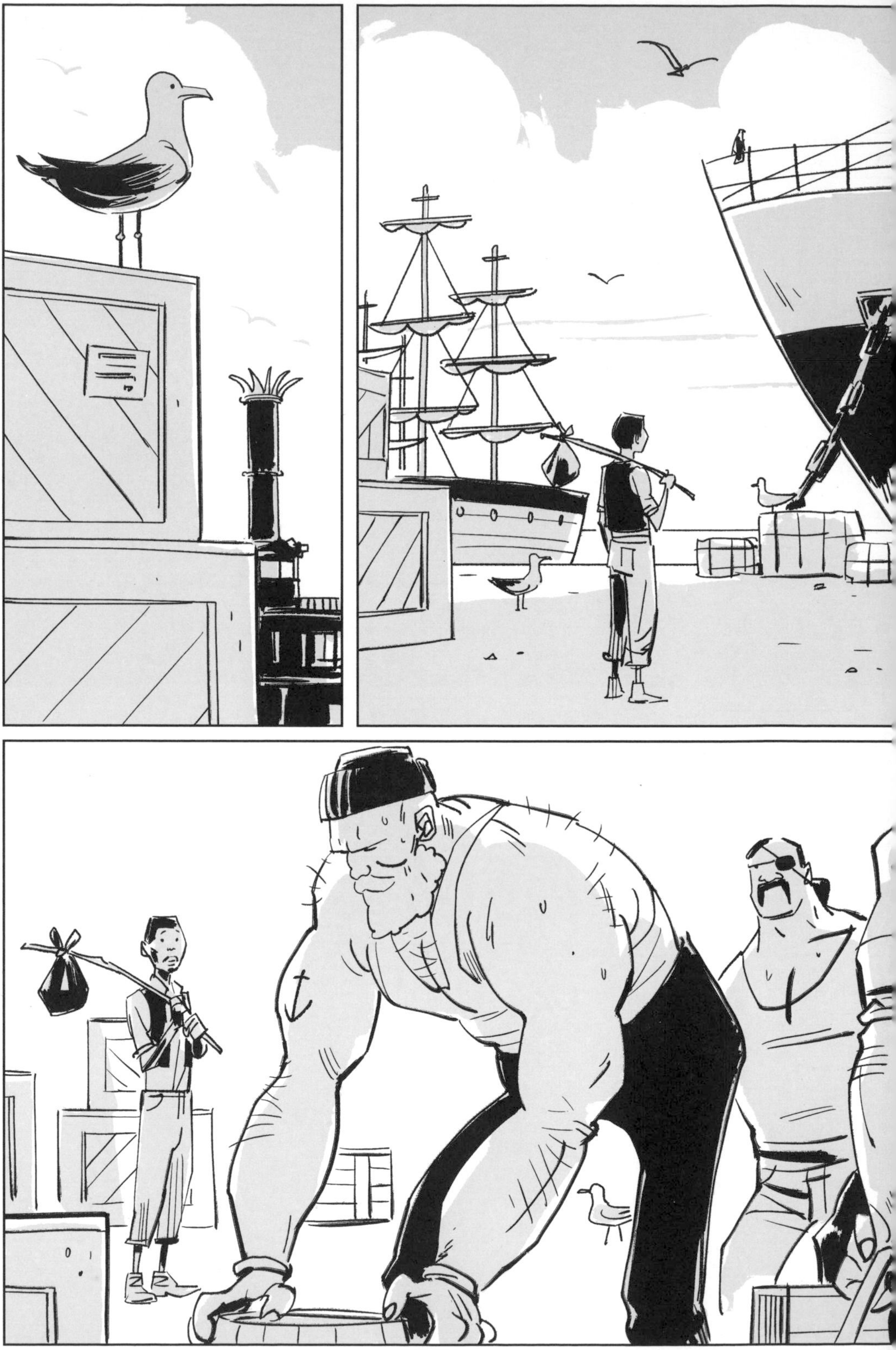

CHAPTER 4

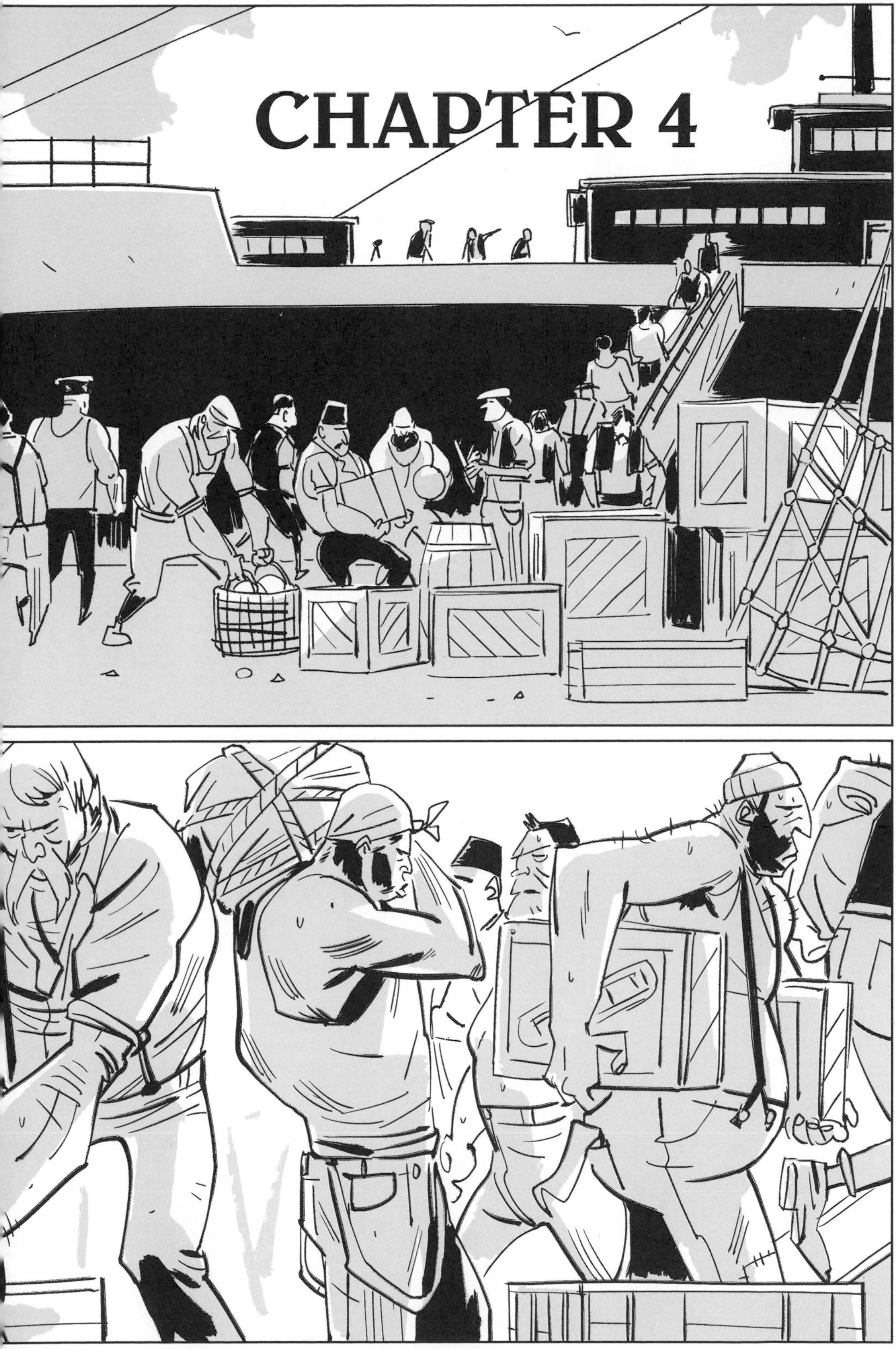

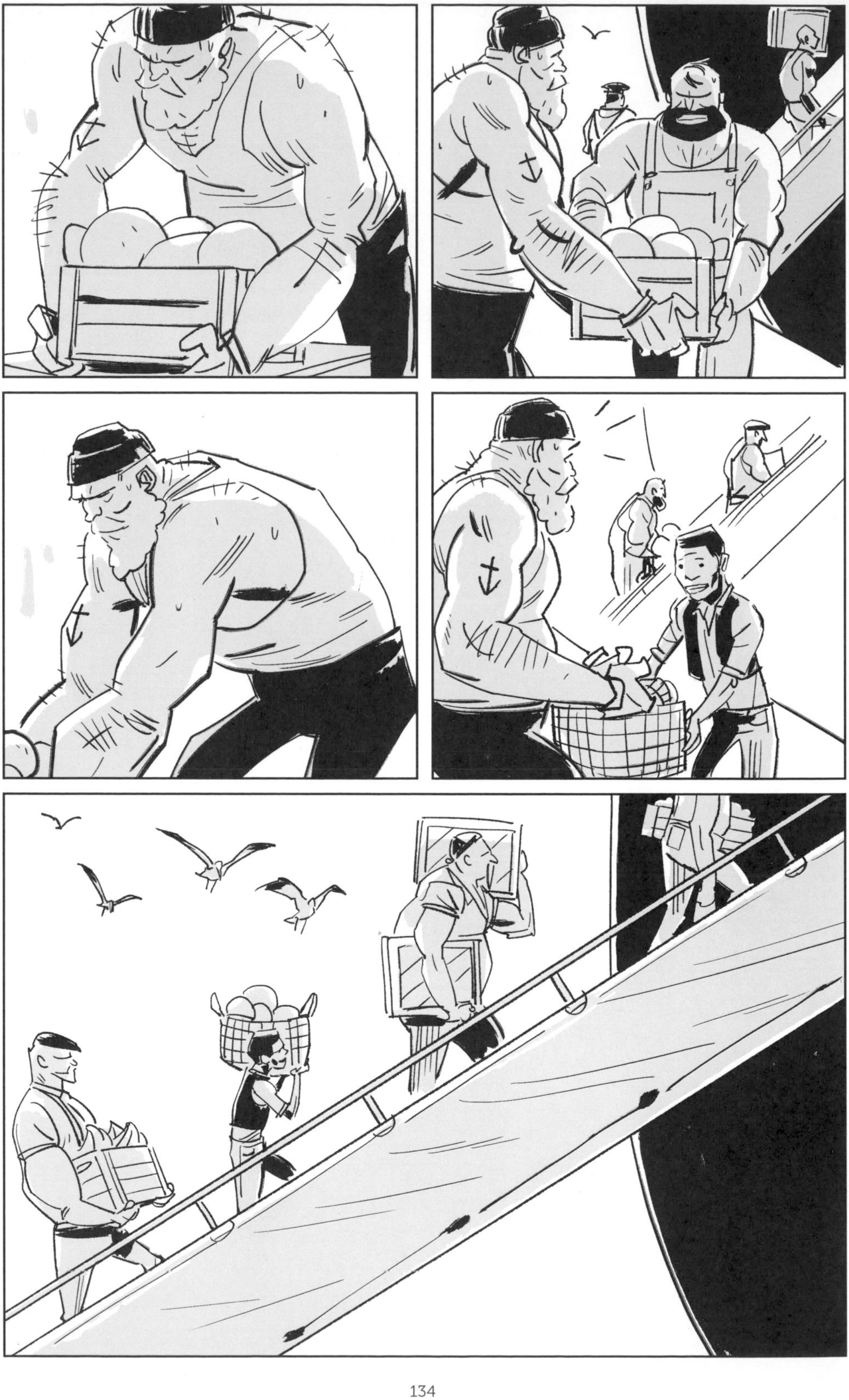

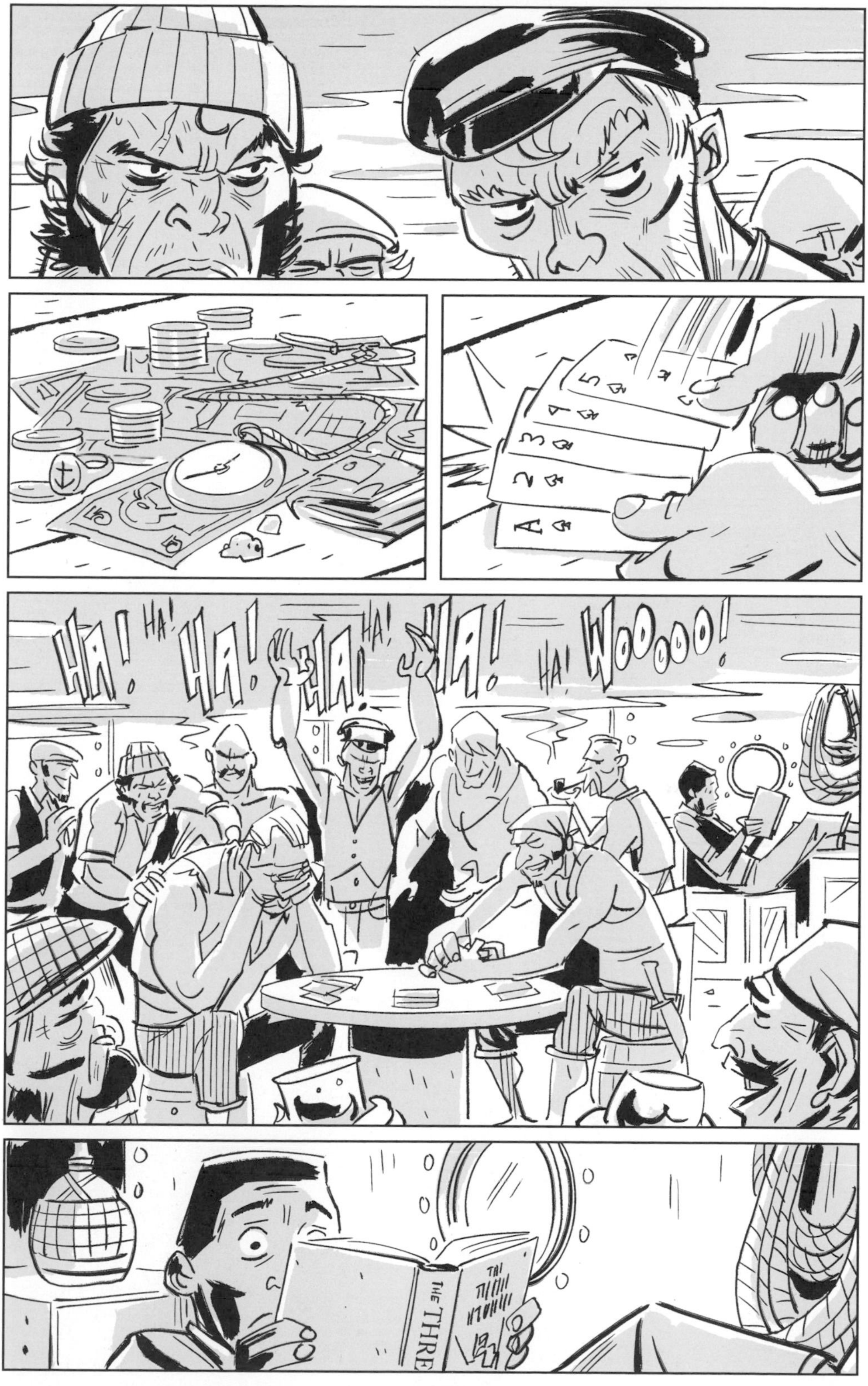
HA! HA! HA! HA! HA! HA! HA! WOOOOO!
HA!
THE THRE

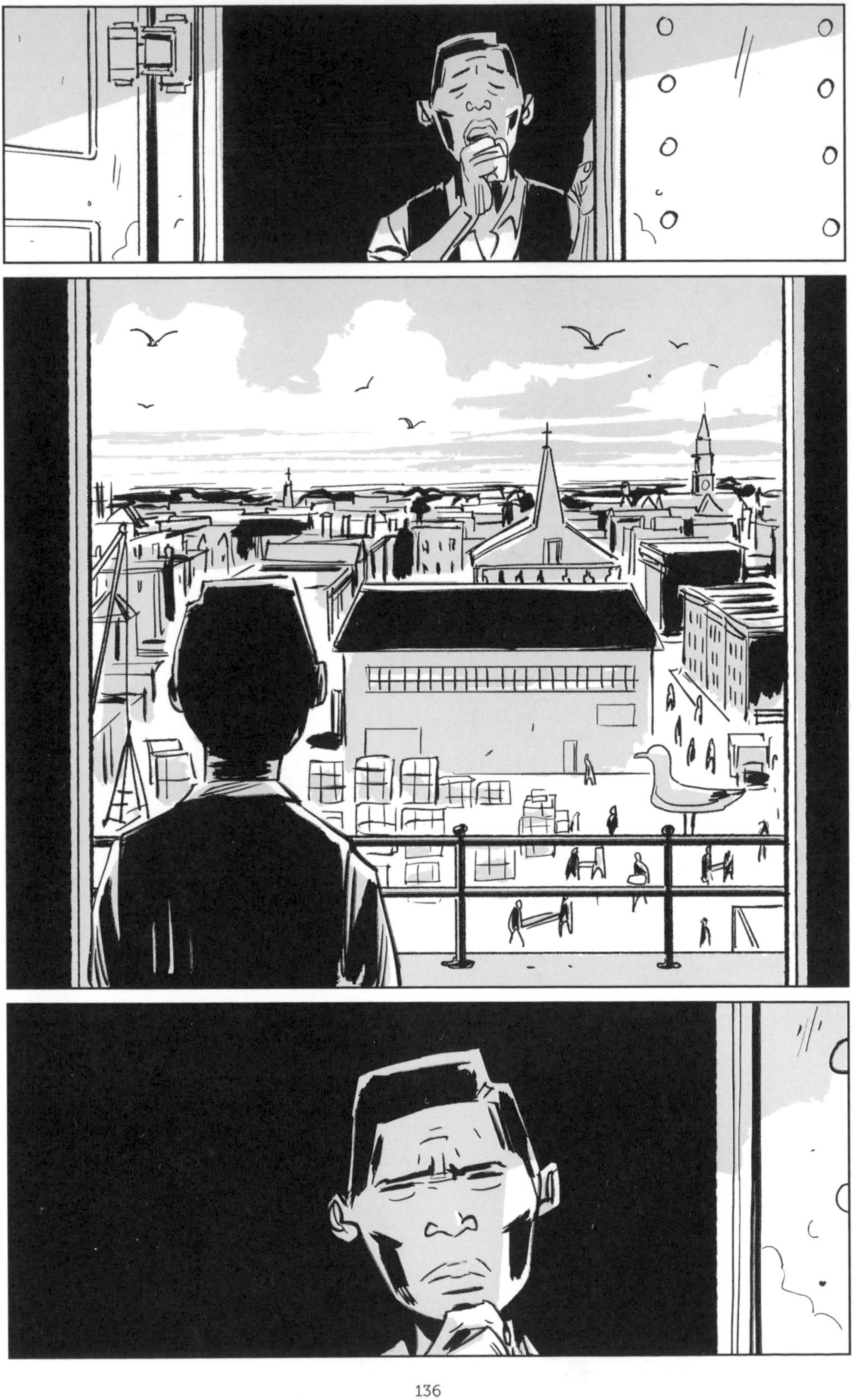

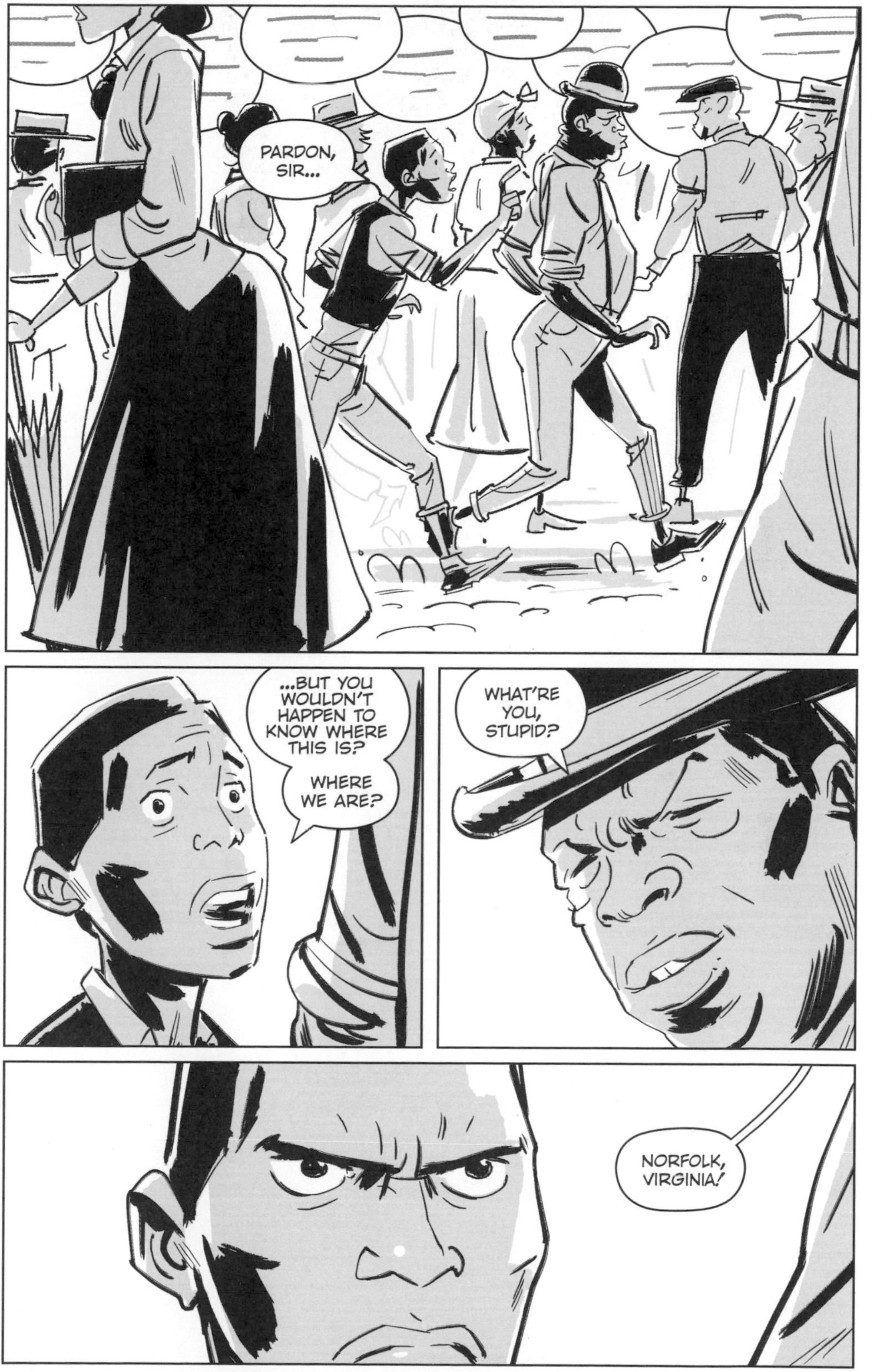
PARDON, SIR...
...BUT YOU WOULDN'T HAPPEN TO KNOW WHERE THIS IS?
WHERE WE ARE?
WHAT'RE YOU, STUPID?
NORFOLK, VIRGINIA!

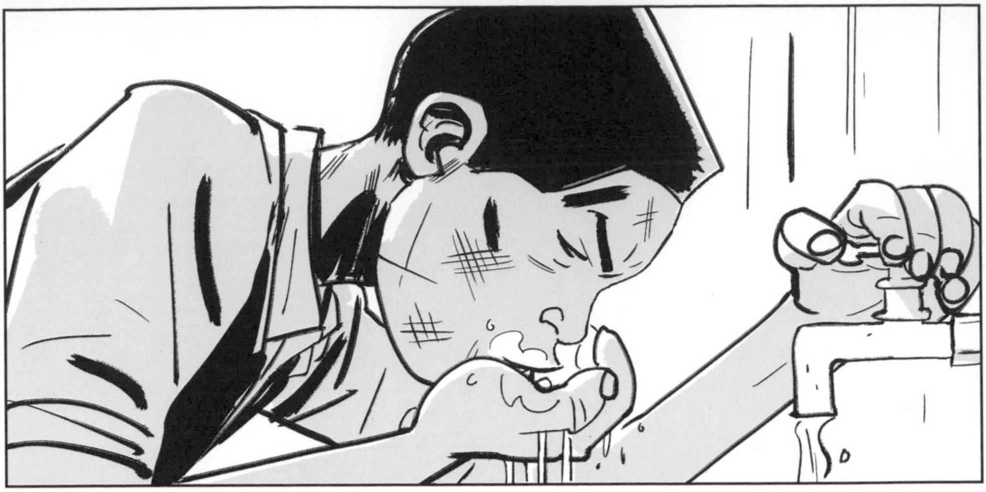

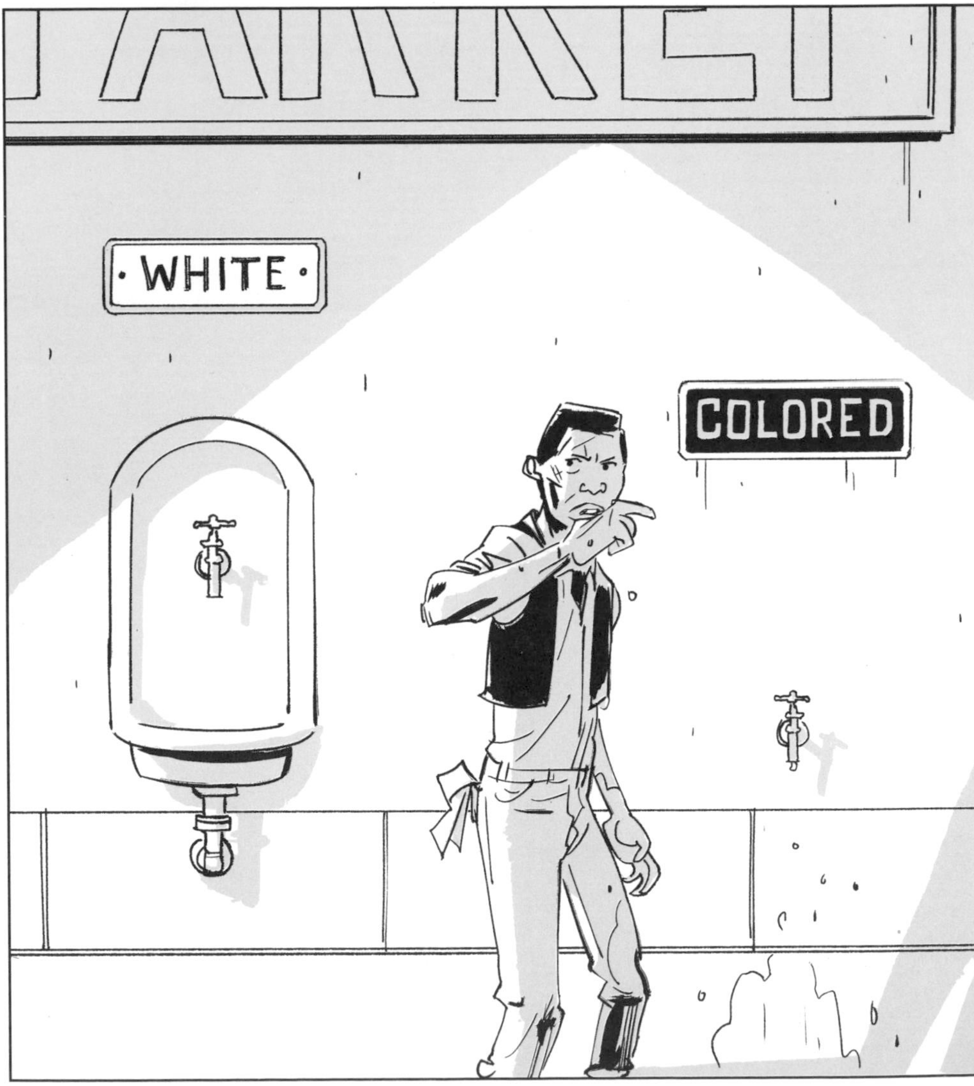
WHITE
COLORED

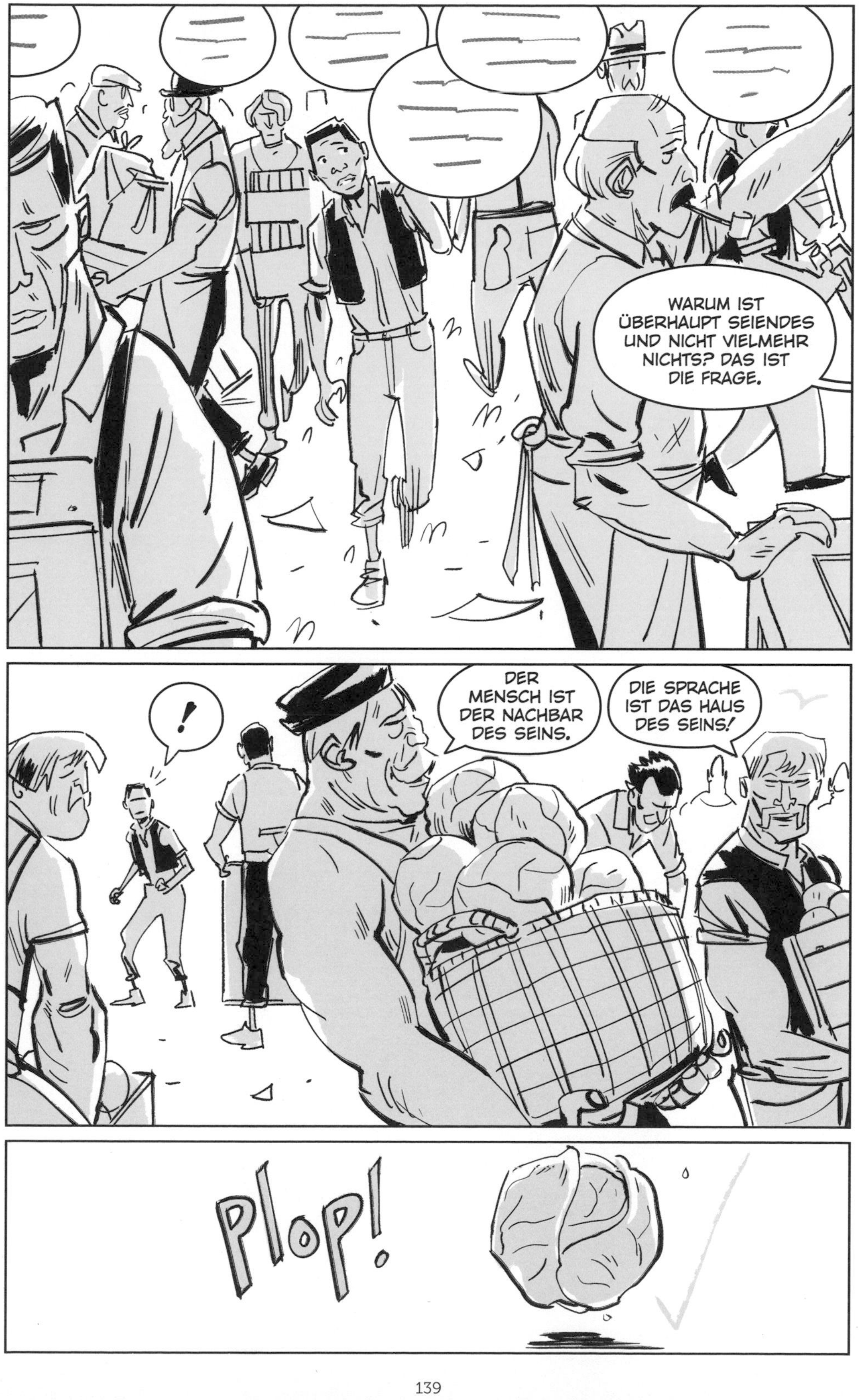
WARUM IST ÜBERHAUPT SEIENDES UND NICHT VIELMEHR NICHTS? DAS IST DIE FRAGE.
!
DER MENSCH IST DER NACHBAR DES SEINS.
DIE SPRACHE IST DAS HAUS DES SEINS!
Plop!

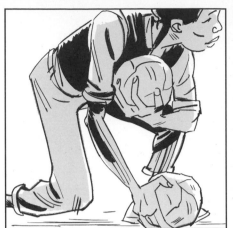

OH, DANKE...

HEY, PAL, LET ME GIVE YOU A HAND.

AH! ZANK YOU.

MARTA RUSS

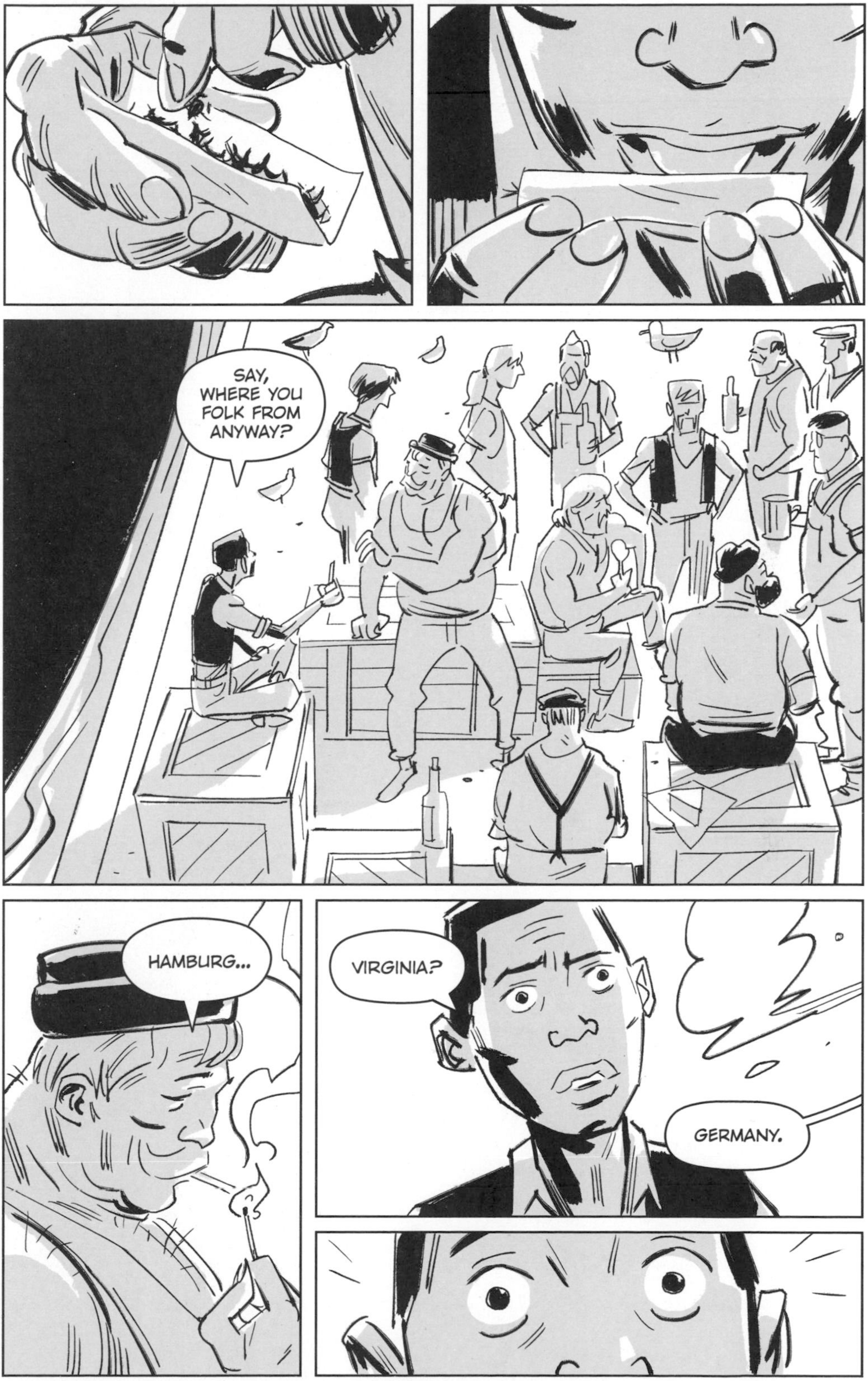
SAY, WHERE YOU FOLK FROM ANYWAY?
HAMBURG...
VIRGINIA?
GERMANY.

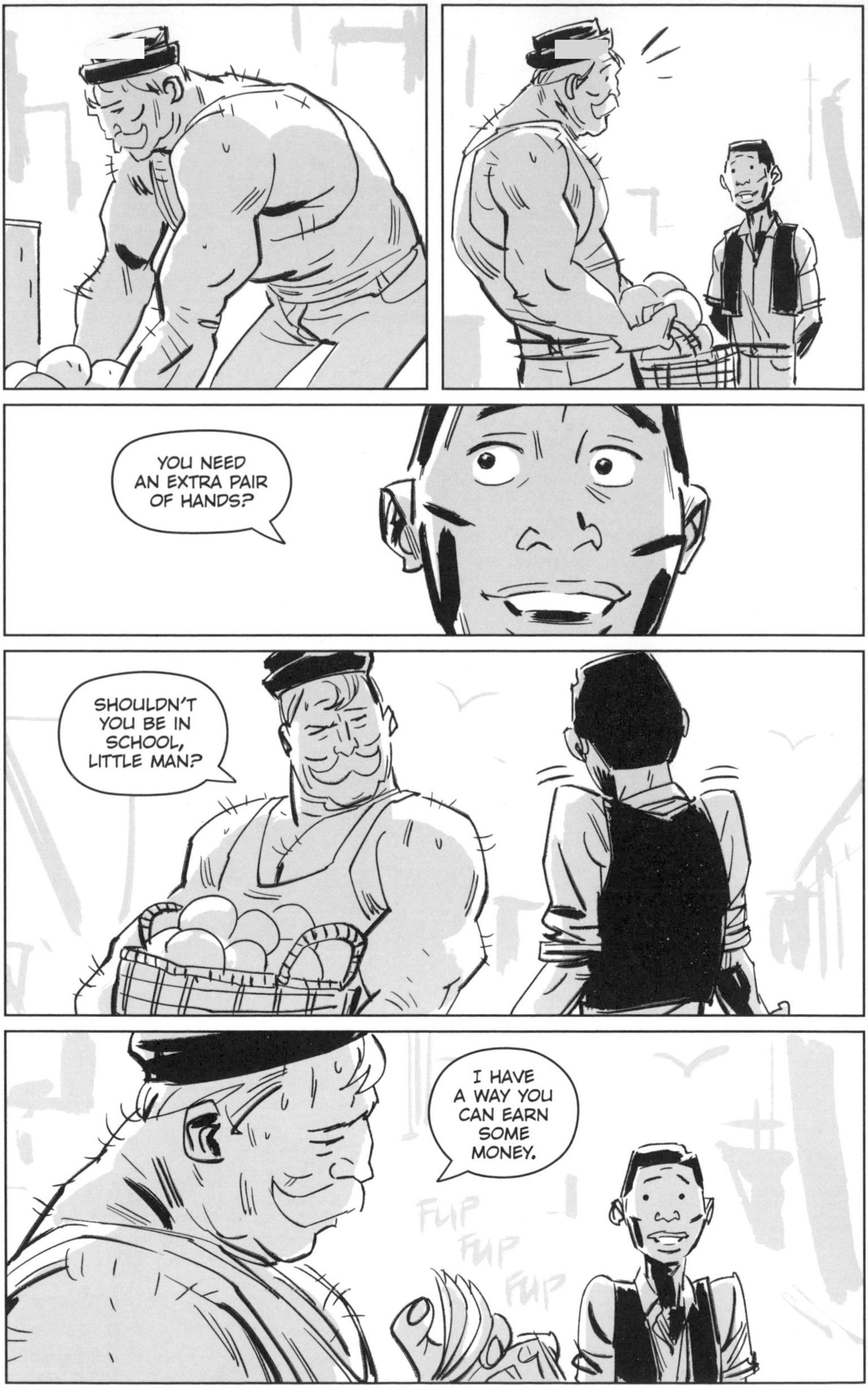
YOU NEED AN EXTRA PAIR OF HANDS?
SHOULDN'T YOU BE IN SCHOOL, LITTLE MAN?
I HAVE A WAY YOU CAN EARN SOME MONEY.
FLIP
FLIP
FLIP

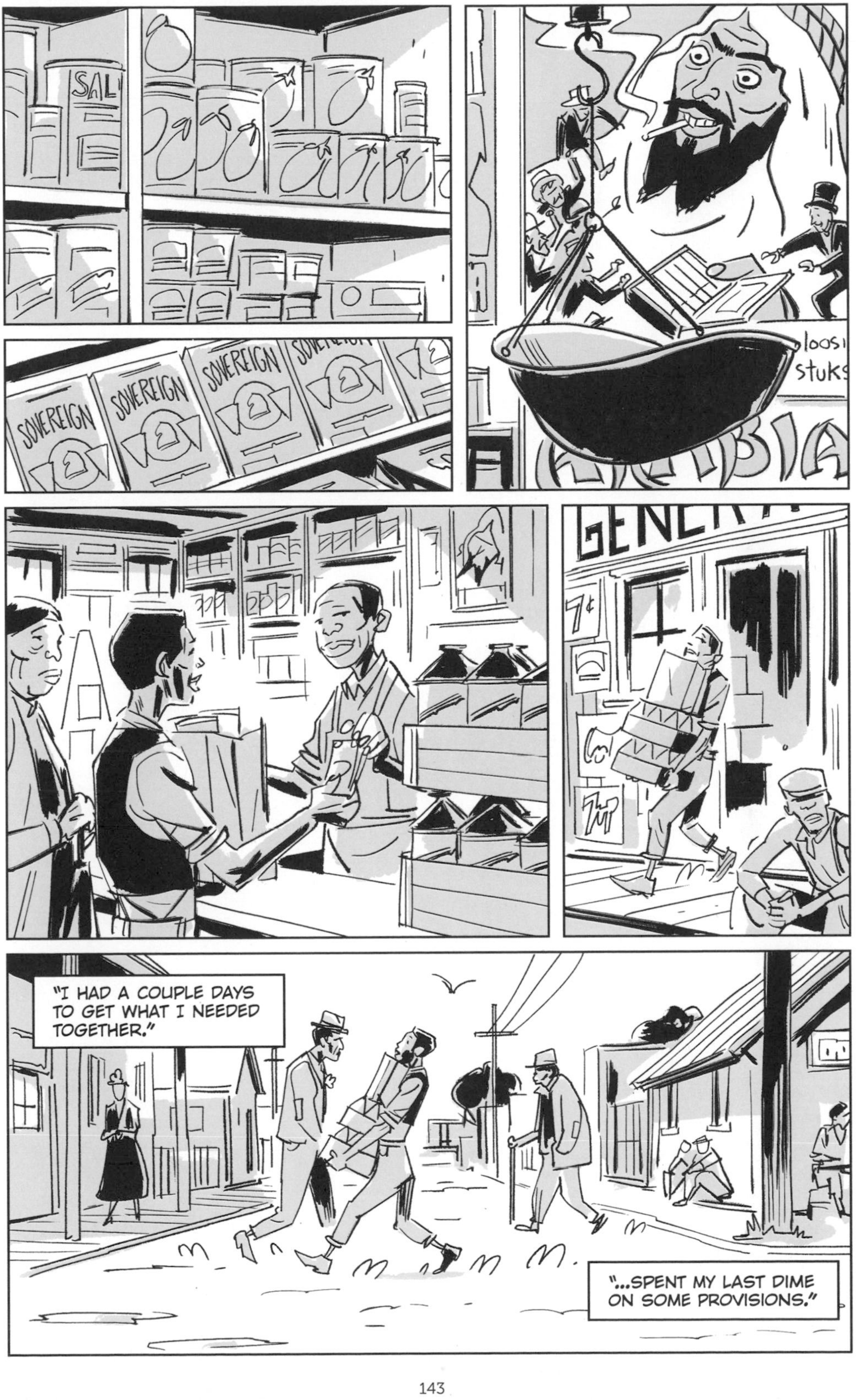
SAL
SOVEREIGN
SOVEREIGN
SOVEREIGN
SOVEREIGN
loosi
stuks
"I HAD A COUPLE DAYS TO GET WHAT I NEEDED TOGETHER."
"...SPENT MY LAST DIME ON SOME PROVISIONS."

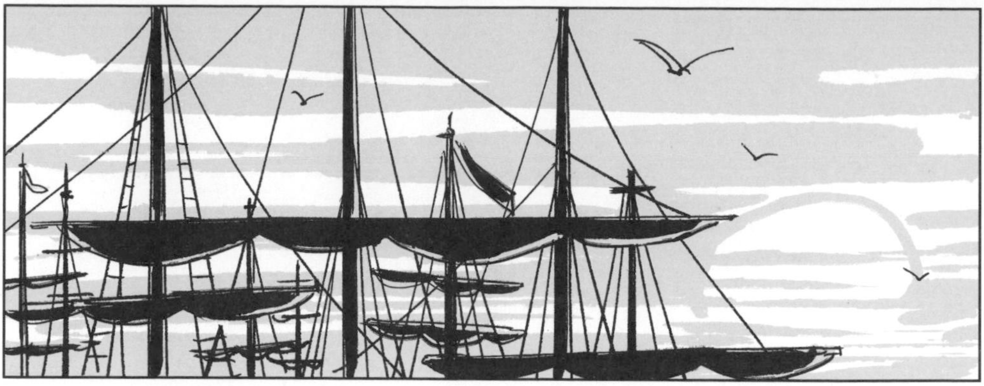

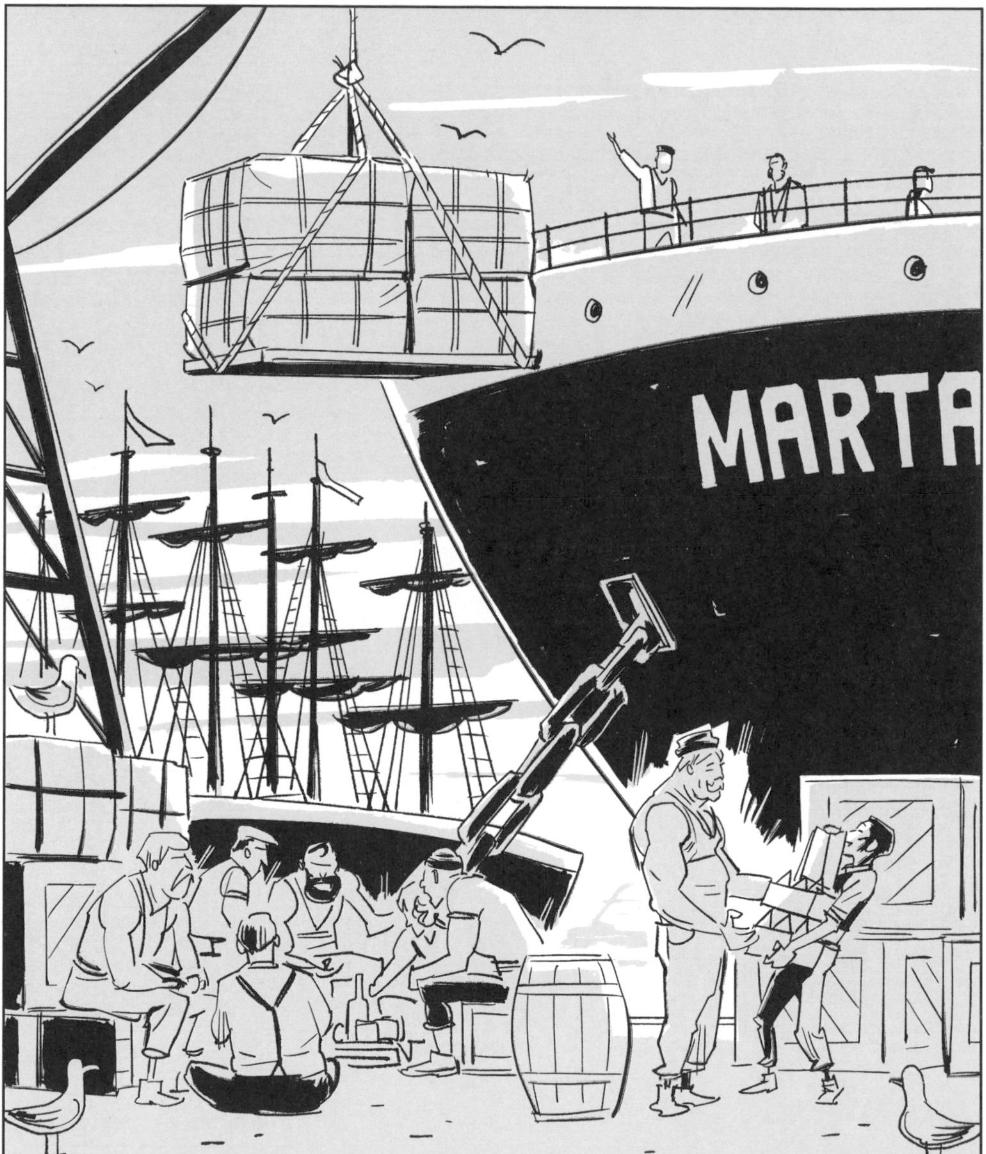
MARTA

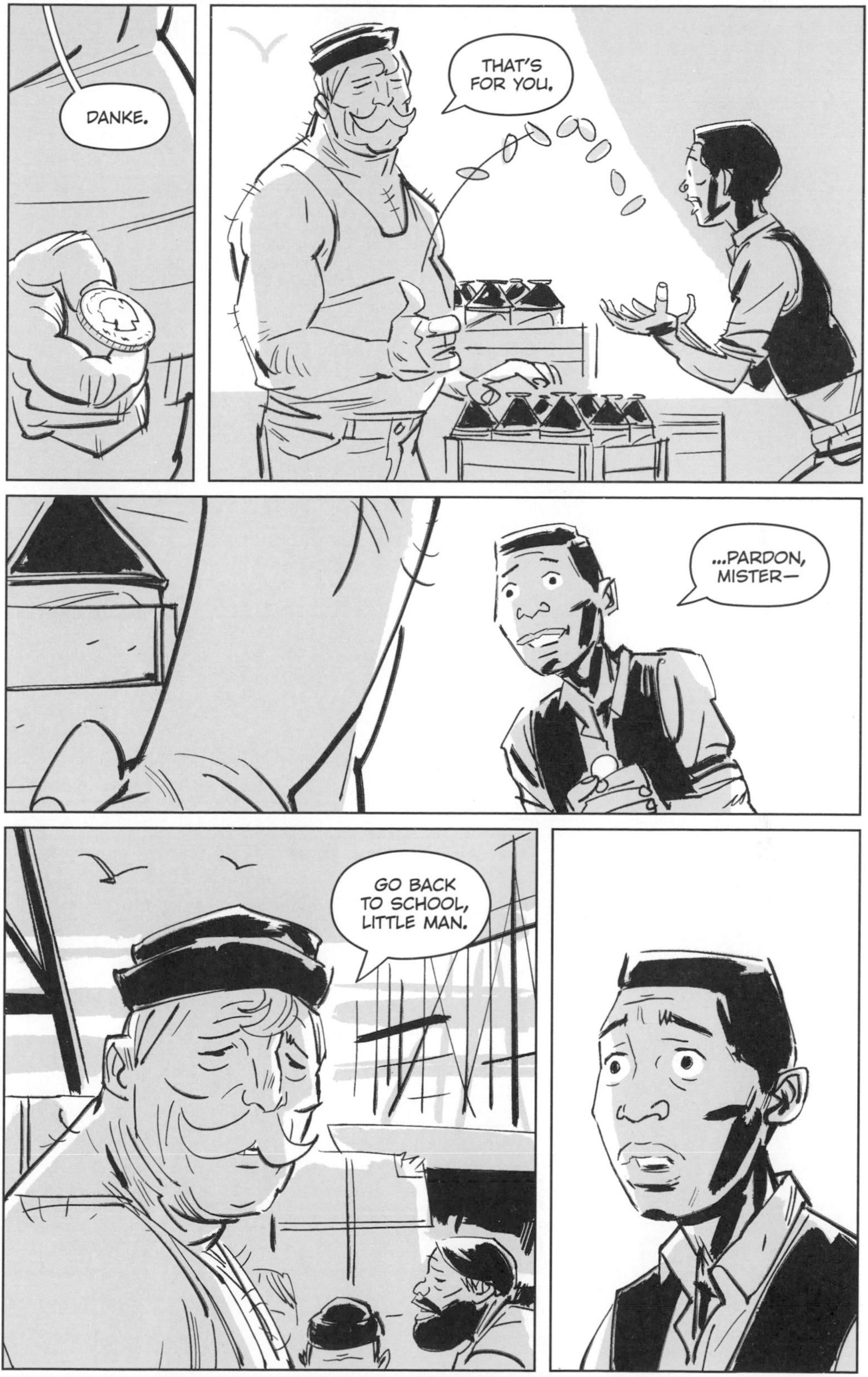
DANKE.
THAT'S FOR YOU.
...PARDON, MISTER—
GO BACK TO SCHOOL, LITTLE MAN.

"AND WHEN NOBODY WAS LOOKING..."

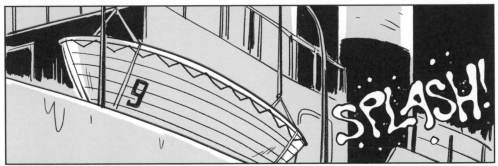

SPLASH!

DIE FRAGE NACH DEM SINN VON SEIN SOLL GESTELLT WERDEN.

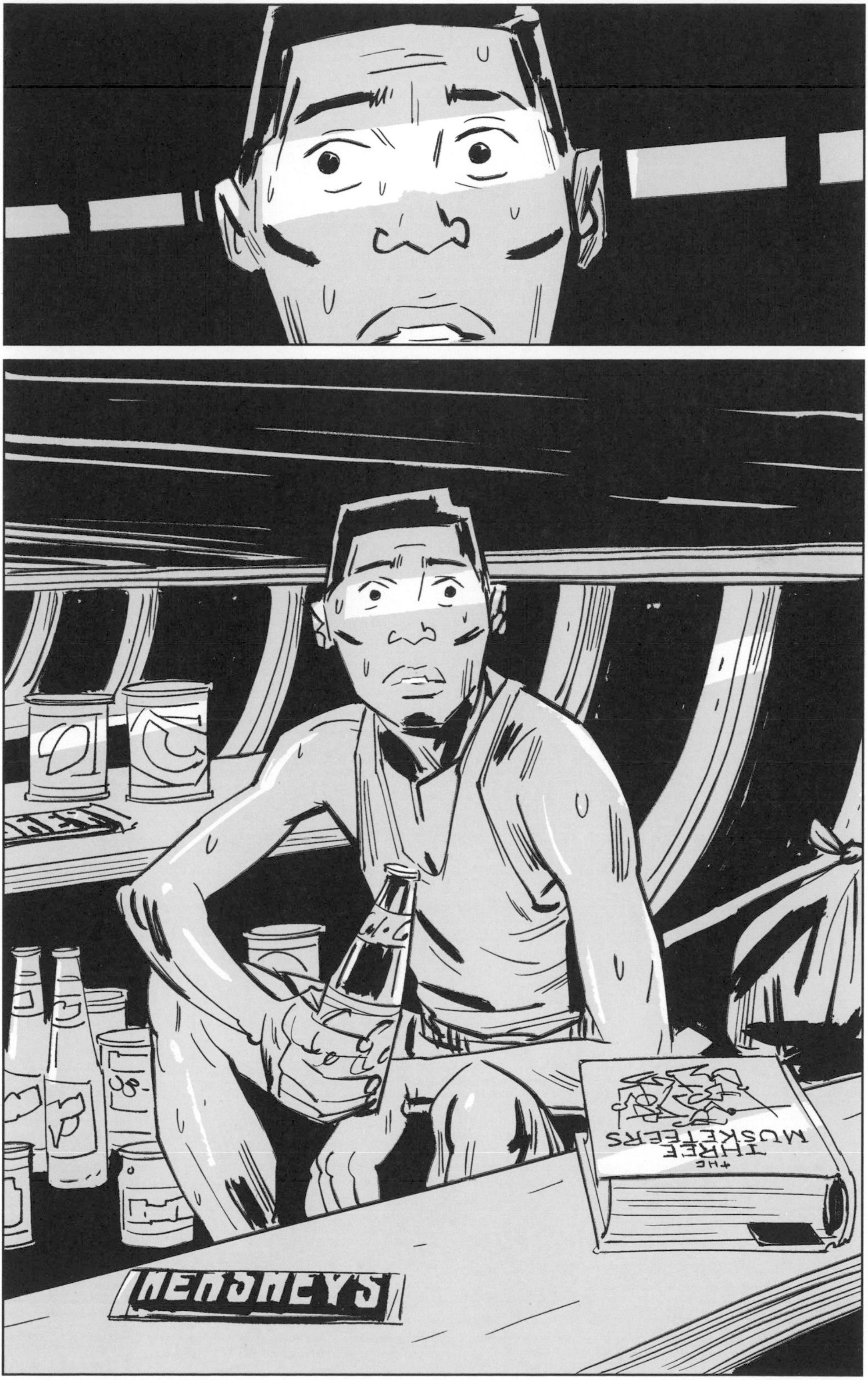
THE THREE MUSKETEERS
HERSHEY'S

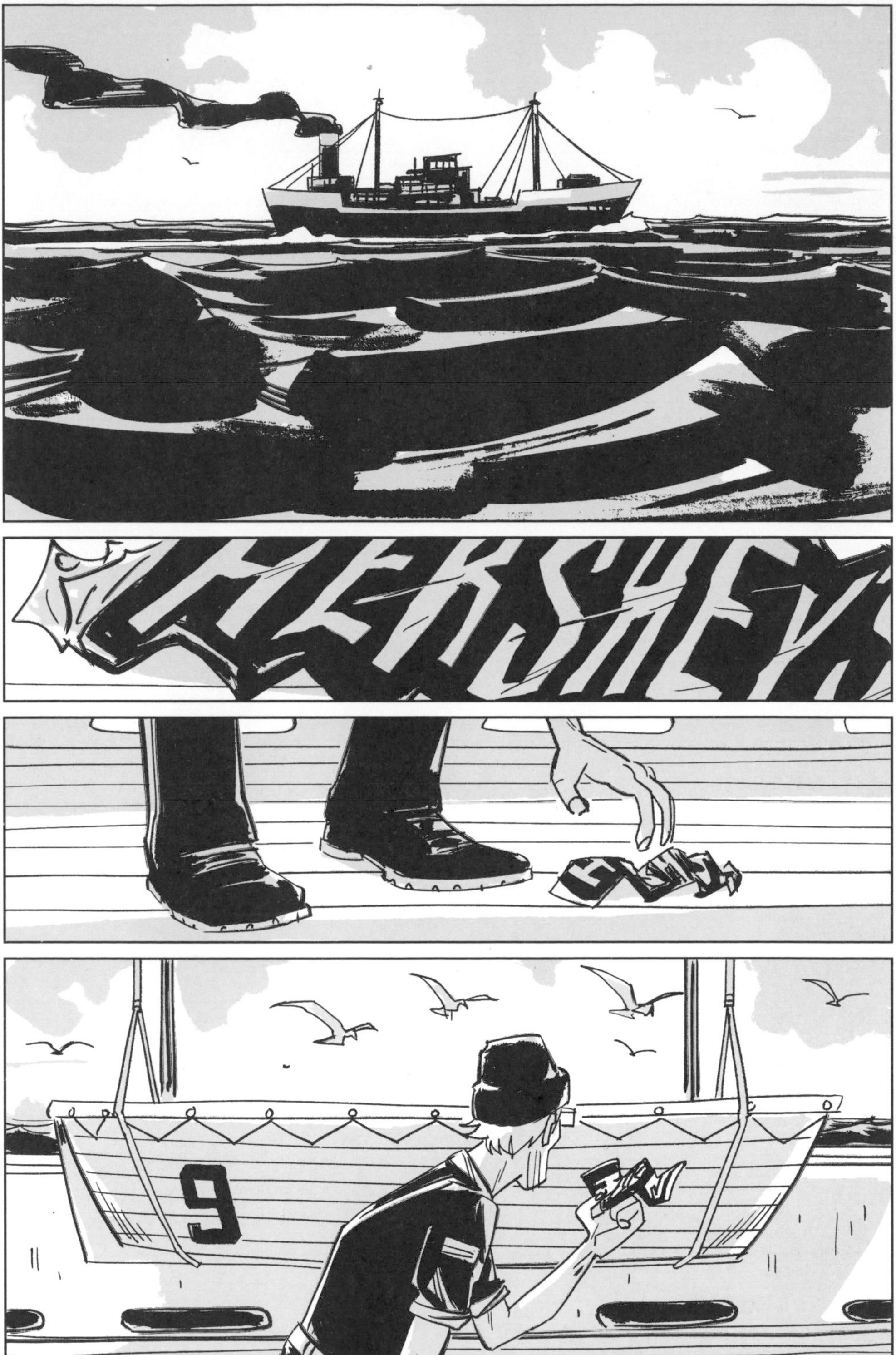
9

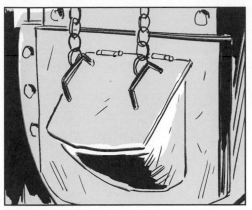

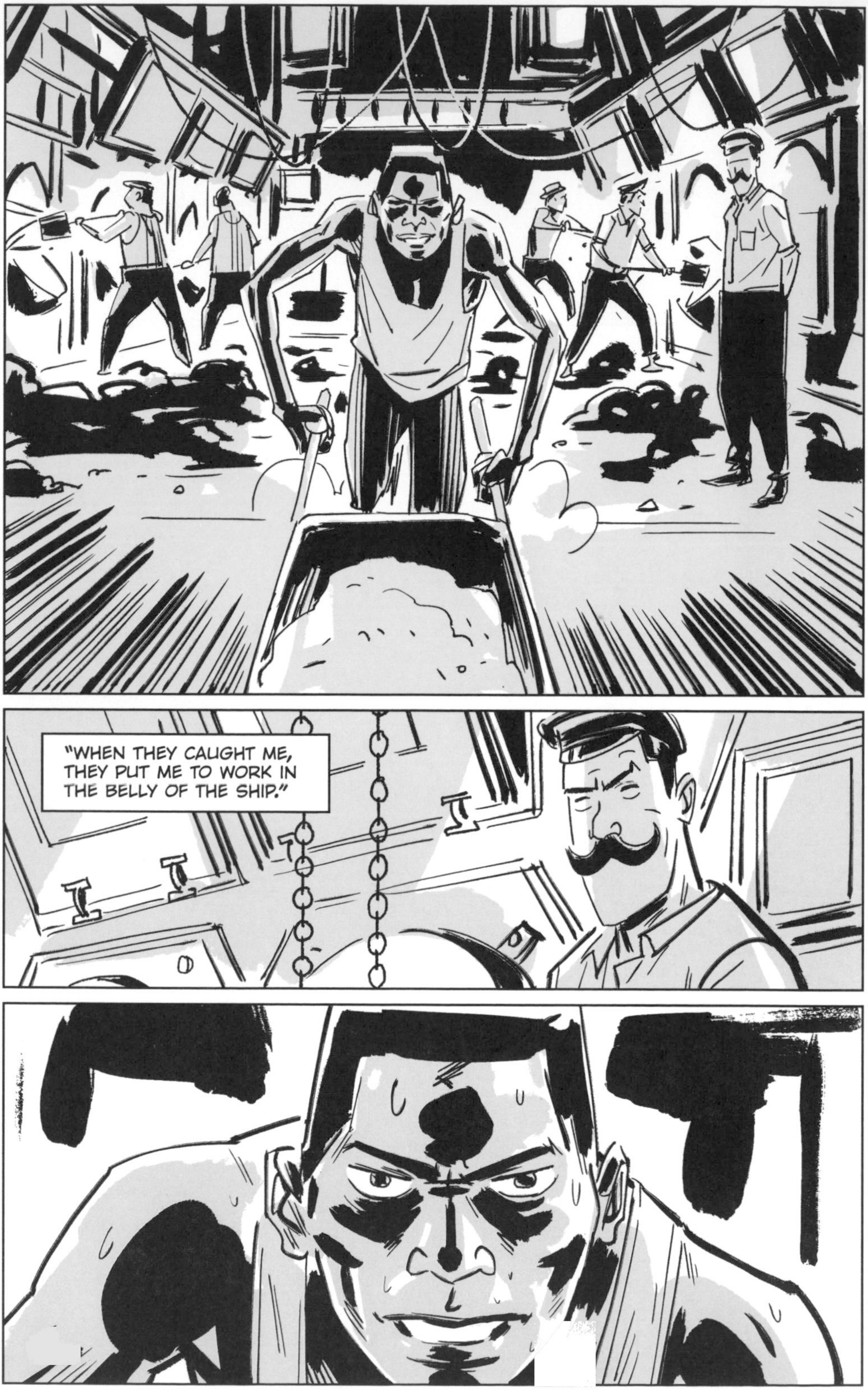
"WHEN THEY CAUGHT ME, THEY PUT ME TO WORK IN THE BELLY OF THE SHIP."

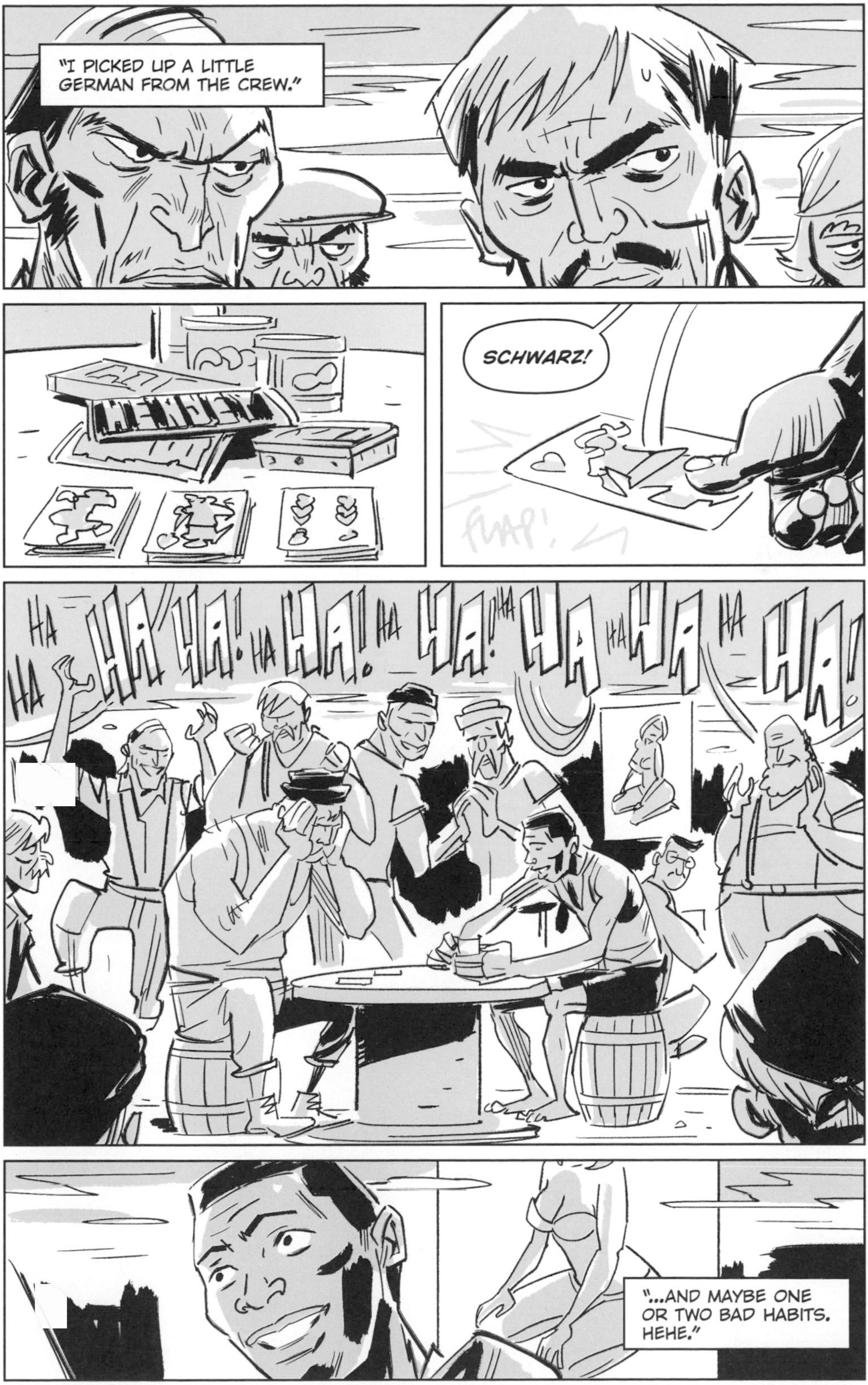
"I PICKED UP A LITTLE GERMAN FROM THE CREW."
SCHWARZ!
FLAP!
HA HA HA! HA! HA HA! HA HA! HA HA HA HA HA! HA HA!
"...AND MAYBE ONE OR TWO BAD HABITS. HEHE."

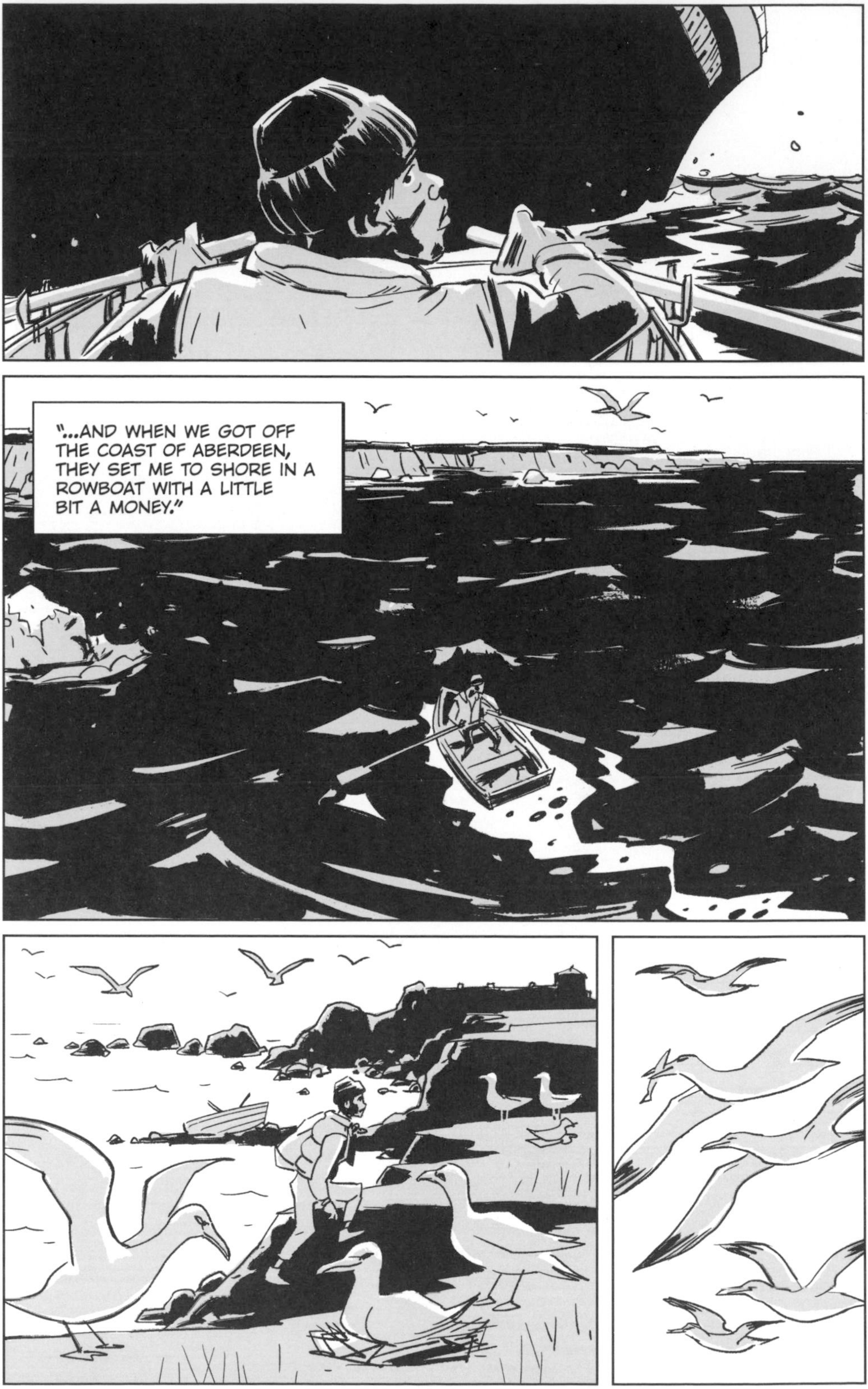
"...AND WHEN WE GOT OFF THE COAST OF ABERDEEN, THEY SET ME TO SHORE IN A ROWBOAT WITH A LITTLE BIT A MONEY."

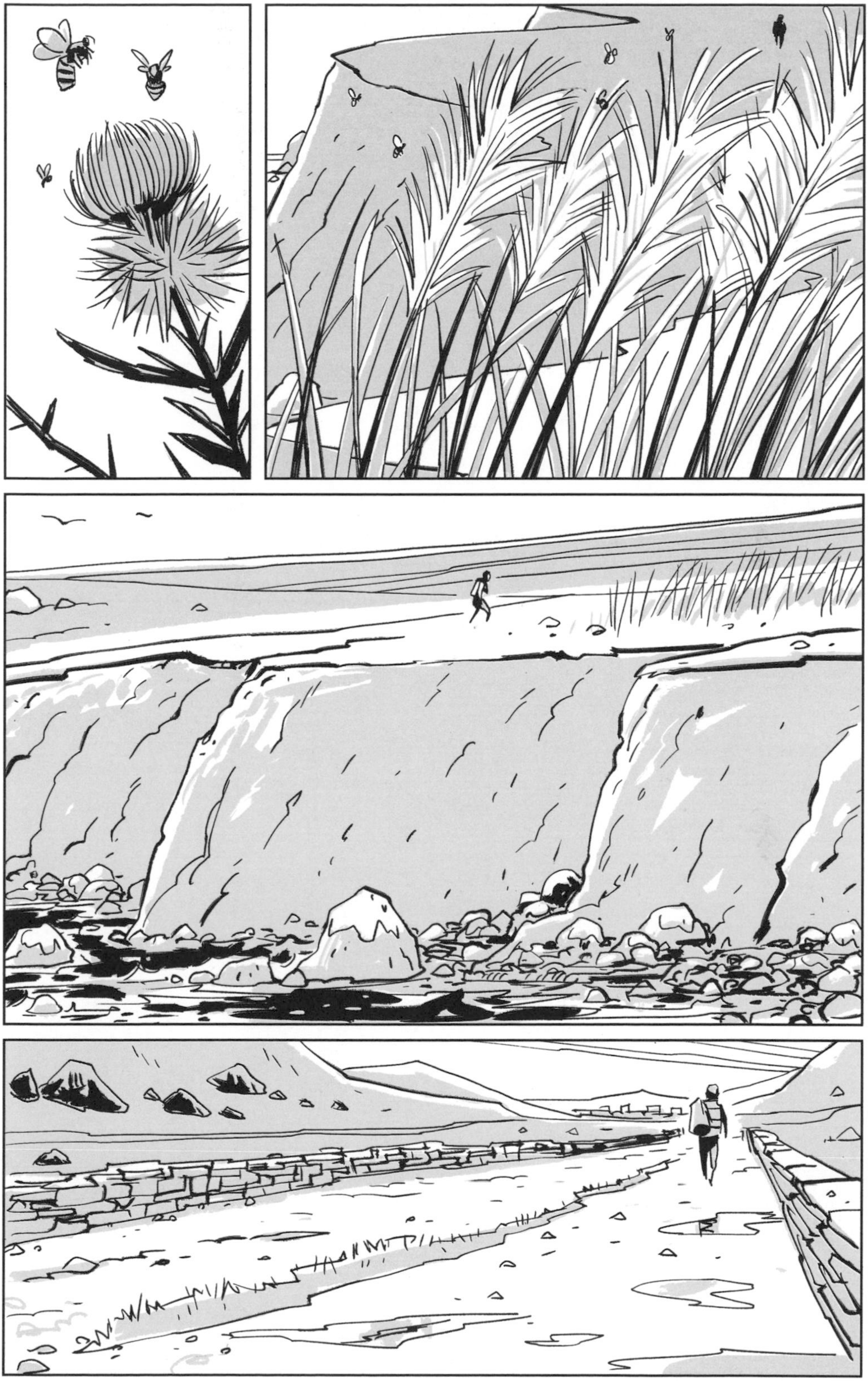

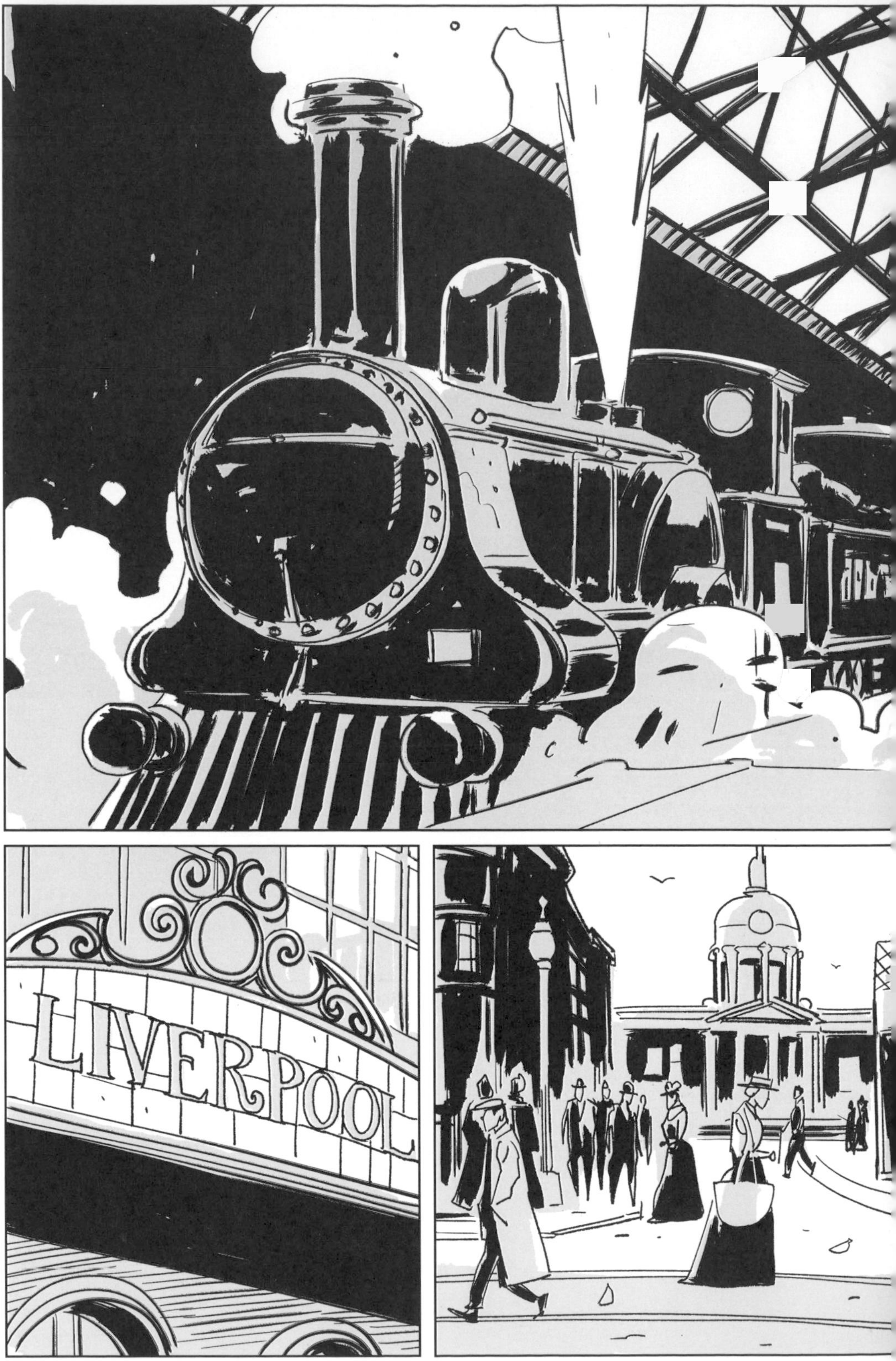
LIVERPOOL

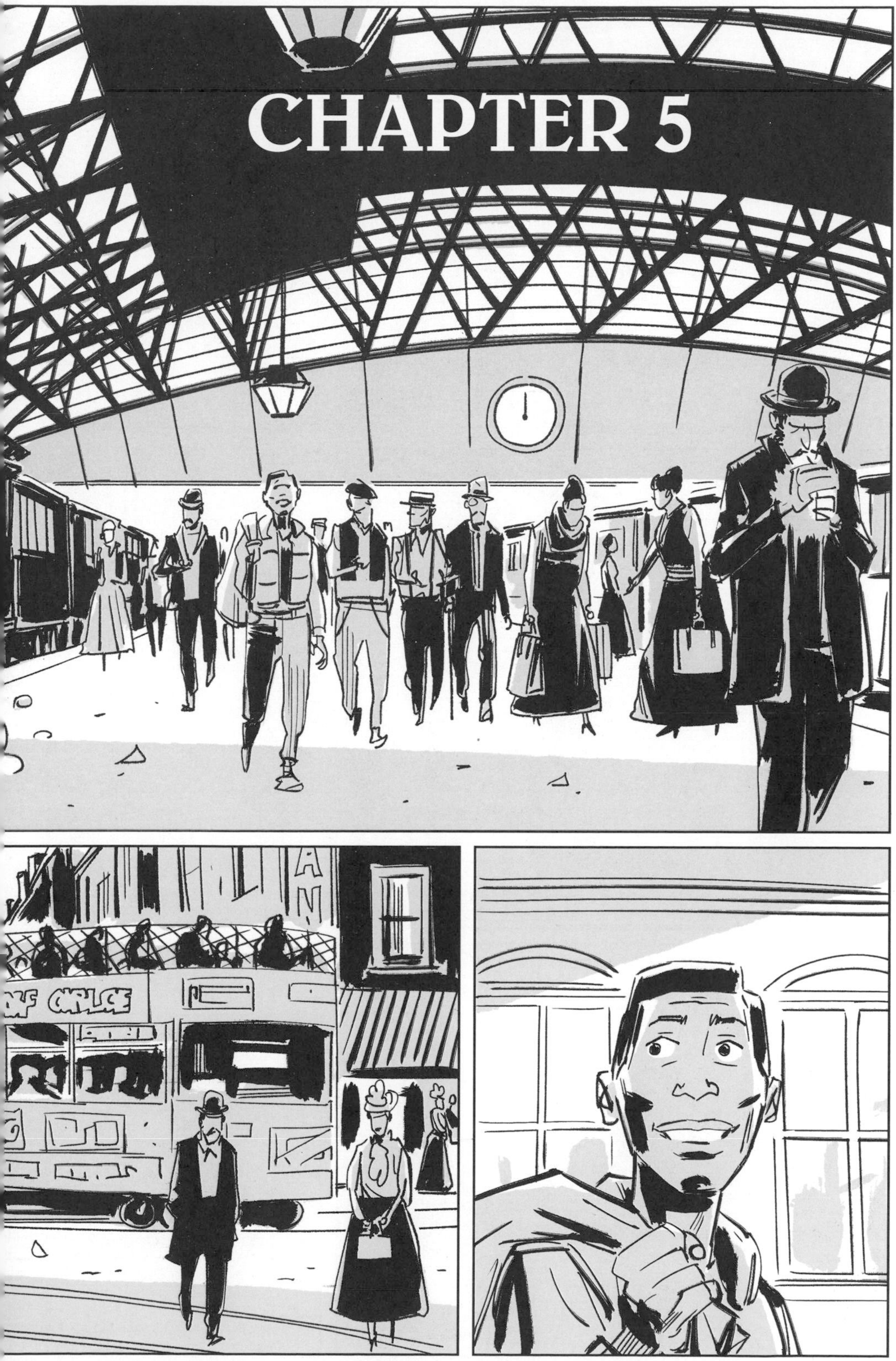
CHAPTER 5

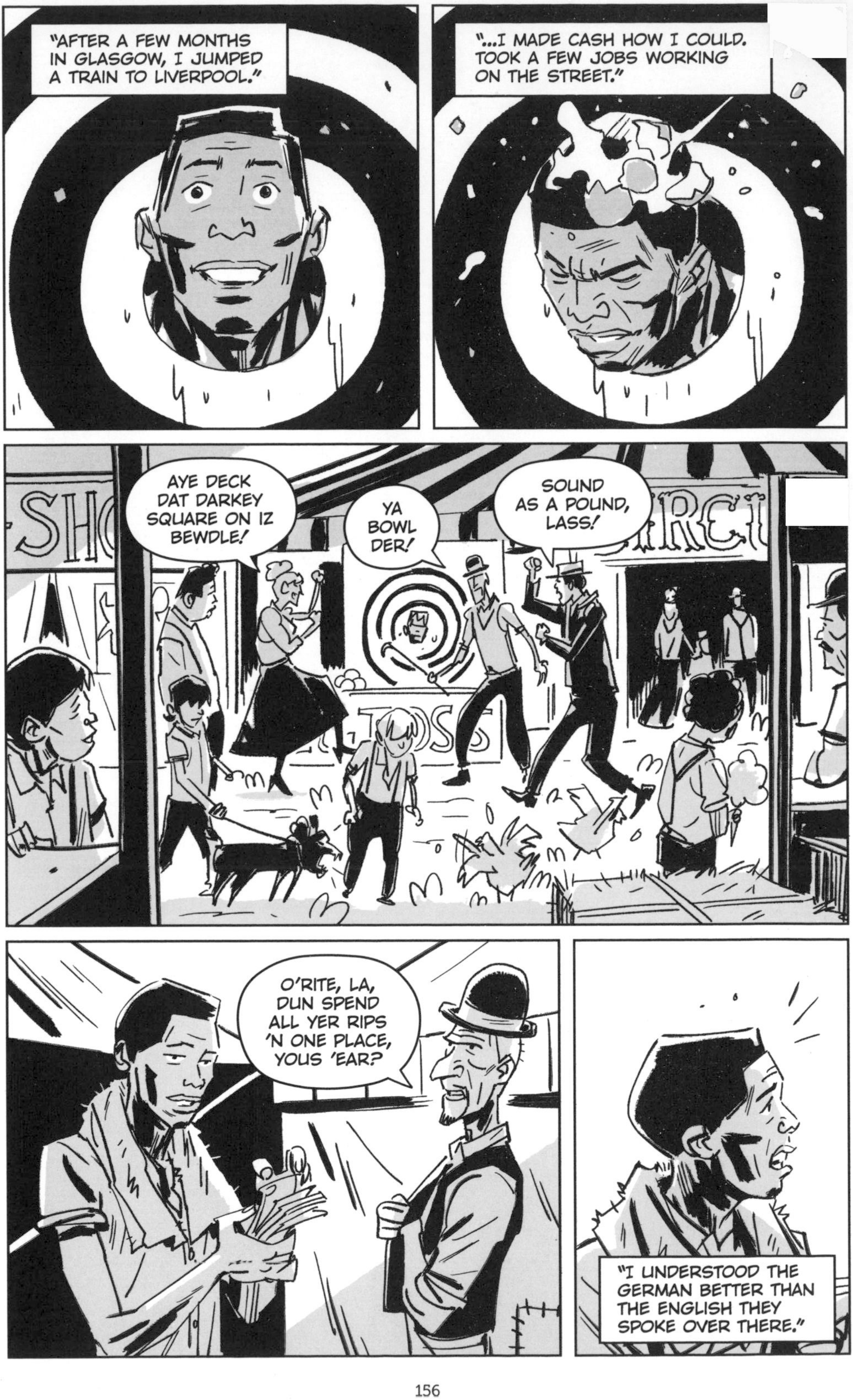
"AFTER A FEW MONTHS IN GLASGOW, I JUMPED A TRAIN TO LIVERPOOL."
"...I MADE CASH HOW I COULD. TOOK A FEW JOBS WORKING ON THE STREET."
AYE DECK DAT DARKEY SQUARE ON IZ BEWDLE!
YA BOWL DER!
SOUND AS A POUND, LASS!
SHO
RC
TOSS
O'RITE, LA, DUN SPEND ALL YER RIPS 'N ONE PLACE, YOUS 'EAR?
"I UNDERSTOOD THE GERMAN BETTER THAN THE ENGLISH THEY SPOKE OVER THERE."

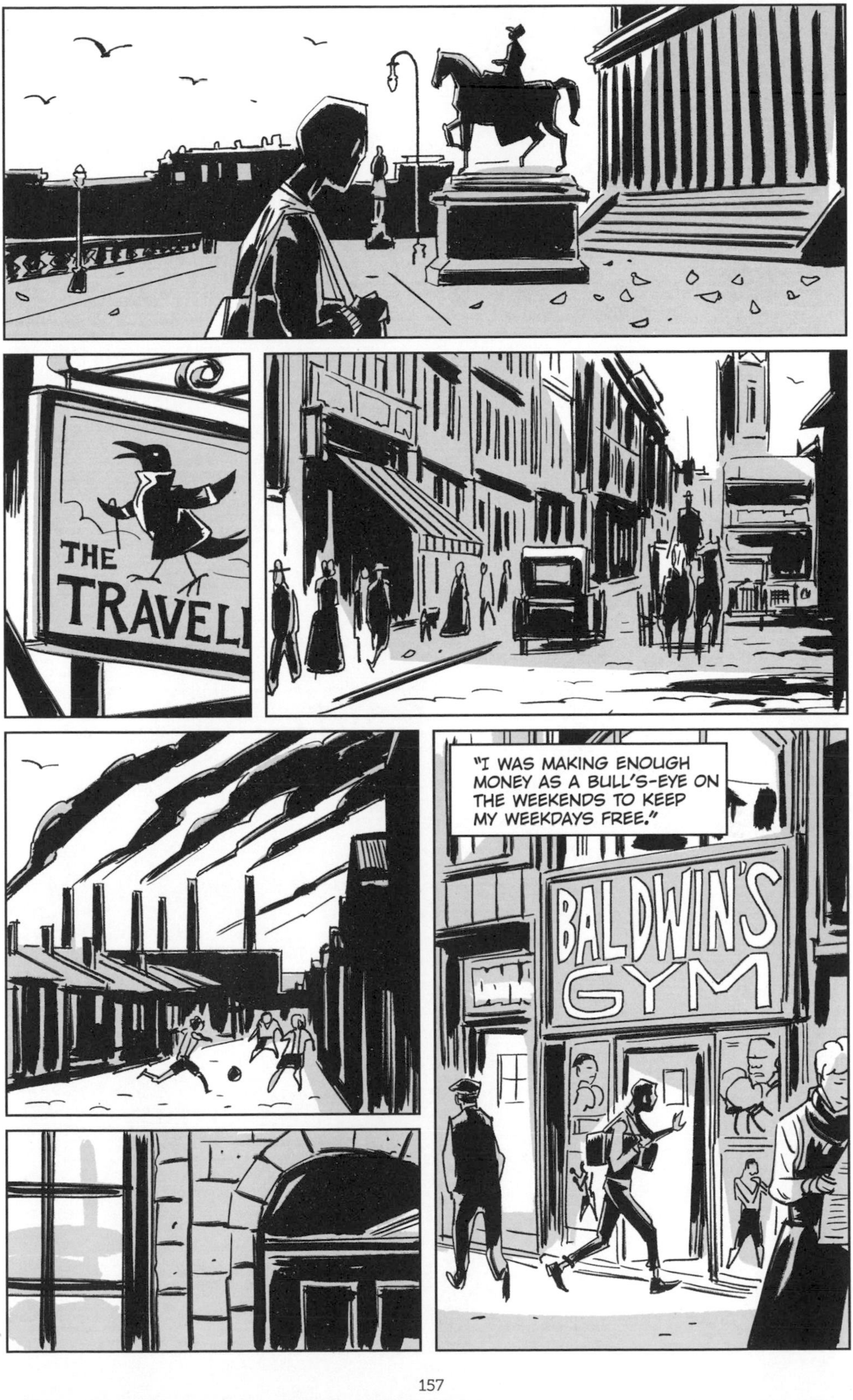
THE
TRAVEL
"I WAS MAKING ENOUGH MONEY AS A BULL'S-EYE ON THE WEEKENDS TO KEEP MY WEEKDAYS FREE."
BALDWIN'S GYM

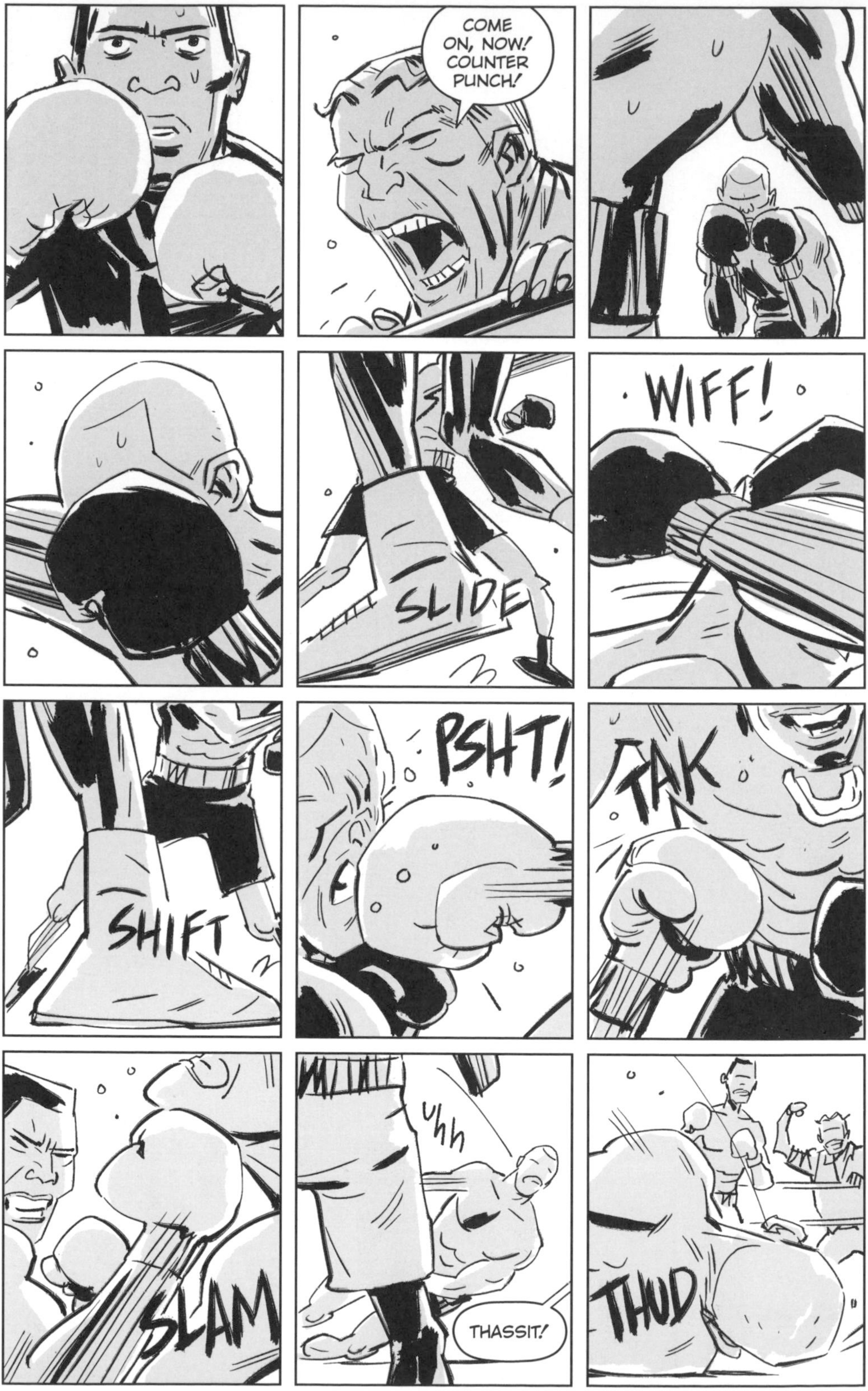
COME ON, NOW! COUNTER PUNCH!
SLIDE
WIFF!
SHIFT
PSHT!
TAK
SLAM
uhh
THASSIT!
THUD

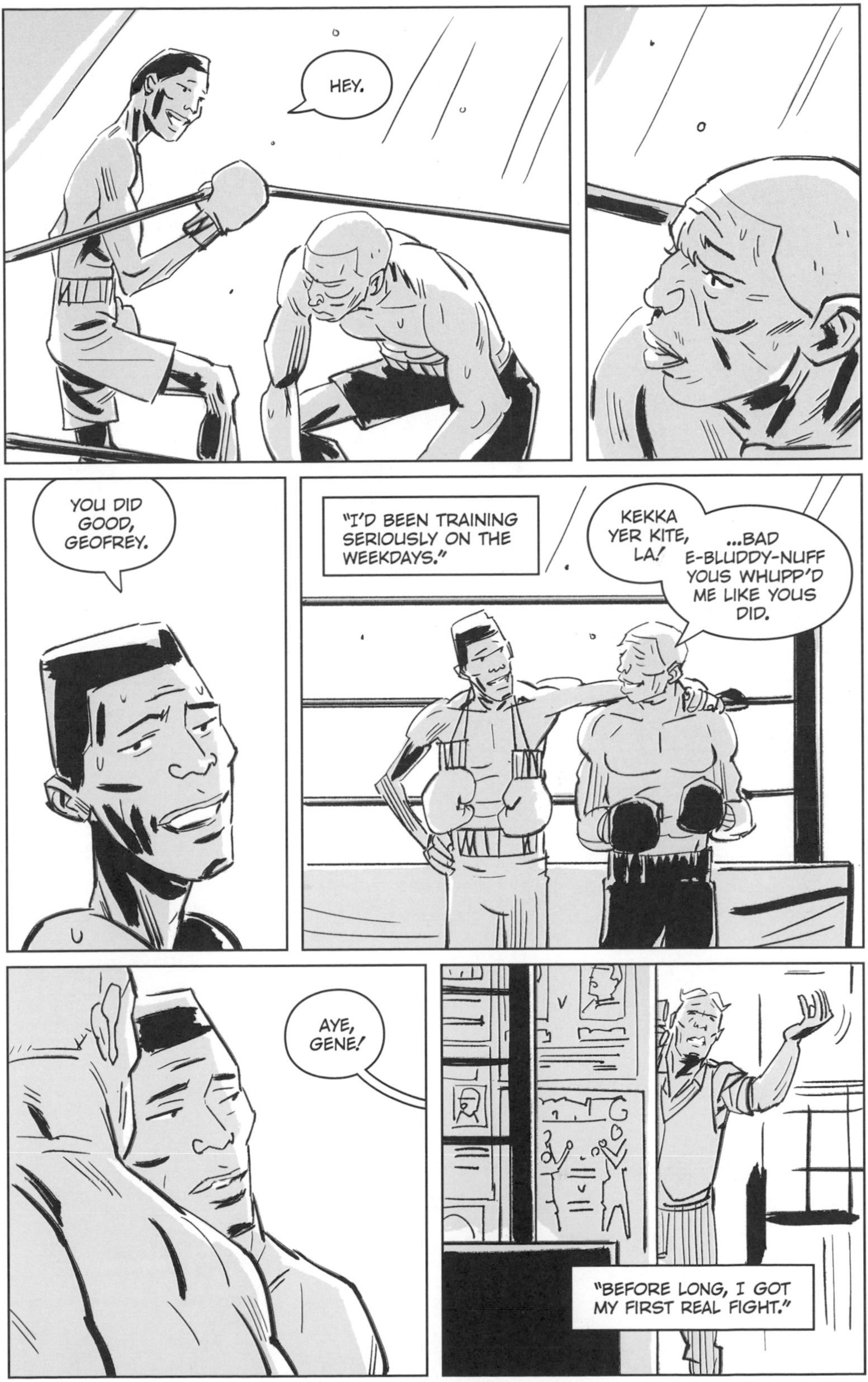
HEY.
YOU DID GOOD, GEOFREY.
"I'D BEEN TRAINING SERIOUSLY ON THE WEEKDAYS."
KEKKA YER KITE, LA!
...BAD E-BLUDDY-NUFF YOUS WHUPP'D ME LIKE YOUS DID.
AYE, GENE!
"BEFORE LONG, I GOT MY FIRST REAL FIGHT."

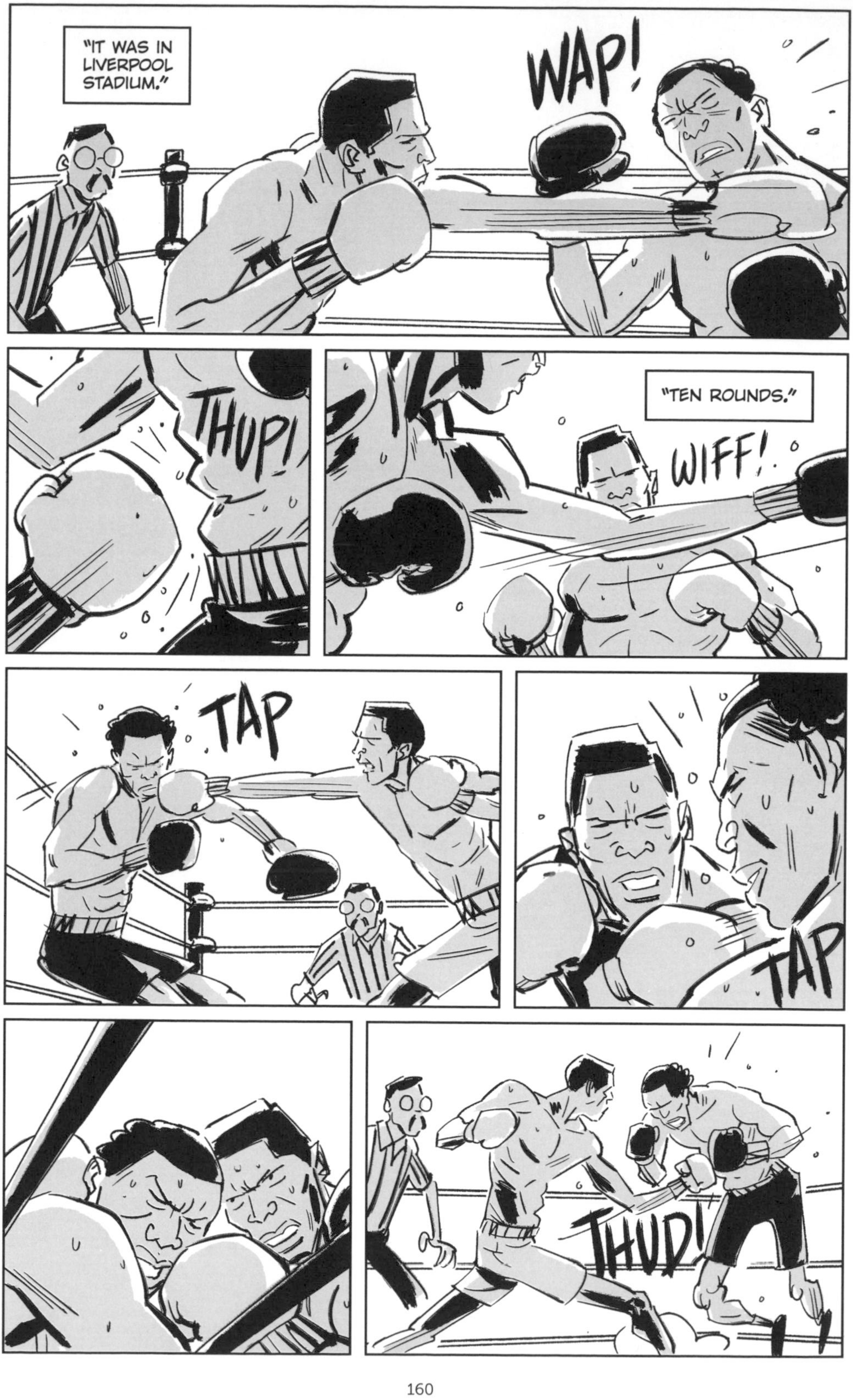
"IT WAS IN LIVERPOOL STADIUM."
WAP!
THUP!
"TEN ROUNDS."
WIFF!
TAP
TAP
THUD!

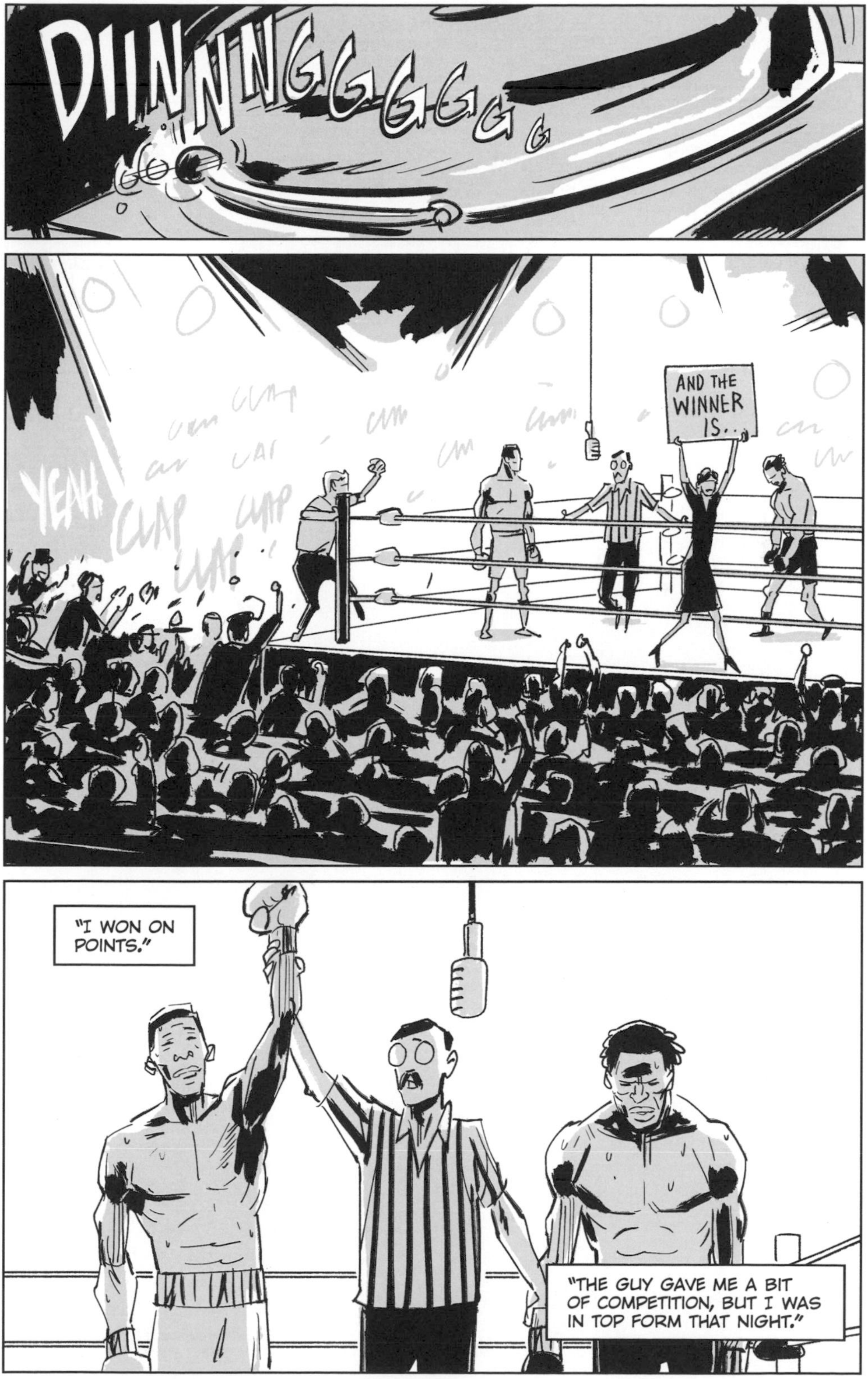
DIINNNGGGGGGG
CLAP CLAP
YEAH!
CLAP
CLAP
CLAP
AND THE WINNER IS...
"I WON ON POINTS."
"THE GUY GAVE ME A BIT OF COMPETITION, BUT I WAS IN TOP FORM THAT NIGHT."

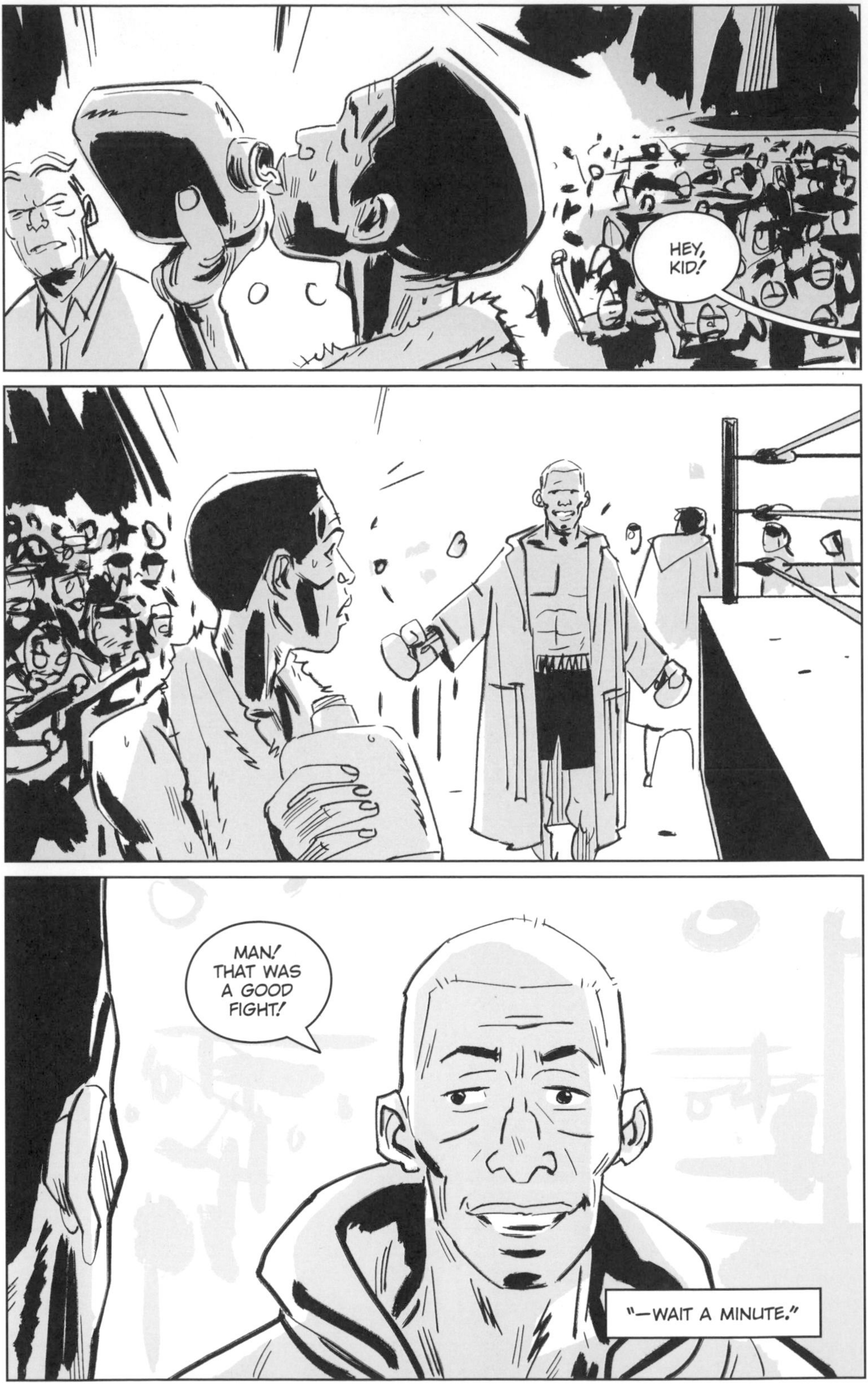
HEY, KID!
MAN! THAT WAS A GOOD FIGHT!
"—WAIT A MINUTE."

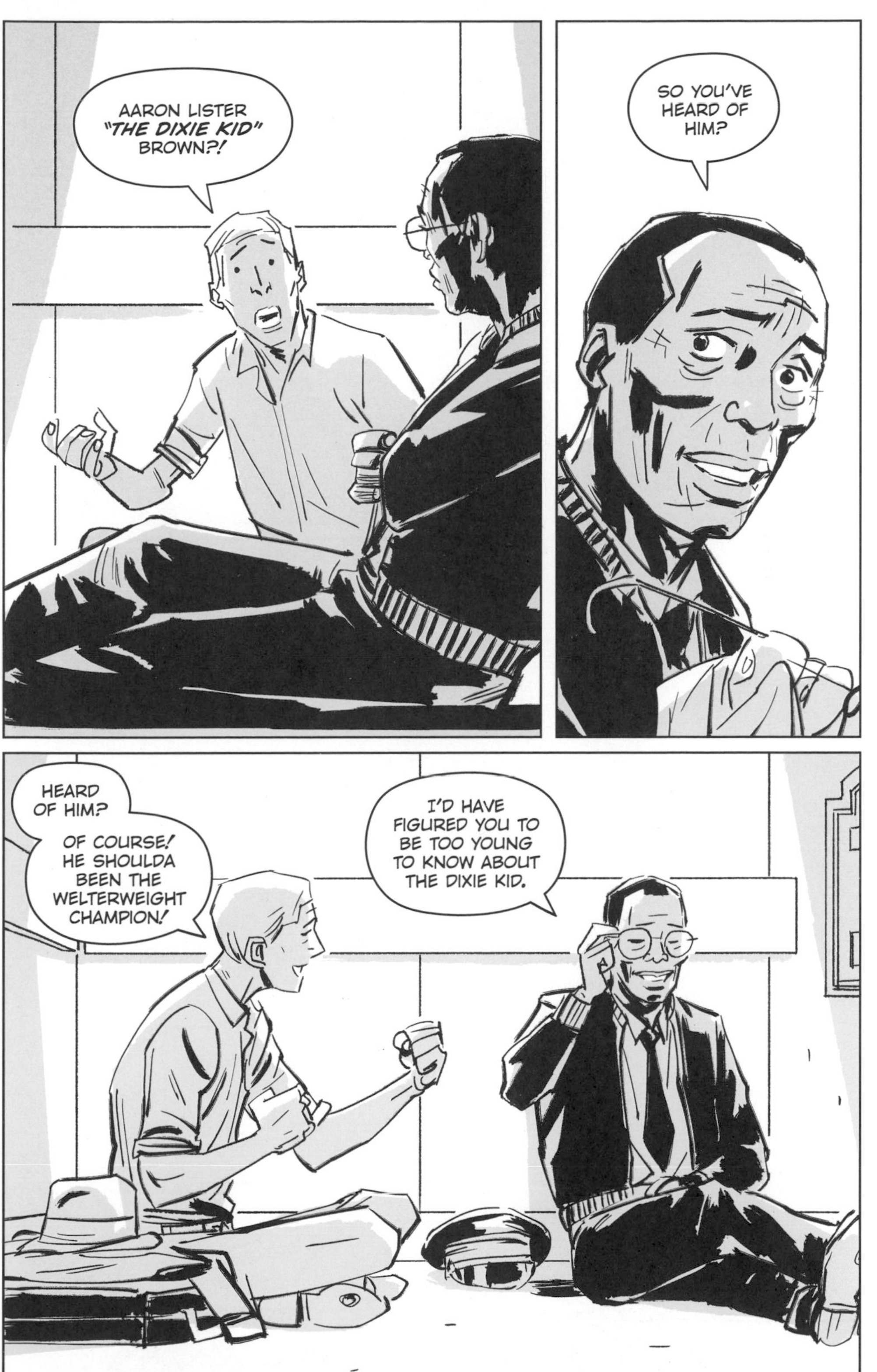
AARON LISTER "THE DIXIE KID" BROWN?!
SO YOU'VE HEARD OF HIM?
HEARD OF HIM?
OF COURSE! HE SHOULDA BEEN THE WELTERWEIGHT CHAMPION!
I'D HAVE FIGURED YOU TO BE TOO YOUNG TO KNOW ABOUT THE DIXIE KID.

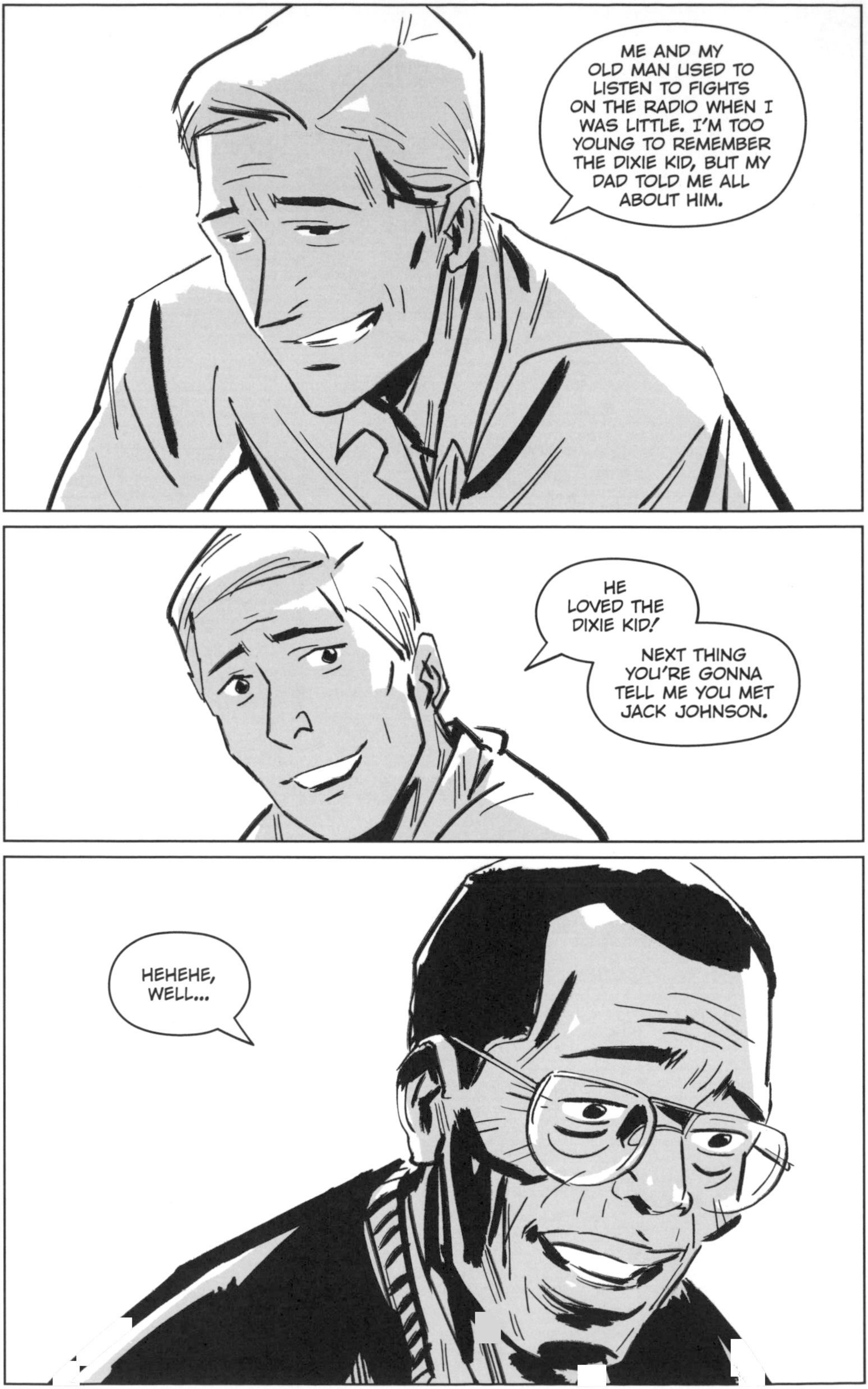
ME AND MY OLD MAN USED TO LISTEN TO FIGHTS ON THE RADIO WHEN I WAS LITTLE. I'M TOO YOUNG TO REMEMBER THE DIXIE KID, BUT MY DAD TOLD ME ALL ABOUT HIM.
HE LOVED THE DIXIE KID!
NEXT THING YOU'RE GONNA TELL ME YOU MET JACK JOHNSON.
HEHEHE, WELL...

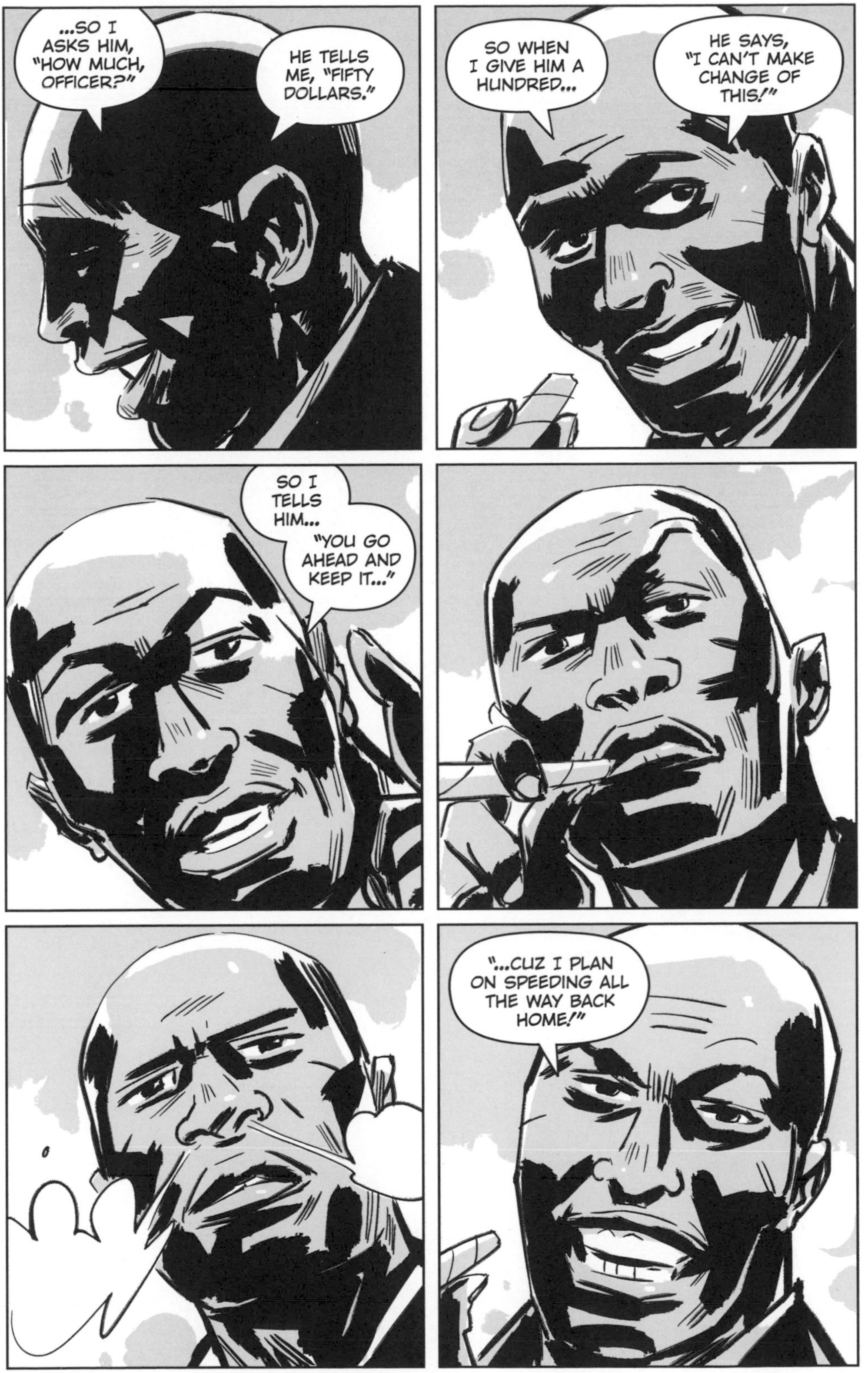
...SO I ASKS HIM, "HOW MUCH, OFFICER?"
HE TELLS ME, "FIFTY DOLLARS."
SO WHEN I GIVE HIM A HUNDRED...
HE SAYS, "I CAN'T MAKE CHANGE OF THIS!"
SO I TELLS HIM...
"YOU GO AHEAD AND KEEP IT..."
"...CUZ I PLAN ON SPEEDING ALL THE WAY BACK HOME!"

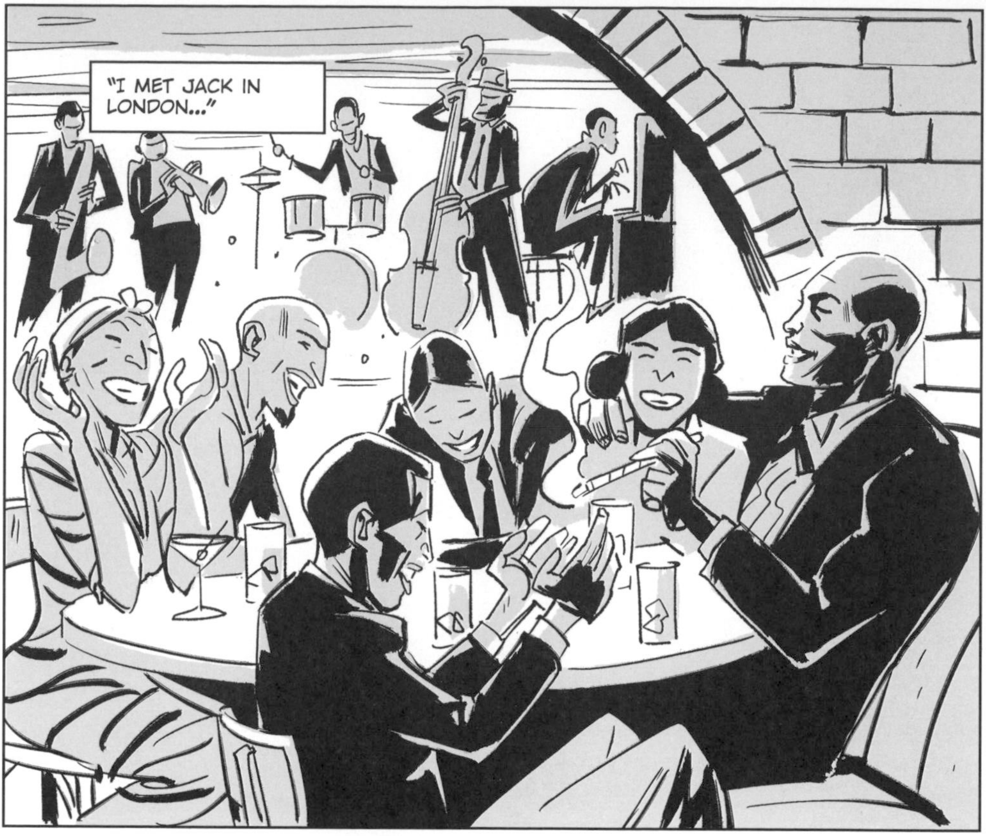
"I MET JACK IN LONDON..."

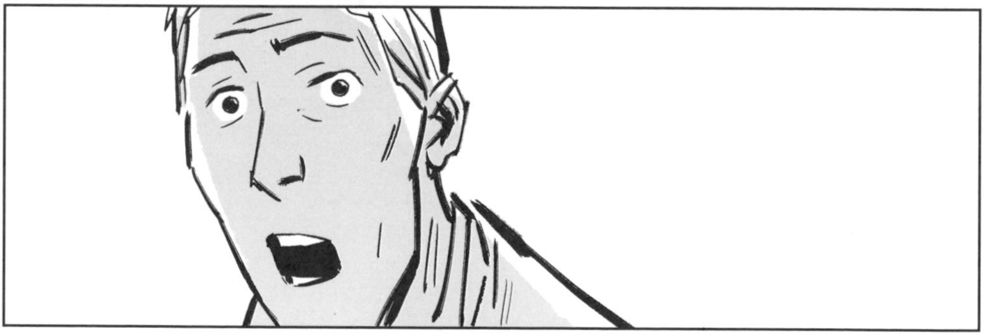

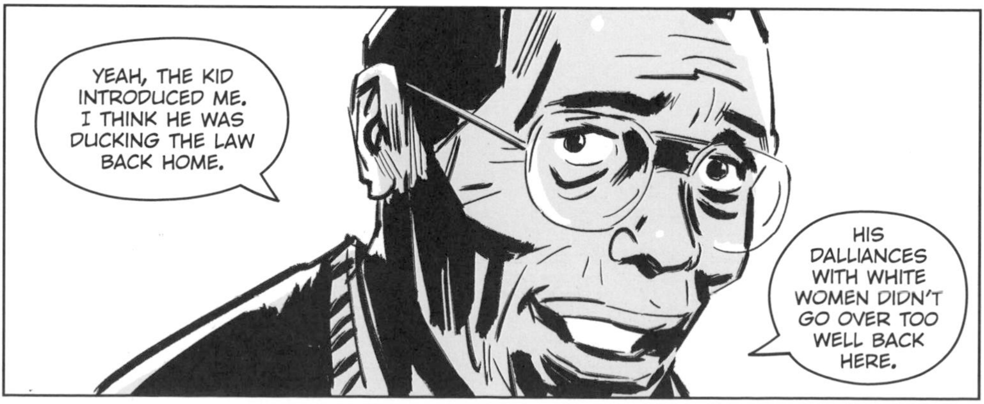
YEAH, THE KID INTRODUCED ME. I THINK HE WAS DUCKING THE LAW BACK HOME.
HIS DALLIANCES WITH WHITE WOMEN DIDN'T GO OVER TOO WELL BACK HERE.

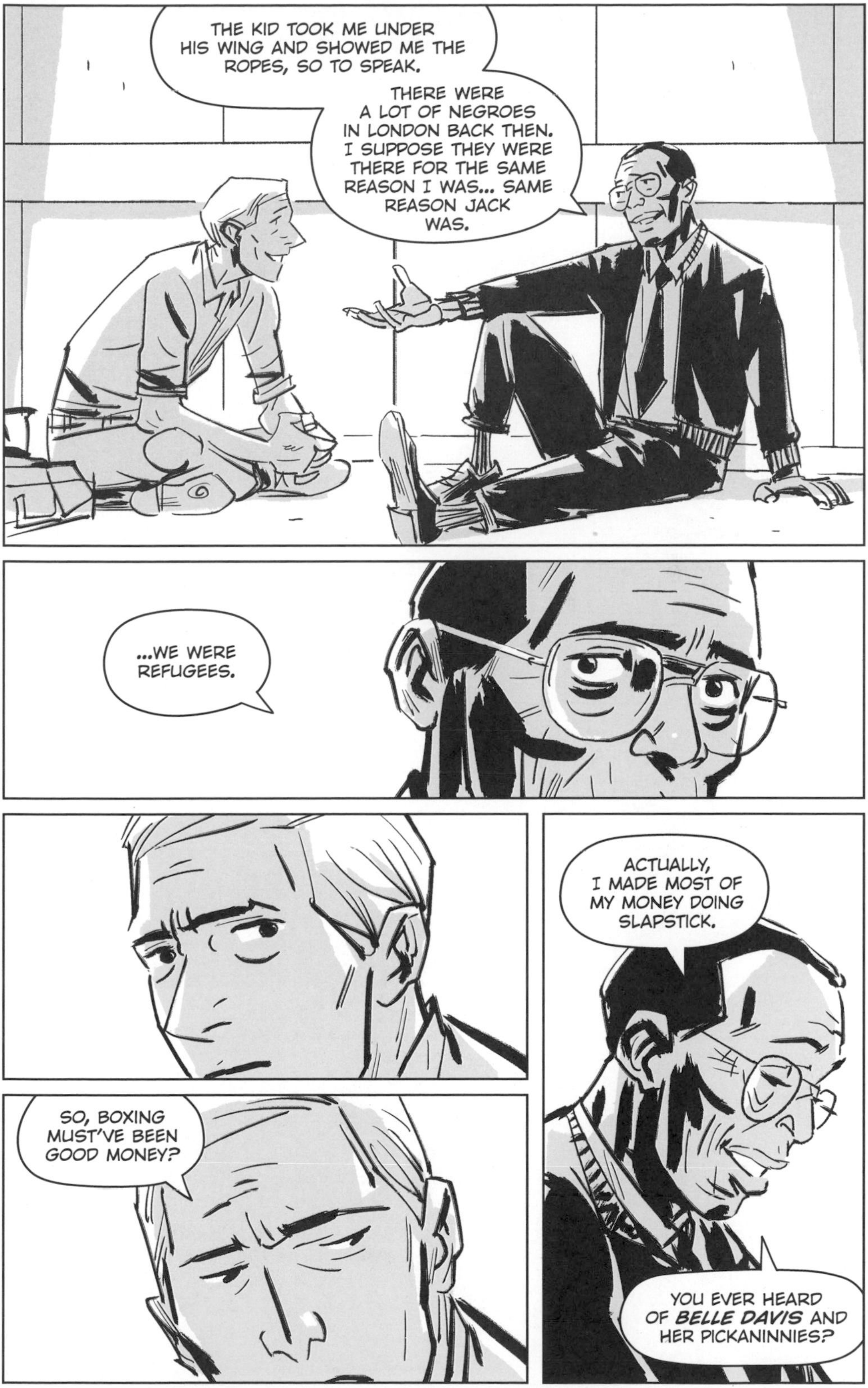
THE KID TOOK ME UNDER HIS WING AND SHOWED ME THE ROPES, SO TO SPEAK.
THERE WERE A LOT OF NEGROES IN LONDON BACK THEN. I SUPPOSE THEY WERE THERE FOR THE SAME REASON I WAS... SAME REASON JACK WAS.
...WE WERE REFUGEES.
SO, BOXING MUST'VE BEEN GOOD MONEY?
ACTUALLY, I MADE MOST OF MY MONEY DOING SLAPSTICK.
YOU EVER HEARD OF ***BELLE DAVIS*** AND HER PICKANINNIES?

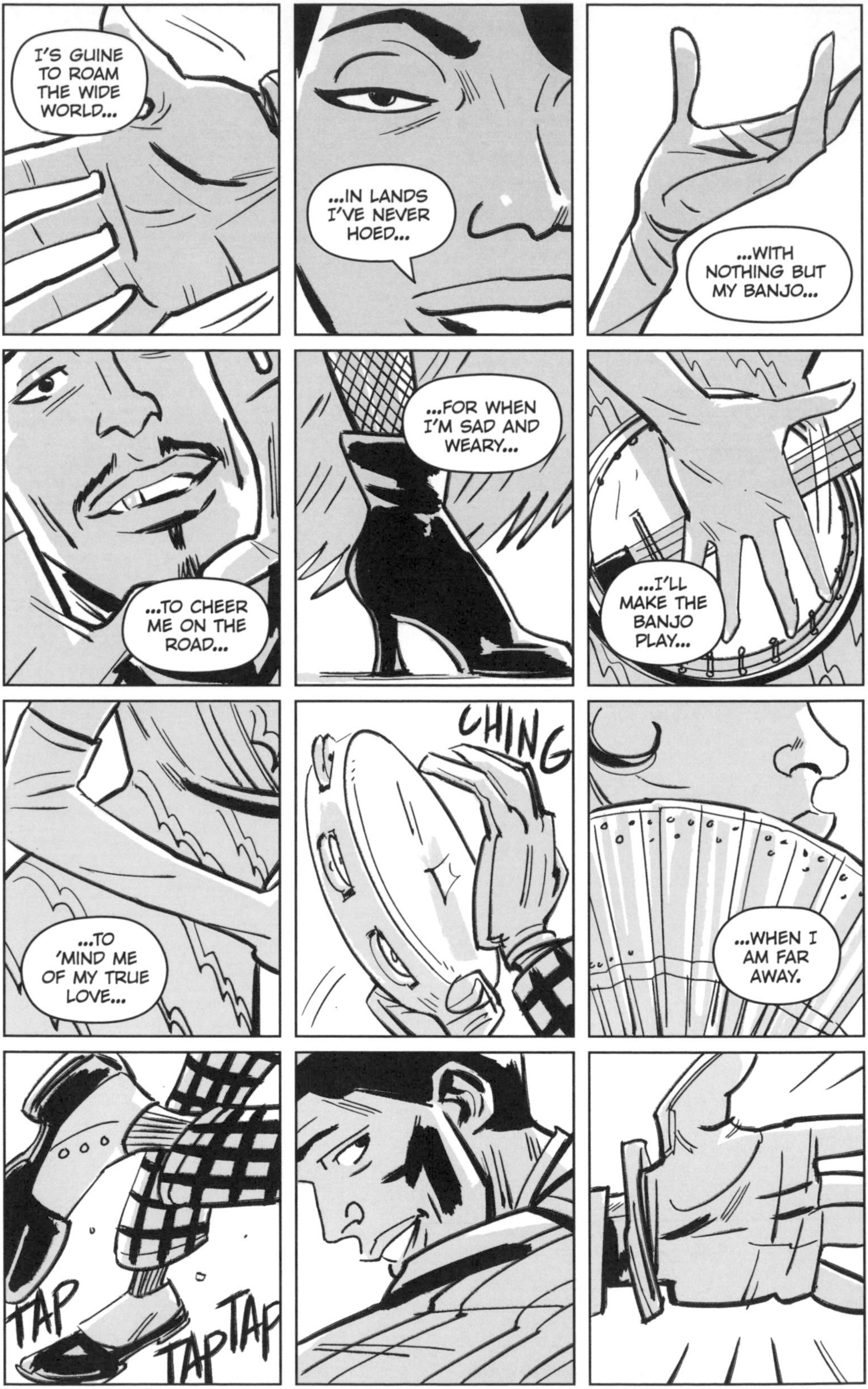
I'S GUINE TO ROAM THE WIDE WORLD...
...IN LANDS I'VE NEVER HOED...
...WITH NOTHING BUT MY BANJO...
...TO CHEER ME ON THE ROAD...
...FOR WHEN I'M SAD AND WEARY...
...I'LL MAKE THE BANJO PLAY...
...TO 'MIND ME OF MY TRUE LOVE...
CHING
...WHEN I AM FAR AWAY.
TAP
TAP TAP

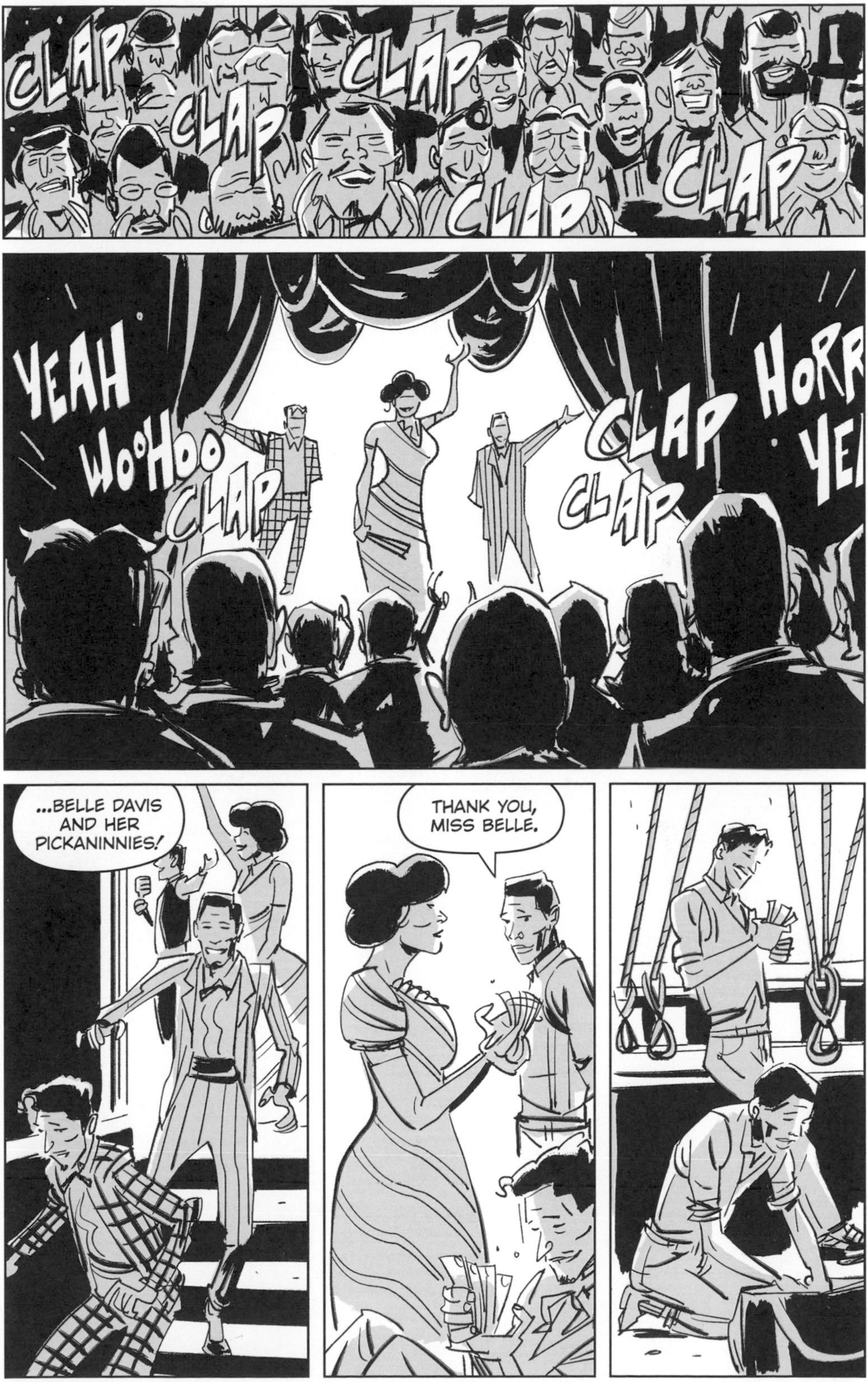
CLAP
CLAP
CLAP
CLAP
CLAP
CLAP
YEAH
WOOHOO
CLAP
CLAP
CLAP
...BELLE DAVIS AND HER PICKANINNIES!
THANK YOU, MISS BELLE.

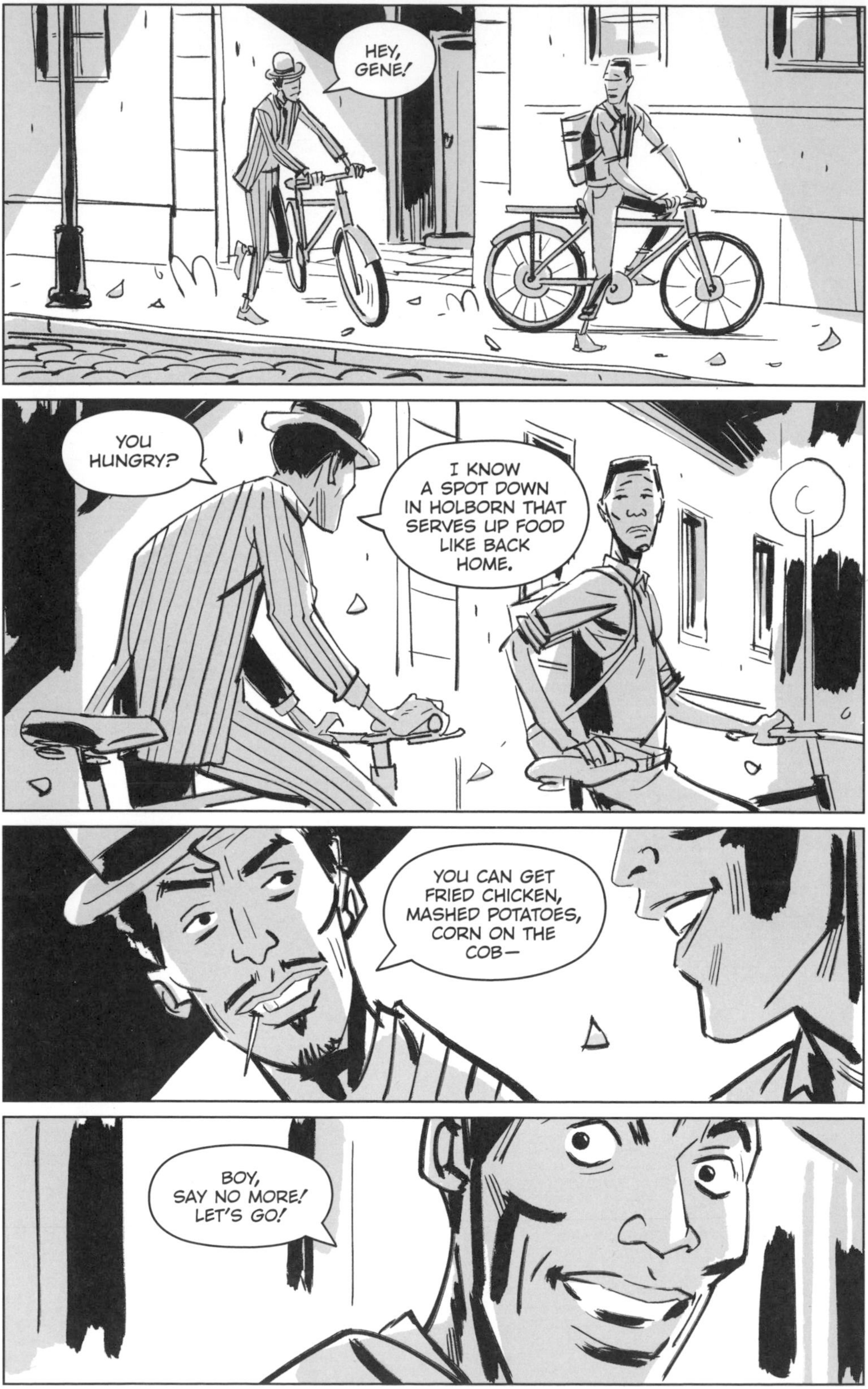
HEY, GENE!
YOU HUNGRY?
I KNOW A SPOT DOWN IN HOLBORN THAT SERVES UP FOOD LIKE BACK HOME.
YOU CAN GET FRIED CHICKEN, MASHED POTATOES, CORN ON THE COB—
BOY, SAY NO MORE! LET'S GO!

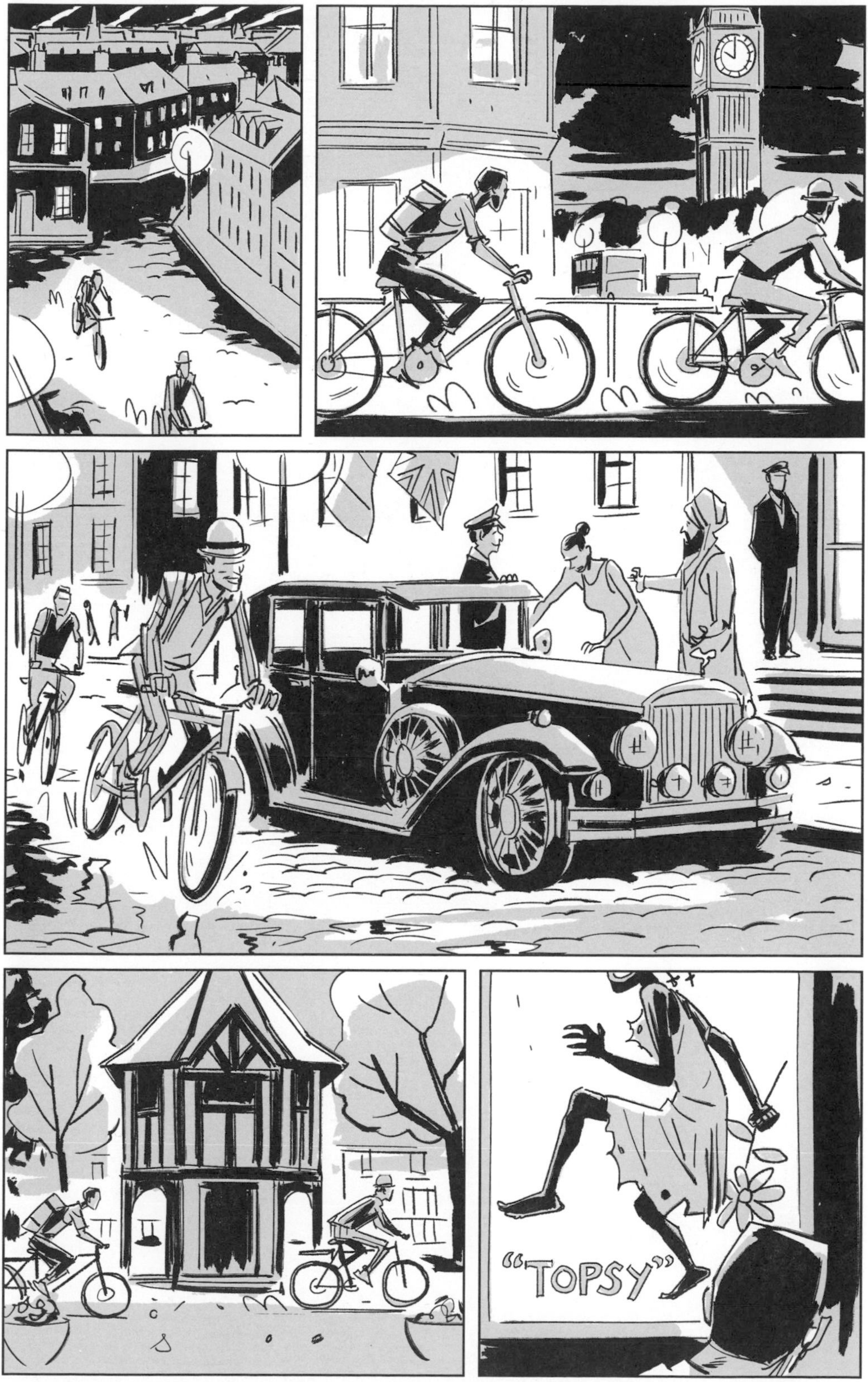
"TOPSY"

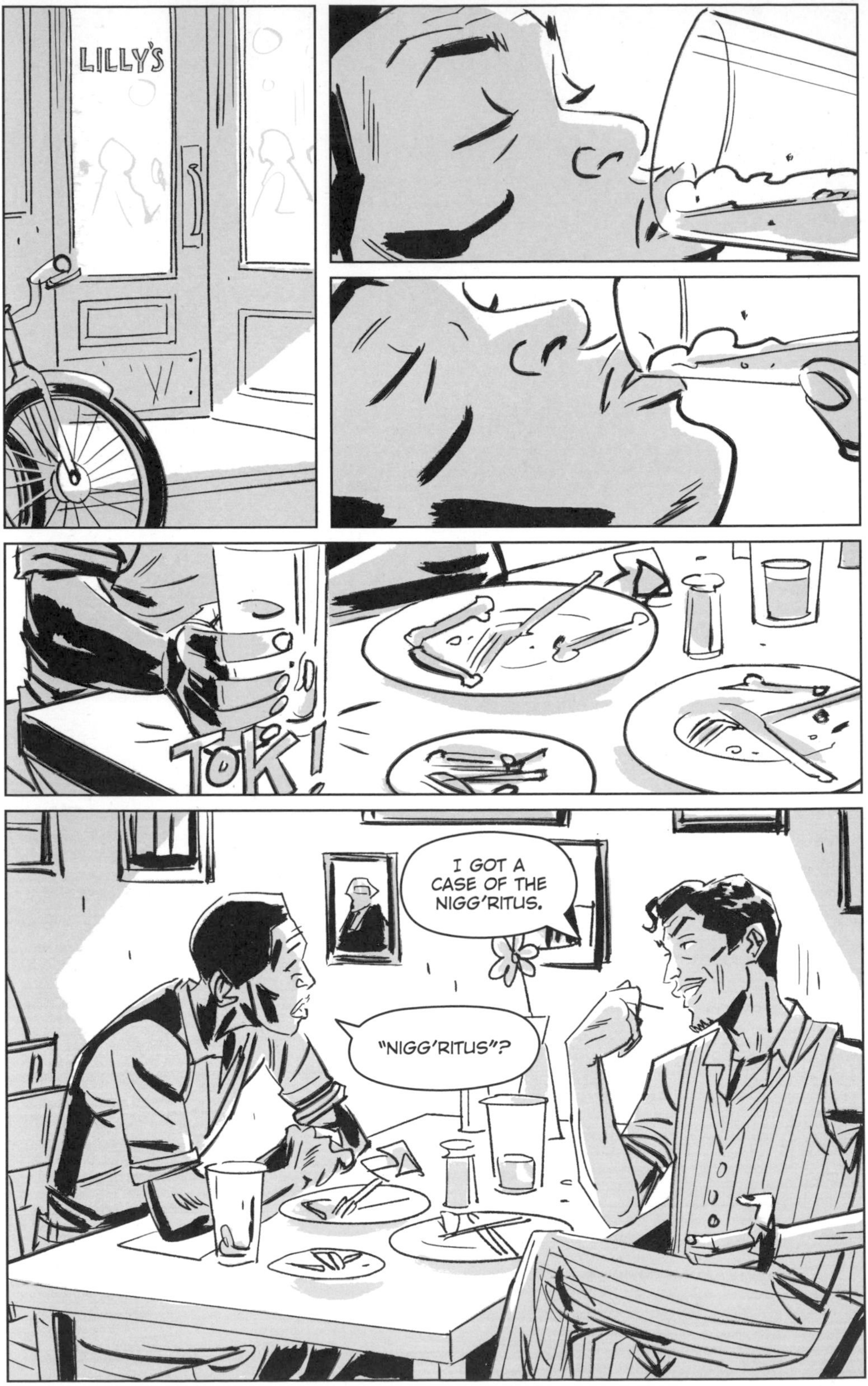
LILLY'S
TOK!
I GOT A CASE OF THE NIGG'RITUS.
"NIGG'RITUS"?

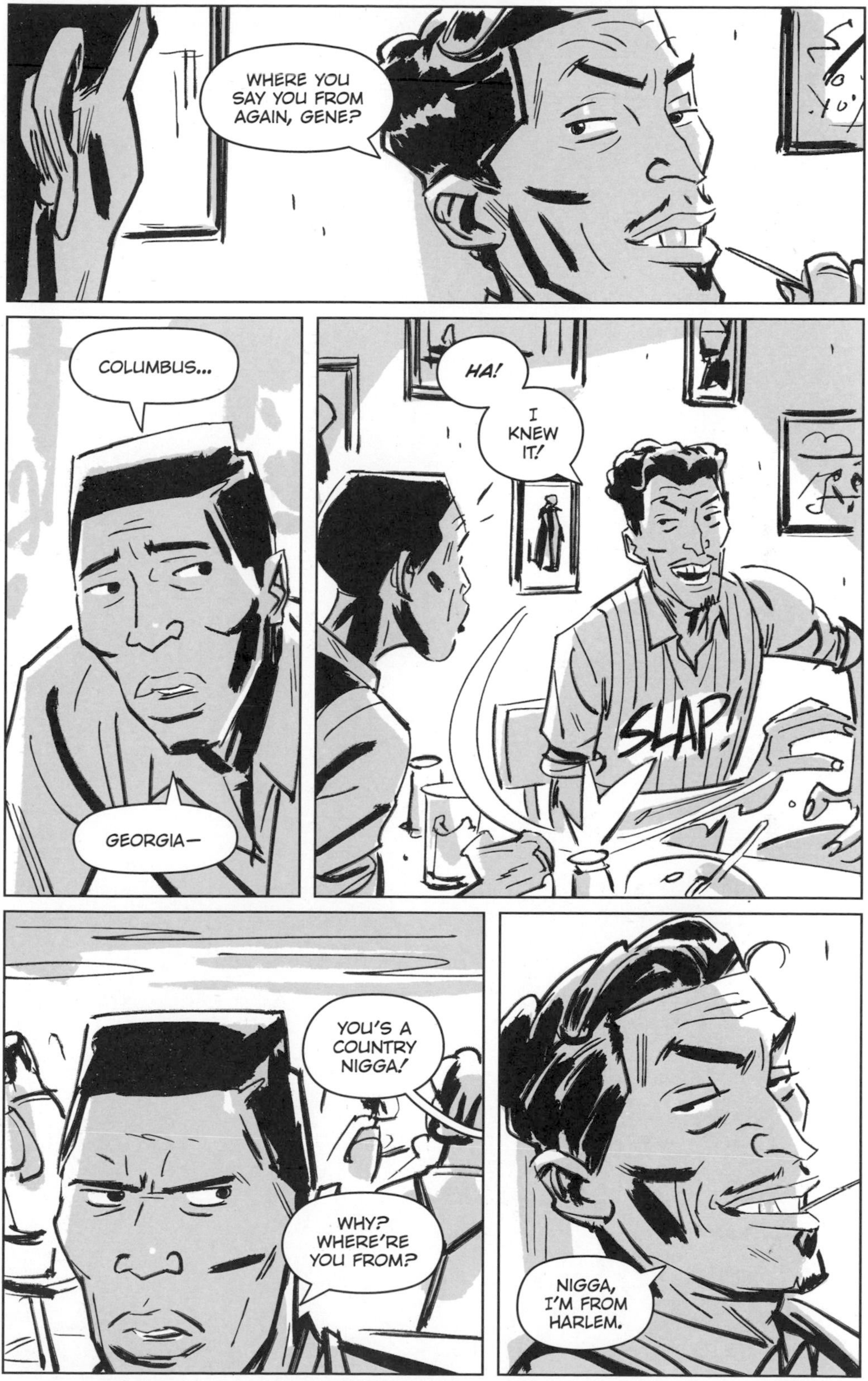
WHERE YOU SAY YOU FROM AGAIN, GENE?
COLUMBUS...
GEORGIA—
HA!
I KNEW IT!
SLAP!
YOU'S A COUNTRY NIGGA!
WHY? WHERE'RE YOU FROM?
NIGGA, I'M FROM HARLEM.

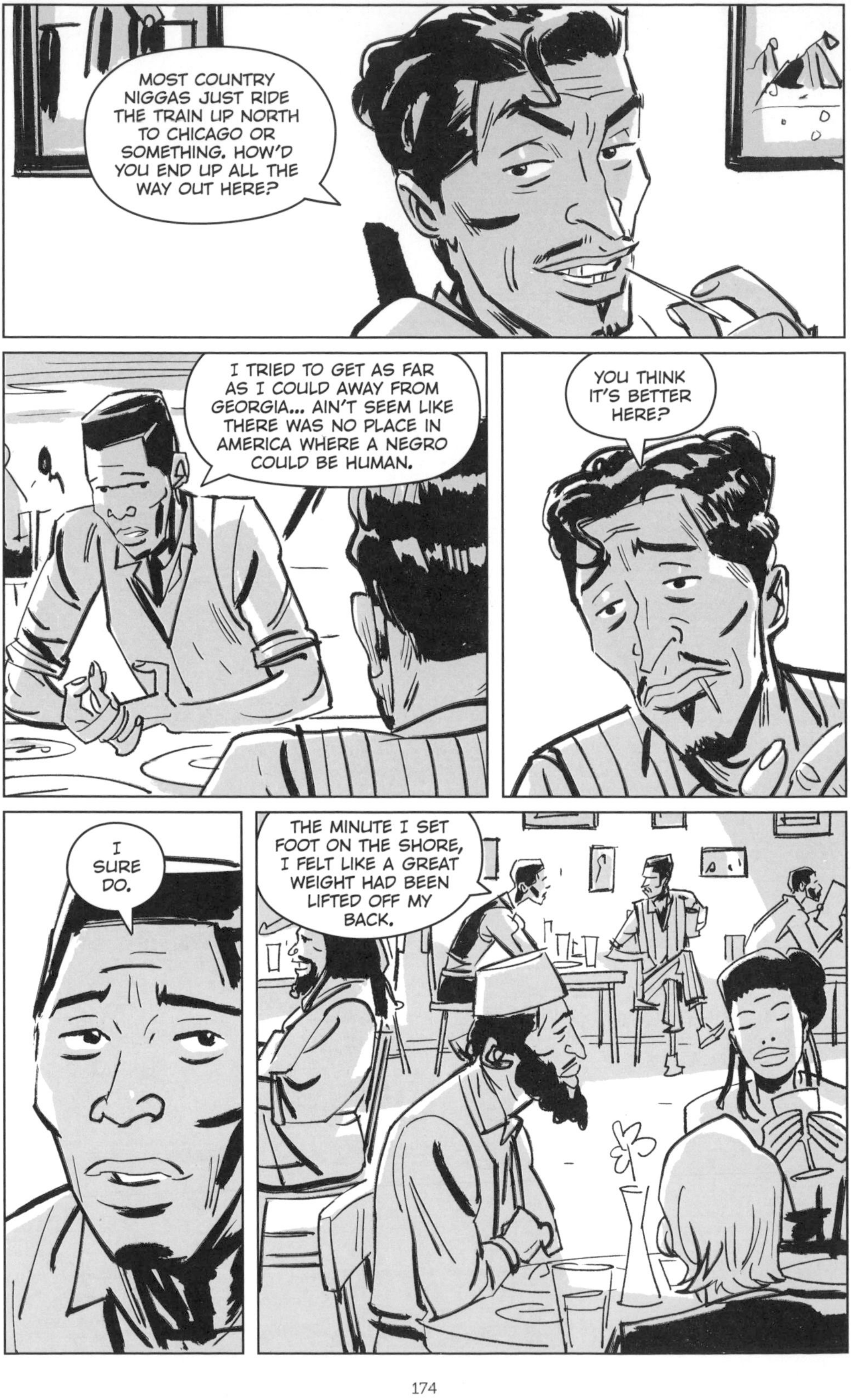
MOST COUNTRY NIGGAS JUST RIDE THE TRAIN UP NORTH TO CHICAGO OR SOMETHING. HOW'D YOU END UP ALL THE WAY OUT HERE?
I TRIED TO GET AS FAR AS I COULD AWAY FROM GEORGIA... AIN'T SEEM LIKE THERE WAS NO PLACE IN AMERICA WHERE A NEGRO COULD BE HUMAN.
YOU THINK IT'S BETTER HERE?
I SURE DO.
THE MINUTE I SET FOOT ON THE SHORE, I FELT LIKE A GREAT WEIGHT HAD BEEN LIFTED OFF MY BACK.

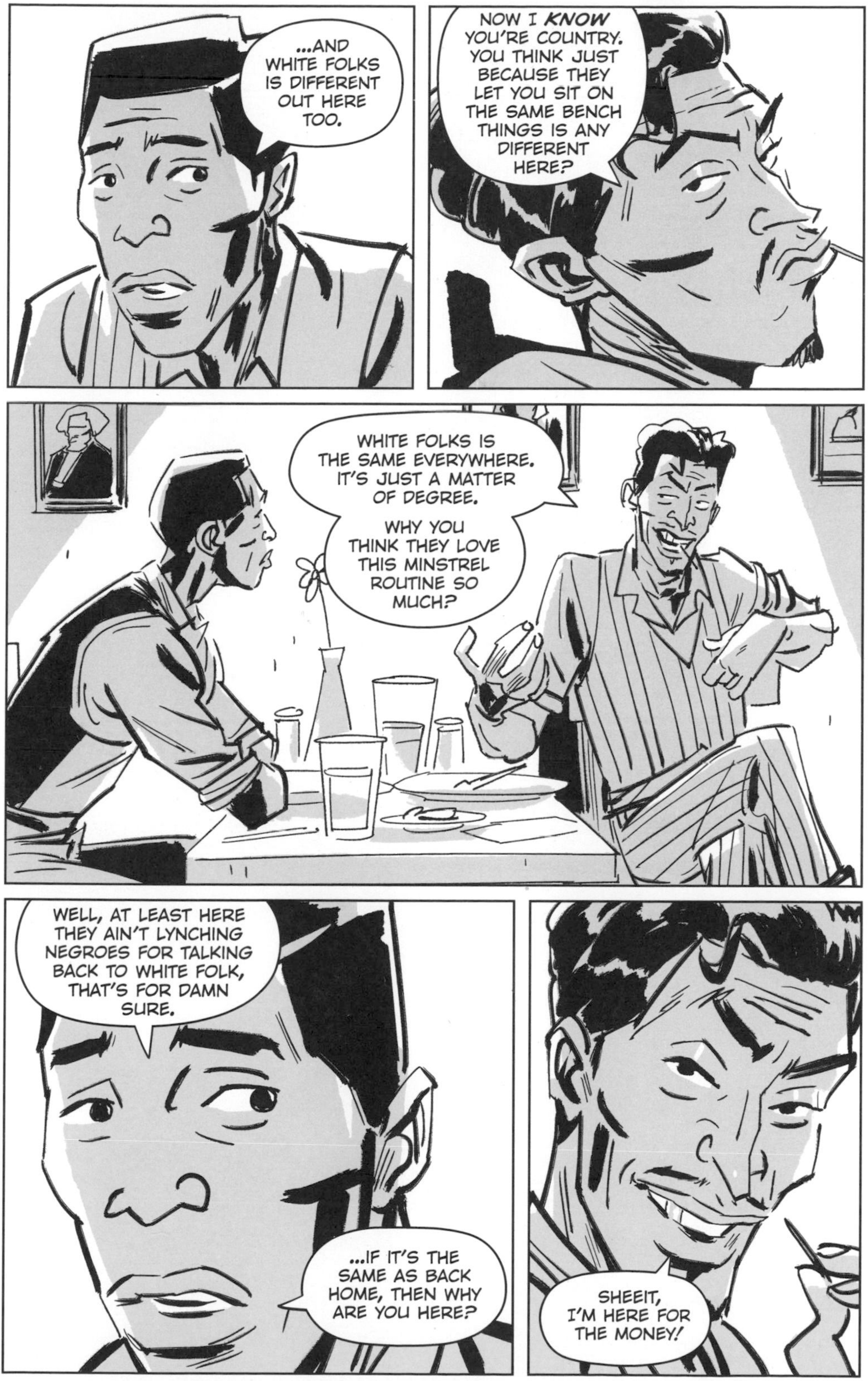
...AND WHITE FOLKS IS DIFFERENT OUT HERE TOO.
NOW I *KNOW* YOU'RE COUNTRY. YOU THINK JUST BECAUSE THEY LET YOU SIT ON THE SAME BENCH THINGS IS ANY DIFFERENT HERE?
WHITE FOLKS IS THE SAME EVERYWHERE. IT'S JUST A MATTER OF DEGREE.
WHY YOU THINK THEY LOVE THIS MINSTREL ROUTINE SO MUCH?
WELL, AT LEAST HERE THEY AIN'T LYNCHING NEGROES FOR TALKING BACK TO WHITE FOLK, THAT'S FOR DAMN SURE.
...IF IT'S THE SAME AS BACK HOME, THEN WHY ARE YOU HERE?
SHEEIT, I'M HERE FOR THE MONEY!

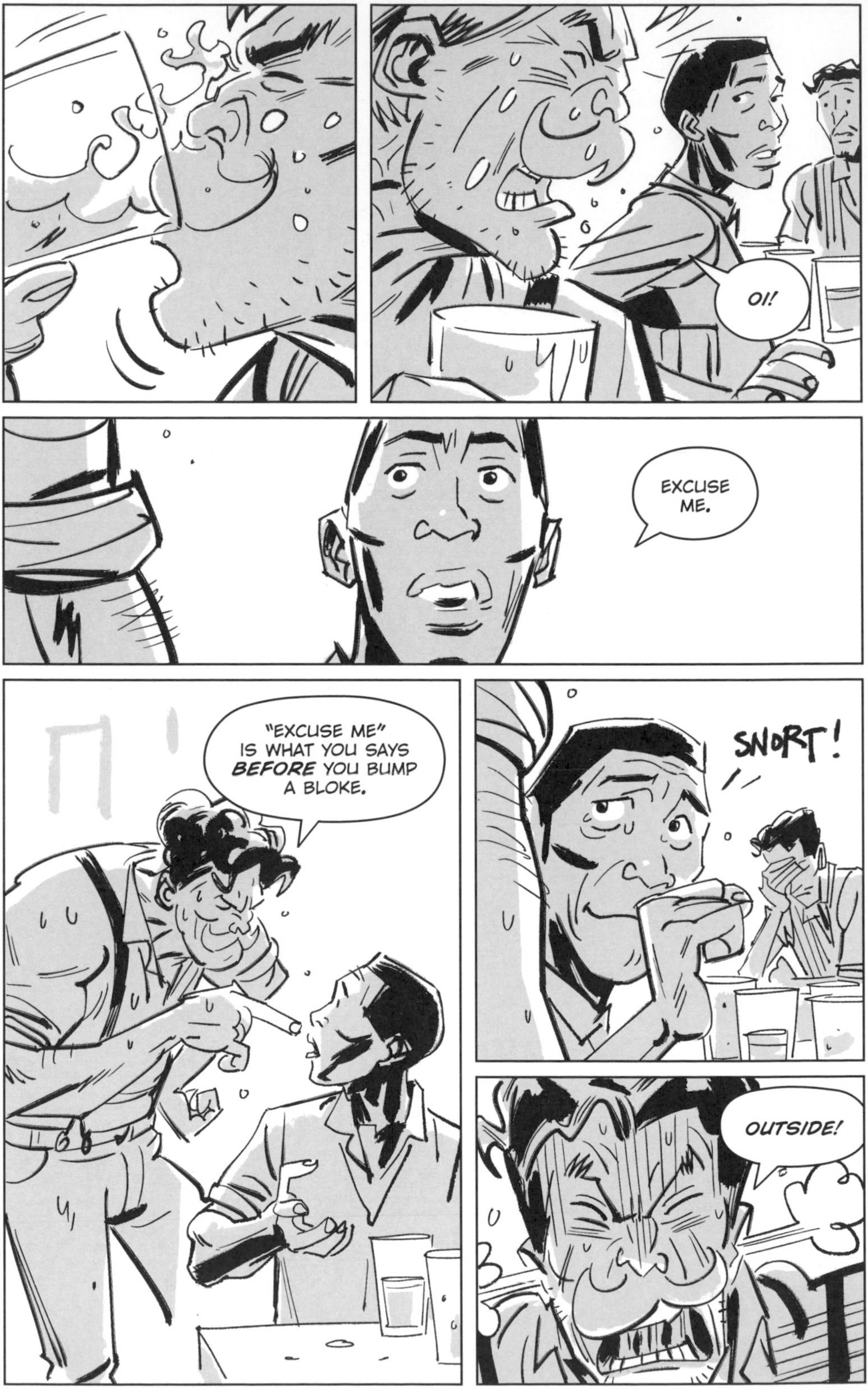
OI!
EXCUSE ME.
"EXCUSE ME" IS WHAT YOU SAYS *BEFORE* YOU BUMP A BLOKE.
SNORT!
OUTSIDE!

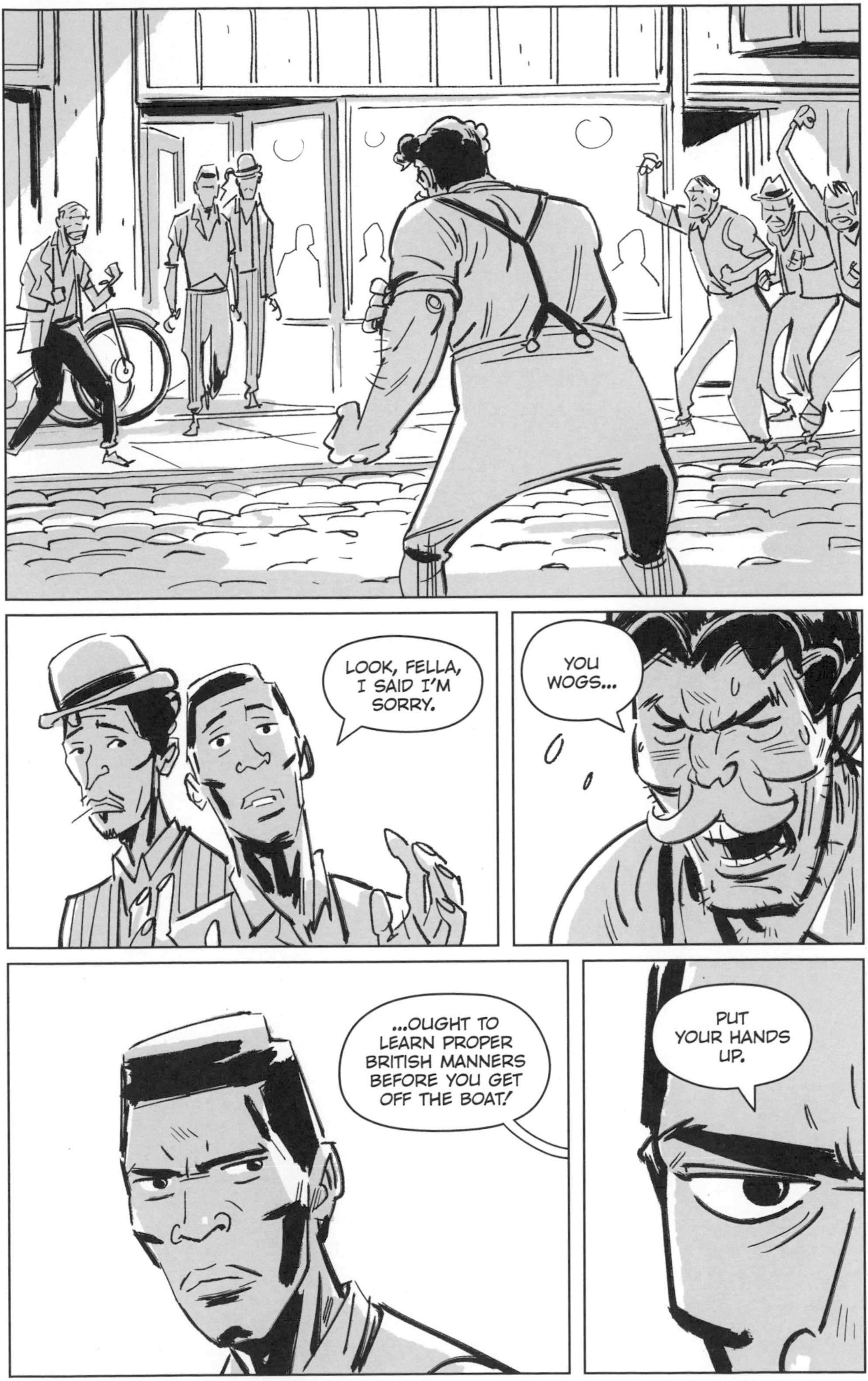
LOOK, FELLA, I SAID I'M SORRY.
YOU WOGS...
...OUGHT TO LEARN PROPER BRITISH MANNERS BEFORE YOU GET OFF THE BOAT!
PUT YOUR HANDS UP.

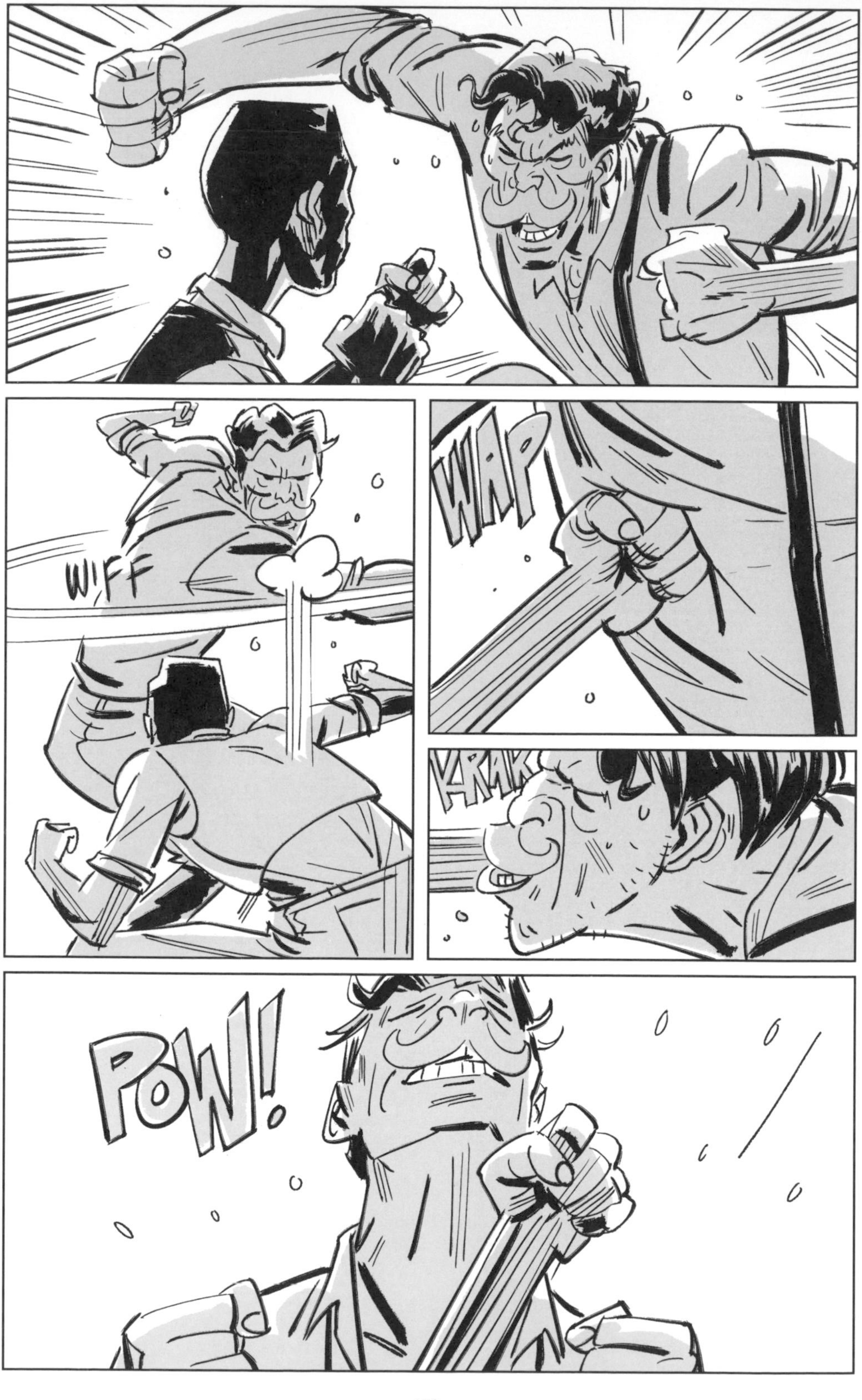
WIFF
WAP
KRAK
POW!

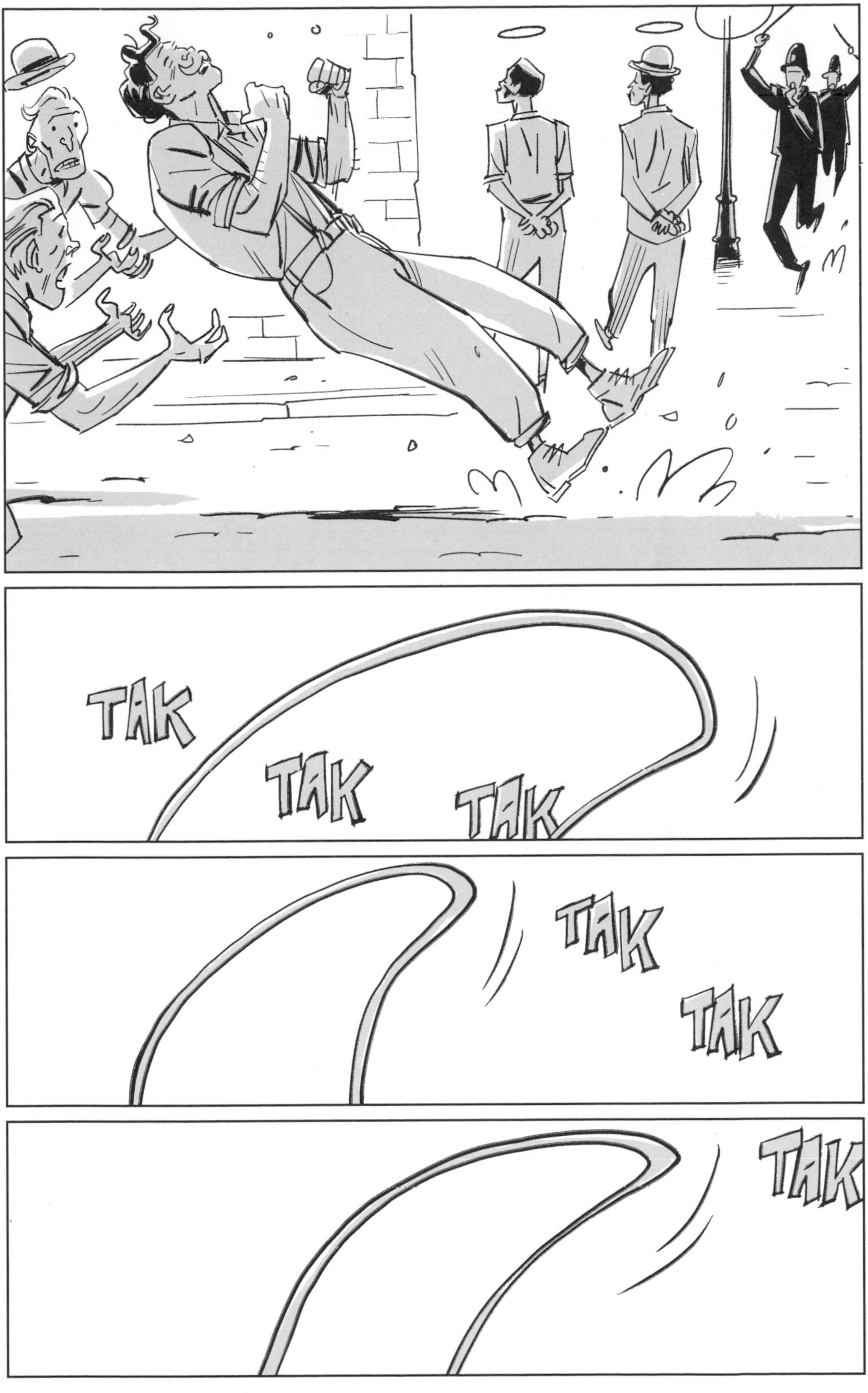
TAK
TAK
TAK
TAK
TAK
TAK

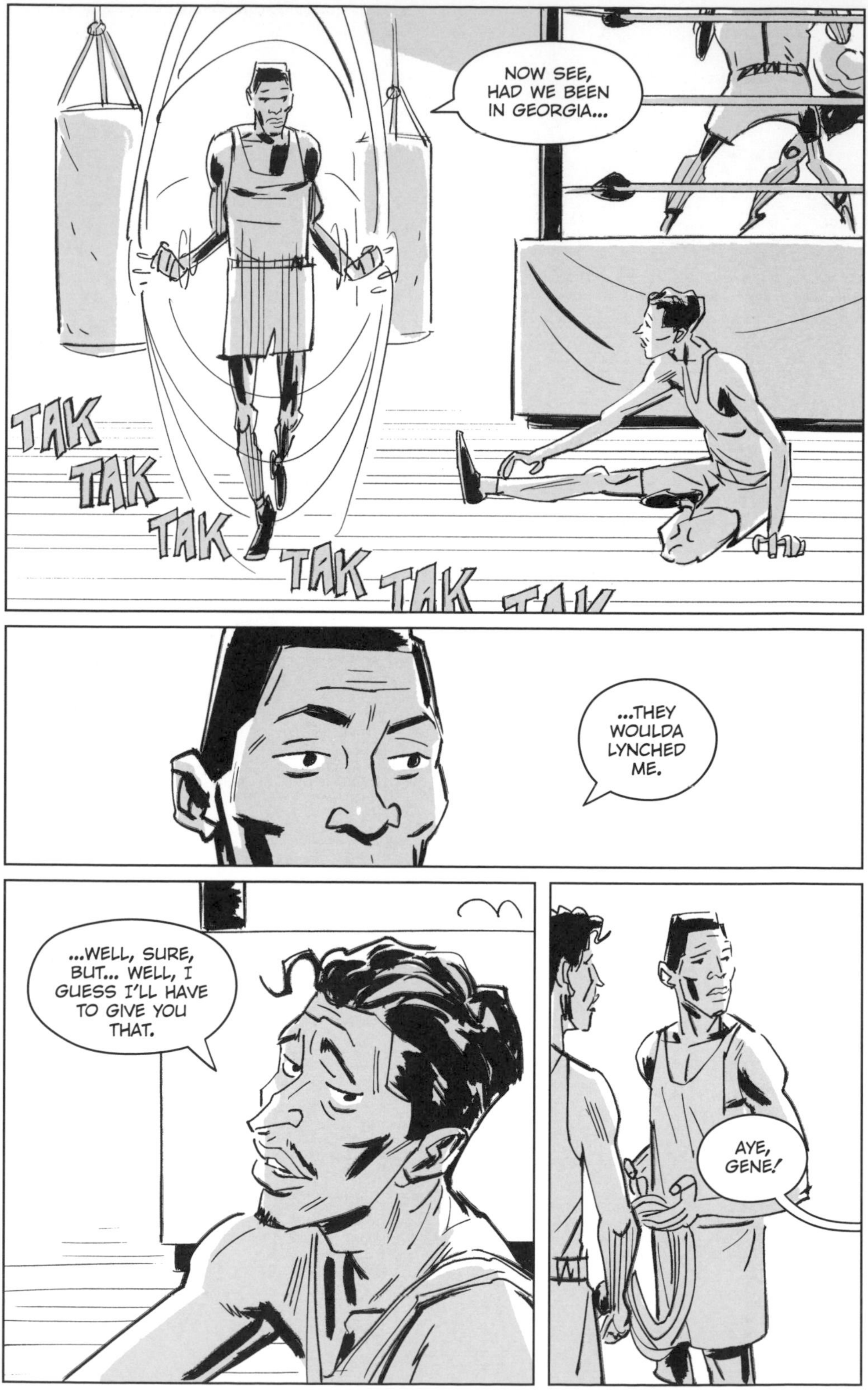
NOW SEE, HAD WE BEEN IN GEORGIA...
TAK TAK TAK TAK TAK
...THEY WOULDA LYNCHED ME.
...WELL, SURE, BUT... WELL, I GUESS I'LL HAVE TO GIVE YOU THAT.
AYE, GENE!

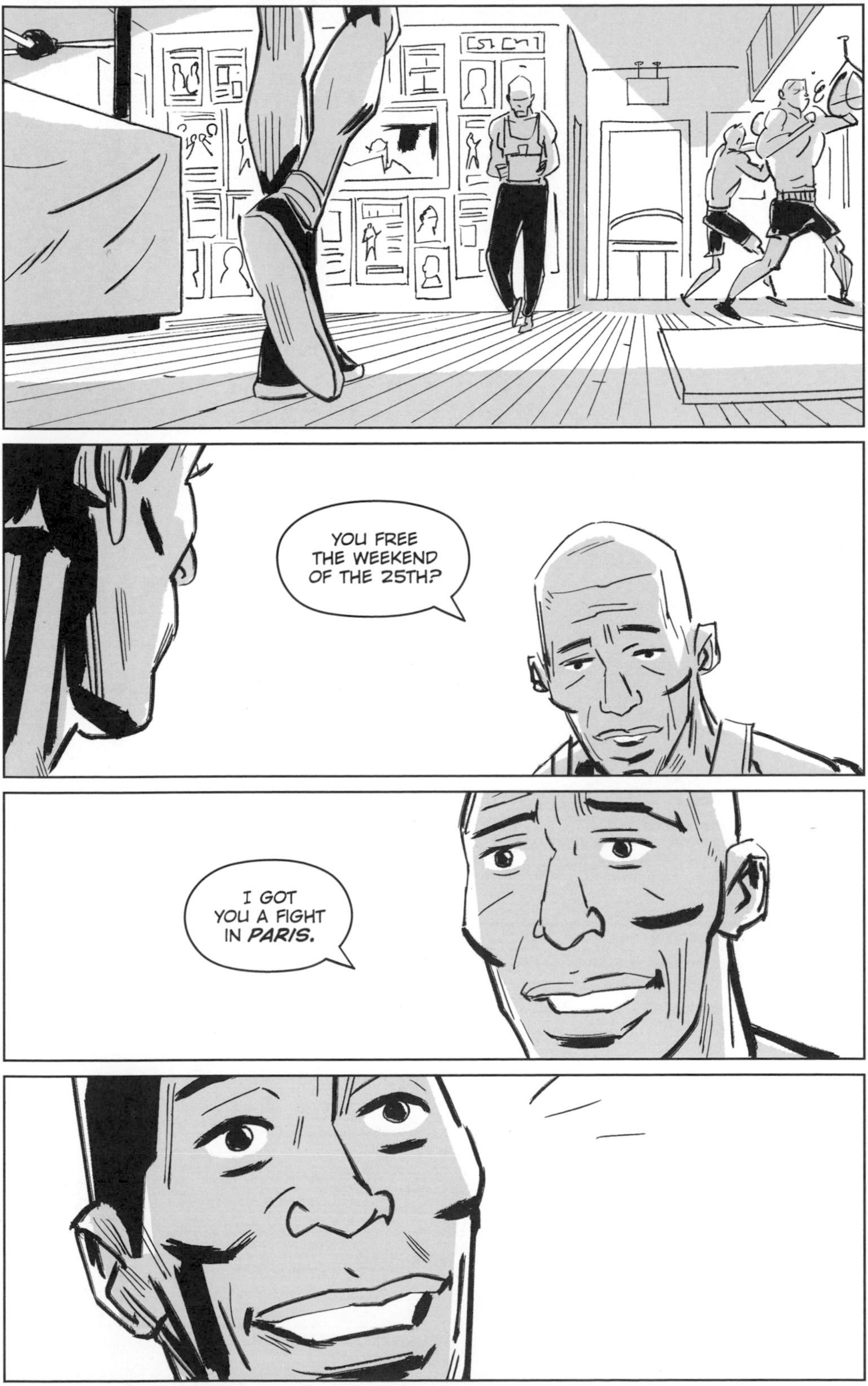
YOU FREE THE WEEKEND OF THE 25TH?
I GOT YOU A FIGHT IN *PARIS.*

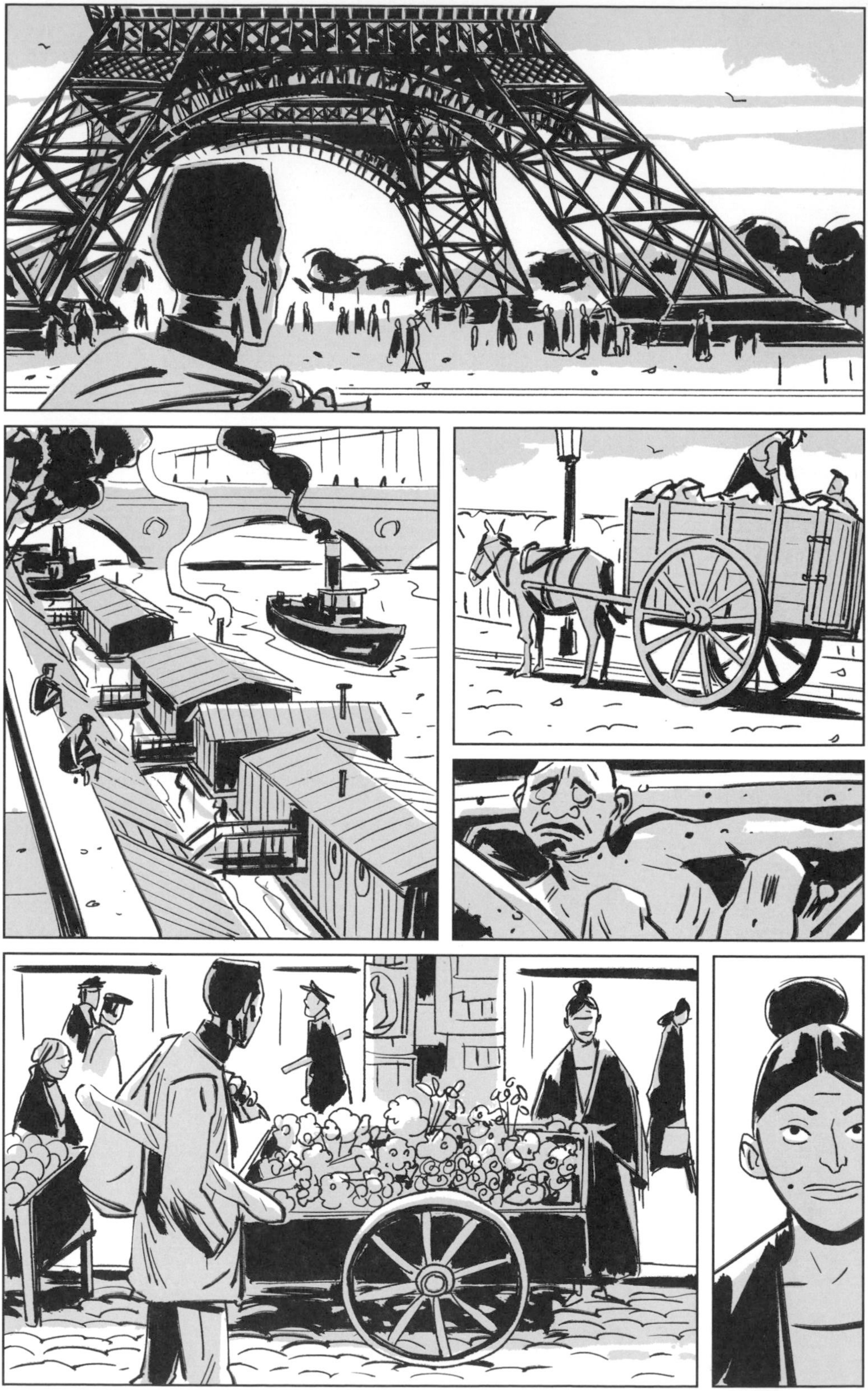

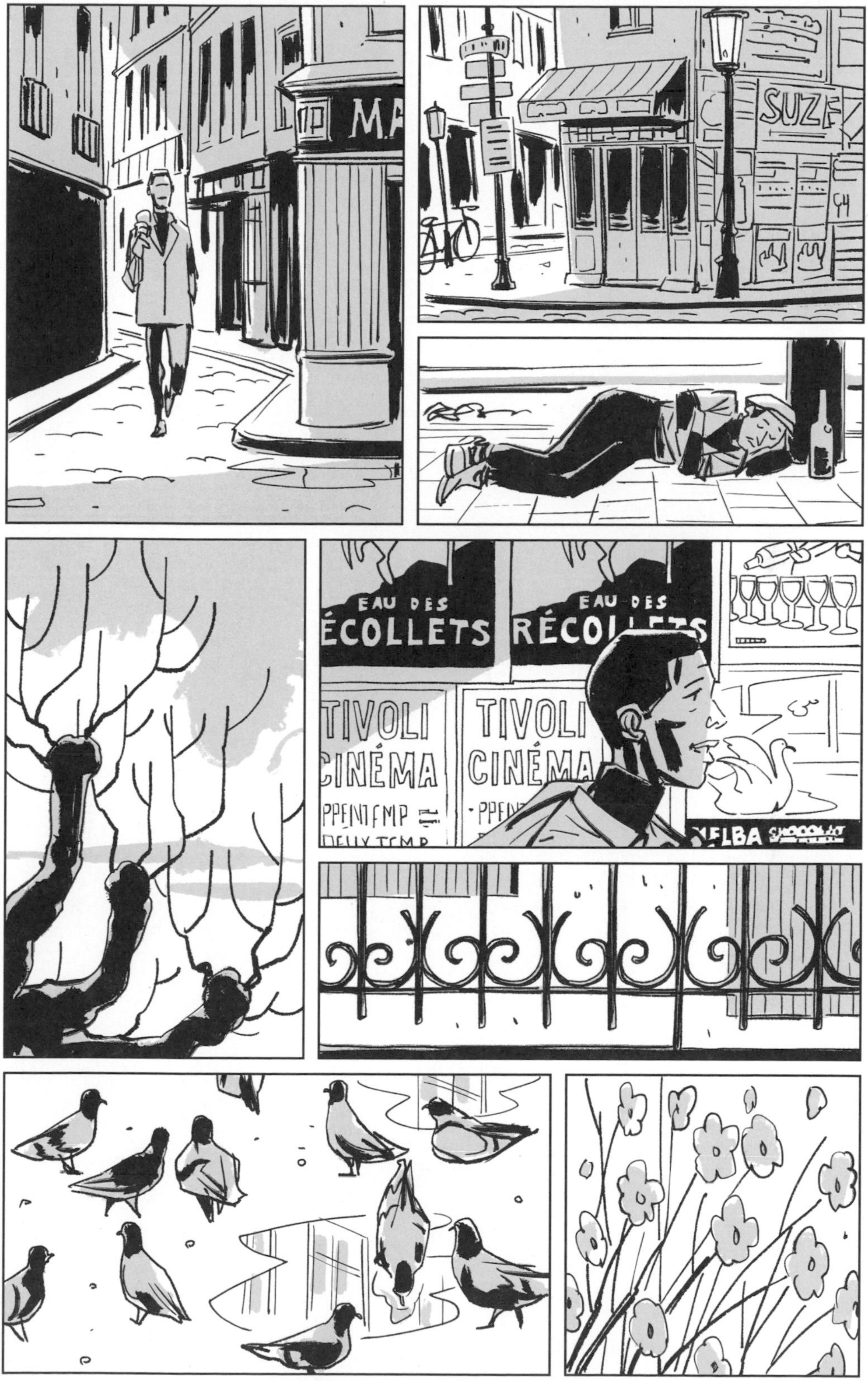
SUZE
EAU DES
RÉCOLLETS
EAU DES
RÉCOLLETS
TIVOLI
CINÉMA
TIVOLI
CINÉMA

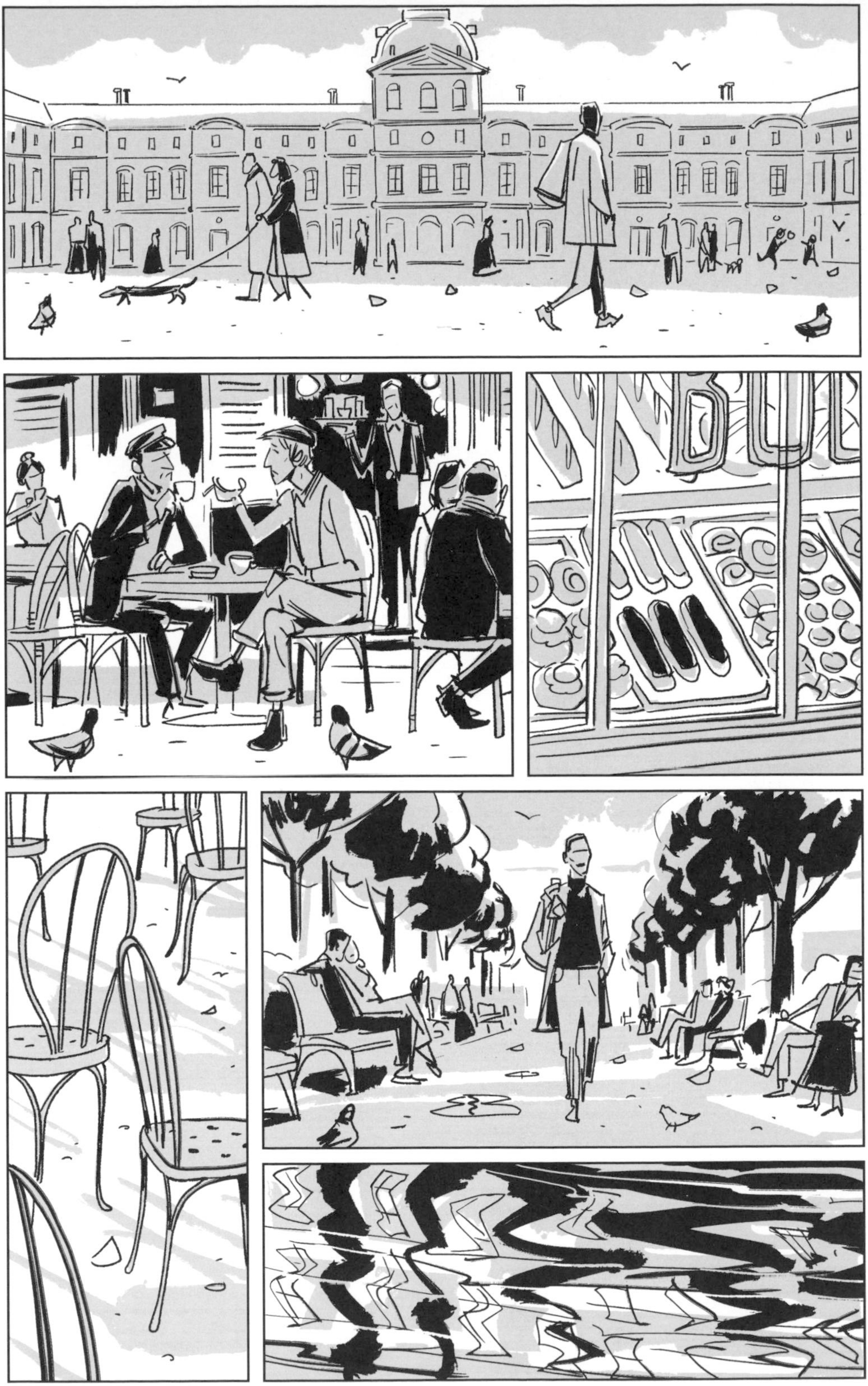

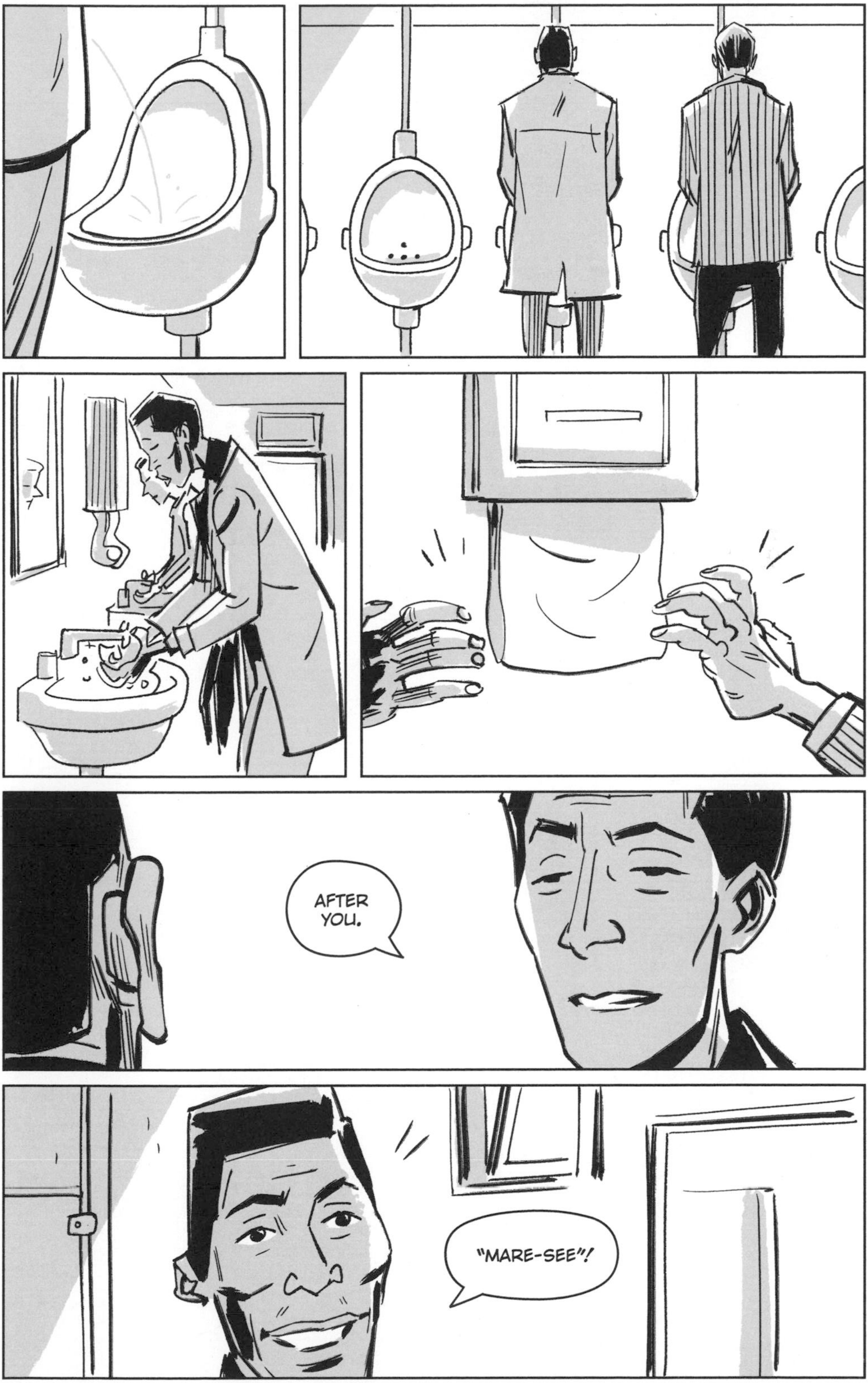
AFTER YOU.
"MARE-SEE"!

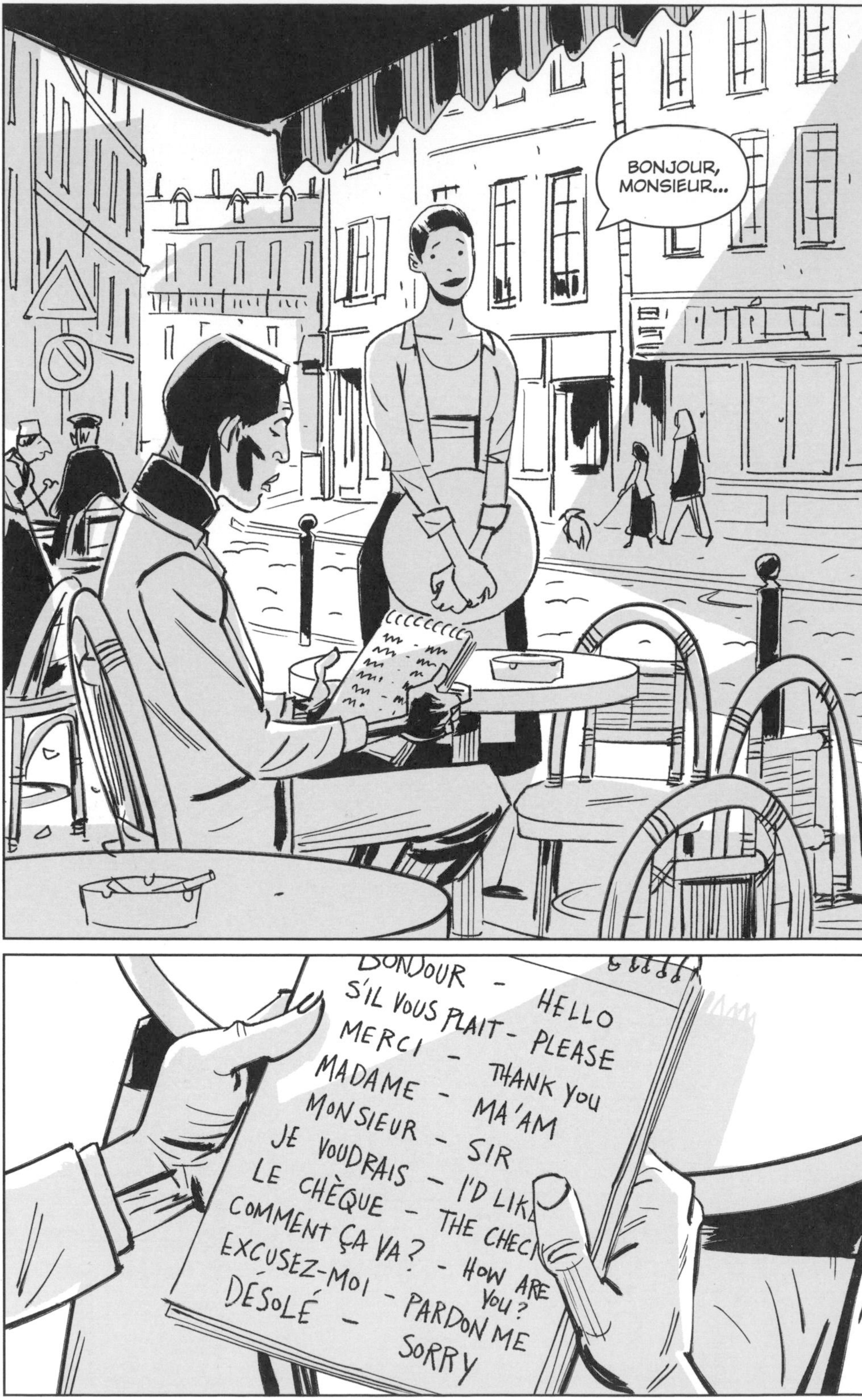
BONJOUR, MONSIEUR...
BONJOUR - HELLO
S'IL VOUS PLAIT - PLEASE
MERCI - THANK YOU
MADAME - MA'AM
MONSIEUR - SIR
JE VOUDRAIS - I'D LIK
LE CHÈQUE - THE CHEC
COMMENT ÇA VA? - HOW ARE YOU?
EXCUSEZ-MOI - PARDON ME
DÉSOLÉ - SORRY

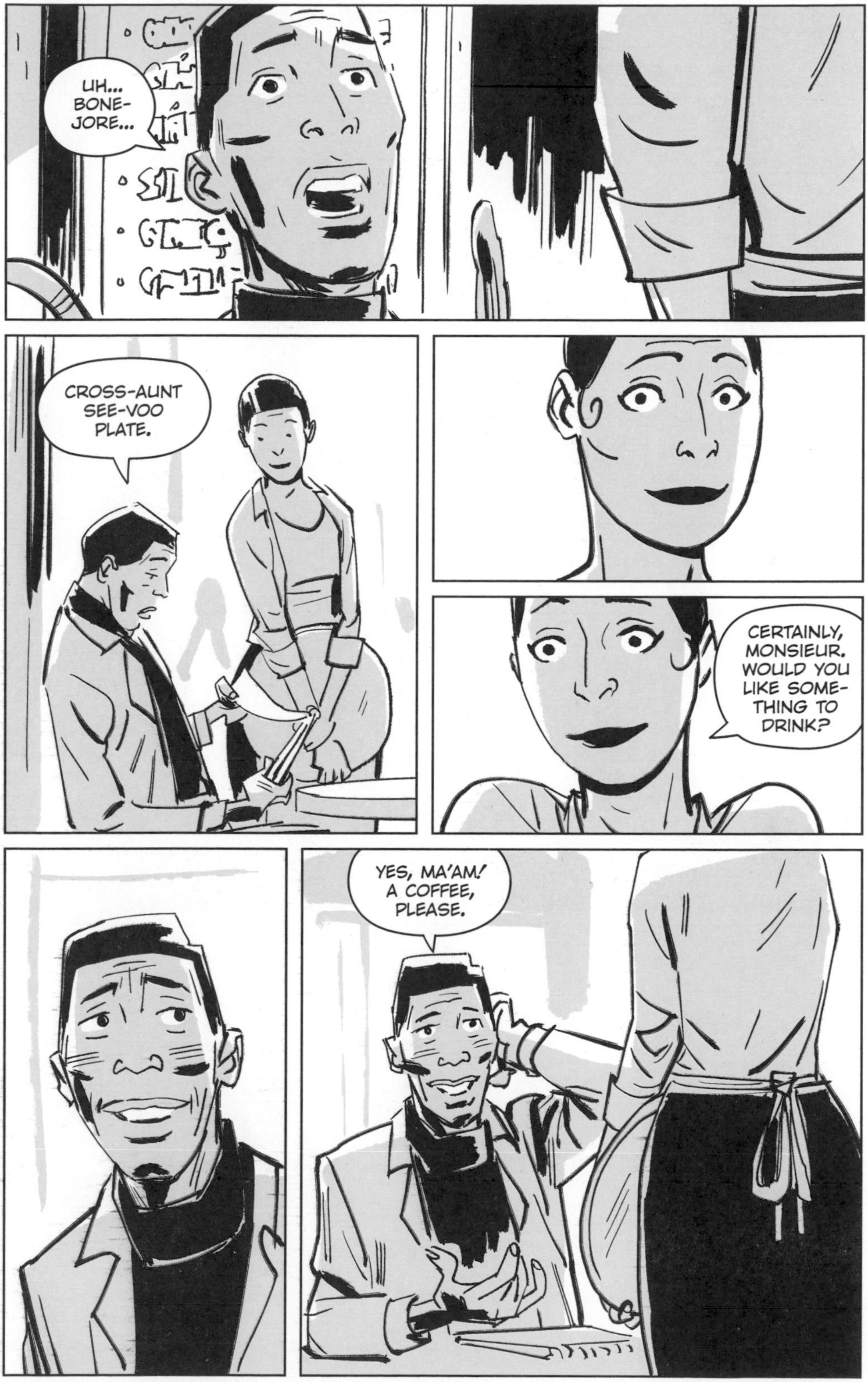
UH... BONE-JORE...
CROSS-AUNT SEE-VOO PLATE.
CERTAINLY, MONSIEUR. WOULD YOU LIKE SOME-THING TO DRINK?
YES, MA'AM! A COFFEE, PLEASE.

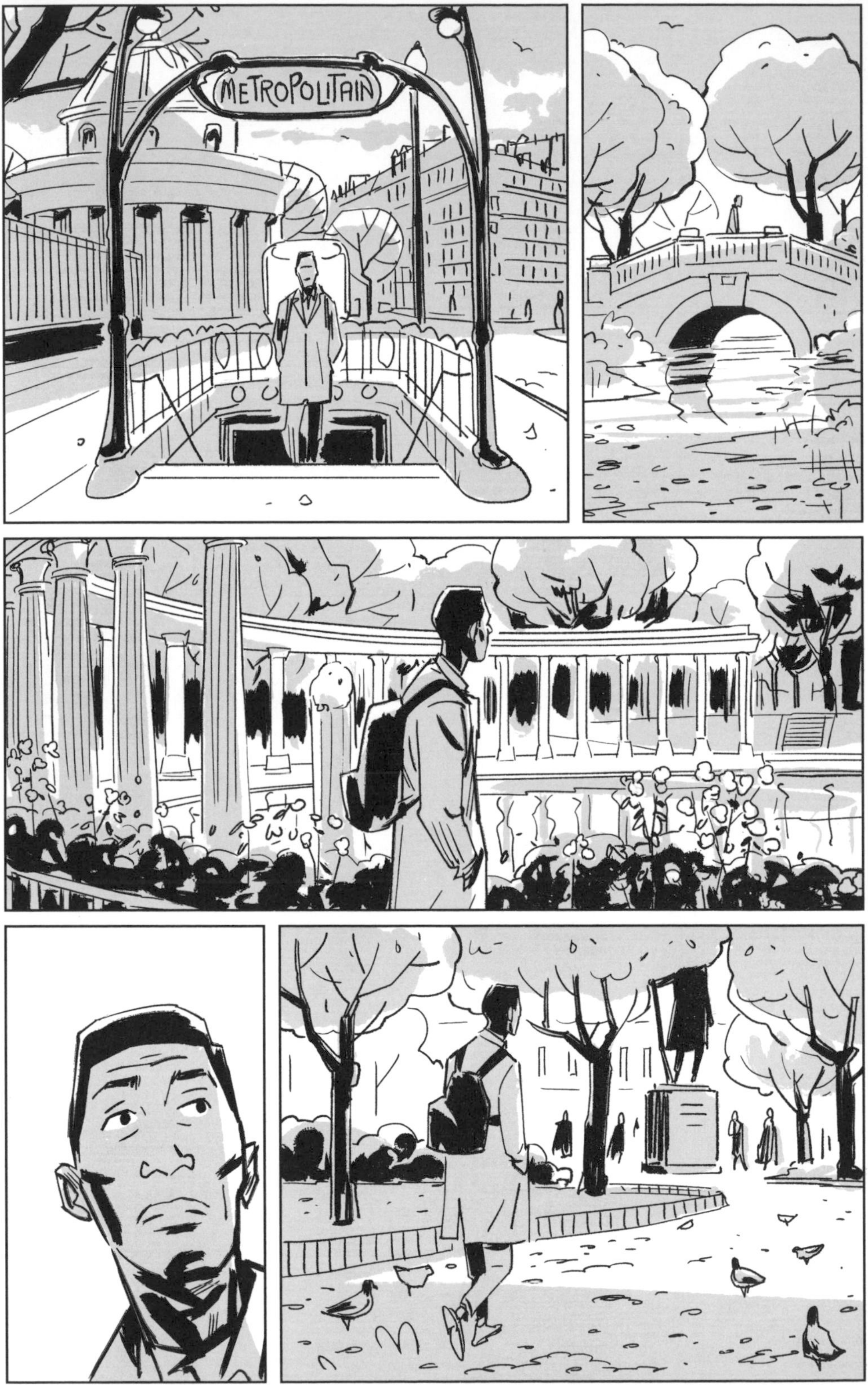
METROPOLITAIN

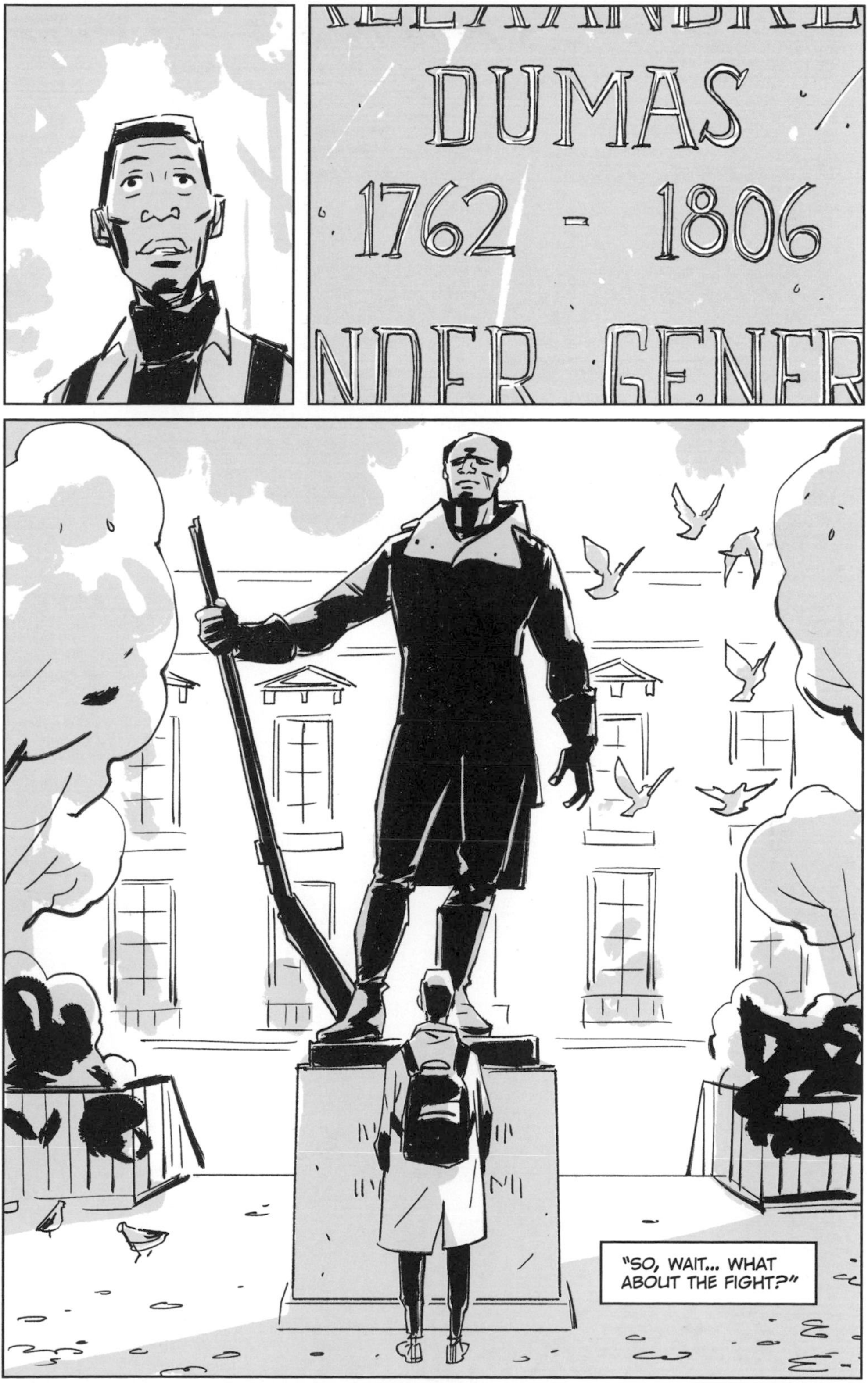
DUMAS
1762 - 1806
"SO, WAIT... WHAT ABOUT THE FIGHT?"

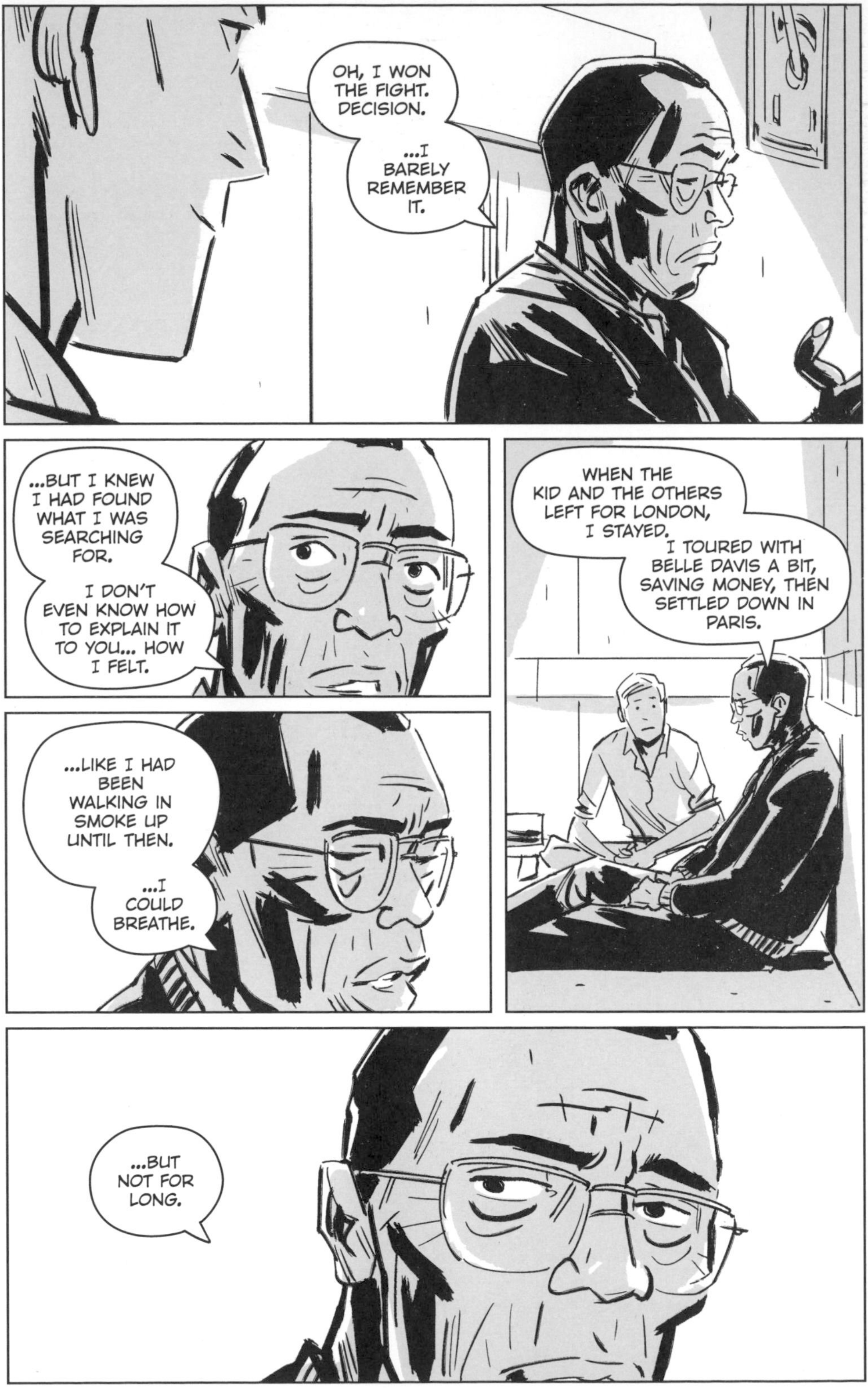
OH, I WON THE FIGHT. DECISION.
...I BARELY REMEMBER IT.
...BUT I KNEW I HAD FOUND WHAT I WAS SEARCHING FOR.
I DON'T EVEN KNOW HOW TO EXPLAIN IT TO YOU... HOW I FELT.
WHEN THE KID AND THE OTHERS LEFT FOR LONDON, I STAYED.
I TOURED WITH BELLE DAVIS A BIT, SAVING MONEY, THEN SETTLED DOWN IN PARIS.
...LIKE I HAD BEEN WALKING IN SMOKE UP UNTIL THEN.
...I COULD BREATHE.
...BUT NOT FOR LONG.

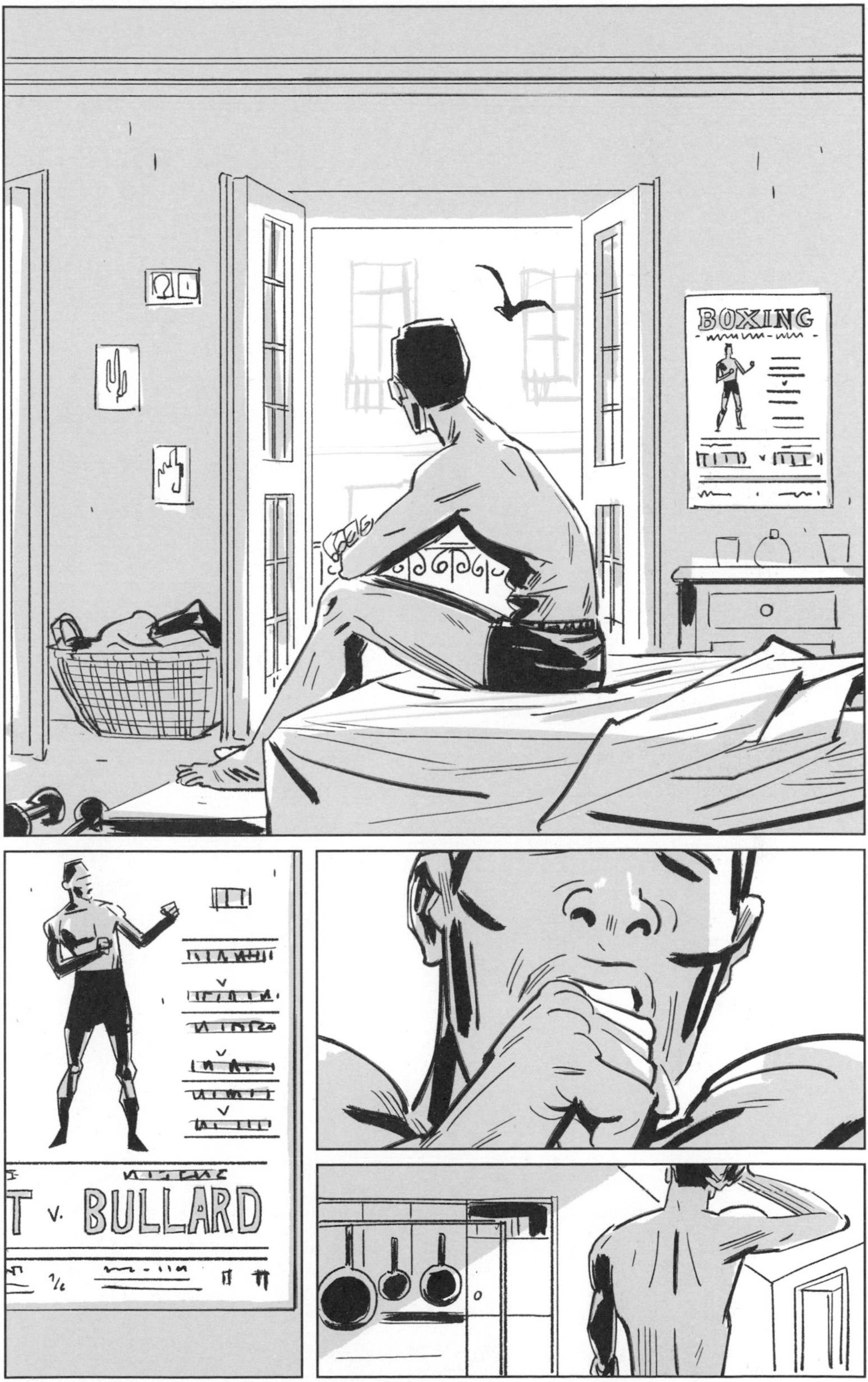
BOXING
T v. BULLARD

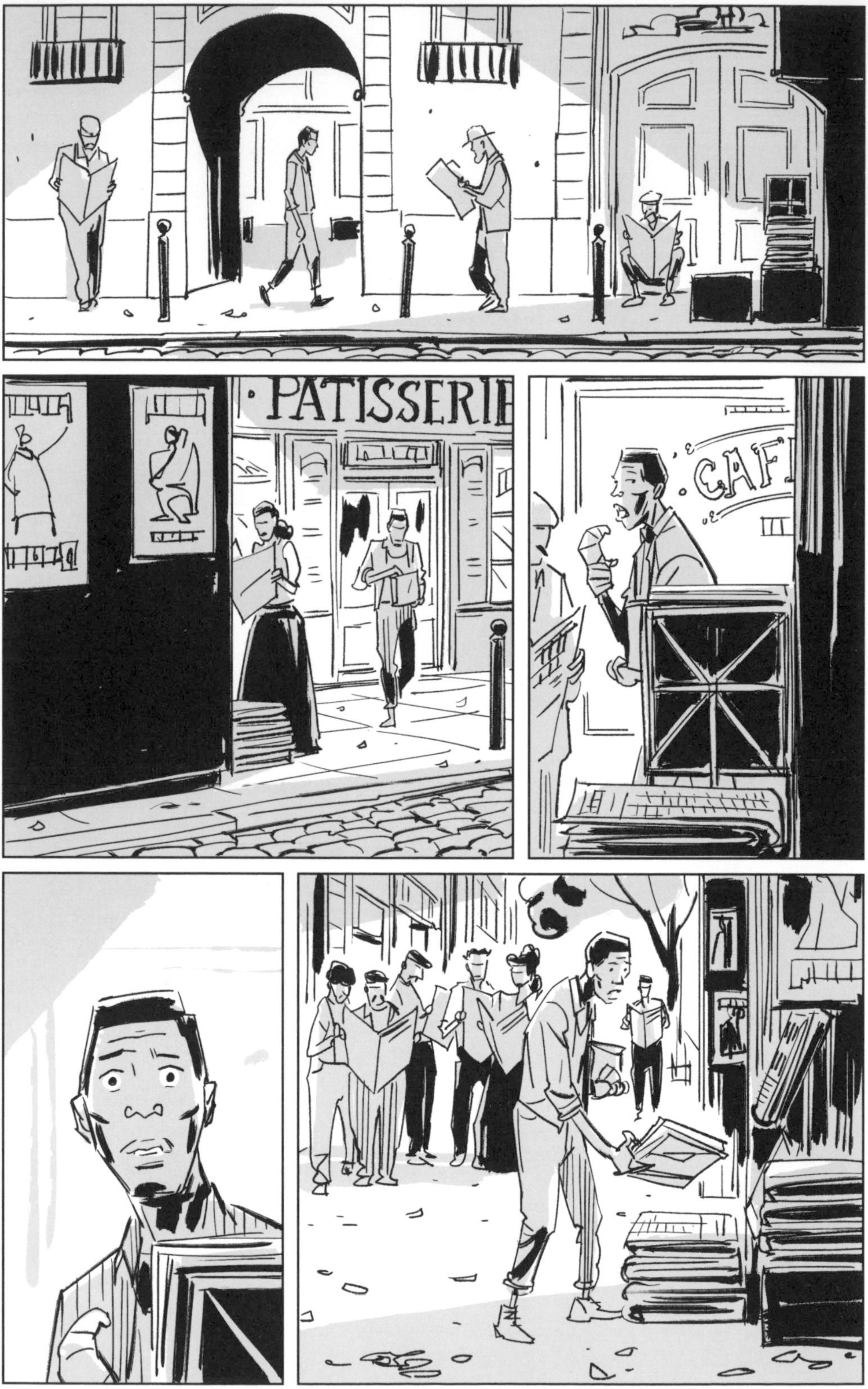
PATISSERI
CAF

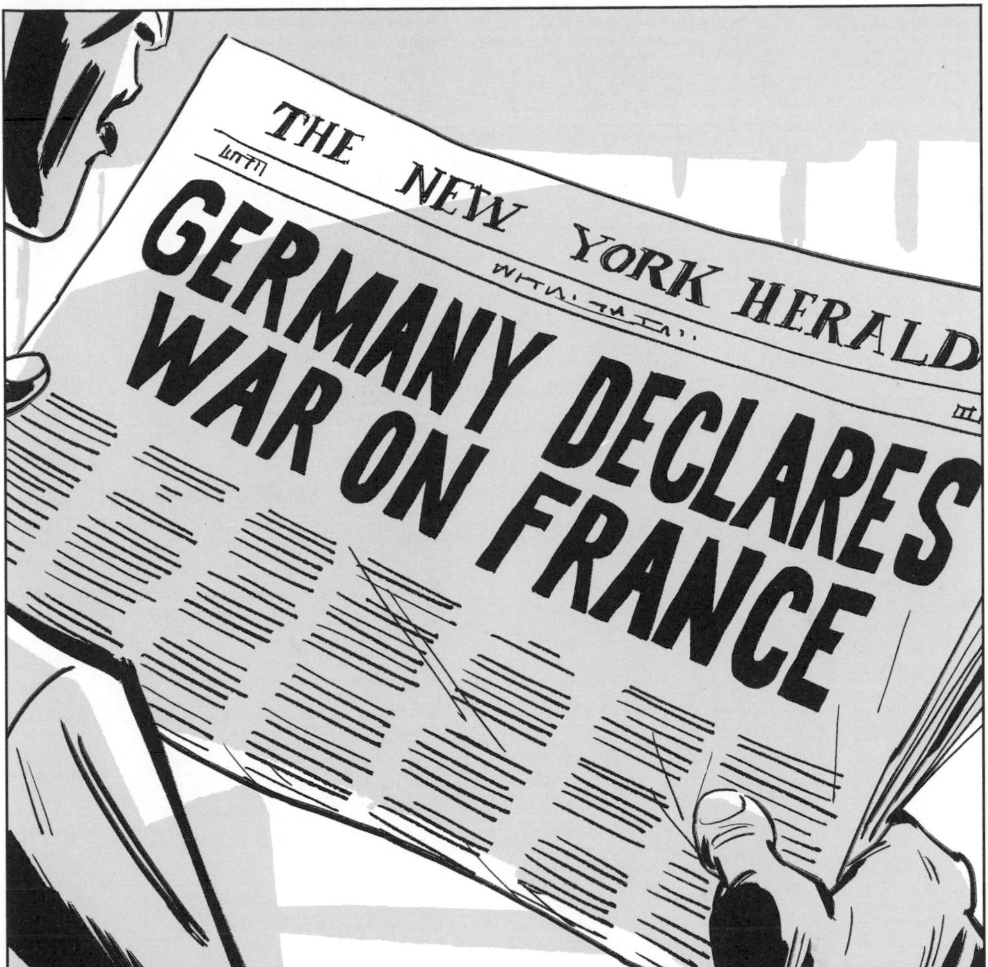
THE NEW YORK HERALD
GERMANY DECLARES WAR ON FRANCE

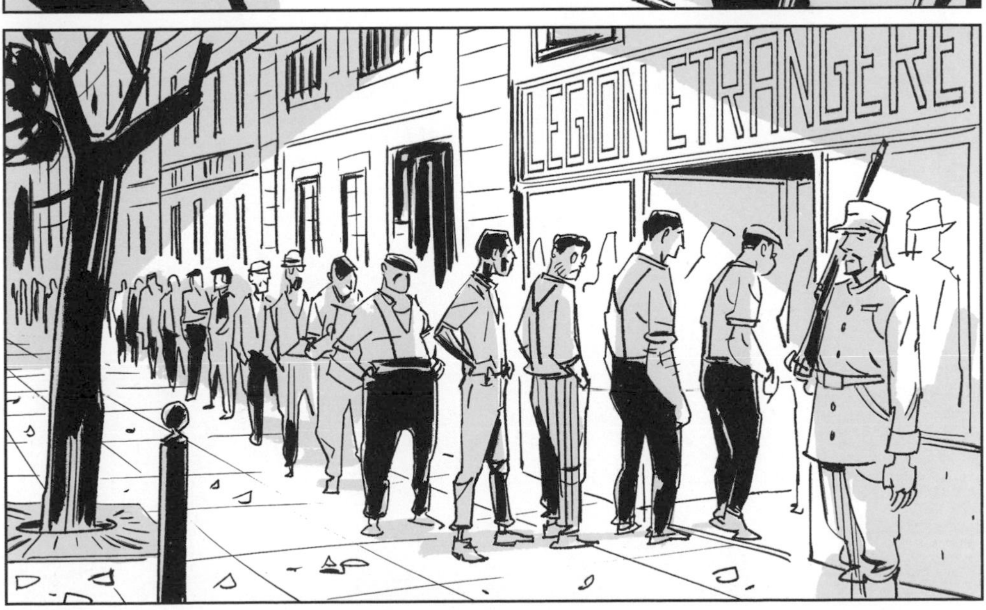
LEGION ETRANGERE

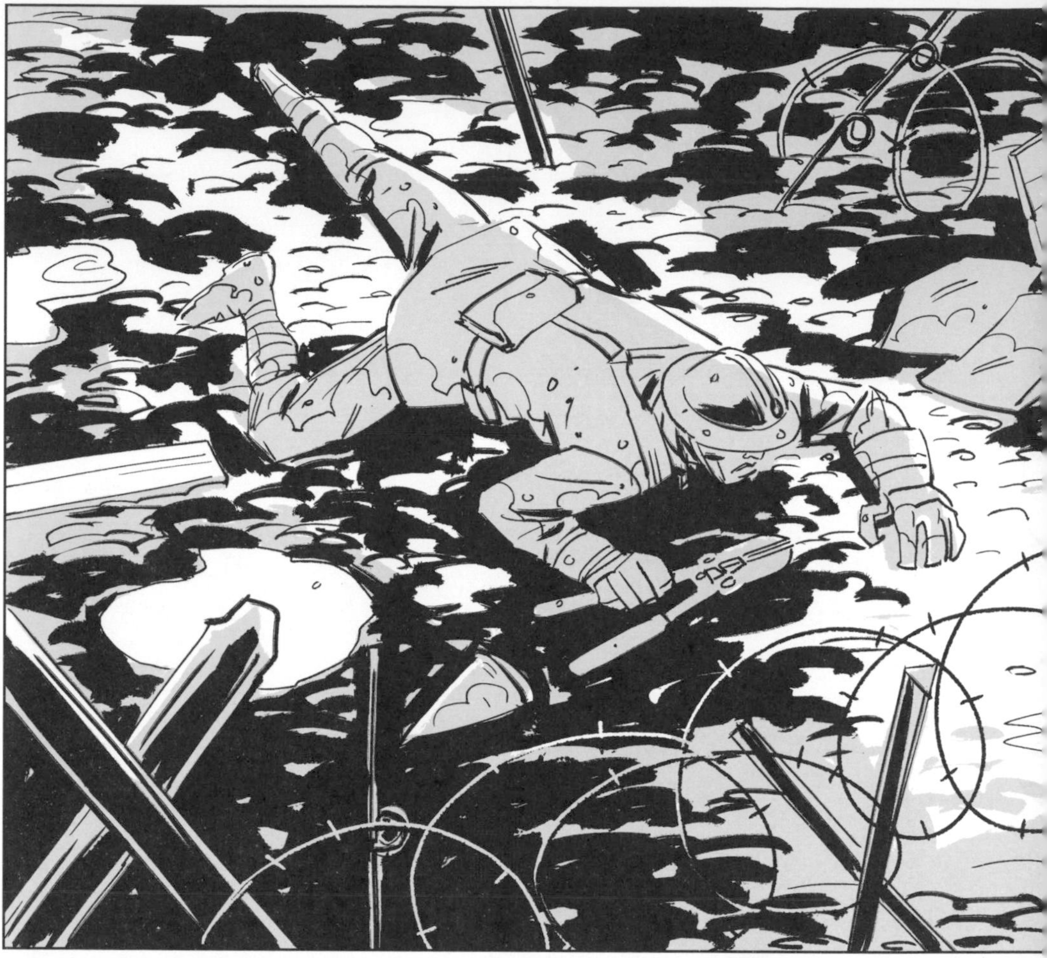

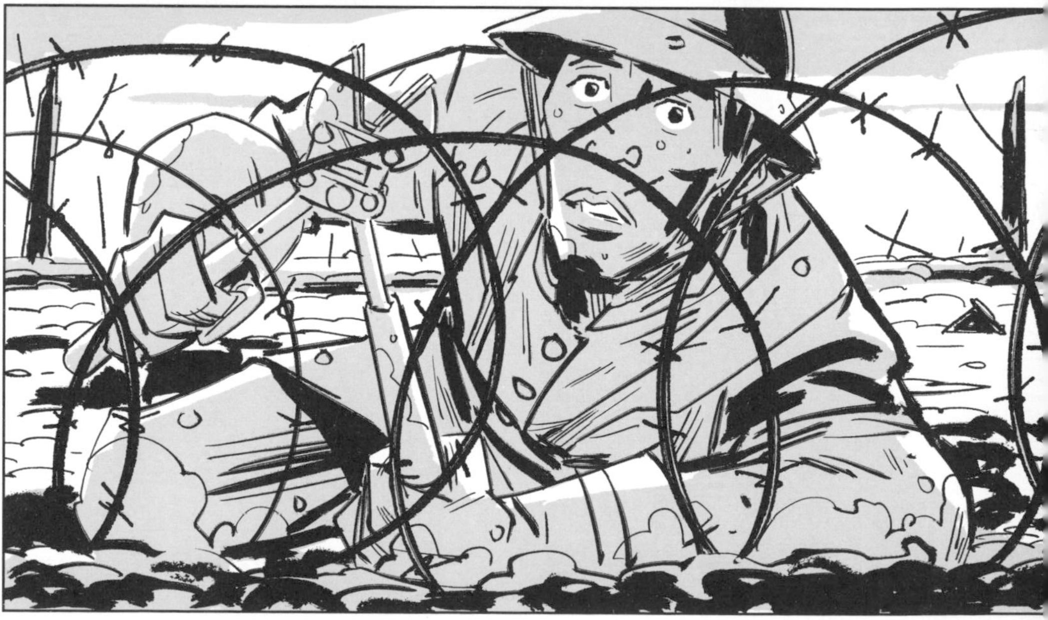

CHAPTER 6

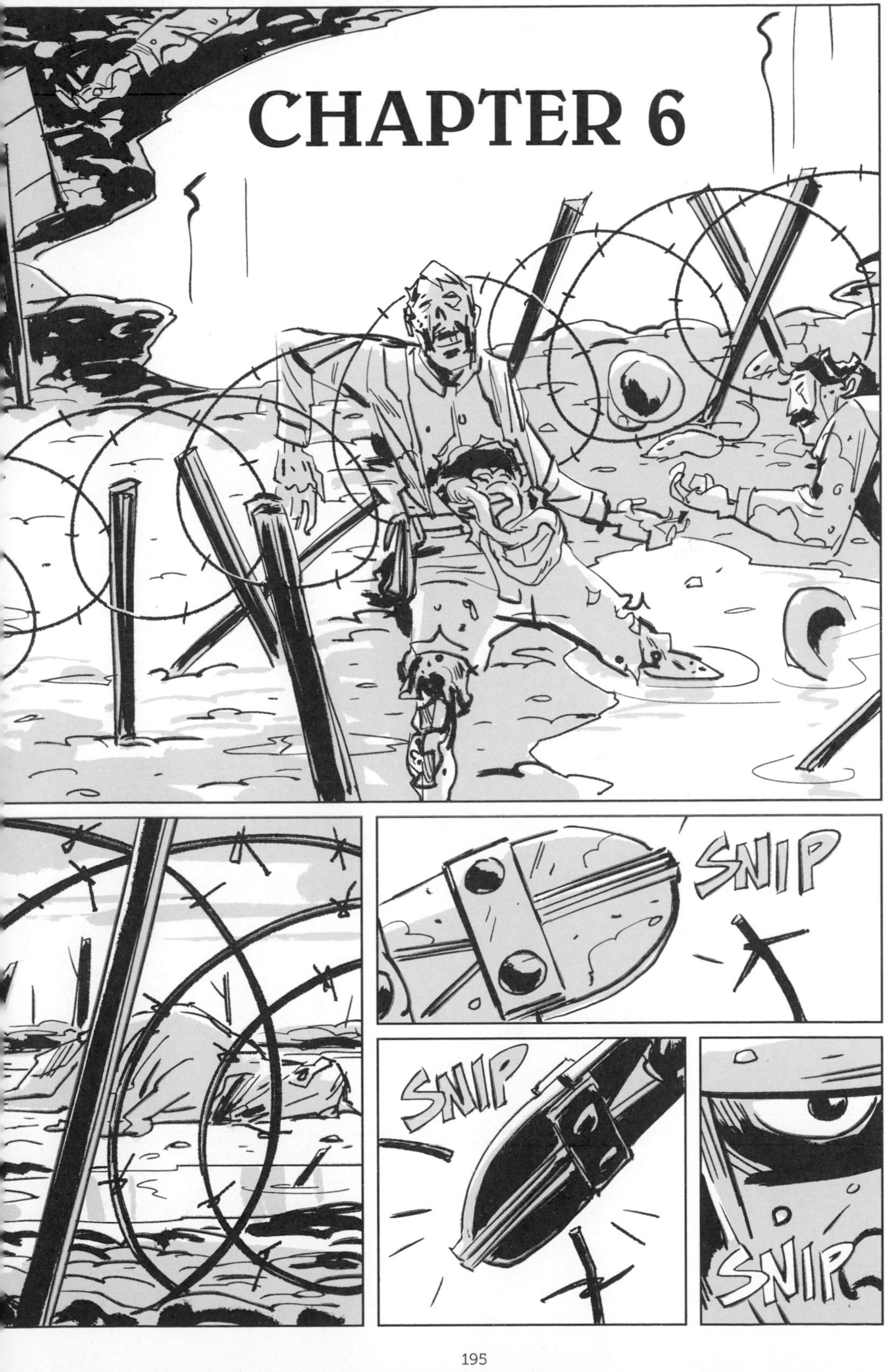
SNIP
SNIP
SNIP

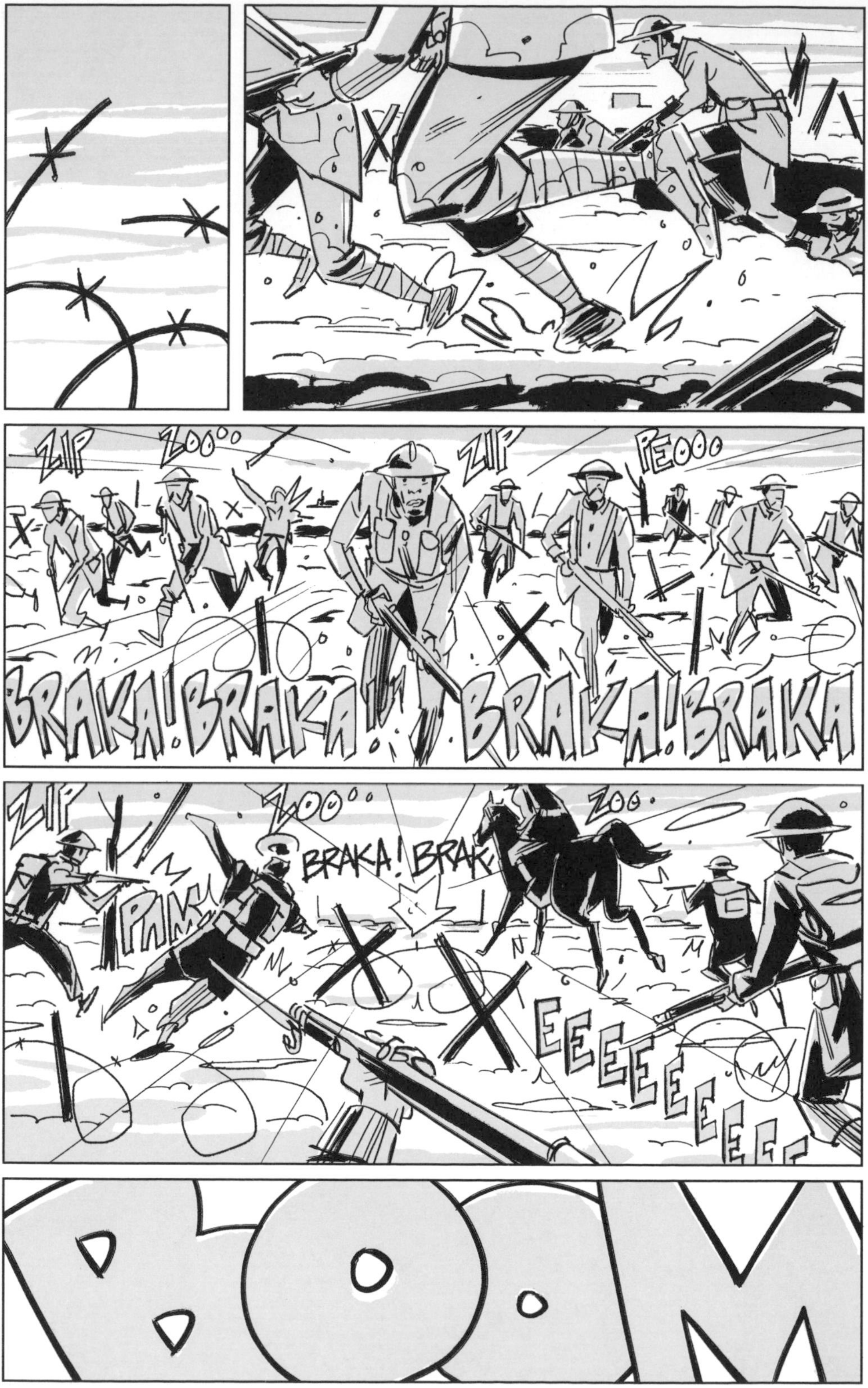
ZIP
ZOOOO
ZIP
PEOOO
BRAKA! BRAKA! BRAKA! BRAKA
ZIP
ZOOOO
ZOO
PAM
BRAKA! BRAK
EEEEEEEEE
BOOM

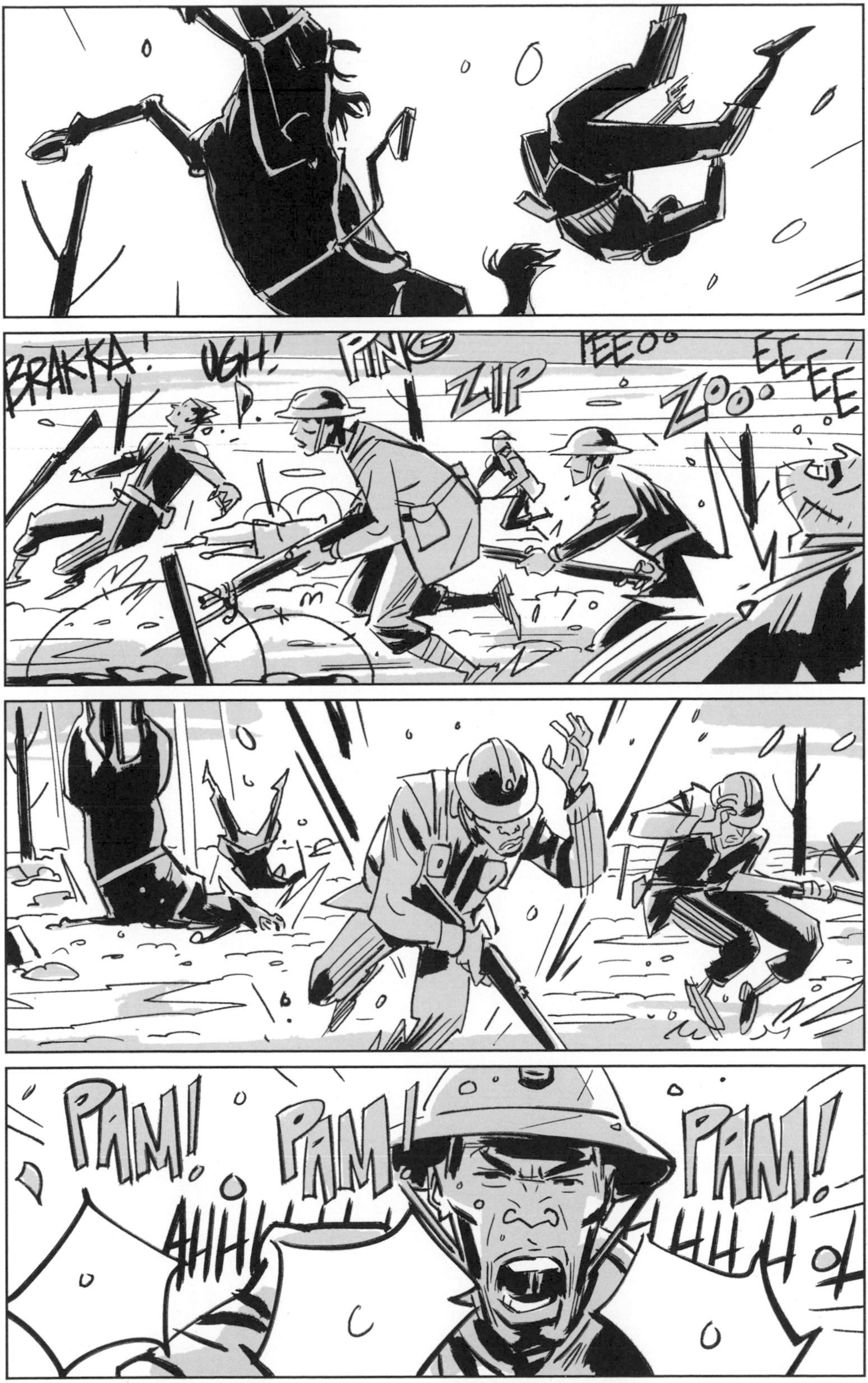
BRAKKA!
UGH!
PING
ZIP
PEEOO
ZOO
EEEEE
PAM!
PAM!
PAM!
AHH!

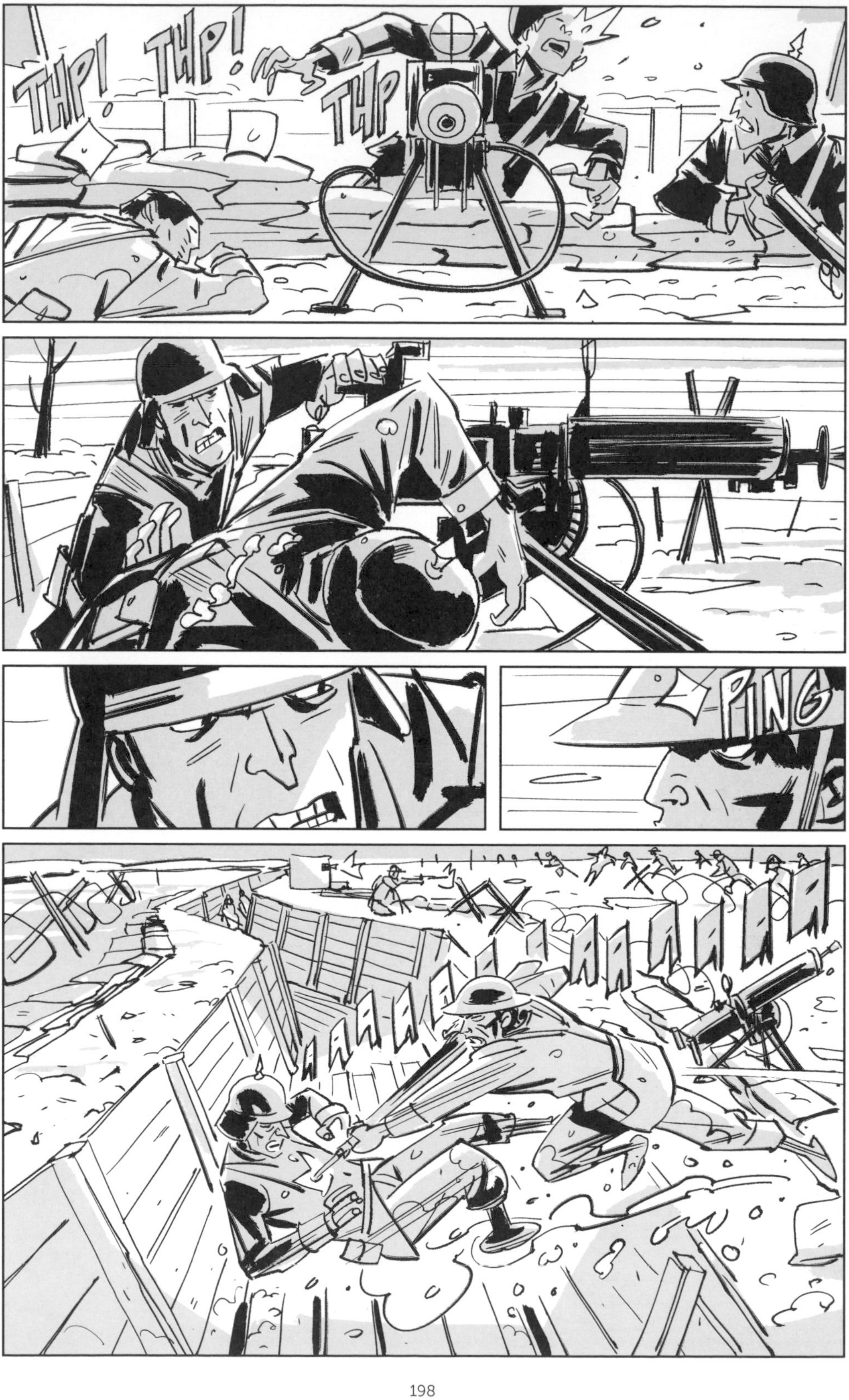
THP! THP!
THP
PING

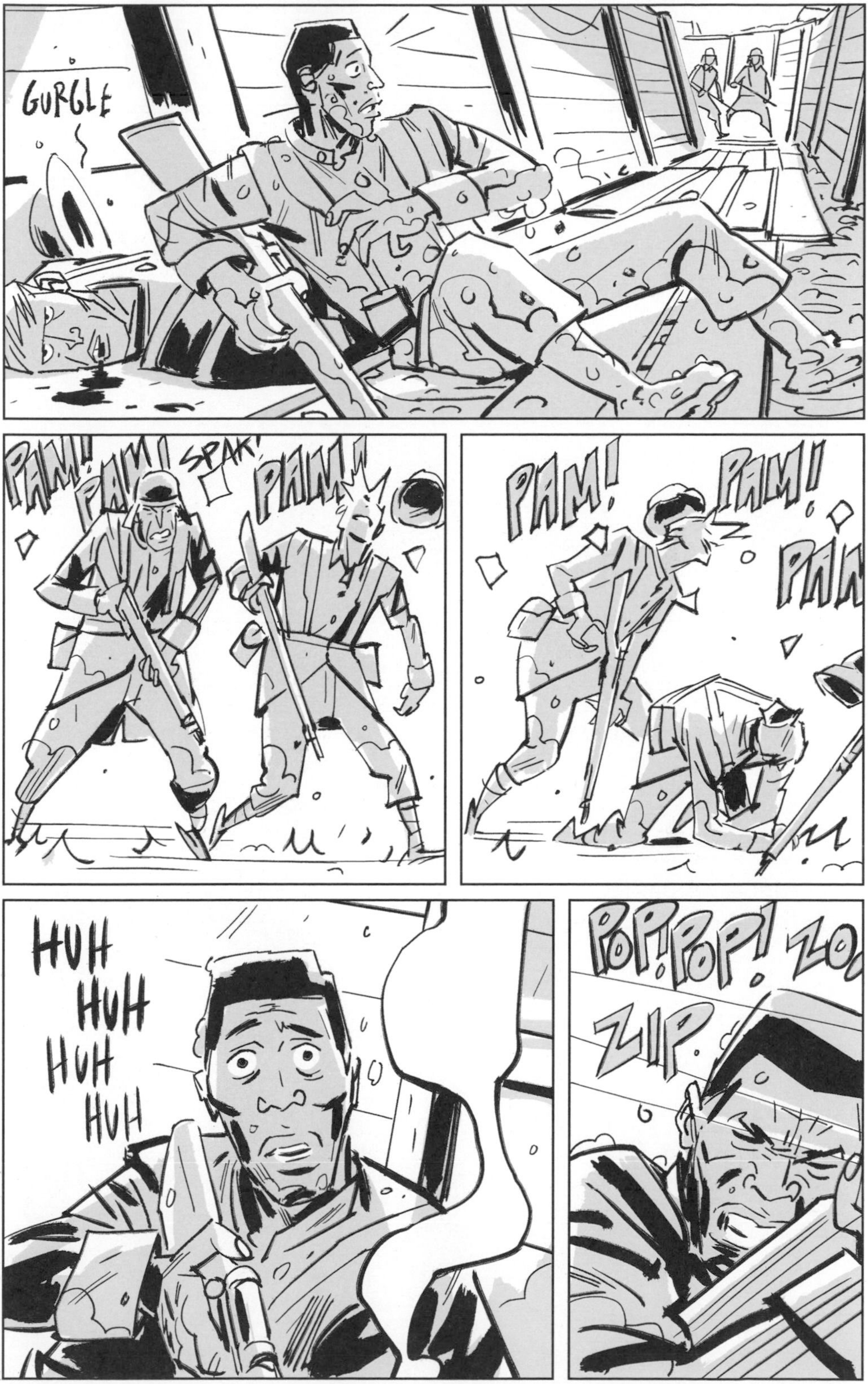
GURGLE
PAM!
PAM!
SPAK!
PAM!
PAM!
PAM!
PA
HUH
HUH
HUH
HUH
POP!
POP!
ZIP

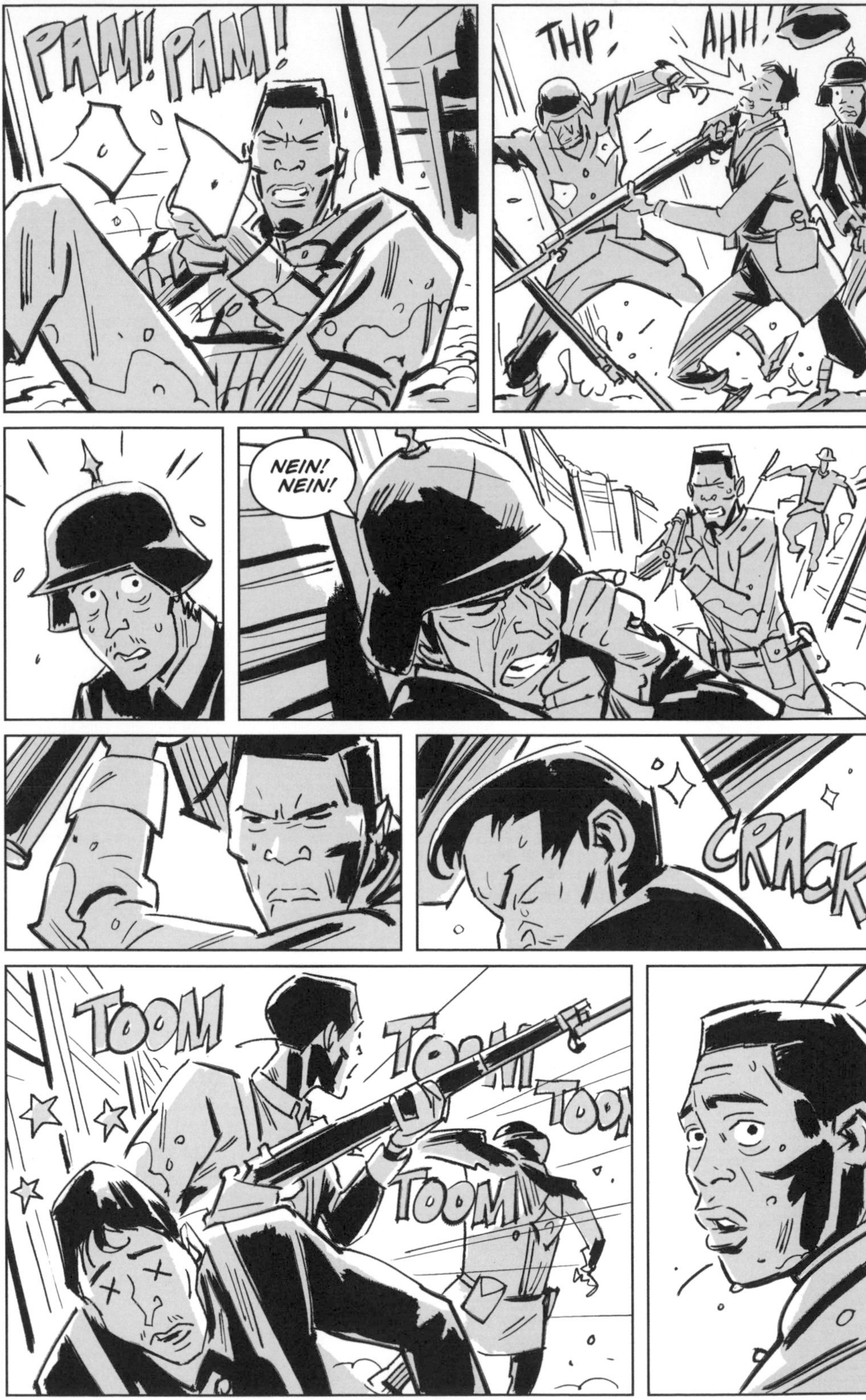
PAM! PAM!
THP!
AHH!
NEIN! NEIN!
CRACK
TOOM
TOOM
TOOM
TOOM

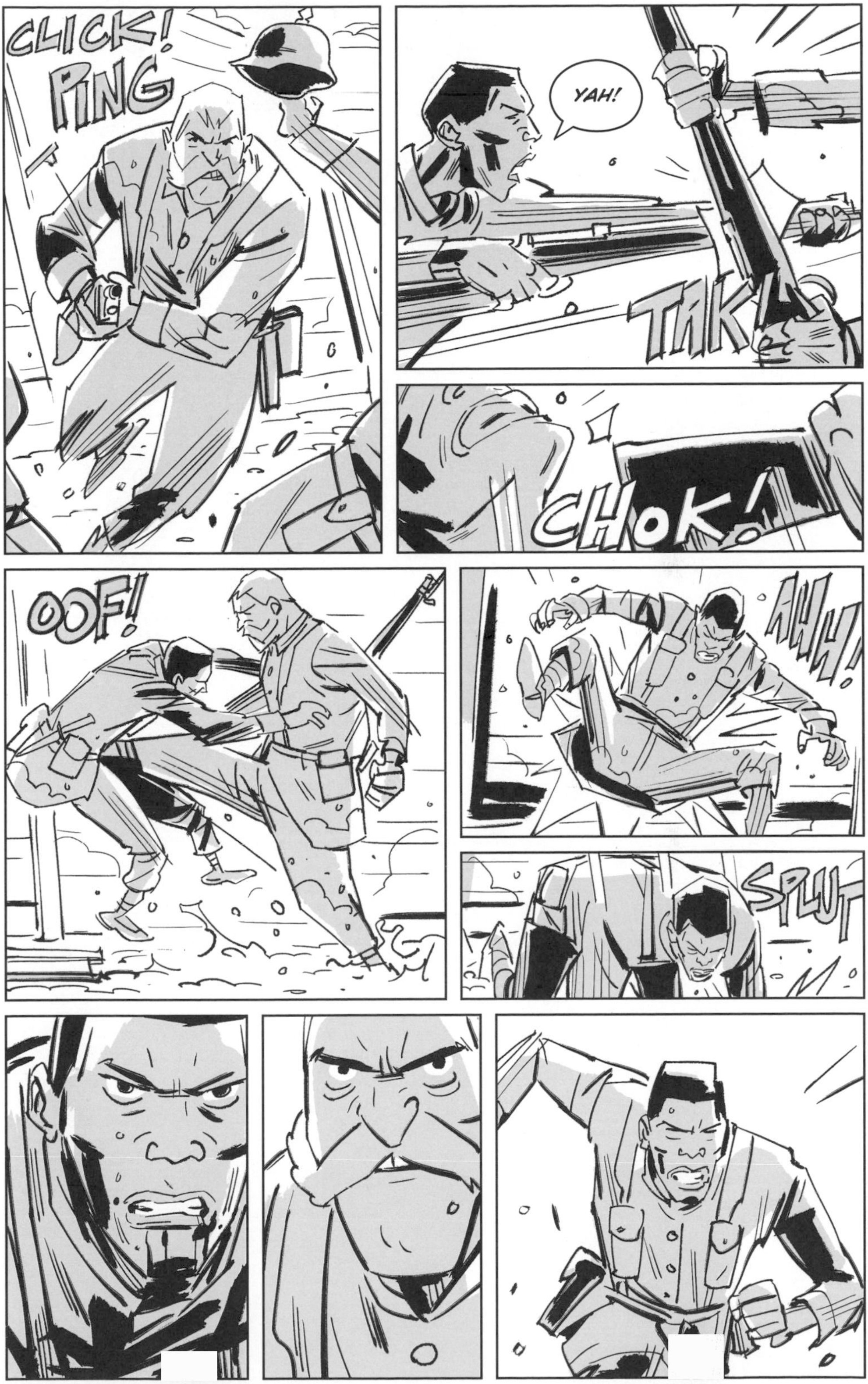
CLICK!
PING
YAH!
TAK!
CHOK!
OOF!
AHH!
SPLUT

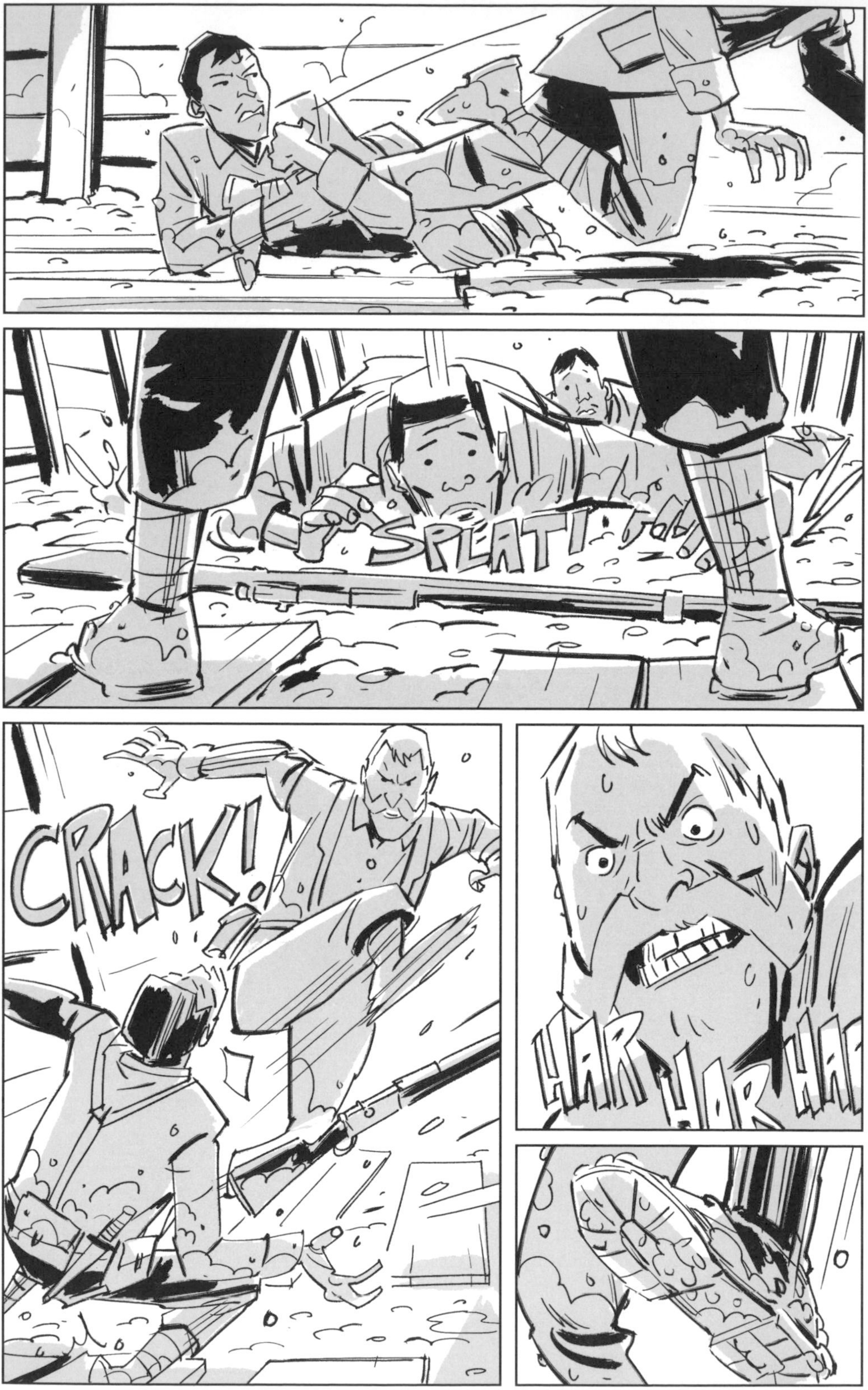
SPLAT!
CRACK!
HAR HAR HA

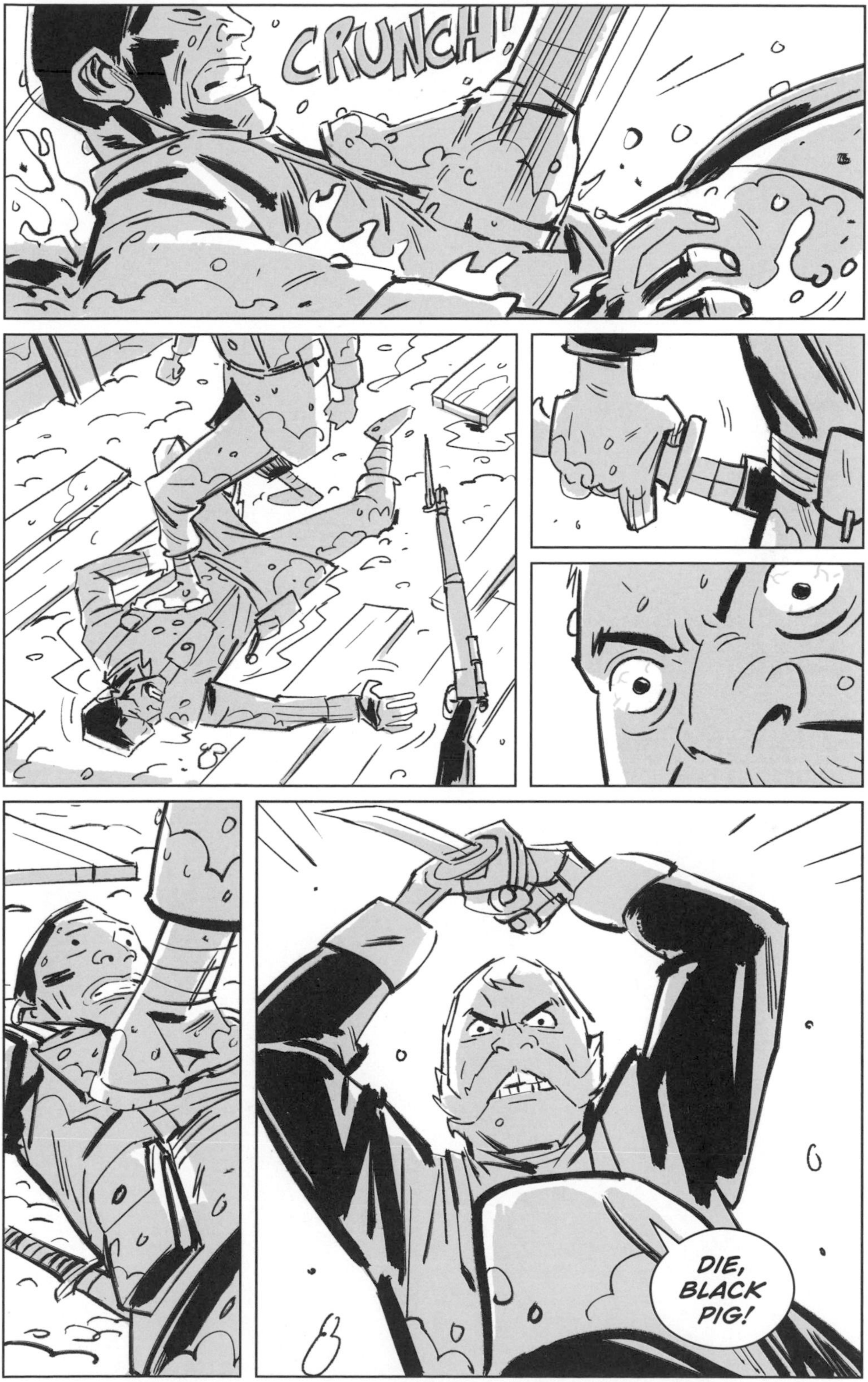
CRUNCH!
DIE, BLACK PIG!

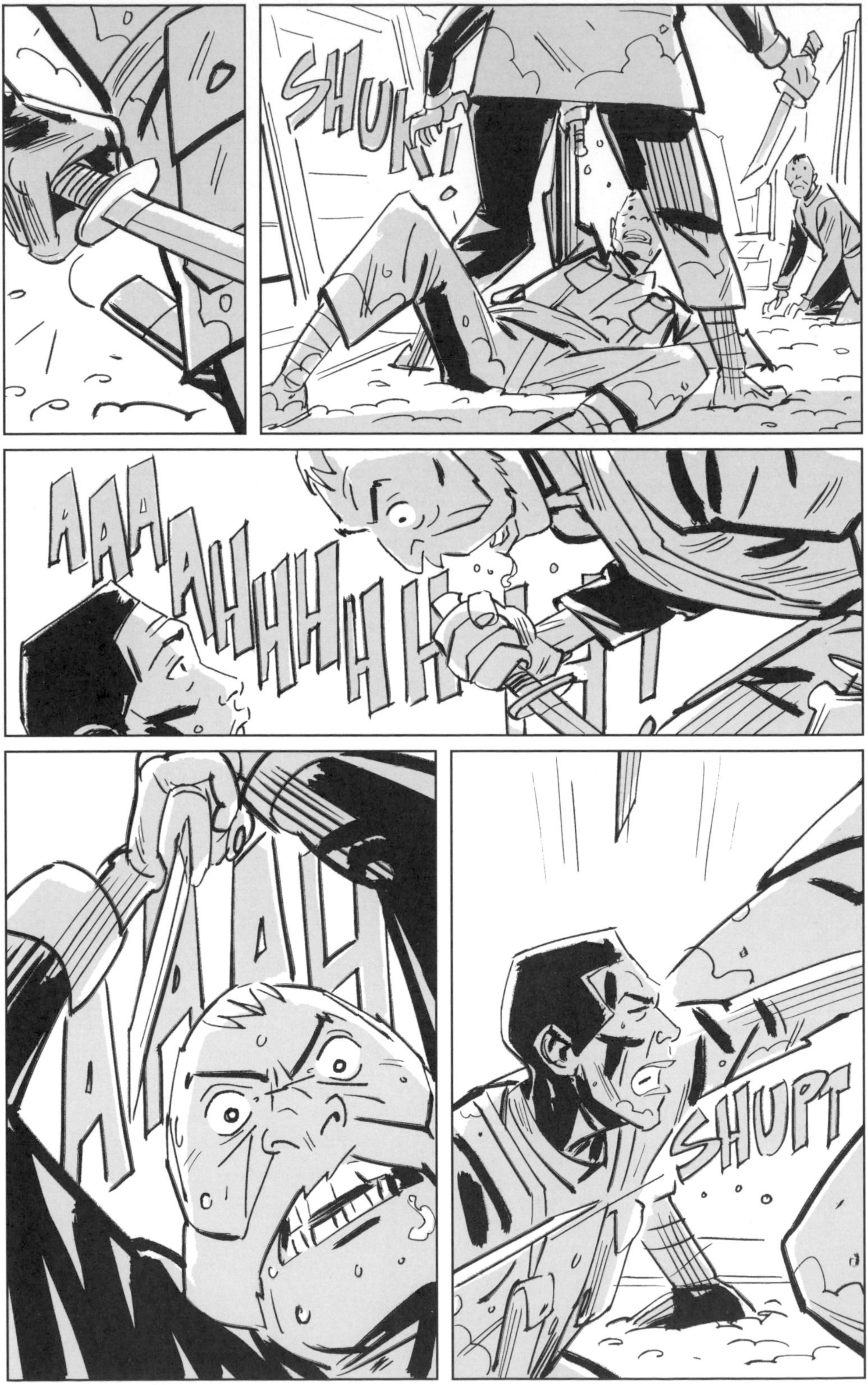
SHUKT
AAAAHHHHHH
AAAAH
SHUPT

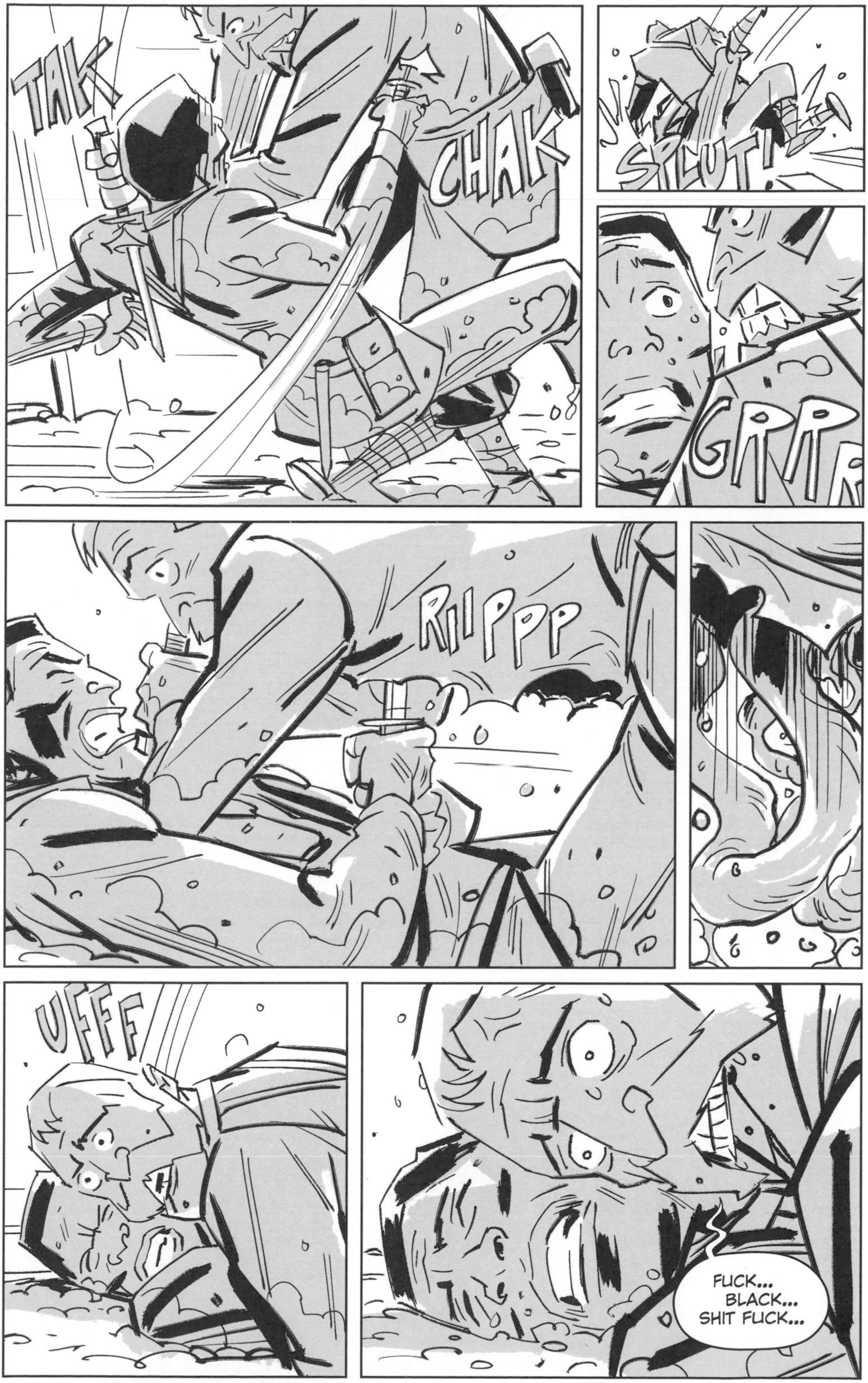
TAK
CHAK
SPLUT
GRRR
RIPPP
UFFF
FUCK... BLACK... SHIT FUCK...

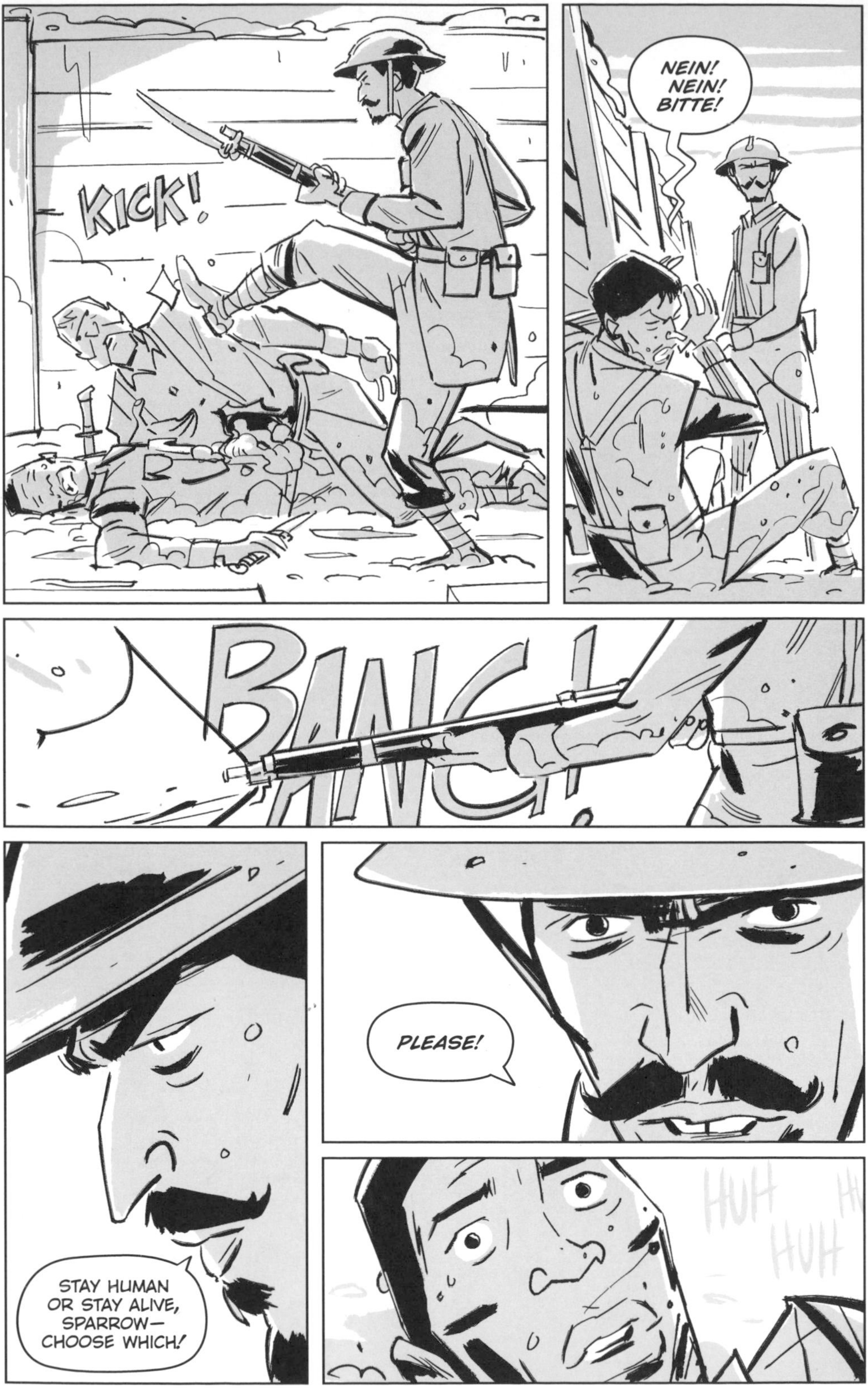
KICK!
NEIN! NEIN! BITTE!
BANG!
PLEASE!
STAY HUMAN OR STAY ALIVE, SPARROW—CHOOSE WHICH!
HUH HUH HUH

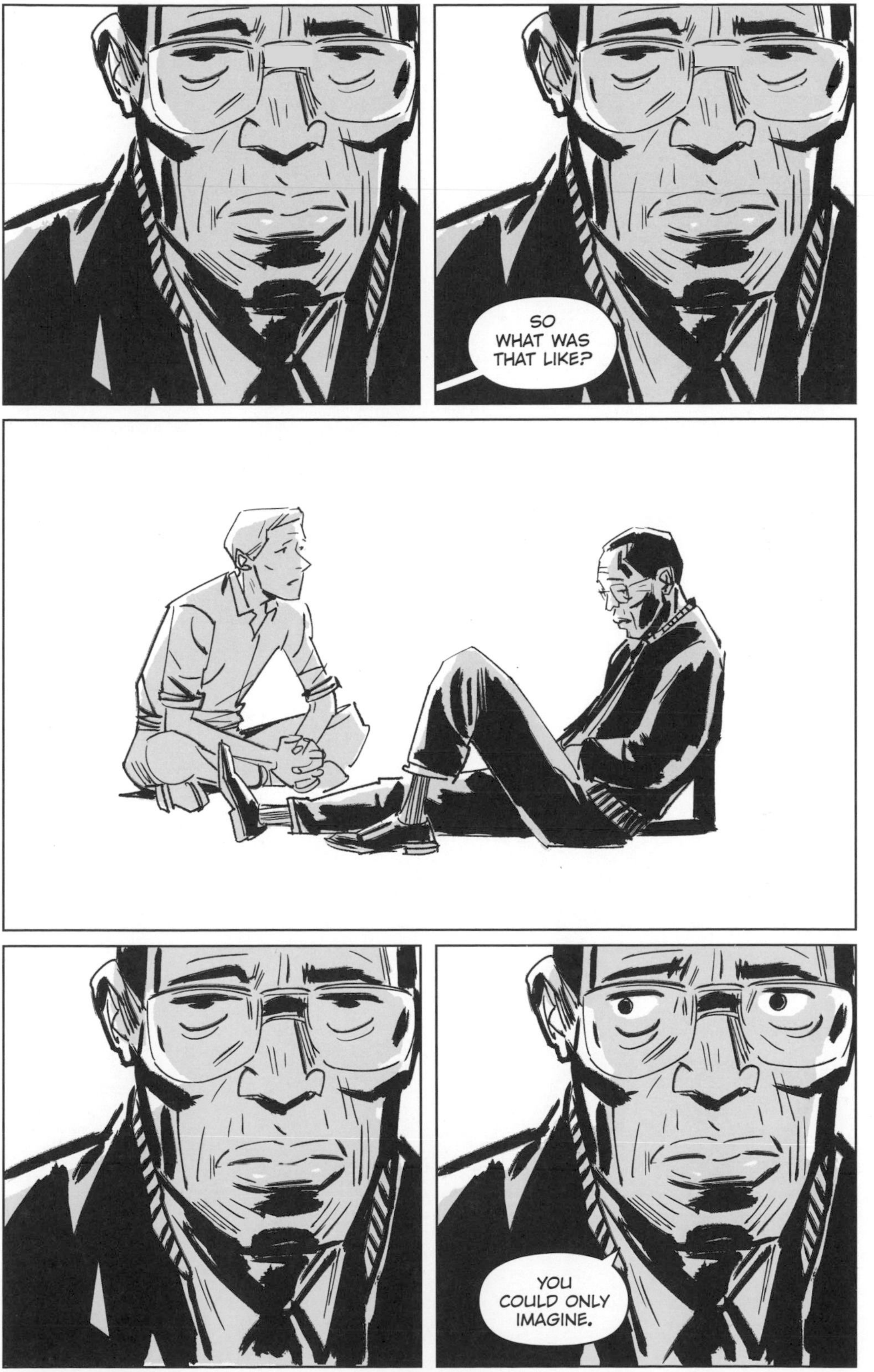
SO WHAT WAS THAT LIKE?
YOU COULD ONLY IMAGINE.

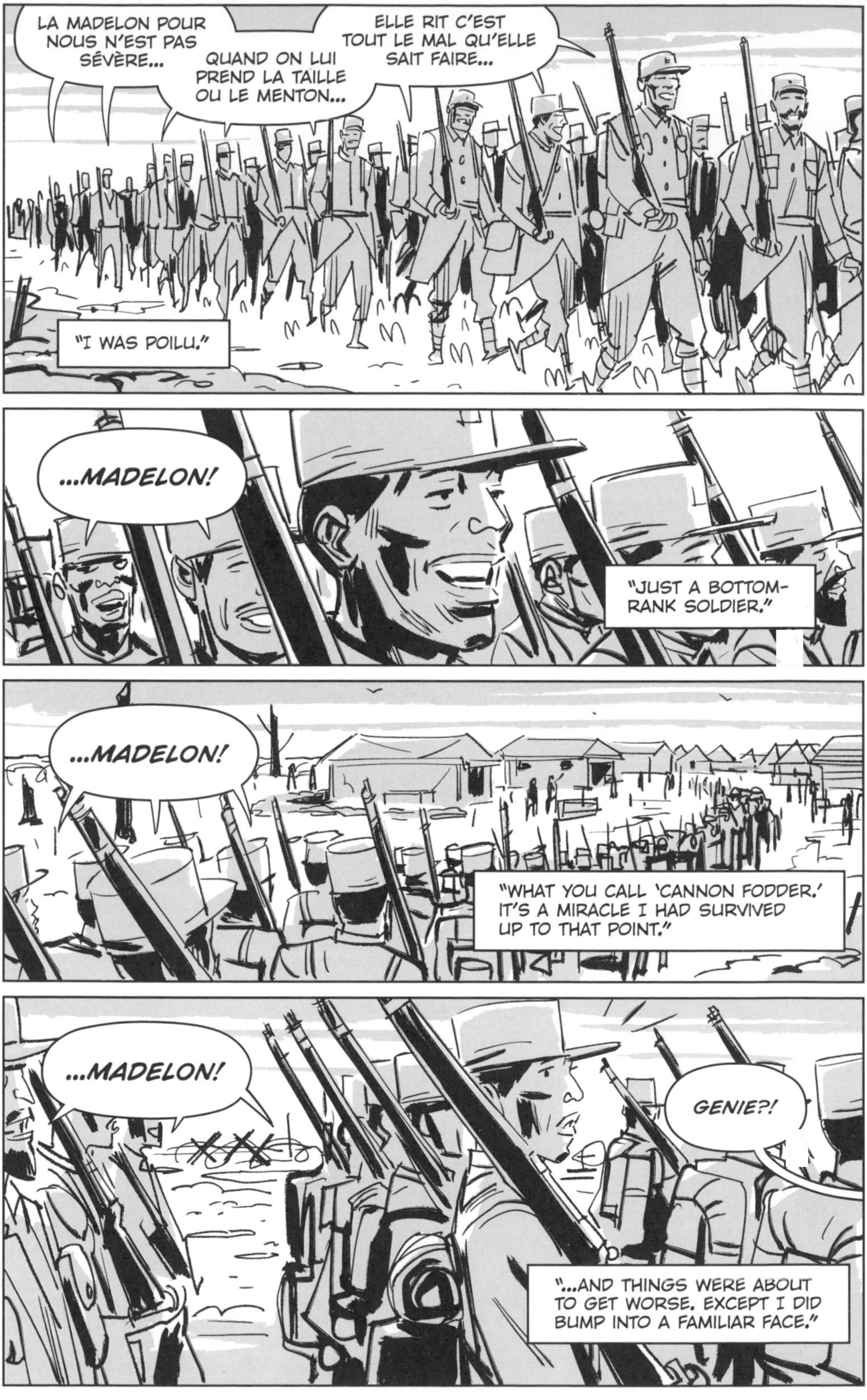
LA MADELON POUR NOUS N'EST PAS SÉVÈRE...
QUAND ON LUI PREND LA TAILLE OU LE MENTON...
ELLE RIT C'EST TOUT LE MAL QU'ELLE SAIT FAIRE...
"I WAS POILU."
...MADELON!
"JUST A BOTTOM-RANK SOLDIER."
...MADELON!
"WHAT YOU CALL 'CANNON FODDER.' IT'S A MIRACLE I HAD SURVIVED UP TO THAT POINT."
...MADELON!
GENIE?!
"...AND THINGS WERE ABOUT TO GET WORSE. EXCEPT I DID BUMP INTO A FAMILIAR FACE."

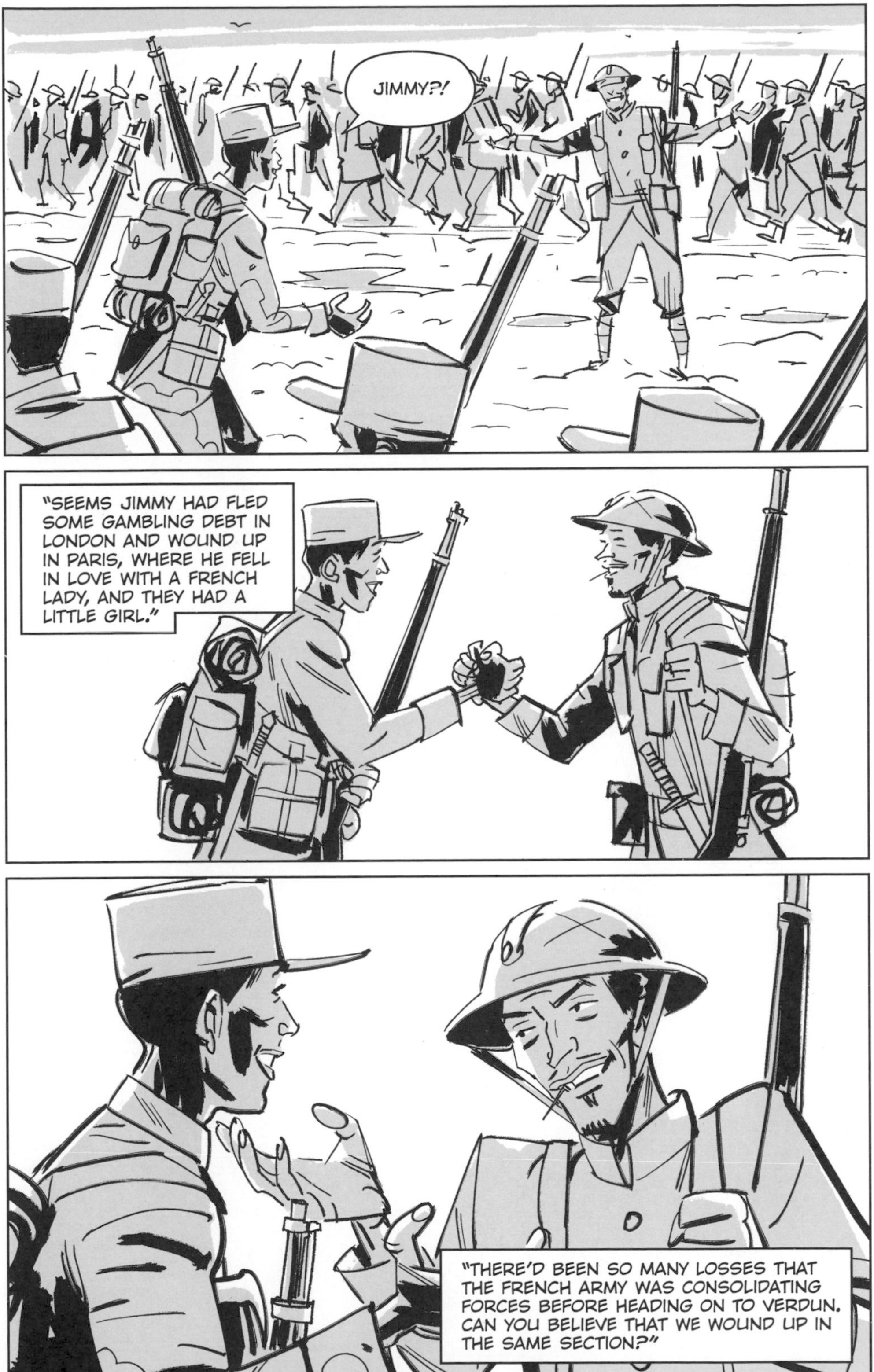
JIMMY?!
"SEEMS JIMMY HAD FLED SOME GAMBLING DEBT IN LONDON AND WOUND UP IN PARIS, WHERE HE FELL IN LOVE WITH A FRENCH LADY, AND THEY HAD A LITTLE GIRL."
"THERE'D BEEN SO MANY LOSSES THAT THE FRENCH ARMY WAS CONSOLIDATING FORCES BEFORE HEADING ON TO VERDUN. CAN YOU BELIEVE THAT WE WOUND UP IN THE SAME SECTION?"

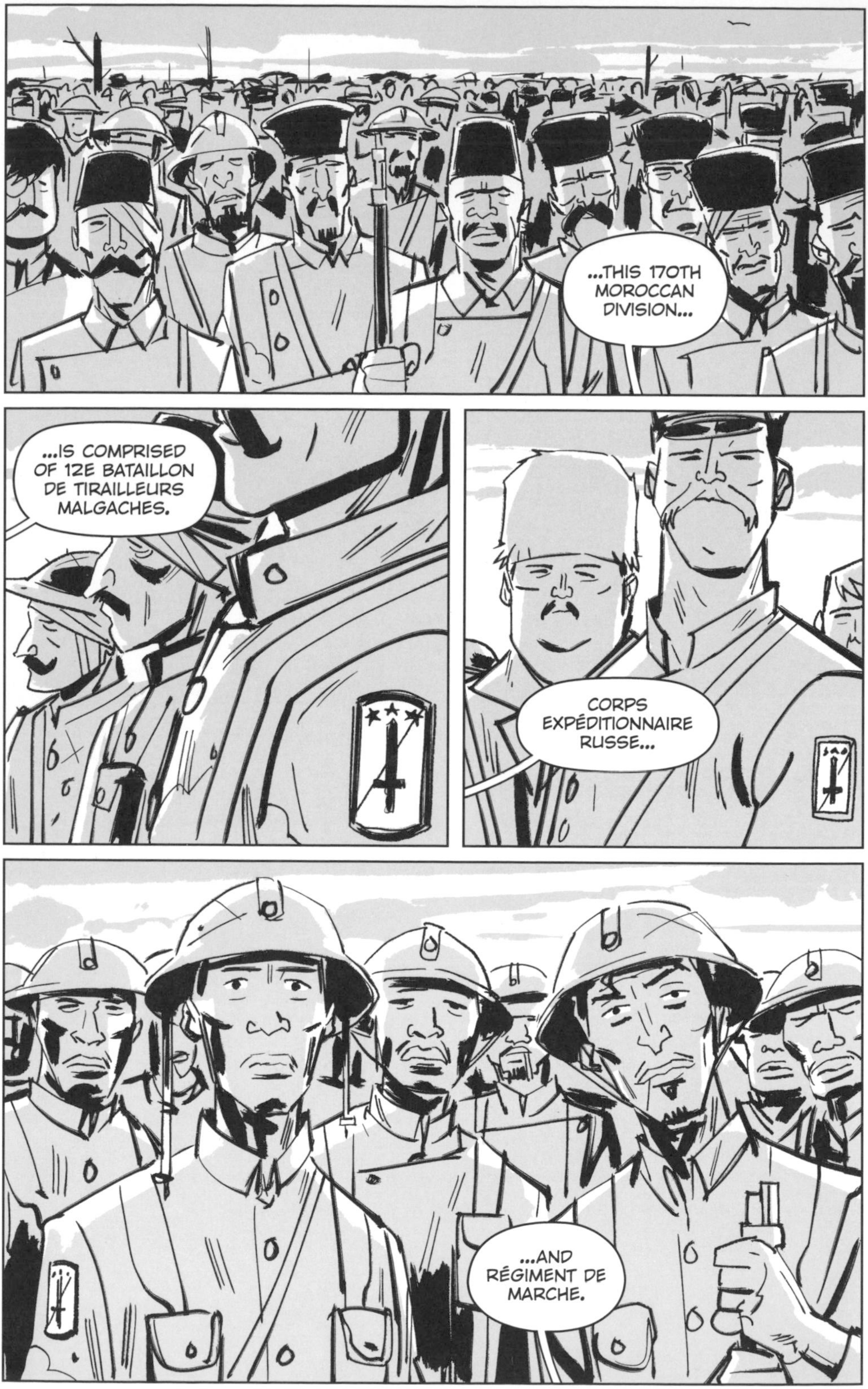
...THIS 170TH MOROCCAN DIVISION...
...IS COMPRISED OF 12E BATAILLON DE TIRAILLEURS MALGACHES.
CORPS EXPÉDITIONNAIRE RUSSE...
...AND RÉGIMENT DE MARCHE.

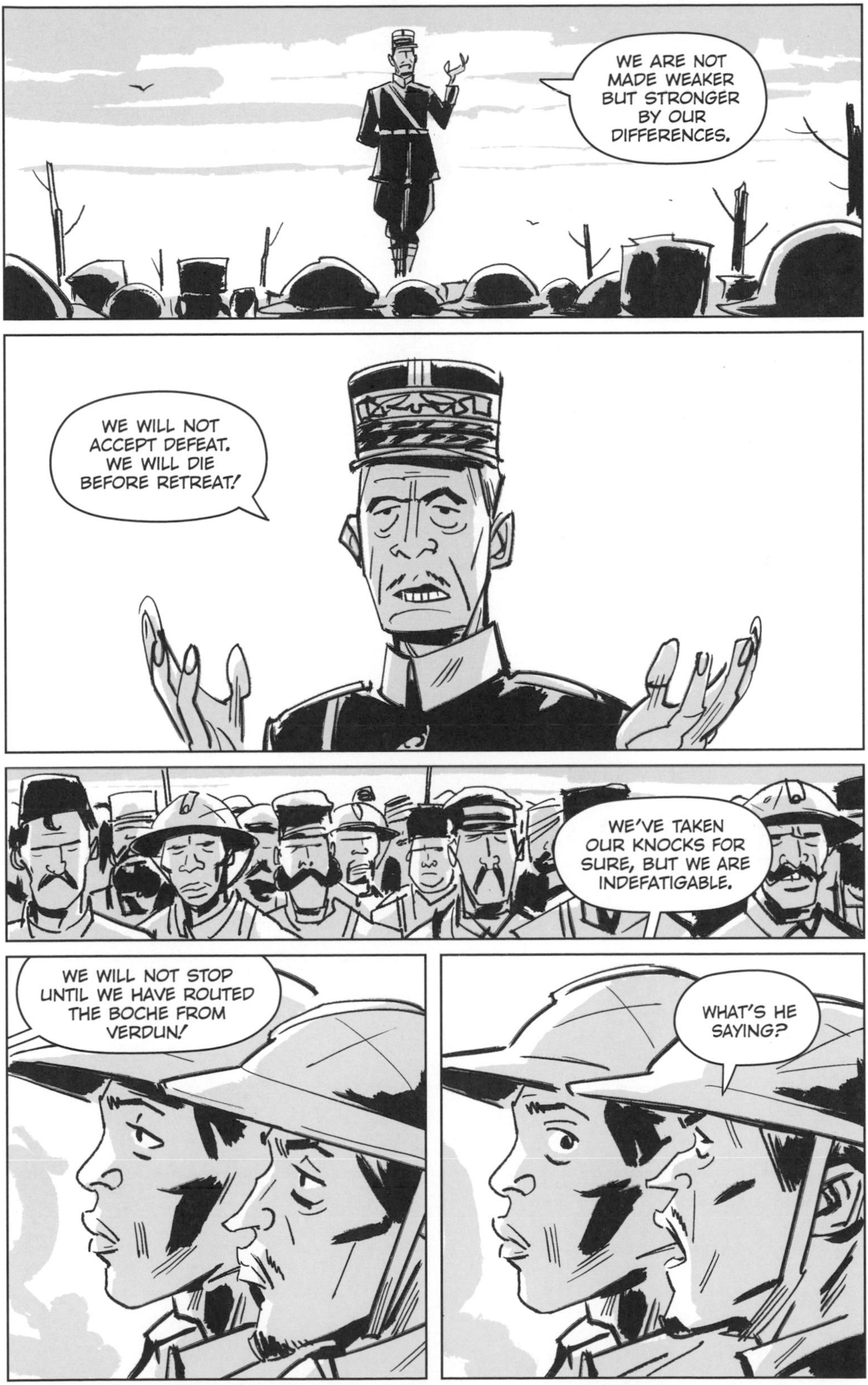
WE ARE NOT MADE WEAKER BUT STRONGER BY OUR DIFFERENCES.
WE WILL NOT ACCEPT DEFEAT. WE WILL DIE BEFORE RETREAT!
WE'VE TAKEN OUR KNOCKS FOR SURE, BUT WE ARE INDEFATIGABLE.
WE WILL NOT STOP UNTIL WE HAVE ROUTED THE BOCHE FROM VERDUN!
WHAT'S HE SAYING?

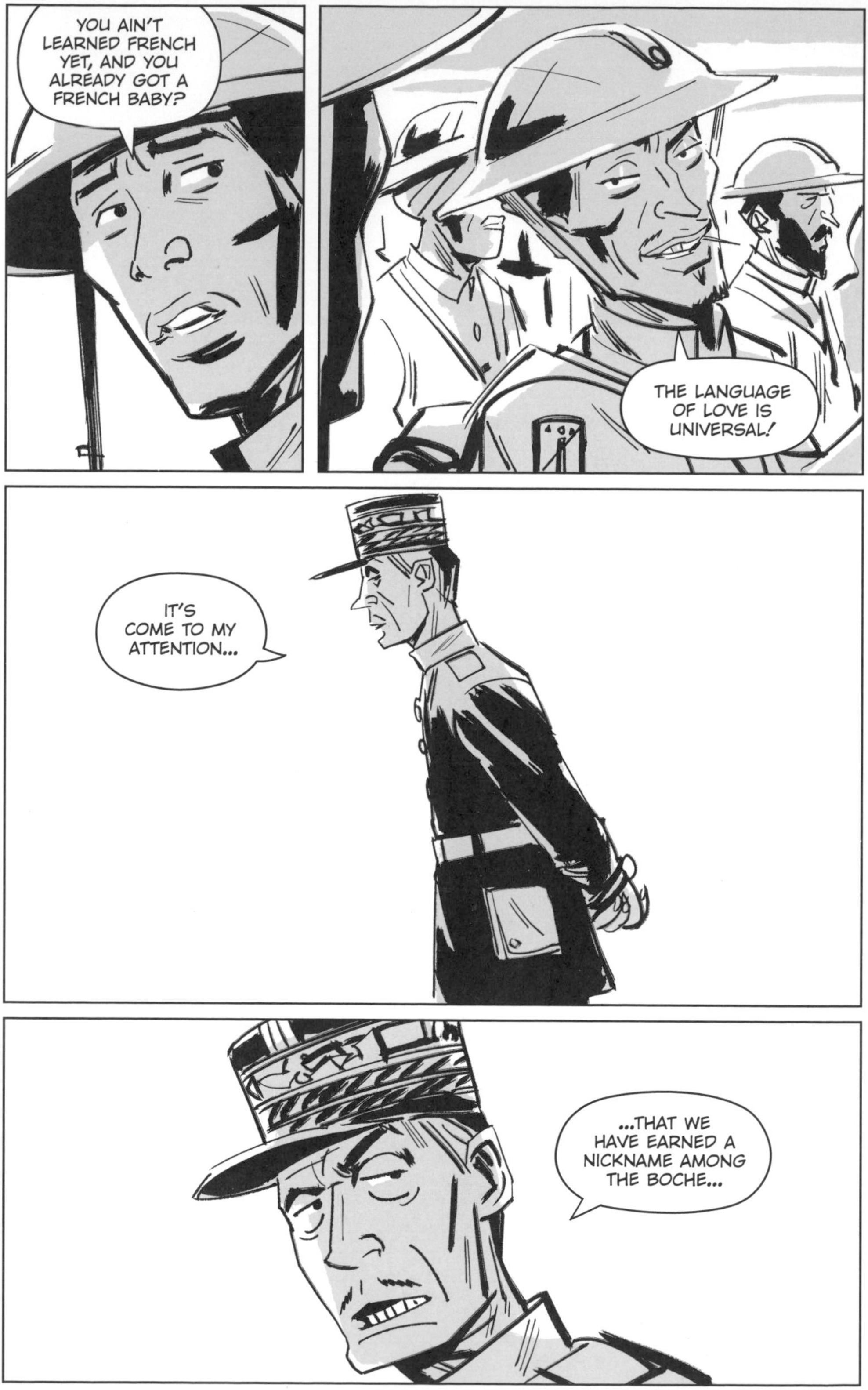
YOU AIN'T LEARNED FRENCH YET, AND YOU ALREADY GOT A FRENCH BABY?
THE LANGUAGE OF LOVE IS UNIVERSAL!
IT'S COME TO MY ATTENTION...
...THAT WE HAVE EARNED A NICKNAME AMONG THE BOCHE...

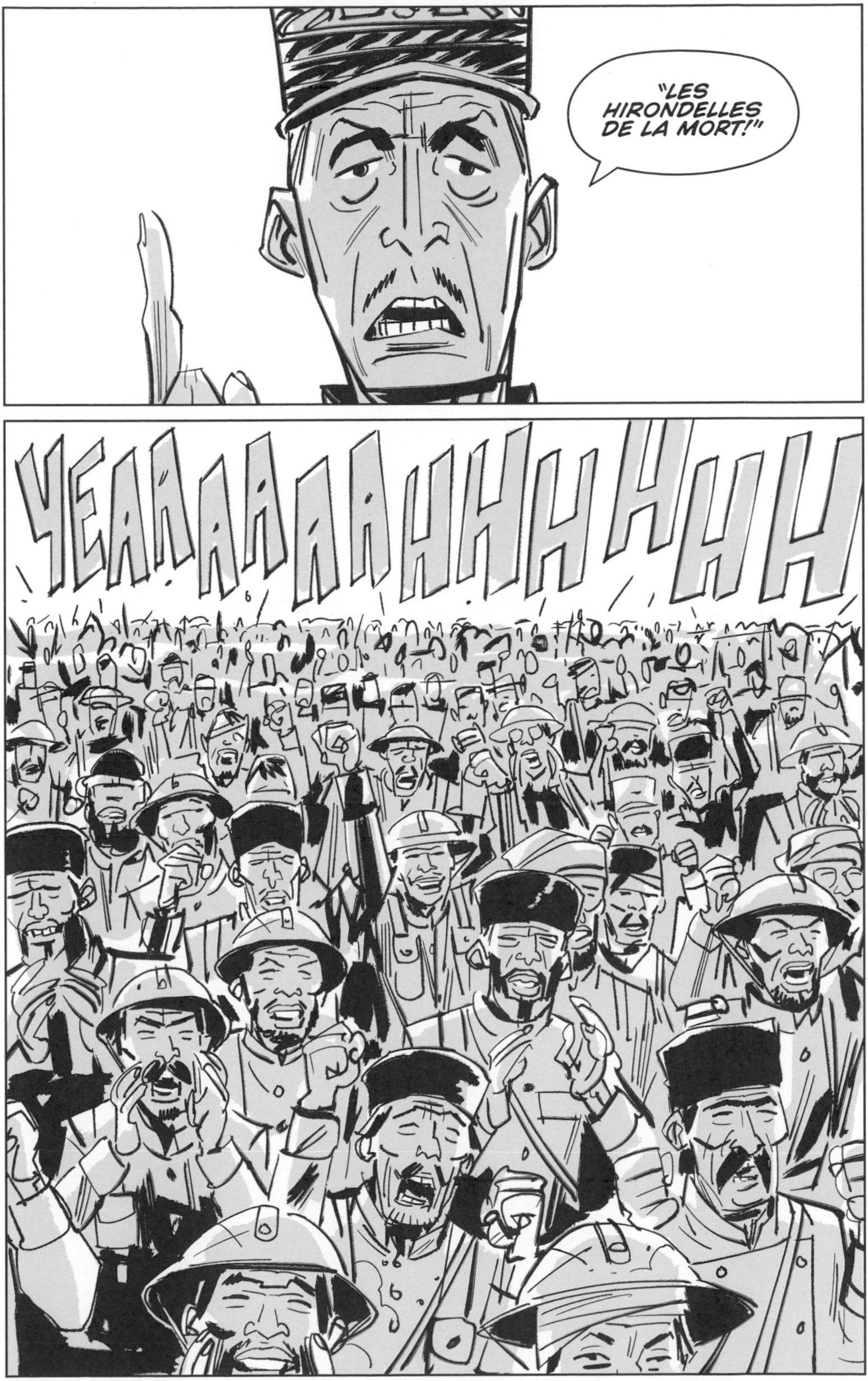
"LES HIRONDELLES DE LA MORT!"
YEAAAAAAHHHHHHHH

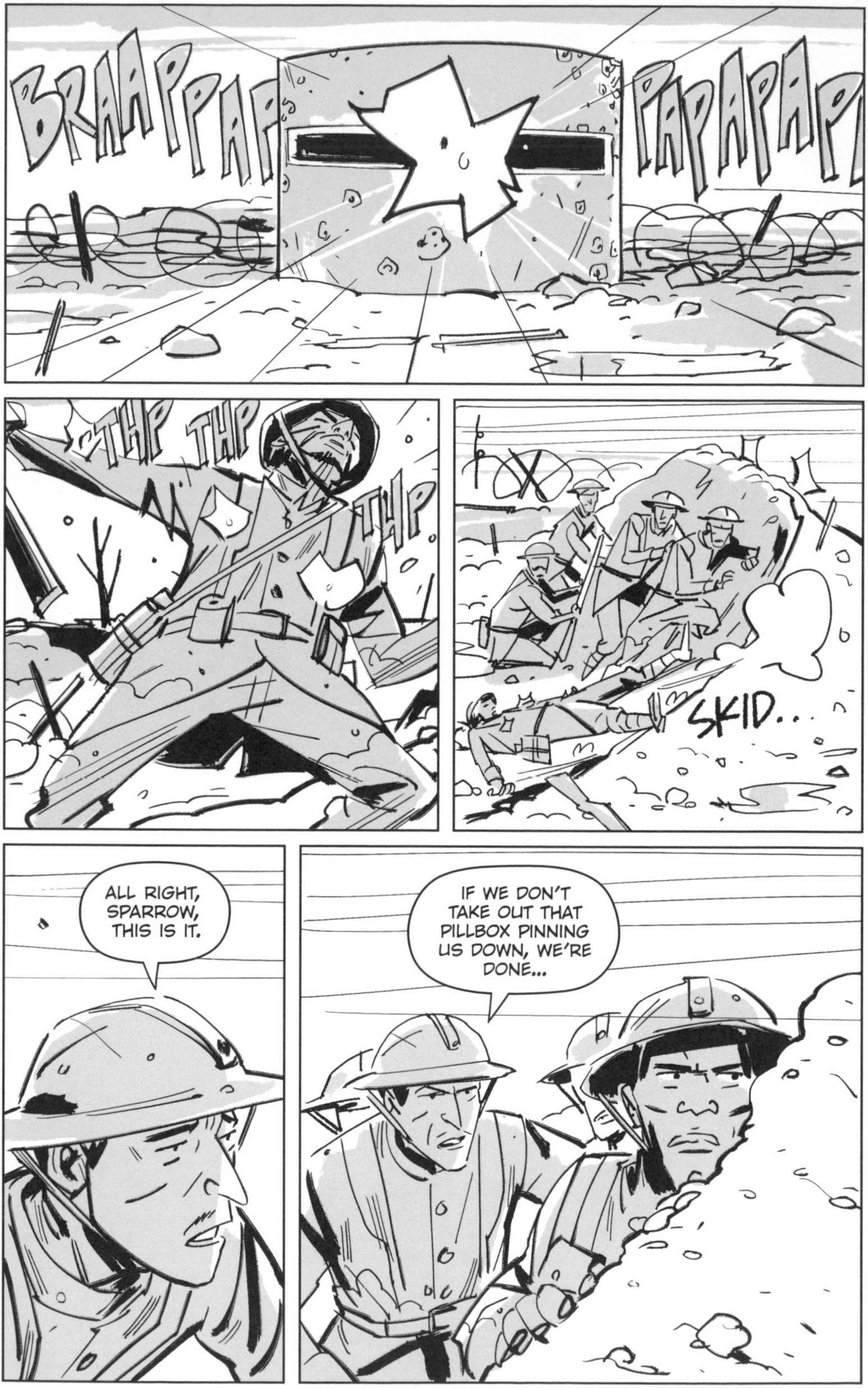
BRAAPPAP
PAPAPAP
THP THP
THP
SKID...
ALL RIGHT, SPARROW, THIS IS IT.
IF WE DON'T TAKE OUT THAT PILLBOX PINNING US DOWN, WE'RE DONE...

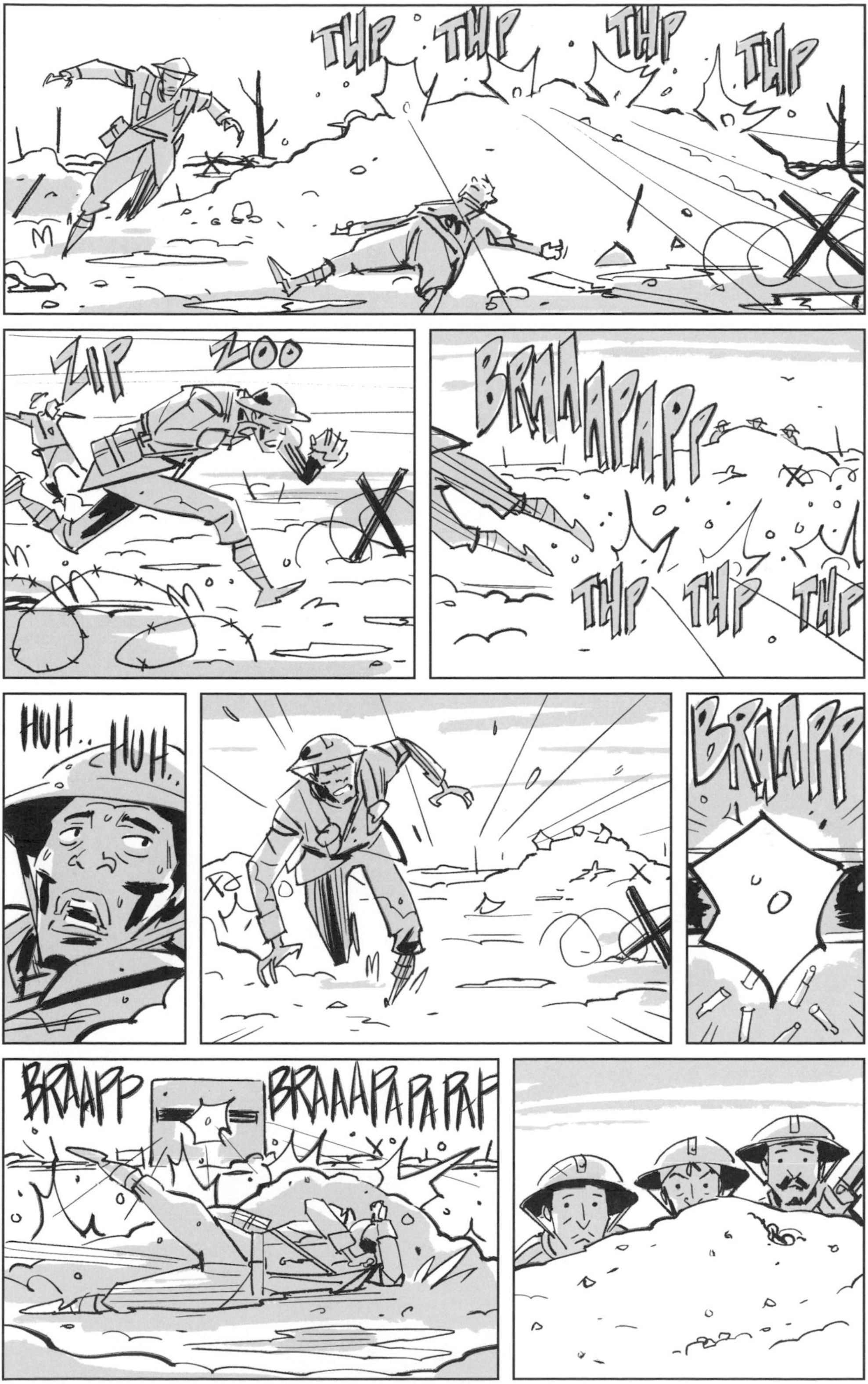
THP THP THP THP
ZIP ZOO
BRAAAAPAPP
THP THP THP
HUH.. HUH..
BRAAPP
BRAAPP BRAAAPAPAPAF

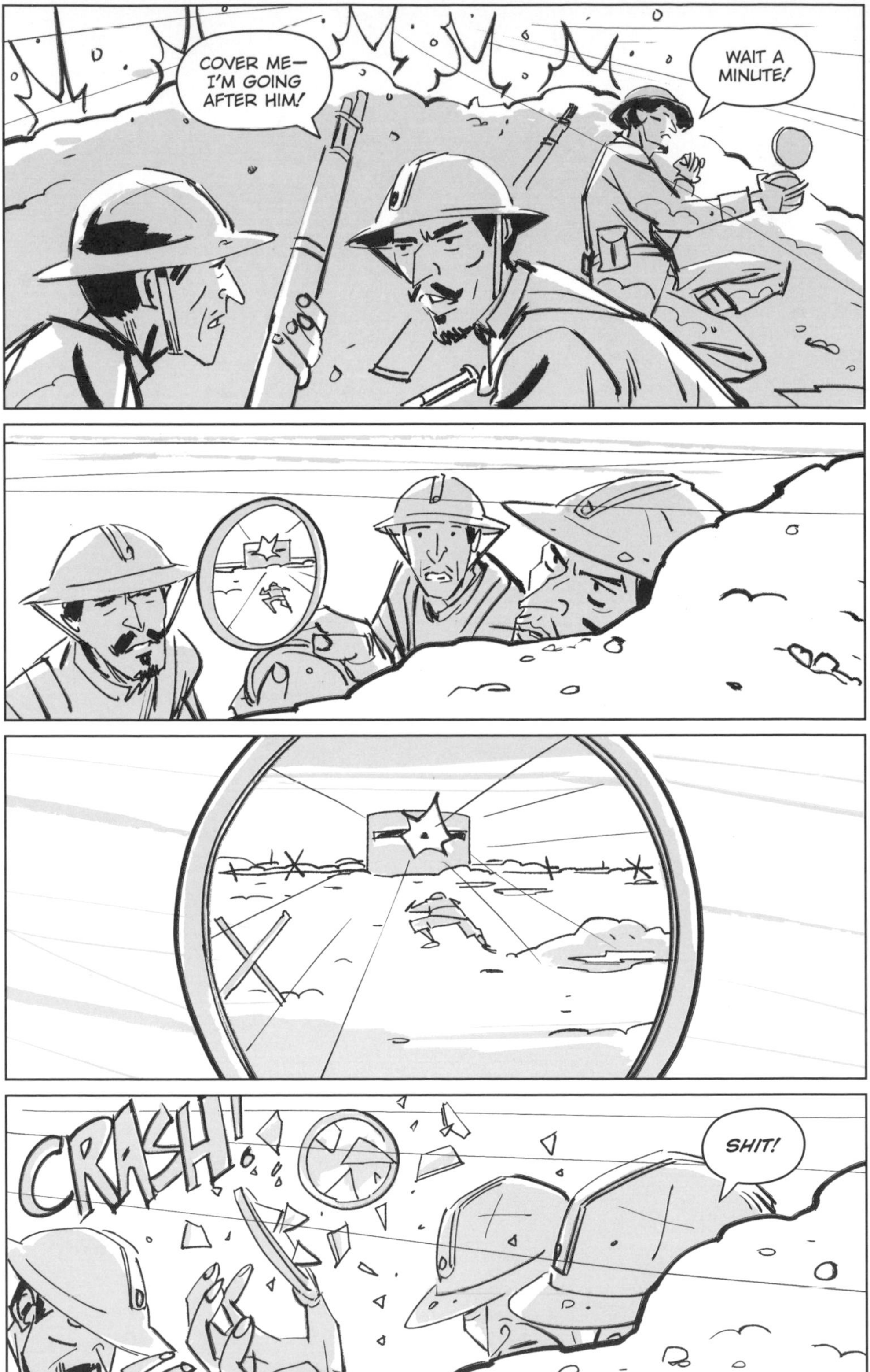
COVER ME— I'M GOING AFTER HIM!
WAIT A MINUTE!
CRASH!
SHIT!

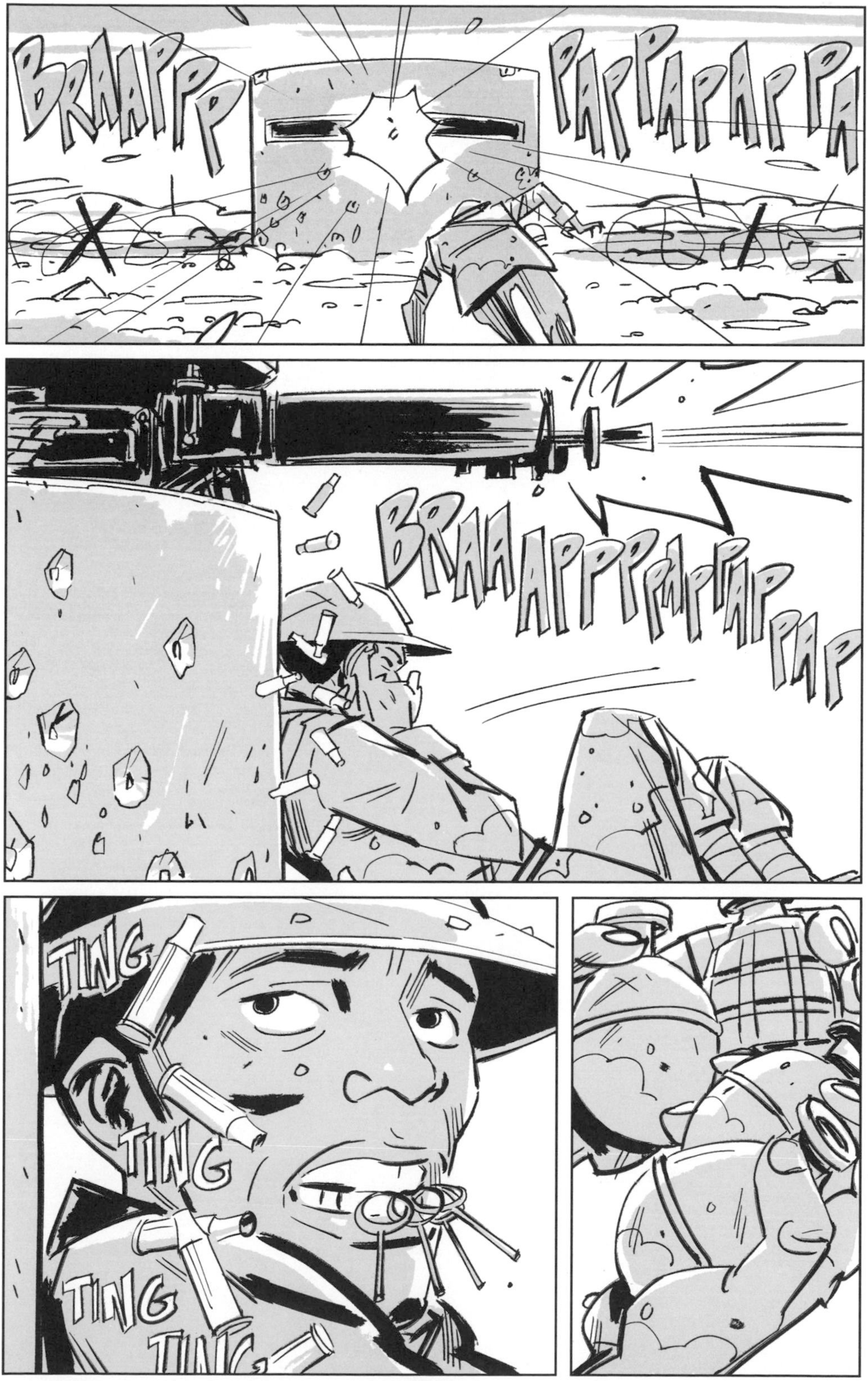
BRAAPPP
PAPPAPAPPAPPA
BRAAAPPPPAPPAPPAP
TING
TING
TING

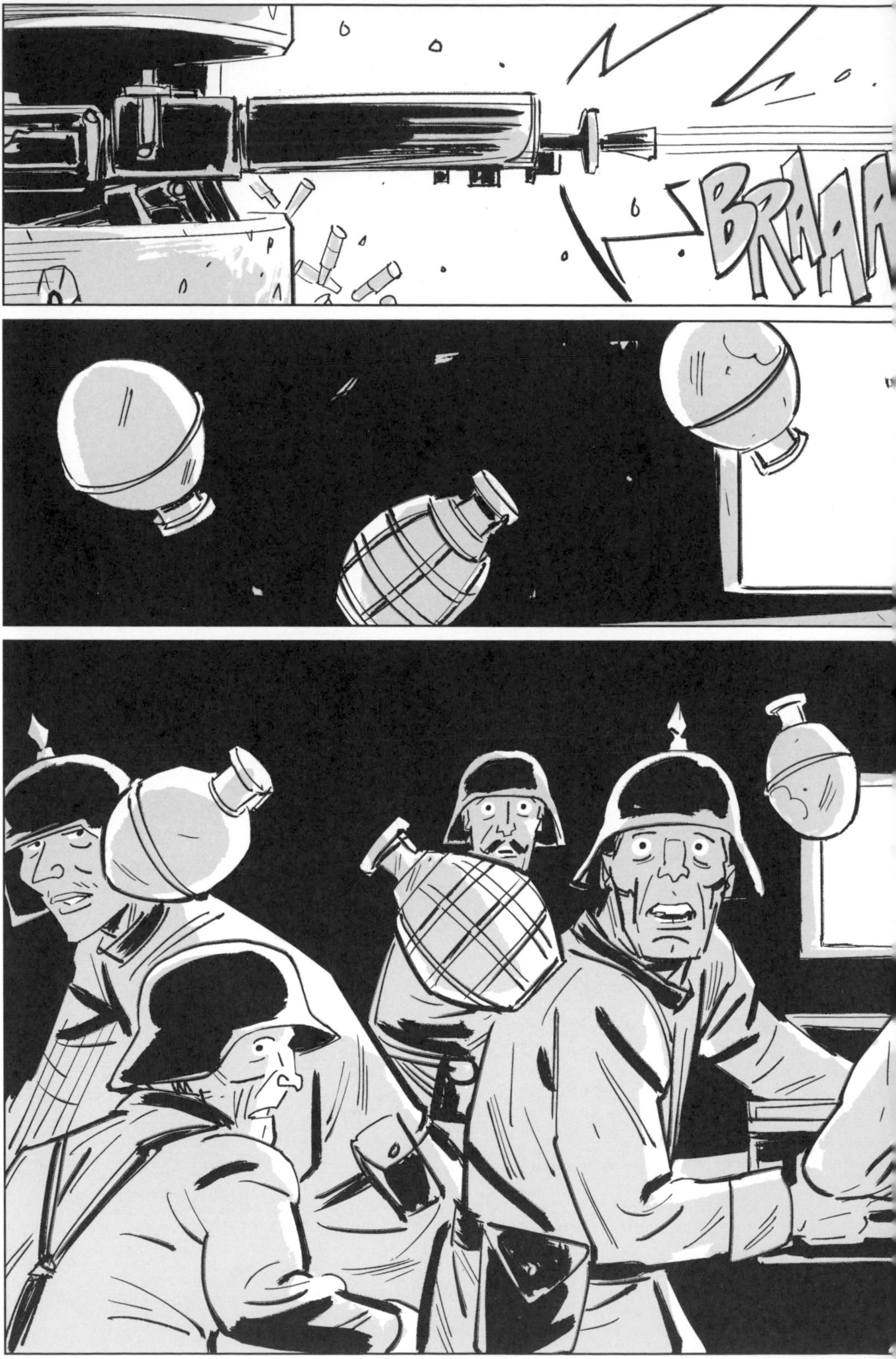
BRAAA

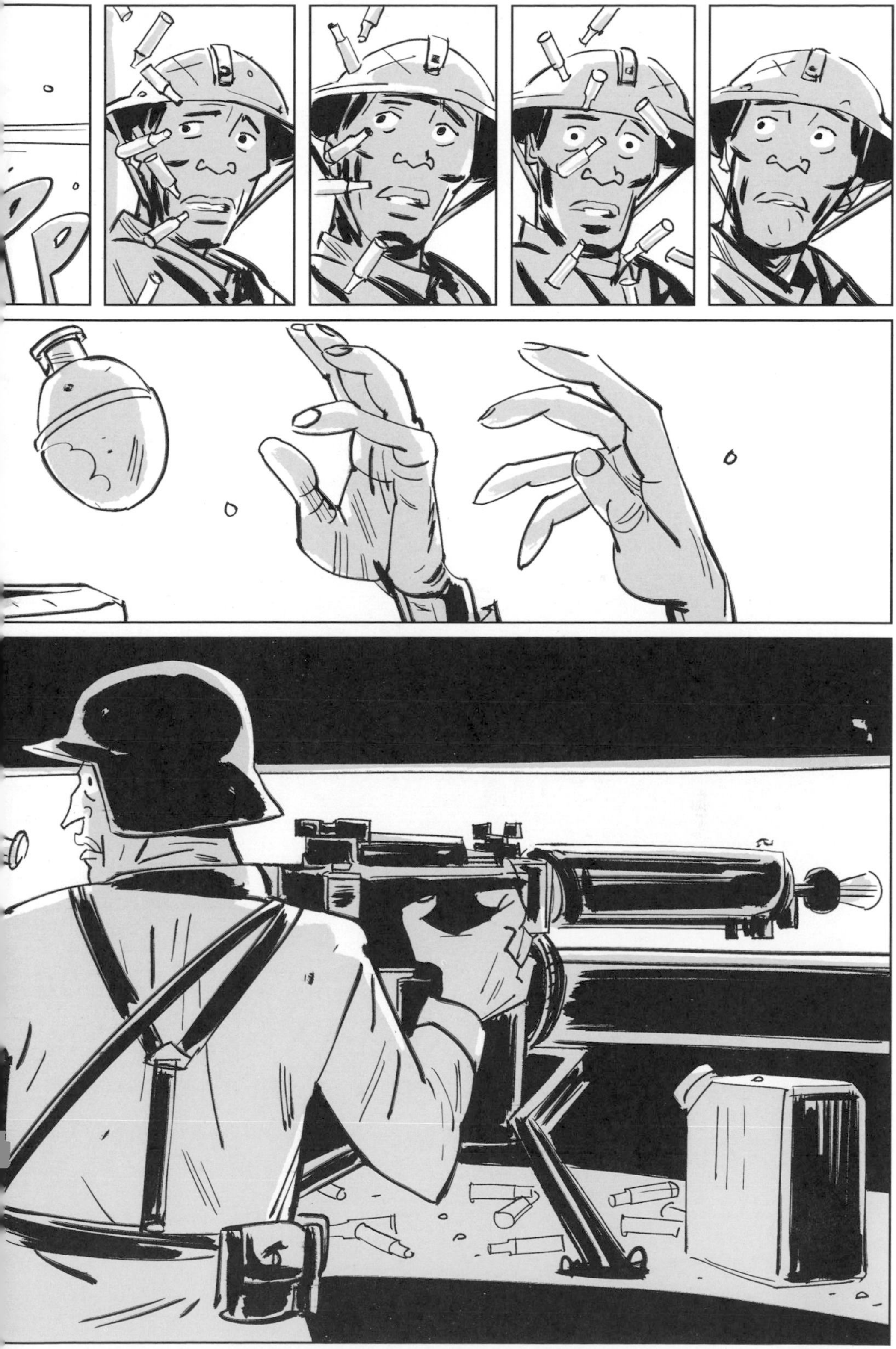

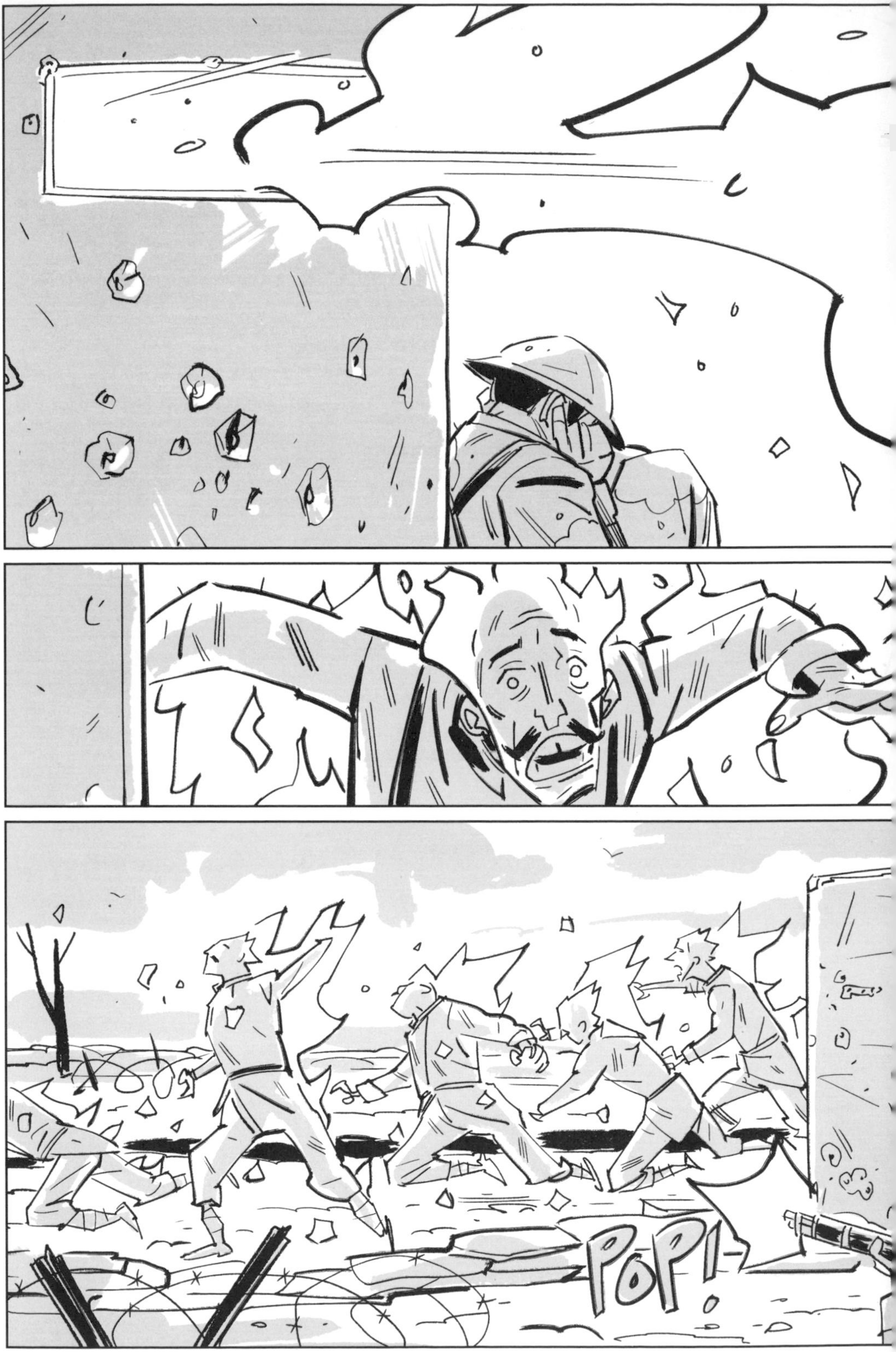
POP!

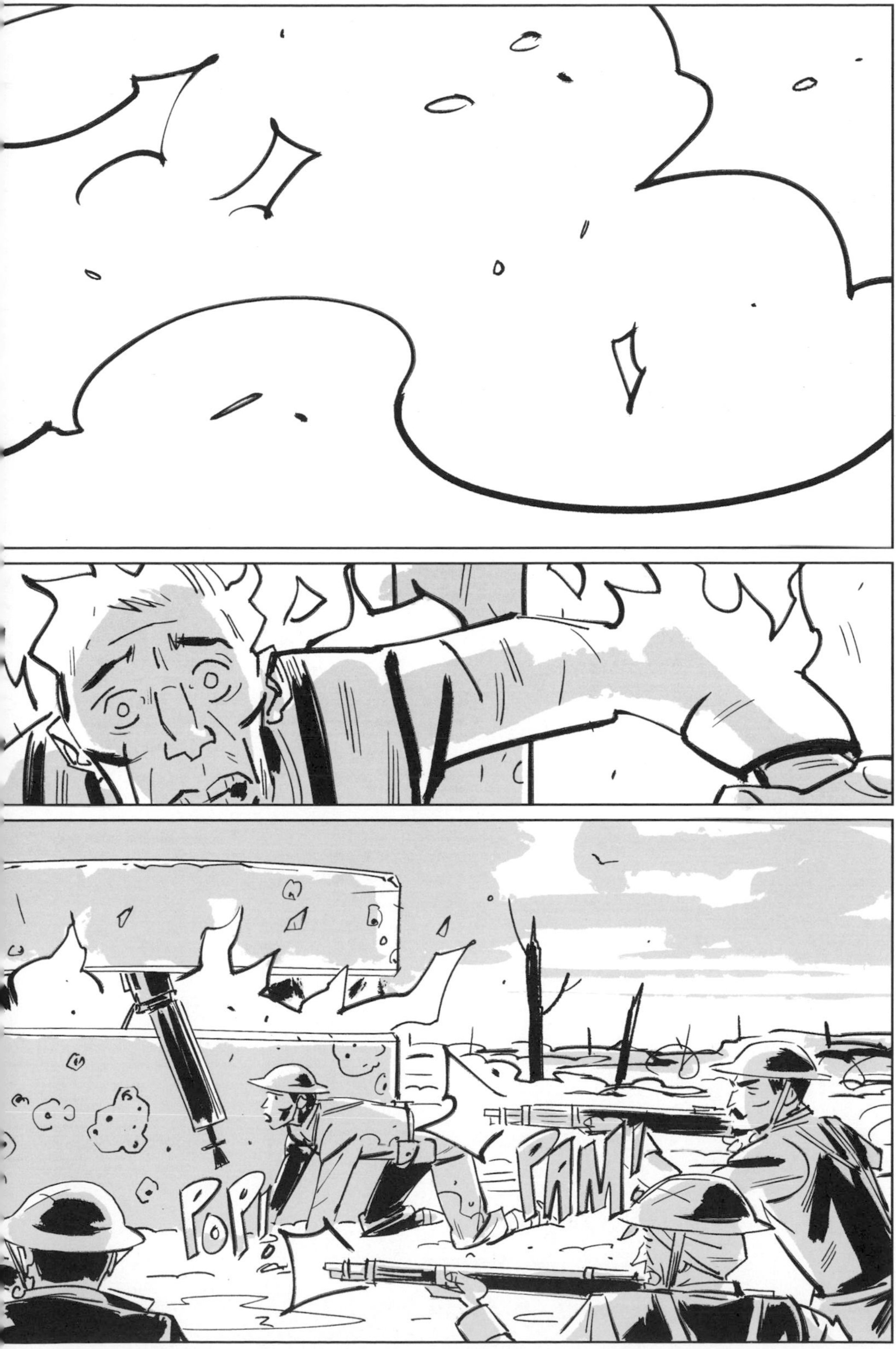
POP!
PAM!

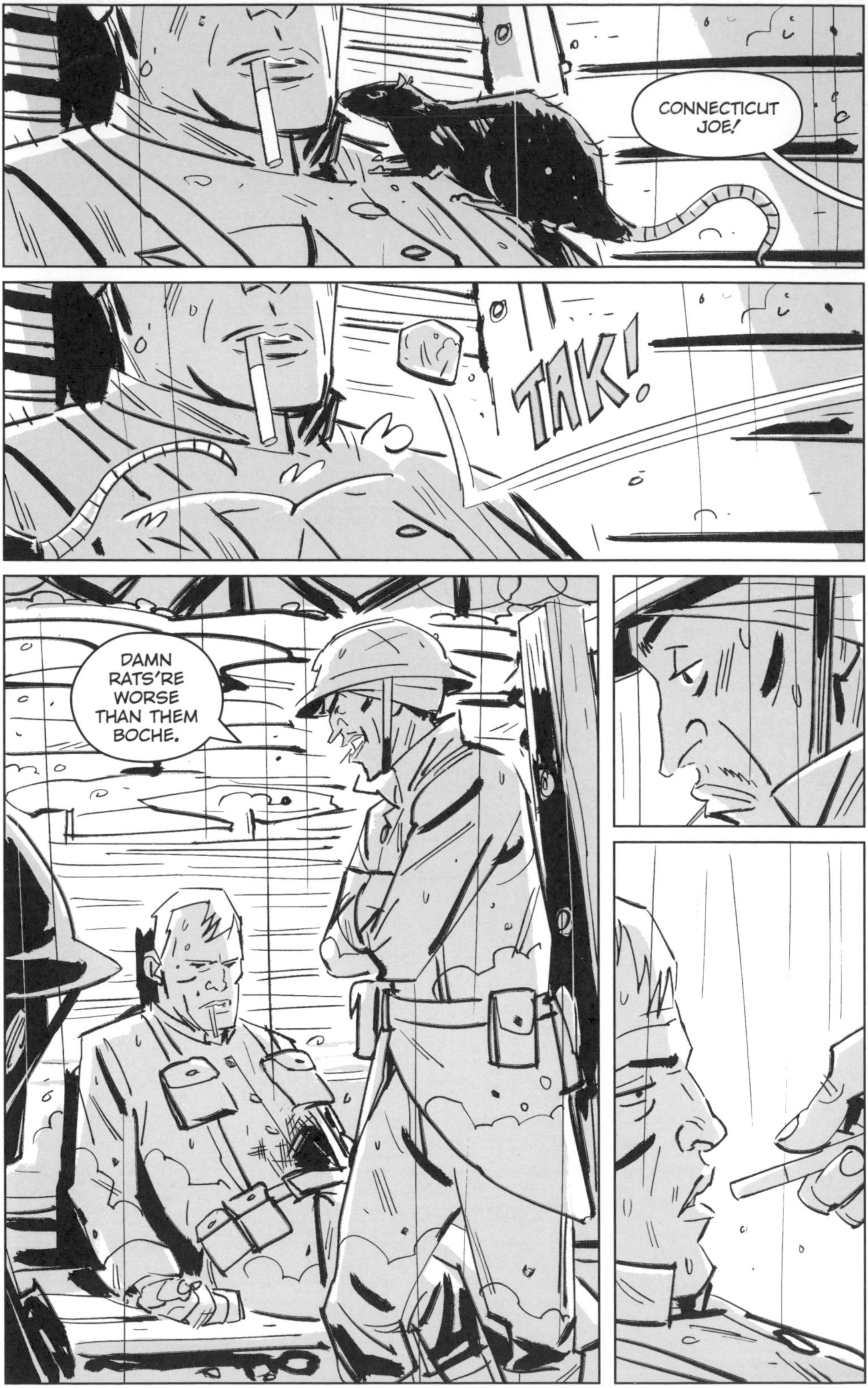
CONNECTICUT JOE!
TAK!
DAMN RATS'RE WORSE THAN THEM BOCHE.

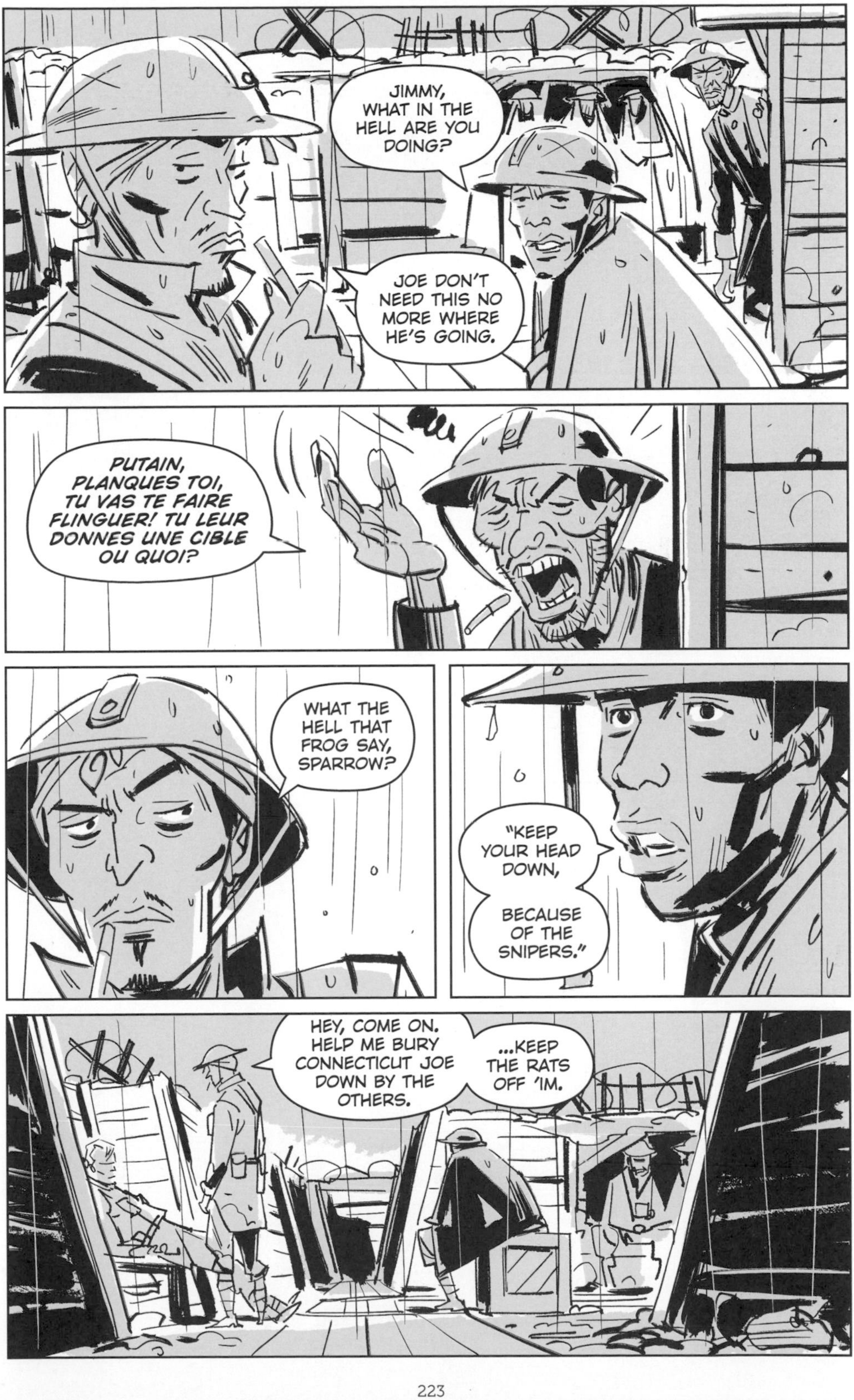
JIMMY, WHAT IN THE HELL ARE YOU DOING?
JOE DON'T NEED THIS NO MORE WHERE HE'S GOING.
PUTAIN, PLANQUES TOI, TU VAS TE FAIRE FLINGUER! TU LEUR DONNES UNE CIBLE OU QUOI?
WHAT THE HELL THAT FROG SAY, SPARROW?
"KEEP YOUR HEAD DOWN,
BECAUSE OF THE SNIPERS."
HEY, COME ON. HELP ME BURY CONNECTICUT JOE DOWN BY THE OTHERS.
...KEEP THE RATS OFF 'IM.

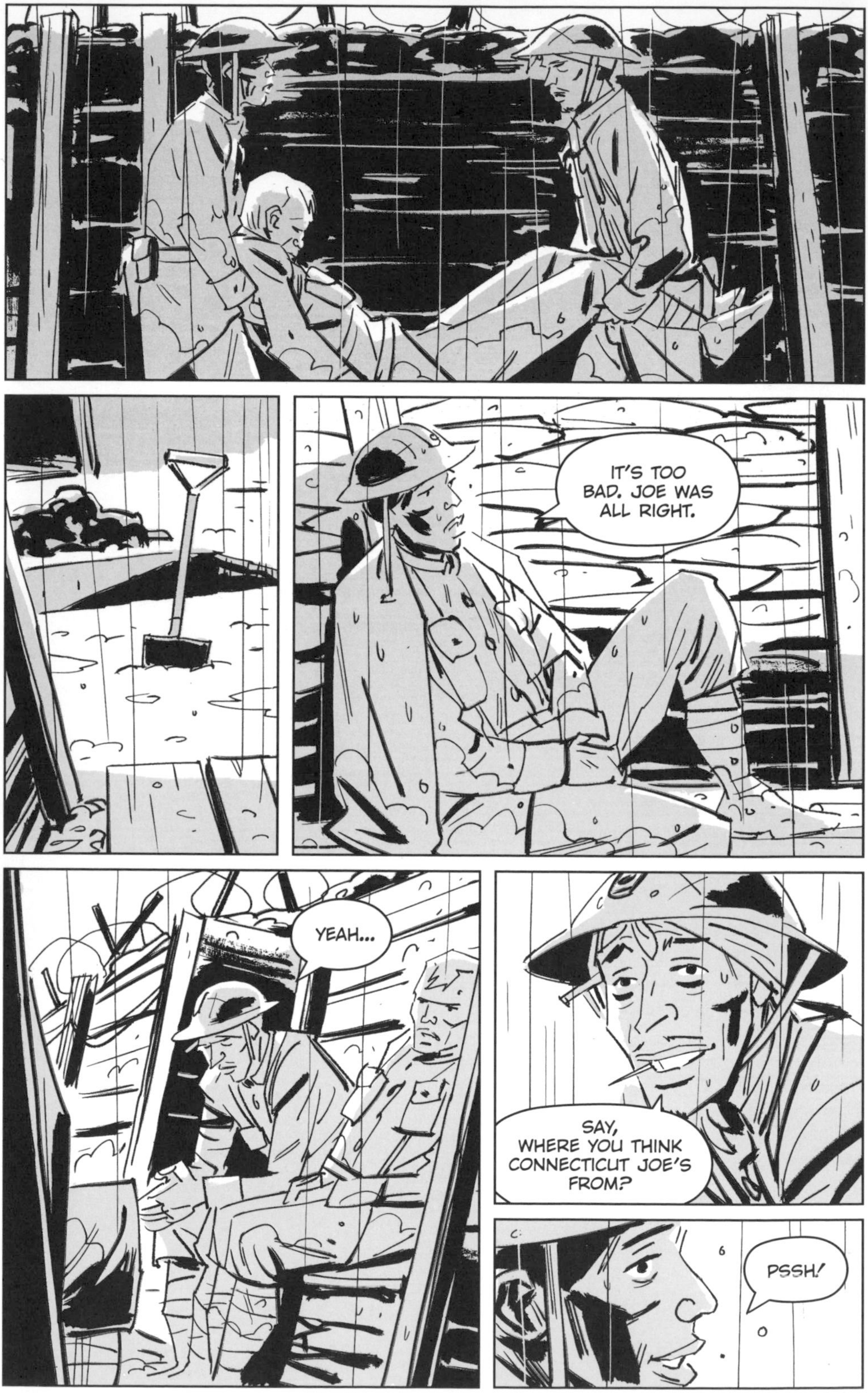
IT'S TOO BAD. JOE WAS ALL RIGHT.
YEAH...
SAY, WHERE YOU THINK CONNECTICUT JOE'S FROM?
PSSH!

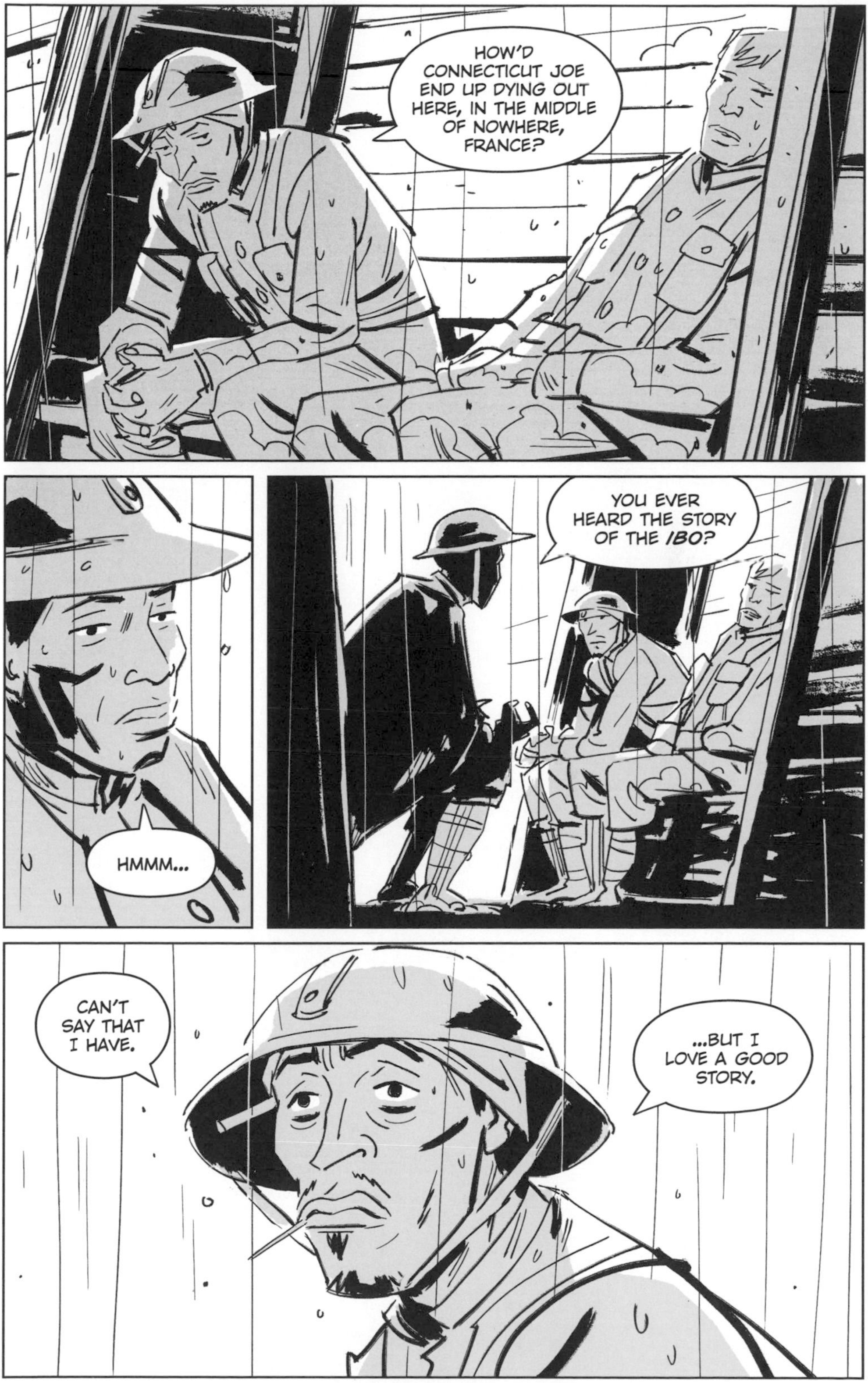
HOW'D CONNECTICUT JOE END UP DYING OUT HERE, IN THE MIDDLE OF NOWHERE, FRANCE?
HMMM...
YOU EVER HEARD THE STORY OF THE *IBO?*
CAN'T SAY THAT I HAVE.
...BUT I LOVE A GOOD STORY.

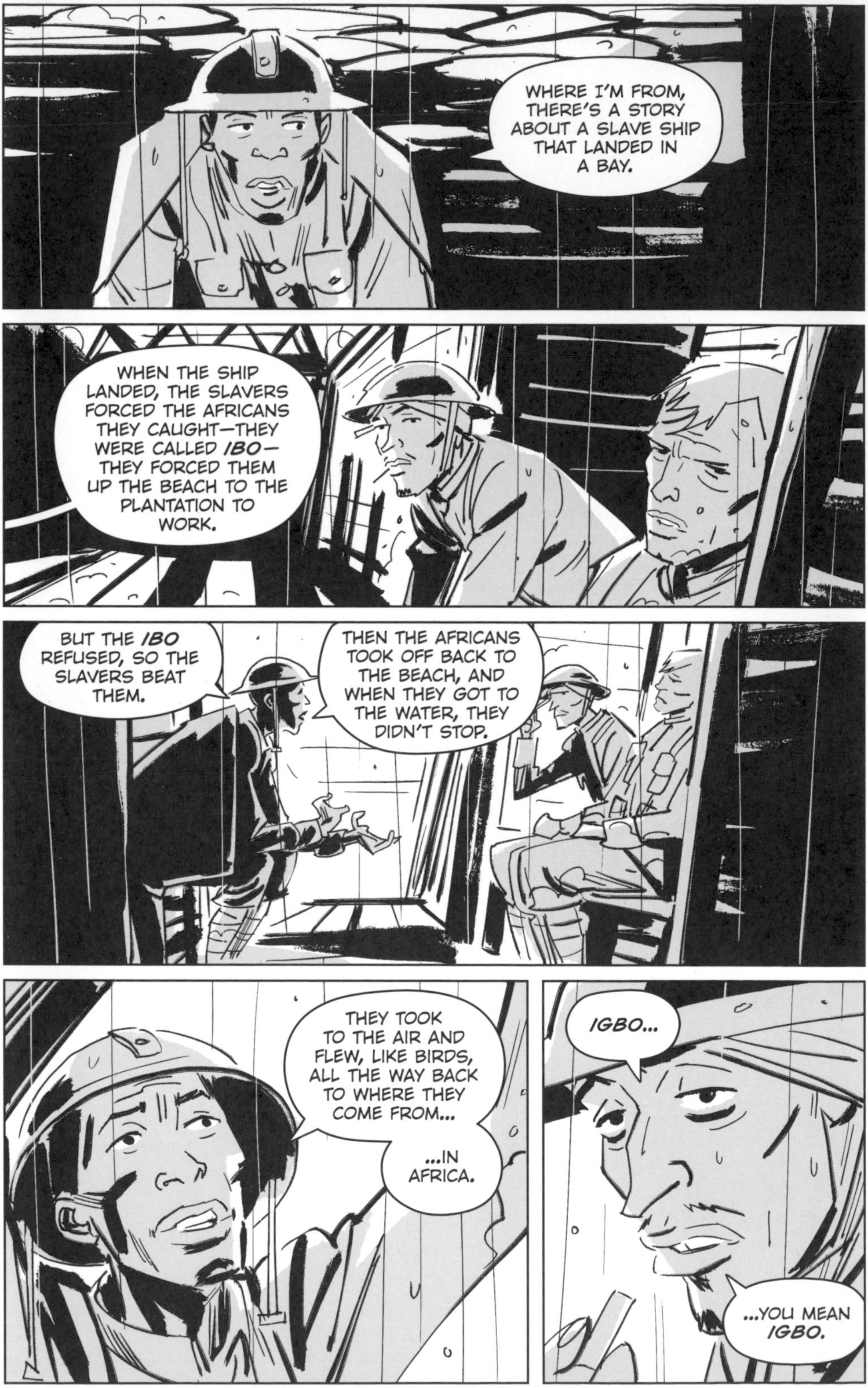
WHERE I'M FROM, THERE'S A STORY ABOUT A SLAVE SHIP THAT LANDED IN A BAY.
WHEN THE SHIP LANDED, THE SLAVERS FORCED THE AFRICANS THEY CAUGHT—THEY WERE CALLED *IBO*—THEY FORCED THEM UP THE BEACH TO THE PLANTATION TO WORK.
BUT THE *IBO* REFUSED, SO THE SLAVERS BEAT THEM.
THEN THE AFRICANS TOOK OFF BACK TO THE BEACH, AND WHEN THEY GOT TO THE WATER, THEY DIDN'T STOP.
THEY TOOK TO THE AIR AND FLEW, LIKE BIRDS, ALL THE WAY BACK TO WHERE THEY COME FROM...
...IN AFRICA.
IGBO...
...YOU MEAN *IGBO.*

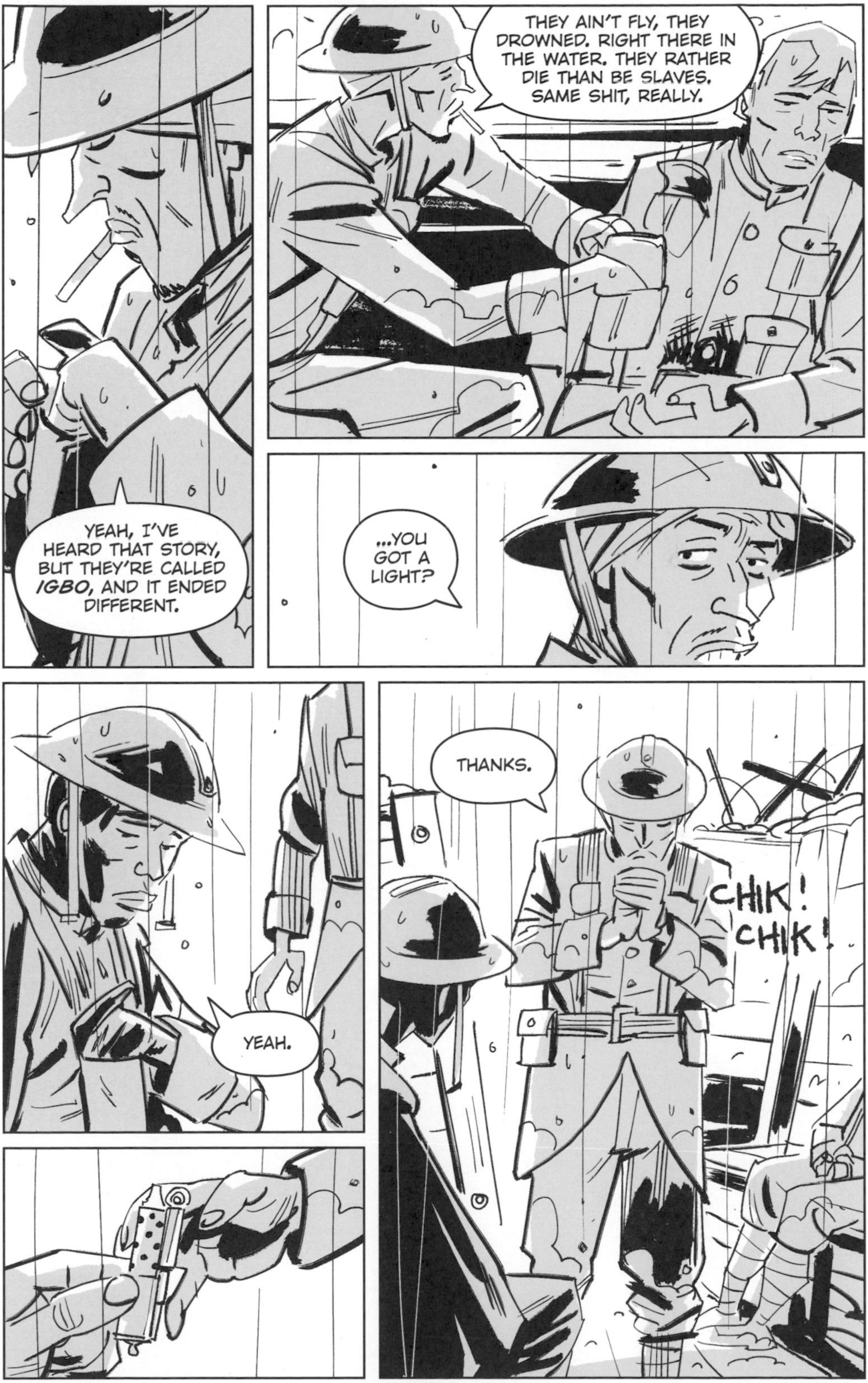
THEY AIN'T FLY, THEY DROWNED. RIGHT THERE IN THE WATER. THEY RATHER DIE THAN BE SLAVES. SAME SHIT, REALLY.
YEAH, I'VE HEARD THAT STORY, BUT THEY'RE CALLED *IGBO*, AND IT ENDED DIFFERENT.
...YOU GOT A LIGHT?
YEAH.
THANKS.
CHIK! CHIK!

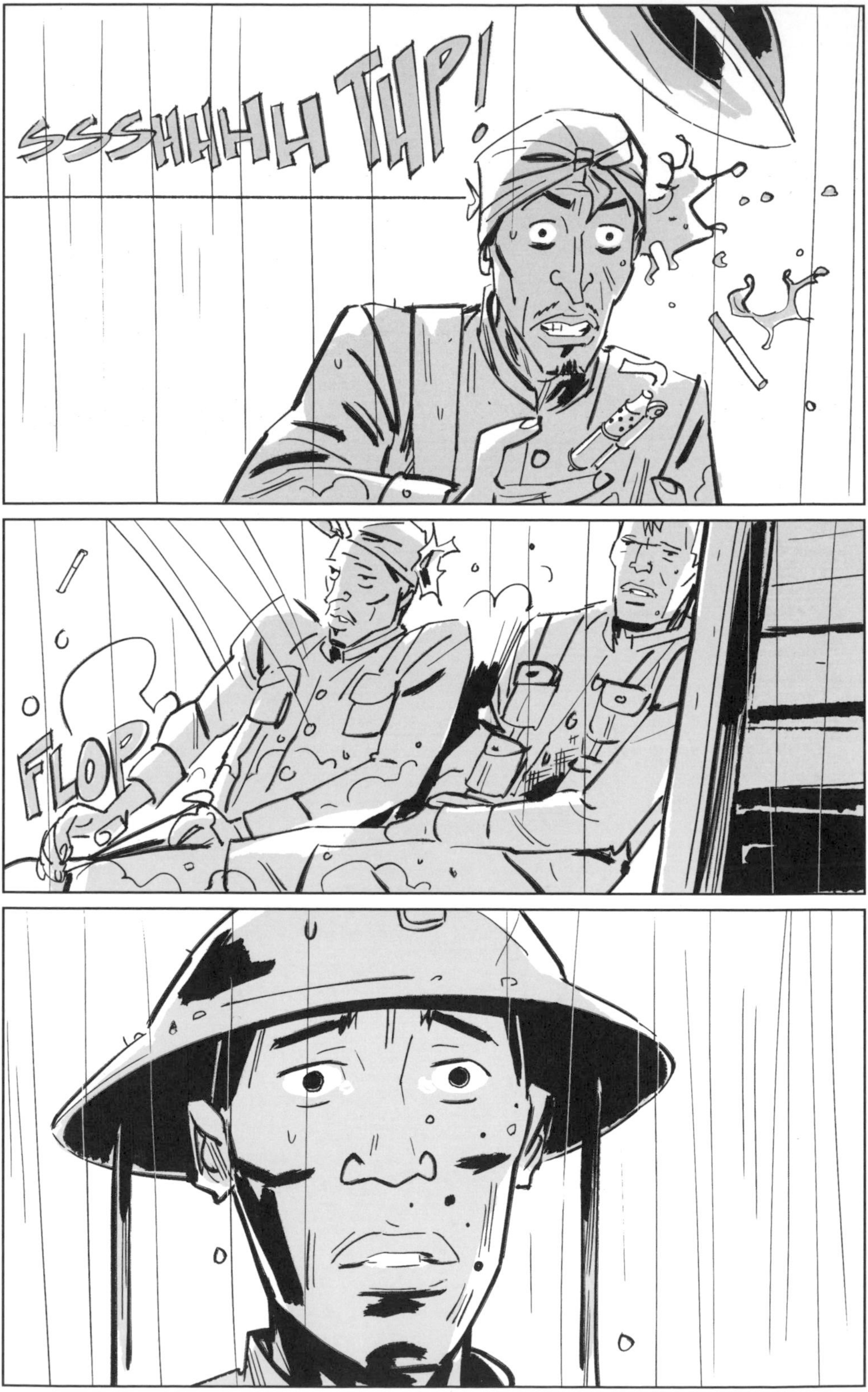
SSSHHHH THP!
FLOP

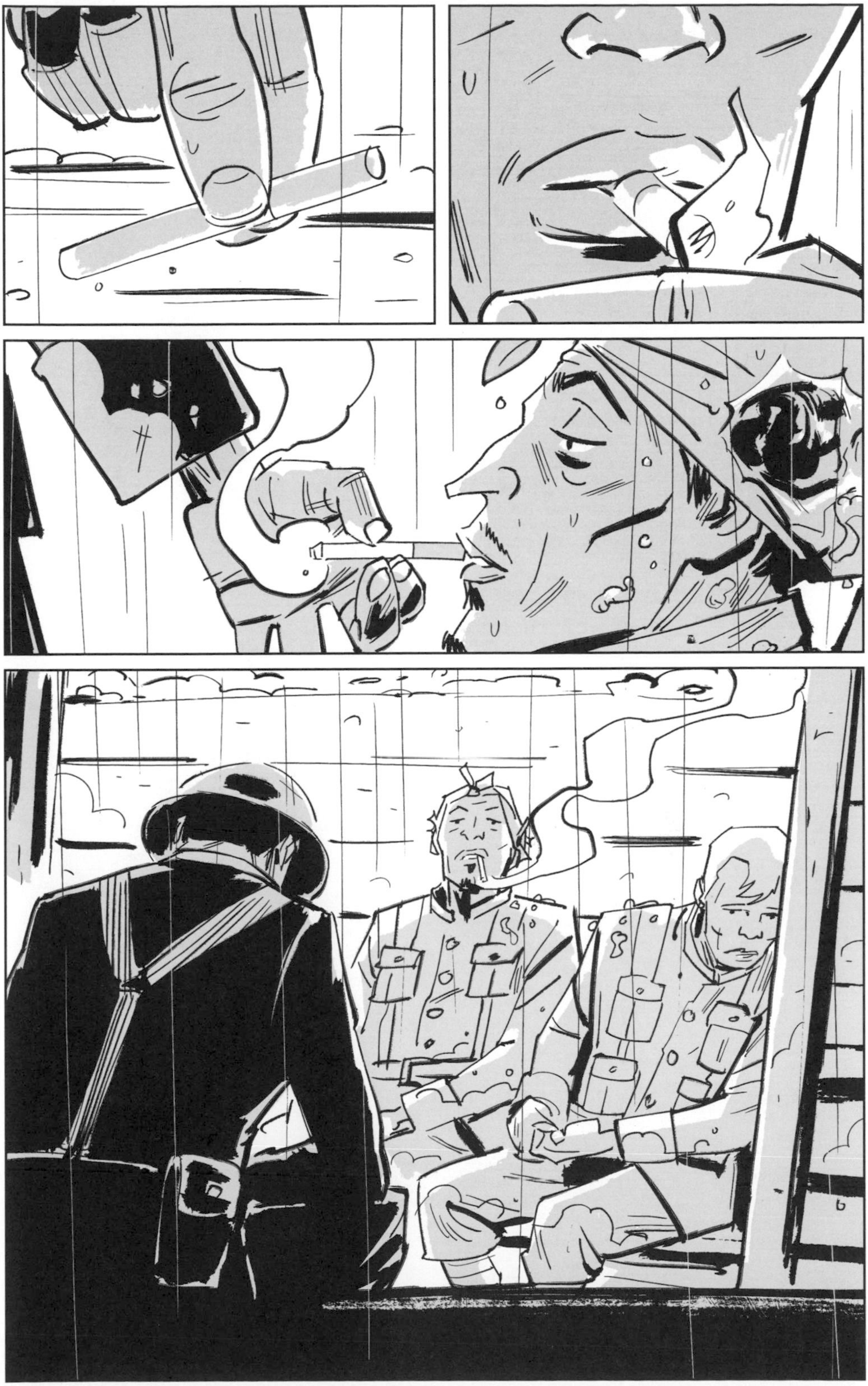

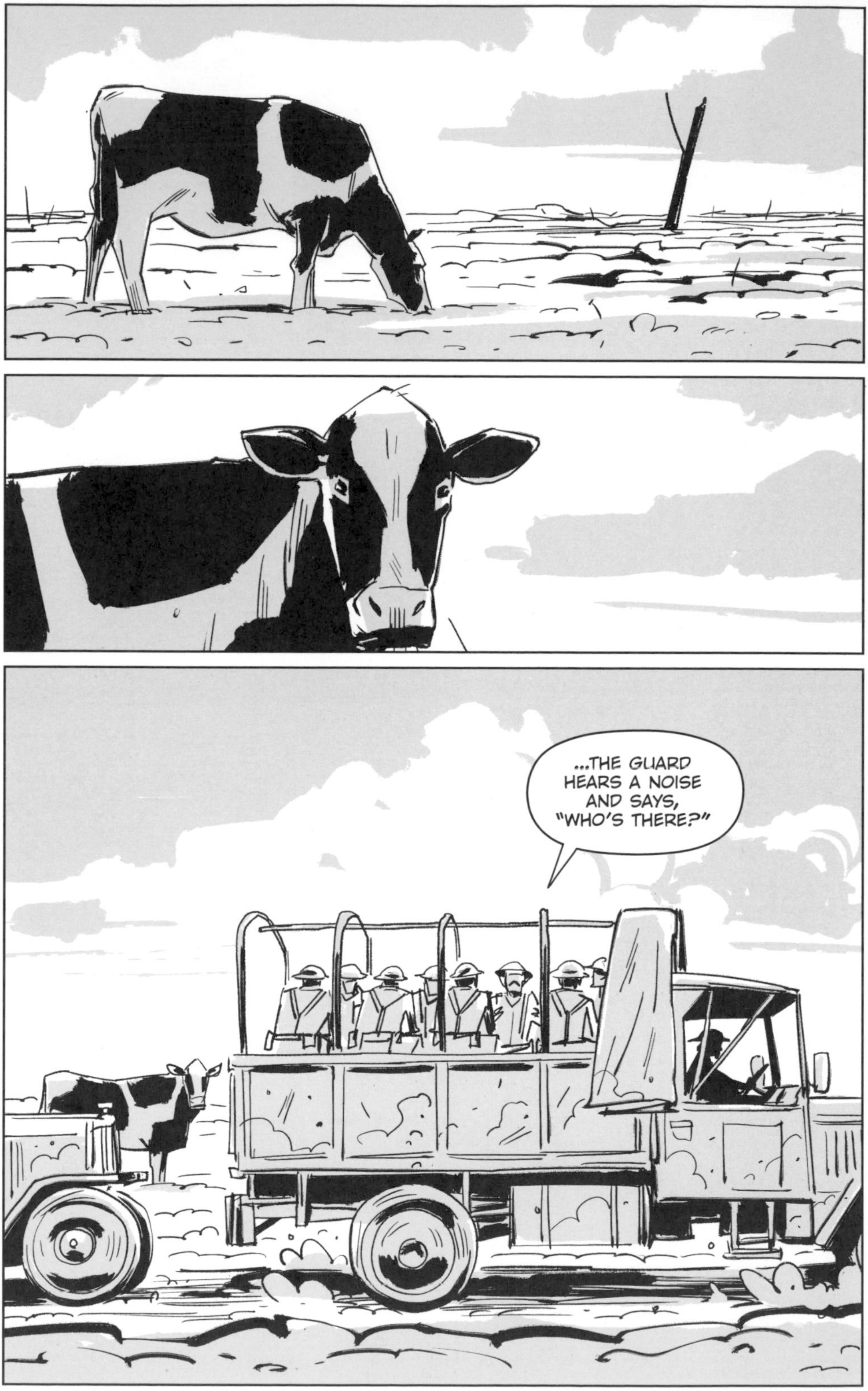
...THE GUARD HEARS A NOISE AND SAYS, "WHO'S THERE?"

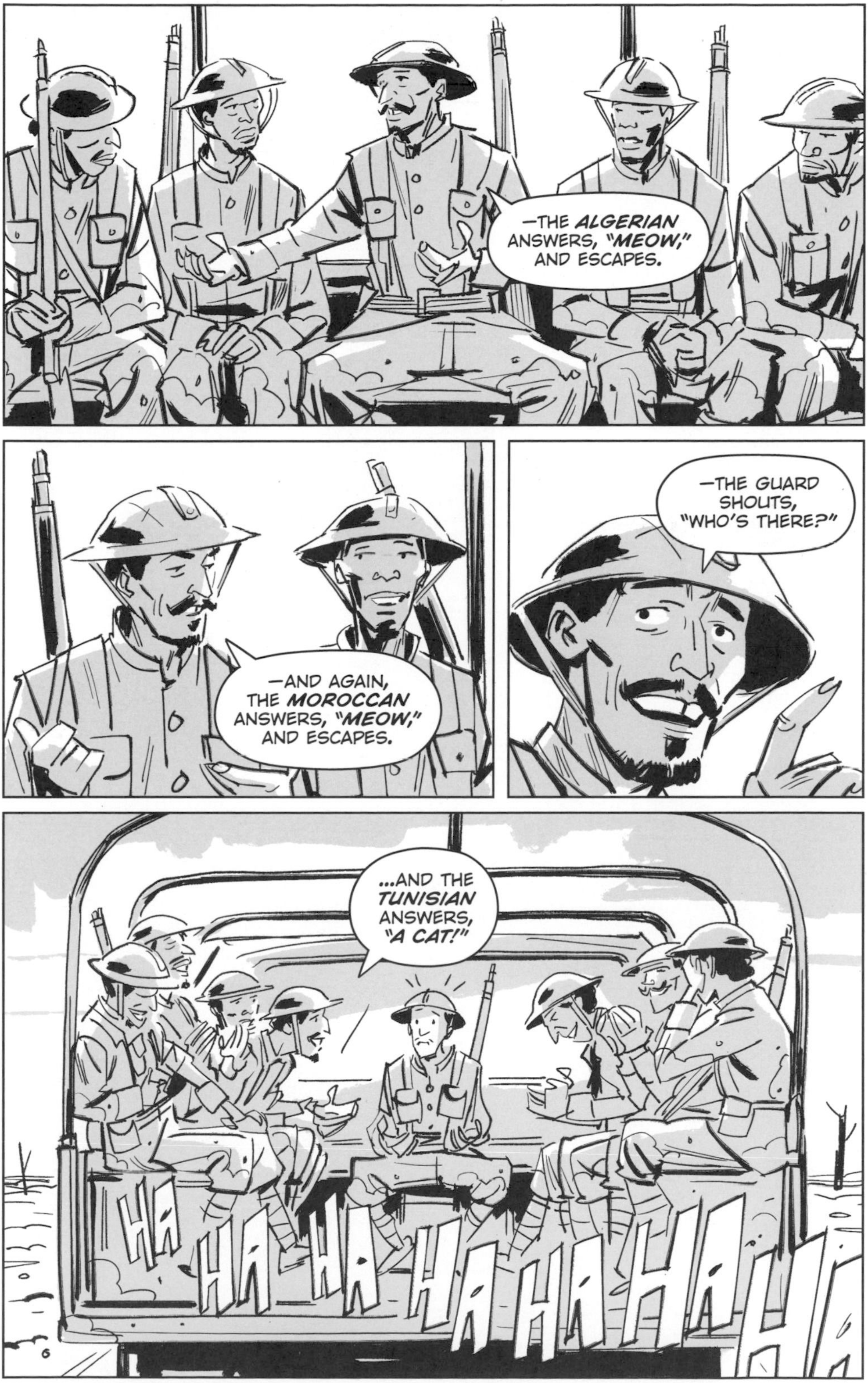
—THE *ALGERIAN* ANSWERS, *"MEOW,"* AND ESCAPES.
—AND AGAIN, THE *MOROCCAN* ANSWERS, *"MEOW,"* AND ESCAPES.
—THE GUARD SHOUTS, "WHO'S THERE?"
...AND THE *TUNISIAN* ANSWERS, *"A CAT!"*
HA HA HA HA HAHAHAHAHA

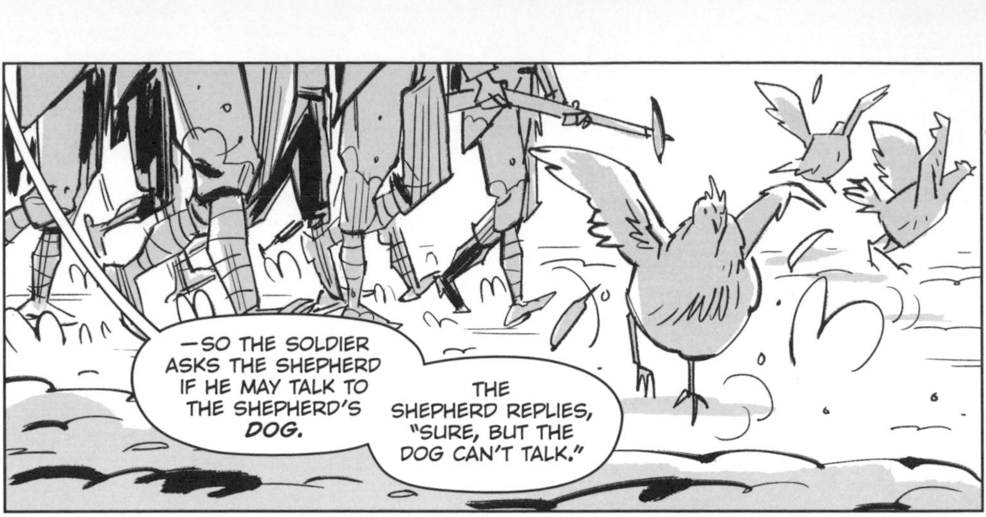
—SO THE SOLDIER ASKS THE SHEPHERD IF HE MAY TALK TO THE SHEPHERD'S DOG.
THE SHEPHERD REPLIES, "SURE, BUT THE DOG CAN'T TALK."

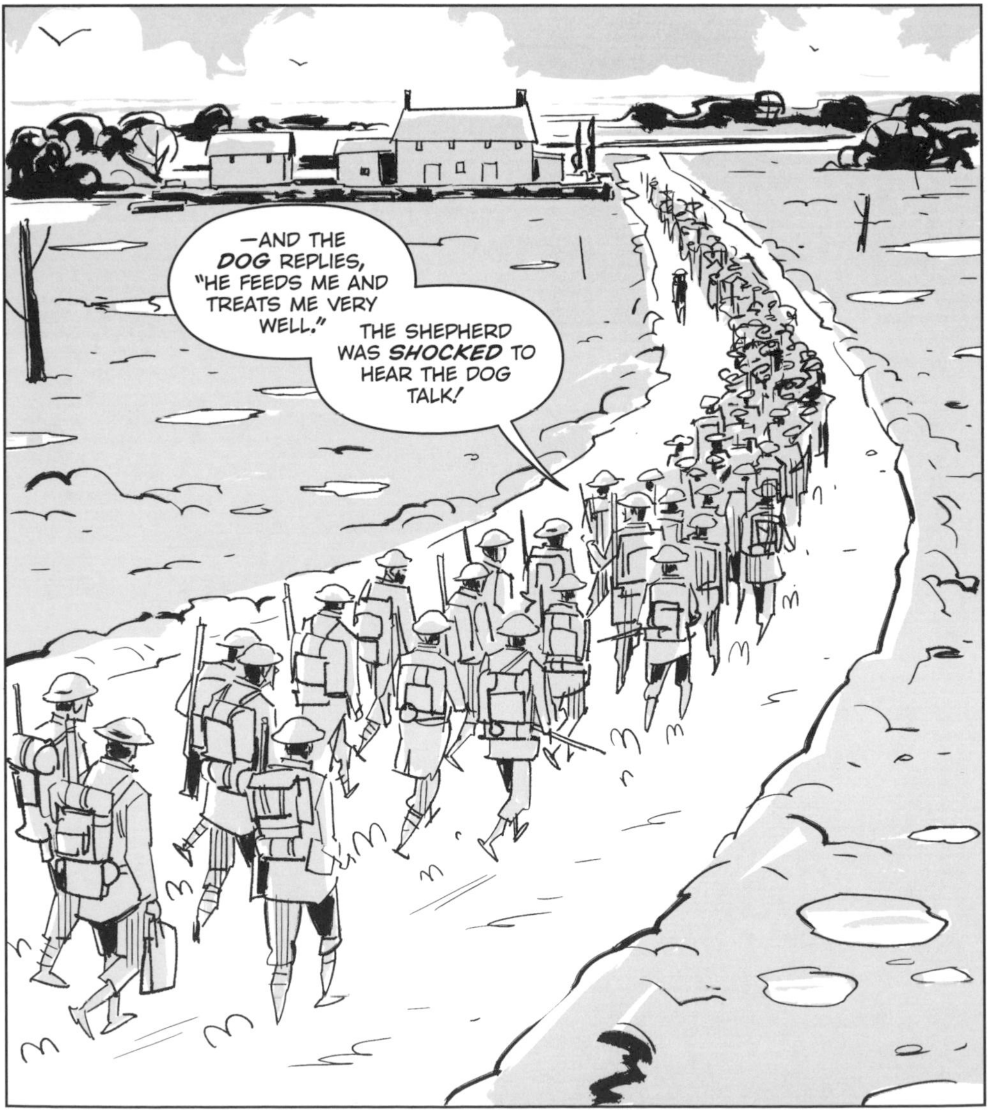
—AND THE DOG REPLIES, "HE FEEDS ME AND TREATS ME VERY WELL."
THE SHEPHERD WAS SHOCKED TO HEAR THE DOG TALK!

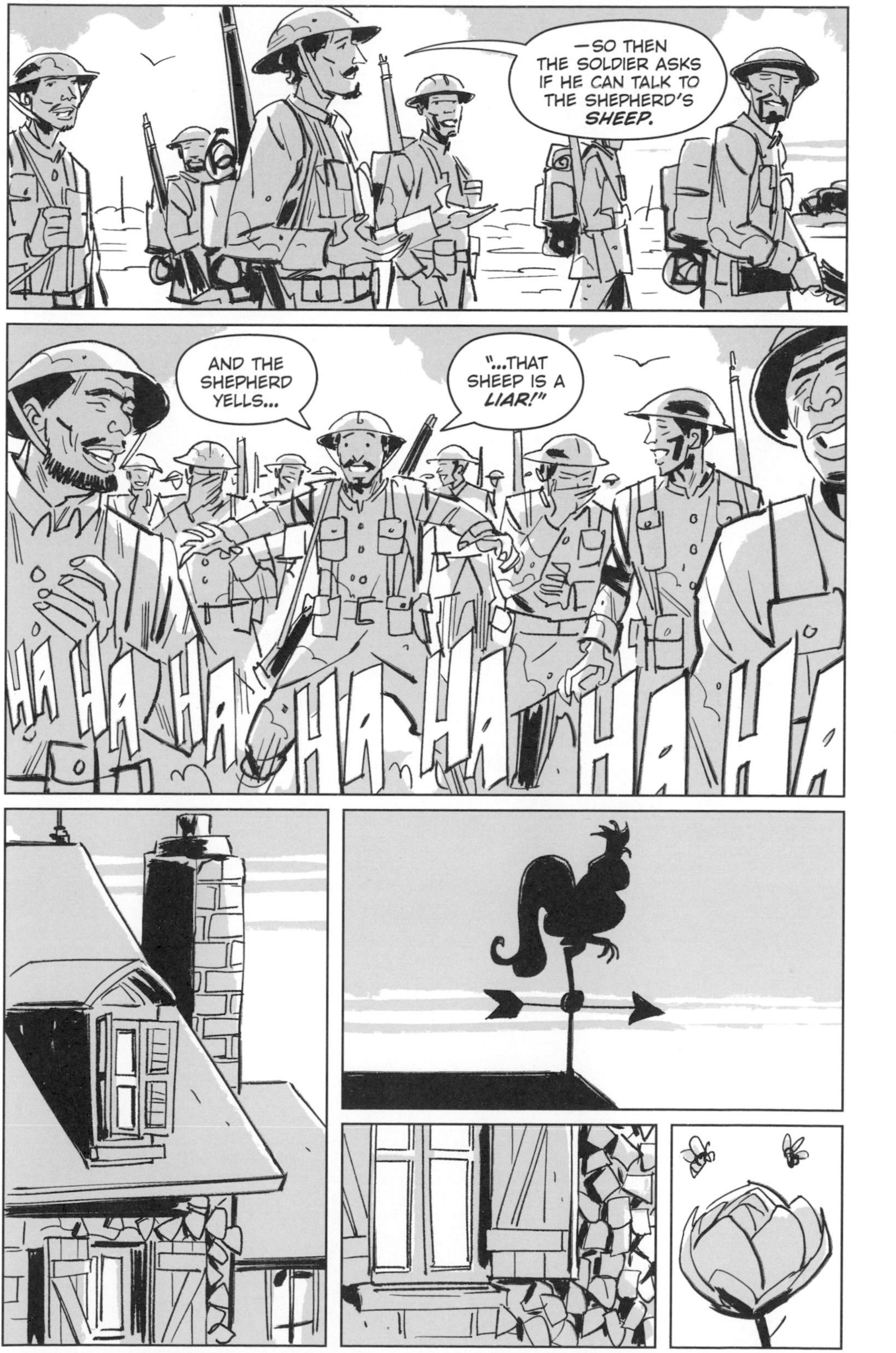
—SO THEN THE SOLDIER ASKS IF HE CAN TALK TO THE SHEPHERD'S *SHEEP.*
AND THE SHEPHERD YELLS...
"...THAT SHEEP IS A *LIAR!*"
HA HA HA HA HA HA HA HA HA HA HA HA

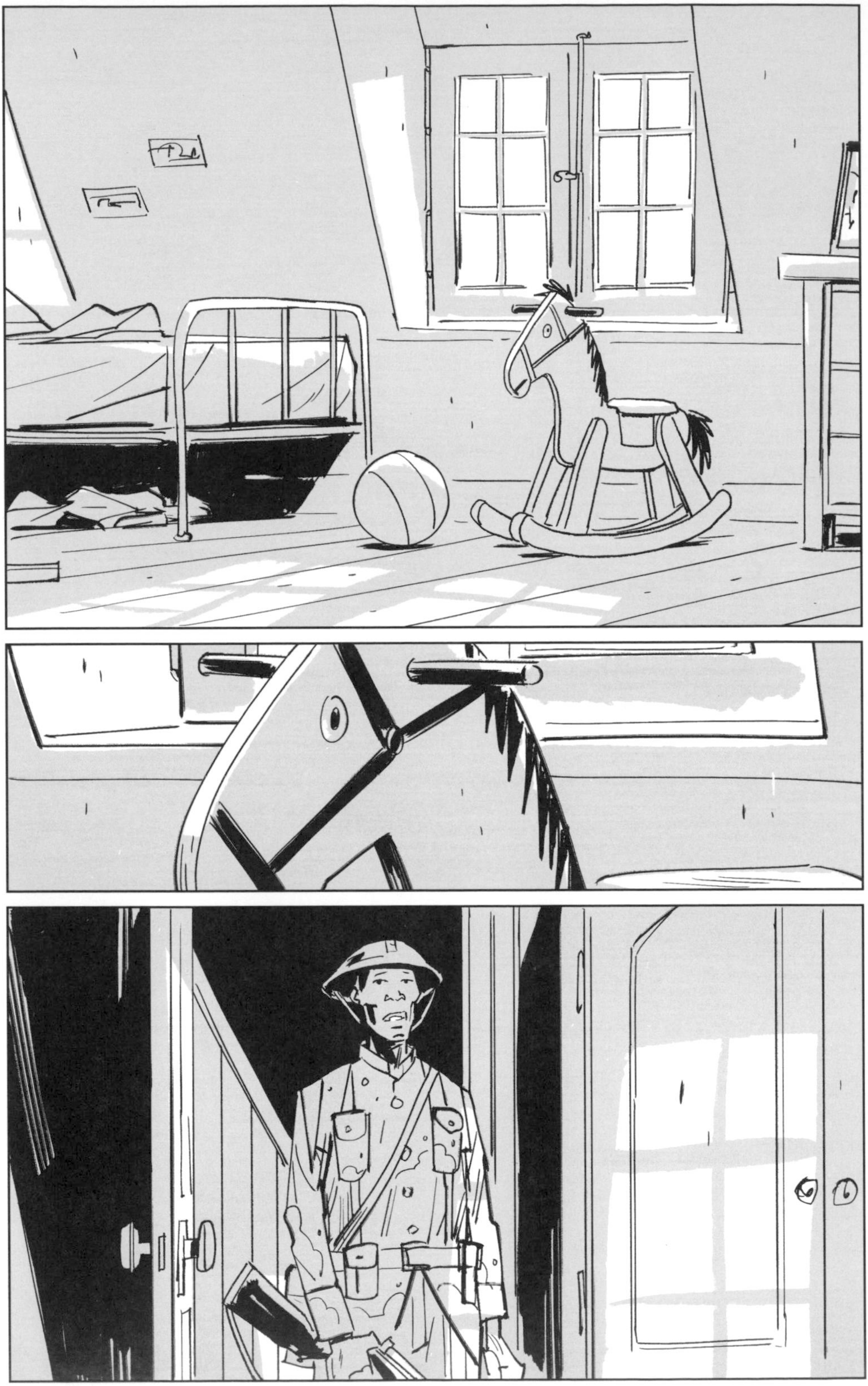

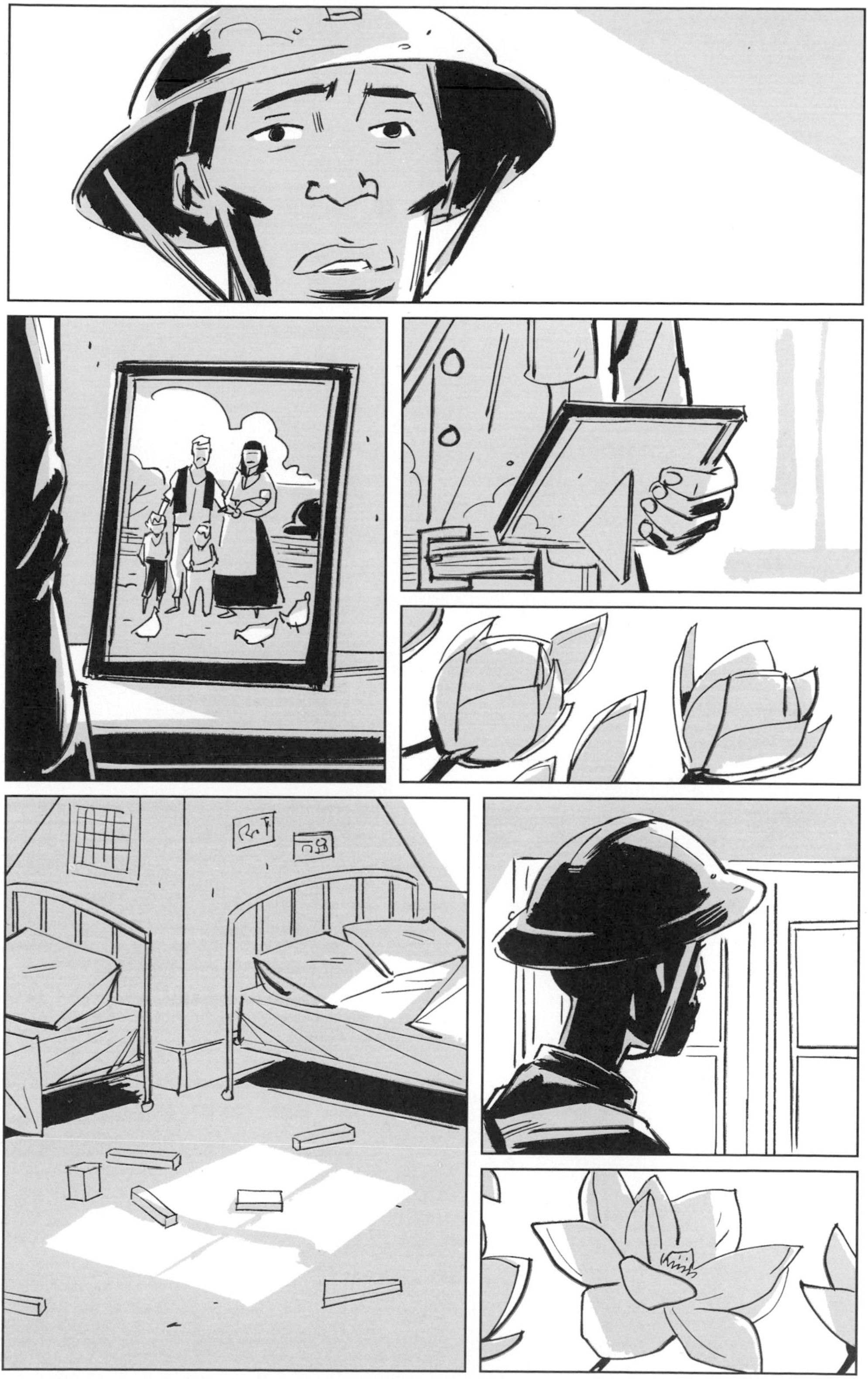

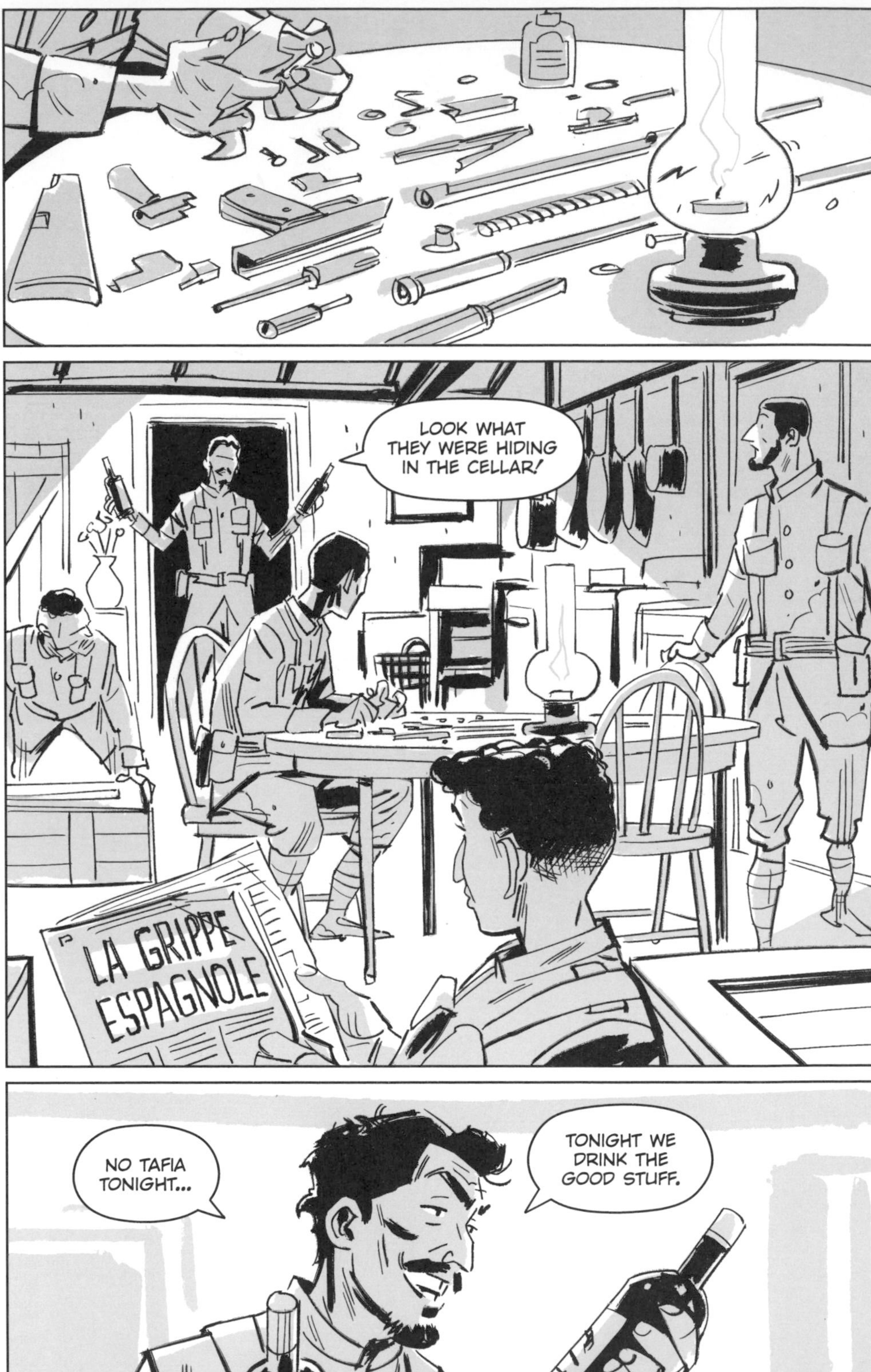
LOOK WHAT THEY WERE HIDING IN THE CELLAR!
LA GRIPPE ESPAGNOLE
NO TAFIA TONIGHT...
TONIGHT WE DRINK THE GOOD STUFF.

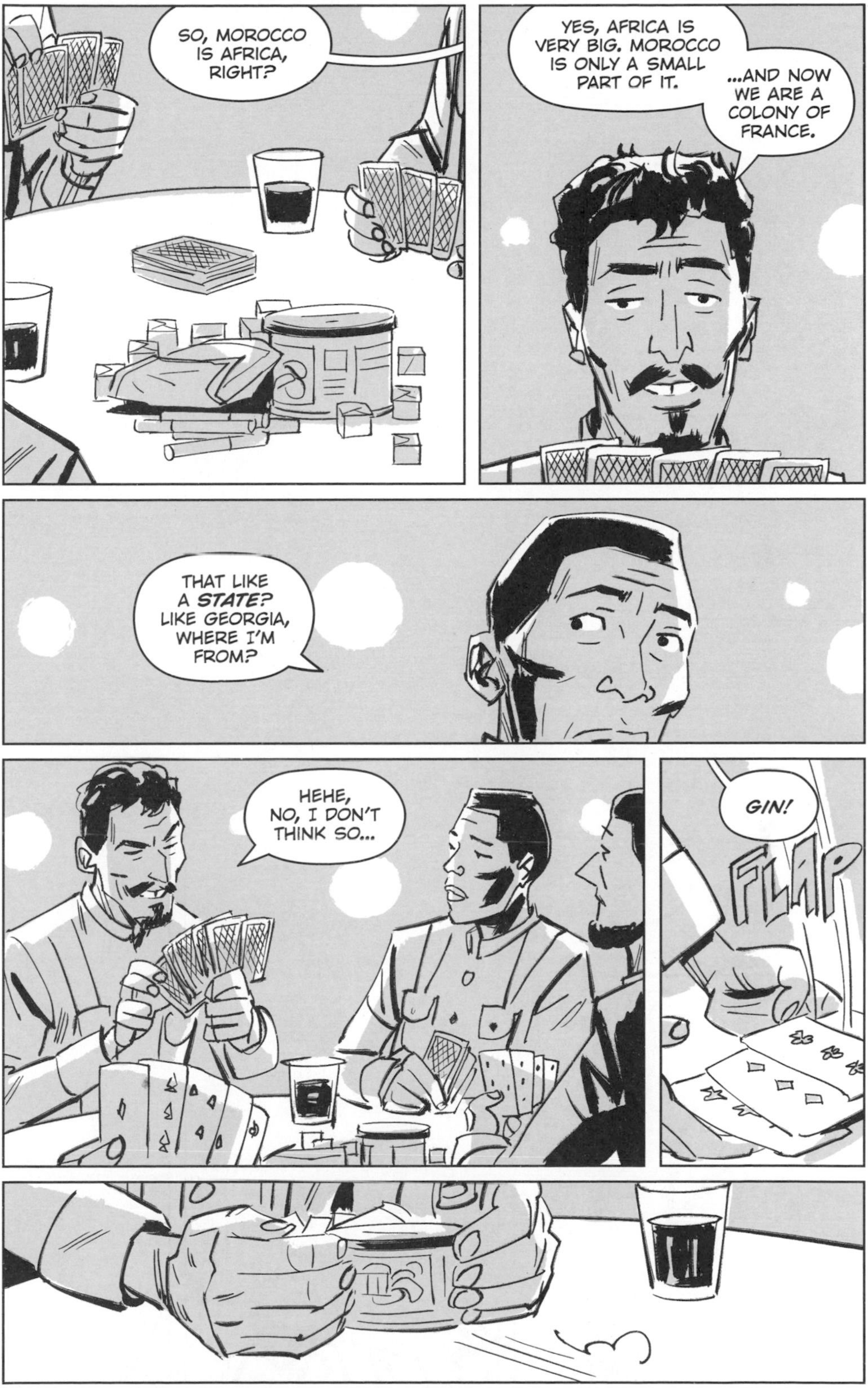
SO, MOROCCO IS AFRICA, RIGHT?
YES, AFRICA IS VERY BIG. MOROCCO IS ONLY A SMALL PART OF IT.
...AND NOW WE ARE A COLONY OF FRANCE.
THAT LIKE A *STATE?* LIKE GEORGIA, WHERE I'M FROM?
HEHE, NO, I DON'T THINK SO...
GIN!
FLAP

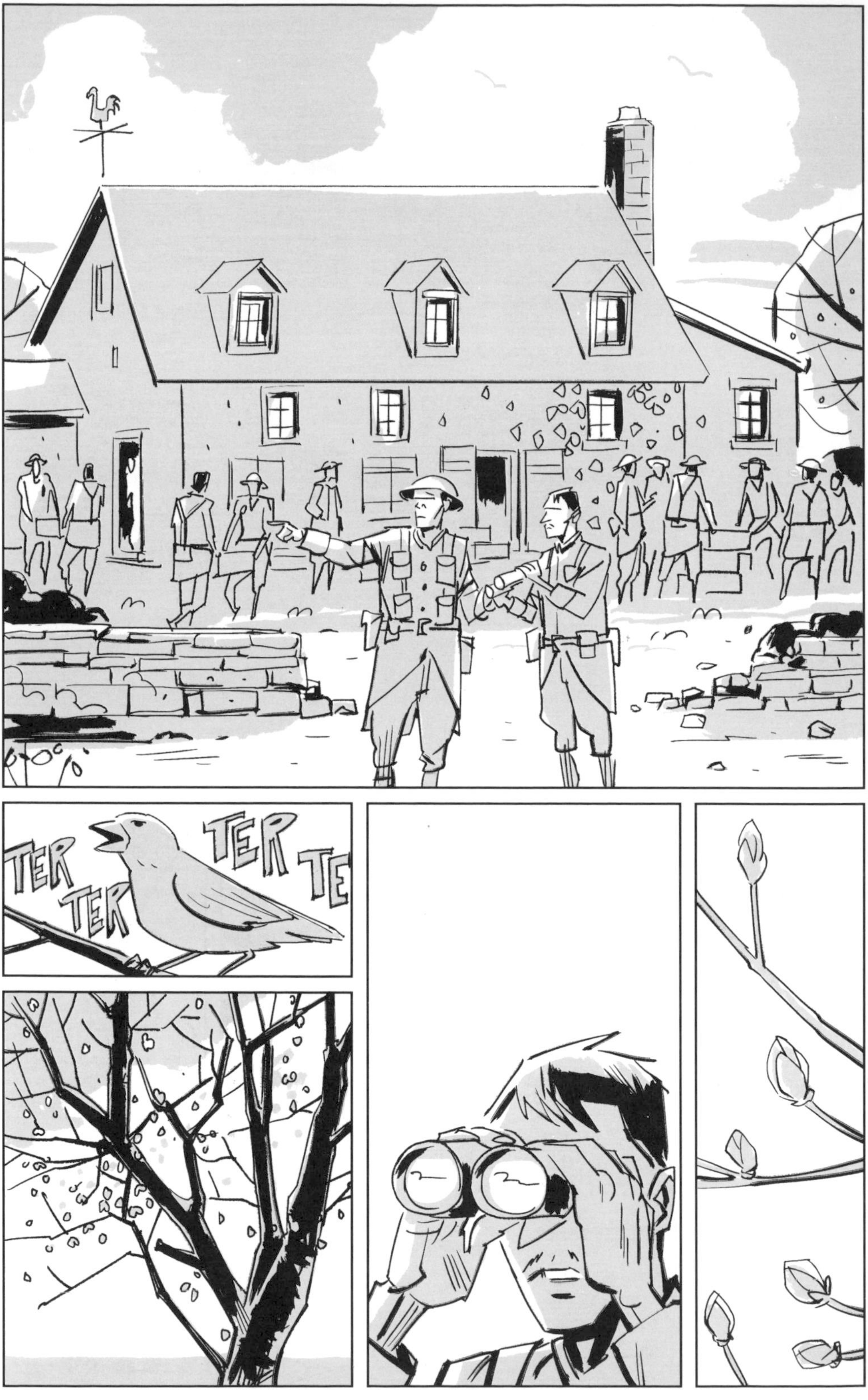
TER
TER
TER
TER
TE

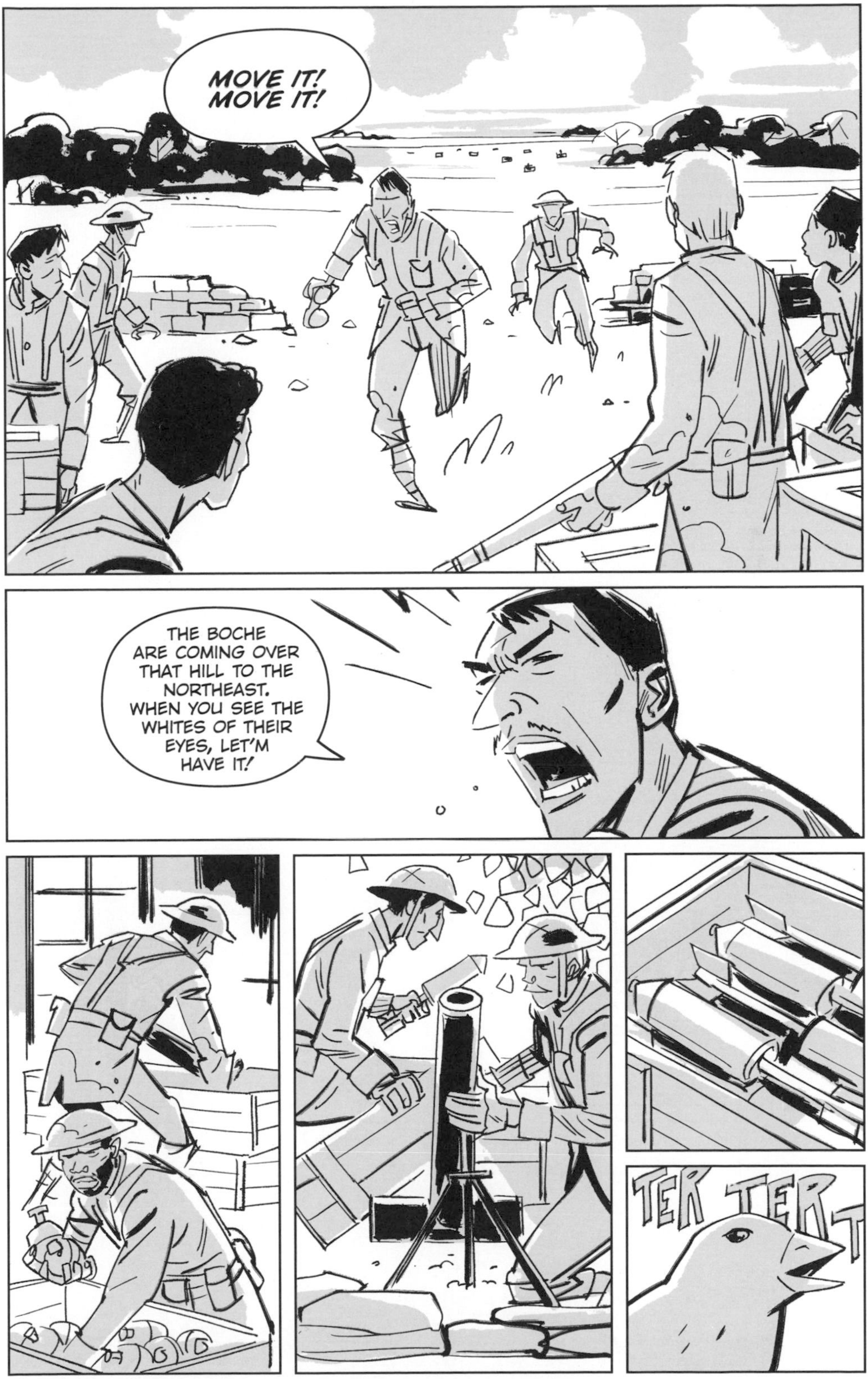
MOVE IT! MOVE IT!
THE BOCHE ARE COMING OVER THAT HILL TO THE NORTHEAST. WHEN YOU SEE THE WHITES OF THEIR EYES, LET'M HAVE IT!
TER TER

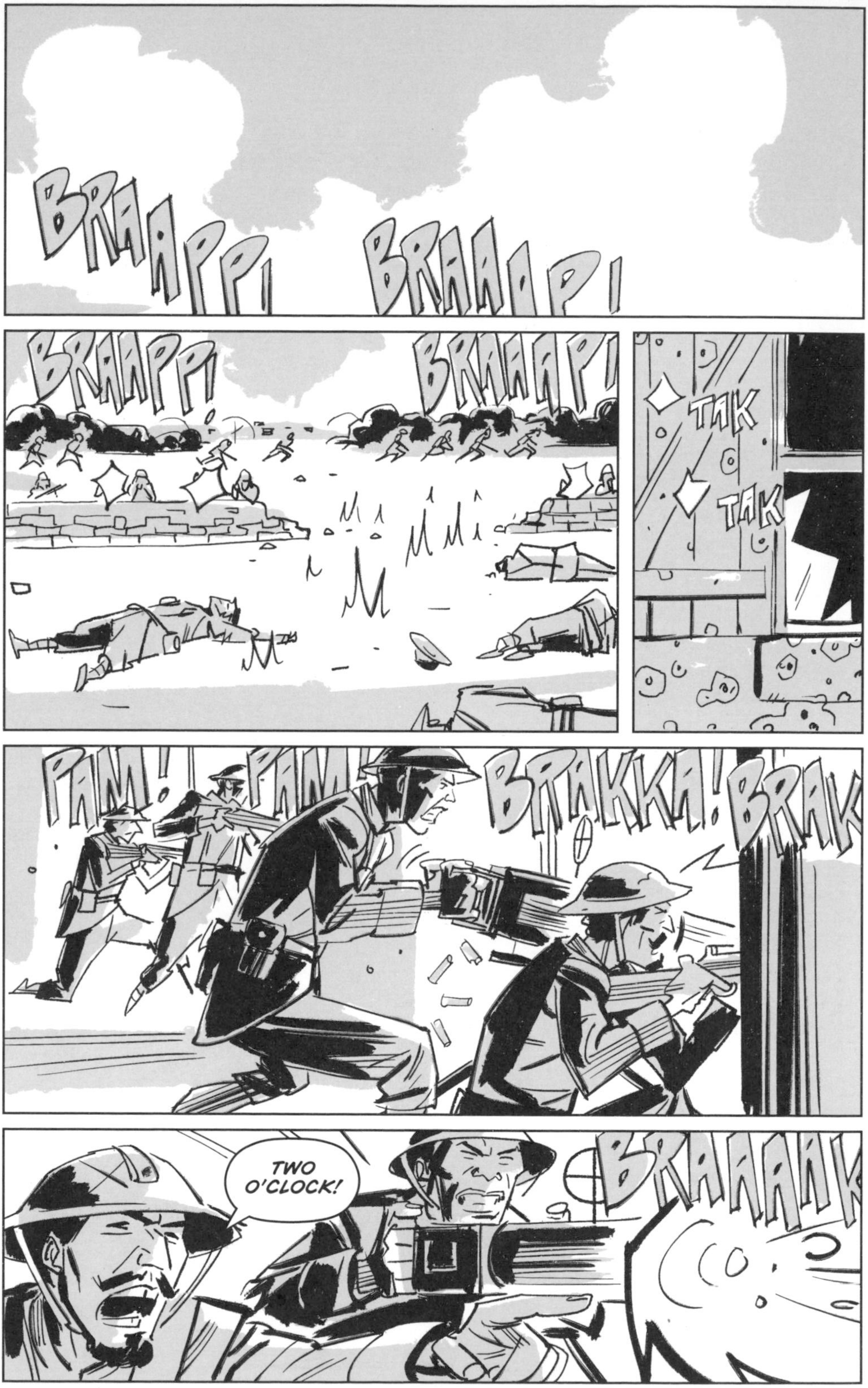
BRAAPP! BRAAAP!
BRAAPP! BRAAAAP!
TAK
TAK
PAM! PAM! BRAKKA! BRAK
TWO O'CLOCK!
BRAAAAK

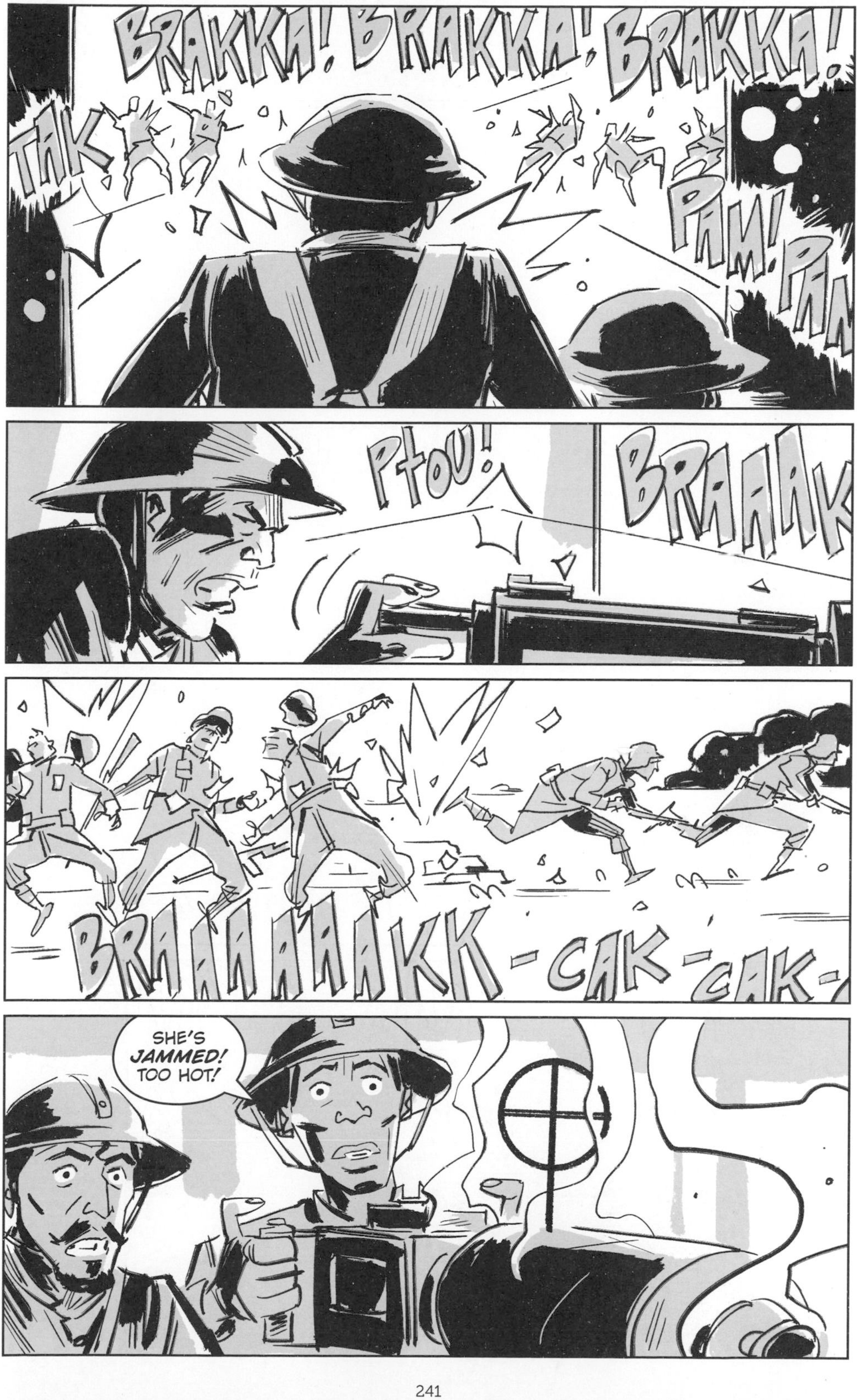
BRAKKA! BRAKKA! BRAKKA!
TAK
PAM! PAM
PTOU!
BRAAAK
BRAAAAAAKK-CAK-CAK-
SHE'S *JAMMED!* TOO HOT!

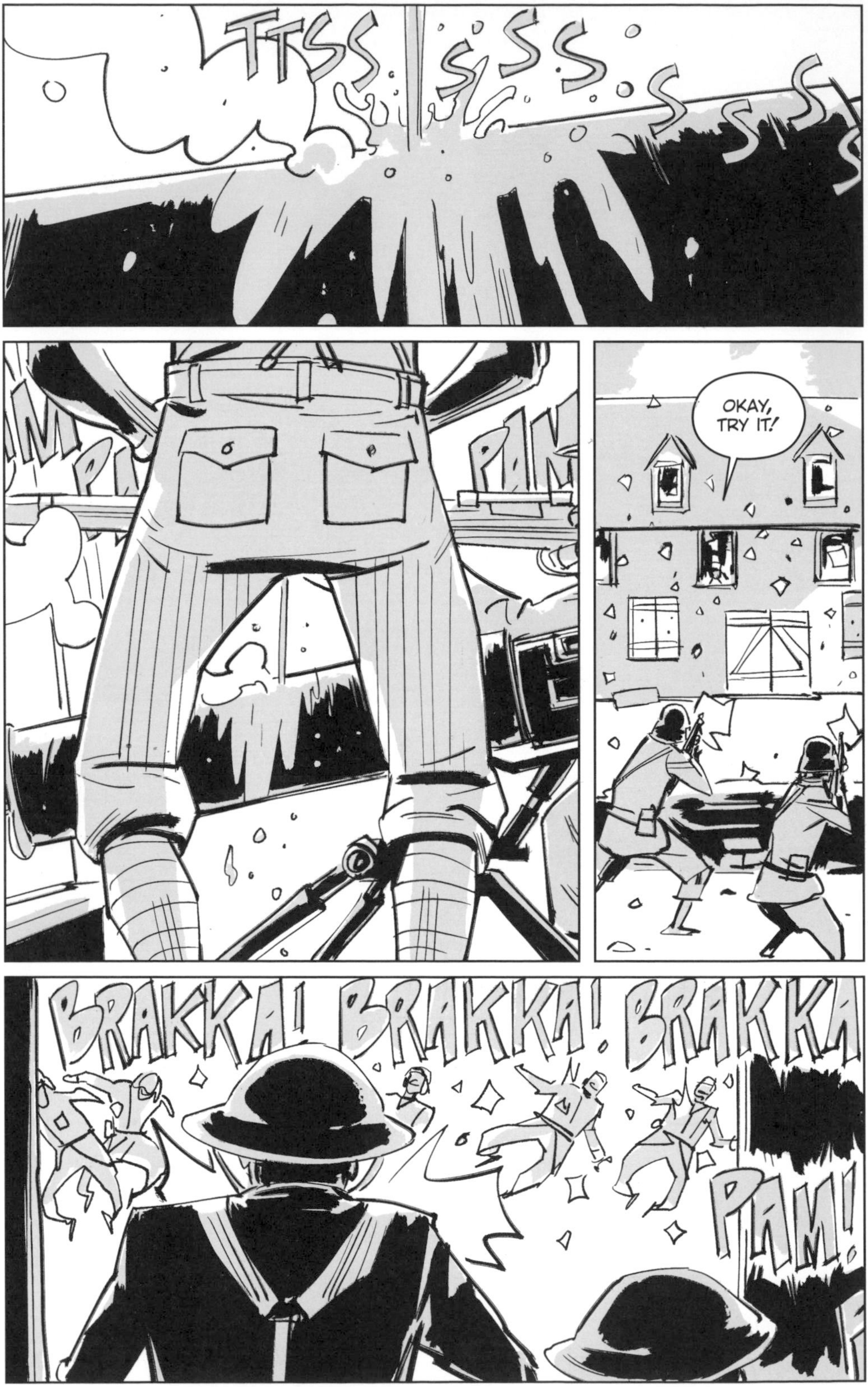
OKAY, TRY IT!
BRAKKA! BRAKKA! BRAKKA
PAM!

BRAAAPP!

THP THP THP

TINC

TINC

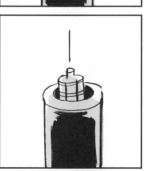
RATTTLL

THOOMP!

EEEEEEEE EEEE EE

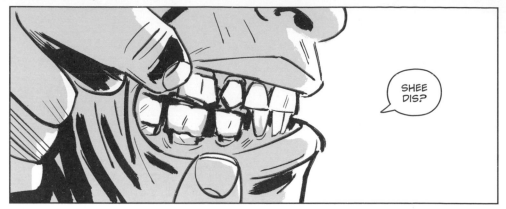

SHEE DIS?

JESUS!

I LOST ALL BUT FOUR OF MY TEETH.

...AHMAD DIDN'T MAKE IT.

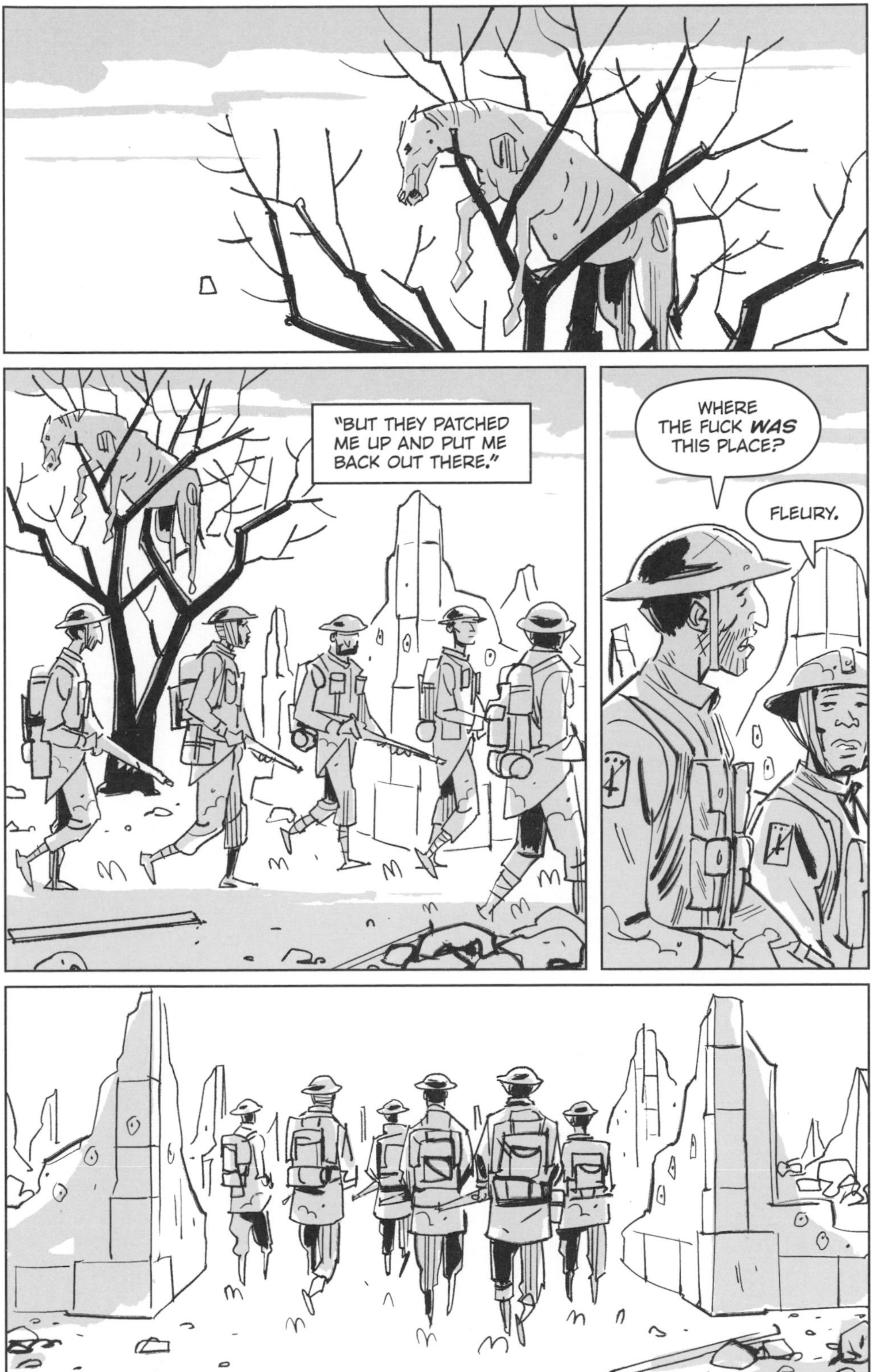
"BUT THEY PATCHED ME UP AND PUT ME BACK OUT THERE."
WHERE THE FUCK **WAS** THIS PLACE?
FLEURY.

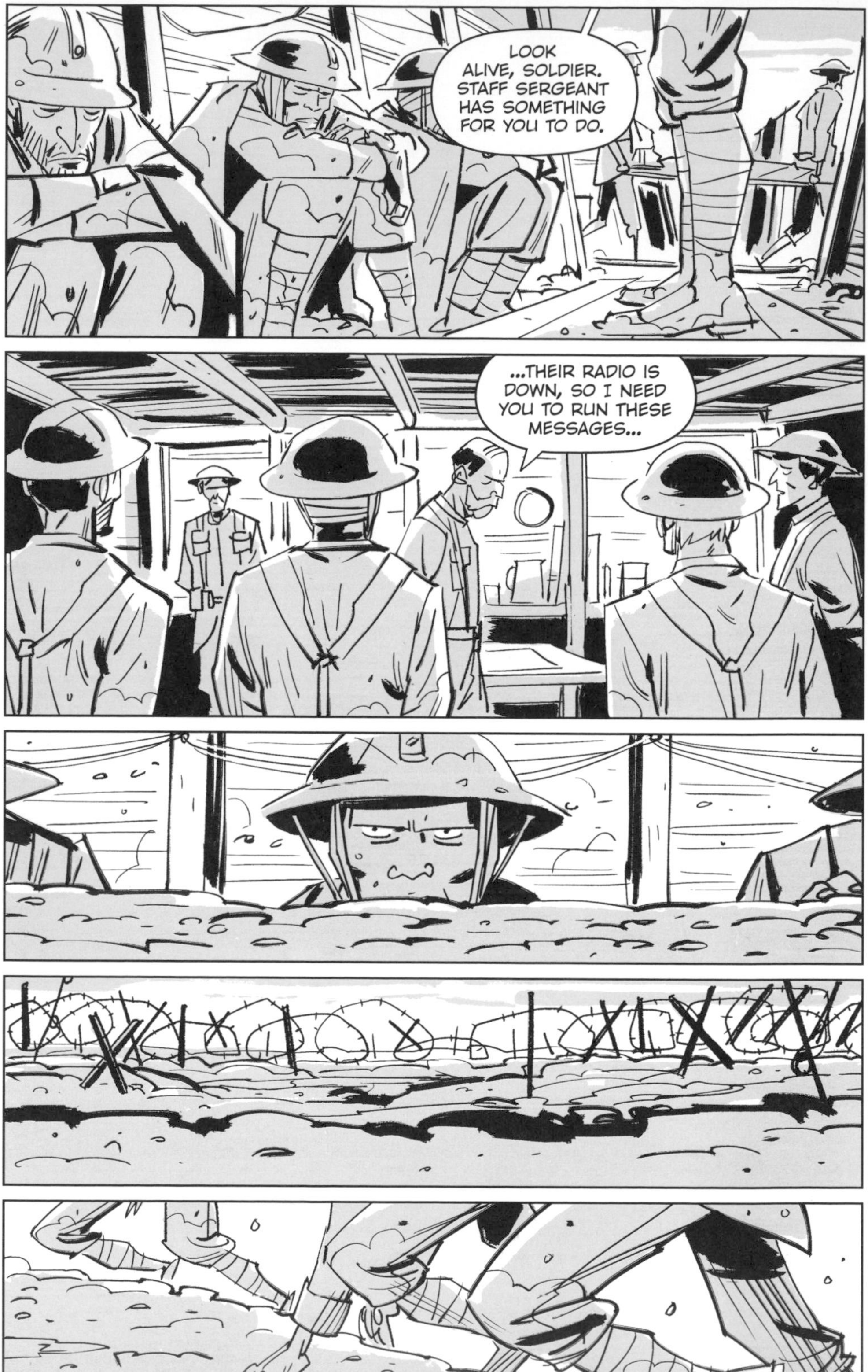
LOOK ALIVE, SOLDIER. STAFF SERGEANT HAS SOMETHING FOR YOU TO DO.
...THEIR RADIO IS DOWN, SO I NEED YOU TO RUN THESE MESSAGES...

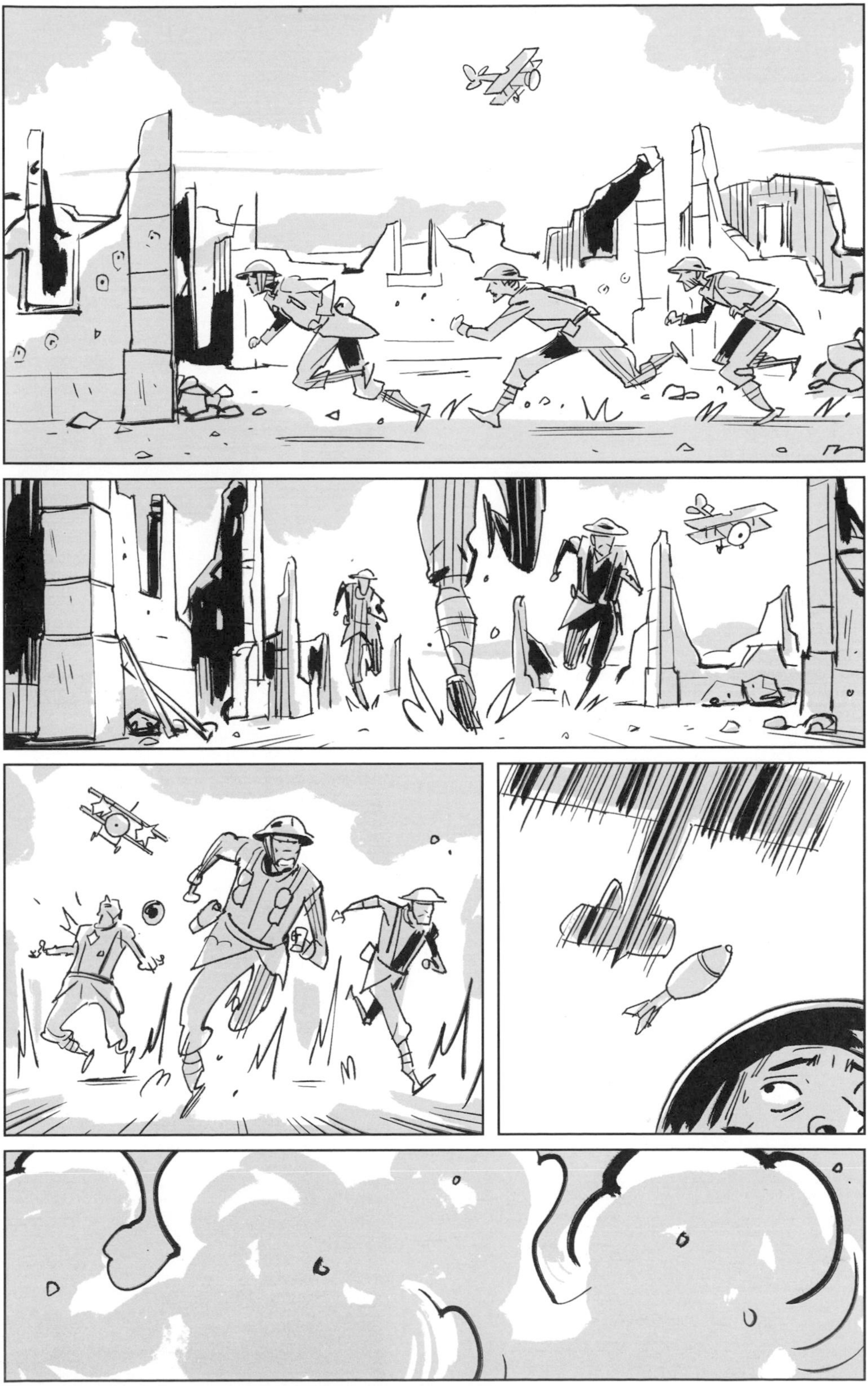

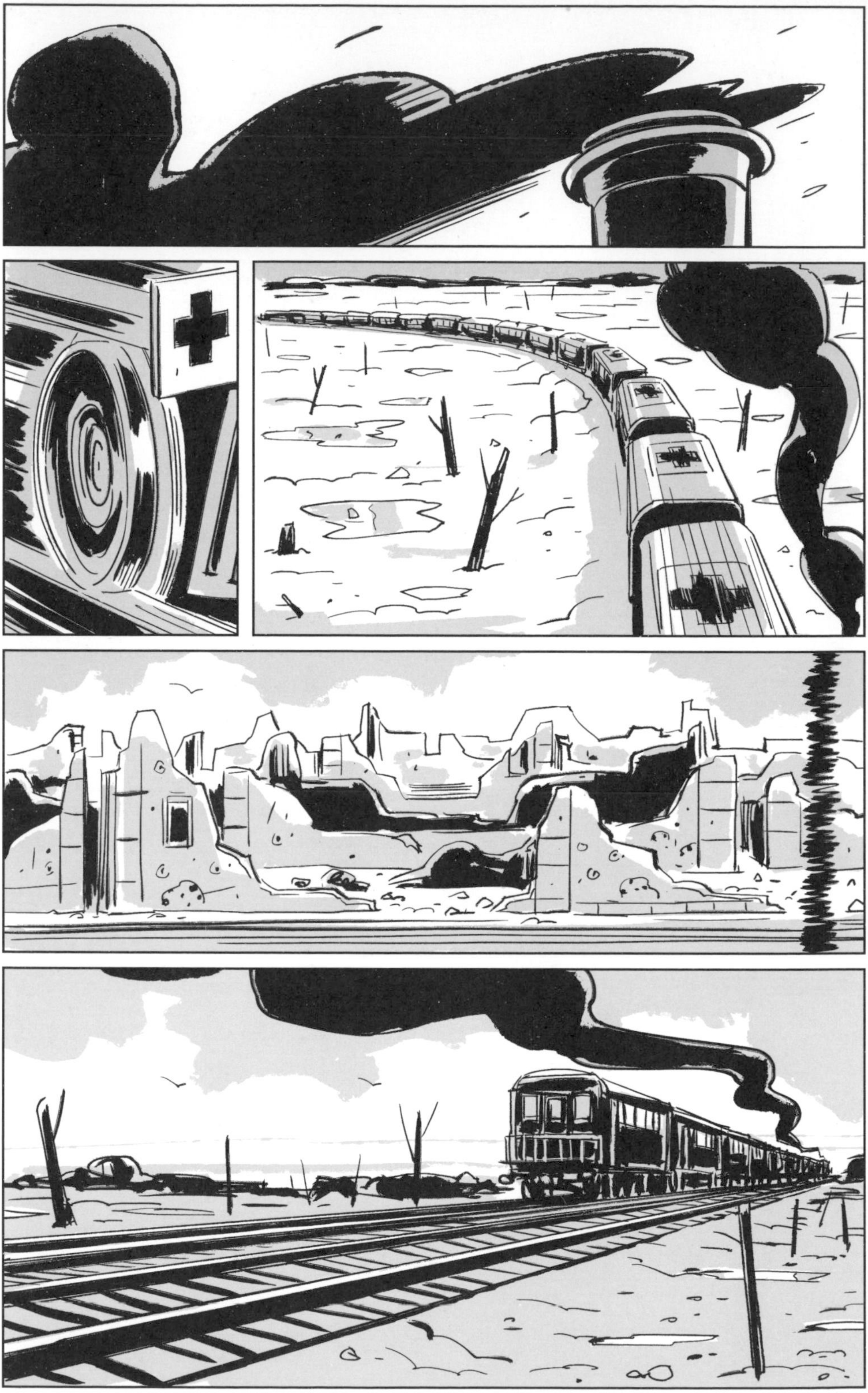

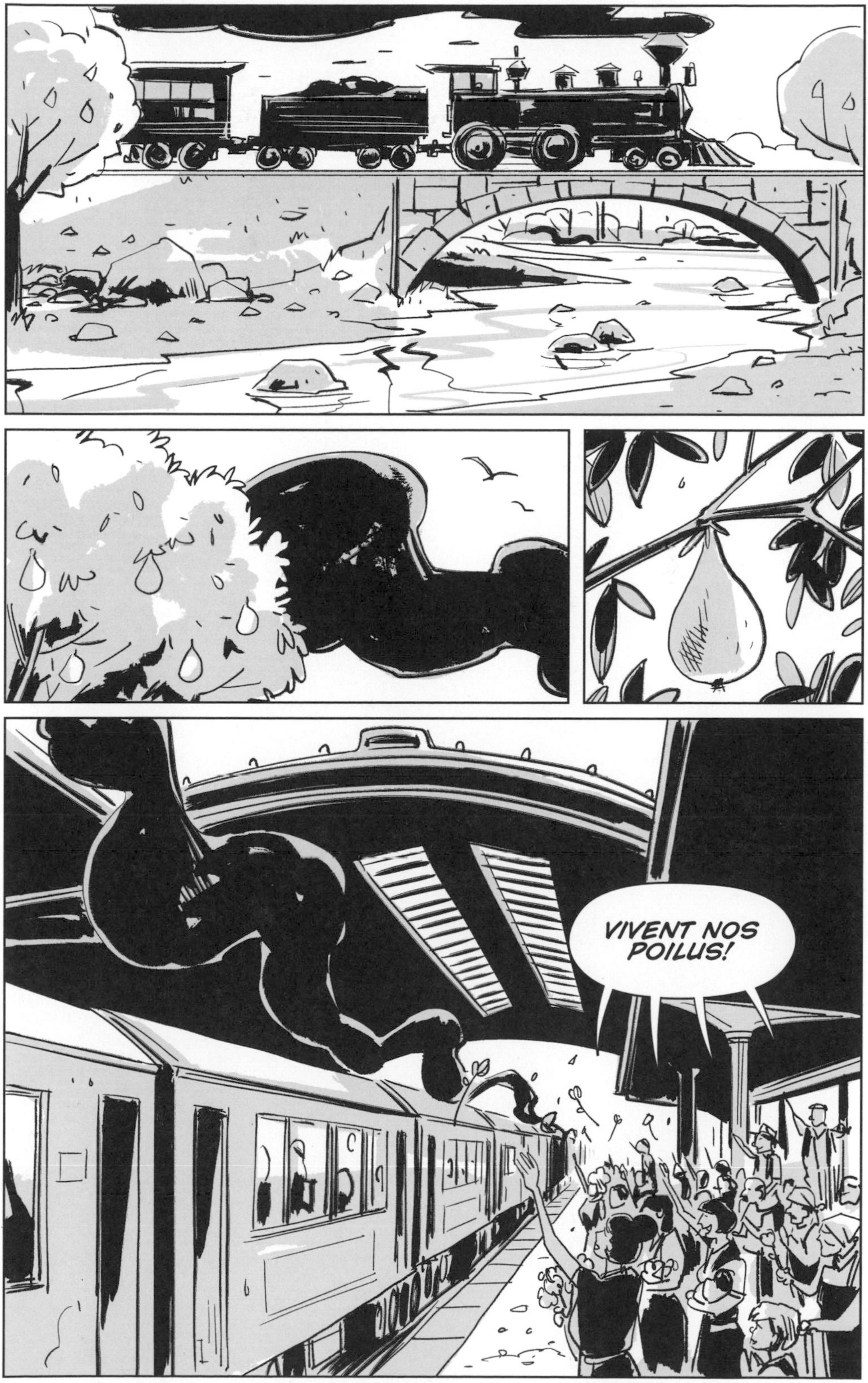
VIVENT NOS POILUS!

WELCOME TO LYON!

GAULOISES
CAPORAL

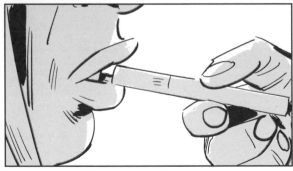

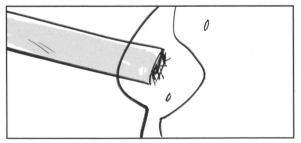

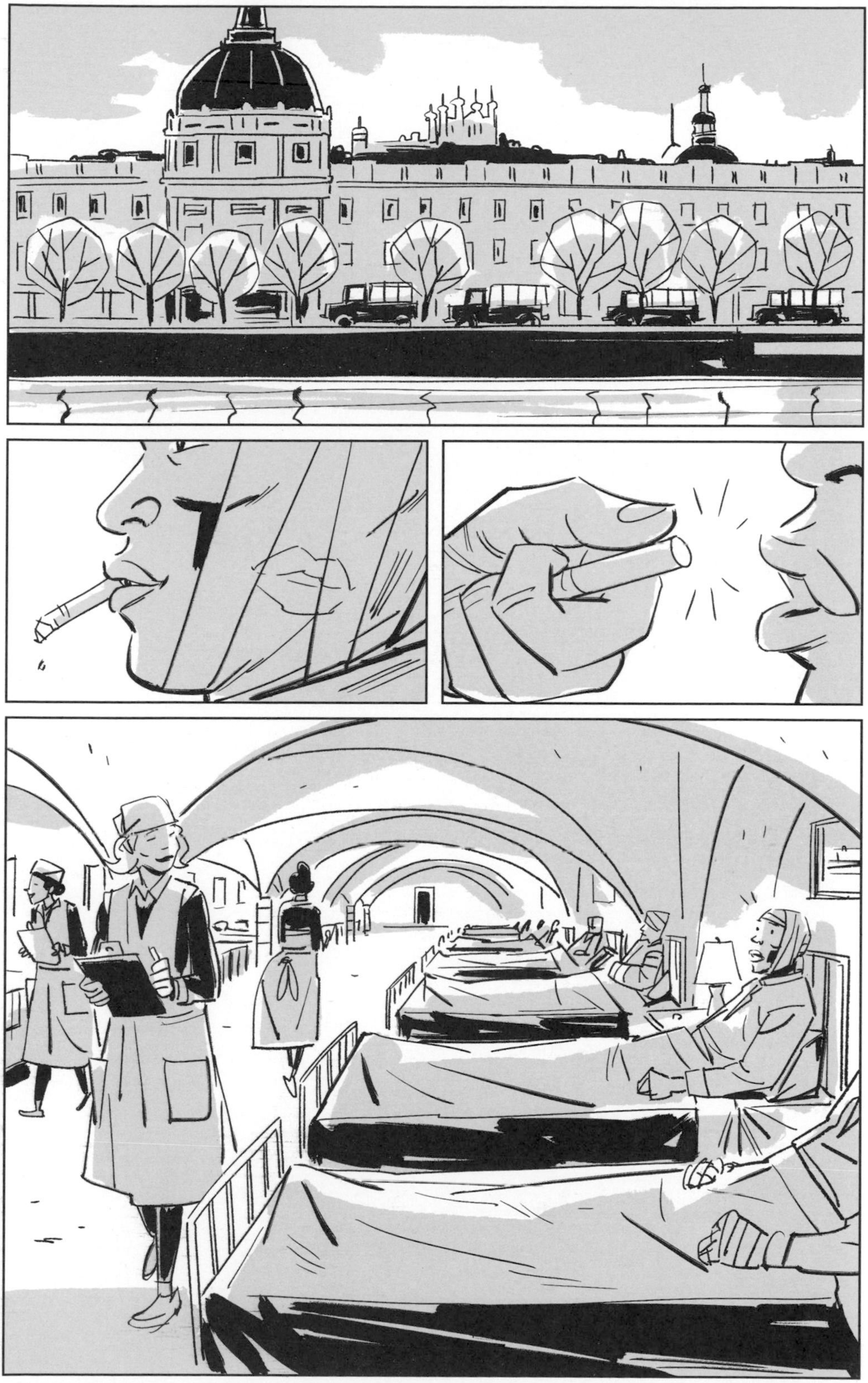

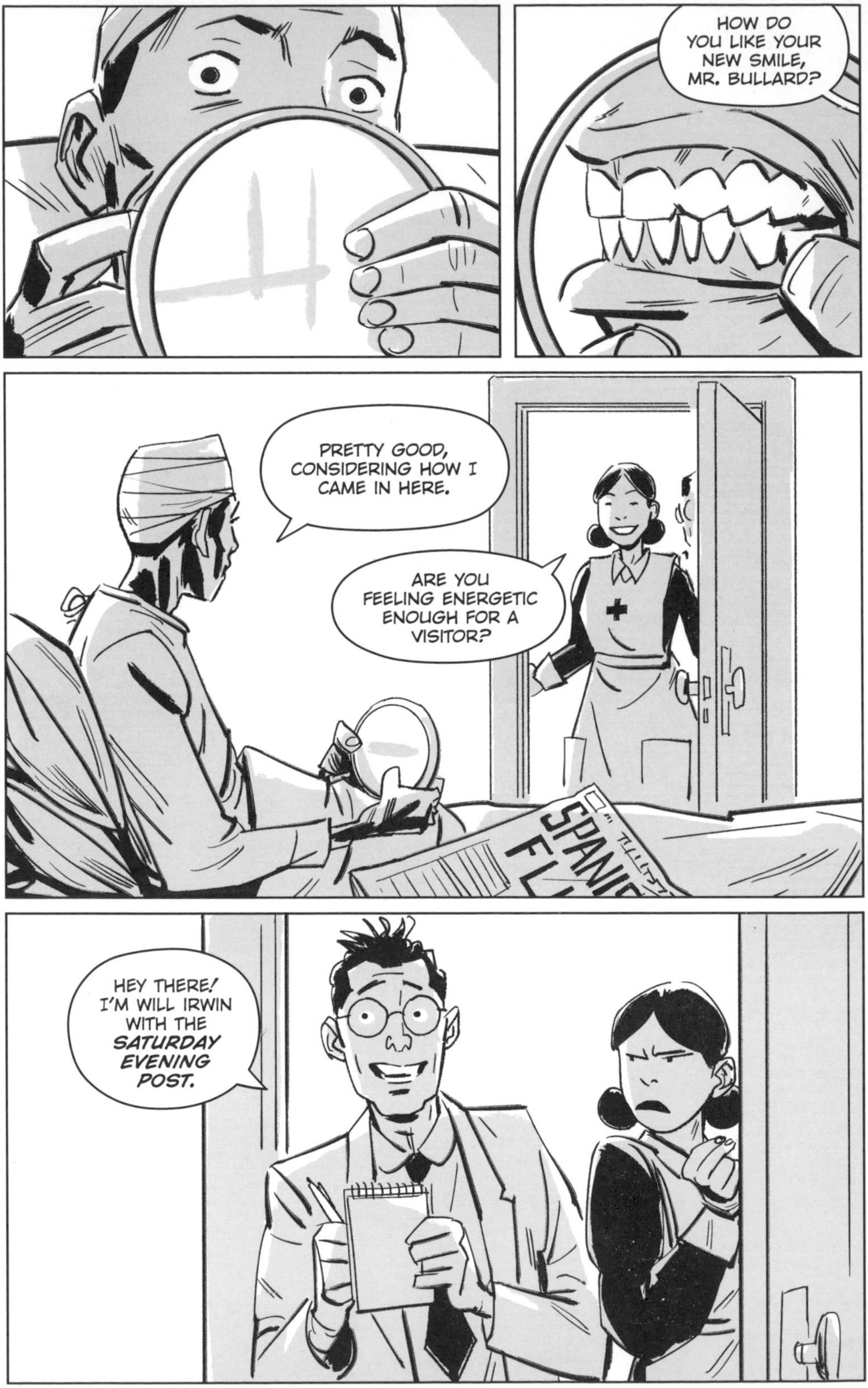
HOW DO YOU LIKE YOUR NEW SMILE, MR. BULLARD?
PRETTY GOOD, CONSIDERING HOW I CAME IN HERE.
ARE YOU FEELING ENERGETIC ENOUGH FOR A VISITOR?
HEY THERE! I'M WILL IRWIN WITH THE *SATURDAY EVENING POST.*

Flashes From the War Zone

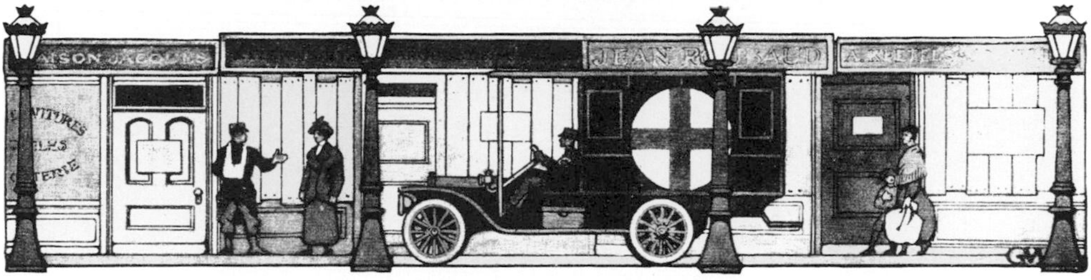

By WILL IRWIN

The Voice of Her Fallen Son

THE proprietor of the jewelry shop next door, who had dropped in to gossip with the petshop man, looked after her and asked in the argot:

"Strapped? Broke?"

"No," said the proprietor, gently scratching the head of Coco, who sat ruffling his feathers; "no, she told me about it when she came to make the bargain. She had one son. He and Coco—they were brought up together. He taught this bird to talk; it is a famous talker, and can whistle three tunes. The son, he is dead at Verdun. And Coco talks with the voice of the dead—you see? Listen!" For Coco had started his gurgle, preliminary to speaking.

"Where are my shoes, *Maman?*" he said.

"How would you like it if——" began the petshop man. Then he stopped dead. For the jeweler had turned and was looking out of the window. And he wore a crêpe band about his left arm.

They told the United States consul of this French hospital town that they had a wounded American in Hospital No. 16; so the consul drifted over, on his first spare afternoon, to see what he could do. At the hospital they referred him to Bed 10, Row 2, Ward 4, where he found his man asleep, the blankets drawn up over his head. The consul touched him.

"Who dah?" exploded a voice from beneath the blankets. Off came the cover, revealing a comely black head and a row of teeth like new gravestones.

"Why you ornery, no-account black hound!" exploded the consul affectionately. "What the blazes are you doing here?"

"Fo' the lawd's sake, mars!" said the wounded American with surprise and gratitude; "you'se from de Souf, ain't you?"

When, a little later, first-class Private Eugene So-and-So, of the this-or-that infantry regiment, grew convalescent, he used to get leave as often as he could so that he might hobble into town on his crutches and visit the consul. I also was a persistent visitor at the consulate; and so on many an afternoon we three—Southerner, Southern negro and Northerner—sat and talked war. A year and a half at the front had made a strange creature of Private Gene. He was, to begin with, a great, young black Hercules, a monument of trained muscle. When the war broke he had been making his living in England by boxing and foot-racing. But he wasn't at all the negro we know at home. War and heroism had given him that air of authority common to all soldiers of the line. He looked you in the eye and answered you straight with replies that carried their own conviction of truth. The democracy of the French Army had brushed off onto him; he had grown accustomed to looking on white men as equals. His race, they say, has a talent for spoken languages. Already there was a trace of French accent in his rich, Southern negro speech; and when he grew excited he would fall into French phrases.

He had held a machine gun during the first terrible days of the Verdun battle, when the Brandenburgers were fighting for Fort Douaumont. For something he did there—a matter of going to the rescue of wounded under fire—he had been mentioned in orders, which is the first step toward the Croix de Guerre. He was going to work hard for that decoration when they sent him back.

He had fought at Arras; he had been in the charges for Notre Dame de Lorette; he had been wounded in the blasted terrain of Champagne. But all memories of those glorious and horrible old actions seemed to have been dimmed by that terrific fighting at Verdun, and especially by that day when his company held off a German charge until man could hold no more, until he knew the red rage and the hot sickness of butchery. He described that day in detail, with a wealth of picturesque negro phrasing and flashes of negro wit which no Northerner could possibly transcribe from memory. They expected the charge that day, and so they cleaned guns, got everything shipshape, and had a good dinner of "*singe*" and biscuits. *Singe* means literally "monkey," and is French soldier slang for beef stew. "If I eat much more of that stuff," said Private Gene, "I certainly will climb trees."

And then the German charge commenced. He described it not as a run but as a steady walk—a great crowd of men in gray coming smoothly on. His company had a nervous little sergeant, who was, nevertheless, willing to take advice, Private Gene said. He danced up and down, yelling "*Feu!*" before the Germans got within proper killing range. But the experienced gunners cajoled him, "joshed" him, until the Germans were massed two hundred yards away. And here the narrative of Private Gene—I heard him tell it several times—always grew confused, dropped into a singsong at intervals, and flashed back and forth between French and English. "*Première pièce—feu! Deuxième pièce—feu!* Rat-a-tat tat-tat tat-tat!" he would say, imitating both the sergeant and the guns. "It was like mowing grass, boss, only the grass grew up as fast as you mowed it. When they got a little start on us and you could rightly see them, they was coming on by fours—four here, four there—*toujours quatre, toujours quatre!* You'd mow them down, and four more would be in their places. You'd look again, and one or two would be way forward. You'd slue the gun around and get them, and four more would be just where you'd fired before, but nearer—and you'd mow them down. *Toujours quatre, toujours quatre!* If you hadn't seen the dead where you'd piled them you'd 'a' got plumb disheartened. When you stopped to cool, and the other gun picked up the *feu*, you could see 'em wriggling like worms in the bait box.

"Yassir, I was sick, awful sick! Every time the sergeant yelled '*Feu!*' I got sicker and sicker. They had wives and children, hadn't they?"

An afternoon, during which the drama was repeated again and again; and then they had to abandon the trench—a matter of a military accident which need not be recorded here. Private Gene destroyed his machine gun. "There's a place where you can do it with your hand," he said, "but not if your hand is fumbly, an' I sho' was fumbly." So he opened the breech and kicked it until he destroyed the mechanism. Then it was a confused flight, dodging from shell hole to shell hole, until he reached cover

(Concluded on Page 70)

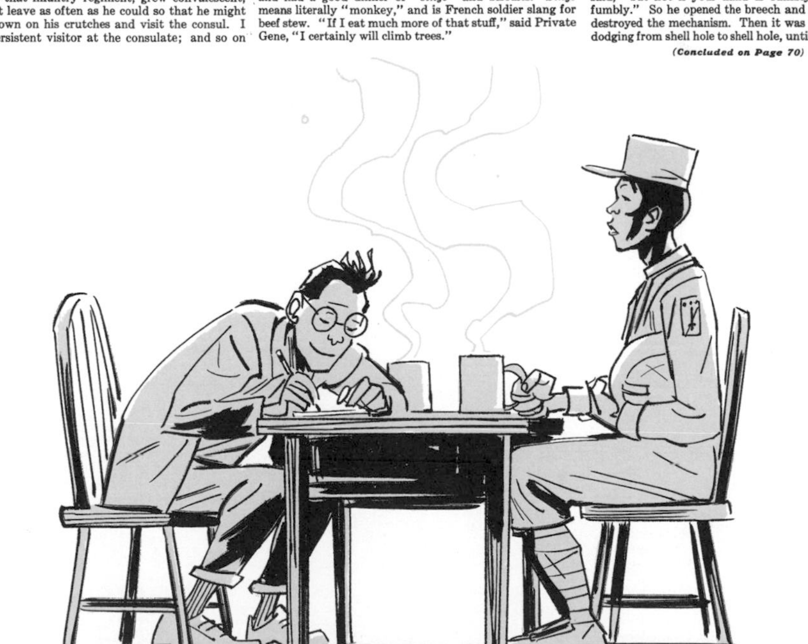

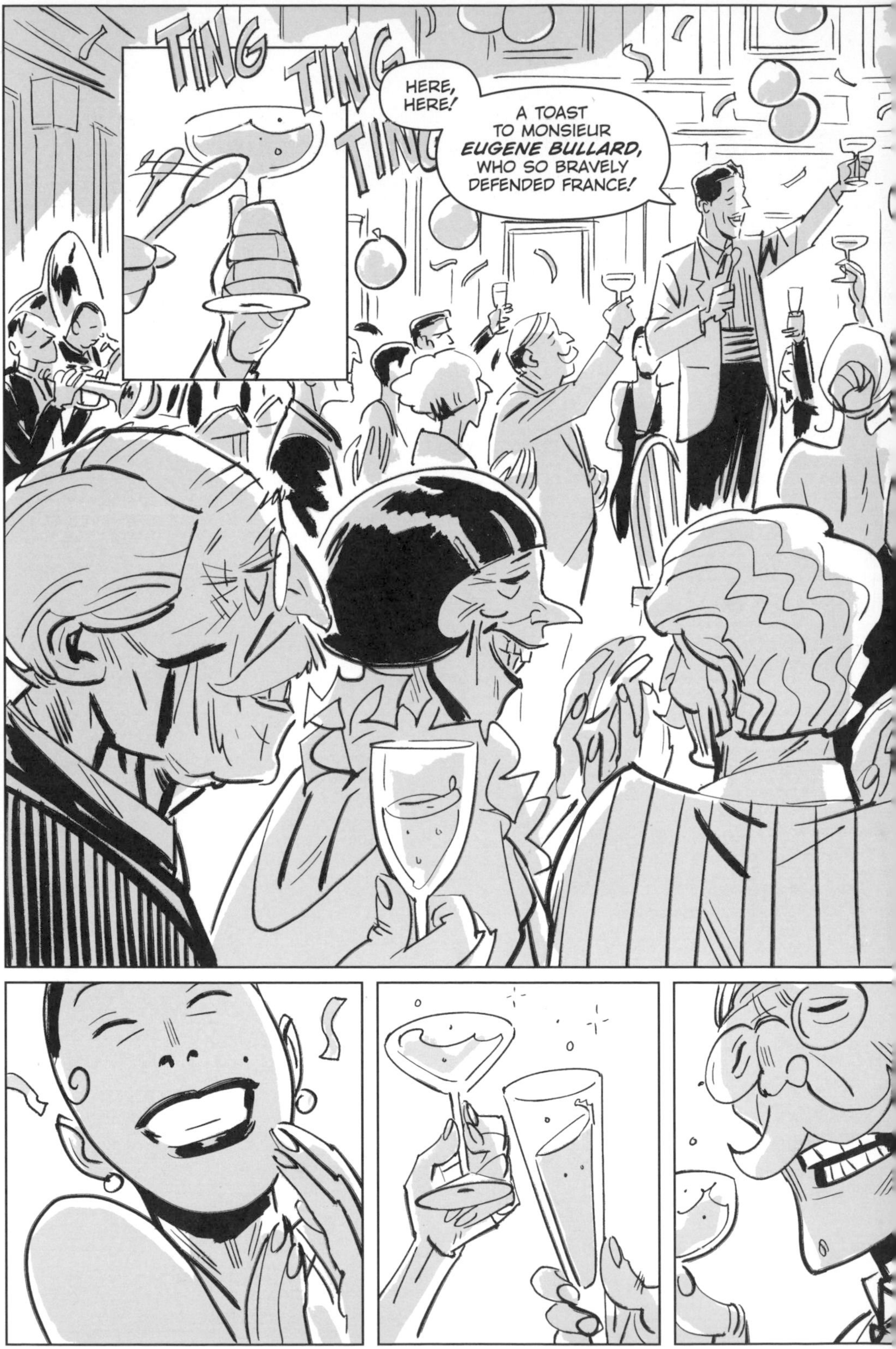
TING TING TING
HERE, HERE!
A TOAST TO MONSIEUR EUGENE BULLARD, WHO SO BRAVELY DEFENDED FRANCE!

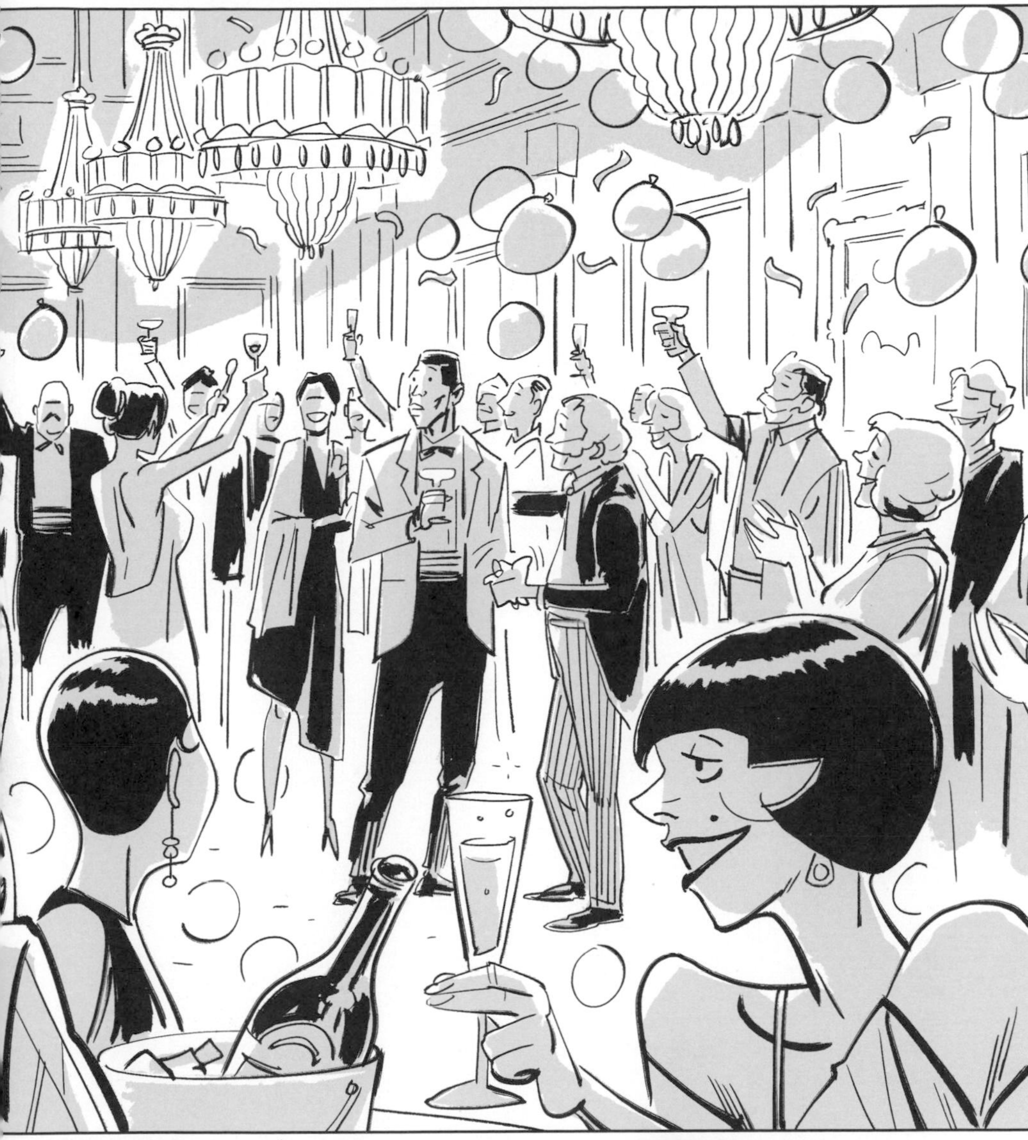
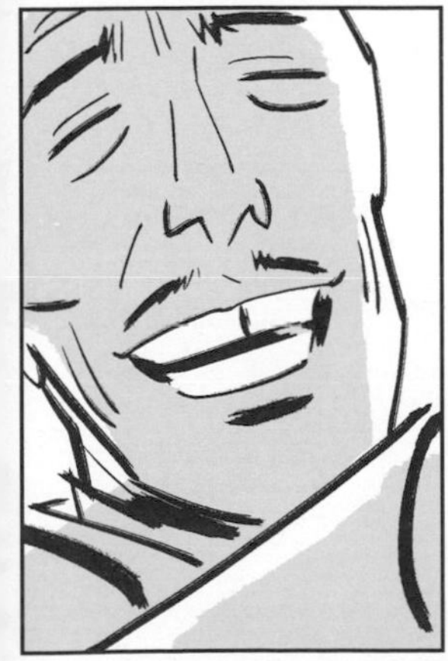
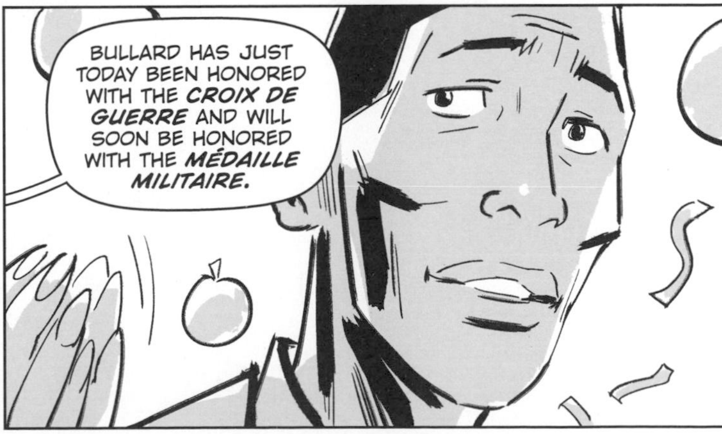
BULLARD HAS JUST TODAY BEEN HONORED WITH THE ***CROIX DE GUERRE*** AND WILL SOON BE HONORED WITH THE ***MÉDAILLE MILITAIRE.***

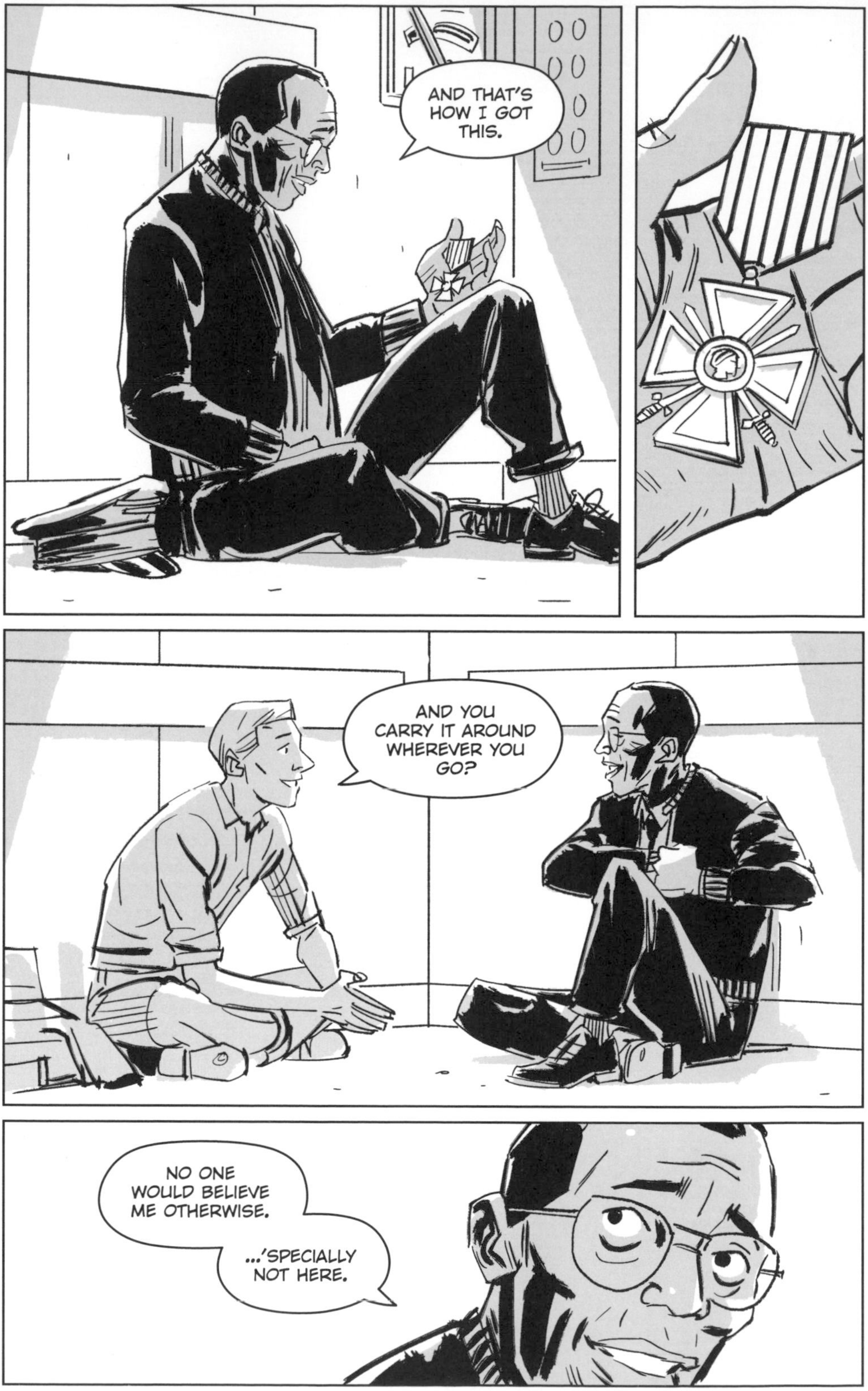
AND THAT'S HOW I GOT THIS.
AND YOU CARRY IT AROUND WHEREVER YOU GO?
NO ONE WOULD BELIEVE ME OTHERWISE.
...'SPECIALLY NOT HERE.

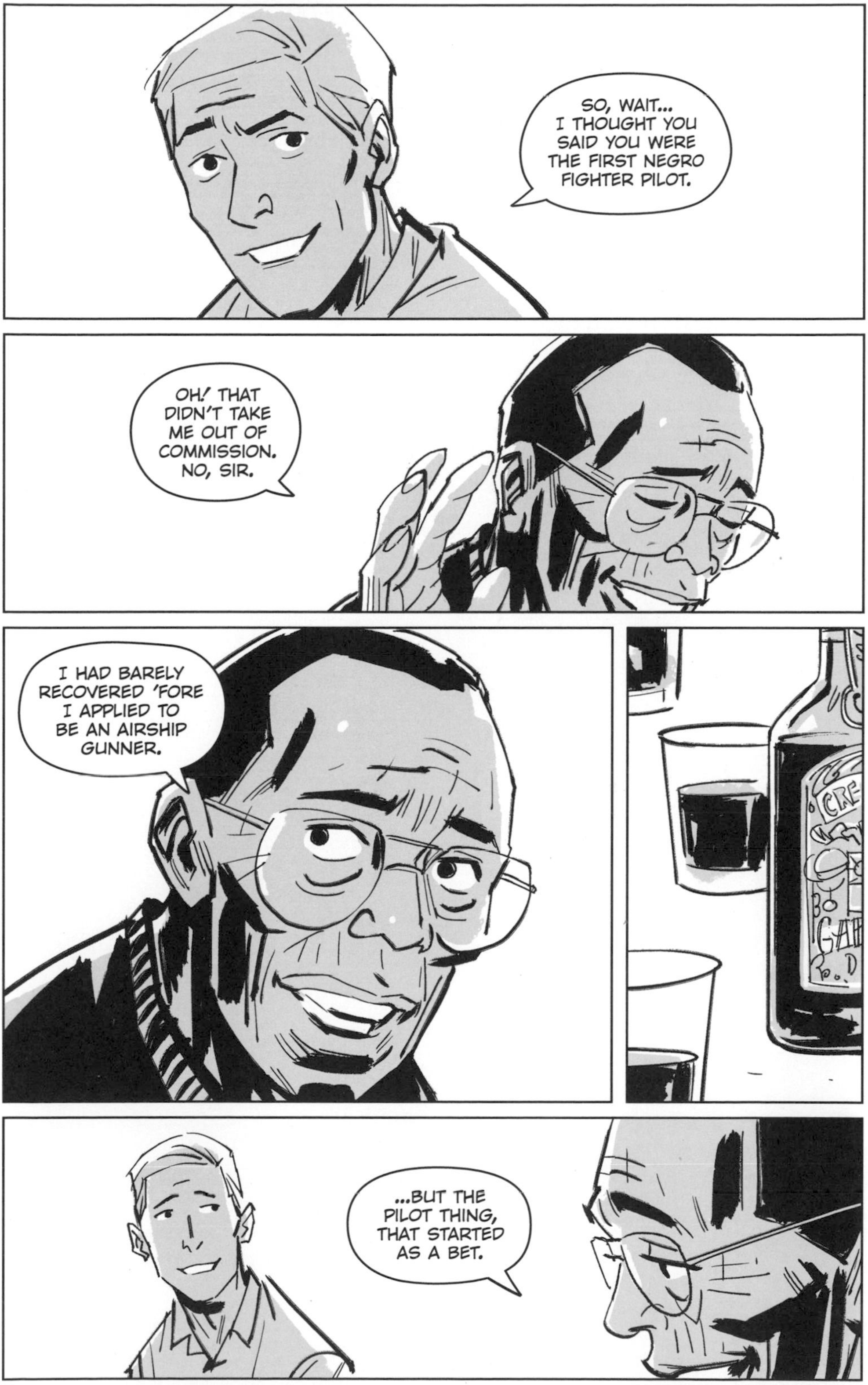
SO, WAIT... I THOUGHT YOU SAID YOU WERE THE FIRST NEGRO FIGHTER PILOT.
OH! THAT DIDN'T TAKE ME OUT OF COMMISSION. NO, SIR.
I HAD BARELY RECOVERED 'FORE I APPLIED TO BE AN AIRSHIP GUNNER.
...BUT THE PILOT THING, THAT STARTED AS A BET.

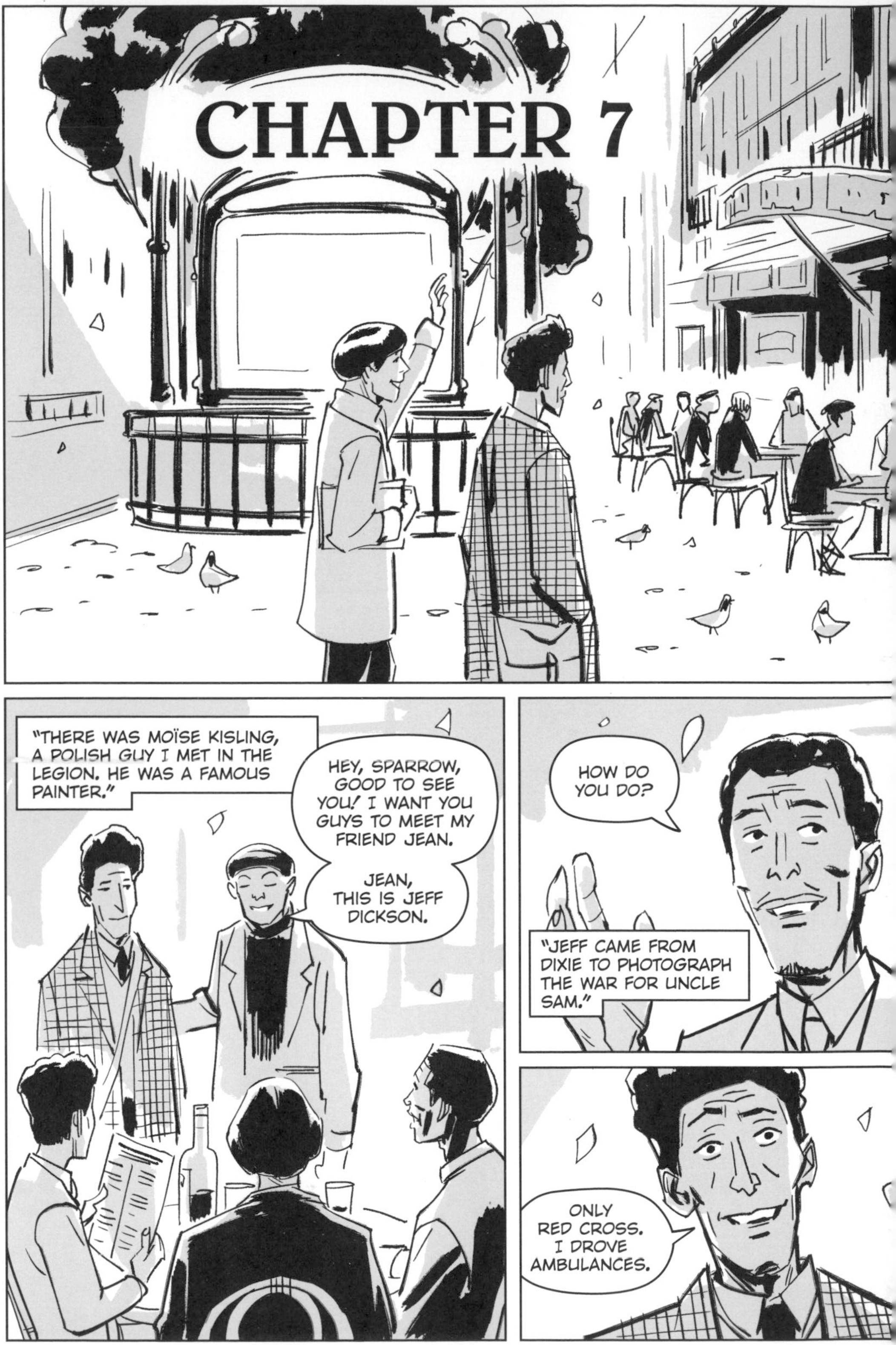
CHAPTER 7
"THERE WAS MOÏSE KISLING, A POLISH GUY I MET IN THE LEGION. HE WAS A FAMOUS PAINTER."
HEY, SPARROW, GOOD TO SEE YOU! I WANT YOU GUYS TO MEET MY FRIEND JEAN.
JEAN, THIS IS JEFF DICKSON.
HOW DO YOU DO?
"JEFF CAME FROM DIXIE TO PHOTOGRAPH THE WAR FOR UNCLE SAM."
ONLY RED CROSS. I DROVE AMBULANCES.

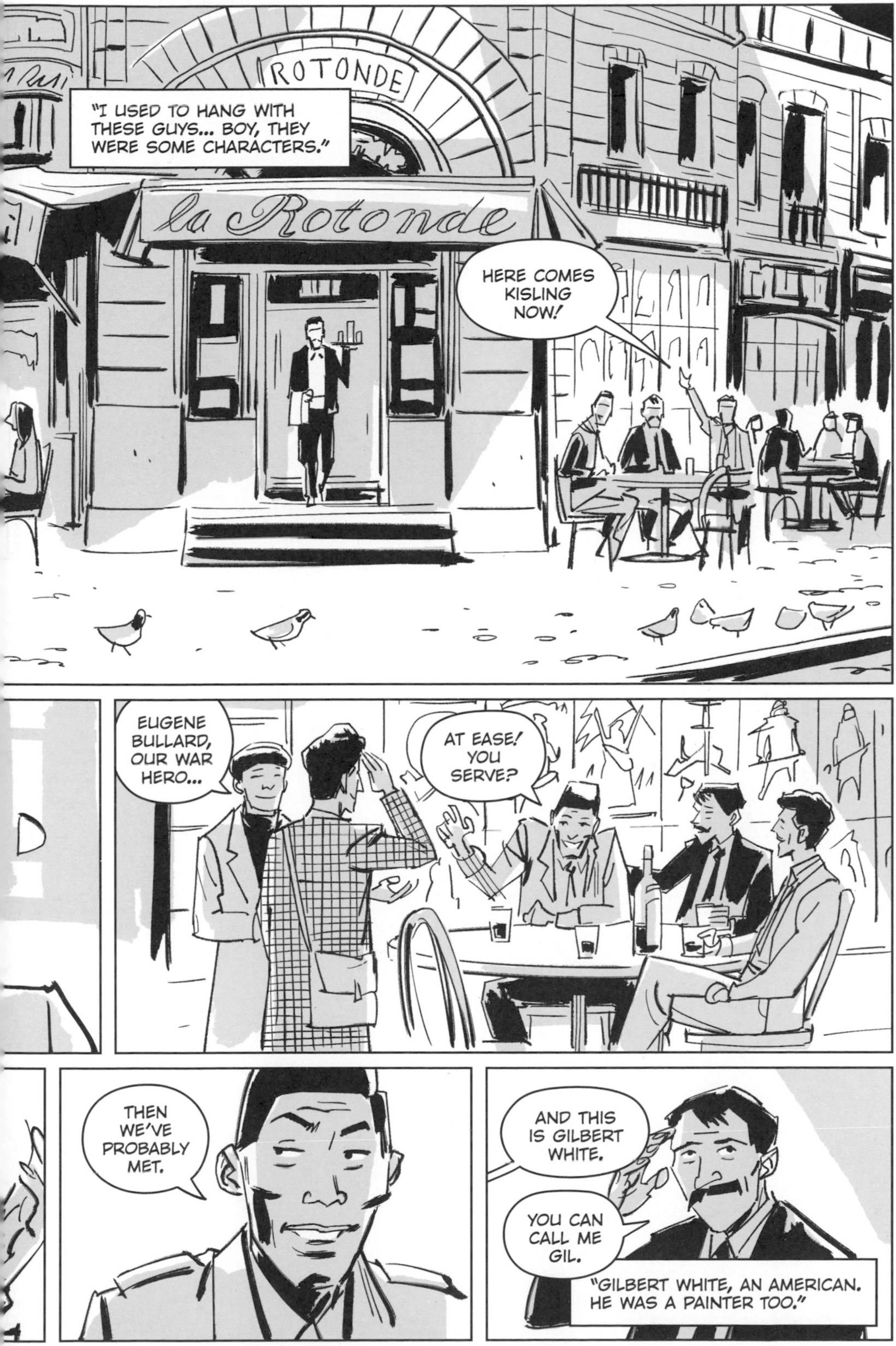
ROTONDE
"I USED TO HANG WITH THESE GUYS... BOY, THEY WERE SOME CHARACTERS."
la Rotonde
HERE COMES KISLING NOW!
EUGENE BULLARD, OUR WAR HERO...
AT EASE! YOU SERVE?
THEN WE'VE PROBABLY MET.
AND THIS IS GILBERT WHITE.
YOU CAN CALL ME GIL.
"GILBERT WHITE, AN AMERICAN. HE WAS A PAINTER TOO."

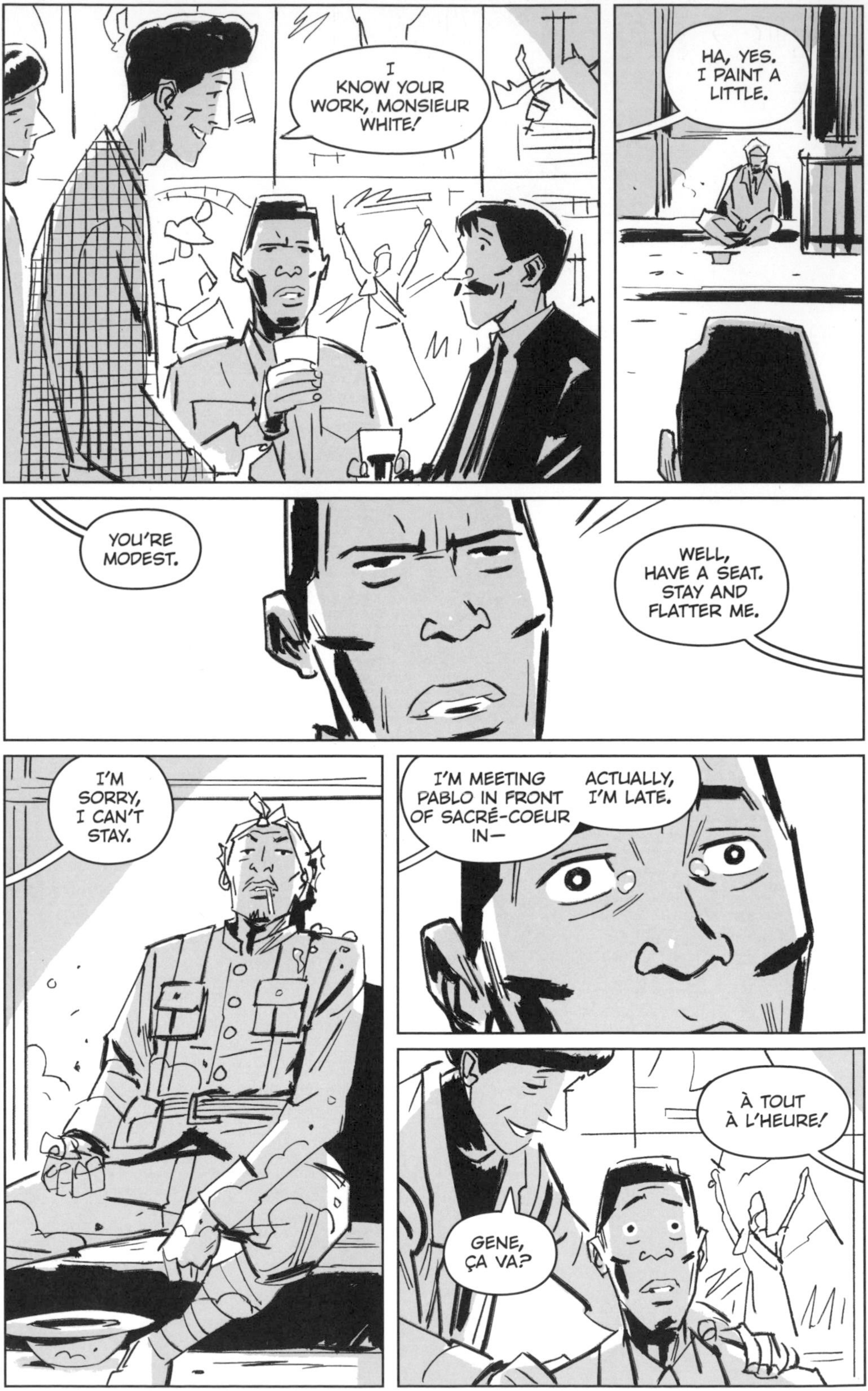
I KNOW YOUR WORK, MONSIEUR WHITE!
HA, YES. I PAINT A LITTLE.
YOU'RE MODEST.
WELL, HAVE A SEAT. STAY AND FLATTER ME.
I'M SORRY, I CAN'T STAY.
ACTUALLY, I'M LATE.
I'M MEETING PABLO IN FRONT OF SACRÉ-COEUR IN—
À TOUT À L'HEURE!
GENE, ÇA VA?

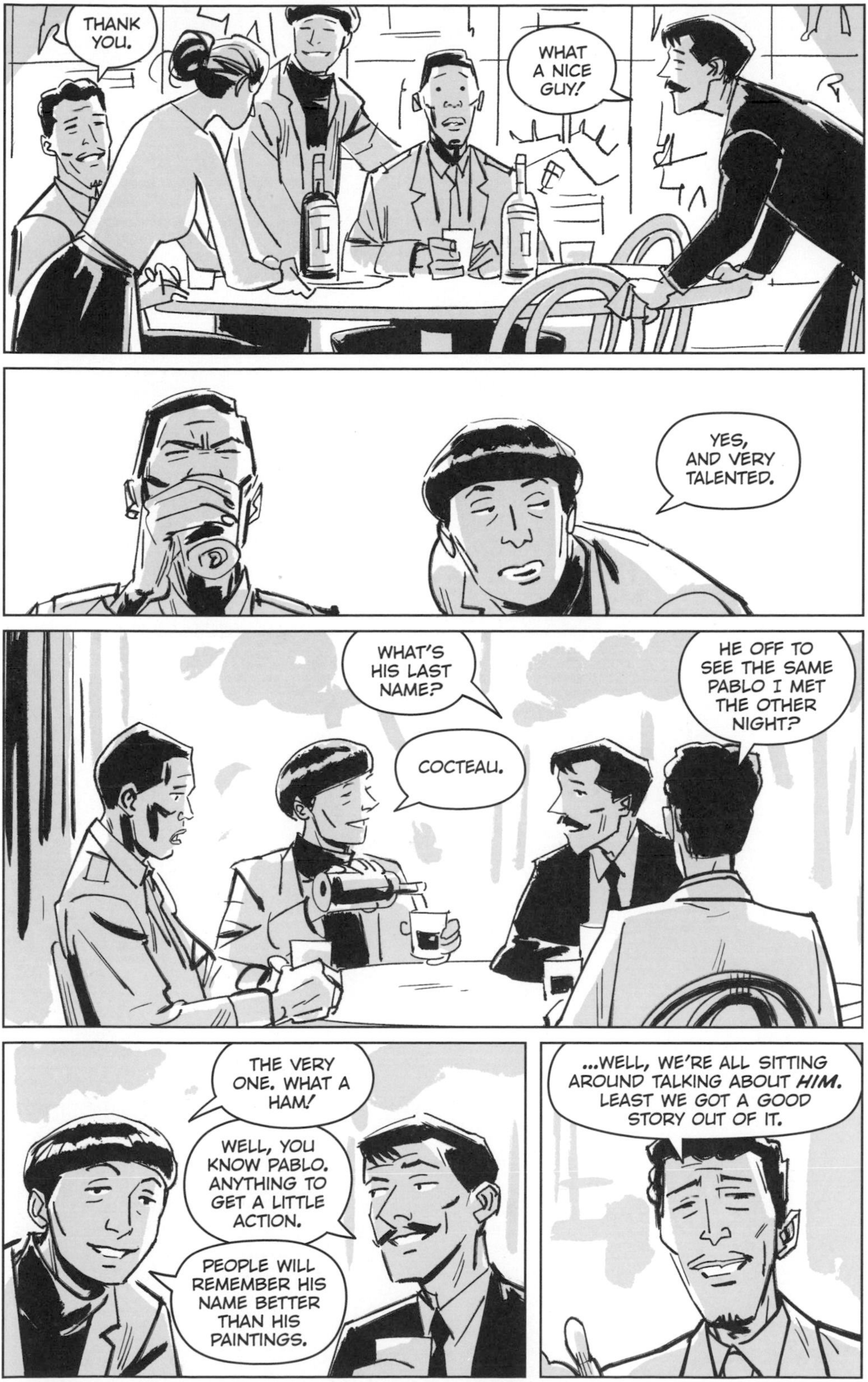
THANK YOU.
WHAT A NICE GUY!
YES, AND VERY TALENTED.
WHAT'S HIS LAST NAME?
COCTEAU.
HE OFF TO SEE THE SAME PABLO I MET THE OTHER NIGHT?
THE VERY ONE. WHAT A HAM!
WELL, YOU KNOW PABLO. ANYTHING TO GET A LITTLE ACTION.
PEOPLE WILL REMEMBER HIS NAME BETTER THAN HIS PAINTINGS.
...WELL, WE'RE ALL SITTING AROUND TALKING ABOUT *HIM*. LEAST WE GOT A GOOD STORY OUT OF IT.

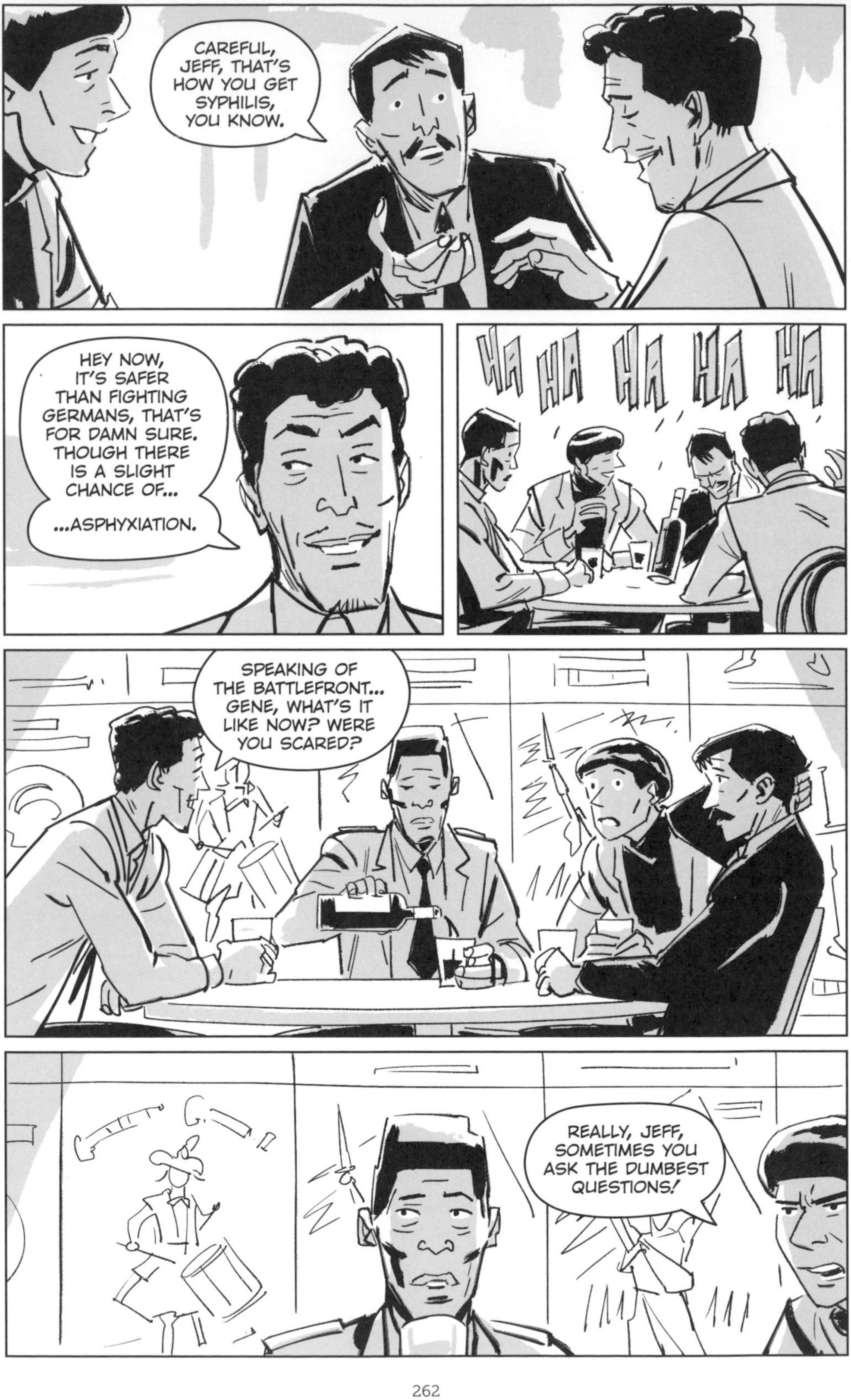
CAREFUL, JEFF, THAT'S HOW YOU GET SYPHILIS, YOU KNOW.
HEY NOW, IT'S SAFER THAN FIGHTING GERMANS, THAT'S FOR DAMN SURE. THOUGH THERE IS A SLIGHT CHANCE OF...
...ASPHYXIATION.
HA HA HA HA HA
SPEAKING OF THE BATTLEFRONT... GENE, WHAT'S IT LIKE NOW? WERE YOU SCARED?
REALLY, JEFF, SOMETIMES YOU ASK THE DUMBEST QUESTIONS!

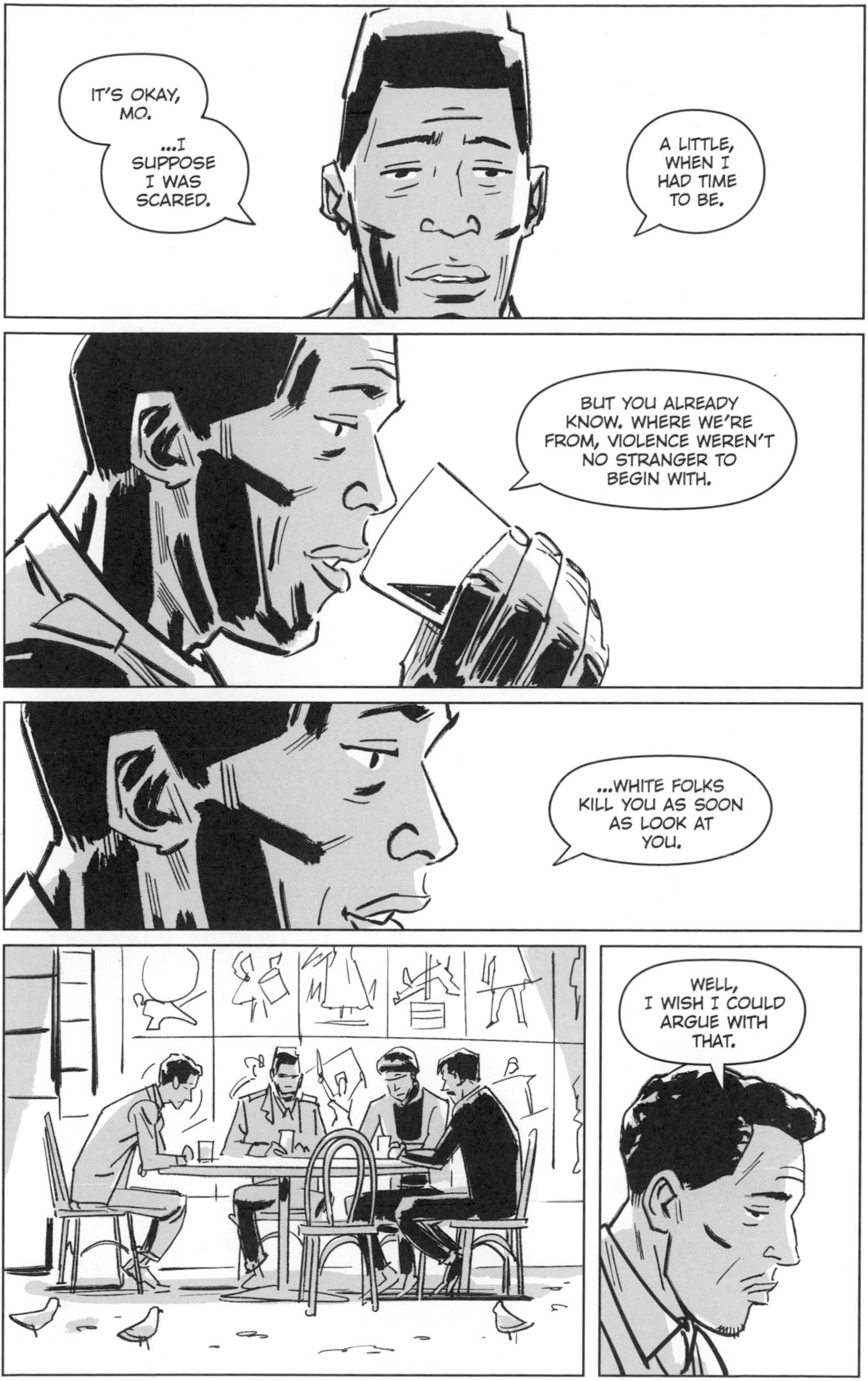
IT'S OKAY, MO.
...I SUPPOSE I WAS SCARED.
A LITTLE, WHEN I HAD TIME TO BE.
BUT YOU ALREADY KNOW. WHERE WE'RE FROM, VIOLENCE WEREN'T NO STRANGER TO BEGIN WITH.
...WHITE FOLKS KILL YOU AS SOON AS LOOK AT YOU.
WELL, I WISH I COULD ARGUE WITH THAT.

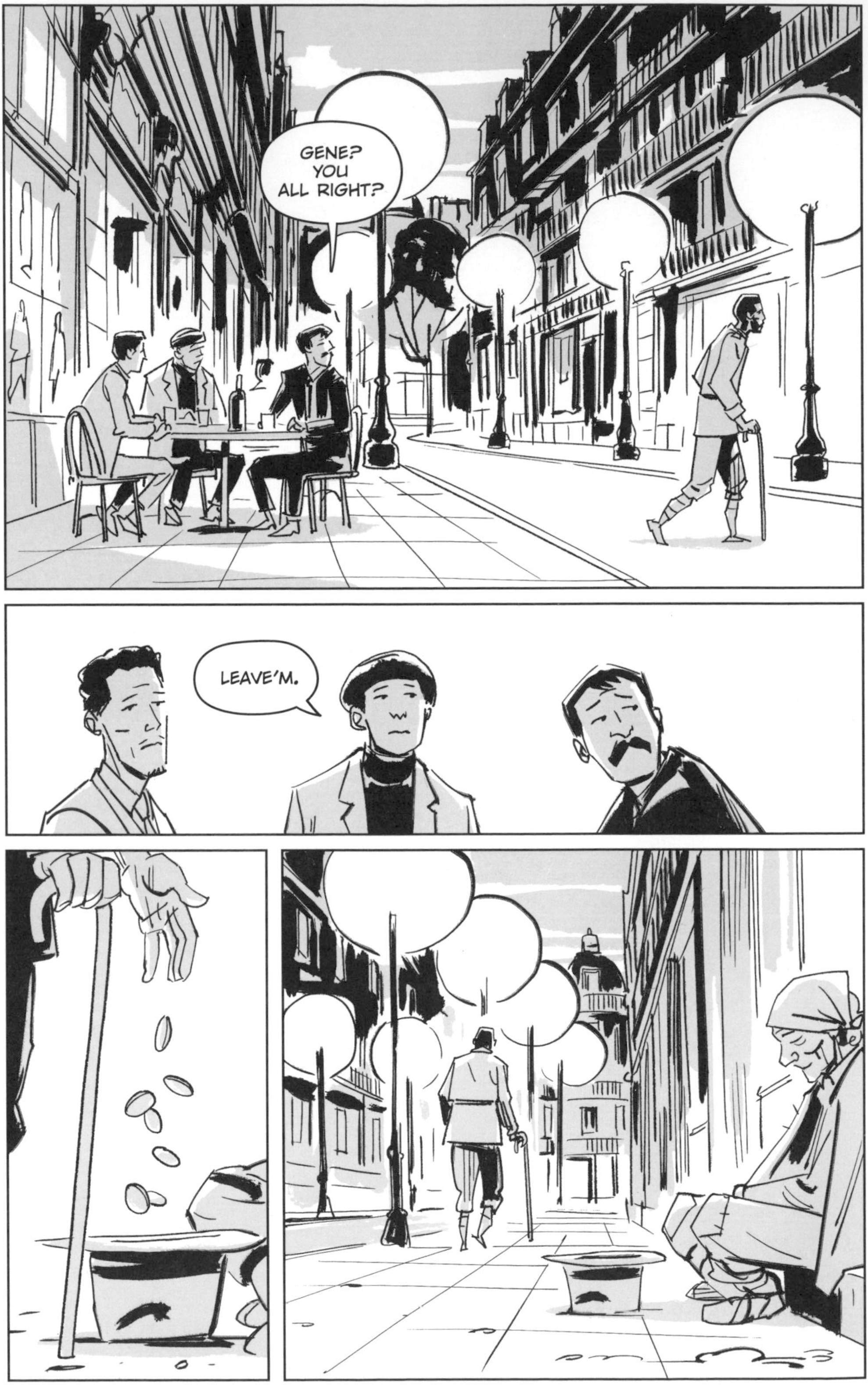
GENE? YOU ALL RIGHT?
LEAVE'M.

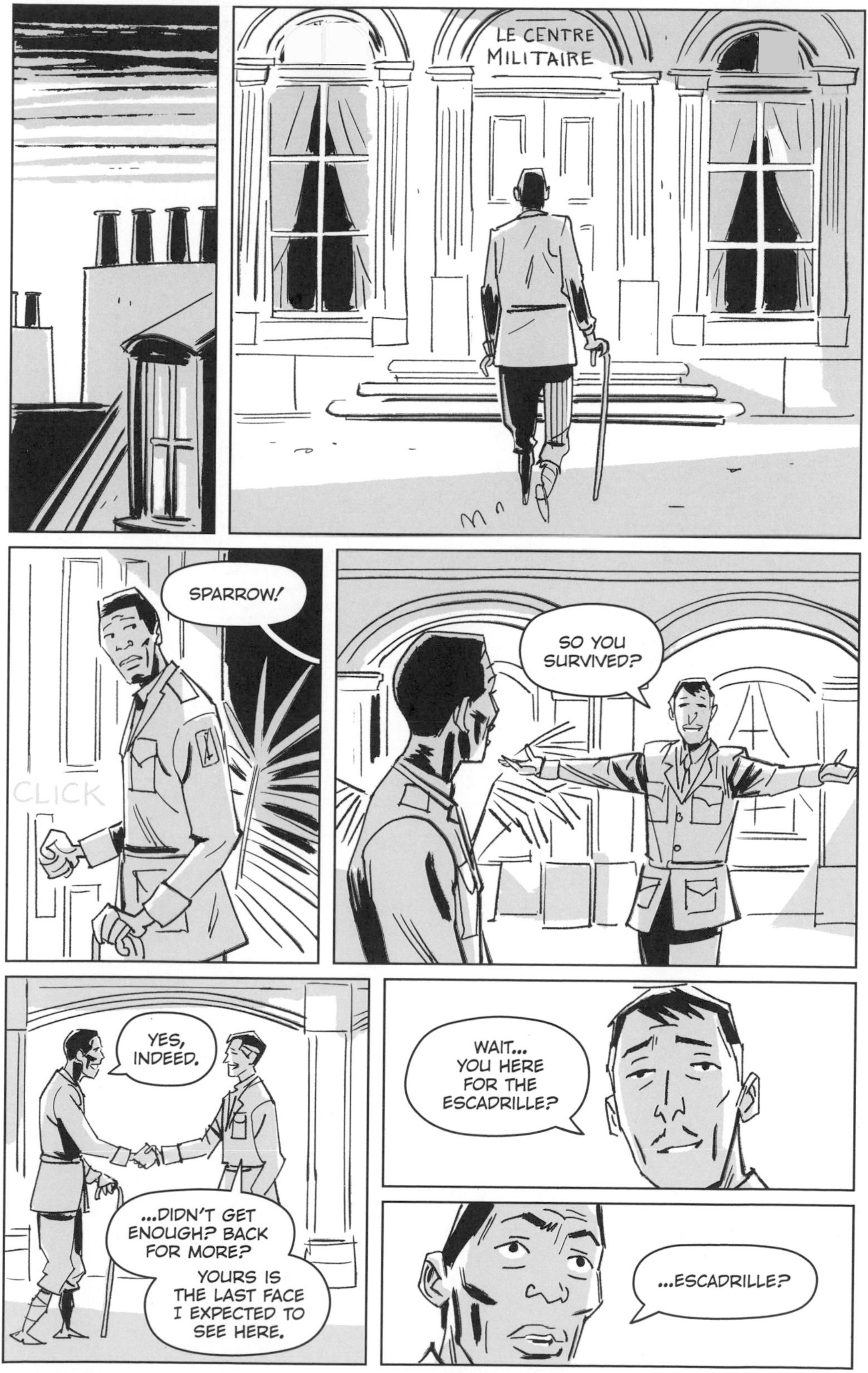
LE CENTRE MILITAIRE
SPARROW!
CLICK
SO YOU SURVIVED?
YES, INDEED.
...DIDN'T GET ENOUGH? BACK FOR MORE?
YOURS IS THE LAST FACE I EXPECTED TO SEE HERE.
WAIT... YOU HERE FOR THE ESCADRILLE?
...ESCADRILLE?

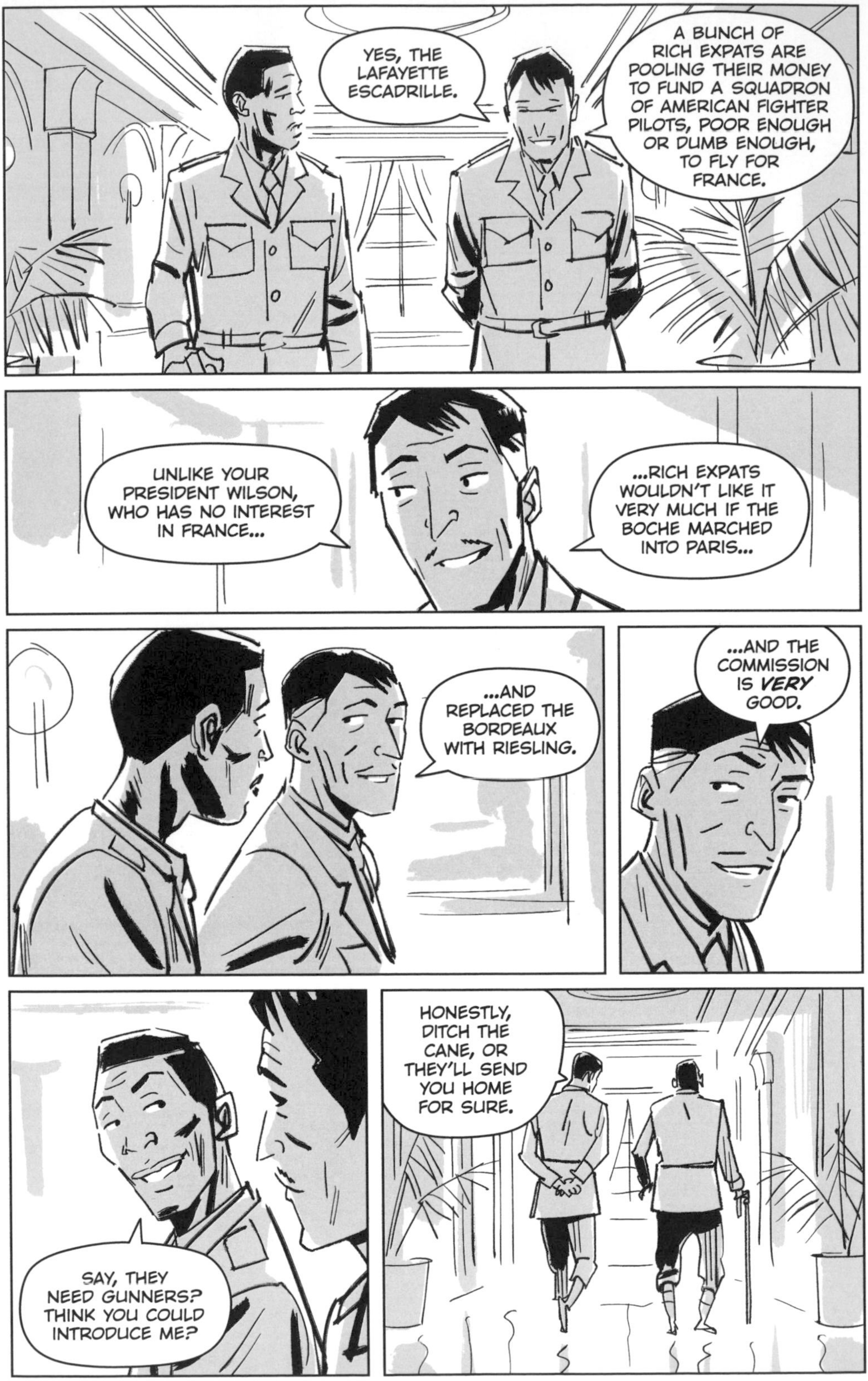
YES, THE LAFAYETTE ESCADRILLE.
A BUNCH OF RICH EXPATS ARE POOLING THEIR MONEY TO FUND A SQUADRON OF AMERICAN FIGHTER PILOTS, POOR ENOUGH OR DUMB ENOUGH, TO FLY FOR FRANCE.
UNLIKE YOUR PRESIDENT WILSON, WHO HAS NO INTEREST IN FRANCE...
...RICH EXPATS WOULDN'T LIKE IT VERY MUCH IF THE BOCHE MARCHED INTO PARIS...
...AND REPLACED THE BORDEAUX WITH RIESLING.
...AND THE COMMISSION IS ***VERY*** GOOD.
SAY, THEY NEED GUNNERS? THINK YOU COULD INTRODUCE ME?
HONESTLY, DITCH THE CANE, OR THEY'LL SEND YOU HOME FOR SURE.

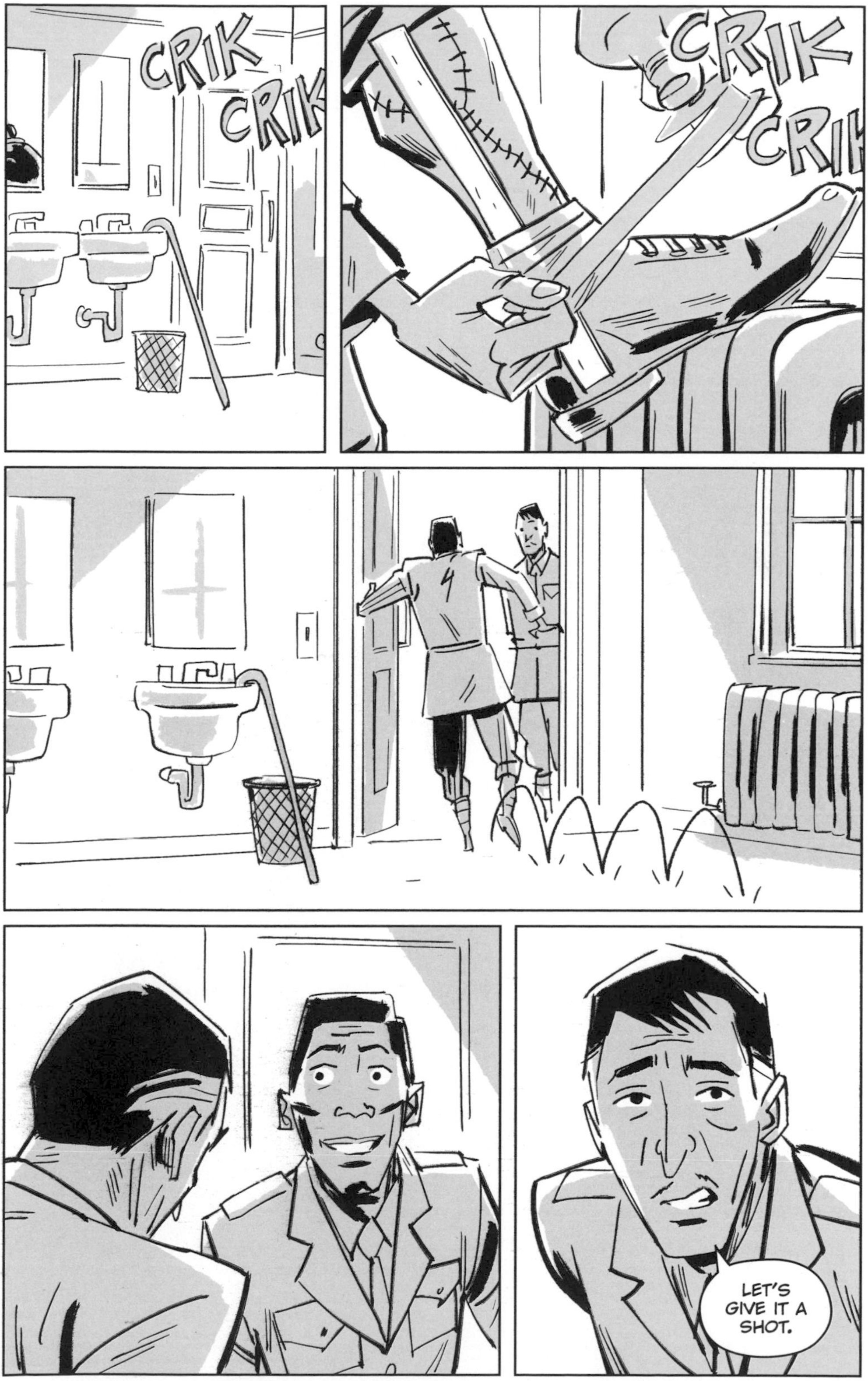
CRIK
CRIK
CRIK
CRIK
LET'S GIVE IT A SHOT.

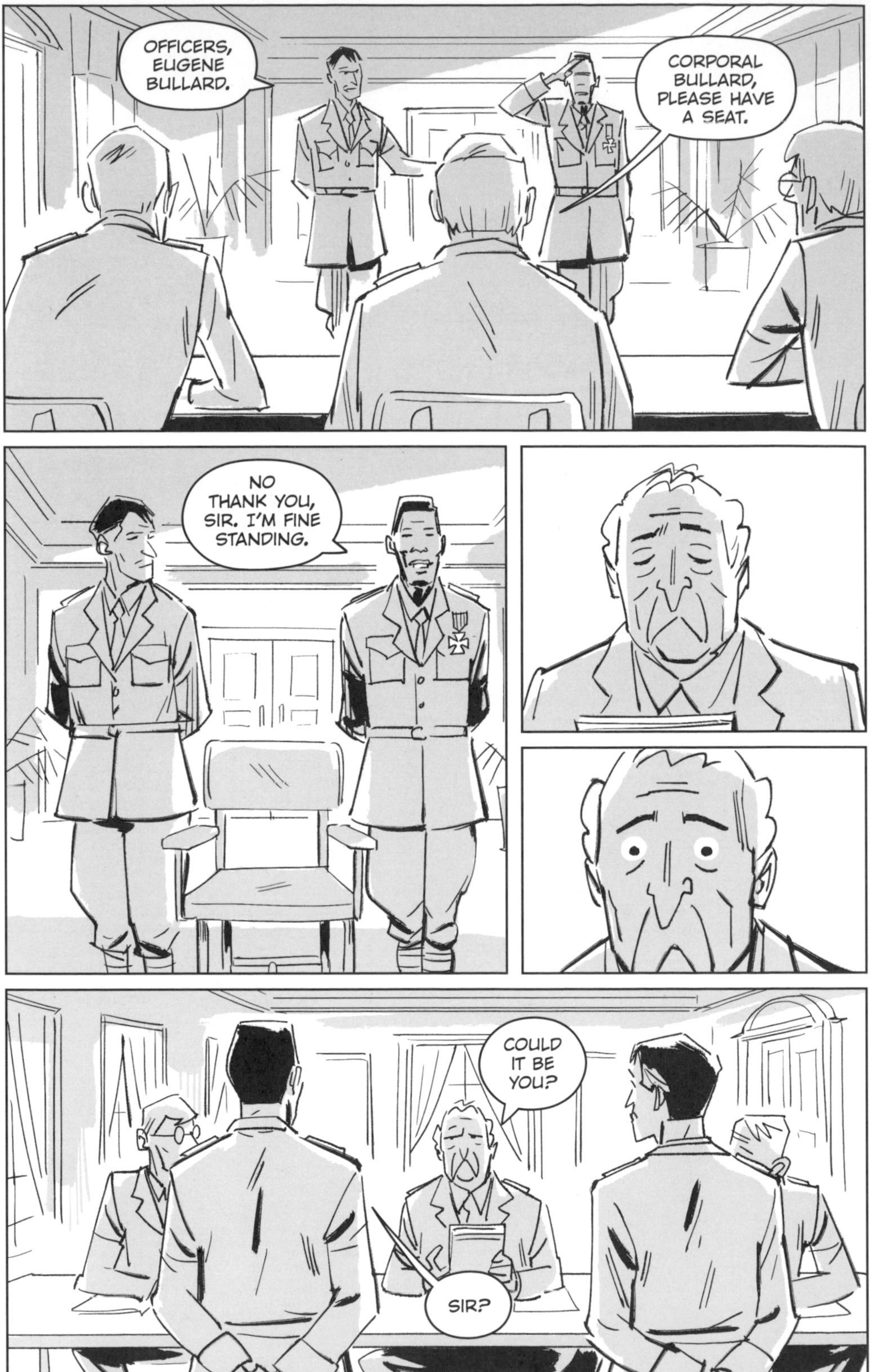
OFFICERS, EUGENE BULLARD.
CORPORAL BULLARD, PLEASE HAVE A SEAT.
NO THANK YOU, SIR. I'M FINE STANDING.
COULD IT BE YOU?
SIR?

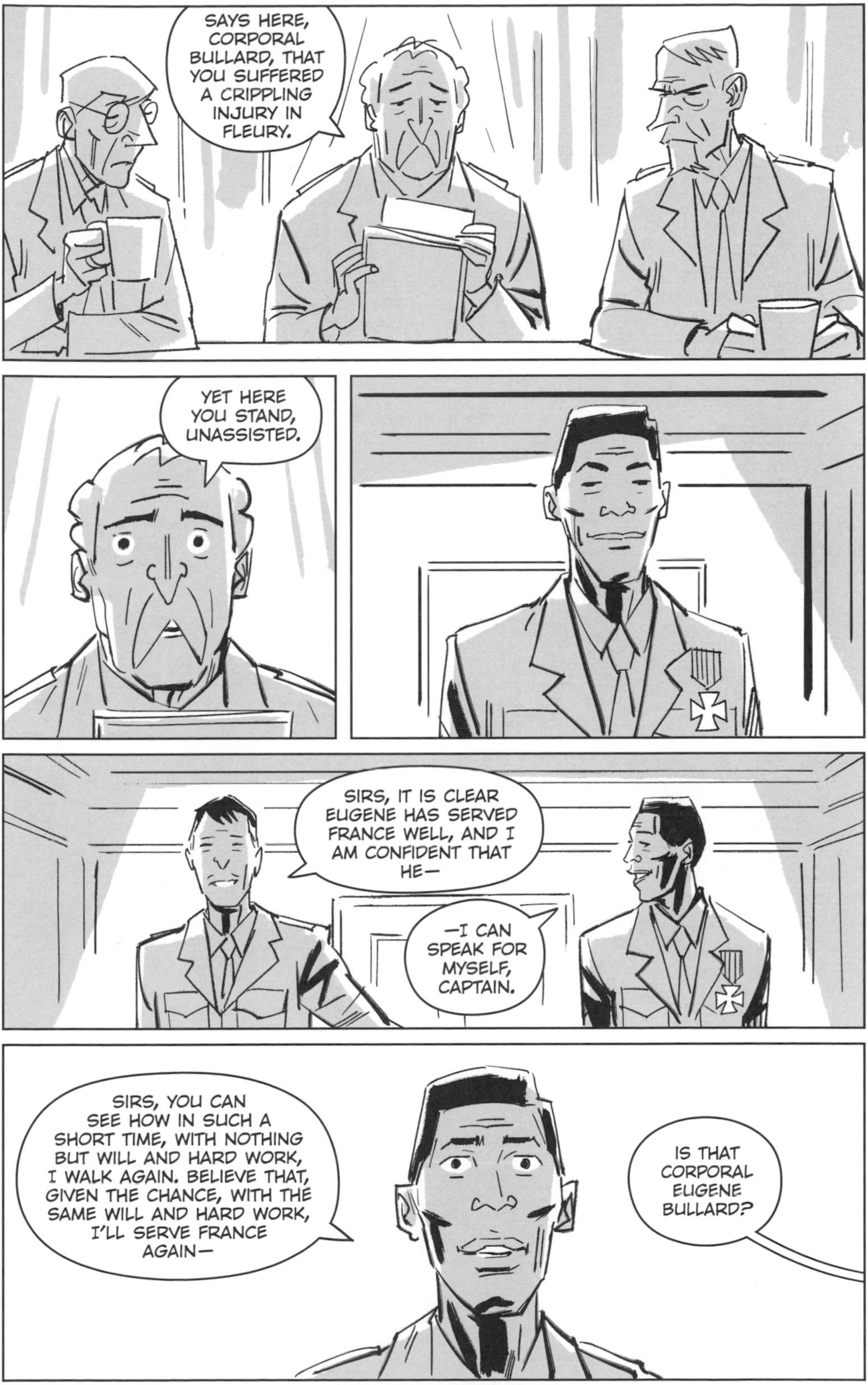
SAYS HERE, CORPORAL BULLARD, THAT YOU SUFFERED A CRIPPLING INJURY IN FLEURY.
YET HERE YOU STAND, UNASSISTED.
SIRS, IT IS CLEAR EUGENE HAS SERVED FRANCE WELL, AND I AM CONFIDENT THAT HE—
—I CAN SPEAK FOR MYSELF, CAPTAIN.
SIRS, YOU CAN SEE HOW IN SUCH A SHORT TIME, WITH NOTHING BUT WILL AND HARD WORK, I WALK AGAIN. BELIEVE THAT, GIVEN THE CHANCE, WITH THE SAME WILL AND HARD WORK, I'LL SERVE FRANCE AGAIN—
IS THAT CORPORAL EUGENE BULLARD?

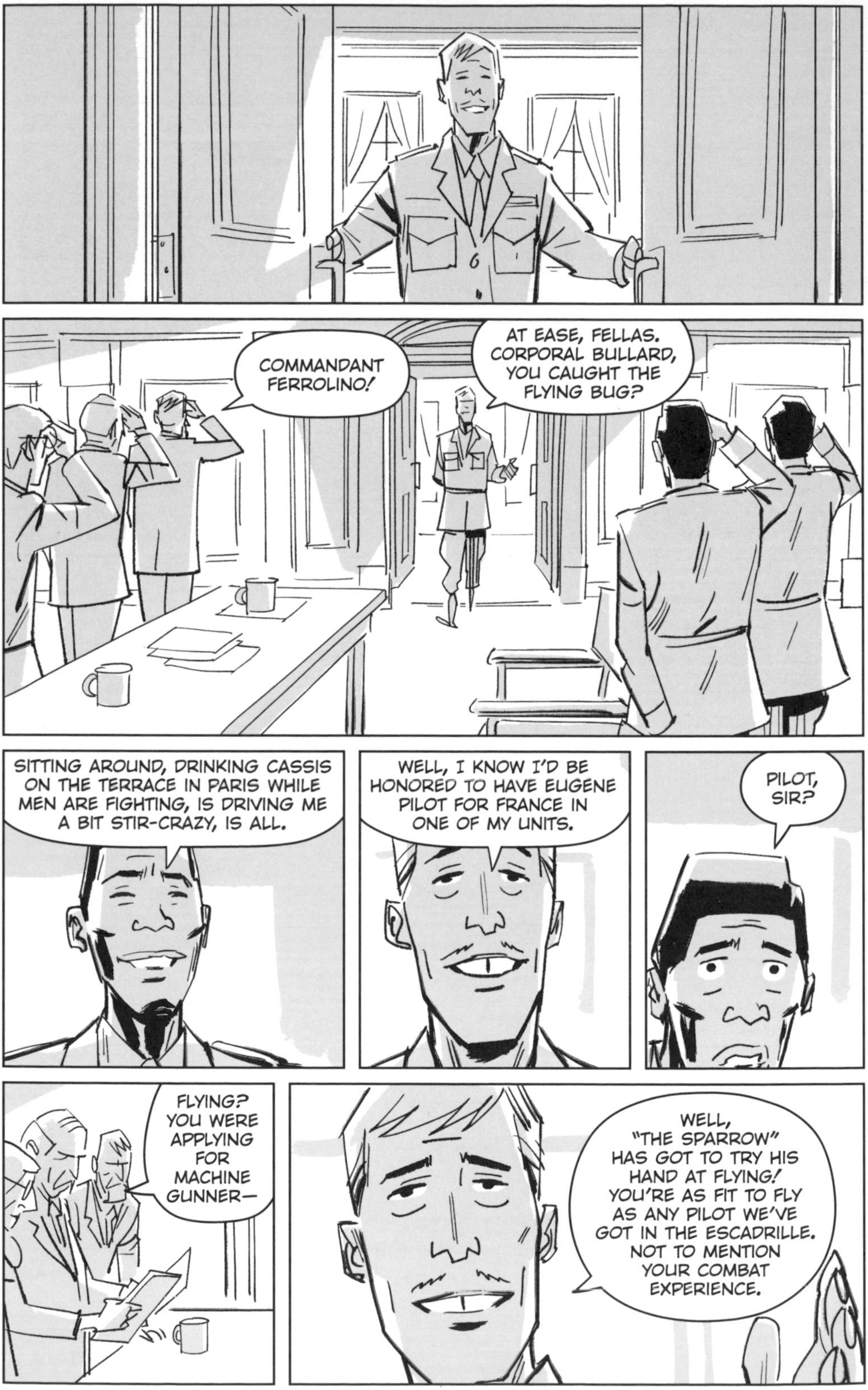
COMMANDANT FERROLINO!
AT EASE, FELLAS. CORPORAL BULLARD, YOU CAUGHT THE FLYING BUG?
SITTING AROUND, DRINKING CASSIS ON THE TERRACE IN PARIS WHILE MEN ARE FIGHTING, IS DRIVING ME A BIT STIR-CRAZY, IS ALL.
WELL, I KNOW I'D BE HONORED TO HAVE EUGENE PILOT FOR FRANCE IN ONE OF MY UNITS.
PILOT, SIR?
FLYING? YOU WERE APPLYING FOR MACHINE GUNNER—
WELL, "THE SPARROW" HAS GOT TO TRY HIS HAND AT FLYING! YOU'RE AS FIT TO FLY AS ANY PILOT WE'VE GOT IN THE ESCADRILLE. NOT TO MENTION YOUR COMBAT EXPERIENCE.

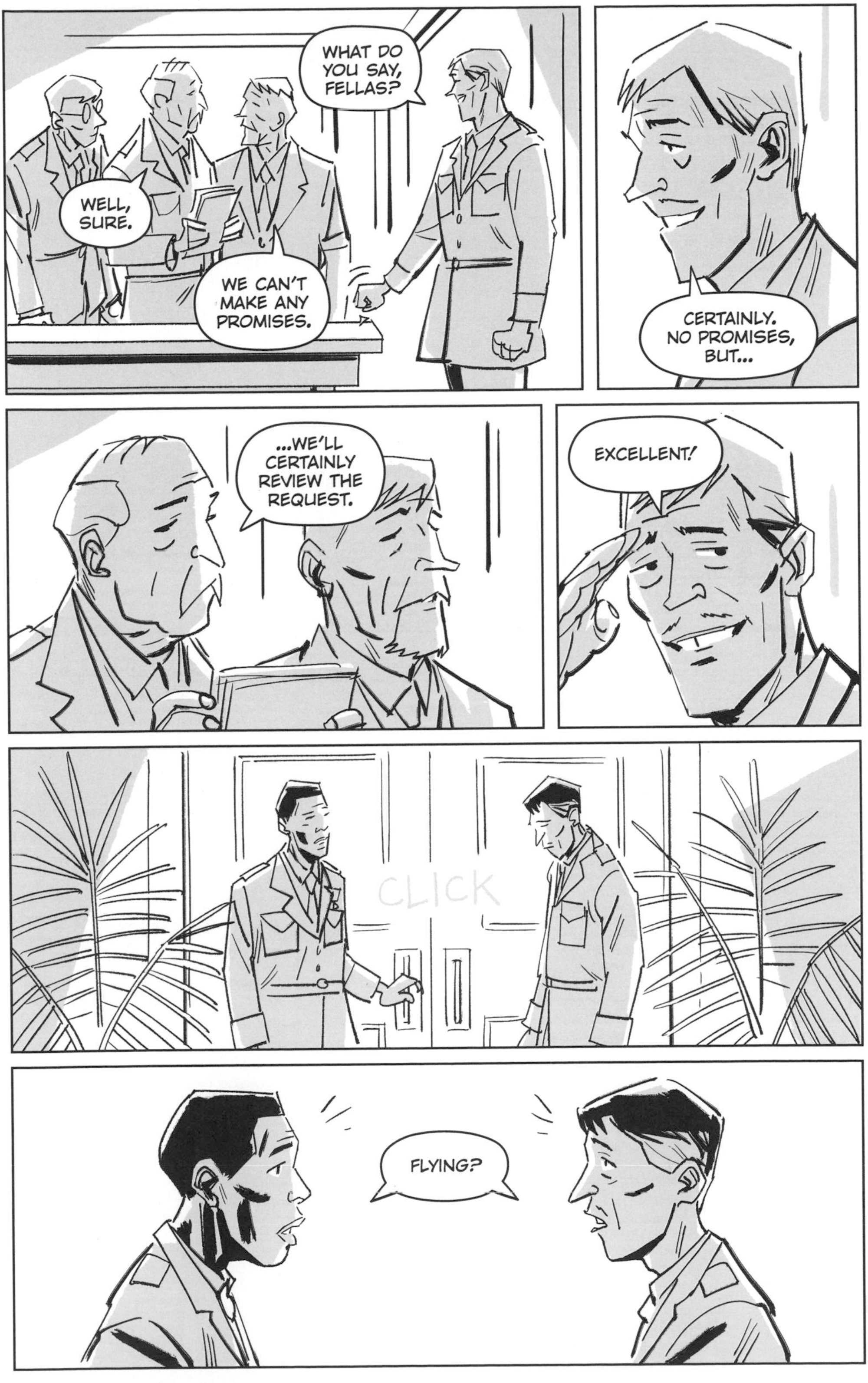
WHAT DO YOU SAY, FELLAS?
WELL, SURE.
WE CAN'T MAKE ANY PROMISES.
CERTAINLY. NO PROMISES, BUT...
...WE'LL CERTAINLY REVIEW THE REQUEST.
EXCELLENT!
CLICK
FLYING?

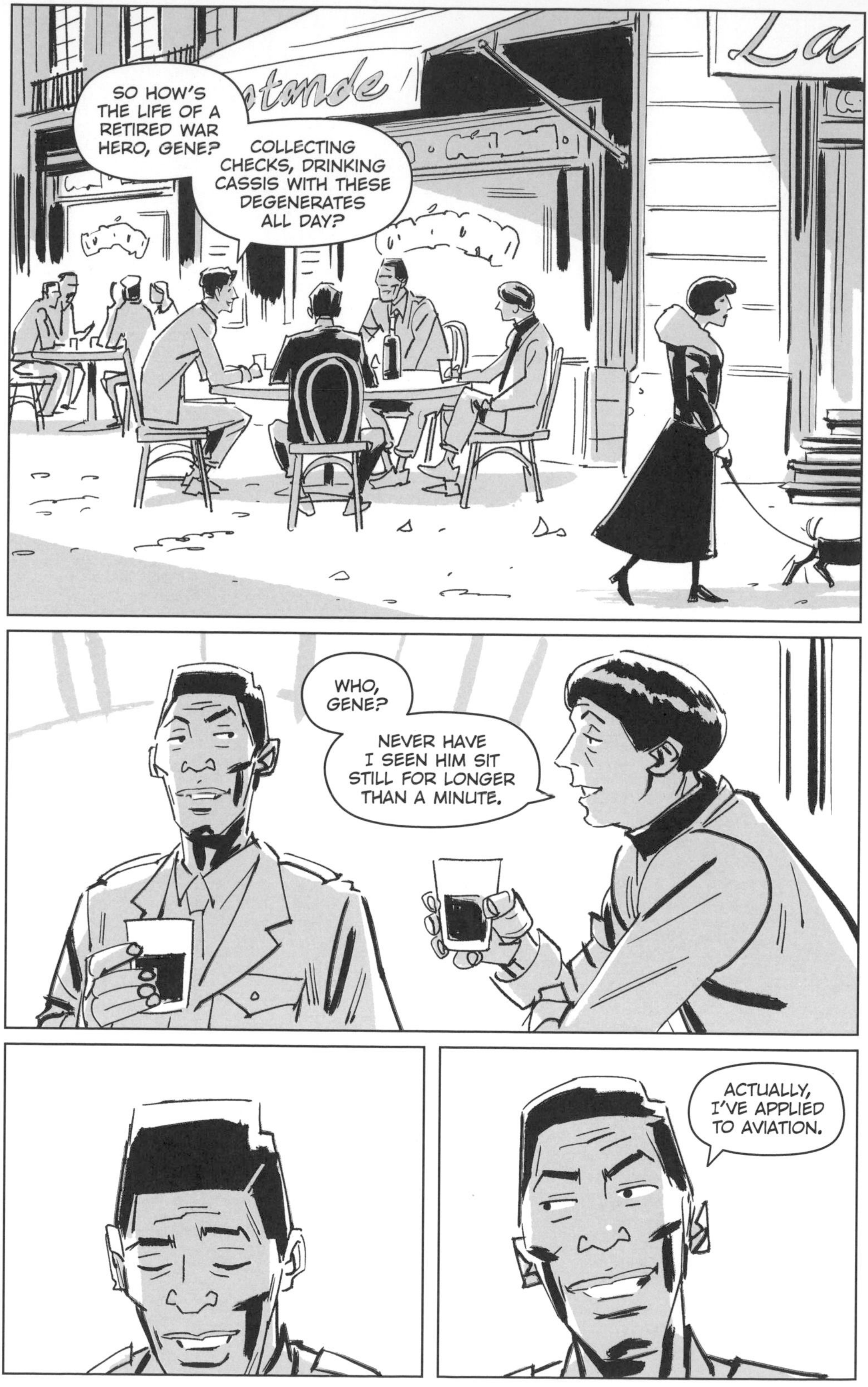

SO HOW'S THE LIFE OF A RETIRED WAR HERO, GENE?
COLLECTING CHECKS, DRINKING CASSIS WITH THESE DEGENERATES ALL DAY?
WHO, GENE?
NEVER HAVE I SEEN HIM SIT STILL FOR LONGER THAN A MINUTE.
ACTUALLY, I'VE APPLIED TO AVIATION.

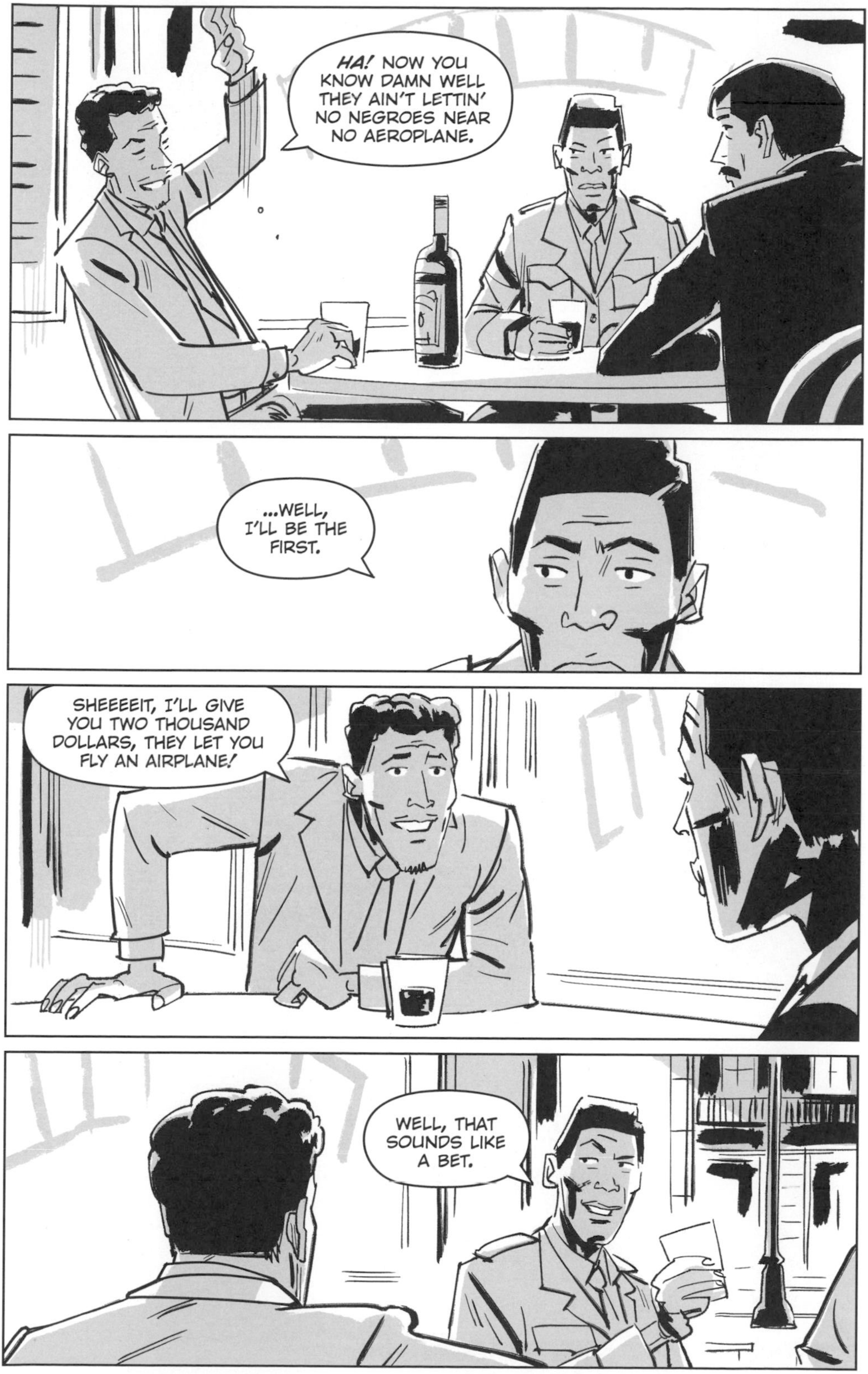
HA! NOW YOU KNOW DAMN WELL THEY AIN'T LETTIN' NO NEGROES NEAR NO AEROPLANE.
...WELL, I'LL BE THE FIRST.
SHEEEEIT, I'LL GIVE YOU TWO THOUSAND DOLLARS, THEY LET YOU FLY AN AIRPLANE!
WELL, THAT SOUNDS LIKE A BET.

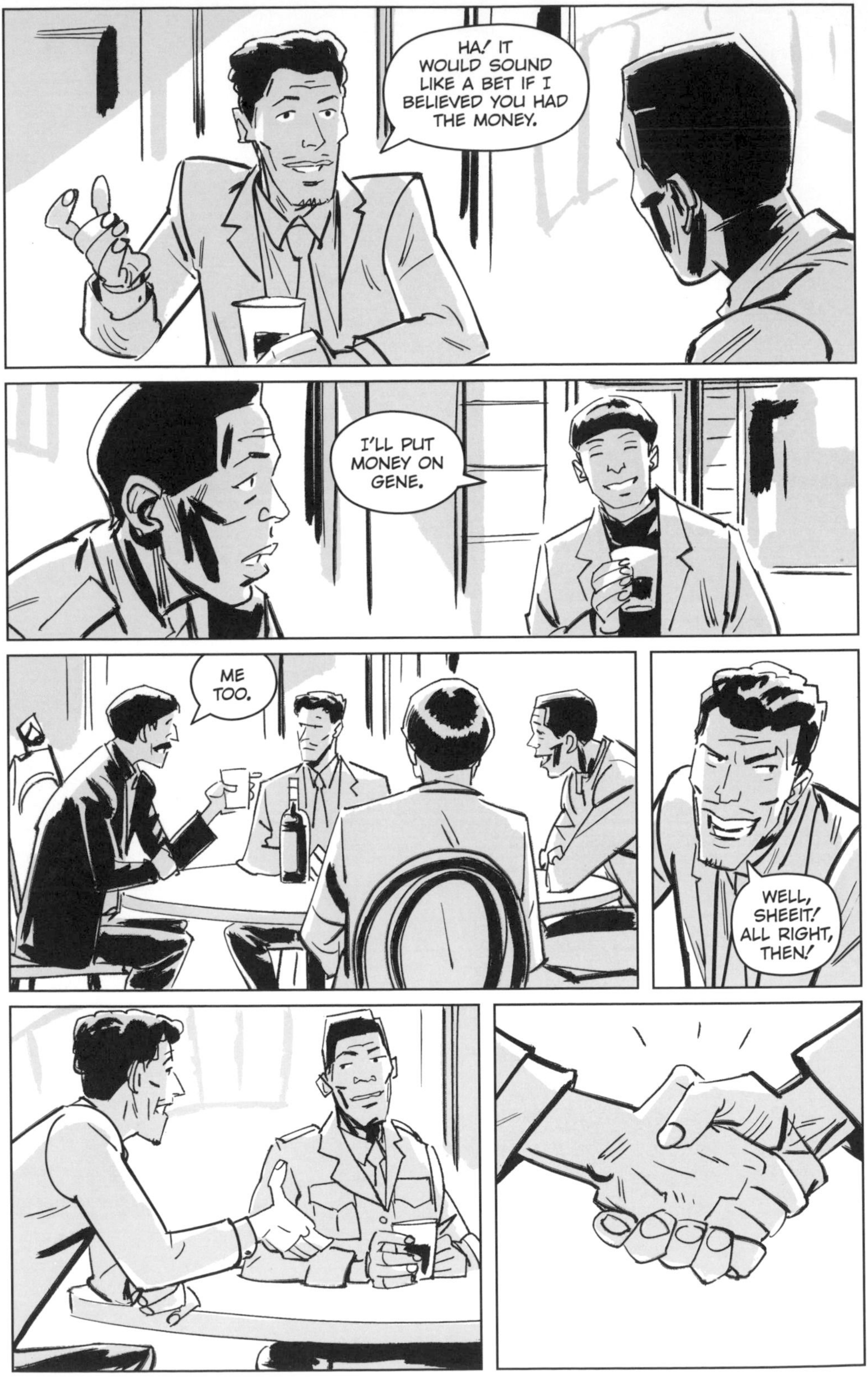
HA! IT WOULD SOUND LIKE A BET IF I BELIEVED YOU HAD THE MONEY.
I'LL PUT MONEY ON GENE.
ME TOO.
WELL, SHEEIT! ALL RIGHT, THEN!

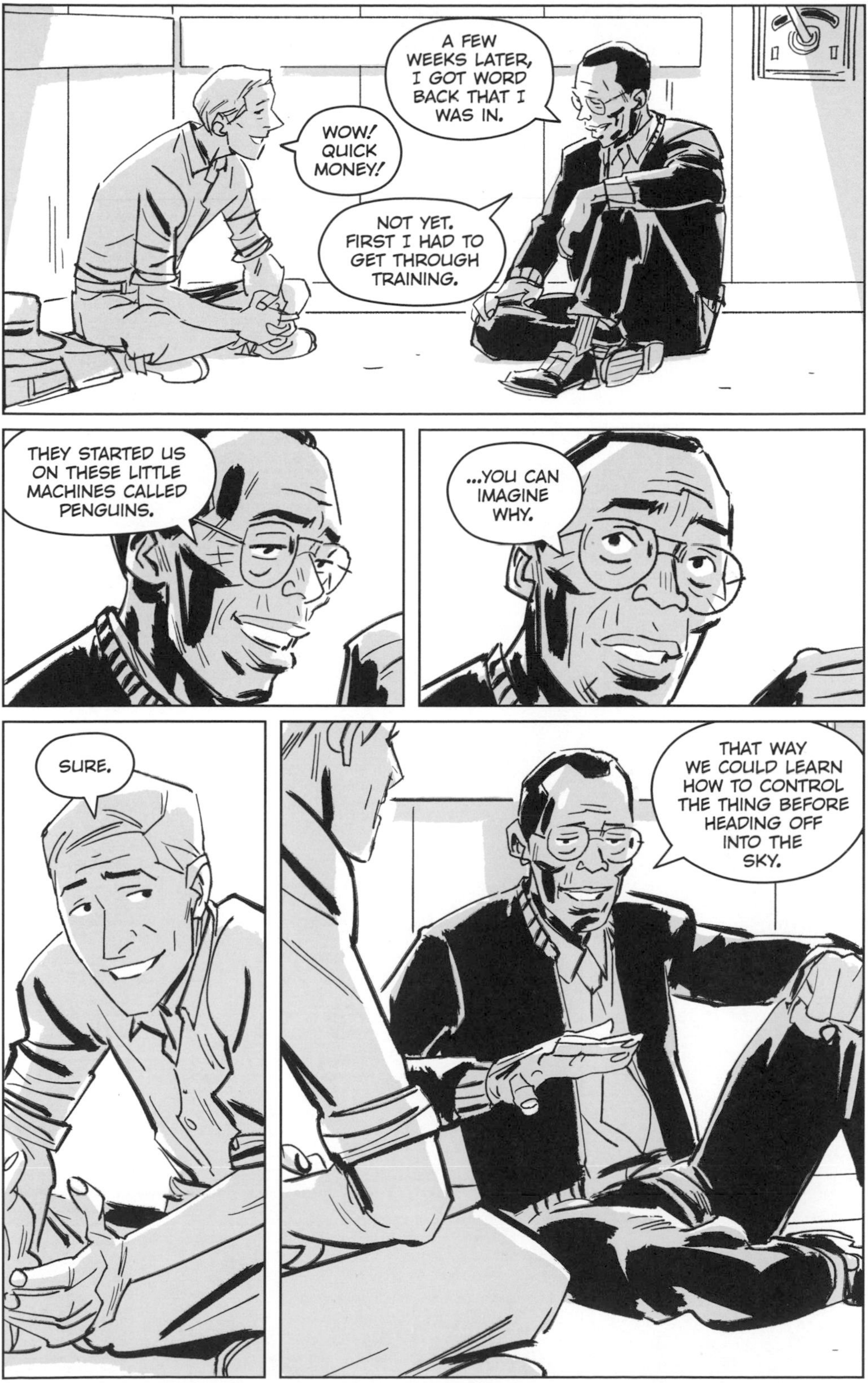
A FEW WEEKS LATER, I GOT WORD BACK THAT I WAS IN.
WOW! QUICK MONEY!
NOT YET. FIRST I HAD TO GET THROUGH TRAINING.
THEY STARTED US ON THESE LITTLE MACHINES CALLED PENGUINS.
...YOU CAN IMAGINE WHY.
SURE.
THAT WAY WE COULD LEARN HOW TO CONTROL THE THING BEFORE HEADING OFF INTO THE SKY.

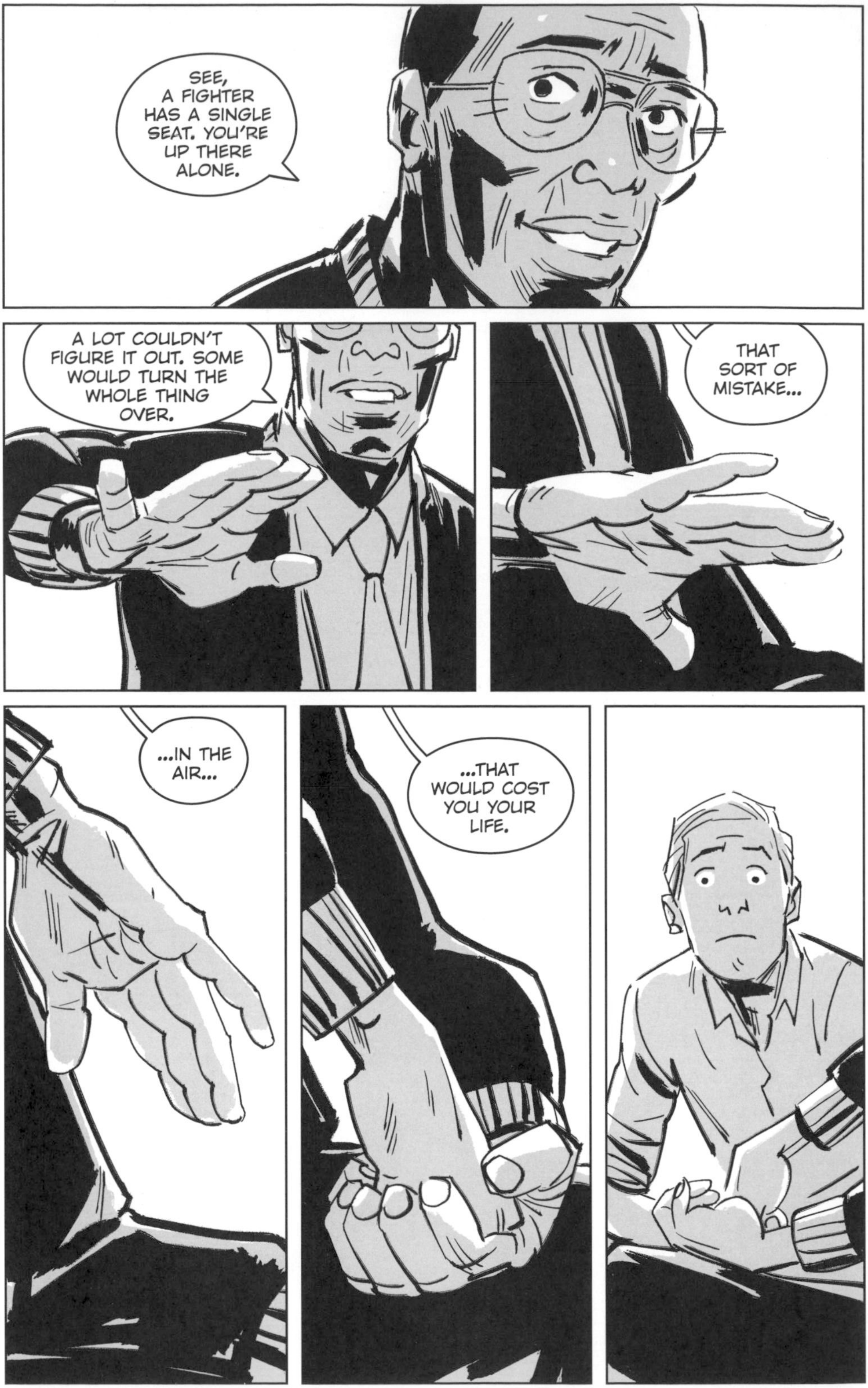
SEE, A FIGHTER HAS A SINGLE SEAT. YOU'RE UP THERE ALONE.
A LOT COULDN'T FIGURE IT OUT. SOME WOULD TURN THE WHOLE THING OVER.
THAT SORT OF MISTAKE...
...IN THE AIR...
...THAT WOULD COST YOU YOUR LIFE.

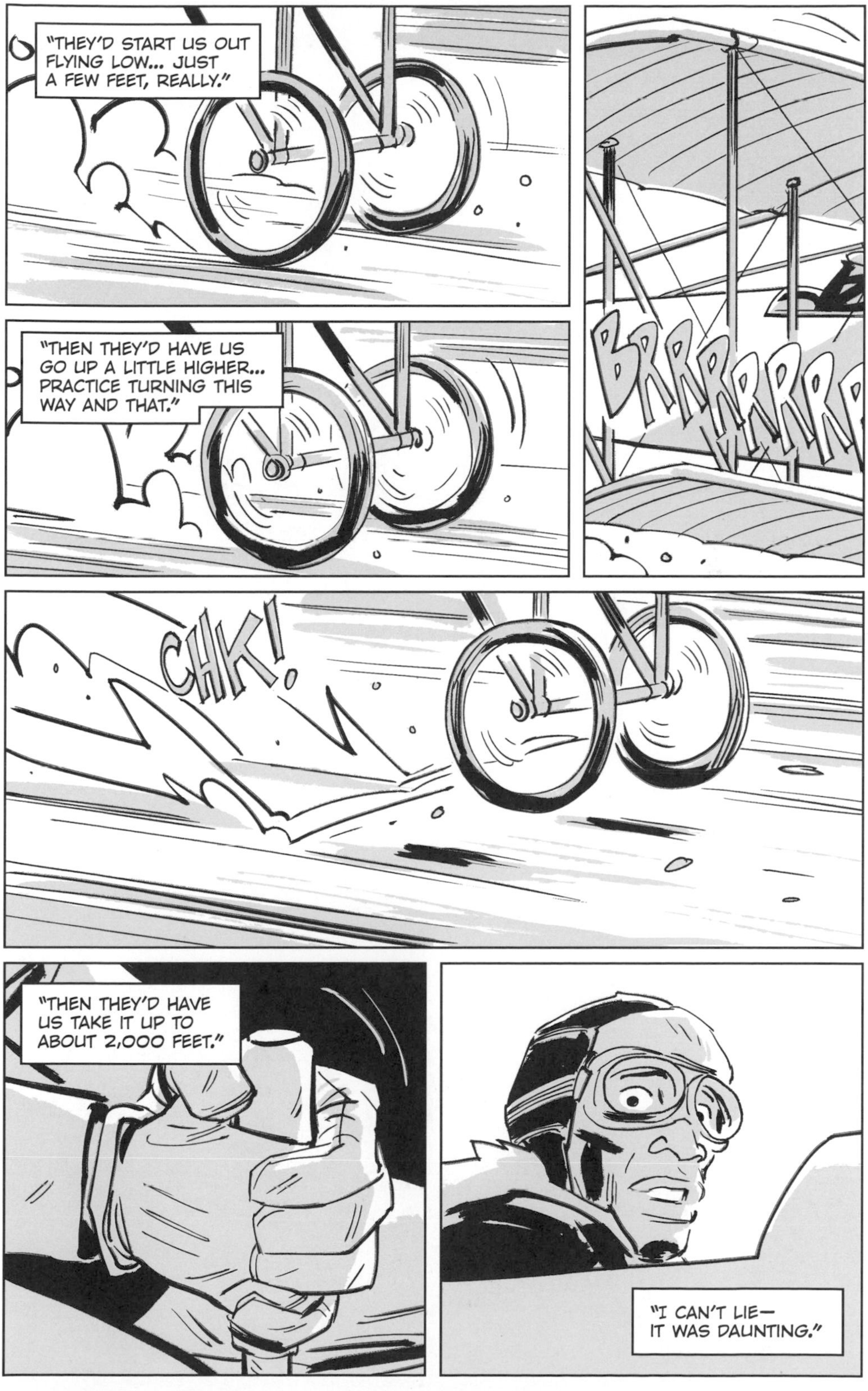
"THEY'D START US OUT FLYING LOW... JUST A FEW FEET, REALLY."
"THEN THEY'D HAVE US GO UP A LITTLE HIGHER... PRACTICE TURNING THIS WAY AND THAT."
BRRRRRRR
CHK!
"THEN THEY'D HAVE US TAKE IT UP TO ABOUT 2,000 FEET."
"I CAN'T LIE— IT WAS DAUNTING."

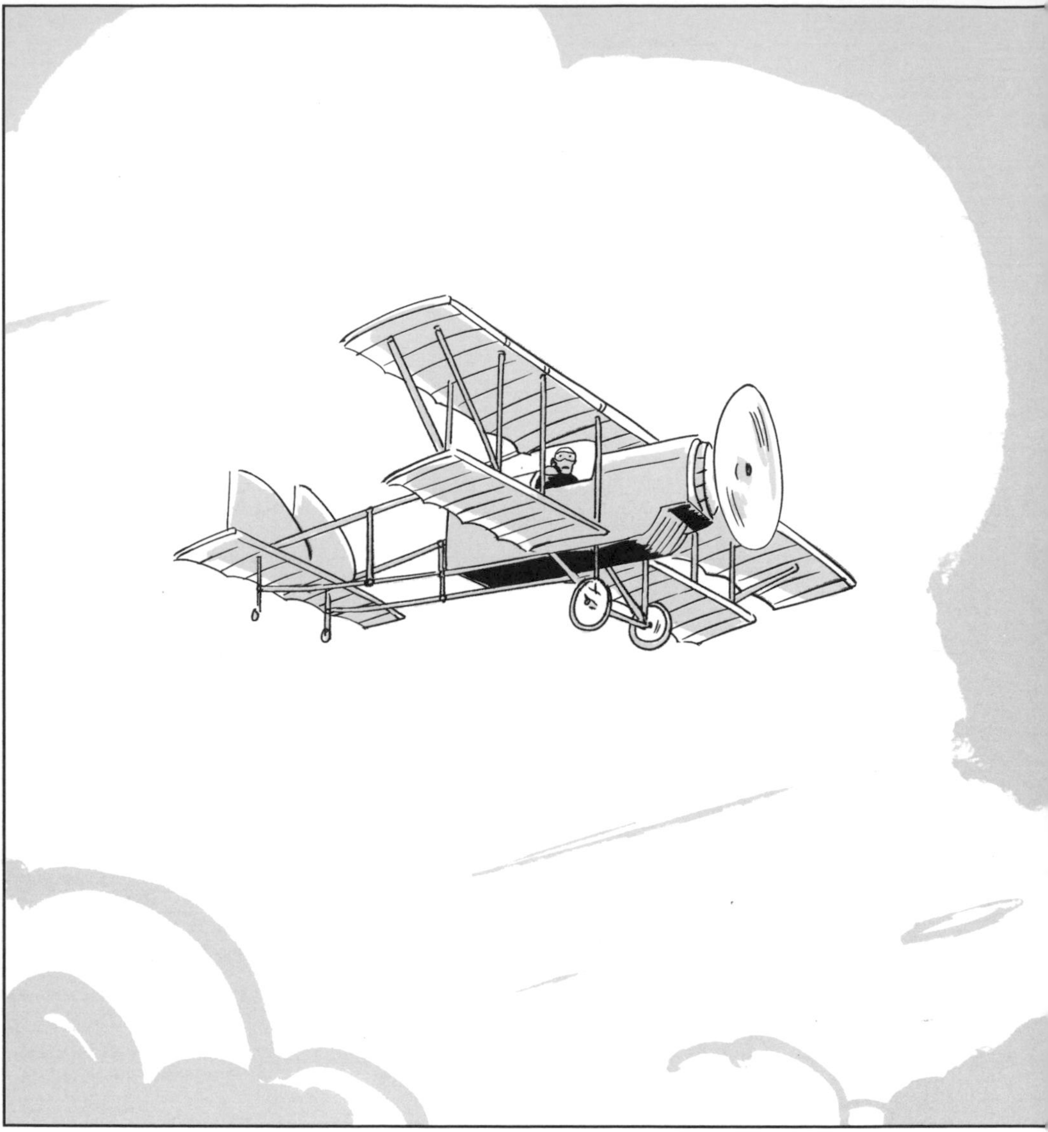

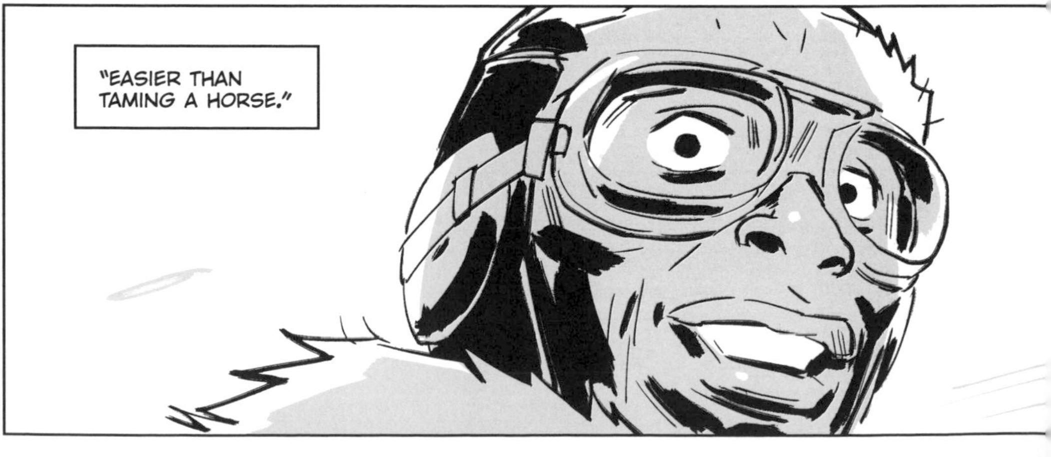
"EASIER THAN
TAMING A HORSE."

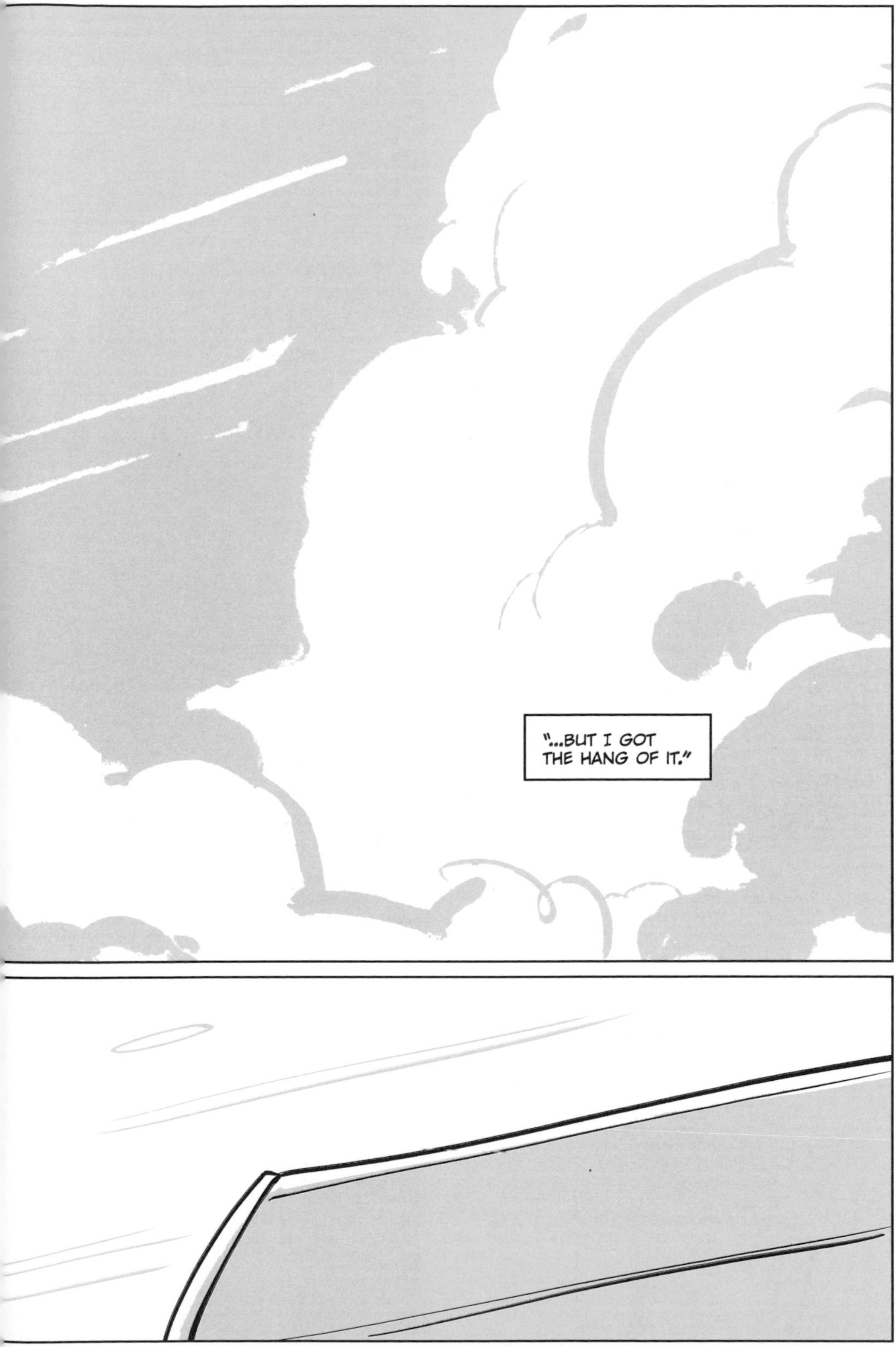
"...BUT I GOT THE HANG OF IT."

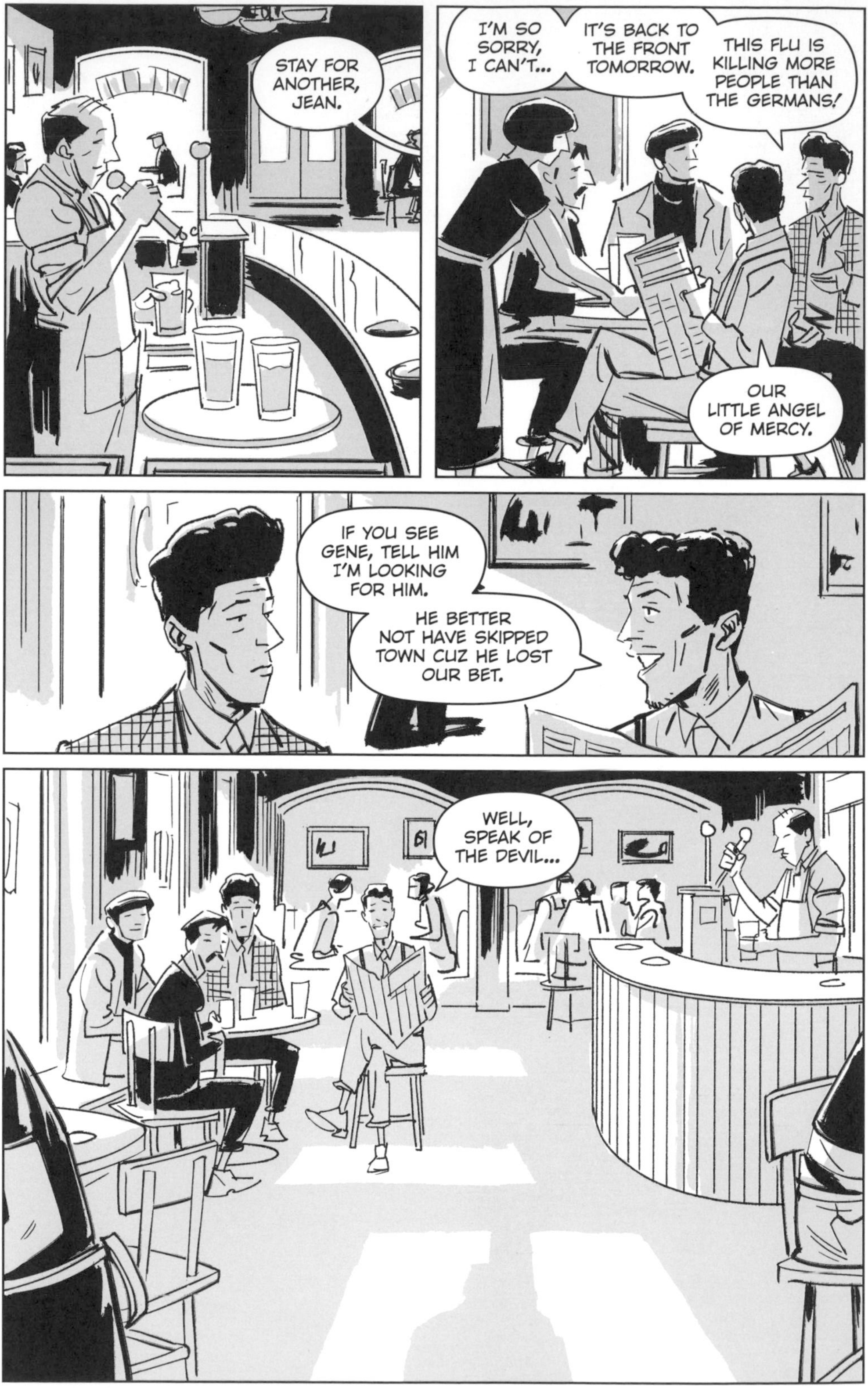
STAY FOR ANOTHER, JEAN.
I'M SO SORRY, I CAN'T...
IT'S BACK TO THE FRONT TOMORROW.
THIS FLU IS KILLING MORE PEOPLE THAN THE GERMANS!
OUR LITTLE ANGEL OF MERCY.
IF YOU SEE GENE, TELL HIM I'M LOOKING FOR HIM.
HE BETTER NOT HAVE SKIPPED TOWN CUZ HE LOST OUR BET.
WELL, SPEAK OF THE DEVIL...

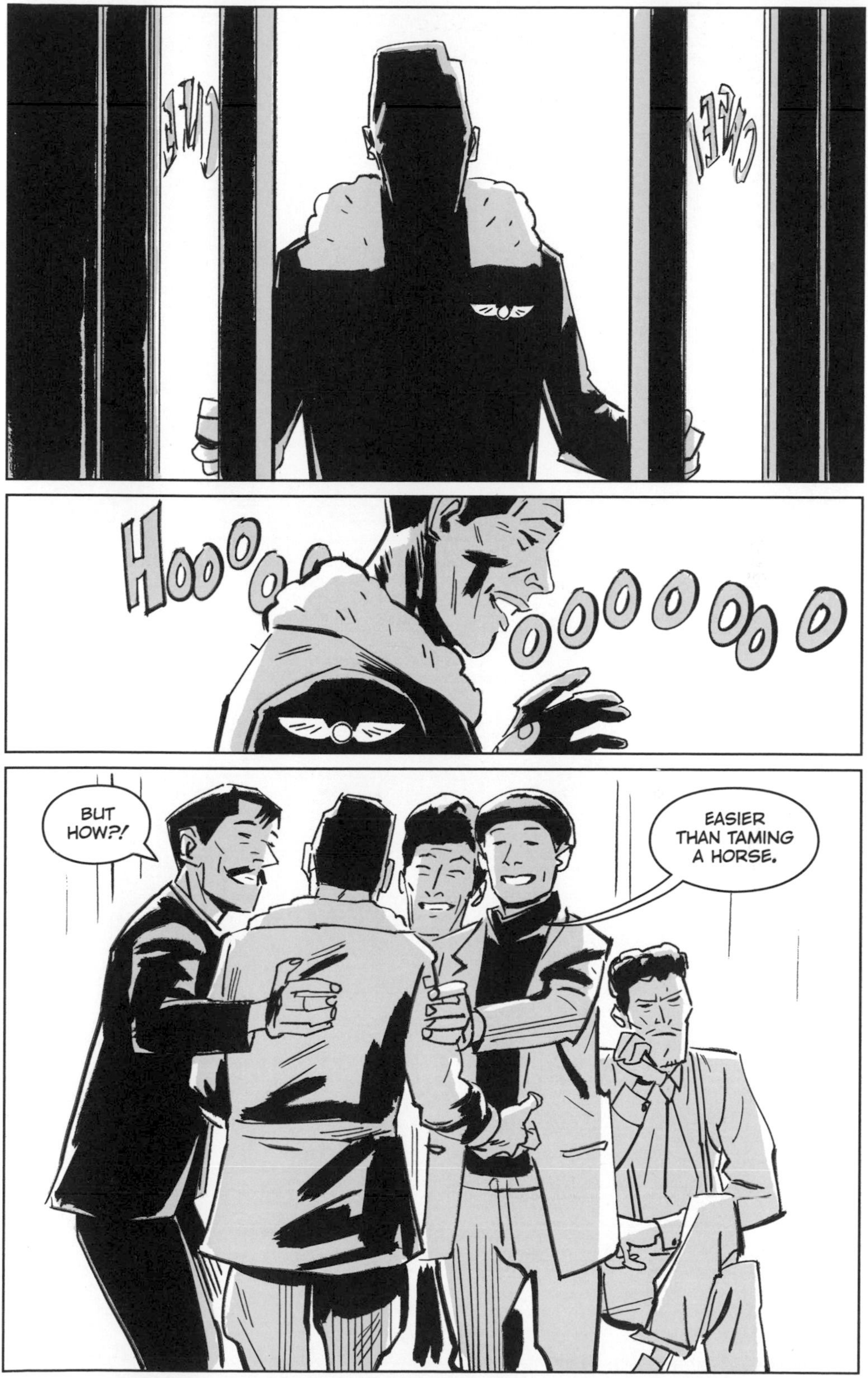
HOOOOOOOOOOOOOO
BUT HOW?!
EASIER THAN TAMING A HORSE.

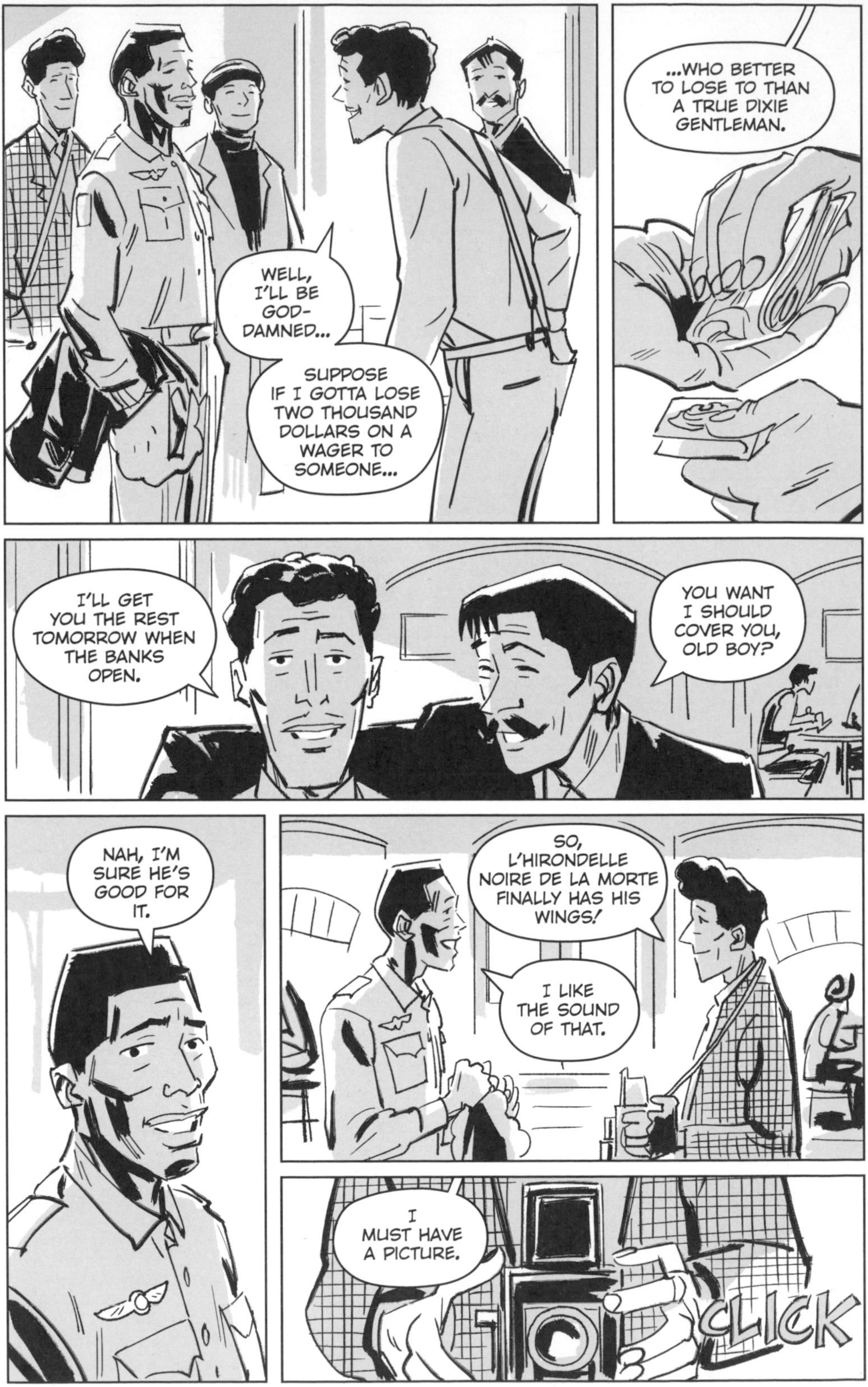
WELL, I'LL BE GOD-DAMNED...
SUPPOSE IF I GOTTA LOSE TWO THOUSAND DOLLARS ON A WAGER TO SOMEONE...
...WHO BETTER TO LOSE TO THAN A TRUE DIXIE GENTLEMAN.
I'LL GET YOU THE REST TOMORROW WHEN THE BANKS OPEN.
YOU WANT I SHOULD COVER YOU, OLD BOY?
NAH, I'M SURE HE'S GOOD FOR IT.
SO, L'HIRONDELLE NOIRE DE LA MORTE FINALLY HAS HIS WINGS!
I LIKE THE SOUND OF THAT.
I MUST HAVE A PICTURE.
CLICK

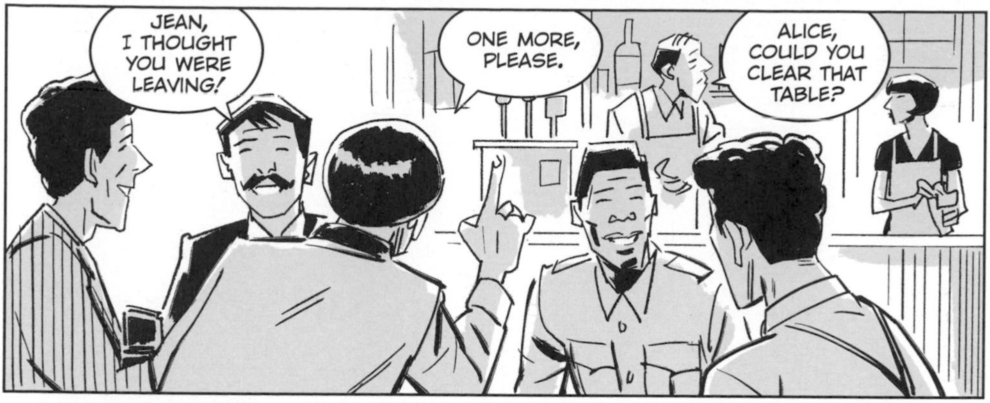
JEAN, I THOUGHT YOU WERE LEAVING!
ONE MORE, PLEASE.
ALICE, COULD YOU CLEAR THAT TABLE?

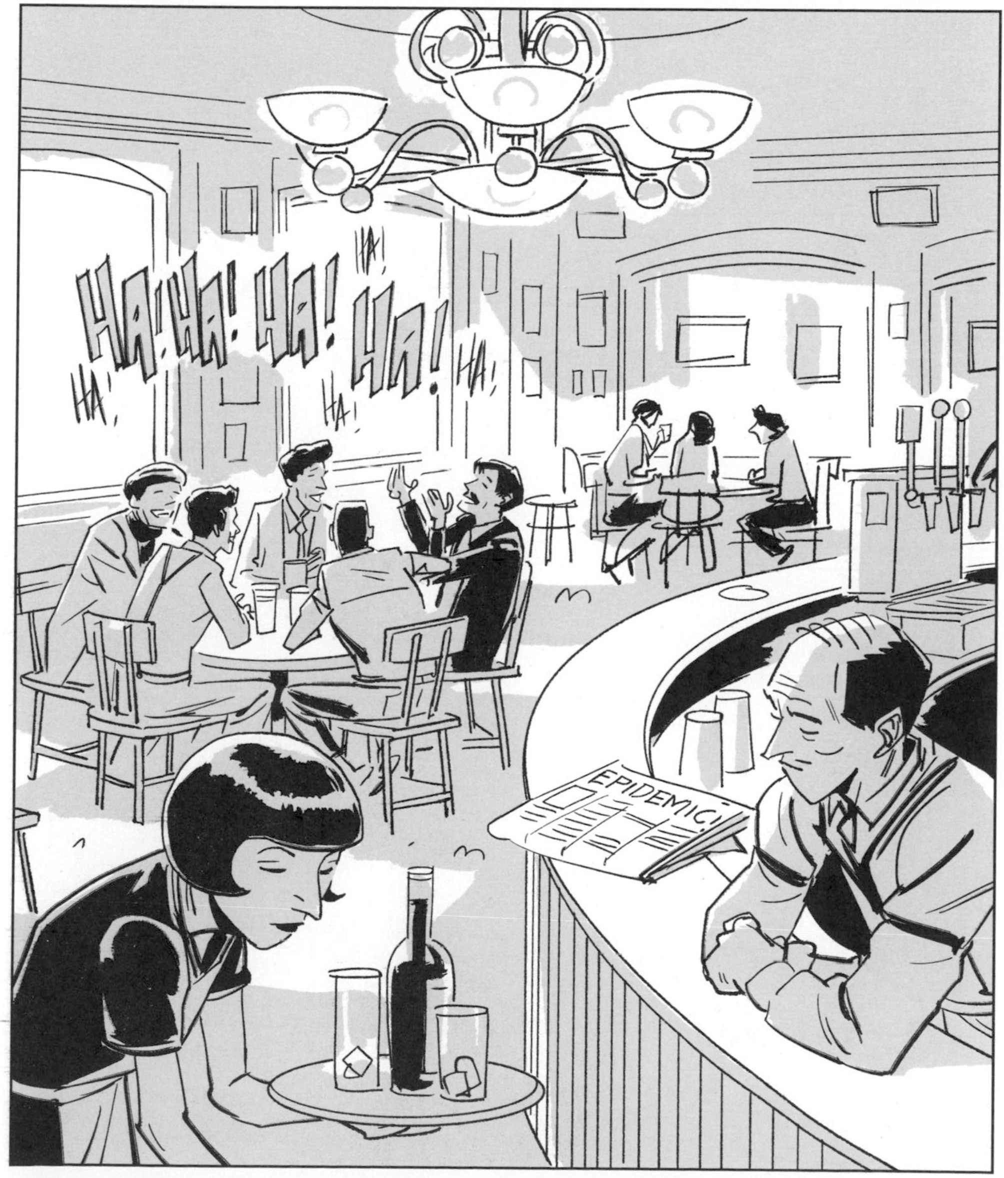
HA! HA! HA! HA! HA! HA! HA! HA!
EPIDEMIC!

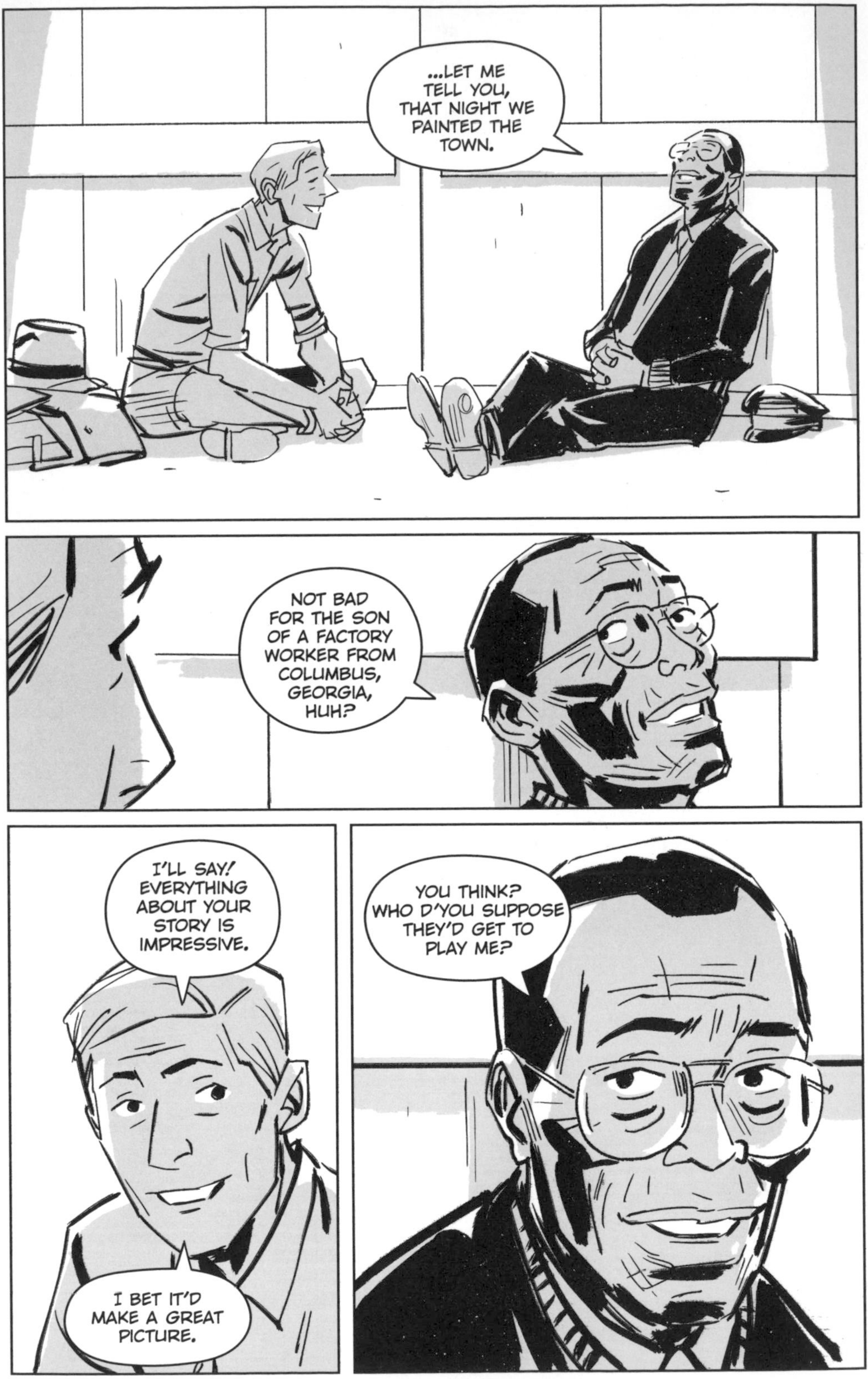
...LET ME TELL YOU, THAT NIGHT WE PAINTED THE TOWN.
NOT BAD FOR THE SON OF A FACTORY WORKER FROM COLUMBUS, GEORGIA, HUH?
I'LL SAY! EVERYTHING ABOUT YOUR STORY IS IMPRESSIVE.
I BET IT'D MAKE A GREAT PICTURE.
YOU THINK? WHO D'YOU SUPPOSE THEY'D GET TO PLAY ME?

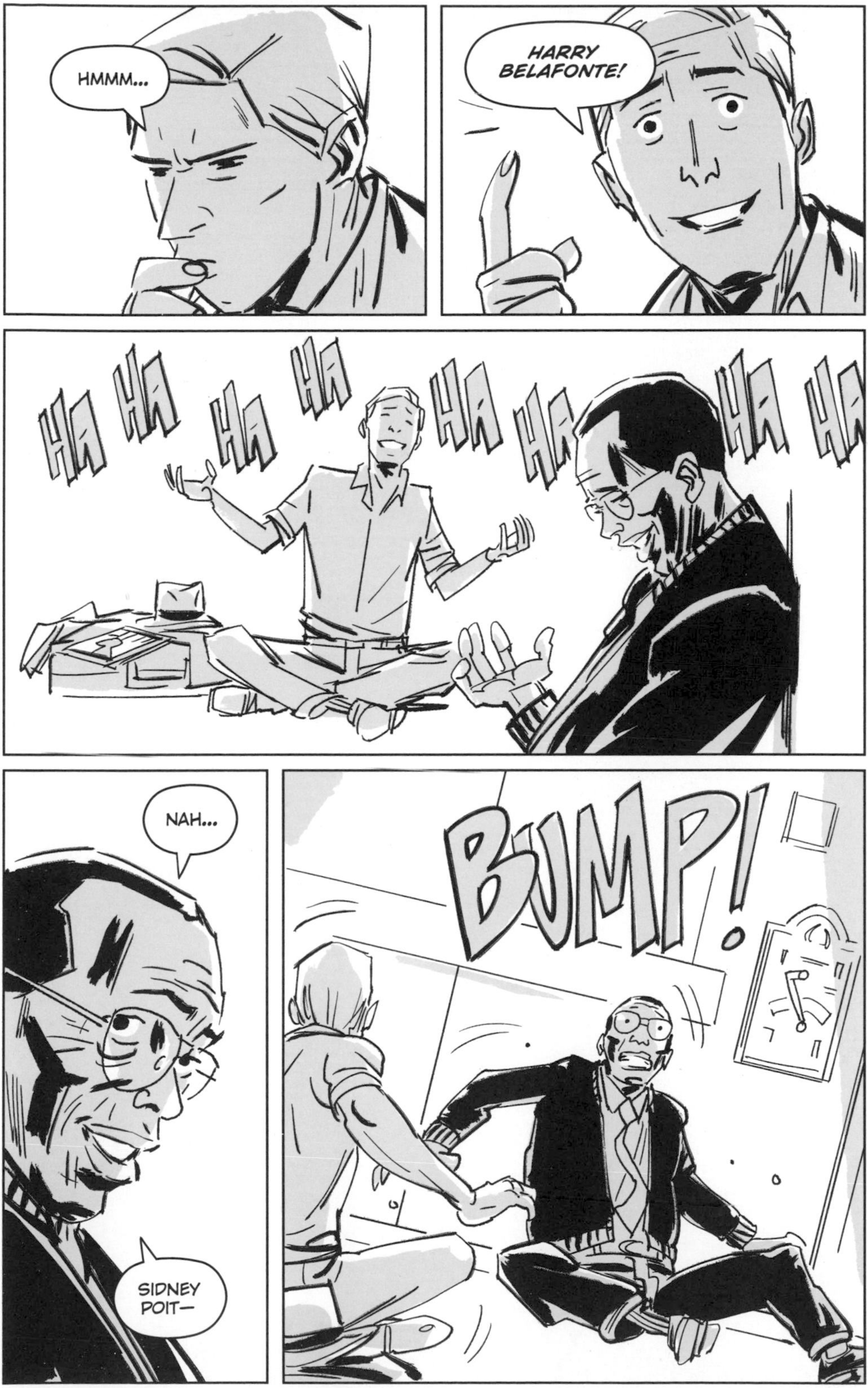
HMMM...
HARRY BELAFONTE!
HA HA HA HA HA HA HA HA
NAH...
SIDNEY POIT—
BUMP!

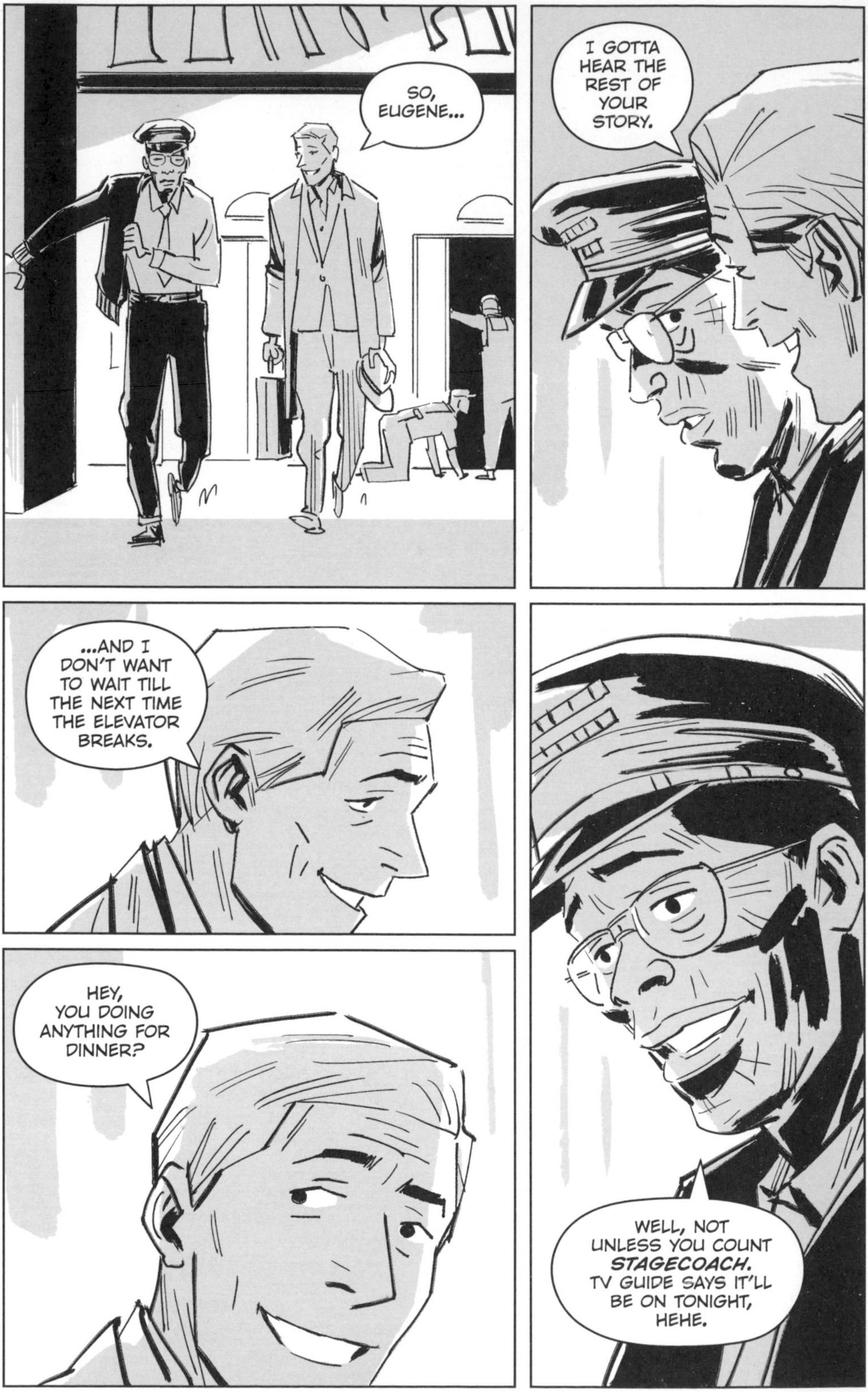
SO, EUGENE...
I GOTTA HEAR THE REST OF YOUR STORY.
...AND I DON'T WANT TO WAIT TILL THE NEXT TIME THE ELEVATOR BREAKS.
HEY, YOU DOING ANYTHING FOR DINNER?
WELL, NOT UNLESS YOU COUNT *STAGECOACH.* TV GUIDE SAYS IT'LL BE ON TONIGHT, HEHE.

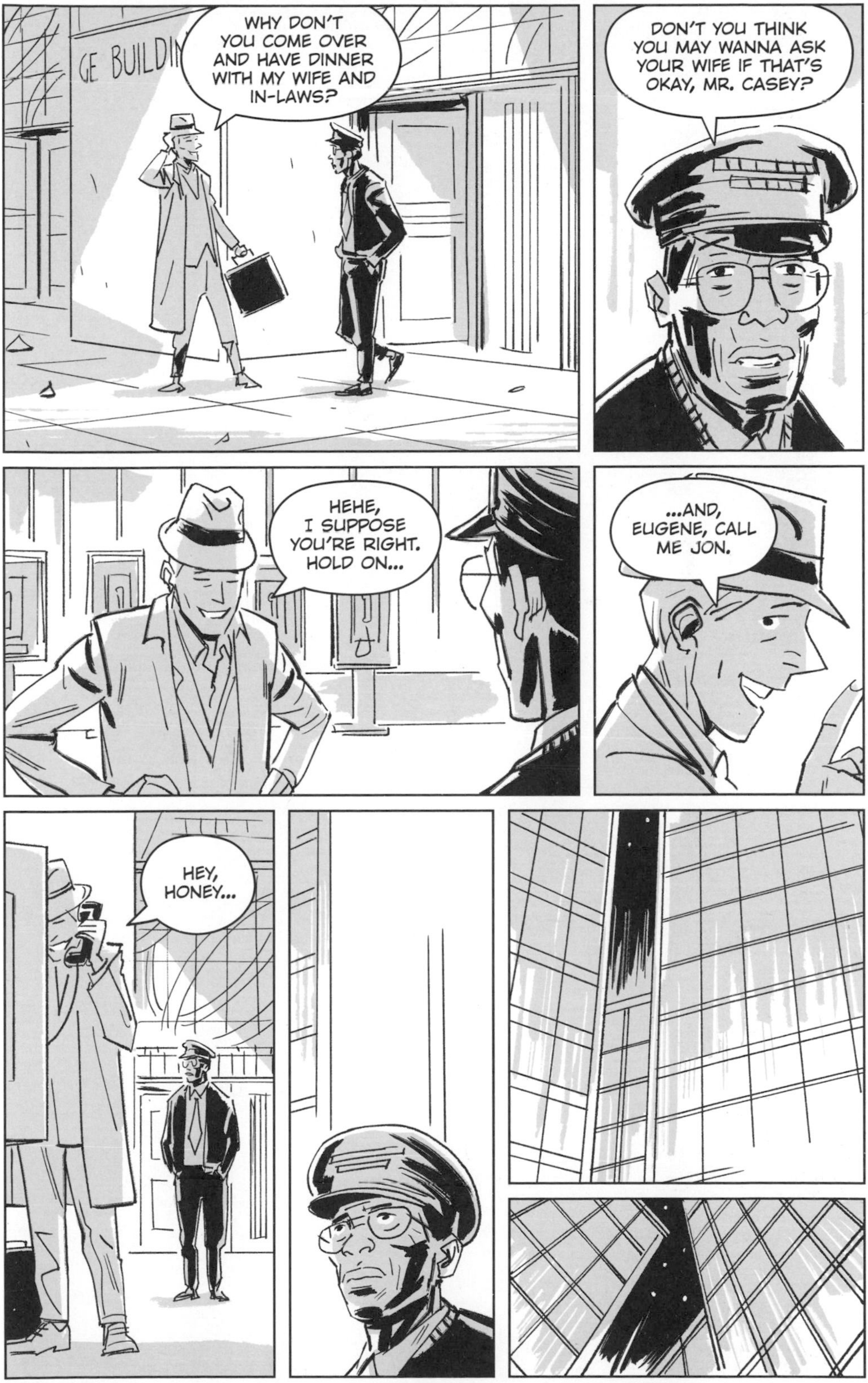
GE BUILDIN
WHY DON'T YOU COME OVER AND HAVE DINNER WITH MY WIFE AND IN-LAWS?
DON'T YOU THINK YOU MAY WANNA ASK YOUR WIFE IF THAT'S OKAY, MR. CASEY?
HEHE, I SUPPOSE YOU'RE RIGHT. HOLD ON...
...AND, EUGENE, CALL ME JON.
HEY, HONEY...

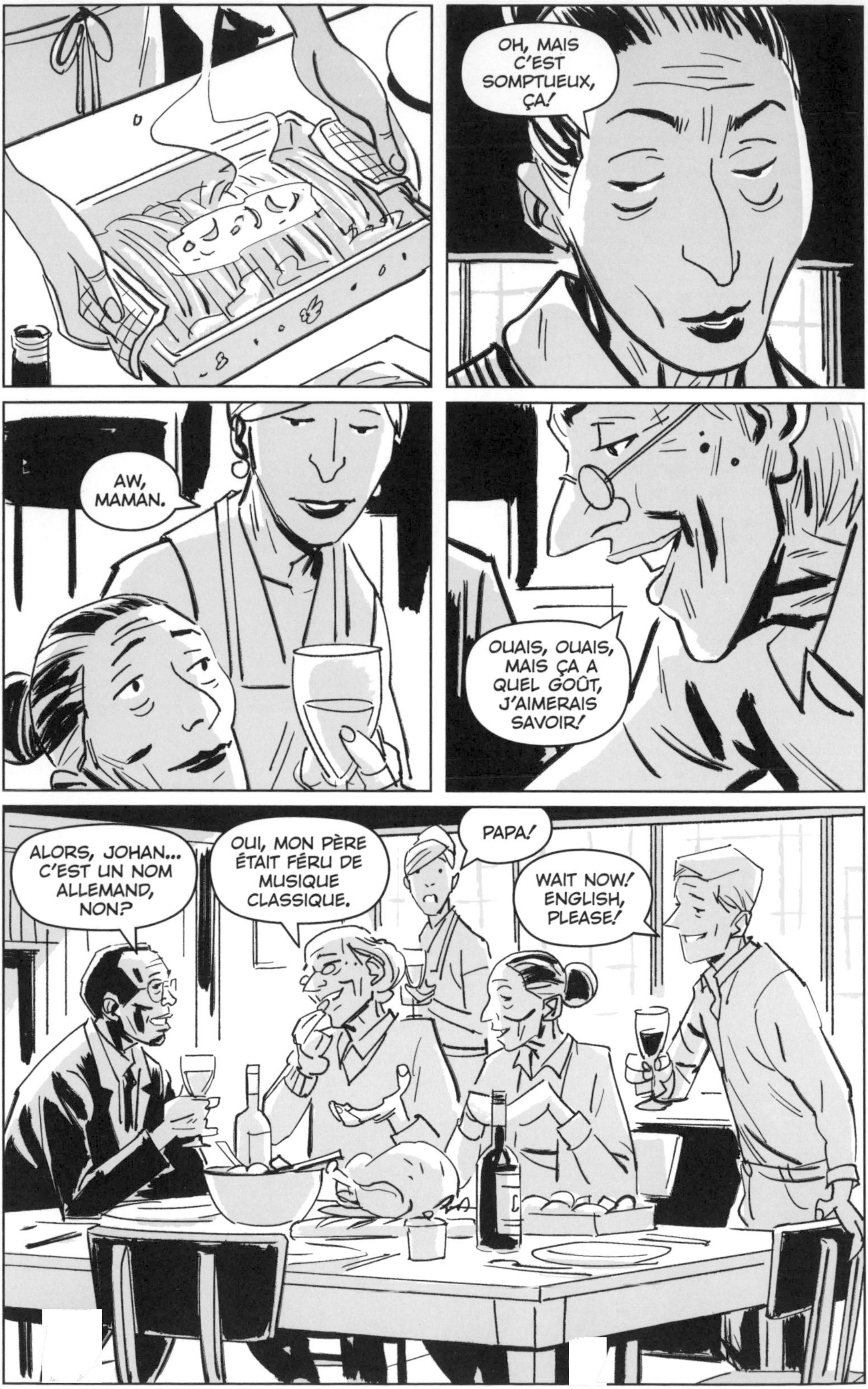
OH, MAIS C'EST SOMPTUEUX, ÇA!
AW, MAMAN.
OUAIS, OUAIS, MAIS ÇA A QUEL GOÛT, J'AIMERAIS SAVOIR!
ALORS, JOHAN... C'EST UN NOM ALLEMAND, NON?
OUI, MON PÈRE ÉTAIT FÉRU DE MUSIQUE CLASSIQUE.
PAPA!
WAIT NOW! ENGLISH, PLEASE!

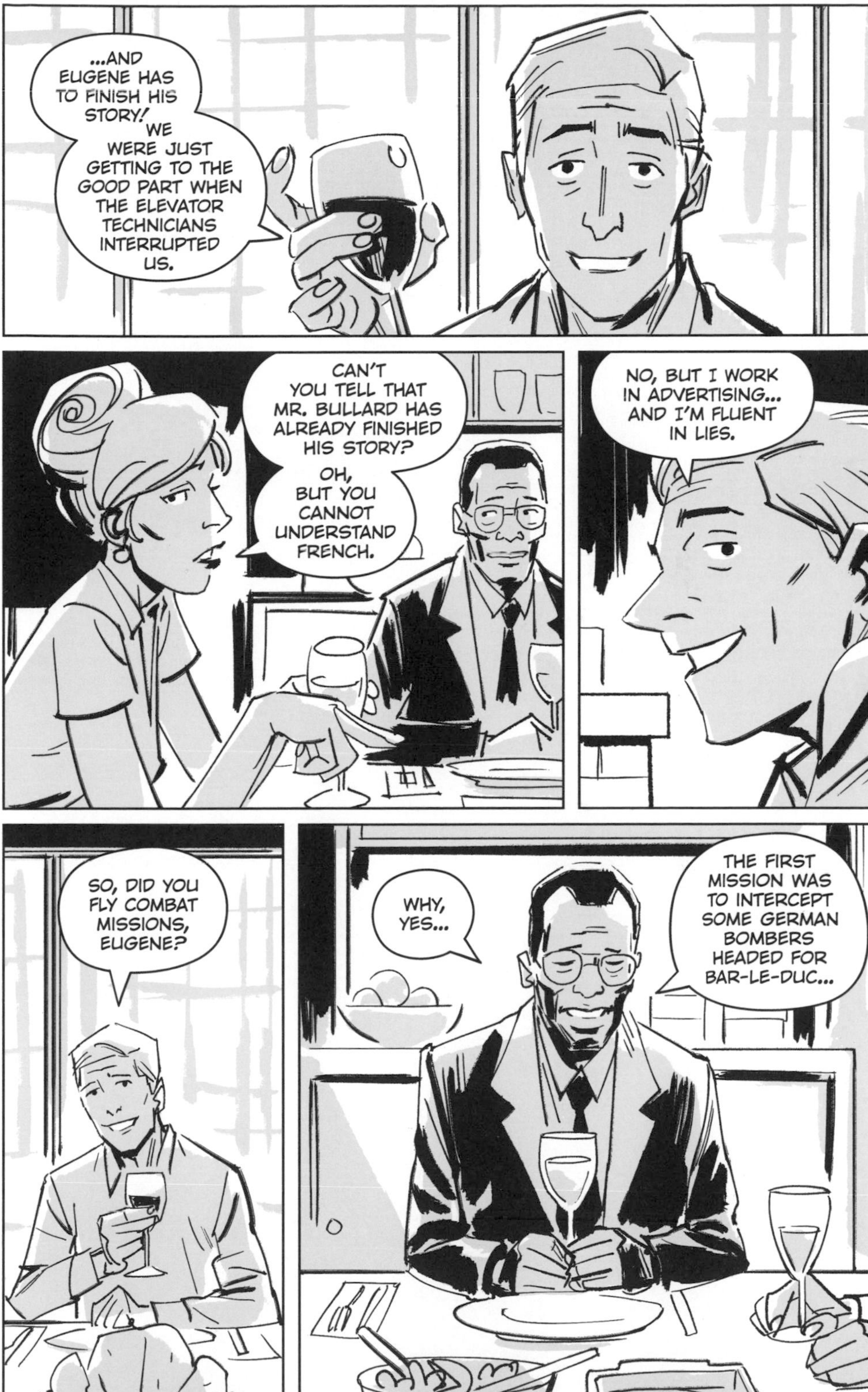
...AND EUGENE HAS TO FINISH HIS STORY! WE WERE JUST GETTING TO THE GOOD PART WHEN THE ELEVATOR TECHNICIANS INTERRUPTED US.
CAN'T YOU TELL THAT MR. BULLARD HAS ALREADY FINISHED HIS STORY?
OH, BUT YOU CANNOT UNDERSTAND FRENCH.
NO, BUT I WORK IN ADVERTISING... AND I'M FLUENT IN LIES.
SO, DID YOU FLY COMBAT MISSIONS, EUGENE?
WHY, YES...
THE FIRST MISSION WAS TO INTERCEPT SOME GERMAN BOMBERS HEADED FOR BAR-LE-DUC...

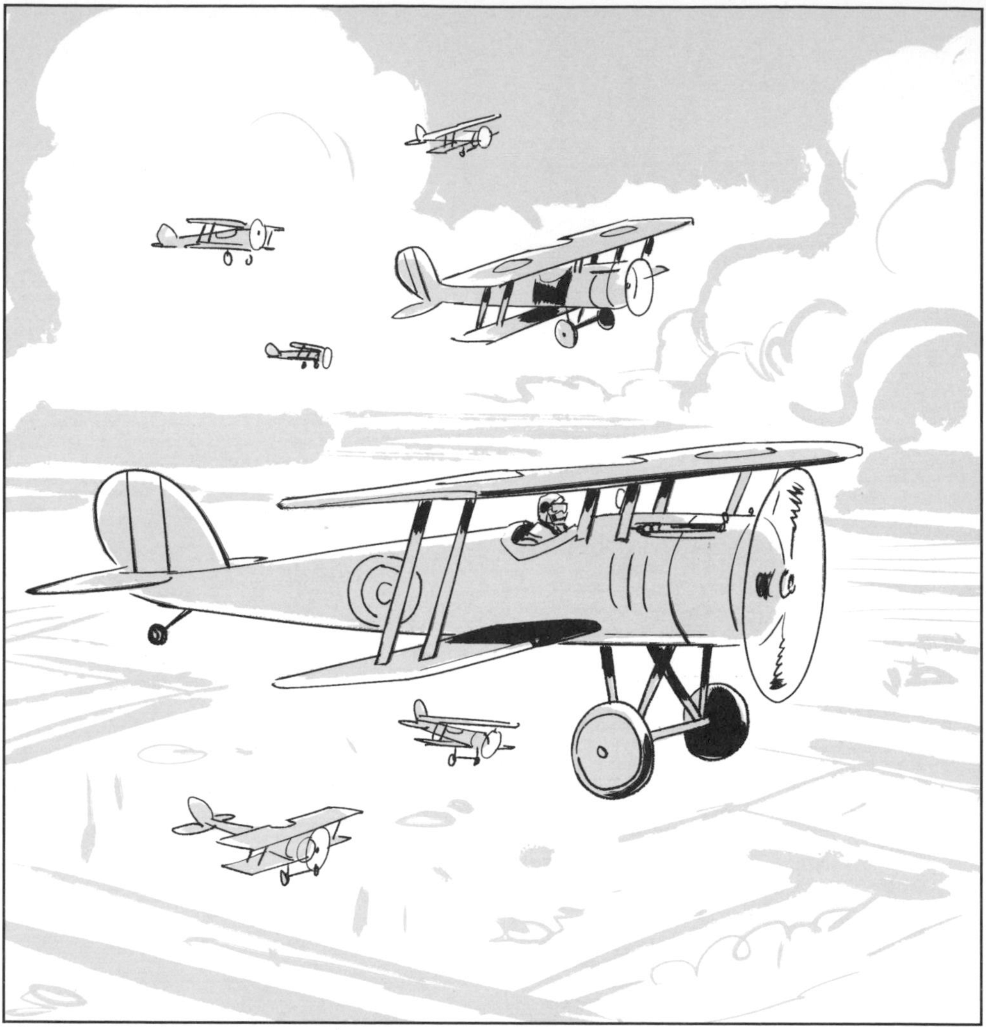

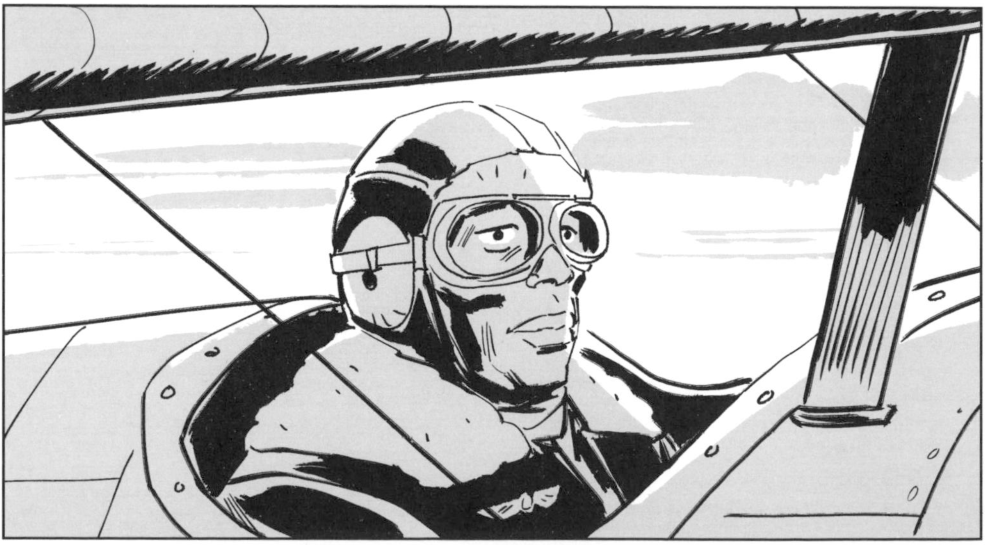

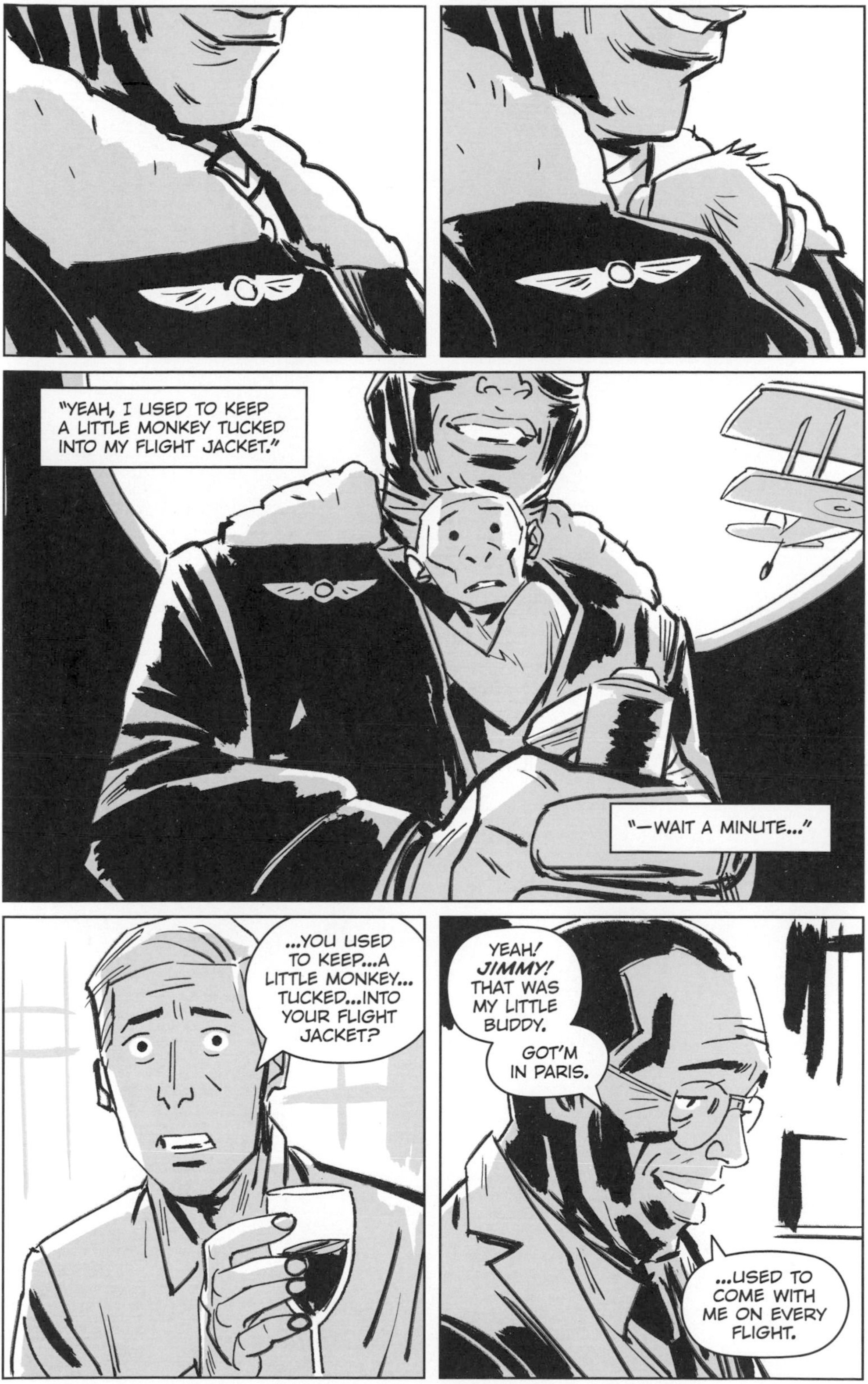
"YEAH, I USED TO KEEP A LITTLE MONKEY TUCKED INTO MY FLIGHT JACKET."
"—WAIT A MINUTE..."
...YOU USED TO KEEP...A LITTLE MONKEY... TUCKED...INTO YOUR FLIGHT JACKET?
YEAH! *JIMMY!* THAT WAS MY LITTLE BUDDY.
GOT'M IN PARIS.
...USED TO COME WITH ME ON EVERY FLIGHT.

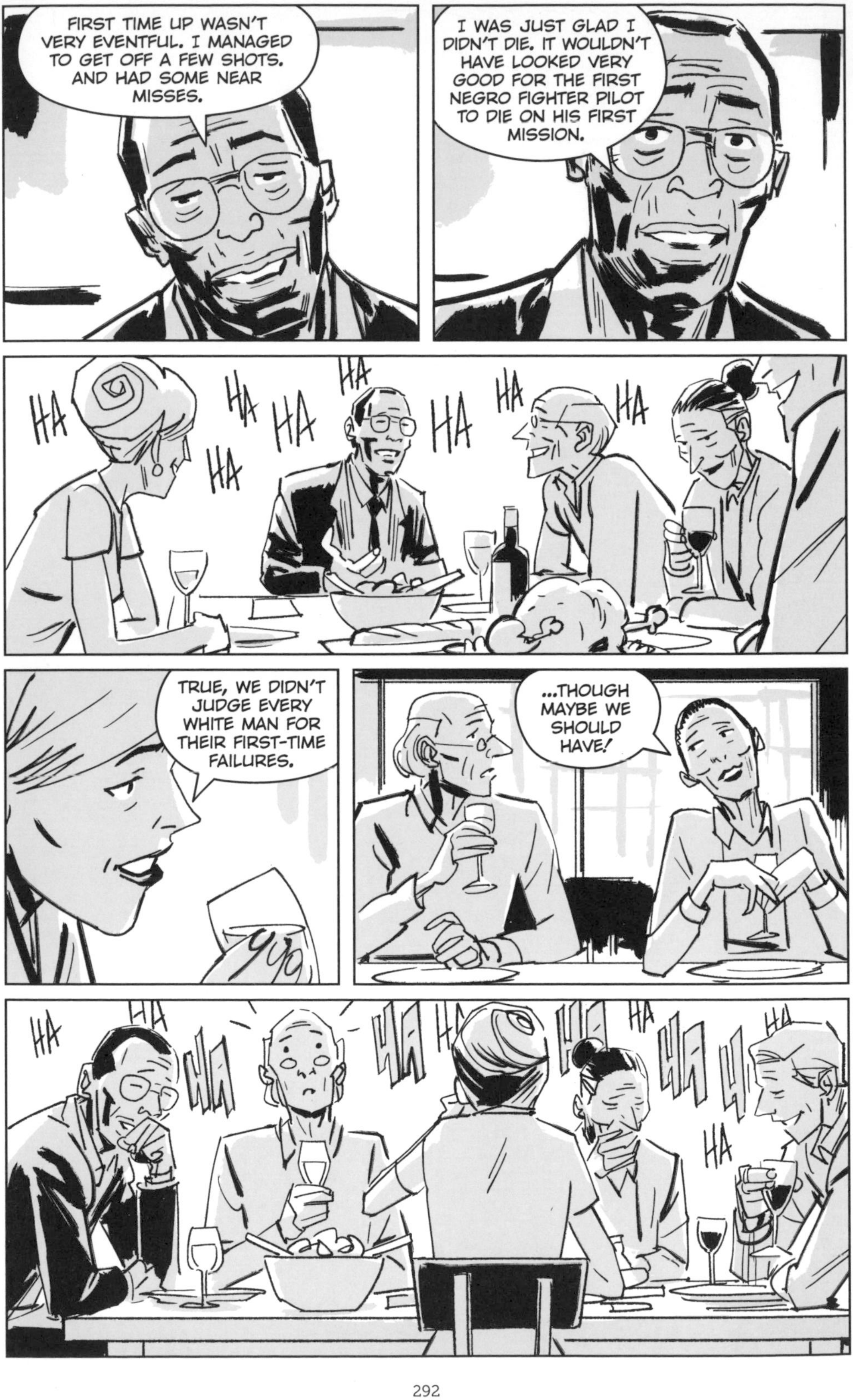
FIRST TIME UP WASN'T VERY EVENTFUL. I MANAGED TO GET OFF A FEW SHOTS. AND HAD SOME NEAR MISSES.
I WAS JUST GLAD I DIDN'T DIE. IT WOULDN'T HAVE LOOKED VERY GOOD FOR THE FIRST NEGRO FIGHTER PILOT TO DIE ON HIS FIRST MISSION.
HA HA HA HA HA HA HA HA HA
TRUE, WE DIDN'T JUDGE EVERY WHITE MAN FOR THEIR FIRST-TIME FAILURES.
...THOUGH MAYBE WE SHOULD HAVE!
HA HA HA HA HA HA HA HA HA

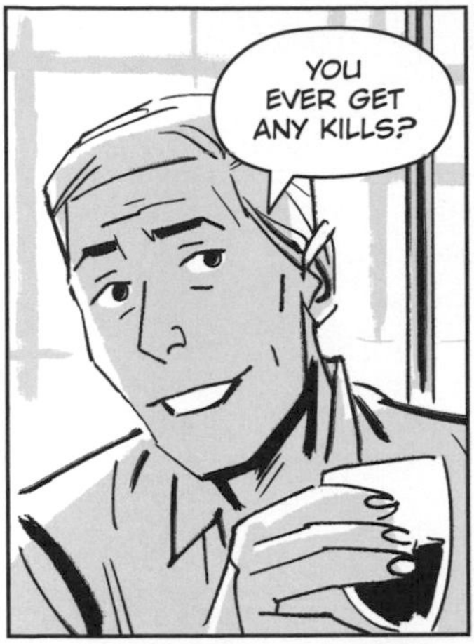
YOU EVER GET ANY KILLS?

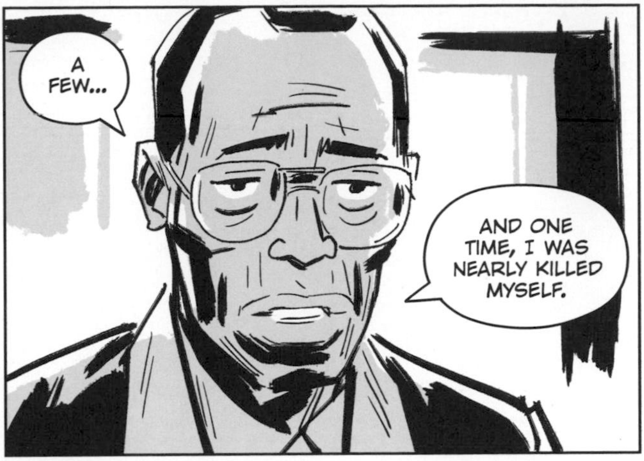
A FEW...
AND ONE TIME, I WAS NEARLY KILLED MYSELF.

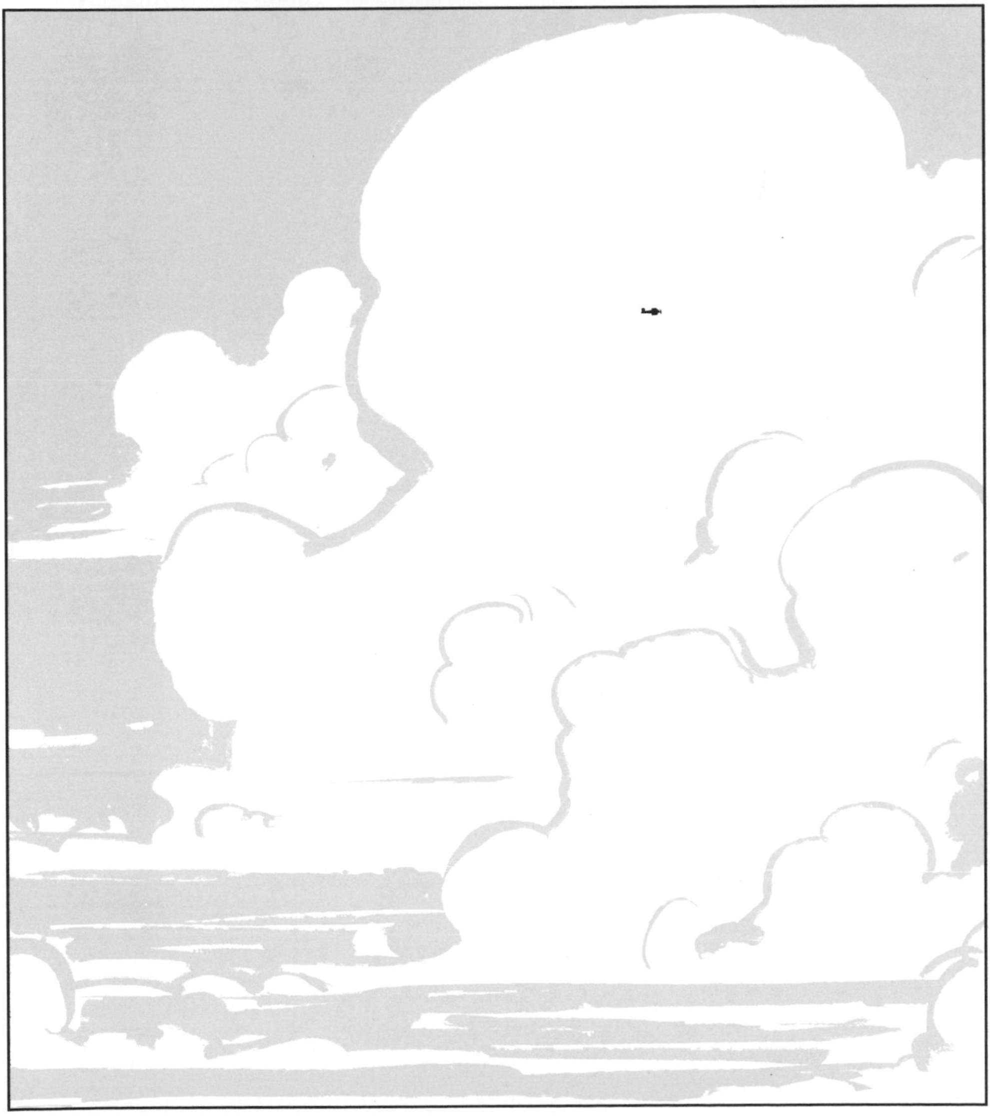

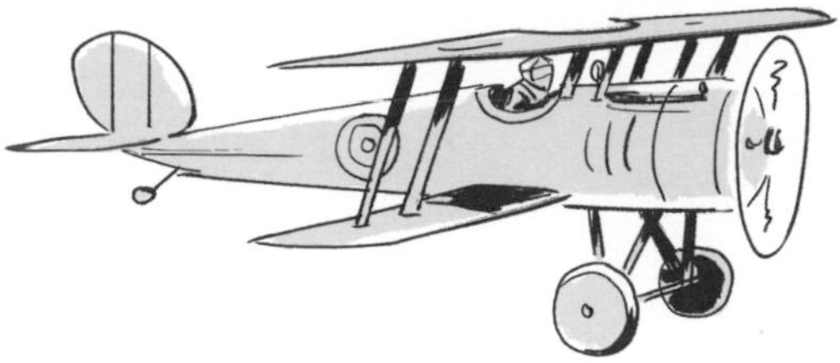

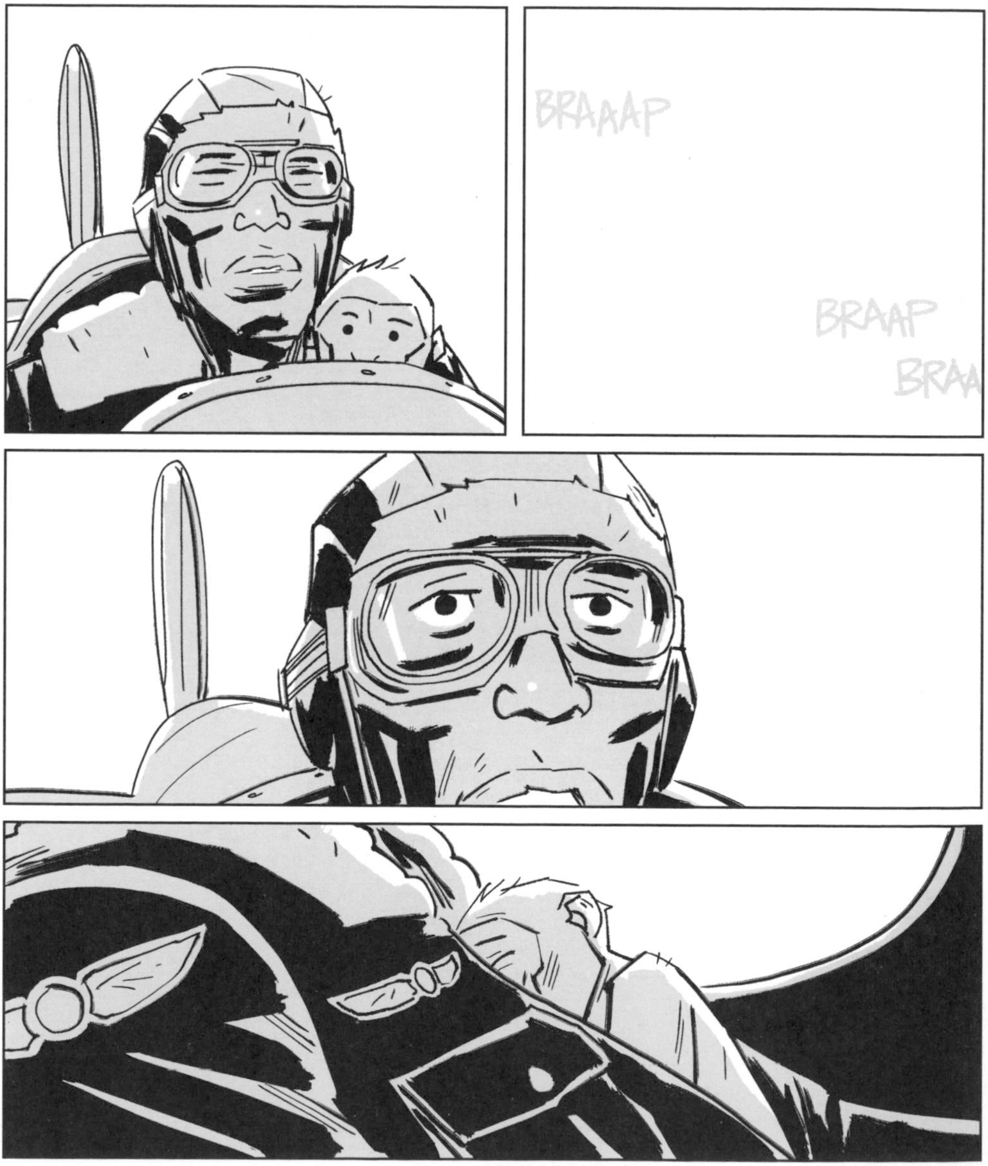
BRAAAP
BRAAP
BRAA

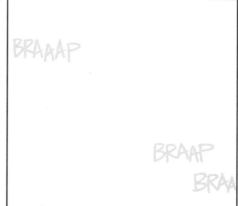

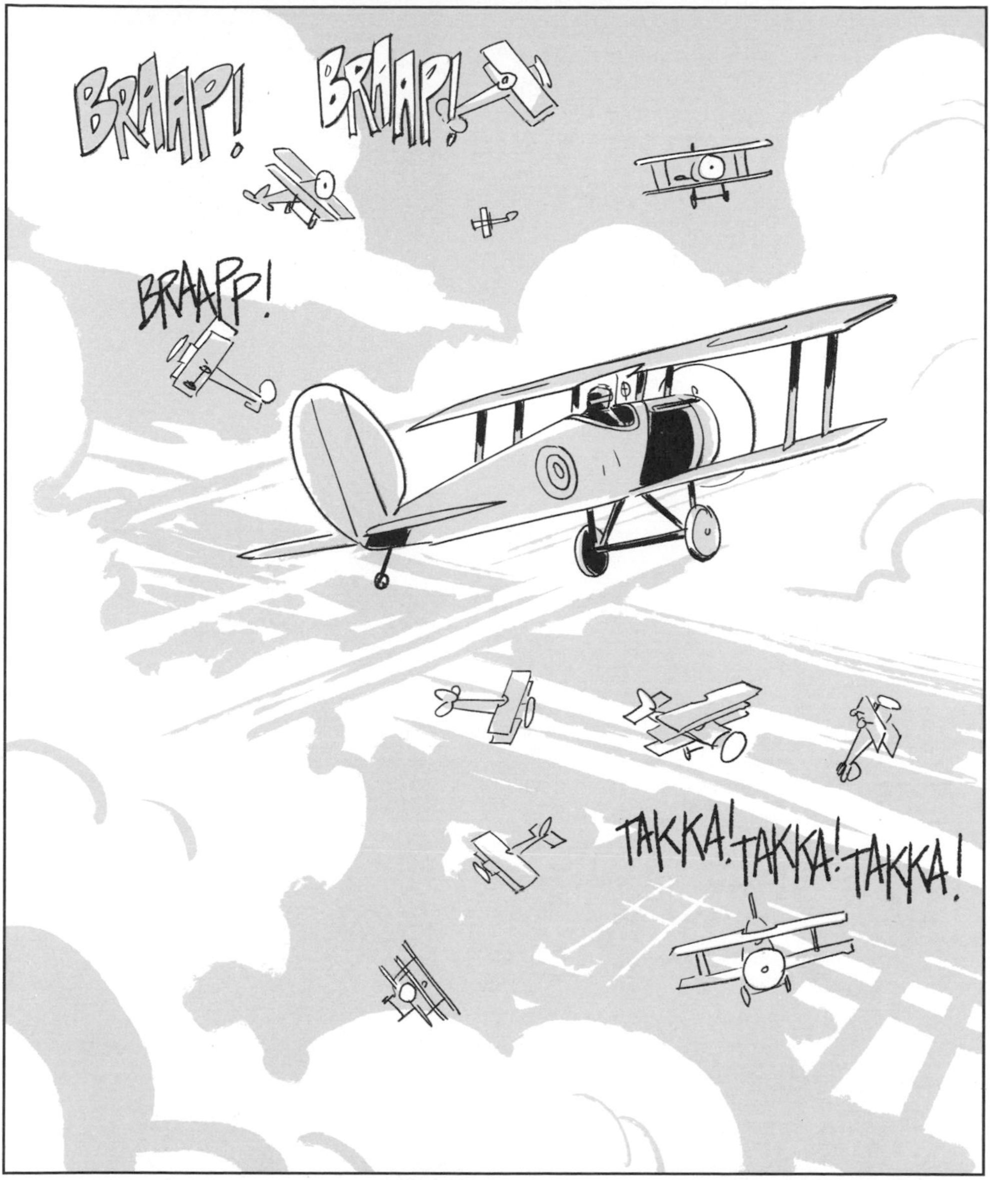
BRAAP! BRAAP!
BRAAPP!
TAKKA! TAKKA! TAKKA!

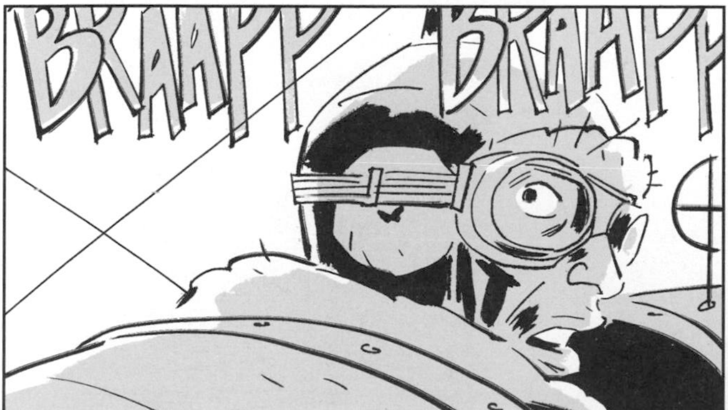
BRAAPP BRAAPP

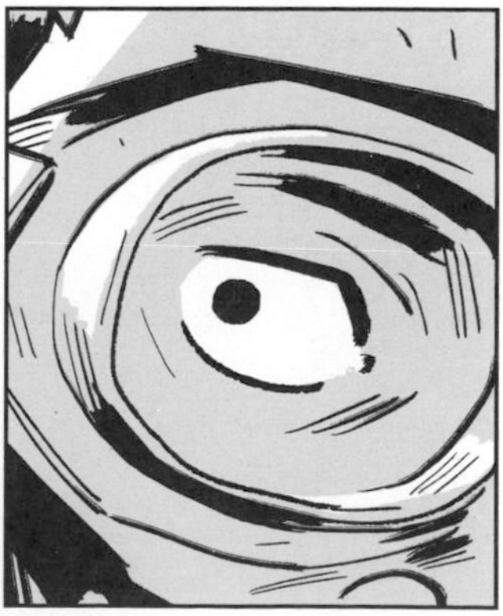

CHAPTER 8

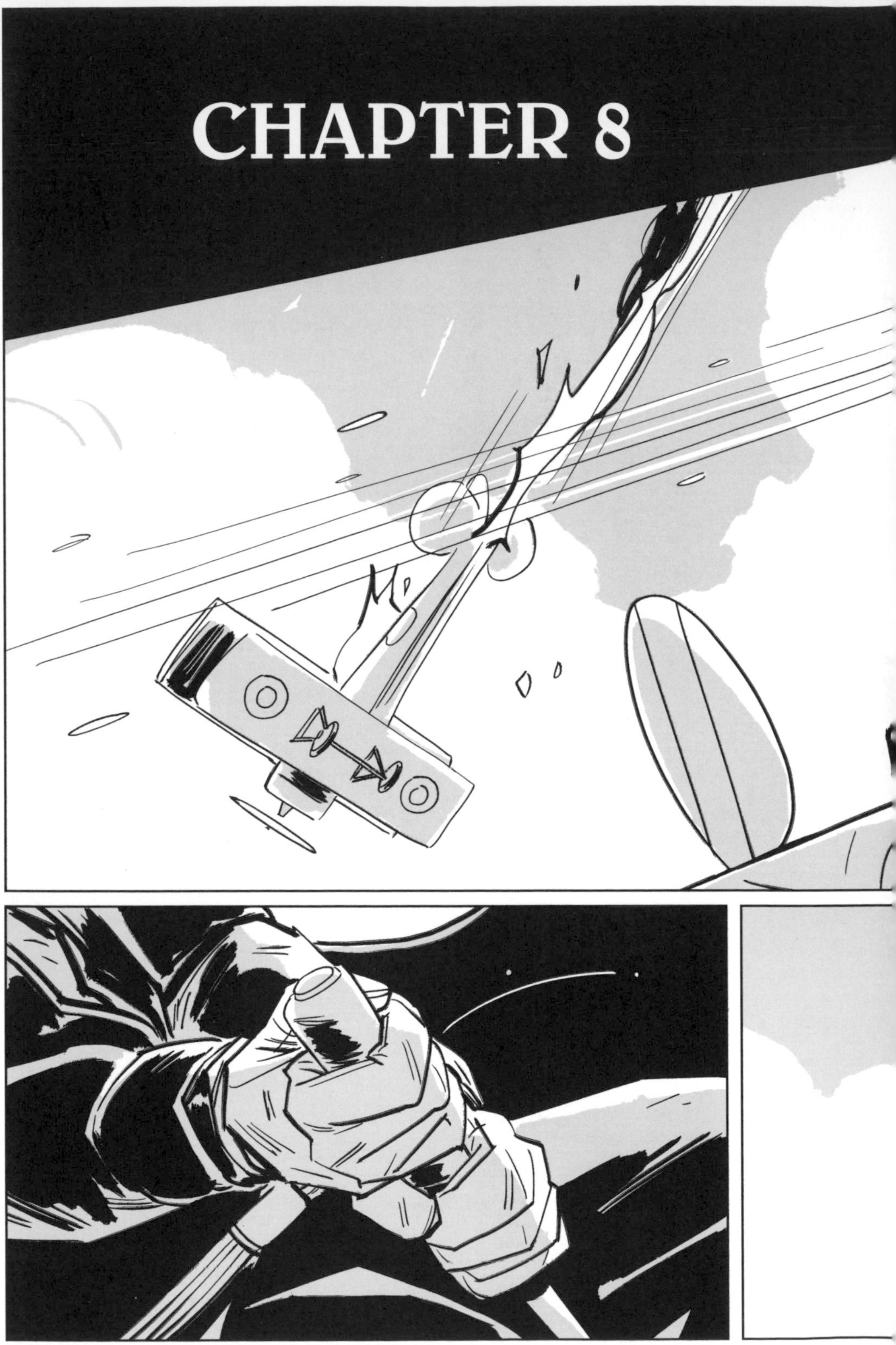

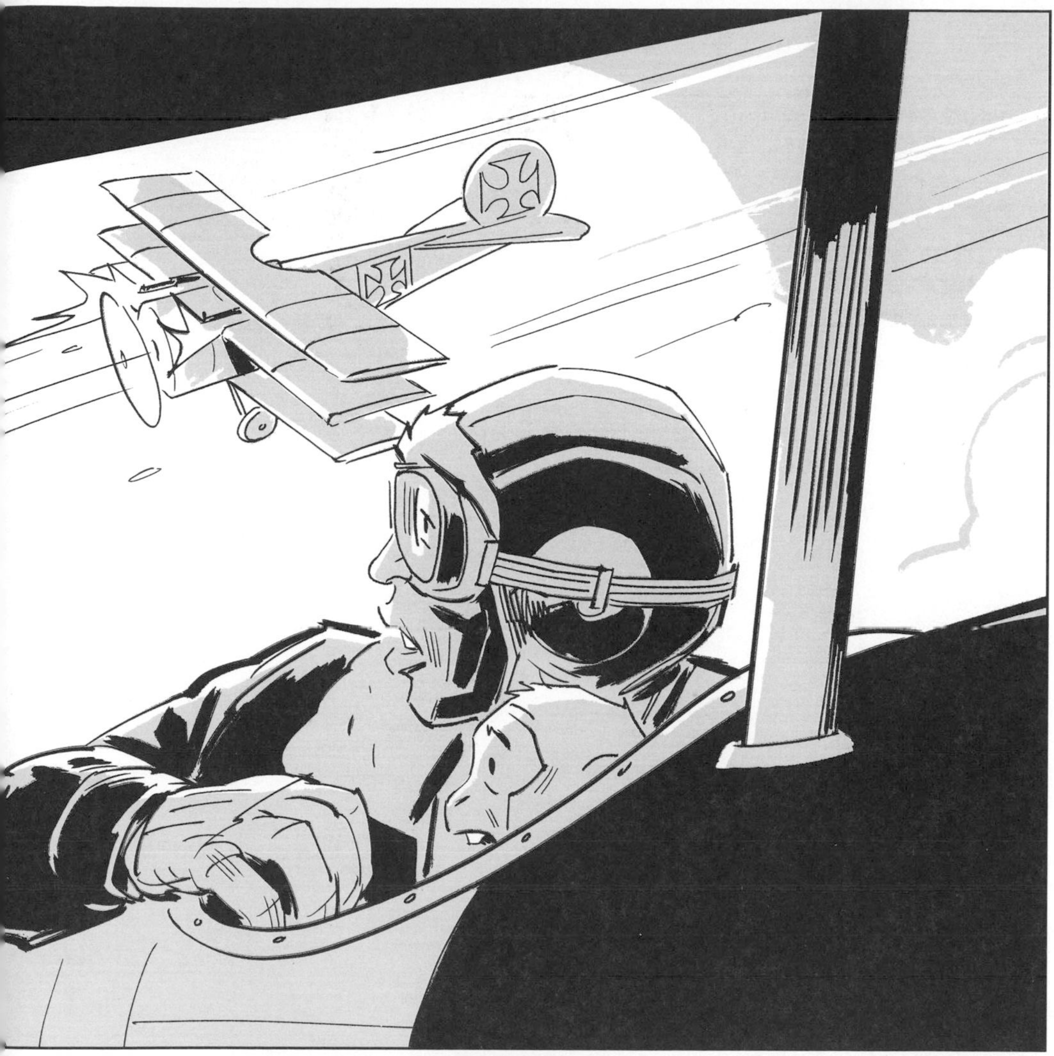

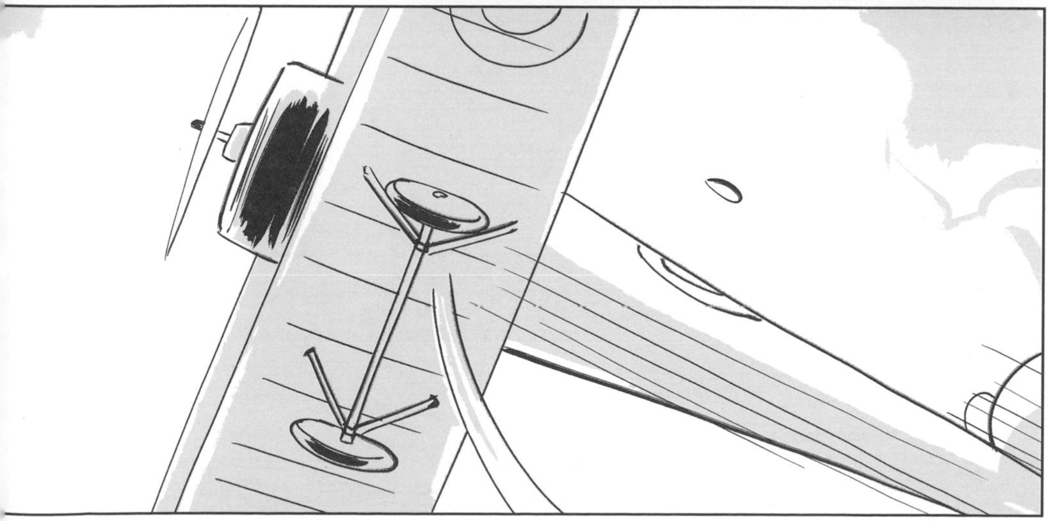

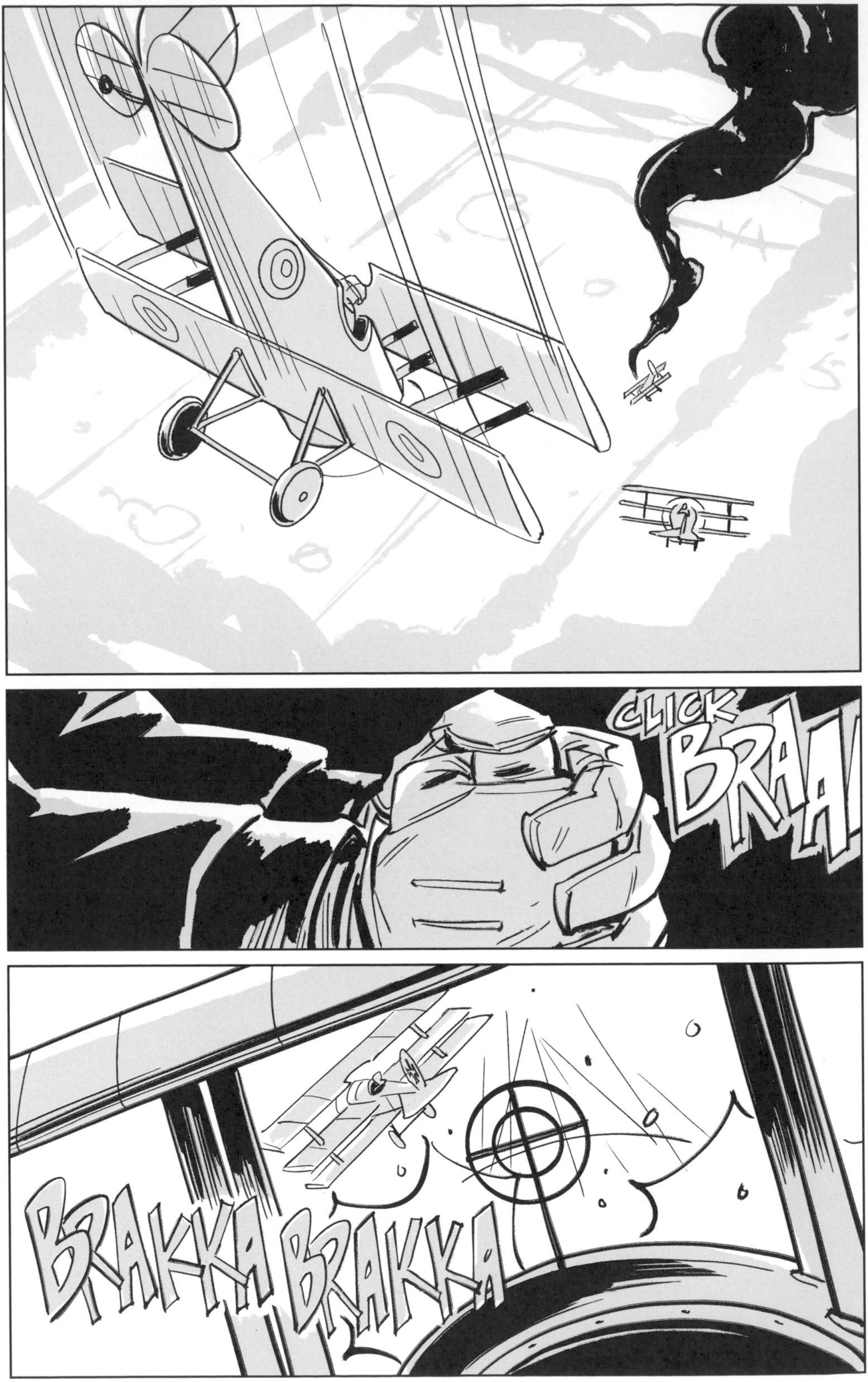
CLICK
BRAA
BRAKKA BRAKKA

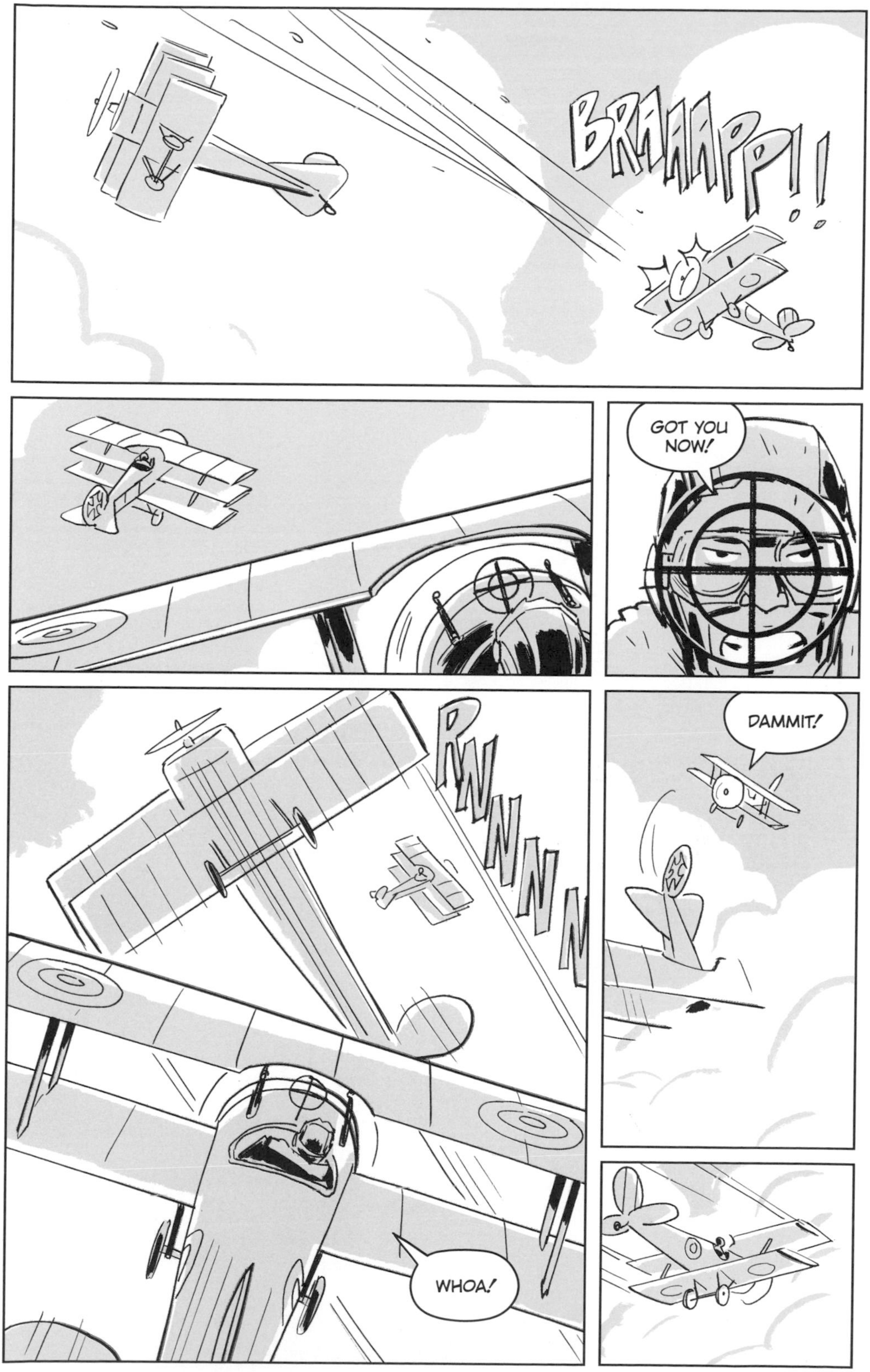
BRAAAPP!!
GOT YOU NOW!
RNNNNN
WHOA!
DAMMIT!

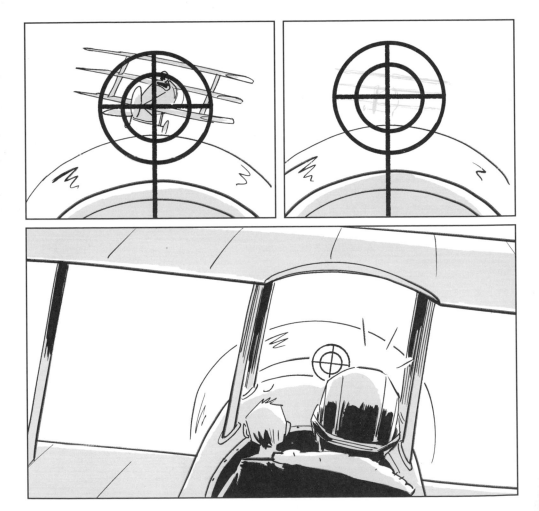

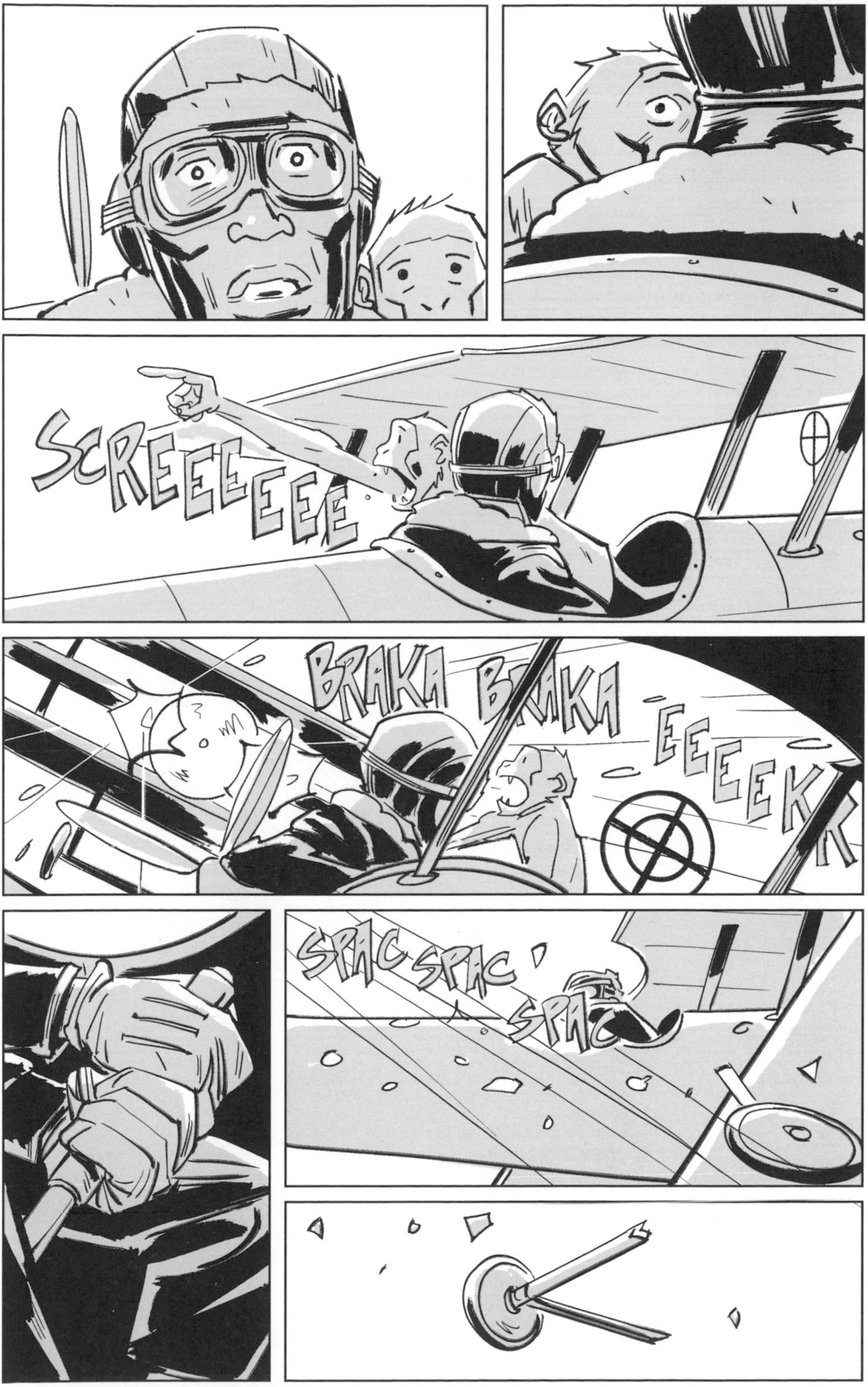
SCREEEEEEE
BRAKA BRAKA
EEEEKK
SPAC SPAC
SPAC

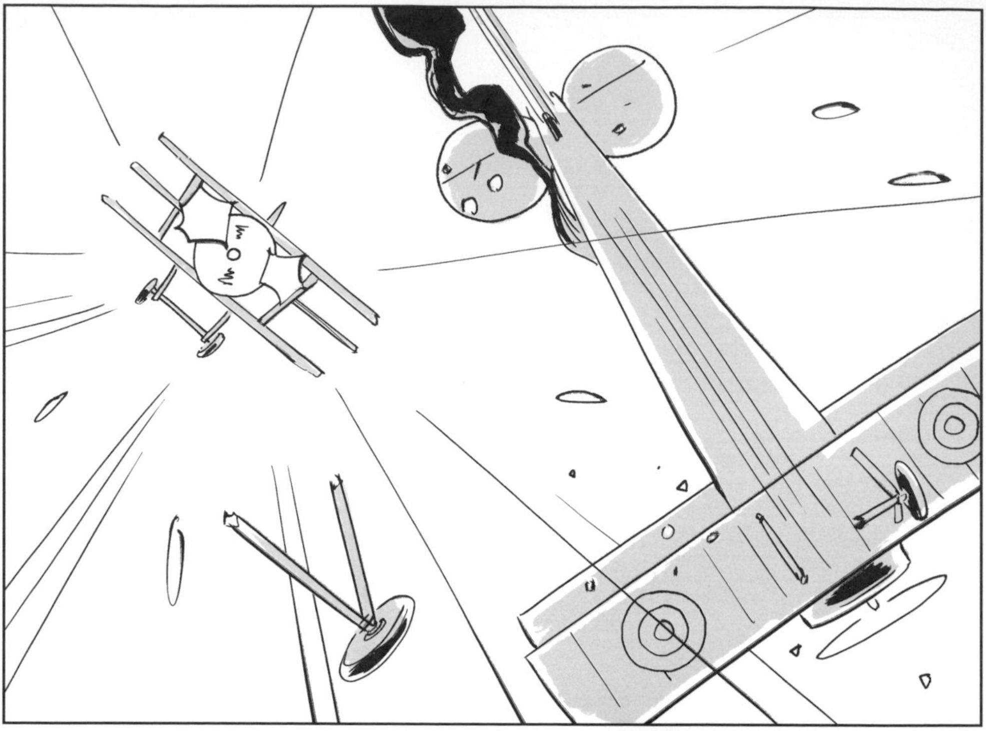

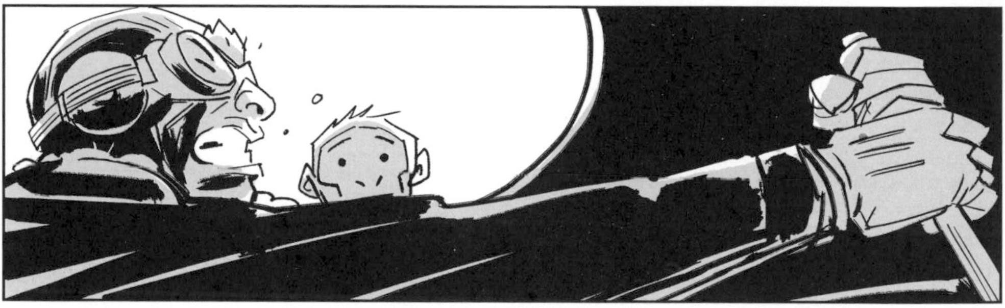

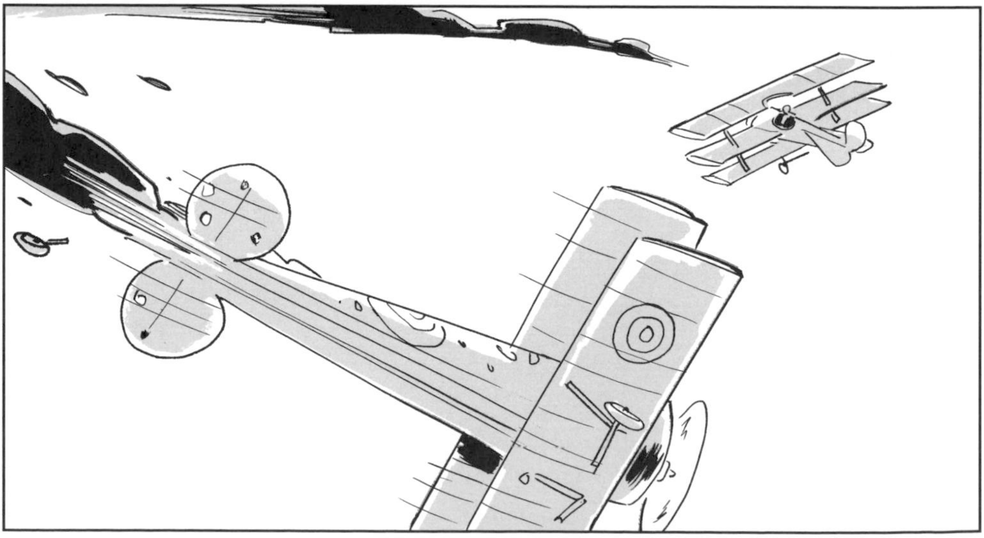

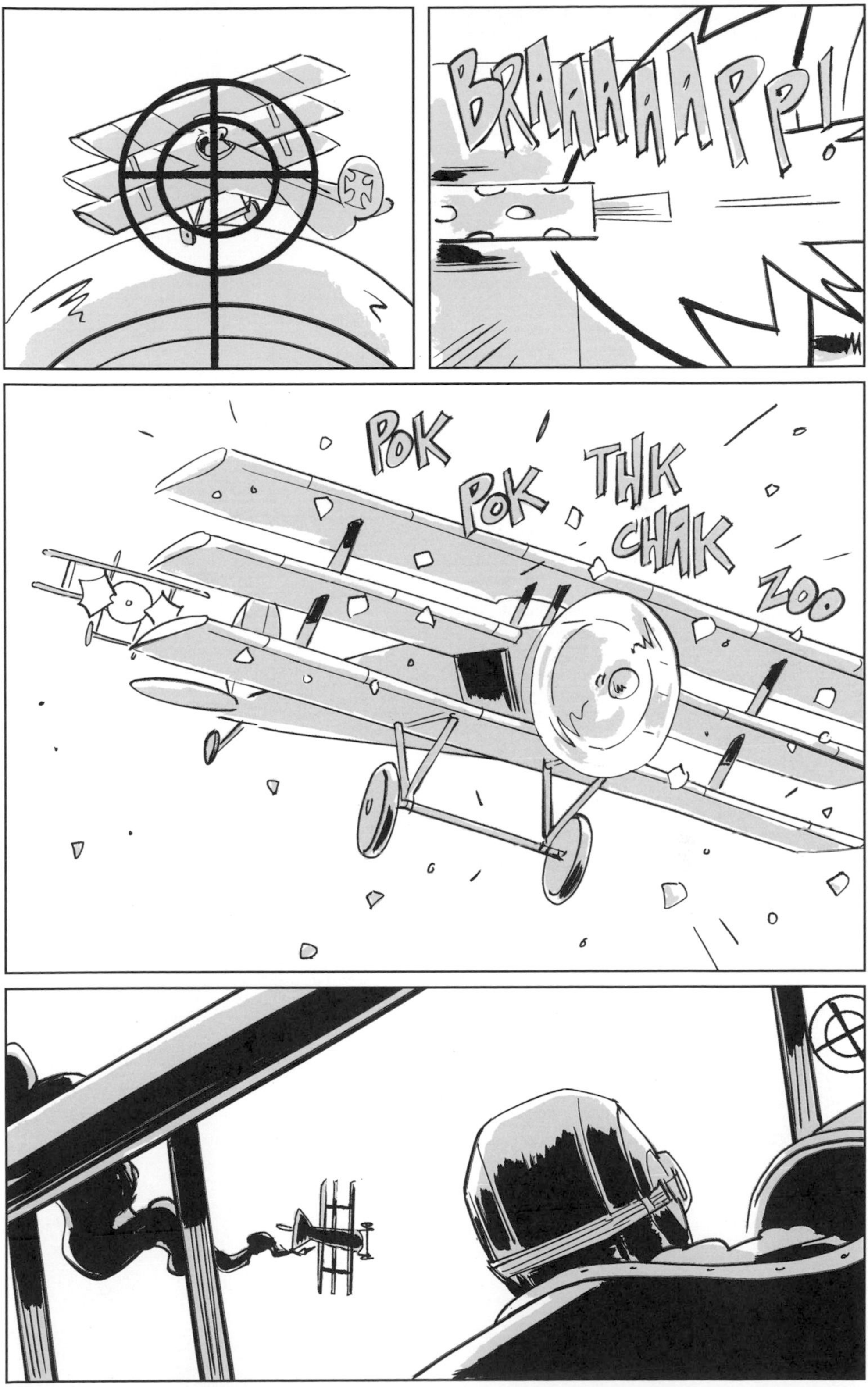
BRAAAAAPP!
POK
POK
THK
CHAK
ZOO

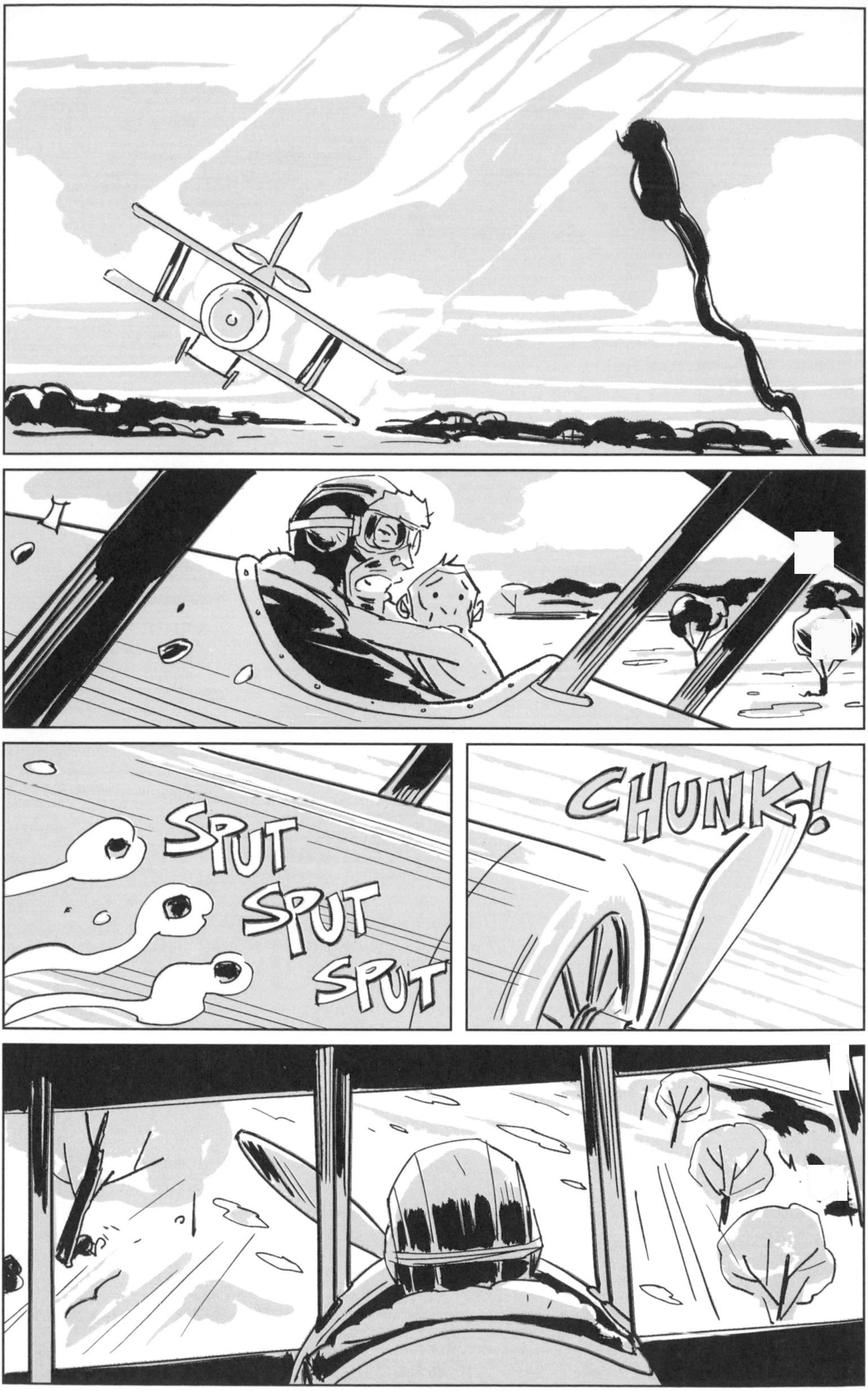
SPUT
SPUT
SPUT
CHUNK!

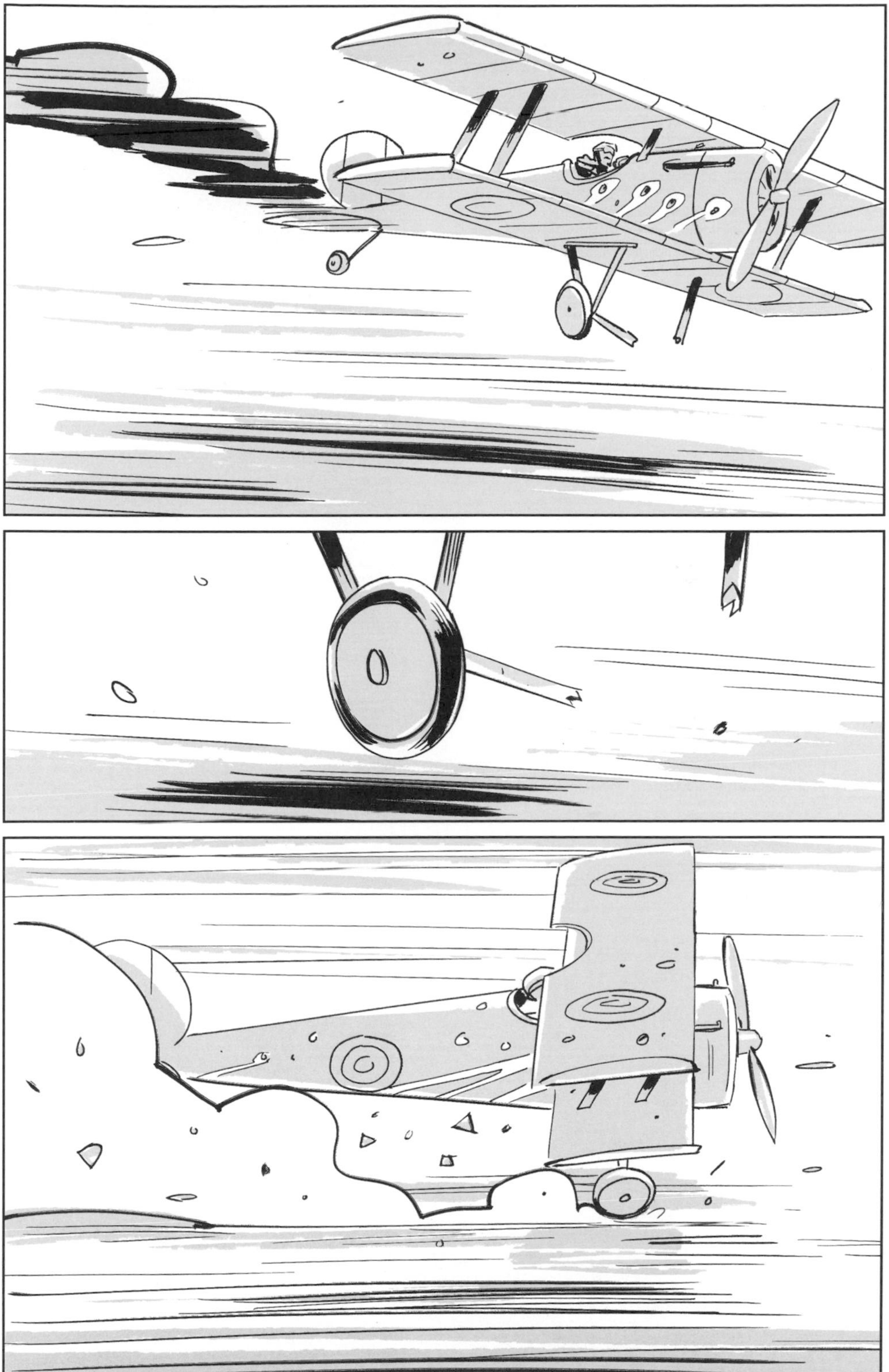

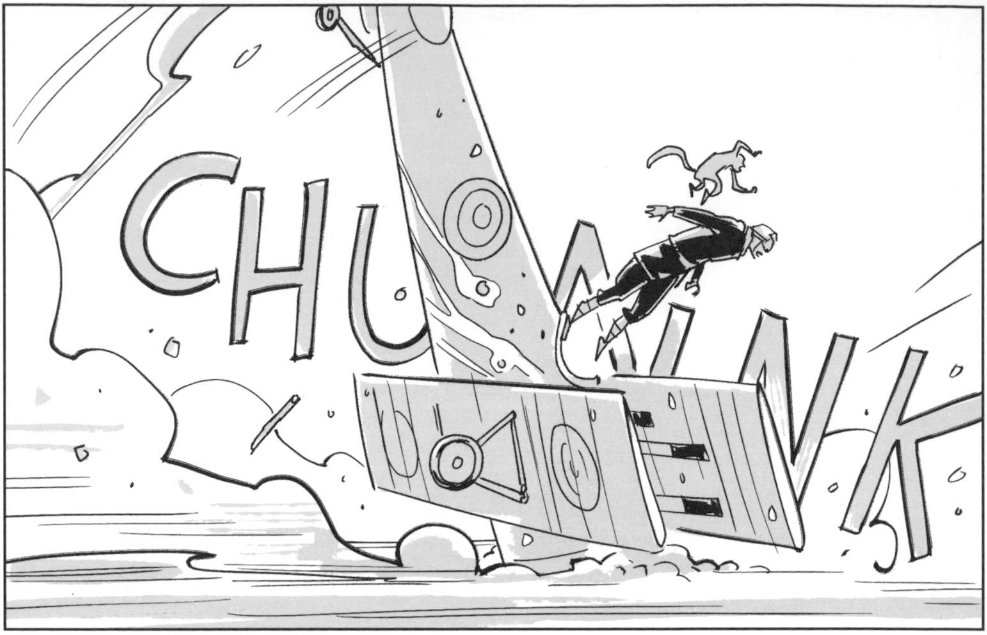
CHU NK

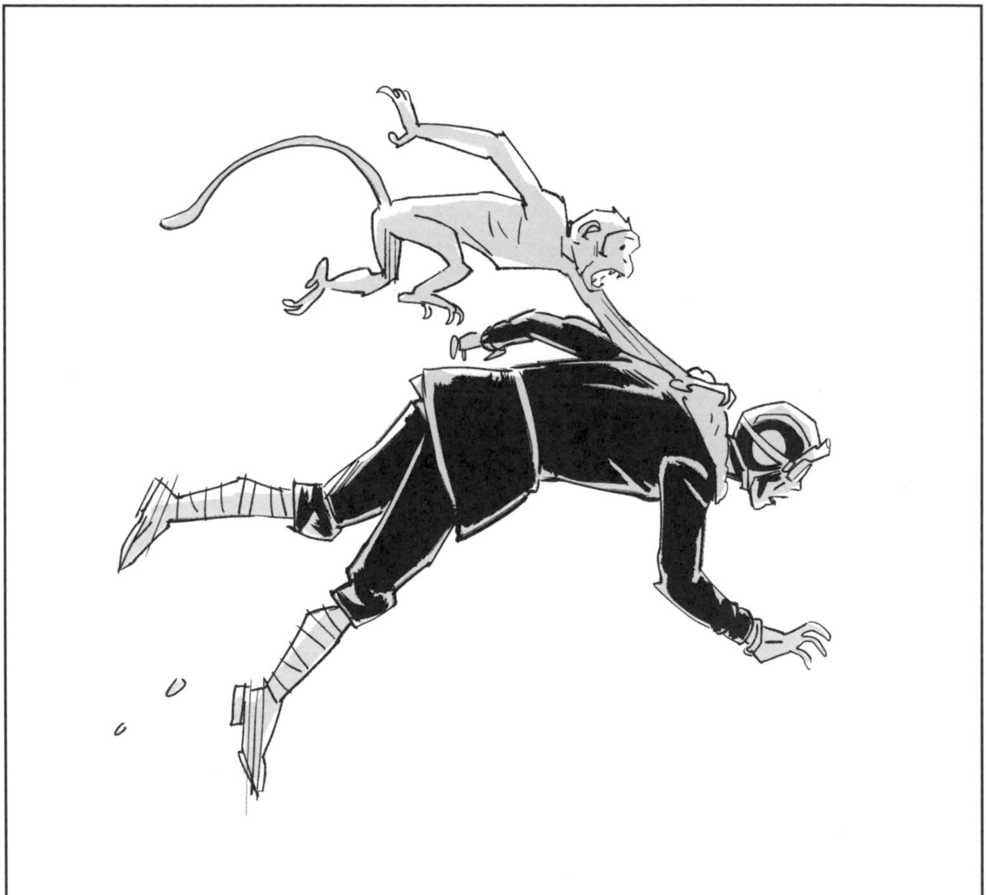

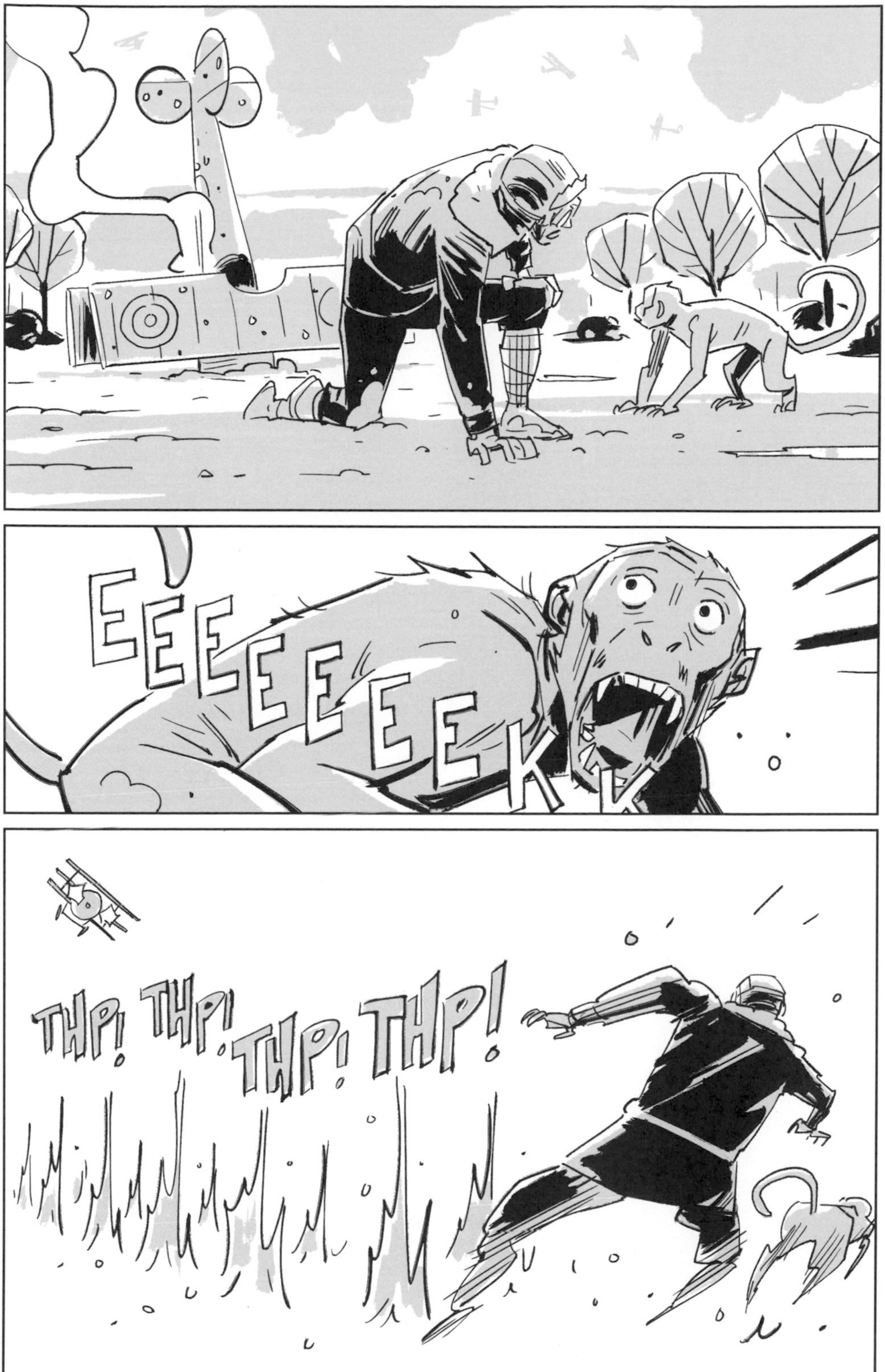
EEEEEEEEKK
THP! THP! THP! THP!

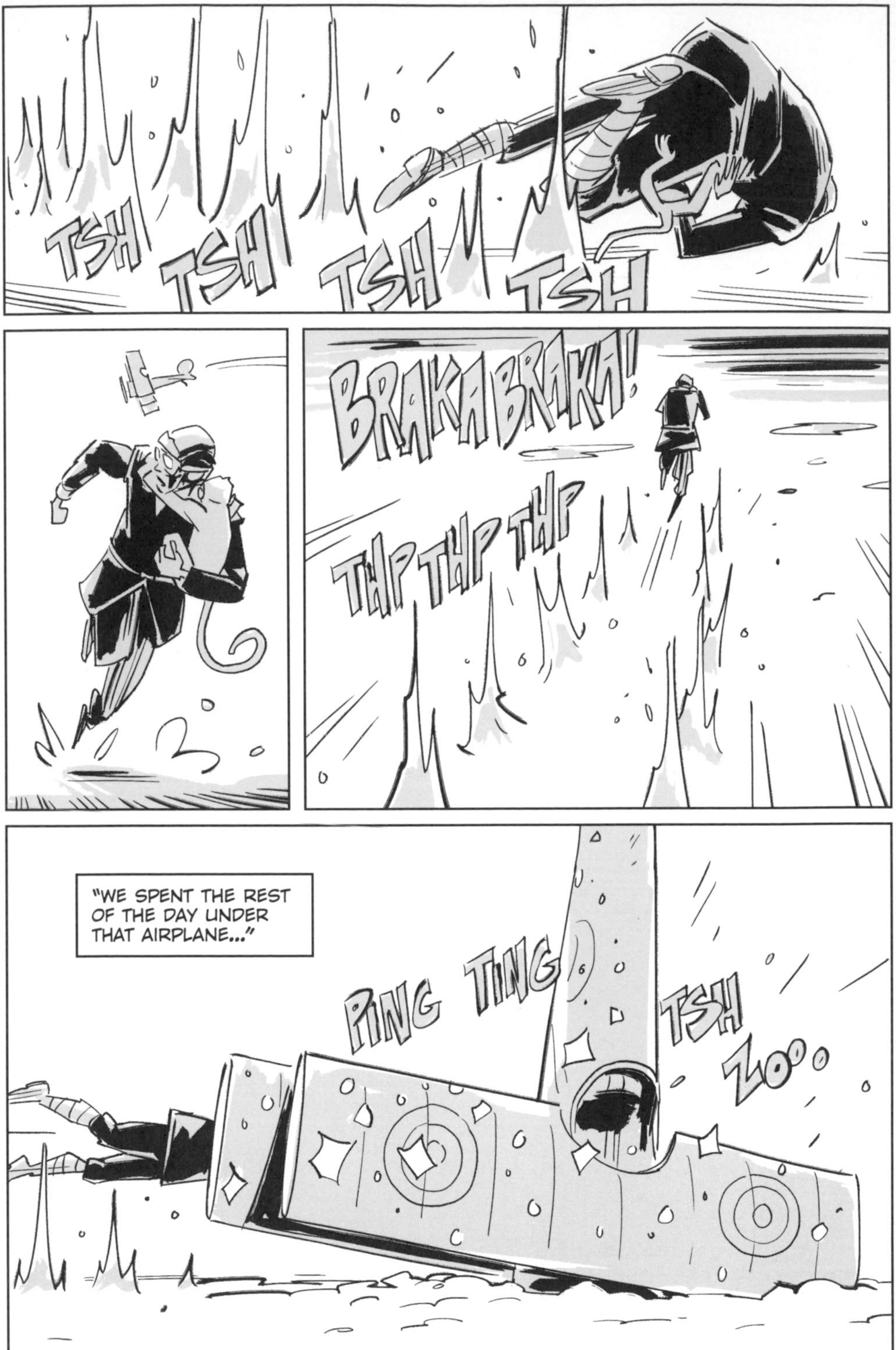

TSH TSH TSH TSH
BRAKA BRAKA!
THP THP THP
"WE SPENT THE REST OF THE DAY UNDER THAT AIRPLANE..."
PING TING TSH
ZOO

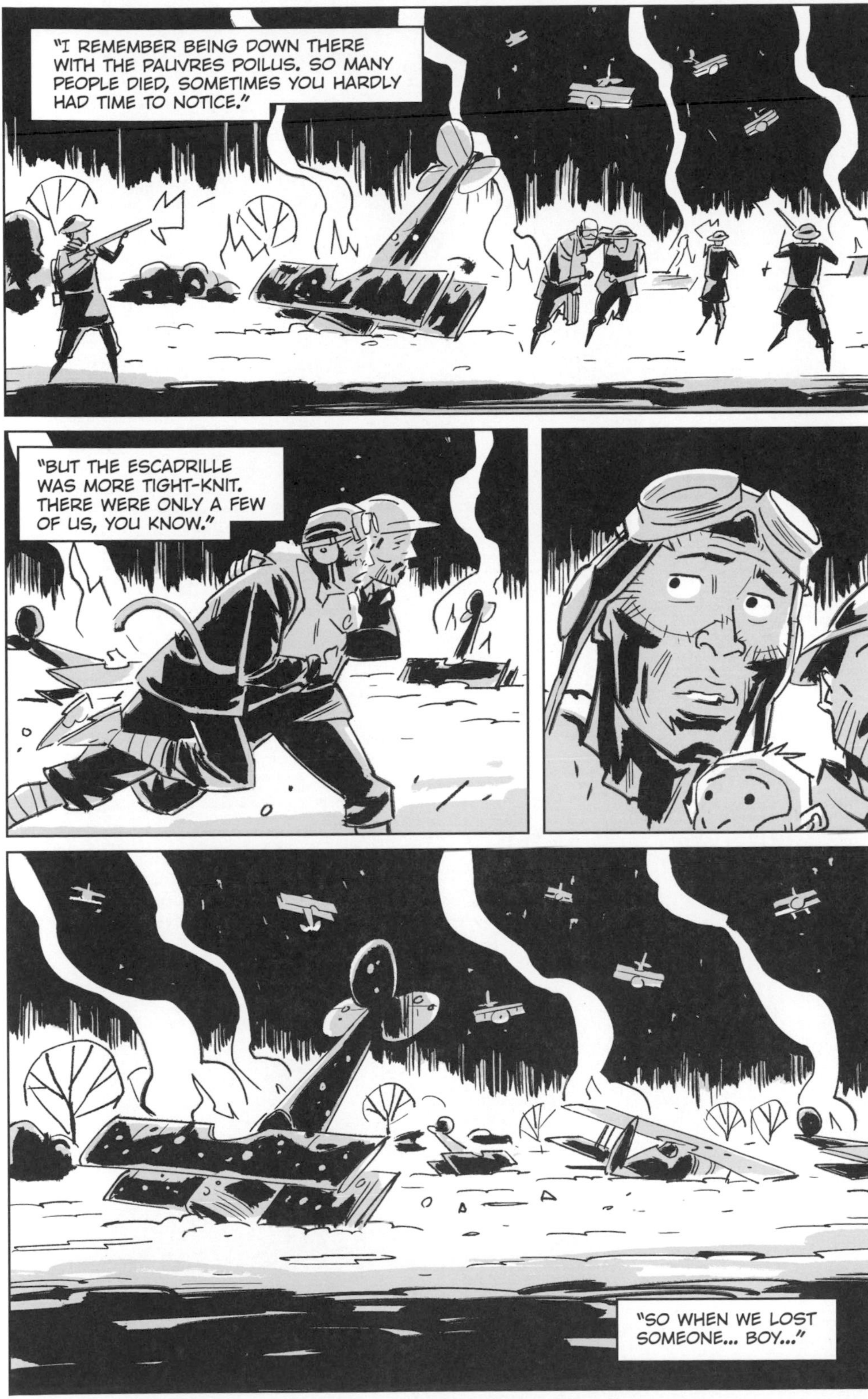
"I REMEMBER BEING DOWN THERE WITH THE PAUVRES POILUS. SO MANY PEOPLE DIED, SOMETIMES YOU HARDLY HAD TIME TO NOTICE."
"BUT THE ESCADRILLE WAS MORE TIGHT-KNIT. THERE WERE ONLY A FEW OF US, YOU KNOW."
"SO WHEN WE LOST SOMEONE... BOY..."

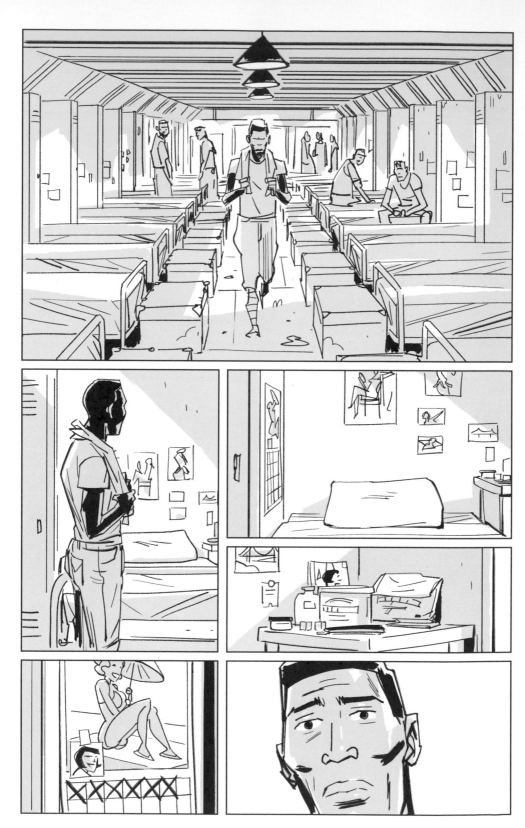

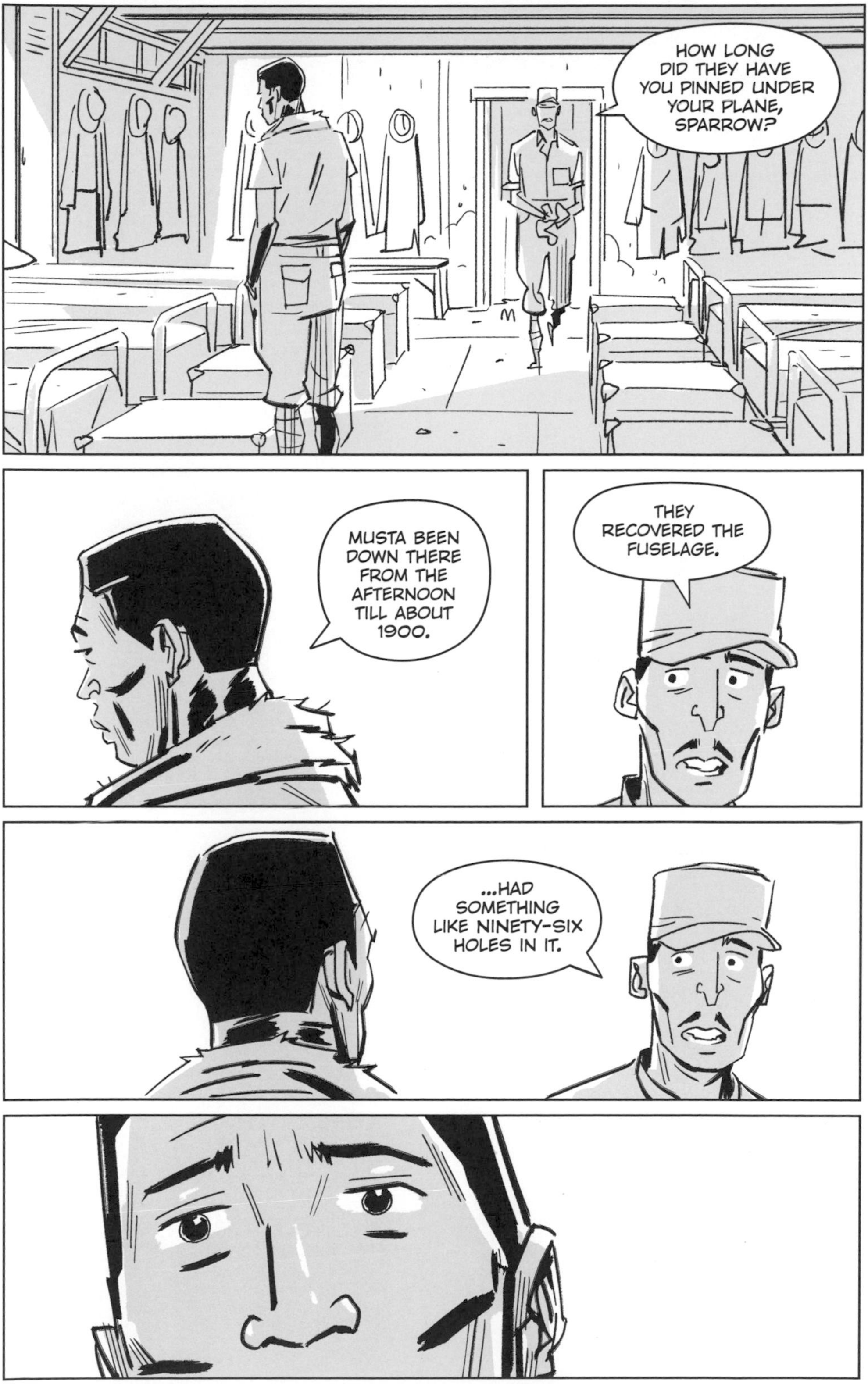
HOW LONG DID THEY HAVE YOU PINNED UNDER YOUR PLANE, SPARROW?
MUSTA BEEN DOWN THERE FROM THE AFTERNOON TILL ABOUT 1900.
THEY RECOVERED THE FUSELAGE.
...HAD SOMETHING LIKE NINETY-SIX HOLES IN IT.

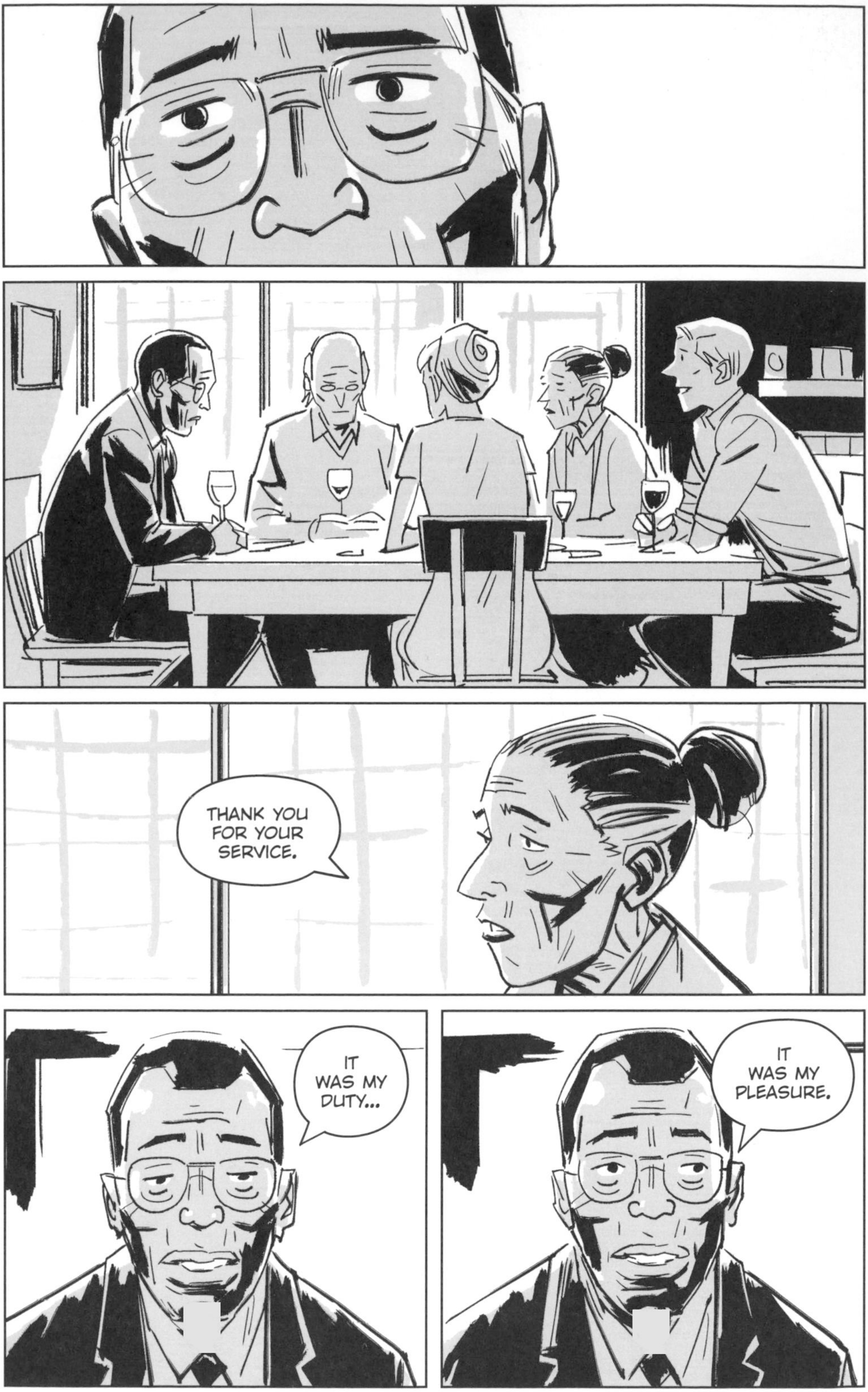
THANK YOU FOR YOUR SERVICE.
IT WAS MY DUTY...
IT WAS MY PLEASURE.

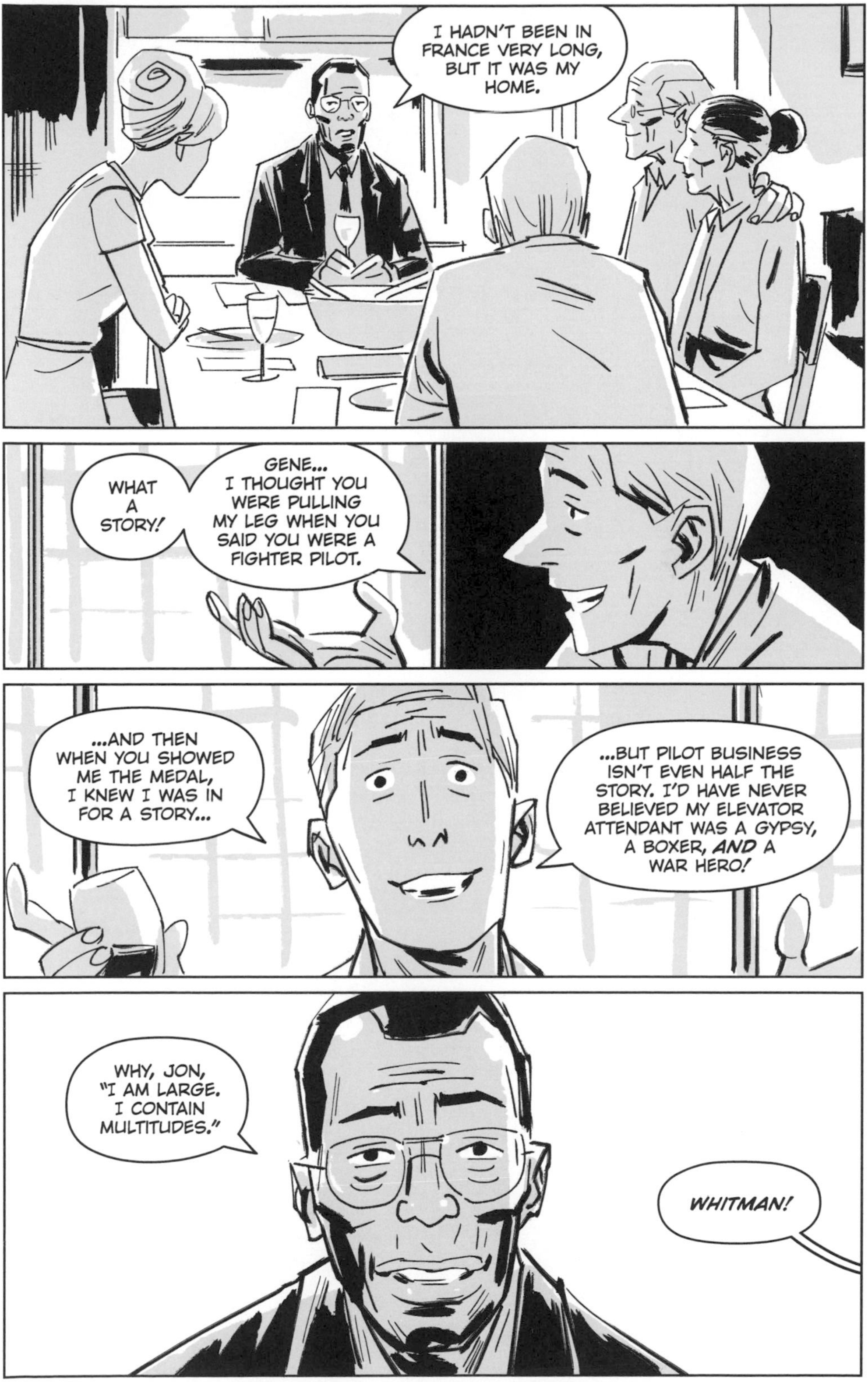
I HADN'T BEEN IN FRANCE VERY LONG, BUT IT WAS MY HOME.
WHAT A STORY!
GENE... I THOUGHT YOU WERE PULLING MY LEG WHEN YOU SAID YOU WERE A FIGHTER PILOT.
...AND THEN WHEN YOU SHOWED ME THE MEDAL, I KNEW I WAS IN FOR A STORY...
...BUT PILOT BUSINESS ISN'T EVEN HALF THE STORY. I'D HAVE NEVER BELIEVED MY ELEVATOR ATTENDANT WAS A GYPSY, A BOXER, AND A WAR HERO!
WHY, JON, "I AM LARGE. I CONTAIN MULTITUDES."
WHITMAN!

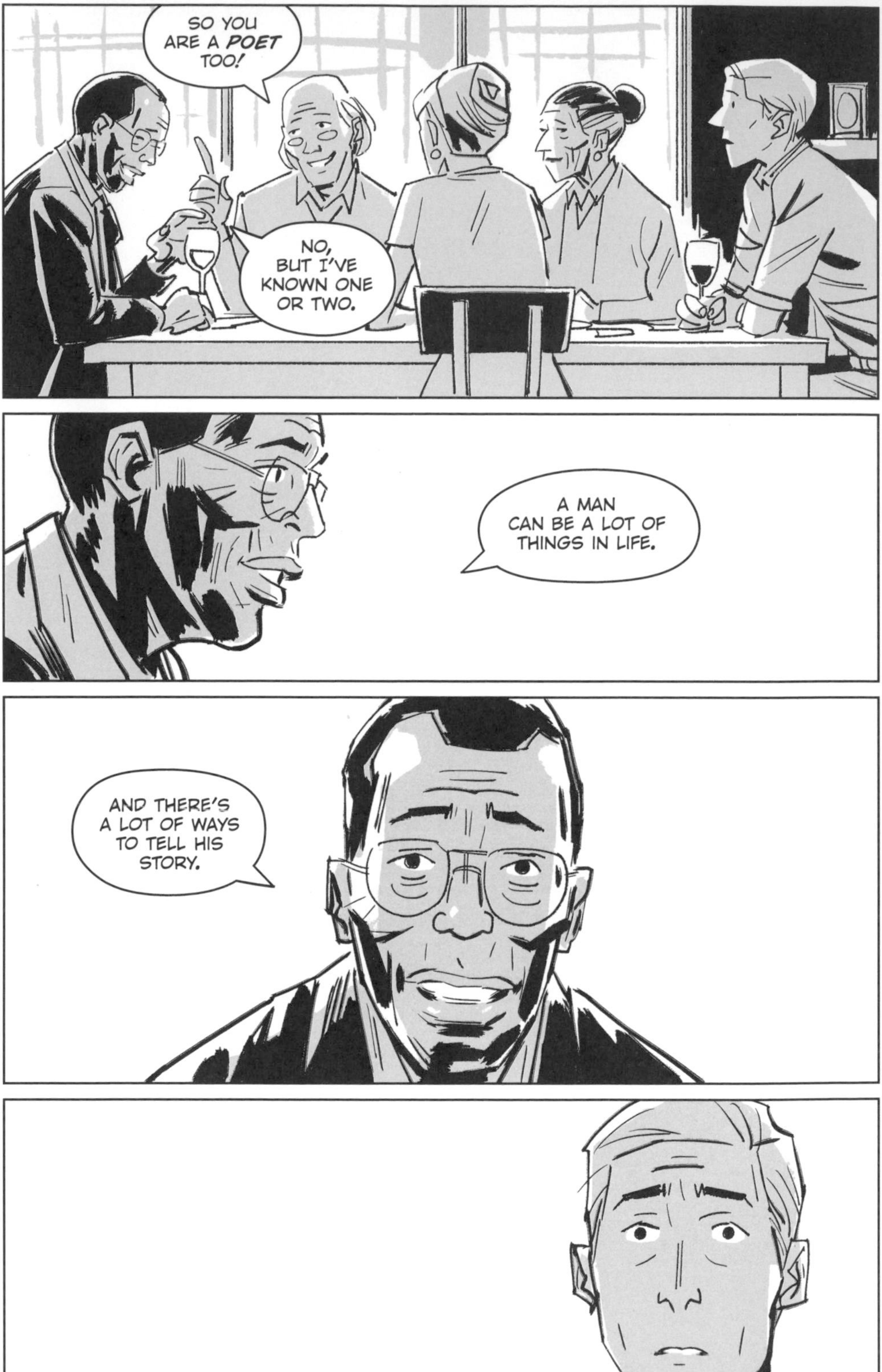
SO YOU ARE A POET TOO!
NO, BUT I'VE KNOWN ONE OR TWO.
A MAN CAN BE A LOT OF THINGS IN LIFE.
AND THERE'S A LOT OF WAYS TO TELL HIS STORY.

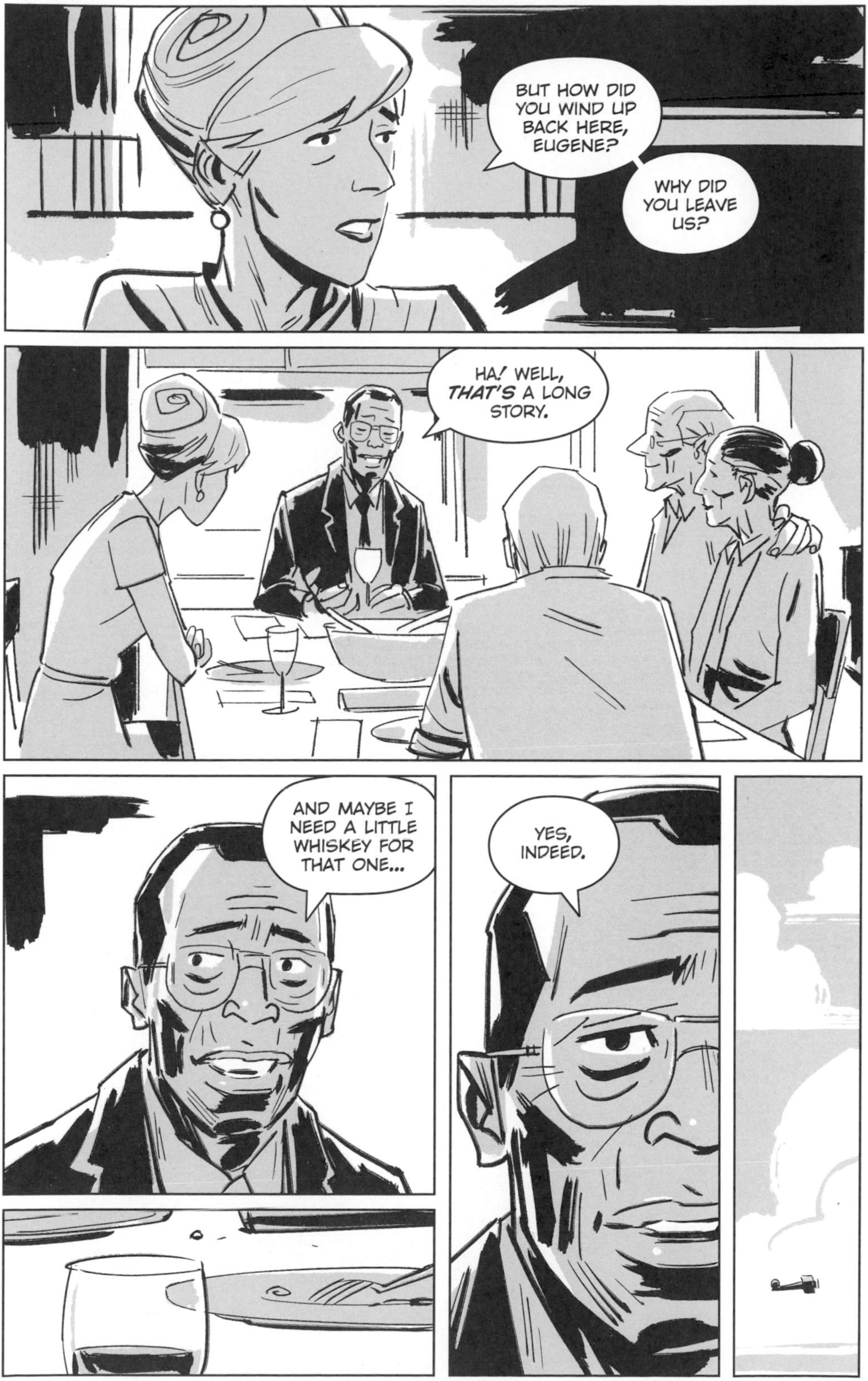
BUT HOW DID YOU WIND UP BACK HERE, EUGENE?
WHY DID YOU LEAVE US?
HA! WELL, *THAT'S* A LONG STORY.
AND MAYBE I NEED A LITTLE WHISKEY FOR THAT ONE...
YES, INDEED.

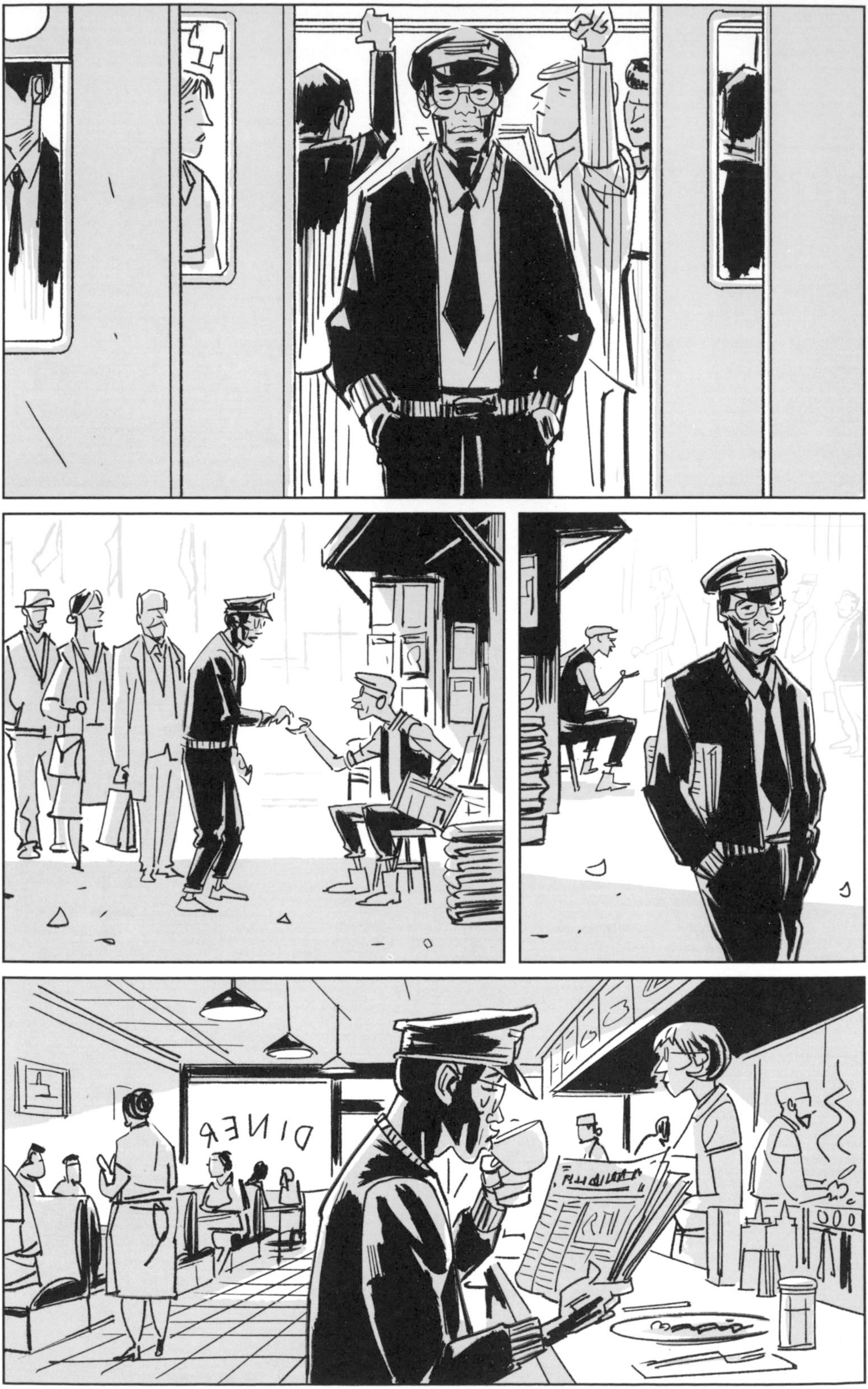
DINER

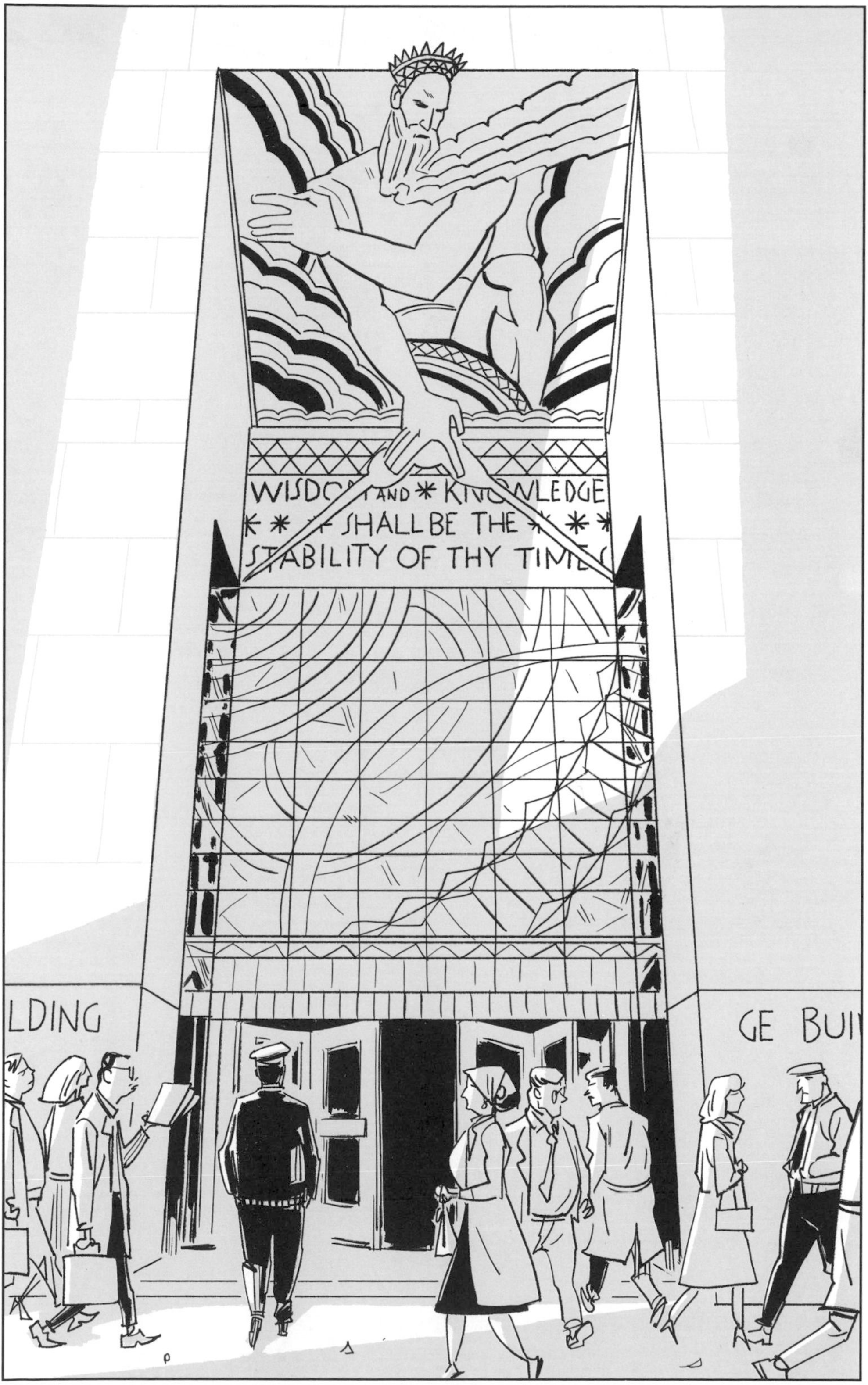
WISDOM AND KNOWLEDGE
SHALL BE THE
STABILITY OF THY TIMES
LDING
GE BUI

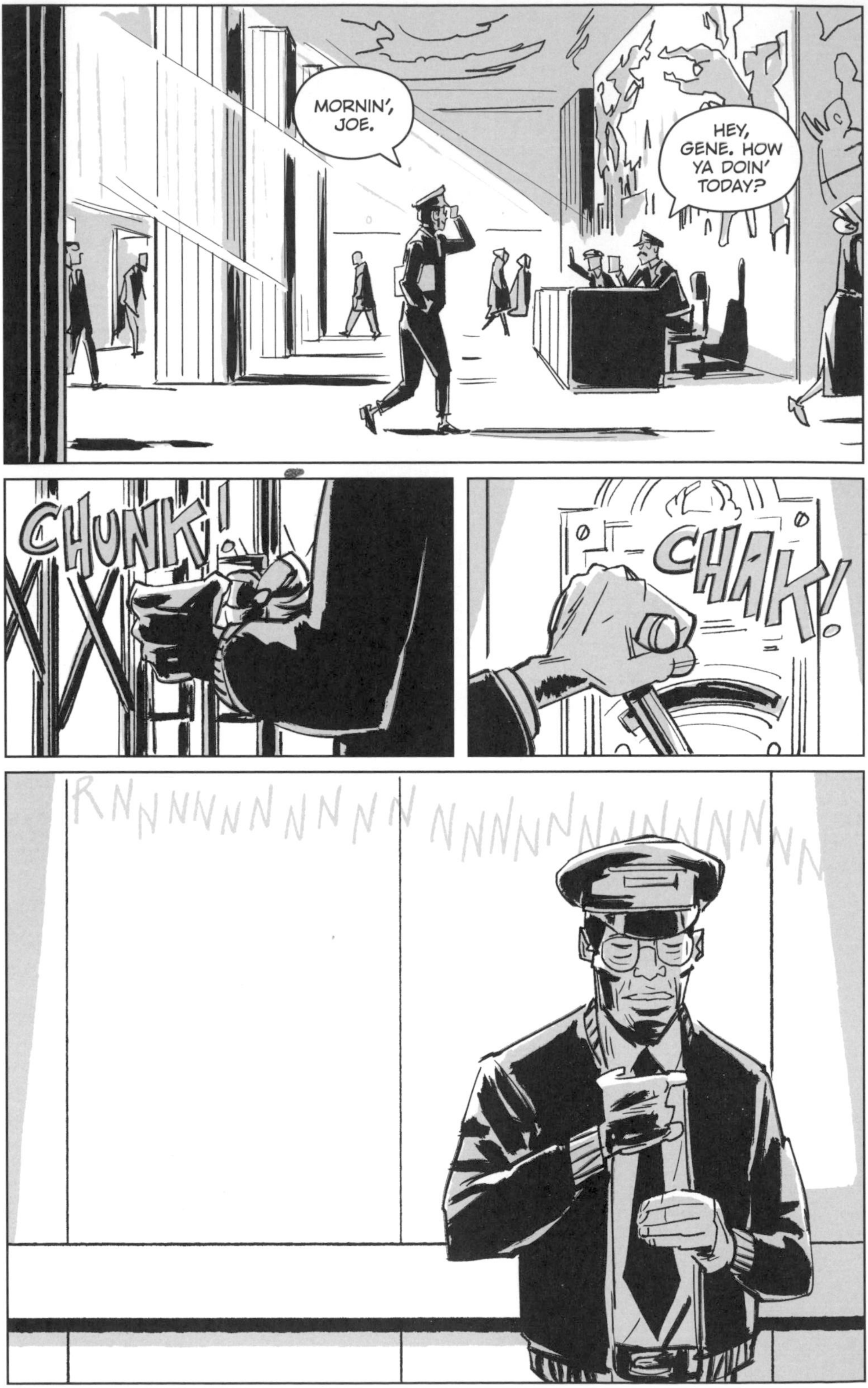
MORNIN', JOE.
HEY, GENE. HOW YA DOIN' TODAY?
CHUNK!
CHAK!
RNNNNNNNNNNNNNNNNNNNNNNNNN

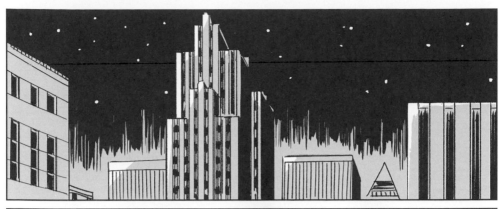

ANOTHER LATE NIGHT, MR. CASEY?

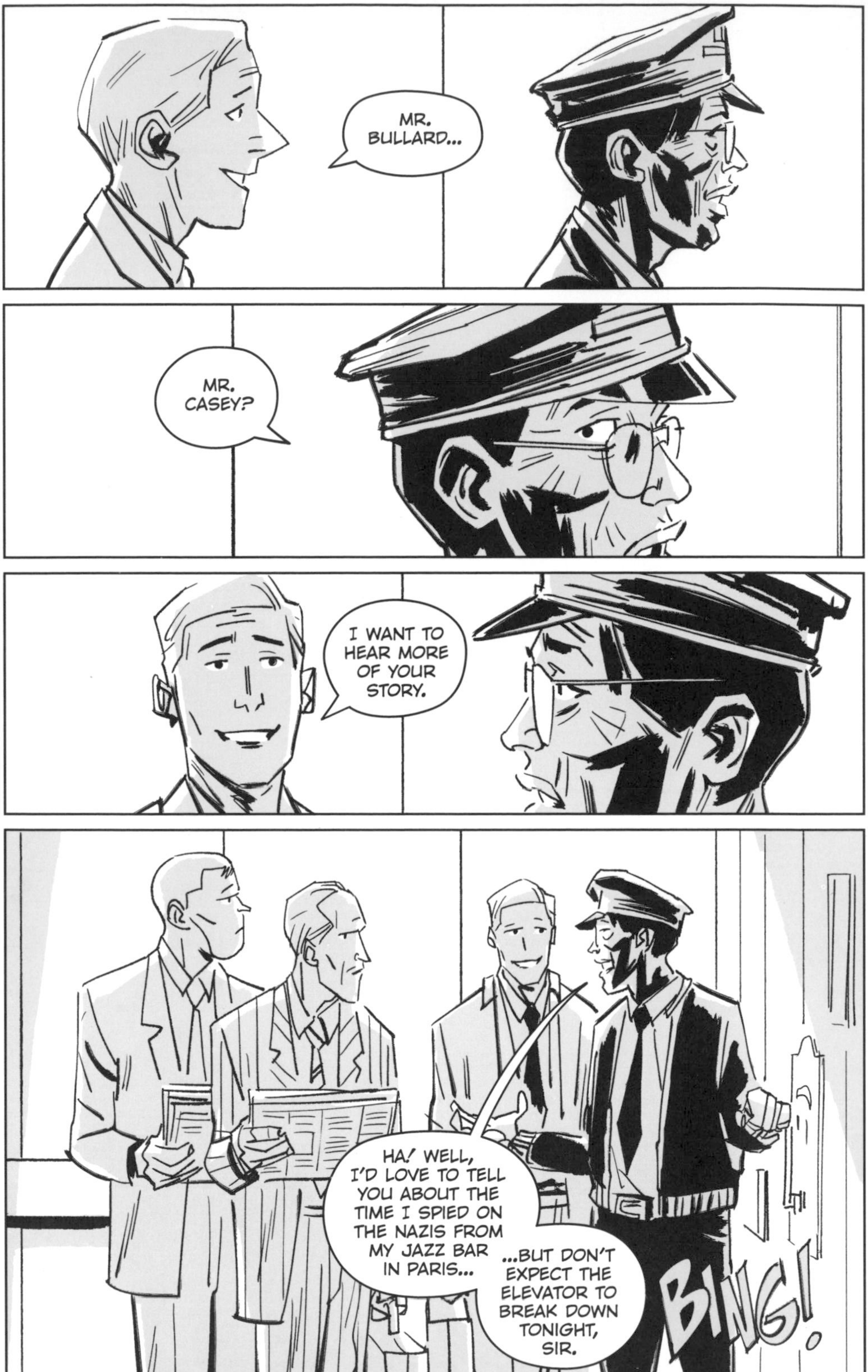

MR. BULLARD...
MR. CASEY?
I WANT TO HEAR MORE OF YOUR STORY.
HA! WELL, I'D LOVE TO TELL YOU ABOUT THE TIME I SPIED ON THE NAZIS FROM MY JAZZ BAR IN PARIS...
...BUT DON'T EXPECT THE ELEVATOR TO BREAK DOWN TONIGHT, SIR.
BING!

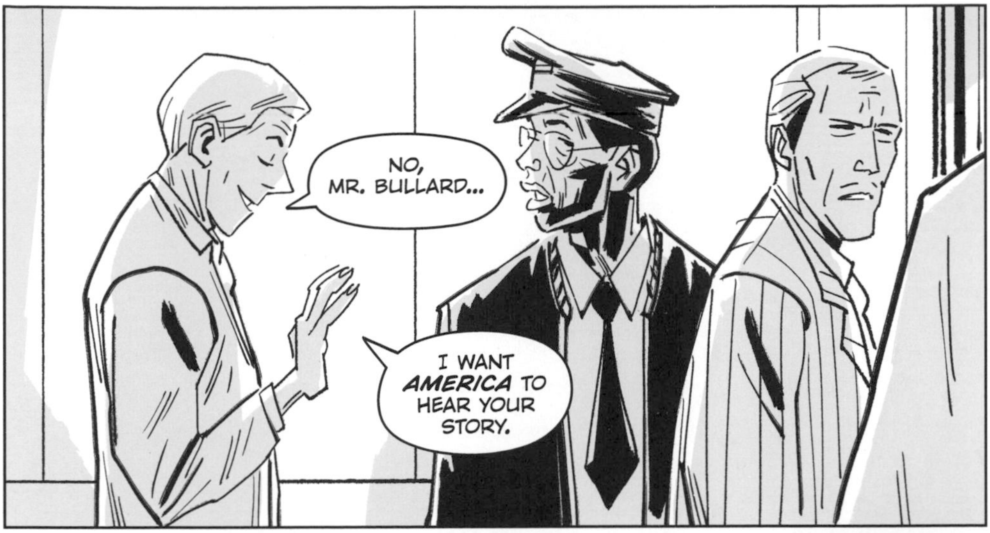
NO, MR. BULLARD...
I WANT *AMERICA* TO HEAR YOUR STORY.

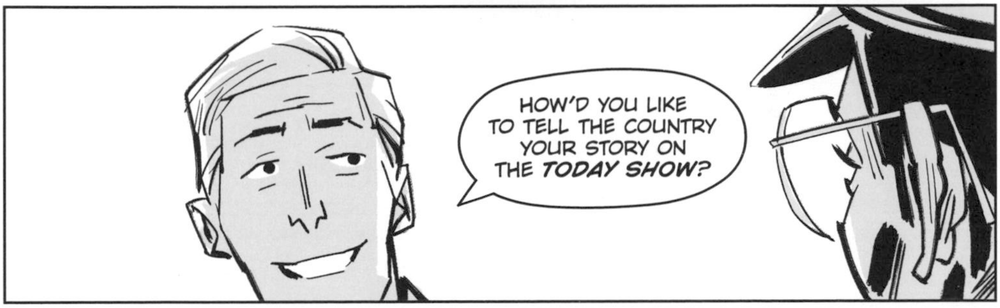
HOW'D YOU LIKE TO TELL THE COUNTRY YOUR STORY ON THE *TODAY SHOW*?

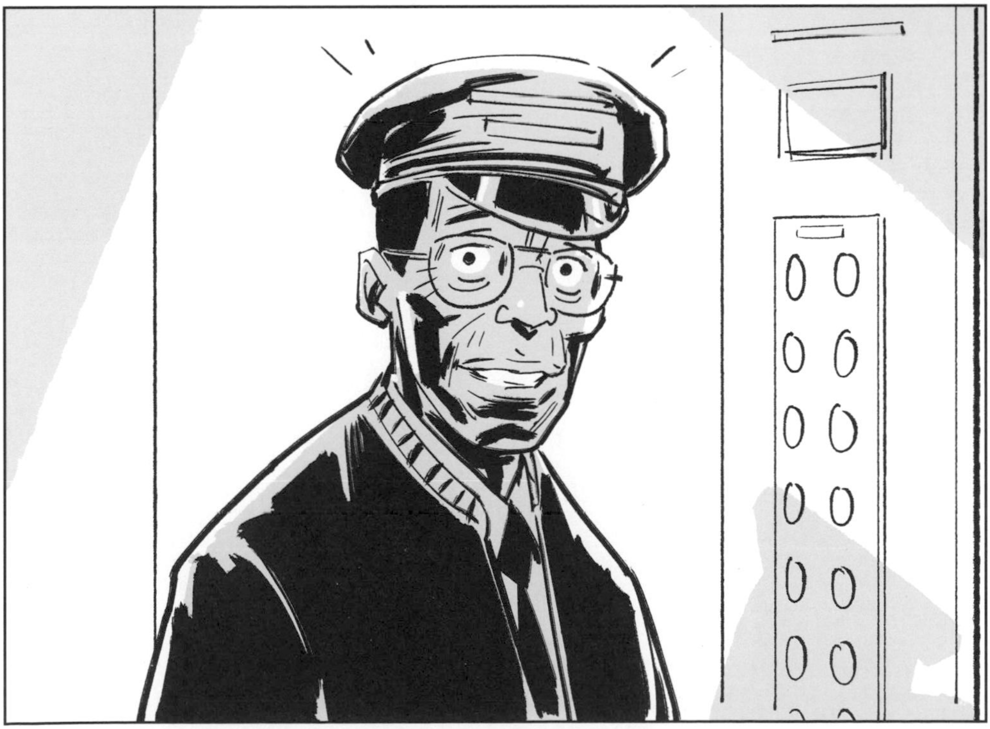

DAVE GARROWAY AND EUGENE BULLARD
ON NBC'S *TODAY SHOW*, DECEMBER 22, 1959

After the war, Eugene Bullard would settle in and make Paris his home.

As a member of the vanguard of Black American expats in Paris, he'd play an important role in the lives of others seeking refuge from American white supremacist terrorism—refugees like Langston Hughes and Josephine Baker.

Bullard would continue to fight for a place to call home, even as white nationalist movements swept Europe. And once again, he'd take up arms to fight for France.

...But that's another story.

BIBLIOGRAPHY

Carisella, P. J., and James W. Ryan. *The Black Swallow of Death: The Incredible Story of Eugene Jacques Bullard, the World's First Black Combat Aviator*. Boston: Marlborough House, 1972.

Keith, Phil, and Tom Clavin. *All Blood Runs Red: The Legendary Life of Eugene Bullard—Boxer, Pilot, Soldier, Spy*. New York: Hanover Square Press, 2019.

Lloyd, Craig. *Eugene Bullard: Black Expatriate in Jazz-Age Paris*. Athens: University of Georgia Press, 2000.

Lloyd, Craig. "The Challenge of a Memoir in Biographical Research: Eugene Bullard's 'All Blood Runs Red.'" *Proceedings and Papers of the Georgia Association of Historians* 12 (1991): 126–142. https://archives.columbusstate.edu/docs/gah/1991/126-142.pdf.

Published by First Second
First Second is an imprint of Roaring Brook Press,
a division of Holtzbrinck Publishing Holdings Limited Partnership
120 Broadway, New York, NY 10271
firstsecondbooks.com

Library of Congress Control Number: 2022904703

Our books may be purchased in bulk for promotional, educational, or business use. Please
contact your local bookseller or the Macmillan Corporate and Premium Sales Deparment at
(800) 221-7945 ext. 5442 or by email at MacmillanSpecialMarkets@macmillan.com.

First edition, 2023
Edited by Mark Siegel, Whitney Taylor, and Tess Banta
Cover design by Kirk Benshoff
Interior book design by Molly Johanson
Production editing by Kat Kopit
French translation assistance by Mark Siegel

Penciled, inked, and colored in Photoshop using Kyle T. Webster's brushes.
Word balloons created in Clip Studio Paint. Lettered with Wild And Crazy font from Comicraft.

Printed in China

ISBN 978-1-62672-852-3
10 9 8 7 6 5 4 3 2 1

Don't miss your next favorite book from First Second!
For the latest updates go to firstsecondnewsletter.com and sign up for our enewsletter.